T0331846

Handbook of Research on Information Security in Biomedical Signal Processing

Chittaranjan Pradhan
KIIT University, India

Himansu Das
KIIT University, India

Bighnaraj Naik
Veer Surendra Sai University of Technology (VSSUT), India

Nilanjan Dey
Techno India College of Technology, India

A volume in the Advances in Information Security, Privacy, and Ethics (AISPE) Book Series

Published in the United States of America by
    IGI Global
    Information Science Reference (an imprint of IGI Global)
    701 E. Chocolate Avenue
    Hershey PA, USA 17033
    Tel: 717-533-8845
    Fax: 717-533-8661
    E-mail: cust@igi-global.com
    Web site: http://www.igi-global.com

Copyright © 2018 by IGI Global. All rights reserved. No part of this publication may be reproduced, stored or distributed in any form or by any means, electronic or mechanical, including photocopying, without written permission from the publisher. Product or company names used in this set are for identification purposes only. Inclusion of the names of the products or companies does not indicate a claim of ownership by IGI Global of the trademark or registered trademark.

Library of Congress Cataloging-in-Publication Data

Names: Pradhan, Chittaranjan, editor.
Title: Handbook of research on information security in biomedical signal
  processing / Chittaranjan Pradhan, Himansu Das, Bighnaraj Naik, and
  Nilanjan Dey, editors.
Description: Hershey, PA : Information Science Reference, [2018] | Includes
  bibliographical references.
Identifiers: LCCN 2017035887| ISBN 9781522551522 (h/c) | ISBN 9781522551539
  (ebook)
Subjects: LCSH: Signal processing--Security measures--Handbooks, manuals,
  etc. | Imaging systems in medicine--Security measures--Handbooks, manuals,
  etc. | Medical informatics.
Classification: LCC R857.S47 I54 2018 | DDC 610.28--dc23 LC record available at https://lccn.loc.gov/2017035887

This book is published in the IGI Global book series Advances in Information Security, Privacy, and Ethics (AISPE) (ISSN: 1948-9730; eISSN: 1948-9749)

British Cataloguing in Publication Data
A Cataloguing in Publication record for this book is available from the British Library.

All work contributed to this book is new, previously-unpublished material. The views expressed in this book are those of the authors, but not necessarily of the publisher.

For electronic access to this publication, please contact: eresources@igi-global.com.

Advances in Information Security, Privacy, and Ethics (AISPE) Book Series

Manish Gupta
State University of New York, USA

ISSN:1948-9730
EISSN:1948-9749

Mission

As digital technologies become more pervasive in everyday life and the Internet is utilized in ever increasing ways by both private and public entities, concern over digital threats becomes more prevalent.

The **Advances in Information Security, Privacy, & Ethics (AISPE) Book Series** provides cutting-edge research on the protection and misuse of information and technology across various industries and settings. Comprised of scholarly research on topics such as identity management, cryptography, system security, authentication, and data protection, this book series is ideal for reference by IT professionals, academicians, and upper-level students.

Coverage

- CIA Triad of Information Security
- Security Classifications
- Device Fingerprinting
- Cookies
- Data Storage of Minors
- Cyberethics
- Risk Management
- Global Privacy Concerns
- Network Security Services
- Computer ethics

IGI Global is currently accepting manuscripts for publication within this series. To submit a proposal for a volume in this series, please contact our Acquisition Editors at Acquisitions@igi-global.com or visit: http://www.igi-global.com/publish/.

The Advances in Information Security, Privacy, and Ethics (AISPE) Book Series (ISSN 1948-9730) is published by IGI Global, 701 E. Chocolate Avenue, Hershey, PA 17033-1240, USA, www.igi-global.com. This series is composed of titles available for purchase individually; each title is edited to be contextually exclusive from any other title within the series. For pricing and ordering information please visit http://www.igi-global.com/book-series/advances-information-security-privacy-ethics/37157. Postmaster: Send all address changes to above address. Copyright © 2018 IGI Global. All rights, including translation in other languages reserved by the publisher. No part of this series may be reproduced or used in any form or by any means – graphics, electronic, or mechanical, including photocopying, recording, taping, or information and retrieval systems – without written permission from the publisher, except for non commercial, educational use, including classroom teaching purposes. The views expressed in this series are those of the authors, but not necessarily of IGI Global.

Titles in this Series

For a list of additional titles in this series, please visit: www.igi-global.com/book-series

Multidisciplinary Perspectives on Human Capital and Information Technology Professionals
Vandana Ahuja (Jaypee Institute of Information Technology, India) and Shubhangini Rathore (IBS Gurgaon, India)
Information Science Reference • copyright 2018 • 400pp • H/C (ISBN: 9781522552970) • US $215.00 (our price)

Security, Privacy, and Anonymization in Social Networks Emerging Research and Opportunities
B. K. Tripathy (VIT University, India) and Kiran Baktha (VIT University, India)
Information Science Reference • copyright 2018 • 176pp • H/C (ISBN: 9781522551584) • US $155.00 (our price)

Critical Research on Scalability and Security Issues in Virtual Cloud Environments
Shadi Aljawarneh (Jordan University of Science and Technology, Jordan) and Manisha Malhotra (Chandigarh University, India)
Information Science Reference • copyright 2018 • 341pp • H/C (ISBN: 9781522530299) • US $225.00 (our price)

The Morality of Weapons Design and Development Emerging Research and Opportunities
John Forge (University of Sydney, Australia)
Information Science Reference • copyright 2018 • 216pp • H/C (ISBN: 9781522539841) • US $175.00 (our price)

Advanced Cloud Computing Security Techniques and Applications
Ihssan Alkadi (Independent Researcher, USA)
Information Science Reference • copyright 2018 • 350pp • H/C (ISBN: 9781522525066) • US $225.00 (our price)

Algorithmic Strategies for Solving Complex Problems in Cryptography
Kannan Balasubramanian (Mepco Schlenk Engineering College, India) and M. Rajakani (Mepco Schlenk Engineering College, India)
Information Science Reference • copyright 2018 • 302pp • H/C (ISBN: 9781522529156) • US $245.00 (our price)

Information Technology Risk Management and Compliance in Modern Organizations
Manish Gupta (State University of New York, Buffalo, USA) Raj Sharman (State University of New York, Buffalo, USA) John Walp (M&T Bank Corporation, USA) and Pavankumar Mulgund (State University of New York, Buffalo, USA)
Business Science Reference • copyright 2018 • 360pp • H/C (ISBN: 9781522526049) • US $225.00 (our price)

701 East Chocolate Avenue, Hershey, PA 17033, USA
Tel: 717-533-8845 x100 • Fax: 717-533-8661
E-Mail: cust@igi-global.com • www.igi-global.com

List of Contributors

Table of Contents

Section 1
Security Requirements for Biomedical Signals

Takhellambam Gautam Meitei, NERIST, India
Sinam Ajitkumar Singh, NERIST, India
Swanirbhar Majumder, Tripura University, India

Suchetha M., VIT University, India
Jagannath M., VIT University, India

Tariq Javid, Hamdard University, Pakistan

Amutha S., Dayananda Sagar College of Engineering, India
Ramesh Babu D. R., Dayananda Sagar College of Engineering, India

Satya Ranjan Dash, KIIT University, India
Asim Syed Sheeraz, KIIT University, India
Annapurna Samantaray, Indraprastha Institute of Information Technology Delhi (IIIT-D),
India

Section 2
Security Over Wireless Sensor Networks and Distributed Systems

Section 3
Security Through Machine Learning Techniques and Watermarking Techniques

Detailed Table of Contents

Section 1
Security Requirements for Biomedical Signals

Takhellambam Gautam Meitei, NERIST, India
Sinam Ajitkumar Singh, NERIST, India
Swanirbhar Majumder, Tripura University, India

These days the wide usage of data has opened security vulnerabilities everywhere. This has led to research in the biometrics area for improving security. Presently with wide development of technology different forms of biometrics are being used in various applications. Thus, fingerprint and face are no longer the only ones being used in this field. The authors have concentrated on PCG as a biometric in this chapter. A very few sources are available in this area deeming it to be nascent. Recent proposals were examined, and it was observed that PCG reduces the risks of vulnerability faced by other biometric system. A simple biometric system would consist of steps like preprocessing, segmentation, feature extraction, and comparison or matching phase. In this chapter, some pre-processing steps as implemented by various authors using wavelets and other feature extraction techniques, implemented for the PCG biometric system by various researchers, are reviewed. Later, in the matching phase, Euclidean distance, GMM, FSR, VQ method are examined.

Suchetha M., VIT University, India
Jagannath M., VIT University, India

The main aim of ECG signal enhancement is to separate the required signal components from the unwanted artifacts. Adaptive filter-based ECG enhancement helps in detecting time varying potentials and also helps to track the dynamic variations of the signals. LMS-based adaptive recurrent filter is used to obtain the impulse response of normal QRS complexes. It is also used for arrhythmia detection in ambulatory ECG recordings. Adaptive filters self-modify its frequency response to change the behavior in time. This property of adaptive filter allows it to adapt its response to change in the input signal characteristics.

A major problem in adaptive filtering is the computational complexity of adaptive algorithm when the unknown system has a long impulse response and therefore requires a large number of taps. The wavelet transform is a time-scale representation method with a basis function called mother wavelet. In wavelet transform, the input signal is subsequently decomposed into subbands. Wavelet transform thresholding in the subband gives better performance of denoising.

This chapter introduces a framework for secure access to biomedical images. Biomedical images are acquired using a vast array of imaging techniques depending upon the specific application. A magnetic resonance spatial domain image is acquired by taking inverse weighted Fourier transform of raw frequency domain data generated by the modality. After correction, these images are stored in a standard format. The access to these stored images is typically subjected to authorization. Medical information in biomedical images needs to be protected in both stored form and in transmission. Encryption technologies are used to secure information whereas compression technologies are used to reduce the information without affecting the contents. In this chapter, a cryptocompression system is proposed which integrates both encryption and compression to fulfill the requirements of electronic protected health information records.

Chapter 4

Breast cancer is the second leading cause of death among women according to Cancer Facts and Figures. In order to increase the survival rate of women due to breast cancer, early and accurate detection of breast cancer is very essential. The quality of the image acquired through different breast imaging modalities: mammography, ultrasonography, and magnetic resonance imaging (MRI) have drawbacks which reduces the efficiency of accurate detection. As per the literature survey, the quality of the image acquired through the breast imaging modalities is not optimal for the accurate detection of cancer at the early stage. Digital image enhancement methods have been widely used in radiology in order to enhance the image quality. Considerable research has been undertaken in the development of enhancement of the image to assist radiologists in the identification of breast abnormalities. In order to further improve the efficiency of detection, diagnosis, and treatment of cancer, the quality of the image has to be improved.

Chapter 5

Electrocardiogram (ECG) is a kind of process of recording the electrical activity/signals of the heart with respect to the time. ECG conveys a wide amount of information related to the structure and functions of the heart, its electrical conduction processes. ECG is a diagnostic tool that the doctors and medical professionals use to measure patients' heart activity by paying attention to the electric current flowing in the heart. Due to the presence of noises, it needs to carry out the filtration process. Filtration is the process of keeping the components of the signals of desired frequencies by setting up an "fc" value and removing the components apart from the said "fc" frequency. It is required to eliminate the noise level from the ECG signal, such that the resultant ECG signal must be free from noises. All these techniques and algorithms have their advantages and limitations which are discussed in this chapter.

This chapter introduces two mathematical transforms—wavelet and curvelet—in the field of biomedical imaging. Presenting the theoretical background with relevant properties, the applications of the two transforms are presented. The biomedical applications include heart sound analysis, electrocardiography (ECG) characterization, positron emission tomography (PET) image analysis, medical image compression, mammogram enhancement, magnetic resonance imaging (MRI) and computer tomography (CT) image denoising, diabetic retinopathy detection. The applications emphasize the development of algorithms to diagnose human diseases, thereby rendering fast and reliable support to the medical personnel. The transforms—one classical (wavelet) and another contemporary (curvelet)—are selected to focus the difference in architecture, limitation, evolution, and application of individual transform. Two joint applications are addressed to compare their performance. This survey is also supplemented by a case study: mammogram denoising using wavelet and curvelet transforms with the underlying algorithms.

Pulse rate, body temperature, blood pressure, and respiratory rate are four vital signs indicating health status of a patient. Oxygen saturation of arterial blood (SaO2) is regarded as fifth vital sign of health status. Pulse oximeters are used in post-operative intensive care units for monitoring pulse rate and SaO2. They make non-invasive simultaneous estimation of pulse rate and SaO2 using photoplethysmogram (PPG) signals captured at red and IR wavelengths. This chapter describes the concept of oximetry, importance of non-invasive medical measurements, principle of pulse oximetry, and the block diagram approach for the design of pulse oximeters. It also presents an exhaustive review on various methods in-vogue for SaO2 estimation, identifies the problems associated with pulse oximeters. The critical limitation is that commercial pulse oximeters are as accurate as their calibration curves. Finally, it presents state-of-the-art research aimed at performance enhancement of pulse oximeters and directions for future work.

Section 2
Security Over Wireless Sensor Networks and Distributed Systems

Information technology has benefitted the society enormously in all spheres of life. Medical sciences have not been left untouched, rather it is using information technology extensively for storing, retrieving, transmitting, and manipulating data. There are various simulators and software designed using virtual reality explicitly to train the medical students like computer-assisted learning (CAL). Biomedical science is a discipline that connects information science, computer science, and healthcare. Biomedical science is critically analyzing, understanding, and knowing the human body. Real-time monitoring can help studying and analyzing the chronic diseases and managing it before the adverse events. Information technology has been proven as a boon in all areas, but it has certain limitations, making it vulnerable to attacks. Information security is a matter of great concern, especially when the data is traveling through the internet, which is an insecure channel. This chapter focuses on varied attacks and their countermeasures.

Chapter 9

The emergence of new innovations in technology changes the rate of data generated in health-related institutions and the way data should be handled. As such, the amount of data generated is always on the increase, which demands the need of advanced, automated management systems and storage platforms for handling large biomedical data. Cloud computing has emerged as the promising technology for present and future that can handle large amount of data and enhance processing and management of the data remotely. One of the disturbance concerns of the technology is the security of the data. Data in the cloud is subject to security threats, and this has highlighted the need for exploring security measures against the threats. The chapter provides detailed analysis of cloud computing deployment strategies and risks associated with the technology and tips for biomedical data storage and processing through cloud computing services.

Intrusion detection in wireless sensor network (WSN) has been a critical issue for the stable functioning of the networks during last decade. Wireless sensors are small and cheap devices that have a capacity to sense actions, data movement, and communicate with each other. It is a self-governing network that consists of sensor nodes deployed in a particular environment, which has wide applications in various areas such as data gathering, military surveillance, transportation, medical system, agriculture, smart building, satellite communication, and healthcare. Wormhole attack is one of the serious attacks, which is smoothly resolved in networks but difficult to observe. There are various techniques used to detect the malicious node such as LITEWORP, SAM, DelPHI, GRPW, and WRHT. This chapter focuses on detection methods for wormhole attacks using trust-based systems in WSN.

Wireless sensor network is an emerging area in which multiple sensor nodes are present to perform many real-time applications like military application, industrialized automation, health monitoring, weather forecast, etc. Sensor nodes can be organized into a group which is led by a cluster head; this concept is known as clustering. Clustering of wireless sensor network is used when sensor nodes want to communicate simultaneously in a single network. The author organizes the sensor nodes by applying UWDBCSN (underwater density-based clustering sensor network) clustering approach in which routing of the packets is controlled by cluster head. The author also considers the security of sensor nodes which are harmful to different types of mischievous attacks like wormhole attack, denial of service attack, replication or cloning attack, blackhole attack, etc. Node replication is one of the types in which an attacker tries to capture the node and generate the replica or clone of that node in the same network. So, this chapter describes how to deal with these types of attacks. The author used the intrusion detection process to deal with this type of attack. All the detection procedure is combined with sleep/wake scheduling algorithm to increase the performance of sensor nodes in the network.

Chapter 12

S. Selva Nidhyananthan, Mepco Schlenk Engineering College, India
Joe Virgin A., Mepco Schlenk Engineering College, India
Shantha Selva Kumari R., Mepco Schlenk Engineering College, India

Security is the most notable fact of all computerized control gadgets. In this chapter, a voice ID computerized gadget is utilized for the security motivation using speech recognition. Mostly, the voices are trained by extracting mel frequency cepstral coefficient feature (MFCC), but it is very sensitive to noise interference and degrades the performance; hence, dynamic MFCC is used for speech and speaker recognition. The registered voices are stored in a database. When the device senses any voice, it cross checks with the registered voice. If any mismatches occur, it gives an alert to the authorized person through global system for mobile communication (GSM) to intimate the unauthorized access. GSM works at a rate of 168 Kb/s up to 40 km and it operates at different operating frequencies like 800MHz, 900MHz, etc. This proposed work is more advantageous for the security systems to trap the unauthorized persons through an efficient communication.

Section 3
Security Through Machine Learning Techniques and Watermarking Techniques

Chapter 13

Anuradha Chetan Phadke, Maharashtra Institute of Technology, India
Priti P. Rege, College of Engineering Pune, India

Mammography is a popular imaging modality currently in use for routine screening of breast. Radiologists look for some of the significant signs of breast cancer while examining the mammogram visually. These signs are bounded masses, clusters of micro-calcifications, spiculations, and architectural distortions. Developing computer-aided algorithms for the detection and classification of abnormalities in mammograms is an extremely challenging task because of significant variableness in the type, size, shape, texture variation of abnormal region, and variability in the structure of surrounding tissues of the breast. The main objective of this chapter is to introduce dominant features of various signs of abnormalities and to discuss techniques to detect various abnormalities in mammograms. This knowledge will help to develop a system that is useful for the early detection and classification of breast cancer.

A new method is proposed to classify the lung nodules as benign and malignant. The method is based on analysis of lung nodule shape, contour, and texture for better classification. The data set consists of 39 lung nodules of 39 patients which contain 19 benign and 20 malignant nodules. Lung regions are segmented based on morphological operators and lung nodules are detected based on shape and area features. The proposed algorithm was tested on LIDC (lung image database consortium) datasets and the results were found to be satisfactory. The performance of the method for distinction between benign and malignant was evaluated by the use of receiver operating characteristic (ROC) analysis. The method achieved area under the ROC curve was 0.903 which reduces the false positive rate.

Chapter 15

Brain tumor and intracerebral hemorrhage are major causes for death among the people. Brain tumor is the growth of abnormal cells multiplied in an uncontrolled manner in brain. Magnetic resonance imaging (MRI) technique plays a major role for analysis, diagnosis, and treatment planning of abnormalities in the brain. Bleed is detected manually by radiologists, but it is laborious, time-consuming, and error prone. The automatic detection method was performed to detect the tumor as well as bleed in brain under a single system. The proposed method includes image acquisition, pre-processing, patch extraction, feature extraction, convolutional neural network (CNN) classification, and fuzzy inference system (FIS) to detect the abnormality with reduced classification loss percentage. This chapter is compared with the existing system of tumor detection using convolution neural network based on certain features such as skewness, kurtosis, homogeneity, smoothness, and correlation.

Currently the industry is focused on managing, retrieving, and securing massive amounts of data. Hence, privacy preservation is a significant concern for those organizations that publish/share personal data for vernacular analysis. In this chapter, the authors presented an innovative approach that makes use of information gain of the quasi attributes with respect to sensitive attributes for anonymizing the data, which gives the fruitfulness of an attribute in classifying the data elements, which is a two-way correlation among attributes. The authors show that the proposed approach preserves better data utility and has lesser complexity than former methods.

Chapter 17
A Hybrid Watermarking Technique for Copyright Protection of Medical Signals in
Rohit M. Thanki, C. U. Shah University, India
Surekha Borra, K. S. Institute of Technology, India
Komal Borisagar, Atmiya Institute of Technology and Science, India

Today, an individual's health is being monitored for diagnosis and treatment of diseases upon analyzing various medical data such as images and signals. Modifications of this medical data when it is transferred over an open communication channel or network leads to deviations in diagnosis and creates a serious health issue for any individual. Digital watermarking techniques are one of the solutions for providing protection to multimedia contents. This chapter gives requirements and various techniques for the security of medical data using watermarking. This chapter also demonstrates a novel hybrid watermarking technique based on fast discrete curvelet transform (FDCuT), redundant discrete wavelet transform (RDWT), and discrete cosine transform (DCT). This watermarking technique can be used for securing medical various types of medical images and ECG signals over an open communication channel.

Chapter 18
Ajita Sahay, KIIT University, India
Chittaranjan Pradhan, KIIT University, India
Amandip Sinha, West Bengal University of Technology, India

This chapter explores medical signal security enhancement using chaotic map and watermarking techniques. This new approach provides security to both the medical image and also maintains the confidentially of both the patient and doctor. Medical image encryption is done by using 2D Gaussian iterated map and BARCODE ECC200. Personal data is encoded in barcode. The encrypted image and barcode are embedded using DCT and DWT, which provides high PSNR values and higher NC value, which help to provide more security.

Preface

INTRODUCTION

Information security has got the edge over the other computations due to heavy traffic based on digital information transmission. Specially, the protection of biomedical data are very sensitive and prime objective as compared to other data. Biomedical data science deals with the storage, retrieval and transmission of the biomedical data. When these data are transmitted, their owner's information plays a vital role for the copyright and copy protections. Similarly, the company's information can be embedded within the transmitting data along with the owner's information. So, there is a need of robust and secure mechanism to transfer the medical images and signals over Internet. This book will focus on advanced models and algorithms in information security for biomedical image and signal processing.

OBJECTIVE OF THE BOOK

Recent advancements and innovations of medical image and signal processing have led to great revolution in biomedical signal processing. It emphasizes on data security and content protection in modern health care system. It is essential to unite the watermarking concept with steganography and digital forensic, which plays a crucial role in the copyright protection. This work can be verified during the data transmission as well as at the receiver's end. Since biomedical data are very sensitive in nature, its security is highly required for the accurate reading and further processing. For the legal verification of the original owner in an efficient optimized techniques are highly required. Even though the attacker gets access to the data transmitted, still there remains a challenge in breaking the copyright content. This book explores the development of the intelligent techniques for the information security in the area of biomedical image and signal processing.

ORGANIZATION OF THE BOOK

The book contains 18 chapters that are organized in three sections as shown below. The first section includes seven chapters dealing with the security requirements and solutions for the biomedical signals. The next five chapters outline the various security mechanisms over the wireless sensor networks and distributed systems. The last section deals with four machine learning approaches to deal with the biomedical data and two watermarking techniques dealing with the biomedical signals.

Section 1: Security Requirements for Biomedical Signals (Chapters 1-7)

This section elaborates the different techniques to handle biomedical signals such as biometrics, images and ECG signals. This section also deals with the secure access to the biomedical images. Conversion of signal from spatial domain to frequency domain also has been discussed here.

Chapter 1

This chapter focusses on the biometric through PCG. Based on the results of recent approaches, it was observed that PCG reduces the risks of vulnerability faced by other biometric systems like fingerprint, face etc. In this chapter, some pre-processing steps as implemented by various authors using wavelets and other feature extraction techniques, implemented for the PCG biometric system by various researchers are reviewed in this chapter. Later, in the matching phase, Euclidean distance, GMM, FSR, VQ method are examined.

Chapter 2

This chapter focuses on adaptive filter based ECG enhancement which helps in detecting time varying potentials and also helps to track the dynamic variations of the signals. LMS based adaptive recurrent filter is used to obtain the impulse response of normal QRS complexes. It is also used for arrhythmia detection in ambulatory ECG recordings. Adaptive filters self-modify its frequency response to change the behavior in time, which allows it to adapt its response to change in the input signal characteristics. A major problem in adaptive filtering is the computational complexity of adaptive algorithm when the unknown system has a long impulse response and therefore requires a large number of taps. Wavelet transform thresholding in the subband gives better performance of denoising.

Chapter 3

This chapter introduces a framework for secure access to biomedical images. Biomedical images are acquired using a vast array of imaging techniques depending upon the specific application. In this chapter, a crypto compression system is proposed which integrates both encryption and compression to fulfil the requirements of electronic protected health information records.

Chapter 4

This chapter focuses on the increased survival rate of women due to breast cancer. As per the Literature Survey, the quality of the image acquired through the breast imaging modalities is not optimal for the accurate detection of cancer at the early stage. Digital image enhancement methods have been widely used in radiology in order to enhance the image quality. Considerable research has been undertaken in the development of enhancement of the image to assist radiologists in the identification of breast abnormalities. In order to further improve the efficiency of detection, diagnosis and treatment of cancer, the quality of the image has to be improved.

Chapter 5

This chapter presents the filtration and classification of ECG (Electrocardiogram) signals. ECG conveys a wide amount of information related to the structure and functions of the heart, its electrical conduction processes. Filtration is the process of keeping the components of the signals of desired frequencies by setting up an 'fc' value and removing the components apart from the said 'fc' frequency. While in this process the authors need to eliminate the Noise level from the ECG Signal, such that the resultant ECG signal must be free from Noises. All these techniques and algorithms have their advantages and limitations which has discussed in this chapter.

Chapter 6

This chapter introduces two mathematical transforms- wavelet and curvelet in the field of biomedical imaging. The biomedical applications include heart sound analysis, electrocardiography (ECG) characterization, positron emission tomography (PET) image analysis, medical image compression, mammogram enhancement, magnetic resonance imaging (MRI) and computer tomography (CT) image denoising, diabetic retinopathy detection. The applications emphasize the development of algorithms to diagnose human diseases, thereby rendering fast and reliable support to the medical personnel. The transforms – one classical (wavelet) and another contemporary (curvelet) are selected to focus the difference in architecture, limitation, evolution and application of individual transform. This survey is also supplemented by a case study- mammogram denoising using wavelet and curvelet transforms with the underlying algorithms.

Chapter 7

This chapter describes the concept of oximetry, importance of non-invasive medical measurements, principle of pulse oximetry and the block diagram approach for the design of pulse oximeters. It also presents an exhaustive review on various methods in-vogue for arterial blood (SaO2) estimation, identifies the problems associated with pulse oximeters. The critical limitation is that commercial pulse oximeters are as accurate as their calibration curves. Finally, it presents current state-of-the-art research aimed at performance enhancement of pulse oximeters and directions for future work.

Section 2: Security Over Wireless Sensor Networks and Distributed Systems (Chapters 8-12)

This section contains five chapters in the wireless sensor network (wsn) and distributed computing environment. It also deals with the security risks, attacks and solutions in this domain. Lastly, this section focuses on the enhancement of the speech recognition.

Chapter 8

This chapter focuses on the various attacks and the counter measures for medical signals. Medical sciences have not left untouched, rather it is using information technology extensively for storing, retrieving, transmitting and manipulating data. Biomedical Sciences is critically analyzing, understanding and knowing the human body. Real-time monitoring can help studying and analyzing the chronic diseases and managing it before the adverse events. Information technology has been proven as a boon in all areas, but it has certain limitations making it vulnerable to attacks. Information security is a matter of great concerns especially when the data is traveling through the internet; which is an insecure channel.

Chapter 9

The chapter provides detailed analysis of cloud computing deployment strategies and risks associated with the technology and tips for biomedical data storage and processing through cloud computing services. Cloud computing has emerged as the promising technology for present and future that can handle large amount of data and enhance processing and management of the data remotely. One of the disturbance concerns of the technology is the security of the data. Data in the cloud is subject to security threats and this has highlighted the need for exploring security measures against the threats.

Chapter 10

This chapter focuses on detection methods for wormhole attack using trust based system in WSN. Wireless sensor is small and cheap devices which has a capacity to sense actions, data movement and communicate with each other nodes. It is a self-governing network which consists of sensor nodes deployed in a particular environment, which has wide application in various areas such as data gathering, military surveillance, transportation, medical system, agriculture, smart building and satellite communication and health care etc. Wormhole attack is one of the serious attacks, which is smoothly resolved in networks but difficult to observe. There are numbers of various techniques are used to detect the malicious node such as LITEWORP, SAM, DelPHI, GRPW and WRHT etc.

Chapter 11

This chapter focuses on the organizations of the sensor nodes by applying UWDBCSN (under-water density based clustering sensor network) clustering approach in which routing of the packets is controlled by cluster head. Sensor nodes can be organized into a group which is leading by a cluster head, this concept is known as clustering. Clustering of wireless sensor network is used when sensor nodes want to communicate simultaneously in a single network.

Chapter 12

This chapter discusses the utilization of voice ID computerized gadget for the security motivation using Speech Recognition. Mostly, the voices are trained by extracting Mel Frequency Cepstral Coefficient feature (MFCC) but it is very sensitive to noise interference and degrades the performance hence Dynamic MFCC is used for speech and speaker recognition. The registered voices are stored in database. When the device senses any voice it cross checks with the registered voice. If any mismatches occur, it gives an alert to the authorized person through Global System for Mobile Communication (GSM) to intimate the unauthorized access. This proposed work is more advantageous for the security systems to trap the unauthorized persons through an efficient communication.

Section 3: Security Through Machine Learning Techniques and Watermarking Techniques (Chapters 13-18)

This section deals with the application of machine learning for the biomedical signals. This section also discusses the auto detection of tumours and focuses on the privacy preservation of medical data. This section also contains two chapters dealing with the application of watermarking techniques for biomedical data.

Chapter 13

Developing computer aided algorithms for the detection and classification of abnormalities in mammograms is an extremely challenging task because of significant variableness in the type, size, shape, texture variation of abnormal region and variability in the structure of surrounding tissues of the breast. The main objective of this chapter is to introduce dominant features of various signs of abnormalities and to discuss techniques to detect various abnormalities in mammograms. This knowledge will help to develop a system which is useful for the early detection and classification of breast cancer.

Chapter 14

This chapter proposes a new method to classify the lung nodules as benign and malignant. The method is based on analysis of lung nodule shape, contour and texture for better classification. The data set consists of 39 lung nodules of 39 patients which contain 19 benign and 20 malignant nodules. Lung regions are segmented based on morphological operators and lung nodules are detected based on shape and area features. The proposed algorithm was tested on LIDC (Lung Image Database Consortium) datasets and the results were found to be satisfactory.

Chapter 15

This chapter proposes a method, which includes image acquisition, pre-processing, patch extraction, feature extraction, Convolutional Neural Network (CNN) classification and Fuzzy Inference System (FIS) to detect the abnormality with reduced classification loss percentage. The proposed work is compared with the existing system of tumour detection using convolution neural network based on certain features such as skewness, kurtosis, homogeneity, smoothness and correlation.

Chapter 16

This chapter presents an innovative approach that make use of Information Gain of the quasi attributes with respect to sensitive attributes, for anonymizing the data, which gives the fruitfulness of an attribute in classifying the data elements, which is a two way correlation among attributes. The authors have shown that the proposed approach preserve better data utility and have lesser complexity than former methods.

Chapter 17

This chapter gives requirements and various techniques for the security of medical data using watermarking. This chapter also demonstrates a novel hybrid watermarking technique based on Fast Discrete Curvelet Transform (FDCuT), Redundant Discrete Wavelet Transform (RDWT) and Discrete Cosine Transform (DCT). This watermarking technique can be used for securing medical various types of medical images and ECG signals over an open communication channel.

Chapter 18

This chapter discusses a new approach which provides security to both the medical image as well as also maintain the confidentially about the personal information about the patient and doctor. Medical Image encryption is done by using 2D Gaussian iterated map and BARCODE ECC200 and personal data is encoded in barcode, Then the encrypted image and barcode are embedded using DCT and DWT which provides high PSNR values higher NC value which helps to provides more security.

Chittaranjan Pradhan
KIIT University, India

Himansu Das
KIIT University, India

Bighnaraj Naik
Veer Surendra Sai University of Technology (VSSUT), India

Nilanjan Dey
Techno India College of Technology, India

Acknowledgment

We would like to thank everyone who participated in this project and made this book into a reality. In particular, we would like to acknowledge the hard work of authors and their cooperation during the revisions of their chapters.

We would also like to acknowledge the valuable comments of the reviewers which have enabled us to select these chapters out of the so many chapters we received and also improve the quality of the chapters.

Lastly, we appreciate the IGI Global team for their continuous support throughout the entire process of publication. Our gratitude is extended to the readers, who gave us their trust, and we hope this work guides and inspires them.

Chittaranjan Pradhan
KIIT University, India

Himansu Das
KIIT University, India

Bighnaraj Naik
Veer Surendra Sai University of Technology (VSSUT), India

Nilanjan Dey
Techno India College of Technology, India

Section 1
Security Requirements for Biomedical Signals

Chapter 1
PCG–Based Biometrics

Takhellambam Gautam Meitei
NERIST, India

Sinam Ajitkumar Singh
NERIST, India

Swanirbhar Majumder
Tripura University, India

ABSTRACT

These days the wide usage of data has opened security vulnerabilities everywhere. This has led to research in the biometrics area for improving security. Presently with wide development of technology different forms of biometrics are being used in various applications. Thus, fingerprint and face are no longer the only ones being used in this field. The authors have concentrated on PCG as a biometric in this chapter. A very few sources are available in this area deeming it to be nascent. Recent proposals were examined, and it was observed that PCG reduces the risks of vulnerability faced by other biometric system. A simple biometric system would consist of steps like preprocessing, segmentation, feature extraction, and comparison or matching phase. In this chapter, some pre-processing steps as implemented by various authors using wavelets and other feature extraction techniques, implemented for the PCG biometric system by various researchers, are reviewed. Later, in the matching phase, Euclidean distance, GMM, FSR, VQ method are examined.

INTRODUCTION

Latest advancements in technologies have driven us for the need of a secure identification of a particular person for security purposes. Various frauds and cybercrimes have led us to look out for a secure identification purpose. Previously people used passwords (something uniquely known only to us) or a token (proving we own something unique to identify ourselves). The chances of a password or a token getting stolen or shared are high, so Biometrics was introduced to reduce the vulnerabilities.

DOI: 10.4018/978-1-5225-5152-2.ch001

Copyright © 2018, IGI Global. Copying or distributing in print or electronic forms without written permission of IGI Global is prohibited.

Biometrics plays an important role in securing our identity. It can be understood as a process or the ability of a system to identify a particular person based on some unique biological features or patterns such as fingerprints, facial recognition, DNAs, voice, eye- iris and retina, palm prints, signatures, etc. The data obtained are compared to a previously stored reference data or templates, and determines if the newly generated data could have been generated by the same person. So, a biometric authentication comprises of two phases, Enrollment phase and Authentication phase. In enrollment phase, as shown below in figure 1(a), a set of databases is created by capturing the patterns or features that provides information about each individual. In the authentication phase, the newly captured feature searches the template for a match. Biometric authentication runs in two modes, depending upon the application used, i.e., identification and verification modes.

1. **Identification Mode:** It takes in information about the unique traits of a user, i.e. it captures the biometric information and searches the whole database for a match, to the captured information. Here, the classification module is trained previously with various sets of extracted features. The features of the input data from the user is then compared with the extracted features stored while training. The general block diagram of identification mode is shown below, Figure 1(b). After classification, the biometric system decides as to whose features does the input sample matches to.
2. **Verification Mode:** This is similar to the identification mode, except for the classifier used. The identification mode classifier uses a 1:N classifier, while the classifier used here is 1:1 classifier. i.e. it is basically a yes or no decision. The system compares the captured data with previously stored information about the same individual and authenticates the particular individual. The block diagram for verification mode is shown below, Figure 1(c).

Pre-processing steps are employed here to minimize noise, making it ready for a better segmentation of the PCG signal, which will provide clear features in the feature extraction process. The extracted features will be stored in a database in the enrollment phase. During authentication, after the preprocessing steps, the feature extraction stage gives the unique information of an individual and finally in the classification stage, the data is compared to the previously stored information in in the template, as shown in the block diagrams in Figure 1.

The biometrics mentioned above is without any doubt better than the methods used previously (passwords and tokens), but they all share a common problem of being duplicated. For example, the authors in (Matsumoto, Matsumoto, Yamada, & Hoshino, 2002) proved that finger prints can be duplicated. About 65-100% accuracy rate was achieved by using gummy fingers on 11 different commercial fingerprint systems. Facial recognition has also been studied to be easy to spoof using 3D printed face models. Voice can be recorded without the consent of the person. Signatures can be copied and duplicated, in fact, there are professional people who can copy and provide exact signatures. DNAs are easy to acquire. With all the advancement in technologies, there is always someone or something that will provide a weakness over a system. So, we look for an alternative, where the problems faced above are minimum. PCG (Phonocardiogram) is one of the emerging techniques that uses the heart sound and has a particular set of features, that can help overcome or reduce the problems faced above. The first use of heart sound as a biometric was introduced by (Beritelli & Serrano, 2007).

Figure 1. General block diagrams of (a) Enrollment phase (b) Identification phase (c) Verification phase

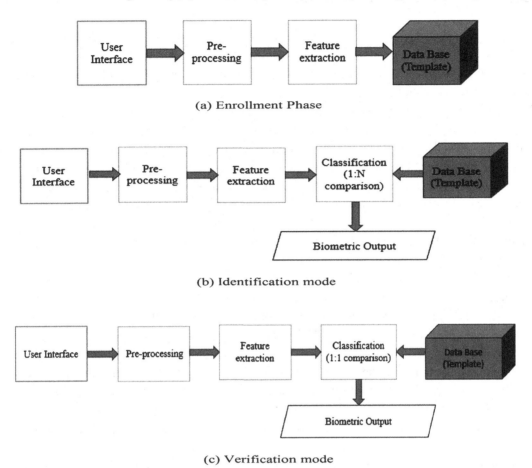

(a) Enrollment Phase

(b) Identification mode

(c) Verification mode

Since PCG biometric uses the sound of the heart, the problem of duplication face by other biometric systems is minimum here. PCG signals are hard to duplicate as each person gives out a unique signal due to various difference in sizes, position, anatomy and chest configuration. So, if we tried duplicating a PCG signal manually without the user's consent, we would have to construct an artificial heart having the same size, configurations and traits exactly similar to that of the user in order to produce the exact signal. As PCG signals are not exposed, and has low frequency range, they cannot be captured from a distance. They can only be recorded or generated by only placing a sensor on the chest surface of the user. In a proper way, PCG signals are easy to generate from a person as the heart sound is one-dimensional with low frequency range. The acquired will be compared to a previously stored data in the biometric system. If the data is found as a match with the previously stored data, the biometric authenticates the user. We shall see how the PCG can be used as a biometric in the next section, and in another we shall see how the processes are done to the heart sounds, segmentations and a few feature extractions using transforms.

PCG (PHONOCARDIOGRAM) AS A BIOMETRIC

Our heart produces two signals, an ECG (Electroencephalograph) signal and a PCG (Phonocardiogram) signal. The ECG signal is a result of the electrical activities of the heart, while the PCG signal is a result of the sounds produced by the heart. The ECG signal has also been studied for the use in biometric systems. We will deal with the PCG signal in this chapter.

Biometrics deals with two attributes, behavioral and physiological. Behavioral attributes are those like a signature, the way of walking or a voice etc., which deals with the behavior of an individual. PCG falls under the physiology attributes as they are unique and varying. Phonocardiography is the process of recording the sound produced during the cardiac cycle. This sound is the cardiac acoustic vibrations and are measured using a digital stethoscope. According to (Phua, Chen, Dat, & Shue, 2008), PCG signals are unique for each person, and satisfies certain biometric requirements as shown below.

1. **Universal**: Each and every person has a heart, that beats and produces PCG signals, until death, i.e., everybody possesses it.
2. **Measurable:** They can be easily captured and recorded using an electronic stethoscope.
3. **Uniqueness:** Heart sound is unique for each person as they are different for each person as it depends upon the size, anatomy, chest configuration, position of the heart. Even for two persons having the same heart diseases, the PCG signals are different.
4. **Vulnerability:** PCG signal, as seen, cannot be duplicated as easy as the other biometrics. Producing a signal exactly similar to the original would be very difficult as the heart sounds depends mainly on the size, position, chest configurations, anatomy of the heart and few other traits.
5. **Acceptability:** This property depends upon the extent up to which people can accept and trust this biometric system to be used in our daily lives, without affecting the privacy of a person. The uniqueness and its low vulnerability, will help in making this biometric acceptable.
6. **Usability:** With the development in technologies, wearable computing devices are available that can be placed to capture the PCG signals on the user even if they are involved in some other tasks. These wearable technologies can read and transmit the signal to the biometric system wirelessly, which will authenticate the user even before the person reaches the destination.
7. **Performance:** The performance of this biometric system will be determined by how accurate and at what rate can it generate positive result. As PCG signals are easy to read and generate, the system should be quite fast. Two parameters in particular define the performance of a biometric system. FRR (False reject rate), which give us the amount of rejection rate by the system upon the same individual and FAR (False accept rate), which gives us the amount of acceptance rate of a different individual upon a reference provided by another individual.

We shall now see the various heart sounds and their properties, and how they are used as a biometric. A human heart consists of four chambers as shown in the figure below. Two upper chambers called left atria and right atria and two lower chambers called left ventricle and right ventricle. Valves are present in between the upper and the lower chambers. These valves controls pumping of blood as they open and close periodically, producing heart sounds, and keeps the blood flowing in one direction. The pumping of heart can be divided in two phases, Systole and Diastole. In systolic, a sudden increase in pressure occurs, as the left and the right ventricles contracts. The Mitral and Tricuspid valves are closed while opening the Pulmonary and Aortic valves as they pump out the blood. The Diastolic phase starts with relaxation of the ventricles. The blood flows from the left atrium to left ventricles and from the right atrium to the right ventricles. As the heart starts relaxing, the Mitral and the Tricuspid valves opens allowing the blood to flow from the atria to the ventricles. The atria contracts at the end of diastole phase to pump all the blood from the atria to the ventricles.

As we have observed above, the valves are major contributors of heart sounds. The heart sound contains four different sounds known as of now, S1, S2, S3 and S4. The first heart sound S1 is caused by the closing of Mitral valve and Tricuspid valve. S2 is due to the closing of Aortic valve and Pulmonary valve. A third, S3 and fourth, S4 sound may be heard sometimes, as they occur rarely. S3 is not produced by the valves, instead they are produced at the beginning of diastole, after S2, as the blood rushes in the left ventricle causing vibrations. S3 is common in children but disappears as we grow old. S3 is also called protodiastolic gallop. Reappearance of S3 in the later stage of life might indicate a failure in left ventricle. The fourth sound, S4 also occurs after the atrial contraction, and are also known as presystolic gallop. Usually, the appearance of S4 generally indicates a pathological state of left ventricular.

The main components of a heart sound are S1 and S2. They are louder and occurs at every heartbeat. S3 and S4 are less loud and rarer than S1 and S2. Hence, we will give more importance on S1 and S2 as the heart always produces them. According to the authors in (Phua, Chen, Dat, & Shue, 2008), S1 has a duration of 0.15secs with a frequency of 25-45 Hz, giving the sound "lubb". S2 has a duration of 0.12secs with a frequency of 50 Hz, giving the sound "dub". So, the sound of the heart, as heard by a common ear comes as "lubb-dub".

The heart also produces various other sounds like a heart murmur, which is a resultant sound of the blood rushing into a heart valve, and they can be picked up by a simple stethoscope. These heart murmurs help us to understand if a heart is defective or not. Murmurs can be either a normal (physiological)

Figure 2. A human Heart showing their chambers

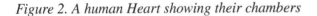
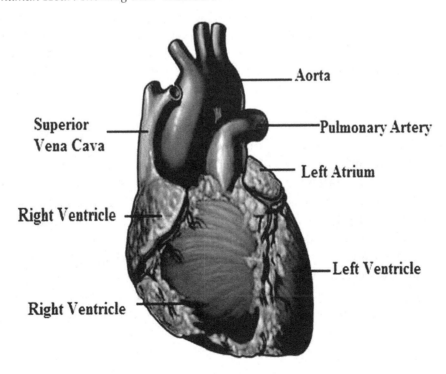

Figure 3. A simple PCG input signal as obtained via auscultation

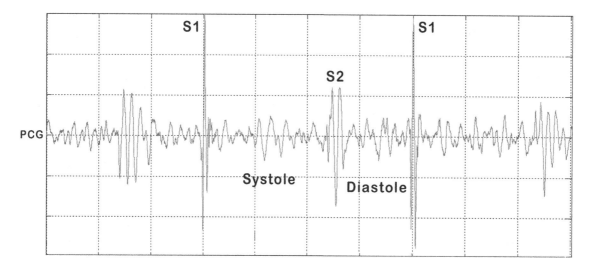

or defective (pathological). Sometimes, murmurs arise due to a leakage in the heart. It should be noted that a defective heart produces an even better PCG signals than a normal heart. As the blood flows in systolic period or diastolic period, the murmurs are differentiated w.r.t. to their timings. They are also characterized by their location (where the sound can be heard clearly.), shape (The shape of the signal it generates), quality (the uniqueness of the signal that is produced with the particular murmur.), radiation (i.e. where the sound is coming from and it is mostly in the direction of the blood flow.), pitch (gives if the signal has high, medium or low pitch) and intensity (gives how loud the sound is produced.). These sounds are recorded using an electronic stethoscope by auscultation.

Auscultation is done on 4 major points of the heart, i.e., Aortic, Pulmonary, Mitral and Lower Sternal Border. Some has suggested that, the best site for recording the heart sound is from the pulmonary site. The sensor in the stethoscope picks up the sounds, and the signal processing is done on the primary sounds, S1 and S2. Segmentations are done to separate the primary sounds, S1 and S2, from other sounds present. The data acquired are stored in mp3 or wav (waveform audio file) formats. As PCG signals are mono-dimensional and has low frequency range, this makes it easier and faster to authenticate the user. Heart signals of a group of different people have similar signal envelopes, but the details of the time and frequency domain waveforms are relatively different.

According to (Beritelli, & Serrano, 2007), in order to differentiate S1 and S2 from other heart sounds and noises, segmentations are done to the generated heart sound, and it was followed by feature extractions. They used Chirp z-transform for feature extraction and Euclidean distance between test heart sound and template for the matching phase. The authors (Phua, Chen, Dat, & Shue, 2008), did not go for segmentation, and approached for feature extraction. They compared Gaussian Mixture Models (GMM) with Vector Quantization (VQ) classification scheme. They observed that GMM-classification scheme performed better than VQ-scheme. We shall discuss them in detail, in the later section. Before that, we will discuss some basic introductions to wavelet transform and Variational mode decomposition before proceeding to the pre-processing algorithms using them.

SOME RELATED MATHEMATICAL BACKGROUND

Some basic introduction to the Wavelet transforms and Variational mode decomposition (VMD) is discussed here. Both the wavelet
transforms and the VMD method will be used in the preprocessing steps and how they are applied will be discussed in the later section.

1. **Wavelet Transform:** A wavelet transform provides time localized representation of a signal which allows multi-resolution analysis. A special function called mother transform undergoes translation and contraction operations to give wavelets. The wavelet transform equation can be express as,

$$W_x(a,b) = \frac{1}{\sqrt{a}} \int\limits_{-\infty}^{+\infty} x(t)\varphi^* \frac{(t-b)}{a} dt \qquad (1)$$

where $\varphi^*(t)$ is a complex conjugate of mother wavelet $\varphi(t)$. Where a and b are the scaling and translation coefficient respectively.

Continuous wavelet transform is used when no reconstruction of the original PCG signal is required with the help of coefficient. But when reconstruction of original signal is needed, discretization of a and b factors must be carried out. By using a discrete set of wavelet scales and translation which obey some defined rules, DWT is implemented. DWT decomposes the signal into mutually orthogonal sets of wavelets. DWT provides a fast computation of wavelet transform through a series of filters. We have seen that the energy of the digital heart sound is centered at about below 15-200Hz. Hence, decomposition up to 5th level (i=5), of the PCG signal can done using DWT. Here i is the number of levels. A threshold is applied to the wavelet coefficients for denoising purpose. Selecting this threshold depends on the energy, i.e., low and high threshold. From the 5 levels of denoising, this threshold is applied only to 3rd, 4th and 5th level. The equation for the two threshold levels are as follows.

$$TL_i = 0.5 \times RMS(w_i x_d) \qquad (2)$$

$$TH_i = 4 \times RMS(w_i x_d) \qquad (3)$$

Equation (2) gives the low threshold and Equation (3) gives the high threshold for the decomposition level i=3,4 and 5. Here, x_d gives the down sampled digital heart sound and w_i denotes the wavelet coefficients for i-th level. The high thresholds are used in detecting spikes and low threshold is used for suppressing noise components. So, any coefficients that does not fall between the high and the low threshold were set to the mean value, like a bandpass filter. Reconstruction of the denoised signal, after the thresholding is done on the 3rd, 4th and 5th levels.

DWT is realized through the successive low and high pass filtering of a discrete time signal. The following equation shows the one-level decomposition of signal.

$$Y_h[k] = \sum_n S[n].h[2k-n] \tag{4}$$

$$Y_l[k] = \sum_n S[n].l[2k-n] \tag{5}$$

where $Y_h[k]$ and $Y_l[k]$ are the subsampled outputs corresponding to high pass and low pass filter respectively. At every level of decomposition, the filtering and subsampling gives half the number of samples through each successive level.

Wavelet decomposition focuses on the structure of coefficients during main cardiac events. Because of the non-stationary nature of the heart sound and previous results, it is unlikely for a single level decomposition to capture the energy of primary components of heart sound accurately. Sometimes, two detail levels are enough to represent the heart sound. In general, multi-level decomposition is required to represent the various kinds of PCG signals. Choosing the best wavelet for a specific application is an overwhelming task. There are several possibilities, such as orthogonal, biorthogonal and redundant. The search for the best mother wavelet is a non-trivial work. Due to its orthogonality property and its strong resemblance with the main components of the heart sound, the Daubechies wavelet has been chosen.

. The pro of using DWT for segmentation is that, it is a time-frequency analysis. Analyzing the pitch and the timing of the heart sound is crucial in a PCG signal. So, segmentation and extraction in time-frequency domain is significantly advantageous even if murmurs are present, as it provides precise duration of S1 and S2 along with frequency information. We can also use Fast Fourier transform (FFT) for segmentation but, it would provide the information from only the frequency domain and the time domain information would not be present. So, the main drawback of using FFT is that the S1 and S2 frequencies overlap making it difficult to extract important information from the overlapped region.

2. **Variational Mode Decomposition:** It is an algorithmic technique to find and break the signal into principle "modes". The work of this algorithm is to detect the local maxima/minima in the PCG signal, which predicts or estimates the lower or upper envelopes by interpolating the extrema that too recursively, further it removes the mean of the envelopes as "low-pass" middle line, thus isolating the high-frequency frequencies as "modes" of the signal. Sometimes, this shift algorithm decomposes a signal into principal modes, though the resulting decomposition is excessively dependent upon the methods of external points finding, interpolating the external points into high frequency carrier envelopes, also the stopping criteria imposed. Few experiments observation tells that, EMD (Empirical Mode decomposition) shares significant similarities with wavelets and adaptive filter banks. In spite of the limited mathematical understanding and some usual limitations, the EMD method had important influence which is widely used in a comprehensive variety of time-frequency analysis applications, which involves signal decomposition in audio engineering and various flux, respiratory, climate analysis and neuromuscular signal found in medicine and biology.

Variational mode decomposition (VMD) is a newly found adaptive signal decomposition algorithm with a compact hypothetical foundation and decent noise strength in comparison with EMD. Not only this, there is still a problematic algorithm allied with the selection of relevant modes. In EMD description, a mode is defined as a signal whose quantity of local extrema and zero-crossing vary at most by one. The definition is somewhat changed into so-called Intrinsic Mode Function (IMF), grounded on modulation criteria. Intrinsic mode functions are amplitude-modulated –frequency-modulated(AM-FM) signals. The instant significance of the newer IMF definition, instead, is limited to bandwidth, which is crucial assumption that allows mode separation in the proposed variational mode decomposition.

VMD process decomposes the input PCG signal into k number of modes which are dense around the center frequency. The variational problem of input signal u(t) is given as,

$$\min_{(i_N, v_k)} \left\{ \sum_k \left\| \partial_t [(\sigma(t) + \frac{j}{\pi t}) i_k] e^{-jw_k t} \right\|_2^2 \right\} \tag{6}$$

where $\sum_k i_k = u$; i_k (k=1,2,3,......L), and it denotes each decomposed mode and v_k is its center frequency.

Next, to address the reconstruction problem Langrangian multipliers and quadratic term are introduced. Thus, Langrangian arguments Γ is given as follows,

$$\Gamma(i_k, V_k, \lambda) = a \sum_k \left\| \partial_t [(\sigma(t) + \frac{j}{\pi t}) i_k] e^{-jw_k t} \right\|_2^2 + \left\| u - \sum i_k \right\|_2^2 + (\lambda_1 u - \sum i_k) \tag{7}$$

where λ is dual ascent, σ is Dirac distribution and α is Lagrange multiplier.

In the next step i_k^j is update to i_k^{j+1} where j is number of iteration and V_n^j is updated to V_n^{j+1} .

Further, with the help of Parseval Fourier isometry and Hermitian symmetry, the equation is solved in the frequency domain. The resulting equation of i_k and V_k can be expressed as,

$$i_n^{j+1} = (u^\wedge - \sum_{i \neq n} i_i^\wedge + \frac{\lambda^\wedge}{2}) \frac{1}{1 + 2\alpha(V - V_i)^2} \tag{8}$$

The symbol ^ specifies frequency domain variables.and,

$$V_n^{j+1} = \frac{\int_0^\infty V |i_n(V)|^2 \, dv}{\int_0^\infty |i_n(V)|^2 \, dv} \tag{9}$$

Hence, this shows that the input signal is decomposed in the form of i_k around their center frequency V_k .

PREPROCESSING AND SEGMENTATION

As we have discussed about the various sounds originating from the heart, we have seen that S1 and S2 are the primary sounds. We will be concentrating on them, as they are generated periodically at every heartbeat. We have also seen that the heart sounds are mono-dimensional, like audio signal, and hence, some techniques used in processing mono-dimensional signals can be applied up to some extent. So, to differentiate between various noises generated from the heart, segmentation of the heart sound is required. While segmenting the PCG signal, we will also aim at noise reduction. Before segmenting, the signal is made ready for segmentation by down sampling, normalization, whichever is required. The process taken up before segmentation is called pre-processing. The heart sound signals are prone to be polluted by the high-frequency impulsive noise. Therefore, pre-processing is performed before further analysis of the signal. Normalization is done by finding out the maximum absolute value of the signal and then dividing the whole signal by that maximum value. A brief discussion on the segmentation process using wavelet decomposition method and the VMD algorithm as discussed in the above topic will be done here.

1. **Wavelet Decomposition Method:** The basic introduction to wavelet transform that is used is discussed in the above topic. In this section, we will discuss its use in the preprocessing algorithm. The steps taken up for wavelet decomposition method is shown in Figure 4.

From the block diagram, we see our aim is to find our desired peaks, i.e. the S1 and S2 peaks for a given PCG input. The input PCG signal, say S(n), contains the primary heart sounds, F(n), and other heart sounds, O(n), and O(n) contains different heart murmurs C(n), and other noise components, N(n). So,

$$S(n) = F(n) + O(n) \tag{10}$$

where,

$$O(n) = C(n) + N(n) \tag{11}$$

The first step consists in isolating F(n) by running the signal through an adaptive sublevel tracking module. This module is based on a re-iterative process involving wavelet filtering. The 4th order Daubechies

Figure 4. General block diagram representing peak detection using wavelet decomposition

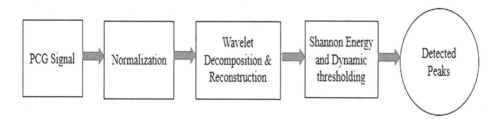

wavelet (db4) is used with 7 levels of decomposition. The approximation and detail coefficients are passed through an adaptive threshold. The threshold in the j-level during the kth iteration is defined as

$$Th_{j,k} = \left| Mean_{j,k} \right| + f_{j,k}.Std_{j,k} \qquad (12)$$

where $Mean_{j,k}$ is the mean value of the coefficients, $f_{j,k}$ is an adjustment factor which is varied between 2 and 3, and $Std_{j,k}$ is the standard deviation of the coefficients for a given level and iteration.

The larger signals (coefficients $> Th_{j,k}$) are kept as part of the signal of interest, and the lower signals (coefficients $< Th_{j,k}$) are passed through the wavelet transform again. The minimum likelihood method is used to adjust the stopping criterion, S_p and is given by,

$$S_p = \left| \frac{E(O_k^2) - E(O_{k-1}^2)}{E(O_k^2)} \right| \qquad (13)$$

where $E(O_k^2)$ is the expected value of square other signal set $O(n)$ at iteration k and $E(O_{k-1}^2)$ denotes the expected value at iteration *k-1*.

To extract the envelope of the signal, the Shannon energy is calculated as given below,

$$E_s = \frac{-1}{N} \sum_{i=1}^{N} H_{norm}^2(i).\log H_{norm}^2(i) \qquad (14)$$

Once the Shannon energy is found, dynamic thresholding is carried out by choosing a threshold value of 75% of maximum valued peak. The peaks which are low in amplitude might be noise or murmurs. So, by neglecting those peaks. The dynamic thresholding is done in order to neglect those peaks. The threshold was taken as 0.75 of the maximum amplitude of the signal in order to neglect the noise and murmurs.

2. **Variational Mode Decomposition Method:** We will now discuss the method performed using VMD. The pre-processed PCG signal is decomposed into 7 modes using VMD. Each of the obtained 7 modes, were analyzed for the input PCG signals. It was observed that the 7th mode exhibited the minimum error among all the 7 modes. The absolute value of the selected 7th mode was normalized and then passed through a tenth order Butterworth low pass filter with cut off frequency 200 Hz. The first heart sounds (*S*1) of the cardiac cycles have frequency less than 200 Hz. The signal obtained is considered for the further analysis. The Shannon's Energy of the processed 7th mode, $\mu7$ of the decomposed signal is calculated because of the advantage of this technique. The step by step process using VMD is shown below,

A dynamic threshold is applied on the obtained Shannon Energy plot in order to find the location of the first heart sound, *S*1. The value of the dynamic threshold is set based on the fact that the processed signal has higher energy at *S*1 locations as compared to the *S*2 locations and other components like mur-

Figure 5. (a) and (b) shows the plot of the Shannon energy before and after dynamic thresholding, and (c) shows the final peaks as detected through wavelet decomposition

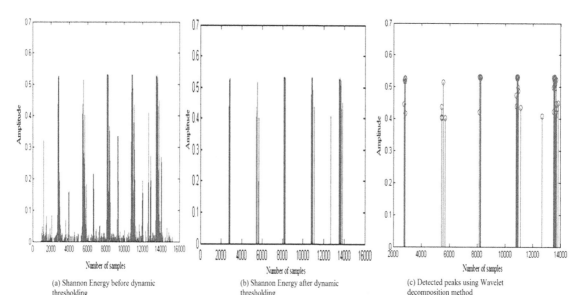

(a) Shannon Energy before dynamic thresholding

(b) Shannon Energy after dynamic thresholding

(c) Detected peaks using Wavelet decomposition method

Figure 6. Block Diagram showing the process applied using VMD

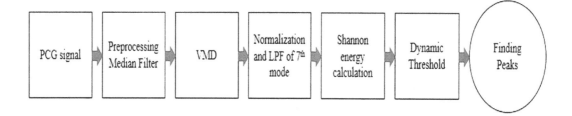

murs. The peaks which are low in amplitude might be noise or murmurs. So, we don't need those peaks. The dynamic thresholding is done in order to neglect those peaks. The threshold is set, approximated about 0.75 of the maximum amplitude of the signal in order to neglect the noise and murmurs. After estimating the peaks, they can be further classified into S1s and S2s using segmentation algorithm. The resultant plots using VMD algorithm is as shown in Figure 7.

Now, that the peaks are detected, an understanding if a peak belongs to S1 or S2 is required. The author in (Banerjee, Mishra & Mukherjee, 2016), followed some steps to neglect inaccurate peaks and detect both S1 and S2. First, they estimated the time duration between two S1 sounds to be about 300ms, and they neglected the peaks between 300ms except for the highest peaks. If two highest peaks are encountered between a short duration, say about 50ms, they are compared and the one having lower amplitude is discarded. This process is followed to get the S1 peaks. For S2 peaks, the locations of a prominent peak between two consecutive S1 peaks are taken into consideration. Also, the information that, the time period between S1 and S2 (systolic) is smaller than the time period between S2 and S1 (diastolic) is considered in determining S2. The S1 and S2 peaks are then given in for further process

Figure 7. Plots (a) and (b) shows the before and after dynamic thresholding and plot (c) shows the peaks as detected via VMD algorithm

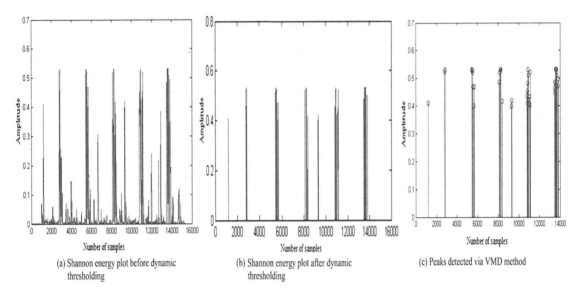

(a) Shannon energy plot before dynamic thresholding

(b) Shannon energy plot after dynamic thresholding

(c) Peaks detected via VMD method

like feature extraction. In the next section, we will discuss various feature extraction processes as used by various authors.

FREQUENCY DOMAIN ANALYSIS

Here we will discuss about various feature extraction models as used by various authors. We have seen how the signals are being segmented. Here we will also see the transformation of the signal from time domain to frequency domain. The limitation with time domain analysis is that various other noises generated by other organs overlaps the heart sound, hence we will undergo our process with frequency analysis. This will also lead to feature extraction of the PCG signal. Feature extraction is required to transform the recorded PCG signal into features that contains each unique information of an individual. These extracted features should be able to help in a simple comparison phase. Analysis of S1 and S2 frequency spectrum of the same person during an interval showed that it produced similar spectrum within the interval, and different for different individual. Some transformations are briefly discussed below.

1. **Chirp Z-Transform:** The benefit of using CZT is that, it can analyze narrow frequency bands under high resolution. CZT is basically the algorithm of fast Fourier transform(FFT) that computes the discrete Fourier transform (DFT) of arbitrary sizes and re-stating the DFT as a convolution.

    The authors in (Beritelli, & Serrano, 2007), performed the feature extraction using Chirp z-transform (CZT). They analyzed the duration of S1 and S2, and then the extracted signals were then maintained at a small frame or window within the durations of S1 and S2, and unwanted samples were set to zero. The time domain peaks as detected were transformed to frequency domain beforehand. The resultant values are then multiplied with Hamming window of similar length. Energy samples of S1 and S2 was observed to be concentrated about 200Hz. CZT values were calculated keeping the frequencies between 20Hz-100Hz and the values obtained is normalized, hence the energy level was attained as the values of each samples is transformed into db. The normalization was done with respect to the square modulus of the values in each frame.

As the energy spectra is unique for each user, recordings from different individual would have different trends. Keeping this in mind, the probability of differentiating a person using S1 and S2 is checked using mean signal energy spectra. The analysis results in showing us that there is enough difference in the curve between different users in their S1 and S2 energy spectra. These obtained signal is then used as the feature vector for the PCG signal, which will be stored in the database or used for comparison in the matching phase.

2. **Short Time Discrete Fourier Transform:** Short Time Discrete Fourier Transform technique is a modified DFT, where we use a shifting window, ω. For a given digital signal, x[n], the STDFT is given by,

$$STDFT\{x[n]\} = X(m, \omega) \tag{15}$$

$$X(m, \omega) = \sum_{n=-\infty}^{\infty} x[n]\omega[n-m]e^{-i\omega n} \tag{16}$$

where, $\omega(n)$ is the window and m denote the shift. The magnitude is carefully chosen and the spectrum is passed through a band pass filter, as shown in the block diagram (Figure 4). The log of the coefficients is taken and Discrete cosine transform is applied to obtain the cepstral coefficients. The cepstrum coefficient is given by,

$$X_k = \sum_{n=0}^{N-1} \{\cos[\frac{\pi}{n}(n + \frac{1}{2})k]\} \times x_n \tag{17}$$

where X_k is our cepstral coefficient.

The authors in (Phua, Chen, Dat, & Shue, 2008), used STDFT for the feature extraction process, without segmentation on the PCG samples. As the heart sound is considered stationary over a short duration, hence the short time stationary property is specified by,

$$X[n, k] = \sum_{m=0}^{N-1} x * w[m + (n-1)S] \exp(-j\frac{2\pi}{N}km)$$

where, n = frame index; k = frequency index; N = frame length; S = frame shift, and w = window.

The window length is expected to be larger, as the heart sound is more stationary, unlike a normal voice sound that vary after every short interval. Ideal window length is approximated to be about 500ms. The steps followed for the feature extraction are as shown in the block diagram below in Figure 3. The phase components are sensitive to noise and they are not considered, instead only the data from spectral magnitude is considered. It is then followed by the Filter bank. Here the PCG signal is processed by passing through a bandpass filter of 20-150Hz range, as the heart sound spectrum is concentrated at the range. The spectrum is passed through a set of filters with the aim of reducing the noise components in the frequency domain. Now, we come across the Dimensional reduction block. Here, compression of spectral magnitude in logarithmic domain is done here, which is then followed by a discrete cosine transform from where the cepstrum coefficients are obtained.

The cepstral component is given by,

$$c[n,k] = \sum_{m=0}^{K-1} \log(|X[n,m]|) \cos(\frac{km\pi}{K})$$

where, k = 1,2,3,...,K, and K is the no of frequency sets in the selected range of 20-150Hz.

Cepstral features with higher coefficients contains lesser information and hence the first 24 coefficient from each frame is selected, also the higher spectrums are produced as a result of excitation process hence they can be neglected. The extracted features, as used by the authors in (Phua, Chen, Dat, & Shue, 2008), are called Linear frequency bands cepstra (LFBC). The process applied is similar to that of a standard Mel Frequency Cepstral Coefficient (MFCC)-feature extraction.

We then come across the spike removal block, where noises arising due to improper handling of stethoscope are controlled. These noises sometimes appear as an impulse and overlaps with the heart sound. In this block, a certain energy threshold is set for removing any segment with higher energy containing the impulsive noise. It is processed by taking the energy of each segment, E[n]. The impulsive noise is given by,

$$10 \log E[n] - \min_{n}(10 \log E[n]) \geq \mu \tag{20}$$

where, n = segment index; μ = threshold

Lastly, we come across the Mean subtractor block. This block deals with reducing the effect of relative transfer function variations. These variations arise as the positioning of a stethoscope varies every time we take in a recording. Using different types of stethoscope also results in transfer function variation and is characterized by the circulation of PCG signal to the recorder. To overcome this variation, cepstral mean subtraction is applied.

Here

$$\log(|X[n,k]|) = \log(|Y[n,k]|) + \log(|Z[k]|) \tag{21}$$

Figure 8. Block diagram showing the steps followed in feature extraction using STDFT

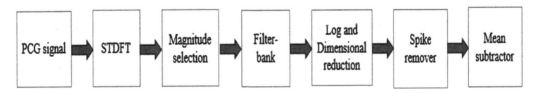

where, X[n,k] is the total transfer function of the process. Y[n,k] is the signal measured in a fixed position (or) the process transfer function and Z[k] is the relative transfer function in frequency domain (or) the average transfer function. Their product is equivalent to the superposition in logarithm domain as shown in Equation (21).

The cepstra of the recorded signal, $c_X[n,k] = c_Y[n,k] + c_Z[n,k]$ (22)

For removing the effects of the channel in the signal, we compute a mean over a range of data and subtract it with the mean of the data. Theoretically, this is supposed to remove the effect of the channel, but practically the effect cannot be completely removed.

The subtraction is as shown below,

$$c_{X,k}\left[n\right] - \left(c_{X,k}\left[n\right]\right) = c_{Y,k}\left[n\right] - \left(c_{Y,k}\left[n\right]\right)$$ (23)

where, $c_{X,k}\left[n\right]$ is the mean over a range and $\left(c_{X,k}\left[n\right]\right)$ is the mean of the *n* no. of data.

3. **Cepstral Analysis With Mel Frequency Cepstral Coefficient (MFCC):** Another method used for feature extraction is Mel frequency cepstral coefficient (MFCC). MFCC has been known to be quite effective in speech and voice recognition applications. Since, PCG is an audio (acoustic) in nature, MFCC can be applied. The basic principle behind MFCC feature extraction is the use of non-linearly space triangular bandpass filter. The block diagram of feature extraction for MFCC is shown in Figure 9.

The relation between Mel-frequency, f_M and linear frequency, f_L is as follows,

$$f_M = 2595\left\{log\left[\frac{1+f_L}{700}\right]\right\}$$ (24)

The coefficients are obtained by computing the magnitude spectrum of the signal, and feeding it to the filter-bank.

The ith coefficient is obtained as shown,

Figure 9. Extraction of MFCC features

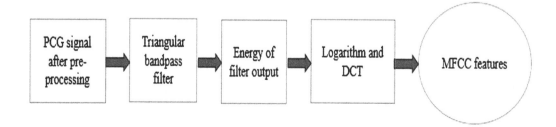

$$MFCC_i = \sum_{k=1}^{K} X_k cos[i(k - \frac{1}{2})\frac{\pi}{K}] i = 0, 1, .., M \qquad (25)$$

X_k = log energy output of the kth filter and M is the number of coefficients that are obtained. The output of this frequency analysis is obtained in matrix form.

4. **First-to-Second (FSR):** In addition to the feature extraction processes in frequency domain, another effective method called First to Second ratio (FSR), is implemented to understand if two PCG signals belongs to one individual in a more efficient way. FSR is a time domain sequence-wise feature. It is calculated as the power ratio of S1 to S2.

So, for N number of S1-S2 cardiac cycles in a PCG sequence, let $\overline{P(S1)}$ represent the average power of all the S1 sound in the acquired sequence, and $\overline{P(S2)}$ for S2. Therefore, they can be written as,

$$\overline{P(S1)} = \frac{1}{N}\sum_{i=1}^{N} P(S1)_i \qquad (26)$$

$$\overline{P(S2)} = \frac{1}{N}\sum_{i=1}^{N} P(S2)_i \qquad (27)$$

where $P(S1)_i$ and $P(S2)_i$ denotes the power of the ith S1 and S2 sound respectively, in the sequence. Hence the FSR can be written as,

$$FSR = \frac{\overline{P(S1)}}{\overline{P(S2)}} \qquad (28)$$

Now, for two PCG sequence h1 and h2, the FSR distance is given by,

$$d_{FSR}(h1, h2) = \left| FSR_{db}(h1) - FSR_{db}(h2) \right| \qquad (29)$$

The d_{FSR} metric helps in improving the rejection of false accepts. They can also be used to find an amplifying factor used in matching phase, as shown.

$$k_{FSR} = max\ \{1,\ (\frac{d_{FSRn}}{t_{FSR}})\} \qquad (30)$$

where, k_{FSR} = the amplifying factor used in matching phase. d_{FSRn} = the normalized d_{FSR} value and t_{FSR} = the threshold that gives minimum Equal Error Rate(ERR).

And so, if $d_{FSRn} < t_{FSR}$, k_{FSR} will have no effect and vice-versa.

Comparison between Chirp-z transform, MFCC, and MFCC with FSR feature extraction based on FRR (False Rejection Rate) against FAR (False Acceptance Rate) showed that MFCC with FSR gave minimum ERR while the maximum ERR was generated by the chirp-z transform.

5. **Modified- Mel Frequency Cepstral Coefficient (MFCC):** In Modified-MFCC, the filter-bank used is modified while the remaining blocks used in a standard MFCC feature extraction is the same. The block diagram is shown in the figure below.

The limitation faced with MFCC is that, the non-linearity increases with increasing mel-frequency, like 1000Hz. Hence, they are more appropriate with speech signal as they have larger frequency range (20 to 800Hz) than a PCG signal (250Hz). At lower frequency range, the MFCC is considered linear. In Equation (24), the 700 in the denominator defines the linearity of the mel-frequency scale. So, the modification in the relation is as follows.

$$f_M = 2595\{log[\frac{1+f_L}{\alpha}]\} \tag{31}$$

As α decreases below 700, the non-linearity increases in the triangular filter.

The feature extraction can be performed using any of the algorithms above. These extracted features are stored in a database during the enrollment phase and used as a comparison piece for the authentication phase.

MATCHING PHASE

We have seen how a PCG signal is recorded and preprocessed for enrollment phase as well as for authentication phase. We have also seen various other ways of feature extraction processes. The final step in a biometric system comes the matching and classification phase, where we compare an input PCG signal with the previously stored feature information in the data base, in order to identify if the previously stored

Figure 10. Block diagram of Modified-MFCC feature extraction

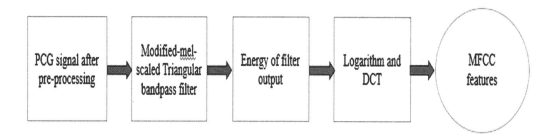

data matches with the given input signal and authenticate the user. This phase depends mostly upon how the segmentation of S1 and S2 is done and also upon the extracted features of the PCG signal. Various algorithms have been introduced to meet the need of the system for faster authentication with accurate authentication. We shall look into and discuss some classification algorithms like Euclidean distance, Gaussian Mixture Models (GMM), Vector Quantization (VQ), GMM/UBM method, as to how they are implemented for a basic PCG biometrics.

1. **Euclidean Distance:** In this algorithm, comparison is done by measuring the distance between the feature set in the template and the feature set of unknown input signal. The authors in (Beritelli, & Serrano, 2007), used the Euclidean distance for matching algorithm. The inter-person and the intra-person distances is computed. Inter-person distance is the distance measured between the features of two different individuals and the intra-person distance is the distance measured between the features of the same individual. The intra-person distance is anticipated to be of lower value than the inter-person distance. We shall denote the Euclidean distance used to measure between two vectors as d_2.

The distances between two input digital heart sound, X and Y, is obtained as follows.

$$d_{S1}(X,Y) = \frac{1}{N^2} \sum_{i,j=1}^{N} d_2\{X_{S1}(i), Y_{S1}(j)\} \tag{32}$$

$$d_{S2}(X,Y) = \frac{1}{N^2} \sum_{i,j=1}^{N} d_2\{X_{S2}(i), Y_{S2}(j)\} \tag{33}$$

where, $d_{S1}(X,Y)$ gives the distance between the S1 of both X and Y. Similarly, $d_{S2}(X,Y)$ gives for S2. So, we are computing the average distance between X and Y for both S1 and S2 in both Equations (32) and (33). $X_{S1}(i)$ and $X_{S2}(i)$ denotes the ith-feature vectors of X heart sound. Similarly, $Y_{S1}(i)$ and $Y_{S2}(i)$ gives the ith-feature vector of the Y heart sound.

Finally, the Euclidean distance between X and Y heart sounds is computed by,

$$d(X,Y) = k_{FSR}\sqrt{(d_{S1}(X,Y)^2 + d_{S2}(X,Y)^2)} \tag{34}$$

Here, k_{FSR} is the amplifying factor defined in the above sub-topics and given in equation (1.30). Minimum ERR as obtained by the MFCC with FSR feature extraction is due to the use of the d_{FSR} and the amplifying factor k_{FSR}. This amplifying factor increases the inter-person distance while the intra-person distance remains unchanged, thereby making the biometric system to improve its performance in correct authentication

2. **Vector Quantization (VQ):** Vector Quantization is effectively used in speech recognition systems. Here, we shall employ a set of algorithms to compare and identify the feature set. The basic prin-

ciple used here is that, we will compute a codebook and partition which will give a minimum average distortion from a given vector source whose statistical properties are known with N number of code vectors and a distortion measure. Here, the large set of cepstral vector is compressed into a smaller set of vector codes. To sum it up, for a given training sequence, τ and N number of code vectors, we find partition of space, P and codebooks, C in such a way that, the average distortion, is minimum.

Supposing a training sequence, τ with M number of vector source having dimension k,

$$\tau = \{x_1, x_2, ..., x_M\} \tag{35}$$

Now, for N number of code vectors, let

$$C = \{c_1, c_2, ..., c_N\} \tag{36}$$

where C represent the codebooks with c_n being the code vector, and the encoding region for each code vector c_n, is given by S_n, and the partition of space, P is given by,

$$P = \{S_1, S_2, ..., S_N\} \tag{37}$$

Now, if a vector source x_m is in the encoding region S_n, then its approximation is c_n.

$$Q(x_m) = c_n; \text{ if } x_m \in S_n \tag{38}$$

where, $Q(x_m)$ is the approximation.

Now, the average distortion,

$$D_{avg} = \frac{1}{Mk} \sum_{m=1}^{M} \left\| x_m - Q(x_m) \right\|^2 \tag{39}$$

Since we are taking approximation, of replacing each feature vector with the nearest code vector, quantization error occurs. To measure the error, the Euclidean distance is used. The authors in (Phua, Chen, Dat, & Shue, 2008), trained the VQ codebook with LBG-algorithm repeatedly to reduce this quantization error. At each repetition, each vector is divided into two new vectors. LBG (Linde-Buzo-Gray) is a VQ algorithm to compute a codebook.

3. **Gaussian Mixture Model (GMM):** Another classification method based on approximation is the Gaussian Mixture Model (GMM). GMM is also an efficient method used in speech recognition algorithms and

The pattern matching using GMM is based on probabilities like conditional probability or the likelihood in the observation for a given model.

The probability of taking a feature vector x from a GMM λ is defined by,

$$p\left(\frac{x}{\lambda}\right) = \sum_{i=1}^{M} w_i . p_i(x) \tag{40}$$

where, x is a D-dimensional random feature vector and M is the number of Gaussian probability density components. w_i is the weight of the ith-component and $p_i(x)$ is the probability density function of the ith-component.

This probability density function $p_i(x)$ is defined by,

$$p_i(x) = \frac{1}{(2\pi)^{D/2} |\Sigma_i|^{1/2}} e^{-\frac{1}{2}(x-\mu_i)^T \Sigma_i (x-\mu_i)}_i; \tag{41}$$

here, μ_i represents the mean vector and Σ_i represents the covariance matrix.

The weight, w_i in equation (1.40) satisfies the limit as, $\sum_{i=1}^{M} w_i = 1$.

Therefore, the Gaussian mixture model, λ is defined by the mean vector, the weights of the mixture and the covariance matrix, and is given by,

$$\lambda = \{w_i, \mu_i, \Sigma_i\}; \text{ for } i=1,2,3,.....,M \tag{42}$$

Assessment of the above parameters is processed using the Expectation-Maximization algorithm. The authors of (Phua, Chen, Dat, & Shue, 2008), implemented GMM by representing each of the input heart sound by a GMM, λ_i. Now each λ_i for each person is trained and tested by referring each signal with each model, λ_i to give the maximum likelihood.

A comparison between VQ and GMM showed that, GMM algorithm gave better accuracy rate with computational cost efficient. GMM works more efficiently when processed with smaller number of components and the performance degrades as the number of components increased, while the VQ algorithm requires large number of components to process as the approximation in the VQ algorithm needs more data points.

Another approach using the GMM was implemented by the authors in (Beritelli & Spadaccini, 2010a). Here, the identification of a given heart sound, s belonging to an individual, I is implemented based on two hypotheses, i.e. H_0, that is a heart sound s belongs to an individual I and H_1, that is a heart sound s does not belong to I.

The conclusion whether the output is an H_0 or H_1 is done using the likelihood computation. We will also make use of a decision threshold, θ in computing the biometric output.

So,

$$S(s,I) = \frac{p(s|H_0)}{p(s|H_1)} \tag{43}$$

Now, if $S(s,I) \geq \theta$, then H_0 is obtained.

And if $S(s,I) < \theta$, then H_1 is obtained.

The probability, $p(s|H_0)$ is obtained using the GMM λ_I, as $(s|\lambda_I)$.

Now,

$$p(s|H_0) = p(s|\lambda_I) = \prod_{j=1}^{K} p(x_j|\lambda_I) \tag{44}$$

Here, the input heart sound s is converted into a set feature vectors x_j, i.e. $s = \{x_1, x_2, \ldots x_K\}$ as $j=1,2,\ldots,K$ with each having D-dimension.

Similarly, $p(s|H_1)$ is computed using background-model λ_W, i.e. a model for all the heart sound of all its expected user.

Hence,

$$p(s|H_1) = p(s|\lambda_W) \tag{45}$$

This model is known as Universal Background Model (UBM). Simply put, the $p(s|H_0)$ is obtained using GMM and $p(s|H_1)$ is obtained using UBM, and hence better known as the GMM/UBM method, (Beritelli & Spadaccini, 2011). In logarithm domain, the final likelihood ratio is expressed as,

$$\wedge(s) = \log S(s,I) = \log p(s|\lambda_I) - \log p(s|\lambda_W) \tag{46}$$

After the matching phase, the Biometric system will provide its result based on its authentication mode used, as discussed above.

CONCLUSION

The importance of biometrics in general and PCG biometric in particular has been discussed here. How they are useful for securing one's identity starting with the basic steps followed in a simple biometric system, like the enrollment phase, authentication phase, along with the identification and verification modes were highlighted. Various short comings of other biometric systems and their vulnerability are also discussed. The various pre-processing steps and feature extraction methods for a PCG signals as implemented by various researchers were referred. The outlines of Wavelet decomposition method and VMD for preprocessing steps have been discussed. Some frequency domain analysis ways and how the features are extracted have been focused upon. Major feature extraction processes like CZT, STDFT, MFCC and FSR were introduced in brief. Going through the cited work it was found that the MFCC+FSR method in feature extraction gave the best features. In future, in order to improve the security level of a biometric system we can combine two biometric system, which in our case can be both ECG and PCG. Finally, we have concluded with various matching phase algorithms that is implemented like Euclidean distance, VQ, GMM, GMM/UBM.

REFERENCES

Abbas, Abo-Zahhad, Ahmed, & Farrag. (2015). *Heart-ID: human identity recognition using heart sounds based on modifying mel-frequency cepstral features*. Academic Press. 10.1049/iet-bmt.2015.0033

Banerjee, S., Mishra, M., & Mukherjee, A. (2016). Segmentation and detection of first and second heart sounds (S1 and S2) using variational mode decomposition. *IEEE EMBS conference on biomedical engineering and science (IECBES)*, 565-570.

Beritelli, F., & Serrano, S. (2007). Biometric Identification based on Frequency Analysis of Cardiac Sounds. *IEEE Transactions on Information Forensics and Security, 2*(3), 596–604. doi:10.1109/TIFS.2007.902922

Beritelli, F., & Spadaccini, A. (2009a). Heart sounds quality analysis for automatic cardiac biometry applications. *Proceedings of the 1st IEEE International Workshop on Information Forensics and Security*. 10.1109/WIFS.2009.5386481

Beritelli, F., & Spadaccini, A. (2009b). Human Identity Verification based on Mel Frequency Analysis of Digital Heart Sounds. *Proceedings of the 16th International Conference on Digital Signal Processing*. 10.1109/ICDSP.2009.5201109

Beritelli, F., & Spadaccini, A. (2010a). An improved biometric identification system based on heart sounds and gaussian mixture models. *Proceedings of the 2010 IEEE Workshop on Biometric Measurements and Systems for Security and Medical Applications*, 31–35 10.1109/BIOMS.2010.5610442

Beritelli, F., & Spadaccini, A. (2010b). A statistical approach to biometric identity verification based on heart sounds. *Proceedings of the Fourth International Conference on Emerging Security Information, Systems and Technologies (SECURWARE2010)*, 93–96. 10.1109/SECURWARE.2010.23

Beritelli, F., & Spadaccini, A. (2011). *Human Identity Verification based on Heart Sounds: Recent Advances and Future Directions*. Academic Press.

Dragomiretskiy, K., & Zosso, D. (2014). Variational Mode Decomposition. IEEE Trans. On Signal Processing, 62(3), 531-544.

Fatemian, S. Z., & Hatzinakos, D. (n.d.). *A Wavelet-Based Approach to Electrocardiogram (ECG) and Phonocardiogram (PCG)* (Ph.D. dissertation). University.

Galbally, J., & Satta, R. (2015). *Three-dimensional and two-and-a-half-dimensional face recognition spoofing using three-dimensional printed models*. IET Biometrics.

Gautam, G., & Kumar, D. (2013). Biometric system for heart sound using wavelet based feature set. *International conference on communication & signal processing (ICCSP)*, 551-555. 10.1109/iccsp.2013.6577115

Jain, A. K., Ross, A. A., & Prabhakar, S. (2004). An introduction to biometric recognition. *IEEE Transactions on Circuits and Systems for Video Technology, 14*(2), 4–20. doi:10.1109/TCSVT.2003.818349

Kouras, N., Boutana, D., & Bendir, M. (2012). Wavelet based segmentation and time-frequency characterization of some abnormal heart sound signals. *24*[th] *International conference on microelectronics (ICM)*, 1-4.

Kumar, D., Carvalho, P., Antunes, M., Henriqus, J., Maldonado, M., Schmidt, R., & Habetha, J. (2006). Wavelet transform and simplicity based on heart murmurs and segmentation. *Computers in Cardiology, 33*, 173–176.

Lima, C. S., & Cardoso, M. J. (2007). *Phonocardiogram segmentation by using Hidden Markov Models.* The 5th IASTED International conference in Biomedical Engineering, BioMED, Austria.

Maji, U., & Pal, S. (2016). Emperical mode decomposiiton vs varaiational mode decomposition on ECG signal processin: A comparative study. *International conference on advance in computing, communications and informatics (ICACCI)*, 1129-1134.

Majumder, S., Pal, S., & Dutta, P. K. (2009). A comparative study for disease identification from heart auscultation using FFT, cepstrum and DCT correlation coefficients. In *13*[th] *International conference on biomedical engineering IFMBE proceedings* (vol. 23). Springer. 10.1007/978-3-540-92841-6_185

Matsumoto, T., Matsumoto, H., Yamada, K., & Hoshino, S. (2002). Impact of artificial gummy fingers on fingerprint systems. *Proceedings of the Society for Photo-Instrumentation Engineers, 4677*, 275–289. doi:10.1117/12.462719

Obaidat, M. S. (1993). Phonocardiogram signal Analysis: Technique and performance comparison. *Journal of Medical Engineering & Technology, 17*(6), 221–227. doi:10.3109/03091909309006329 PMID:8169938

Phua, K., Chen, J., Dat, T. H., & Shue, L. (2008). Heart sound as a biometric. *Pattern Recognition, 41*(3), 906–919. doi:10.1016/j.patcog.2007.07.018

PHYSIONET Homepage. (n.d.). Retrieved from https://physionet.org/physiobank/database/challenge/2016/training.zip

Seshadri, N. P. G., Geethanjali, B., & Kumar, S. P. (2016). Analysis of heart sounds using time-frequency visual representations. *International Journal of Biomedical Engineering and Technology, 21*(3), 205–228. doi:10.1504/IJBET.2016.078283

Sun, H., Chen, W., & Gong, J. (2013). An improved empirical mode decomposition-wavelet algorithm for phonocardiogram signal denoising and its application in the first and second heart sound extraction. *6th International conference on Biomedical Engineering and informatics*, 187-191. 10.1109/BMEI.2013.6746931

Wang, P., Kim, Y., Ling, L. H., & Soh, C. B. (2005). First heart sound detection for phonocardiogram segmentation. *IEEE Engineering in medical and biology 27*[th] *annual conference*, 5519-5522. 10.1109/IEMBS.2005.1615733

Wang, P., Kim, Y., & Soh, C. B. (2005). Feature extraction based on mel-scaled wavelet transform for heart sound analysis. *IEEE Engineering in medicine and biology 27*[th] *annual conference*, 7572-7575. 10.1109/IEMBS.2005.1616264

KEY TERMS AND DEFINITIONS

Chirp Z-Transform: An algorithm for the assessment of z-transform that was developed to overcome the restrictions of Fast Fourier transform evaluating z-transform in a limited contour.

First-to-Second Ratio (FSR): In the study for phonocardiogram signals, it can be explained as the ratio between the average power of the first heart sound and the second heart sound.

Gaussian Mixture Model: It can be looked at as a probabilistic model to label unknown parameters that have similar sets of data within an overall data sets.

Mel Frequency Cepstrum Coefficient: Mel frequency cepstrum coefficient can be defined as the overall coefficients together that makes up an mel frequency cepstrum. The frequency bands in mel frequency cepstrum is similarly set apart on a mel scale.

Short Time Discrete Fourier Transform: A modified discrete Fourier transform, where the signal is analyzed only for a short content of the overall frequency and phase, as the signal is never constant with time, practically.

Variational Mode Decomposition: An algorithm developed to detect the maxima or minima for a signal after breaking up the signal into principle modes.

Vector Quantization: A quantization model that separates a large set of data into smaller sets having similar or approximated data closest to each set.

Wavelet Transform: A transform that characterizes various functions in wavelet. It has a better advantage over Fourier transform as it deconstructs or constructs signal accurately.

Chapter 2
Biosignal Denoising Techniques

Suchetha M.
VIT University, India

Jagannath M.
VIT University, India

ABSTRACT

The main aim of ECG signal enhancement is to separate the required signal components from the unwanted artifacts. Adaptive filter-based ECG enhancement helps in detecting time varying potentials and also helps to track the dynamic variations of the signals. LMS-based adaptive recurrent filter is used to obtain the impulse response of normal QRS complexes. It is also used for arrhythmia detection in ambulatory ECG recordings. Adaptive filters self-modify its frequency response to change the behavior in time. This property of adaptive filter allows it to adapt its response to change in the input signal characteristics. A major problem in adaptive filtering is the computational complexity of adaptive algorithm when the unknown system has a long impulse response and therefore requires a large number of taps. The wavelet transform is a time-scale representation method with a basis function called mother wavelet. In wavelet transform, the input signal is subsequently decomposed into subbands. Wavelet transform thresholding in the subband gives better performance of denoising.

1. INTRODUCTION TO SIGNAL DENOISING TECHNIQUES

Denoising of biological signal is very seminal to recognize the signal features underlying in noise. Researchers strive to develop an optimum model to eliminate noises of any origin. A corrupted signal containing noise can be estimated by designing a filter that reduces the noise while leaving signals relatively unaffected. Recent techniques are developed for denoising the noisy signals with 50Hz, such filters are introduced by Suchetha (2017). The filter designing in the domain of optimal filtering is pioneered by Wiener (1949) and further modified by Kalman (1960) and Bucy (1961). Better understanding of signal and noise components is required for designing the filters, but adaptive filters can automatically adjust its parameters and no prior knowledge of signal or noise description is needed. Widrow (1975) at Stanford University developed an adaptive noise-cancelling system. Its purpose is to cancel power line frequency interference at ECG amplifier output and recorder output. (Widrow & Stearns 1998).

DOI: 10.4018/978-1-5225-5152-2.ch002

Copyright © 2018, IGI Global. Copying or distributing in print or electronic forms without written permission of IGI Global is prohibited.

Traditional adaptive filtering is usually performed in the time domain. Transforms have an important potential for signal processing problems since they can provide a different representation of signals. The Discrete Fourier Transform (DFT) is often used when frequency domain adaptive filtering is applied. However, the DFT is suitable only for stationary signals, for which statistical properties of signals are invariant to a shift of time. Later wavelet transform (WT) has been developed which can be utilised for non-stationary signals analysis. Wavelets come with fast computational algorithms and provide a flexible prototyping environment (Deubechies, 1990; Frazier, 1999). The WT allows extracting features that vary in time, which makes it a useful tool for analysing the signals with transient characteristics. Wavelet shrinkage concepts developed by Donoho and Johnstone (1995) and Bruce and Gao (1996) are the some of the ideas in the field of denoising. Shrinkage analysis analyses the coefficients of empirical wavelet with a threshold and if its magnitude is less than threshold value, then this value is set to zero.

Hard and soft shrinkage functions were developed by Donoho and Johnstone (1995). In case of soft shrinkage case, significant empirical wavelet coefficient values are set as zero (kill) if values lie between $-\lambda$ to $+\lambda$ threshold ranges and will shrink the remaining coefficient values to zero. In hard shrinkage case, wavelet coefficients of insignificant empirical are destroyed if the values lies between $-\lambda$ to $+\lambda$ and remaining coefficient values are used for signal representation. A function for subband adaptive shrinkage was developed for ECG de-noising later. Incorporation of the shrinkage function is done by selecting the proper subband level at vicinity of the power line frequency. The concept of wavelet thresholding depends on the belief that in a wavelet representation, magnitudes of signal will dominate noise, so the wavelet coefficient values can be set as zero in case if magnitudes are fewer compared to threshold value. Another drawback of this method is that this does not naturally match all original signals as the basis functions are fixed.

Another problem with biological signals is the degrading of signal by power line frequency interference (PLFI). The method removes in interference with the help of a notch filter which is tuned to interference frequency. This method has certain drawbacks. For example, when there is a reduction in output noise power, this filter will remove 50 Hz signal components. Also it has a minute roll off which will attenuate remaining bands of frequency. The major problem with finite impulse response notch filter is its large bandwidth, so infinite impulse response (IIR) notch filter is preferred in spite of design complexity. If the notch is required to be very sharp and the interfering sinusoid drifts slowly, it requires an adaptive solution. Simple bandwidth controlling, infinite null, adaptively tracking exact frequency and phase of interference are the major advantages of adaptive notch filter (ANF). An alternate solution was proposed by Widrow et al (1975) that consist of a 90^0 phase shifter and an adaptive filter.

An alternative solution to the problem can be provided by the orthogonal wavelet decomposition signal processing technique. Xu and Yan (2004) developed a wavelet shrinkage approach. To remove the sinusoidal interference and white noise this detail coefficient thresholding was developed. A notch filter was used by Zhi-Dong Zhao and Yu-Quan Chen (2006) for the removing the ECG signal power line interference. But the notch filter will remove the 50Hz frequency irrespective of signal component or noise component because in ECG signal, the spectrum of noise and the ECG is overlapping.

2. SURVEY OF SIGNAL DENOISING TECHNIQUES

The primary aim of denoising is to extract hidden information from an observed noisy signal (Srinath, Rajasekaran, & Viswanathan, 2003). The problem of estimating an unknown signal embedded in Gaussian noise has been dealt in a number of studies and for such problem least square error criterion is used.

2.1 Filters for Denoising Statistically Stationary Signals

Any prior knowledge about a contaminating noise should be used in estimating the hidden signal. When ECG signal represented as x(t) is monitored in a noisy environment where noise is represented as n(t), then the measured signal y(t) can be considered as another random process. In general cases the noise is additive. Obtained signal can be expressed as:

$$y(t) = x(t) + n(t) \tag{2.1}$$

In most practical applications, signal and the noise are uncorrelated. Most types of noises can be eliminated directly in time-domain. An advantage of this method is that signal and noise do not require spectral characterization and they work faster than filtering in frequency domain. Linear filters fail to denoise because the spectrum of signal and noise gets overlapped, so when noise is removed, signal component will also get removed. Ensemble average technique can differentiate the repeating signal from that of noise without altering the signal (Kalman & Bucy, 1961; Tompkins, 1995). Ensemble averaging technique is useful only in those cases were the signal is either statistically quasi periodic or the signal is cyclo-stationary. Signal copies or multiple realizations are accessible and the noise is stationary random process which has zero mean and are uncorrelated with the signal. Signal to noise ratio of the processed signal increases with increase in the number of repetition N. The major advantage of this technique is that as in case with frequency domain filtering, here the signal spectral content is not lost. This technique fails when only one realization of an event is available.

In case of moving average (MA) filtering, temporal statistics are considered. An easy MA filter design for removing noise using the *Hanning filter* was proposed by Tompkins (1995). In this technique, a temporal window of samples is obtained at various time intervals. The MA is a FIR type filter, which has the merits of non-recursive realization, stable and has linear phase. The MA filter is used as a high-pass filter to recover ECG signal. Canan et al (1997) showed that the filtering system will remove the trend mixed to ECG signal. The MA filter recovers the low varying trend and pure ECG signal is obtained by subtracting the recorded data from the trend. The Wiener filtering is useful (Nikolaev, 2000; Rangayyan, 2003) when:

- Signal is in statistically stationary condition.
- Noise is independent of signal and it is a stationary random process.

For designing a filter, prior knowledge about the signal or noise is necessary. Design of notch filter needs very narrow bandwidth. If the notch is required to be very sharp and the interfering sinusoids drift slowly, it requires an adaptive solution.

2.2 Overview of Adaptive Filters for Signal Denoising

When fixed and separate frequency bands are occupied by both signal and noise, then conventional linear filters having fixed coefficients are used for signal extracting. If the characteristics of the filter are variable and it is adaptive to changing characteristics of signal, the coefficients must vary. If the frequency band is unknown adaptive filter can be used. It is also used:

- When there is variable filter characteristics, and adapted to change in conditions;
- When spectral overlap of signal and noise occurs;
- When there is a variable band occupation by noise and it varies with time or it is unknown.

When both signal and noises are stationary, the adaptive filter act like fixed filter and when there is periodic interference, the adaptive filter acts as a notch or comb. These are applicable only when there is additive noise case. Widrow (1975) developed an adaptive noise-cancelling system. Its purpose is to cancel power line frequency interference occurring at the output of ECG amplifier and the recorder (Widrow & Stearns, 1998). One major widely used algorithm for adaptive filtering is least mean square (LMS) algorithm introduced by Widrow and Hoff (1959). This is simple and provides easy computation and it does not require data repetitions or off-line gradient estimations. LMS algorithm can be used in a practical system without averaging, squaring or differentiation. Moreover it is elegant in its simplicity and efficiency. In LMS based adaptive algorithm weights are calculated iteratively to obtain a minimum mean square error.

The weight vector equation from the method of steepest descent is represented by:

$$w(n+1) = w(n) + \frac{1}{2}\mu\left[-\nabla\left(E\left\{e^2(n)\right\}\right)\right]$$

Here step-size parameter is μ. $e^2(n)$ is the mean square error between y(n) and reference signal and can be expressed as:

$$e^2(n) = \left[d*(n) - w^h x(n)\right]^2$$

The gradient vector can be computed using the equation:

$$\nabla_w\left(E\left\{e^2(n)\right\}\right) = -2r + 2Rw(n)$$

The biggest problem in steepest descent method is the calculations of real-time r and R matrices values. LMS algorithm simplifies problem by using instantaneous values of r and R instead of the actual values.

$$R(n) = x(n)x^h(n)$$

$$r\left(n\right) = d*\left(n\right)x\left(n\right)$$

Weight update equation can therefore be written as:

$$w\left(n+1\right) = w\left(n\right) + \mu x\left(n\right)\left[d*\left(n\right) - x^{h}\left(n\right)w\left(n\right)\right]$$

$$= w\left(n\right) + \mu x\left(n\right)e*\left(n\right)$$

$$weight, w\left(n+1\right) = W\left(n\right) + \mu x\left(n\right)e*\left(n\right)$$

LMS algorithm will converge and stay stable for the condition:

$$0 < \mu < 1/\lambda_{max}$$

Here λ_{max} is the highest Eigen value of R, which will be a correlation matrix. Convergence may be very slow when Eigen values are widespread. Eigen value spread of R matrix is determined by calculating the ratio of the highest Eigen value of the matrix to the smallest eigen value. The algorithm converges very slowly if μ is small. A large μ can give a speedy convergence but the problem is it may be less stable around the least value. Many methods are used to decrease the squared error at every instant or cross correlation of input and the error.

In the field of signal detection, there are two major groups of adaptive filters are used, ANC and ALE. The basic ANC model is illustrated in Figure 1.

Here the signal s(n) is corrupted by v(n), which is the additive noise. The reference signal is taken from a noisy environment where signal is very weak. Output of FIR filter can be written as:

Figure 1. Basic ANC Model

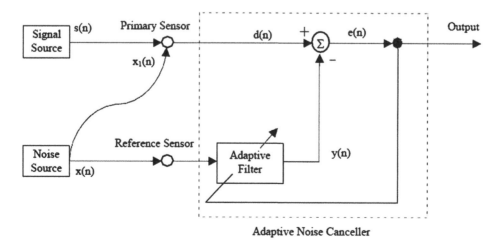

Adaptive Noise Canceller

$$y\left(n\right) = \sum_{m=0}^{N-1} w\left(m\right)x\left(n-m\right)$$

where n represent the number of iterations.

Error can be calculated using the expression:

$$e\left(n\right) = d\left(n\right) - y\left(n\right)$$

Filter weights are modified from e(n) and x(n).

$$w\left(n+1\right) = w\left(n\right) + \mu e\left(n\right)x\left(n\right)$$

where w(n) represents the current weight value vector, w(n+1) the succeeding weight value vector, x(n) the input and e(n) the error vector and μ is the convergence factor.

The adaptive line enhancer (ALE) simply predicts a signal thus it finds a signal hidden in noise. It relies on canceling the noise by extracting the noise obtained signal. This is controlled in an adaptive manner in order to get improved SNR. The ALE is a form of ANC without using reference. The input of the system is the wave with some noise in the background. When a delayed version of that wave is passed through the adaptive filter and by comparing it to the original wave, the output of the filter is going to be the wave and the output of the system will be the background noise. Figure 2 shows the basic model of adaptive noise enhancer and the blocks involved with x(n) as input.

Modern filtering techniques like Independent Component Analysis (ICA), Principal Component Analysis (PCA), and wavelet transform are other solutions. PCA is a variable reduction procedure. A PCA analysis proceeds in this fashion, with each new component computing for getting smaller and smaller amounts of variances. The resulting component after the analysis completion will display the varying degrees of relation with the observed variables. But these are completely uncorrelated with each other. ICA is a source separation method and it is based on probability theory. This is a computational and statistical technique for finding the hidden factors which underlie sets of random variables or signals.

Figure 2. Basic adaptive noise enhancer model

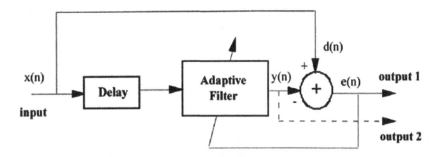

2.3 Transform Domain Filtering for Signal Denoising

Transforms have an important potential for signal processing problems since they can provide a different representation of signals, which are more suitable for processing. Frequency domain (or transform domain) filtering is used, mechanized in a different way to improve the convergence performance of the standard LMS algorithm. This is done by using the orthogonally properties of Discrete Fourier Transform and similar transforms.

When Signal is statistically stationary the frequency domain filtering becomes useful:

- Noise is independent and is a stationary random process.
- The signal spectrum is narrowed to bandwidth.
- Information removed by filter does not strongly affect signal.
- Real-time and on-line filtering is not desired.

Many transforms are available for adaptive filtering algorithms. Discrete cosine transforms (DCT) and DFT are popular orthogonal transforms. The Fourier transform is the most important tool used for analyzing the frequency related components. Short-time Fourier transform (STFT) uses a sliding window to find the spectrogram. Here the problem is that the length of window will reduce the resolution in frequency. Wavelet Transform (WT) is deemed as a solution to this problem. Wavelet Transform helps to extract features that vary in time, which makes it a useful tool for analyzing the signals with transient and non-stationary characteristics.

2.4 Overview of Wavelet Transform Filters for Signal Denoising

A wavelet means a small wave and it is a compactly supported function of time. Morlet, a geophysical engineer in late 1970's, came up with an alternative for STFT. In 1985, Meyer, a pure mathematician developed an orthonormal wavelet with attractive time-frequency localization properties. Mallet (1989), formulated the concept of "multiresolution analysis", which provides a simple algorithm to perform wavelet decomposition. He discovered some relations between the pyramid algorithms, Quadrature Mirror Filters (QMF) and the orthonormal wavelet basis. Meyer in 1989 developed the first non-trivial wavelets. These wavelets are continuously differentiable but this does not have compact support. Later Ingrid Daubechies constructed a set of wavelet orthonormal basis function in 1988. In his findings it is stated that WT can be developed with a pair of FIR filters called QMF pair.

Unlike Fourier Transform, WTs have an infinite set of basis functions, which uses only sine and cosine functions. The wavelet analyses know as continuous wavelet transform is defined as:

$$X_{WT}(\tau, s) = \frac{1}{\sqrt{|s|}} \int x(t) \cdot \psi^* \left(\frac{t - \tau}{s} \right) dt$$

x(t) is decomposed into a set of basis functions called wavelets. s and τ are called the scaling and translation parameters. The Wavelet Transform hardly performs the convolution function and the basis function. This is very useful in executing practical applications.

Wavelet Series is the sampled version of CWT. The computations of it may take more amount time and consumes more resources, according to required resolution. The Discrete Wavelet Transform based on sub band coding will provide fast computation of Wavelet Transform. Computation time and resources required is reduced in this case.

The Discrete Wavelet Transform is performed by the decomposition of high pass filters and scaling is performed by decomposition the low pass filters. As shown in figure 3, DWT is performed by successive filtering of the signals. This is called Mallat-tree decomposition or Mallat algorithm. Its importance is in the way it connects the continuous-time mutiresolution to discrete-time filters. The signal sequence is represented as x[n], where n is an integer. The low pass and high pass filter is denoted by G_0 and H_0. Detailed information, d[n] is produced by the high pass filter at each level. The low pass filter produces coarse approximations a[n].

Until the desired level is reached the filtering and decimation process is continued. The number of levels required depends on the signal length. DWT is obtained by concatenating all the coefficients, a[n] and d[n] of the signals from the last level of decomposition.

Figure 4 shows the reconstruction of the main signal from wavelet coefficients.

Reconstruction is nothing but the reverse of decomposition process. Here approximation and detail coefficients at every level are up sampled.

Wavelet shrinkage concepts developed by Donoho and Johnstone (1995) and the works of Breiman, Bruce, and Gao (1996) provides a new turn to the problem of denoising. Donoho et al. (1995), designed

Figure 3. Three-level wavelet decomposition tree

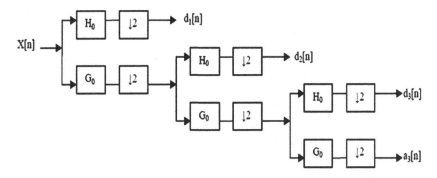

Figure 4. Three-level wavelet reconstruction tree

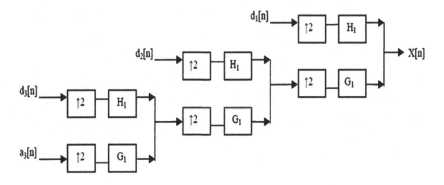

Figure 5. Plot of original signal, noise and noisy signal when noise level is 10%

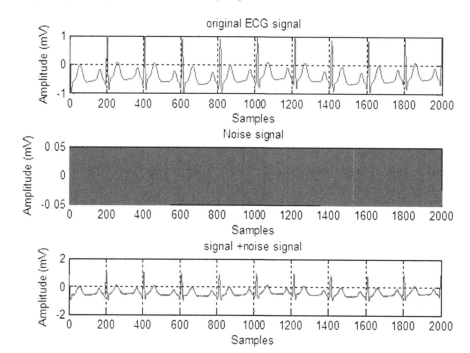

Figure 6. Spectrum of Original and Denoised signal

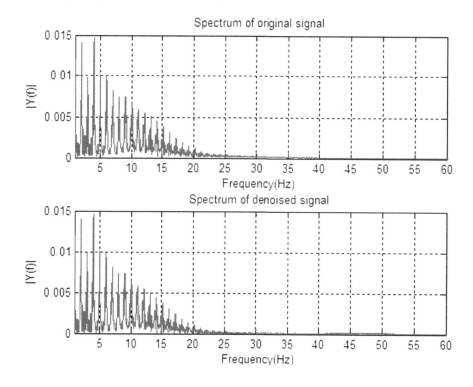

wavelet shrinkage methods for denoising function estimation. These functions are the *hard* and the *soft* shrinkage functions:

Hard Thresholding: $\delta^H(x) = \{\ 0,\ |x| \leq \lambda$

$x,\ |x| > \lambda$

Soft Thresholding: $\delta^S(x) = \{\ 0,\ |x| \leq \lambda$

$x - \lambda,\ x > \lambda$

$x + \lambda,\ x < -\lambda$

where $\lambda \in [0, \infty]$ is the threshold.

3. SIMULATION RESULTS AND DISCUSSION

The problem caused by noise play a major role in biomedical signal processing as they directly degrade the performance characteristic of the signals. Biomedical signals are of very low magnitude ranging from microvolts to few millivolts and frequency range is less than 5 KHz. Original ECG signal and the noisy signal is shown in Figure 5. De-noised signal using wavelet threshold approach is also shown in Figure 5. After denoising the spectrum of both original and denoised signal is compared to see the difference. Notch filter is implemented by selecting the notch frequency at 50Hz. Major problem with the notch filter is that it will remove both the signal component and noise component present at 50 Hz. The Wavelet transform (WT) is applied to noisy ECG signal and different subbands are obtained. These subbands are the approximation and detail coefficients of the signal. Hard and soft thresholding are applied on the noisy counterpart. In this method level dependent threshold is applied by which the coefficients that lies below the threshold is considered as noise and above as signal components. The performance of the proposed method in respect of various noise level and frequency range is showed in Table 1 to 3.

The performance of any denoising algorithm can be compared by estimating the performance parameters. From the analysis it is evident that this method removes the noise component which is spread around the 50 Hz frequency without affecting the signal component. The performance of the denoised

Table 1. Performance parameters at various noise levels (%)- Wavelet Soft Thresholding

Noise Level(%)	SNR	MSE	SNRimp	PRD	PSNR
5	25.194	0.163	25.28	0.3024	4.0168
10	23.09	0.173	23.47	0.4905	1.8366
15	23.66	0.179	24.42	0.4304	2.0438
20	23.8	0.194	24.96	0.4167	1.7654
25	23.46	0.18	25.38	0.4508	2.0187
30	23.25	0.21	25.38	0.4723	1.4653

Table 2. Performance parameters at various noise levels (%)- Wavelet Hard thresholding

Noise Level (%)	SNR	MSE	SNRimp	PRD	PSNR
5	26.68	0.0961	26.76	0.214	4.75
10	24.07	0.1855	24.87	0.3916	3.05
15	24.27	0.1603	25.02	0.374	2.76
20	23.54	0.2031	24.7	0.4416	1.53
25	23.95	0.1819	25.67	0.4018	2.01
30	23.41	0.201	25.75	0.45	1.66

Table 3. Performance parameters at various noise levels (%) - Notch filtering

Noise Level (%)	SNR	MSE	SNRimp	PRD	PSNR
5	32.98	0.03	17.16	0.038	10.87
10	30.45	0.05	20.85	0.033	13.13
15	28.05	0.1	22.49	0.037	13.05
20	25.52	0.15	25.78	0.034	13.05
25	23.12	0.22	27.22	0.037	12.33
30	22.35	0.33	28.47	0.032	13.1

signal is monitored using parameters like signal to noise ratio (SNR), Root mean square (RMS) error, Percentage root mean-square difference (PRD), SNR improvement, and Peak signal to noise ratio (PSNR) to study the quality of the reconstructed signal.

This method of wavelet thresholding gives a higher SNR value when the noise level is low and decreases gradually as the noise level increases. The main advantage is its simplicity in implementation and better accuracy even though the level of noise is varying. It can be applicable to any denoising applications even with a very low frequency range.

REFERENCES

Canan, S., Ozbay, Y., & Karhk. (1997). A Method for Removing Low Varying Frequency Trend from ECG Signal. *Proc. IEEE 2ⁿᵈ International Biomedical Engineering Days*, 144-146.

Daubechies, I. (1998). Orthonormal bases of compactly supported wavelets. *Communications on Pure and Applied Mathematics, 41*(7), 909–996. doi:10.1002/cpa.3160410705

Donoho, D. L. (1995). De-noising by soft thresholding. *IEEE Trans. Inform. Theory, 41*(3), 613–627.

Donoho, D. L., & Johnstone, I. M. (1995). Adapt to unknown smoothness via wavelet shrinkage. *Journal of the American Statistical Association, 90*(432), 1200–1224. doi:10.1080/01621459.1995.10476626

Donoho, D. L., & Johnstone, I. M. (1995). Adapt to unknown smoothness via wavelet shrinkage. *Journal of the American Statistical Association, 90*(432), 1200–1224. doi:10.1080/01621459.1995.10476626

Frazier, M. W. (1999). *An Introduction to Wavelets through Linear Algebra*. Springer.

Kalman, R., & Bucy, R. (1961). New results in linear filtering and prediction theory. *Trans. ASME, Ser. D. Journal of Basic Engineering, 83*(1), 95–107. doi:10.1115/1.3658902

Lee, M. H., Shyu, K. K., Lee, P. L., Huang, C. M., & Chiu, Y. J. (2011). Hardware Implementation of EMD Using DSP and FPGA for Online Signal Processing. *IEEE Transactions on Industrial Electronics, 58*(6), 2473–2481. doi:10.1109/TIE.2010.2060454

Mallet, S. G. (1989). A Theory for Multiresolution Signal Decomposition: The Wavelet Representation. *IEEE Transactions on Pattern Analysis and Machine Intelligence, 11*(7), 674–693. doi:10.1109/34.192463

Meyer, Y. (1993). *Wavelets: Algorithm and Applications*. Philadelphia: Society for Industrial and Applied Mathematics, SIAM.

Nikolaev, N. (2000). Wavelet Domain Wiener Filtering for ECG Denoising using improved Signal Estimate. *Proc. IEEE, 4*, 3578-3581. 10.1109/ICASSP.2000.860175

Srinath, M. D., Rajasekaran, P. K., & Viswanathan, R. (2003). *Introduction to Statistical Signal Processing and Applications*. Pearson Education.

Suchetha. (2017). A comparative analysis of EMD based filtering methods for 50 Hz noise cancellation in ECG signal. *Journal of Medical Informatics Unlocked, 8*(1), 54-59.

Suchetha, M. (2017). A Novel Approach for the Reduction of 50Hz Noise in Electrocardiogram using Variational Mode Decomposition. *International Journal of Current Signal Transduction Therapy, 12*(1), 39–48. doi:10.2174/1574362412666170307092351

Widrow, B., Glover, J. R., McCool, J. M., Kaunitz, J., Williams, C. S., Hearn, R. H., ... Goodlin, R. C. (1975). Adaptive noise canceling: Principles and applications. *Proceedings of the IEEE, 63*(12), 692–1716. doi:10.1109/PROC.1975.10036

Widrow, B., & Stearns, S. D. (2000). *Adaptive Signal Processing*. Englewood Cliffs, NJ: Prentice Hall International.

Wiener, N. (1949). *Extrapolation, Interpolation and Smoothing of Stationary Time Series with Engineering Applications*. Wiley.

Xu, L., & Yan, Y. (2004). Wavelet based Removal of Sinusoidal Interference from a Signal. *Measurement Science & Technology, 15*(9), 1779–1786. doi:10.1088/0957-0233/15/9/015

Zhao, Z.-D., & Chen, Y.-Q. (2006). A New Method for Removal of Baseline Wander and Power Line Interference in ECG Signals. *Machine Learning and Cybernetics, 2006 International Conference on*, 4342-4347. 10.1109/ICMLC.2006.259082

Chapter 3
Secure Access to Biomedical Images

Tariq Javid
Hamdard University, Pakistan

ABSTRACT

This chapter introduces a framework for secure access to biomedical images. Biomedical images are acquired using a vast array of imaging techniques depending upon the specific application. A magnetic resonance spatial domain image is acquired by taking inverse weighted Fourier transform of raw frequency domain data generated by the modality. After correction, these images are stored in a standard format. The access to these stored images is typically subjected to authorization. Medical information in biomedical images needs to be protected in both stored form and in transmission. Encryption technologies are used to secure information whereas compression technologies are used to reduce the information without affecting the contents. In this chapter, a cryptocompression system is proposed which integrates both encryption and compression to fulfill the requirements of electronic protected health information records.

INTRODUCTION

Biomedical images are generally imagined images that are acquired by the application of physical principles. These images are often valuable and typically require implementation of information security measures for authorized access. This chapter introduces a framework for secure access to biomedical images.

Images are acquired, stored, transferred from one place to another, and processed. Information and communication technologies play an important role to accomplish these tasks. Commercial systems use intensive computing resources to apply complex image processing and analysis algorithms in order to produce desired results. These results are useful for further examination by medical experts or computer-based expert systems.

DOI: 10.4018/978-1-5225-5152-2.ch003

Copyright © 2018, IGI Global. Copying or distributing in print or electronic forms without written permission of IGI Global is prohibited.

Biomedical images are acquired using a vast array of imaging techniques depending upon the specific application. A magnetic resonance spatial domain image is acquired by taking inverse weighted Fourier transform of raw frequency domain data generated by the modality. After correction, these images are stored in a standard format. Access to these stored images is typically subjected to authorization.

Information security measures are helpful in order to provide a controlled access to biomedical images. These security measures ensure protection of useful information in images from unauthorized access, manipulation, and deletion. These aspects of information security are referred to as information confidentiality, integrity, and availability – the CIA triad model. The model provides useful insights on how information needs to be protected in the presence of a wide variety of threats.

Encryption and compression standards are useful when images are archived and retrieved over a network medium. Compression is used optionally to lower the impact of encryption overhead. In this chapter, components and function of a proposed cryptocompression system with advanced encryption standard and joint photographic experts group 2000 standard for biomedical image processing are described. The structure and objectives of this chapter are as follows:

- Provide an overview of fundamental security concepts, CIA triad model, framework, and related standards helpful to provide secure access to biomedical images.
- Briefly review information security research that enabled the protection of digital images in general and biomedical images in particular.
- Explain proposed framework components and function.
- Outline challenges and future research trends.

BACKGROUND

Information Security

Information security (INFOSEC) refers to the protection of information contents and information systems against unauthorized access and modification in stored form, during processing, or in transmission channel (Kissel, 2013). It ensures information availability to authorized users by preventing denial of service attacks. It includes security measures that are necessary to detect, document, and counter threats. INFOSEC ensures confidentiality, integrity, and availability of information – known as the confidentiality, integrity, and availability (CIA) triad model. Figure 1 shows the CIA triad model. This model is designed to guide INFOSEC policies in organizations. The model terms are briefly defined with implementation technologies as follows:

- Confidentiality refers to authorized access and is implemented with cryptographic techniques.
- Integrity refers to consistency and is implemented with digital signatures and hash algorithms.
- Availability refers to timely and reliable access and is implemented with secure redundant systems and networks.

Table 1. Acronyms

Acronym	Term
AE	Application Entity
AES	Advanced Encryption Algorithm
AWS	Amazon Web Services
ePHI	Electronic Protected Health Information
CIA	Confidentiality, Integrity, and Availability
CSA	Compressed and Secure Archive
CT	Computed Tomography
DES	Data Encryption Standard
DHCP	Dynamic Host Configuration Protocol
DICOM	Digital Imaging and Communications in Medicine
EHR	Electronic Health Record
FSAMI	Framework for Secure Access to Medical Images
INFOSEC	Information Security
HIPAA	Health Insurance Portability and Accountability Act
HIS	Hospital Information System
HL7	Health Level Seven
ISCL	Integrated Secure Communication Layer
JPEG	Joint Photographic Experts Group
LDAP	Lightweight Directory Access Protocol
MRI	Magnetic Resonance Imaging
NEMA	National Electrical Manufacturers Association
NIST	National Institute of Standards and Technology
PHI	Protected Health Information
PGM	Portable Gray Map
RIS	Radiology Information System
TLS	Transport Layer Security
WAF	Web Application Firewall

Cryptography

Cryptology refers to data storage and communication in a secret manner (Simmons, 2016). It includes both cryptography and cryptanalysis. Cryptography refers to key-controlled transformations of information that is either impossible or computationally infeasible to decipher. Cryptanalysis refers to the art of recovering ciphered information without the knowledge of key. Cryptographic systems are generally classified as cipher systems, key cryptosystems, and block or stream ciphers. A short description of each term is as follows:

- Cipher systems generally use mathematical operations: transpositions and substitutions.

Figure 1. Confidentiality, integrity, and availability (CIA) triad model

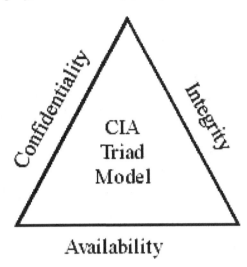

- Key cryptosystems employ either symmetric key or asymmetric keys.
- Block or stream ciphers break plaintext into blocks or streams for encryption.

Encryption at transmitter and decryption at receiver require significant computing resources. An approach to lower the effect of computational overhead is to use compression for data communication. Two main encryption standards are advanced encryption standard (AES) (Daemen & Rijmen, 2011) and data encryption standard (DES) (Paar, & Plzl, 2010). Both AES and DES are block cipher based on symmetric encryption and published as national institute of standards and technology (NIST) standards.

Figure 2 shows a public-private key cryptosystem. The public key of receiving entity is used at transmitter to encrypt plaintext. The receiving entity uses the private key to decrypt the received cipher text. As the name suggests, the public key is available to everyone; however, only receiver has access to the private key to see the information in plaintext.

Compression

Compression refers to data encoding using fewer bits. Data compression is an important area with applications in almost every field. The task is accomplished by identifying and exploiting following principle types of data redundancies (Gonzalez & Woods, 2008).

Figure 2. Public-private key cryptosystem

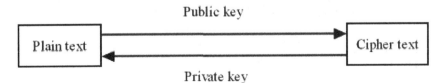

- Coding redundancy is reduced using code words assigned to various symbols.
- Spatial and temporal redundancy is reduced by exploiting similarity in nearby pixels and frames.
- Irrelevant information is reduced by exploiting information ignored by the human visual system.

Compression plays an important role in case of image data storage and transmission. Consider a typical case in which ten times reduction in image size is possible without affecting the information perception. In this case time required for image transmission reduces ten times. This saving is significant especially for a large image data set.

Compression include both lossy and up to lossless techniques. These techniques can be combined to compress part(s) of an image using lossless method whereas the rest of image is compressed in a lossy manner. Figure 3 shows transmission with compressed data. The transmitter sends compressed data which is decompressed at receiver.

Cryptocompression System

A cryptocompression system has both cryptographic and compression modules. The system uses encryption, compression for at transmitter and decryption, decompression at receiver. Such a system is capable of providing both data security and data reduction at the same time. The computational cost is high at both transmitter and receiver. Both transmission time and storage requirements are reduced within a secure environment.

The decryption techniques do not tolerate a bit change in the encrypted cipher text for faithful data recovery. This poses a real constraint on conventional image transmission networks which are designed to preserve image quality without affecting the human perception. The introduction of bit change(s) in the received cryptocompressed data will result in useless decryptocompressed plain text. Therefore reliable transfer is essential requirement for faithful recovery of cryptocompressed data.

Two cryptocompression systems for secure transfer of medical images are proposed by Borie, Puech, and Dumas (2004). Their proposed systems are based on block cipher using tiny encryption algorithm (Wheeler & Needham, 1995) and stream cipher based on Vigenere's ciphering with the compression based on run length coding. Ali, Aziz, Akhtar, and Bhatti (2009) proposed a framework for secure access to medical images (FSAMI). Their developed algorithm used region-of-interest based cryptocompressed data with AES and joint photographic experts group (JPEG) 2000 standard. Figure 4 shows the FSAMI framework.

In FSAMI framework DICOM images are acquired either from modality or from archive. These images are converted to portable gray map (PGM) format. The region-of-interest is marked by the interactive process. The JJ2KEncoder is used to generate the compressed data. The compressed data contains region-of-interest compressed with lossless scheme whereas background is compressed with lossy

Figure 3. Transmission with compressed data

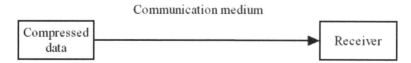

Figure 4. Framework for secure access to medical images (Ali, Aziz, Akhtar, & Bhatti, 2009)

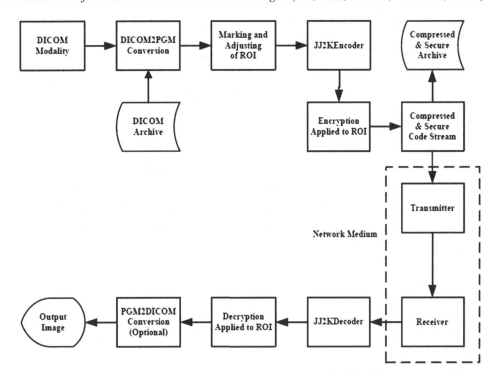

scheme. These encryption schemes are defined in JPEG 2000 standard. After compression step, AES encryption is applied on lossless part. The cryptocompressed data is transmitted. There is an option to save this information in compressed and secure archive. The steps at receiver side are self-explanatory. Figure 5 shows resulting images at various stages of framework.

Biomedical Images

An image is record of a scene captured at specific time. Presently, information shared on social media is mostly in the form of digital images. These images are taken by digital cameras. These cameras have imagining sensors that record incoming light intensity values in the form of an array of numbers. Biomedical images are internal anatomic records that provide biochemical and physiological analysis of tissues and organs (Collection Development Manual of the National Library of Medicine, 2004). These

Figure 5. Resulting images in the FSAMI framework (Ali, Aziz, Akhtar, & Bhatti, 2009)

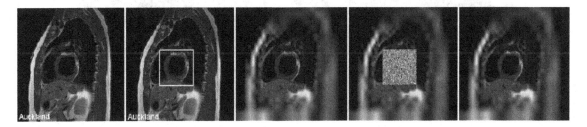

image are obtained by using medical imaging modalities, for example, computed tomography (CT), digital X-ray imaging, magnetic resonance imaging (MRI), molecular and cellular imaging, and scanning microscopies. Figure 6 shows an example of a biomedical image.

Biomedical images are important part of biomedical big data. Depending upon the nature and application, these images may have significant value for an organization. In such a case, there is a need to ensure secure access to authorized users. The security system implements required measures as per INFOSEC definition. Encryption technologies are considered primarily for secure storage and secure communication of important information.

Biomedical images are usually part of a clinical examination conducted by the radiology department of a healthcare organization as per recommendation by the consultant. A study may consist of several hundred images out of which fewer images may have relatively more diagnostic value. These diagnostically important images are marked jointly by the radiographer and medical expert during preparation of the study and at report sign-off by another medical expert. The marked images need to be accessible only to authorized users to ensure privacy of health information.

Figure 6. Example of a biomedical image visualization (Arena, Rueden, Hiner, Wang, Yuan, & Eliceiri, 2016)

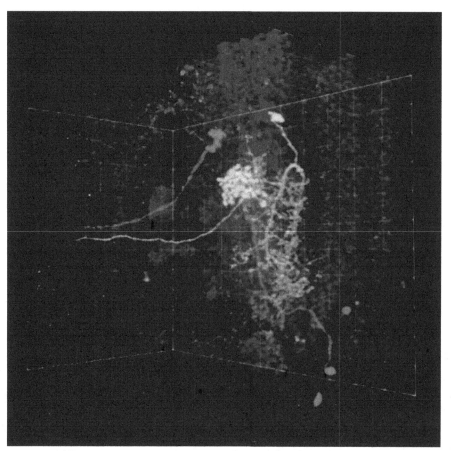

*For a more accurate representation see the electronic version.

Digital Imaging and Communication in Medicine

Digital imaging and communications in medicine (DICOM) standard is developed to facilitate the management and communication of medical images and related health records (NEMA, 2017). The DICOM standard provides interoperability for medical imaging devices and equipment for network communications, syntax and semantics of commands, media communication, and mandatory compliance information. The standard does not outline implementation details, overall set of features and functions, and testing/validation procedure. The standard is developed with an emphasis on diagnostic medical imaging as practiced in cardiology, dentistry, ophthalmology, pathology, radiology, and related disciplines, and image-based therapies such as interventional radiology, radiotherapy and surgery. It is also well suited to a wide range of information exchanged in healthcare environments. Figure 7 shows extracted image from DICOM format in R programming language using oro.dicom package (Whitcher, 2015).

The DICOM standard specify system management and security profiles which are defined by referencing externally developed standard protocols, such as dynamic host configuration protocol (DHCP), lightweight directory access protocol (LDAP), transport layer security (TLS) and integrated secure communication layer (ISCL). These protocols may use security techniques like public keys, public-private keys, and smart cards. There are a number of data encryption standardized available, for example AES and DES. The DICOM standard provides mechanisms that can be used to implement security policies to interchange objects and leaves the responsibility to establish and enforce appropriate policy to secure information on local administrator.

The DICOM standard specifies application specific subsets referred as application profiles used for interchange of medical images and related information on DICOM storage for specific clinical uses. These profiles follow the framework defined in the DICOM standard for the interchange of different types of information. An application profile has associated security settings that enable selection of cryptographic techniques to use with the secure media storage.

The DICOM standard only outlines mechanisms that may be used to implement appropriate security policies with regard to the DICOM objects interchange between application entities. For example, a security policy may enforce some level of access control. The standard assumes that the application entities (AEs) involved in a DICOM interchange have appropriate security policies which include access control, audit trails, physical protection, maintaining the integrity and confidentiality of both image and non-image data, and mechanisms to identify privileged users as per their assigned rights to access data. Essentially, each AE must insure security of local environment before initiating secure communications with other AEs.

Health Level Seven Standards

Health information in electronic form is preferred due ease of access. Health Level Seven International (HL7) is a not-for-profit, ANSI-accredited organization. HL7 standards provide a framework to manage electronic health information. It is applicable on exchange, integration, sharing, and retrieval of such information. The set of standards defines how information is assembled for communication from one host computer to another, language, structure and data types required for interoperability between information systems. Figure 8 shows security labeling service (Jorgenson, Pyette, Davis, Connor, & Blobel, 2014). HL7 standards support clinical practice and the management, delivery of health services and evaluation. These standards are categories in following categories:

Figure 7. DICOM image displayed using R (Javid, 2017)

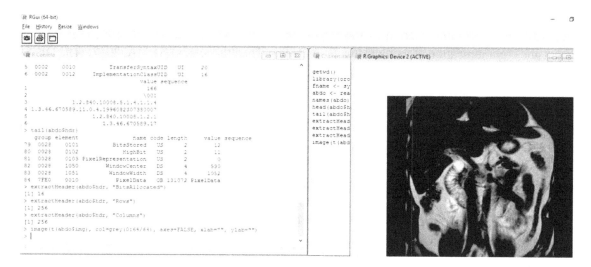

- Primary standards that are more frequently used in health organizations.
- Foundational standards define fundamental tools and building blocks to implement technology.
- Clinical and administrative domains contain messaging and document standards.
- Electronic health record (EHR) profiles provide functional models to manage medical information.
- Implementation guides to support and supplement standards implementation.
- Rules and references provide technical specification and programming structures.
- Education and awareness for adoption of HL7 standards.

Figure 8. HL7 security labeling service (Jorgenson, Pyette, Davis, Connor, & Blobel, 2014)

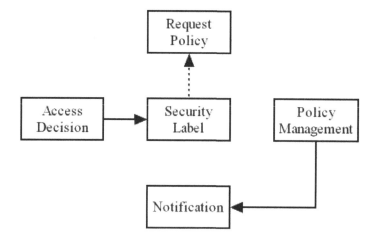

Figure 9. Generic PACS components and basic data flow (Huang, 2014)

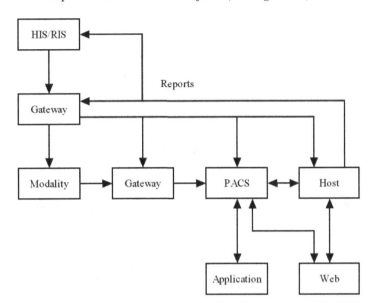

Picture Archiving and Communication System

Picture archiving and communication system (PACS) based on digital, communication, display, and information technologies has revolutionized the practice of radiology and medicine (Huang, 2014). It includes digital imaging modalities to lower patient exposure to radiations, speed-up healthcare delivery, and reduction in overall medical operation costs. A digital radiology department has the following components:

• Radiology information system (RIS) as a subset of hospital information system (HIS).
• Digital imaging system like PACS that includes medical imaging modalities.

PACS contains high volume of radiographic data useful to improve quality patient care services and outcome. The art and science of utilizing this biomedical big data is termed as the imaging informatics discipline. A subset of PACS comes with medical imaging modalities. An integrated or enterprise level PACS deployment is very costly and requires longer deployment time. DICOM standards are necessary requirements for PACS. Figure 9 shows generic PACS components and basic dataflow model.

HIPAA Compliance

Patient confidentiality is a serious concern for medical data and especially for images. This is the mandate of Health Insurance Portability and Accountability Act (HIPAA). The intent behind this act was to reform the healthcare industry by cost reduction, simplification of administrative processes and lowering burdens, and improving the security and privacy of medical health information. HIPAA act provides a conceptual framework for medical records security and integrity and enforce significant penalties in case of noncompliance. However, the guidelines provided by the act do not outline specific technical solutions. There is a consistent emphasis on the need for flexible solutions appropriate for a variety of clinical scenarios. Figure 10 shows an example of Amazon Web Services Web Application Firewall (AWS WAF) which is part of Amazon's HIPPA compliant cloud offerings.

The HIPAA privacy rule focused on the storage, access, and sharing of medical information of any individual. More specifically it outlines security standards to protect electronic health data records. These records are also known as electronic protected health information (ePHI). HIPAA compliance requires the following safeguards in place for ePHI:

- Physical safeguards include facility access and control with authorized access.
- Technical safeguards require access control with unique login credentials and security measures.
- Technical policies to ensure integrity and disaster recovery mechanism.
- Network, or transmission, security to protect information and information system from unauthorized access.

The HIPAA security rule requires covered entities (CEs) that are similar to DICOM AEs to maintain suitable administrative, technical, and physical safeguards for ePHI. Specifically, CEs must have the following measures in place (HHS.gov, 2013):

- Ensure the confidentiality, integrity, and availability of ePHI.
- Identify and protect against security threats.
- Protect against impermissible uses or disclosures.
- Ensure compliance by their workforce.

PROPOSED FRAMEWORK

The proposed cryptocompression system for secure access to biomedical images is based on use of generic PACS components and data flow model in Huang (2014) with the framework for secure access to medical images (FSAMI) by Ali, Aziz, Akhtar, and Bhatti (2009). Figure 11 shows an integrated PACS and FSAMI system that has the ability to use cryptocompressed data for both storage and transmission.

Figure 10. HIPAA compliant Amazon Web Services Web Application Firewall (AWS WAF)

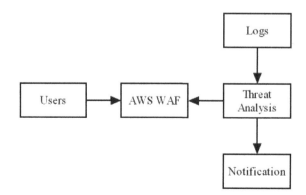

Figure 11. Proposed formulation for secure access to biomedical images with framework for secure access to medical images (FSAMI) and compressed and secure archive (CSA)

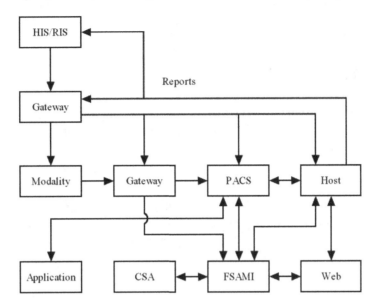

The compressed and secure archive (CSA) is accessible through FSAMI framework. Though other formulations for image data flow with cryptocompression are possible, the focus of discussion here is on the proposed formulation.

The FSAMI framework is connected to the PACS server, host, Web server, and modality. The communication from medical imaging modality is through the acquisition gateway.

Challenges

Data privacy and security is a big challenge and especially when data size is huge. This is especially true for the case of biomedical images. When encryption and compression schemes are applied to large size data, the computation overhead increases considerably.

A number of standards exist to provide guidance on privacy and security of medical information. However, the task to provide authorized access requires considerable efforts due persistent nature of challenges faced primarily due digital nature of biomedical images.

Cryptocompression systems need to be deployed and maintained in physically secure locations with limited physical access. However, the case of software is different. Their protection requires application of updates which are known to have effect on the overall reliability of system.

Both compression and encryption schemes require an ideal communication channel with no loss of information in transit. Loss of a single bit can result in significant quality degradation for complete or part of the image received. The multimedia networks for audio and video are known to tolerate information loss to a certain extent. However, this is not the case for a cryptocompression system.

Medical and radiographic experts are not convinced to use technologies which limit their ability to visualize beyond region-of-interest, compressed in a lossless manner. Author has many discussions with medical experts on use of compression for medical images. Most of them are not convinced to use such technology. The main reason stated was that all parts of a medical image are important at some point in time. The possibility of valuable diagnostic information loss has to be avoided in all cases. This mindset is a big challenge.

FUTURE RESEARCH DIRECTIONS

The proposed formulation is a typical case which is a mere attempt to make the FSAMI framework fit for a hospital PACS deployment. Other formulations to integrate this cryptocompression system within the PACS environment are possible.

The proposed FSAMI framework may be used as a software plugin within PACS server and host workstation.

A hardware implementation of the optimized version of proposed formulation is also possible.

Author was unable to convince a medical expert while at BCBGC-09 conference, Orlando, USA; on why to apply such a technique only on the image part of DICOM file? Medical expert insisted to manipulate the DICOM header information in order to protect privacy. A valuable suggestion still awaited to be explored.

CONCLUSION

This chapter has presented a possible practical implementation of a cryptocompression system for biomedical images. The proposed setup was explained by the introduction of an earlier developed framework for secure access to medical images in a hospital PACS environment. Cryptocompression systems offer an attractive choice to take care of privacy and security part of electronic protected health information. Despite many challenges, the future is promising for both compression and encryption technologies for upcoming biomedical Big Data setups.

ACKNOWLEDGMENT

Author would like to acknowledge Prof. Dr. Vali Uddin, Dean Faculty of Engineering Sciences & Technology, Hamdard University, Karachi Campus, Pakistan for his valuable suggestion toward this work which is closely related to author's research interests and industry experience.

REFERENCES

Ali, T. J., Aziz, A., Akhtar, P., & Bhatti, M. I. (2009). A framework for secure access to medical images. *2009 International Conference on Bioinformatics, Computational Biology, Genomics and Chemoinformatics (BCBGC-09).*

Arena, E. T., Rueden, C. T., Hiner, M. C., Wang, S., Yuan, M., & Eliceiri, K. W. (2016). Quantitating the cell: Turning images into numbers with ImageJ. *Wiley Interdisciplinary Reviews. Developmental Biology*, *6*(2). doi:10.1002/wdev.260 PMID:27911038

Borie, J. C., Puech, W., & Dumas, M. (2004). Crypto-Compression System for Secure Transfer of Medical Images. *2nd Medical Image and Signal Processing.*

Collection Development Manual of the National Library of Medicine. (2004). 4th ed.). Bethesda, MD: U.S. Dept. of Health and Human Services, Public Health Service, National Institutes of Health, National Library of Medicine.

Daemen, J., & Rijmen, V. (2011). *The design of Rijndael: AES - the advanced encryption standard.* Berlin: Springer.

Gonzalez, R. C., & Woods, R. E. (2008). *Digital Image Processing* (3rd ed.). Pearson.

HHS.gov. (2013). *Summary of the HIPAA Security Rule.* Retrieved July 29, 2017, from https://www.hhs.gov/hipaa/for-professionals/security/laws-regulations/index.html

Huang, H. K. (2014). *PACS and Imaging Informatics: Basic Principles and Applications* (2nd ed.). Wiley-Blackwell.

Javid, T. (2017). How to read DICOM in R with oro.dicom? [Web log post]. Retrieved July 30, 2017, from http://tariqjavid72.blogspot.com/2017/07/how-to-read-dicom-in-r-with-orodicom.html

Jorgenson, D., Pyette, P., Davis, J. M., Connor, K., & Blobel, B. (2014). *HL7 Standard: Privacy, Access and Security Services (PASS) - Security Labeling Service, Release 1.0.* Academic Press.

Kissel, R. (Ed.). (2013). *Glossary of key information security terms.* Gaithersburg, MD: U.S. Dept. of Commerce, National Institute of Standards and Technology. doi:10.6028/NIST.IR.7298r2

NEMA PS3 / ISO 12052. (2017). *Digital Imaging and Communications in Medicine (DICOM) Standard.* Rosslyn, VA, USA: National Electrical Manufacturers Association (NEMA). Available at http://medical.nema.org/

Paar, C., & Pelzl, J. (2010). *Understanding Cryptography: A Textbook for Students and Practitioners.* Berlin: Springer Berlin. doi:10.1007/978-3-642-04101-3

Simmons, G. J. (2016). Cryptology. In *Encyclopædia Britannica.* Encyclopædia Britannica, Inc.

Wheeler, D., & Needham, R. (1995). TEA, a tiny encryption algorithm. In *Proceedings of the 1995 Fast Software Encryption Workshop.* Springer-Verlag.

Whitcher, B. (2015). Rigorous - DICOM Input / Output [R package oro.dicom version 0.5.0]. Retrieved July 31, 2017, from https://CRAN.R-project.org/package=oro.dicom

ADDITIONAL READING

Amazon Web Services, Inc. (2017). Architecting for HIPAA Security and Compliance on Amazon Web Services.

Announcing the Advanced Encryption Standard (AES). (2001). United States: National Institute of Standards and Technology.

Dey, N., Das, P., Chaudhuri, S. S., & Das, A. (2012). Feature analysis for the blind-watermarked electro-encephalogram signal in wireless telemonitoring using Alattar's method. *Proceedings of the Fifth International Conference on Security of Information and Networks (SIN'12)*, 87-94. 10.1145/2388576.2388588

Dey, N., Mukhopadhyay, S., Das, A., & Chaudhuri, S. (2012). Analysis of P-QRS-T components modified by blind watermarking technique within the electrocardiogram signal for authentication in wireless telecardiology using DWT. *International Journal of Image, Graphics and Signal Processing, 4*(7).

Dey, N., Roy, A., Das, A., & Chaudhuri, S. (2012). Stationary Wavelet Transformation Based Self-recovery of Blind-Watermark from Electrocardiogram Signal in Wireless Telecardiology. *Recent Trends in Computer Networks and Distributed Systems Security*, 347-357. Introduction to HL7 Standards. (n.d). Retrieved July 29, 2017, from http://www.hl7.org/implement/standards

Dey, N., & Santhi, V. (2017). *Intelligent Techniques in Signal Processing for Multimedia Security*. Cham: Springer International Publishing. doi:10.1007/978-3-319-44790-2

Masmoudi, A., & Puech, W. (2014). Lossless chaos-based crypto-compression scheme for image protection. *IET Image Processing, 8*(12), 671–686. doi:10.1049/iet-ipr.2013.0598

Mhetre, N. A., Deshpande, A. V., & Mahalle, P. N. (2016). Trust Management Model based on Fuzzy Approach for Ubiquitous Computing. *International Journal of Ambient Computing and Intelligence, 7*(2), 33–46. doi:10.4018/IJACI.2016070102

National Institute of Standards and Technology. (1999). *FIPS PUB 46: Data Encryption Standard*. Washington, D.C.: U.S. Dept. of Commerce, National Bureau of Standards.

Sarkar, M., Banerjee, S., Badr, Y., & Sangaiah, A. K. (2017). Configuring a Trusted Cloud Service Model for Smart City Exploration Using Hybrid Intelligence. *International Journal of Ambient Computing and Intelligence, 8*(3), 1–21. doi:10.4018/IJACI.2017070101

Tamane, S., Solanki, V. K., & Dey, N. (2017). *Privacy and security policies in Big Data*. Hershey, PA: IGI Global, Information Science Reference. doi:10.4018/978-1-5225-2486-1

Yamin, M., & Sen, A. A. (2018). Improving Privacy and Security of User Data in Location Based Services. *International Journal of Ambient Computing and Intelligence, 9*(1), 19–42. doi:10.4018/IJACI.2018010102

KEY TERMS AND DEFINITIONS

Application Entity: Application entity is a functional unit in DICOM. The imaging modality, server, or workstation in the PACS have unique application entities.

Cryptocompression System: A system which implements both encryption and compression technologies to generate cryptocompressed text from plain text.

Cryptography: Cryptography refers to key-controlled transformations of information that is either impossible or computationally infeasible to decipher.

Cryptosystem: A system which converts plain text to cipher text or cipher text to plain text by the application of encryption or decryption algorithm. The key generation for encryption and decryption algorithms is also part of a cryptosystem.

Denial of Service (DoS) Attack: A situation in which service is not available to an authorized user. A typical case of in which a malicious software code makes services inaccessible by overloading computing and network resources.

Digital Imaging and Communications in Medicine: Digital imaging and communications in medicine (DICOM) is the standard for the communication and management of medical images and related data.

Distributed DoS Attack: A distributed denial-of-service attack is a botnet attack in which multiple locations are used to attack on a service.

Information Security: Information security (INFOSEC) refers to the protection of information and information systems against unauthorized access and modification of information in storage, processing, or in transit.

National Institute of Standards and Technology: The National Institute of Standards and Technology (NIST) was founded in 1901 and is now part of the U.S. Department of Commerce.

Picture Archiving and Communication System: Picture archiving and communication system (PACS) includes digital imaging modalities to lower patient exposure to radiations, speed-up healthcare delivery, and reduction in overall medical operation costs.

Chapter 4
Early Detection of Breast Cancer Using Image Processing Techniques

Amutha S.
Dayananda Sagar College of Engineering, India

Ramesh Babu D. R.
Dayananda Sagar College of Engineering, India

ABSTRACT

Breast cancer is the second leading cause of death among women according to Cancer Facts and Figures. In order to increase the survival rate of women due to breast cancer, early and accurate detection of breast cancer is very essential. The quality of the image acquired through different breast imaging modalities: mammography, ultrasonography, and magnetic resonance imaging (MRI) have drawbacks which reduces the efficiency of accurate detection. As per the literature survey, the quality of the image acquired through the breast imaging modalities is not optimal for the accurate detection of cancer at the early stage. Digital image enhancement methods have been widely used in radiology in order to enhance the image quality. Considerable research has been undertaken in the development of enhancement of the image to assist radiologists in the identification of breast abnormalities. In order to further improve the efficiency of detection, diagnosis, and treatment of cancer, the quality of the image has to be improved.

1. INTRODUCTION

Primary modality Screening mammography is considered for the diagnosis and screening of breast cancer because Screening Mammography is the easiest and affordable way to diagnose breast cancer (American Cancer Society, 2014; Prannoy Giri, Sara, & Ana Kumar, 2017). For dense tissues the mammogram images are low in contrast and noisy nature. Because of this, difficulties are being faced by radiologists during image interpretations (G¨orgel, 2013). Thus amplifying contrast and removing noise of mammogram images become one of the key objectives. Artificial Neural Networks (ANN) techniques were adopted for breast disease classification (Mehdy, 2017). In order to accomplish contrast enhancement followed

DOI: 10.4018/978-1-5225-5152-2.ch004

Copyright © 2018, IGI Global. Copying or distributing in print or electronic forms without written permission of IGI Global is prohibited.

by removing noise, an approach has been proposed based on Bi-orthogonal Wavelets and Morphological operations. Features necessary for the detection can be extracted using a level dependent soft threshold which separates noise from the image by retaining the valuable information. Presence of calcifications and masses in mammogram images are the main source of abnormalities. They are categorized by the features such as density, size, margin, shape, and contour of the breast. The proposed approach is evaluated by applying it to the images from the archive, *Mammographic Image Analysis Society (MIAS)*. The results are analyzed and evaluated with existing soft threshold techniques: Sure Shrink (SS), Visu Shrink (VS) and Bayes Shrink (BS). The subjective analysis is executed based on radiologist evaluation. Receiver Operating Characteristic (ROC) is drawn for the true positives and the false positives.

Regarding the security aspect of data, a biometric authentication system provides quite a reasonable solution for security because it uses human anatomical or behavioral features for the verification process (Dey, 2013). The multimodal biometric authentication system, which uses a combination of modalities, has advantages over its unimodal counterpart, especially in areas of False Acceptance Rate (FAR) and False Rejection Rate (FRR). Particle swarm optimization (PSO) is a powerful globally accepted evolutionary swarm intelligence method for classification in data mining (Das, 2014).Biomedical signal and information hiding has been written in an easy way to address the need of improvements in data hiding algorithms to ensure authenticity and security of patients' information (Dey, 2014). The Peak Signal to Noise Ratio (PSNR) of the original signal vs. watermarked signal has to correlate well for better performance. Medical images are extremely precious owing to its importance in diagnosis, education, and research.

Recently, telemedicine applications and remote medical education play an imperative role in the advancement and progressiveness of the healthcare industry.

Featuring extensive coverage on areas such as kinetic knowledge, cognitive analytics, and parallel computing in the field of big data has been explained. In particular, accuracy of results vs. privacy degree, privacy vs. performance, and trust between users are open problems and an approach by integration of peer-to-peer (P2P) with the caching technique and dummies from real queries has been addressed by the author (Yamin, 2018). Trust is actually a matter of feeling with which one feels connected with some persons in the form of multicast groups. Multicast Route Reliability (MRR) is purely a probabilistic function of Cartesian product of past relationships and present moving patterns (Tyagi, 2017). Information and technology revolution has brought a radical change in the way data are collected. The data collected is of no use unless some useful information is derived from it. Therefore, it is essential to think of some predictive analysis for analyzing data and to get meaningful information (Acharjya, 2017). Cloud computing becomes popular to internet users in context of smart city, cloud computing is applicable in different Government, public and private sectors (Sarkar, 2017). Biometric identification is a good candidate technology, which can facilitate a trusted user authentication with minimum constraints on the security of the access point (Mohammed Fouad, 2017). Trust management plays an important role in ubiquitous communication. It helps in decision making and to identify risks (Mhetre, 2016) has been addressed by the author (Borty, 2016).

2. PROPOSED APPROACH

In this approach, bi-orthogonal wavelet is used which has two different wavelets separately for reconstruction and decomposition. To get more desirable decomposition and reconstruction, two different scaling functions and wavelet functions with 4 filters are used. Bi-orthogonal wavelet generates symmetric and orthogonal wavelets, which provides scope for anisotropic elements such as boundary discontinuities and curvatures in the image. Under translation the sub band images are invariant and non-aliasing. These properties can restrict unwanted artifacts as motion artifact, software processing artifacts and detector-associated artifacts. For removing noise, thresholding the detailed wavelet coefficient has been accomplished. Soft threshold on each co-efficient level has been adapted to extract the necessary information from the image. Figure 1 explains the approach for mammogram enhancement and denoising.

The threshold was computed at each level based on the Equation (1)

$$T = \left(\frac{j}{2}\right) * log2\left(\max\left(d_j\right)\right)$$

In the above equation, level is represented by 'j' and the wavelet coefficient value by d_j. Coefficients below the threshold T is set to zero considering it as noise and the Coefficients above the threshold T are considered as the information to be retained. Hence it is replaced by the value obtained from subtracting the threshold from the coefficients. In order to extend the complete coverage of the wavelet coefficients,

Figure 1. Approach for mammogram enhancement and denoising.

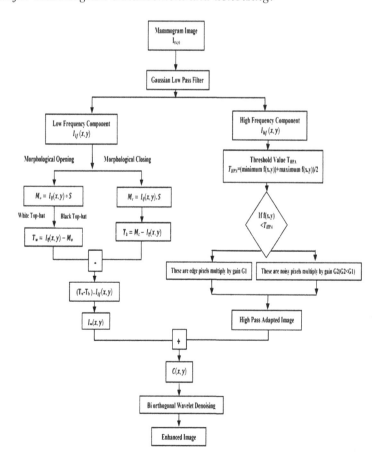

the obtained value including the level information is reduced by half. The soft-threshold, *f(x)*, given by equation (2), in which x is the wavelet coefficient.

$$f(x) = sign(x)(|x| - T) \, if \, |x| > T \text{ else } 0$$

For evaluation, the performance metrics Contrast Improvement Index (CII) and Edge preservation index (EPI) are computed. A personalized test pertaining to the original and enhanced mammograms to assess the medical utility of the algorithm has been performed. A comparative analysis has been made between the adopted technique and other soft-thresholding techniques: Visu Shrink (VS) (Chang, 2000), Bayes Shrink (BS) and Sure Shrink (SS) based on the personalized test and the performance statistics.

Figure 2 gives the results of visual comparison of the original mammograms with the three existing contrast-enhancement methods VS, BS, SS and the proposed method. It is obvious that the adopted method yields better contrast than the existing methods. One more significance of the proposed method is that it avoids saturation of intensities in comparison to the case VS.

The quantitative image processing metric CII is computed based on Equation 3. The ratio of contrast of processed image and the contrast of original image for a 5 x 5 neighborhood is calculated. The above process is executed for all the existing techniques VS BS and SS and also for the proposed technique against the original contrast. Figure 3 shows the CII graph for the mammograms.

$$C = \frac{(Imax - Imin)}{(Imax + Imin)} \tag{3}$$

I_{max} and I_{min} are the maximum and minimum intensities.
The Edge Preservation Index (EPI) is calculated by Equation (4)

$$EPI = \frac{\sum \left(\left| I_{ce}(i, j) - I_{ce}(i+1, j) \right| + \left| I_{ce}(i, j) - I_{ce}(i, j+1) \right| \right)}{\sum \left(\left| I_0(i, j) - I_o(i+1, j) \right| + \left| I_0(i, j) - I_0(i, j+1) \right| \right)} \tag{4}$$

$I_0(i,j)$ is the intensity of the original image and $I_{ce}(i,j)$ is the intensity of the processed image for the pixel index *(i,j)*. A greater value of EPI depicts improved delineation while enhancing the contrast. Hence it is observed that the proposed approach delivers slightly an improved performance than the existing approaches as given by the highest average value of EPI in the group. Figure 3 indicates the EPI plot for the mammograms.

Receiver Operating Characteristics (ROC) analysis is performed by a standard web-ROC tool (Eng, 2014) for diagnosis of breast cancer. The analysis is performed as follows; images from MIAS archive are shuffled which includes mammograms with and without abnormalities like presence of micro calcification and masses are given to the radiologist for evaluation. The radiologist conducted the evaluation on a rating of 1-5regarding the identification and description of the lesion with '1' being certainly negative with full assurance that there is no lesion and '5' being absolutely positive with full assurance that there is a lesion. Figure 5 depicts the ROC plot.

Figure 2. Contrast enhanced images

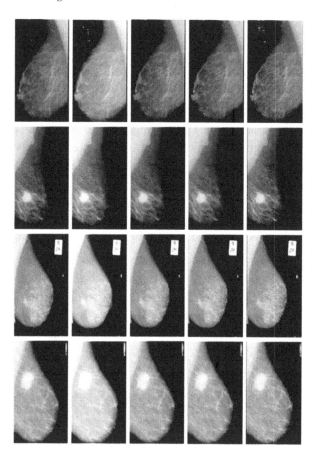

Figure 3. CII graph

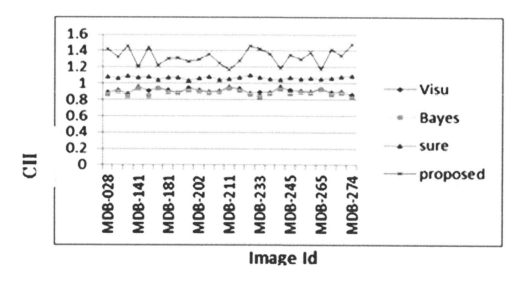

Figure 4. EPI plot

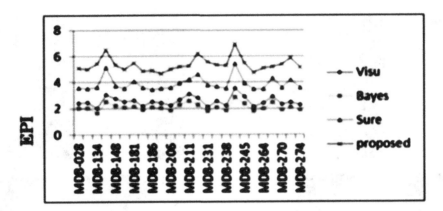

The detection of Region of Interest (ROI) is performed based on grouping of homogeneous regions and differentiating each region with color quantization technique. Each region describes the specific properties which help in identifying the ROI. The ROI is marked for the mammogram images before enhancement and after enhancement. Figure 6 shows the ROI marking for the mammogram images. The ROI marking is effective in the enhanced images than the original images.

Breast Imaging Modality: Ultrasonography

Ultrasonography is another modality to identify and localize the breast lesions. The significance of sonography is it can reveal a mass which is hidden amidst dense tissues in mammography. The advantages of sonography are it is portable, low cost and free from radiation (Dhillon, 2011). Though it has advantage the drawbacks are: less contrast and low resolution (Deka, 2013). Due to these drawbacks it

Figure 5. ROC analysis

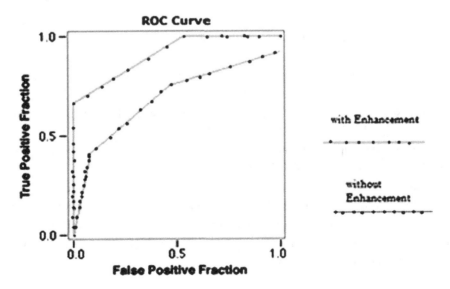

Figure 6. ROI on mammograms (a) Before enhancement; (b) After enhancement

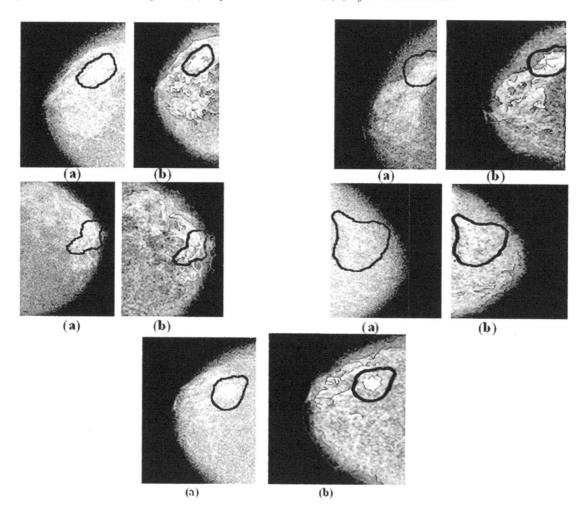

is challenging for the radiologist to understand and analyze the ultrasound image for finding the abnormal features. To overcome the existing drawback there is a necessity of speckle reduction. Speckle is a unique noise that exists in all coherent imaging systems including medical ultrasound images which affects the performance. Speckle is a multiplicative noise which mainly depends on the signal. A technique has been adopted for speckle denoising and edge enhancement of the ultrasound breast images for the segmentation of the Region of Interest (ROI). The technique is verified for the images from the dataset "The Digital Database for Breast Ultrasound Image" DDBUI (Tian, 2008). The effect of the adopted technique is evaluated and compared with the previous techniques: Speckle Reducing Anisotropic Diffusion filter (SRAD), Total Variation (TV) filter.

Daubechies wavelet has been selected for speckle noise removing because of the improvement of better representation of image semantics. The breast ultrasound image is categorized into four sub bands LL, LH, HL, HH where LL is low frequency sub band and LH, HL, HH are the high frequency sub bands. Total Variation (TV) method established on Rudin-Osher-Fatemi (ROF) is adapted for removing noise the LL co-efficient based on the Equation (5):

$$\underset{u}{\overset{inf}{}}\left\{ J\left(u\right) + \left(2\lambda\right)^{-1} f - u^{2}{}_{L^{2}} \right\} \tag{5}$$

In the above expression 'f' denotes the noisy image, 'u' is the component to be extracted from 'f'; λ is the turning parameter with constant value above zero. $J(u) = \int |\nabla u|$ is the total variation. In order to differentiate textures from noise, in the sub bands with high frequency, local variance is adopted. Local variance V (i, j) is computed as per the Equation (6).

$$V\left(i,j\right) = \frac{1}{L^{2}} \sum_{(p,q)\in Z_{ij}} C^{2}{}_{LH}\left(p,q\right) - \frac{1}{L^{4}} \left(\sum_{(p,q)\in Z_{ij}} C_{LH}\left(p,q\right) \right)^{2} \tag{6}$$

In which $Z_{ij} = \left[i - \dfrac{L-1}{2}, i + \dfrac{L-1}{2} \right] \times \left[j - \dfrac{L-1}{2}, j + \dfrac{L-1}{2} \right]$

The coordinates i and j are positive integers. 'L' is the odd size window with middle coordinates (i,j) in the wavelet coefficient CLH. The average of the local variance is computed and fixed as the threshold 'T' for that image. Similarly 'T' is computed for all the images, and if the local variance V (i, j) >T, it is referred as the texture region which contains the necessary information and if V (i, j) ≤ T is related as the noisy components. To reduce the speckle noise, soft thresholding based wavelet shrinkage is applied on high frequency sub bands. The coefficients related to noise are assigned zero value and the coefficient which corresponds to texture is replaced by the value from the Equation (7):

$$C_{LH} = 0, \text{ if } V\ (i, j) \le T \text{ else } C_{LH}\ (i,j) = C_{LH}\ (i,j) - T \tag{7}$$

The above equation specifies the calculation by subtracting the threshold 'T' from the coefficients. Soft threshold is effective because maximum of coefficients are zero and only few coefficients are with greater magnitude.

Soft threshold avoids discontinuities and also it prevents the sudden transition in the image which gives visually pleasing images. Inverse wavelet transform is applied to rebuild the image with the intention to improve the edges which holds the main features of the image. In order to improve the edge continuity and contrast, grouping of homogeneous blocks is applied to the speckle reduced images to get the finer details of the image

With the aim to calculate the performance of the proposed algorithm, forty breast ultrasound images are chosen from the dataset "The Digital Database for Breast Ultrasound Image" DDBUI (Chang, 2000). The database covers breast images with and without lesions. Three categories of breast images which include normal, benign, and malignant are present in the dataset. Three classes of breast images including normal, benign, and malignant are present in the database. Normal class is identified by cases from the patients who came to the hospital for regular checkup and were recognized as healthy. Benign class holds cases from screening test in which suspicious regions were found and was confirmed as benign by biopsy. Malignant class holds cases which were confirmed as malignant by biopsy

All the images in the database are stored in JPEG format with an image size of 450×450 pixels. The algorithm is verified on ultrasound breast images from the database 'DDBUI' and also verified on clinical dataset. The outcomes of speckle noise removing for three breast ultrasound images are displayed in Figure 6. The visual evaluation of the images representevidently that the proposed algorithm is performing well in decreasing the speckles.

The edge enhancement algorithmhave created a visually enhanced quality image for the breast ultrasounds as a consequence, of the proposed edge in which improvement method for the breast ultrasound image with microcalcification as shown in Figure 8. Calcification existence can be evidently seen in the improved image.

Figure 9 shows the outcomes of the edge enhancement algorithm which is been applied on a breast ultrasound image with fine facts of mass which is an evidently seen in the next improved image.

The adopted method which has reasonably improved the quality of the image results in the better identification of region of interest when compared with the existing methods: Speckle Reducing Anisotropic Diffusion (SRAD), Wavelet shrinkage and Total variation method.

Figure 7. Breast images: (a) (c) (e) with speckles; (b) (d) (f) after speckle reduction

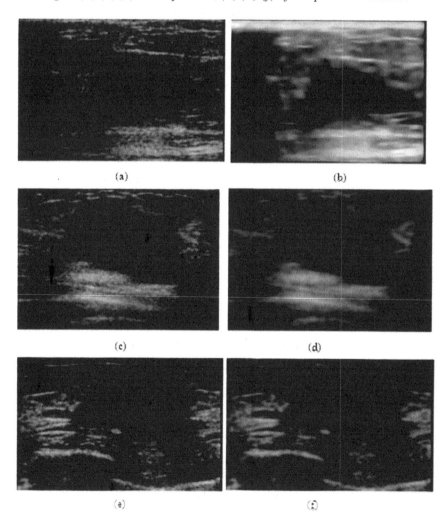

Figure 8. Ultrasound images with microcalcification: (a) (c) Original image; (b) (d) enhanced image

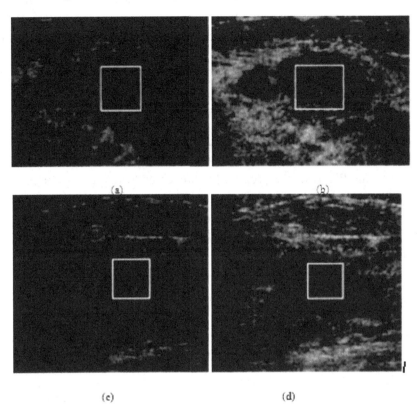

(a)   (b)

(c)   (d)

Figure 9. Ultrasound Breast image with the mass: (a) before enhancement (b) after enhancement by proposed method

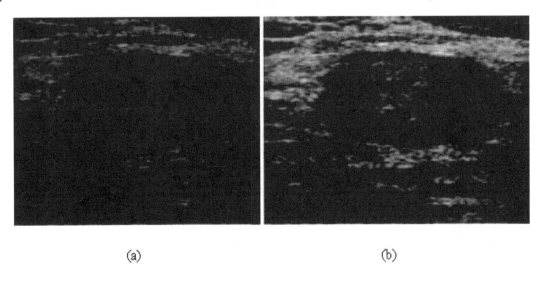

(a)   (b)

The graphical representation in Figure 10 shows MSE values, analyses clearly that the error rate is less in the given proposed method when it was been compared with other the different methods.

The image fidelity is measured by the PSNR and it is calculated based on the Equation (8). PSNR value discloses the closeness of the transformed image with the original image.

$$PSNR = 20.\log_{10}\left(MAX_1\right) - 10.\log_{10}\left(MSE\right) \tag{8}$$

The PSNR value for the images are reconstructed again, in which it is high based on the type of an proposed approach, in which it displays enhanced performance related to it and also gives about plotted graph for values of the PSNR of the proposed approach and the type of comparative methods is displayed in Figure 11.

The parameters like Quality index Q, and also the mathematically modeled to measure the about distortion factor. In Q it reflects about the three different factors: loss of correlation, the luminance distortion, and the contrast distortion factors.

Figure 10. Given MSE plot for the proposed type and comparitive method type in the ultrasound images

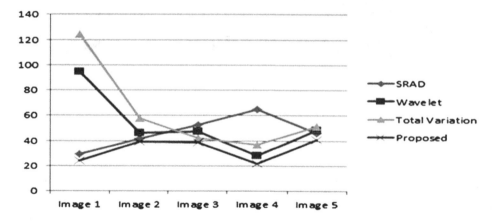

Figure 11. PSNR plots of the proposed and comparative methods in ultrasound images

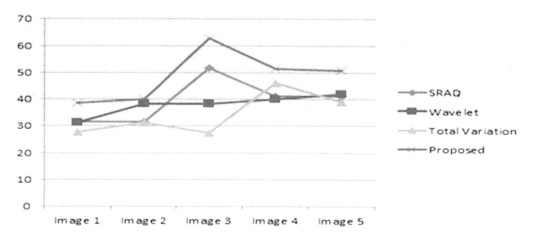

In the graphical representation for the type of 'Q' values of the proposed approach and also the comparative method values are displayed in the Figure 12.

In the analysis of the proposed approach compared to other methods based on the metrics: in MSE, PSNR and Q reveals that the concept of proposed approach is less error with PSNR high values and Q. This results in the significant improvement of the proposed approach in the speckle removing noise.

Also in the individual analysis of the given proposed algorithm has been carried out based on the visual quality of the certain image obtained from the proposed approach and with the three comparative methods like (SRAD, Wavelet, Total variation and proposed method). Figure 13 shows the breast ultrasound image of one patient (referred as Breast ultrasound image 1) with the type of speckle noise present in it and also the noise removed images based on the comparative approaches and the proposed approach to recognize the ROI.

The algorithm is verified on a breast ultrasound image (referred as Breast ultrasound image 2) with speckle noise. Figure 13 shows the image with speckle noise and the noise removed images based on the comparative approaches and also about the proposed approach to mark the ROI.

The individual evaluation of the given proposed algorithm established on the visual quality of the certain image gives improvement inthe image quality.

Breast Imaging Modality: Magnetic Resonance Imaging (MRI)

Magnetic Resonance Imaging (MRI) of the breast image delivers about valuable information about the breast conditions, and that it cannot be obtained by other imaging modalities. Also MRI images are most corrupted by the Rician noise which will not give about clarity of the fine details of the certain image (Manj´on, 2010). Also to reduce Rician noise by conserving information in the breast MRI images, an Optimal Single stage Principal Component Analysis (OSPCA) has been proposed, in which the pixels in the certain image are been first grouped based on the resemblance characteristics called as Local Pixel Grouping (LPG) (Zhang, 2010). After grouping about the pixels, shrinkage is accomplished in the Principal Component Analysis (PCA) domain for removing noise. With respect to preserve and enhance the edges, an edge improvement algorithm established on high passes adaptation technique.

Figure 12. Plot for Q values

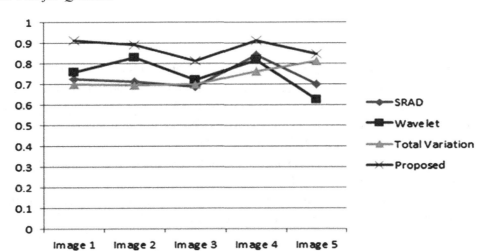

Figure 13. Breast image (1) (a) original (b) SRAD (c) wavelet method (d) Total variation (e) adopted method

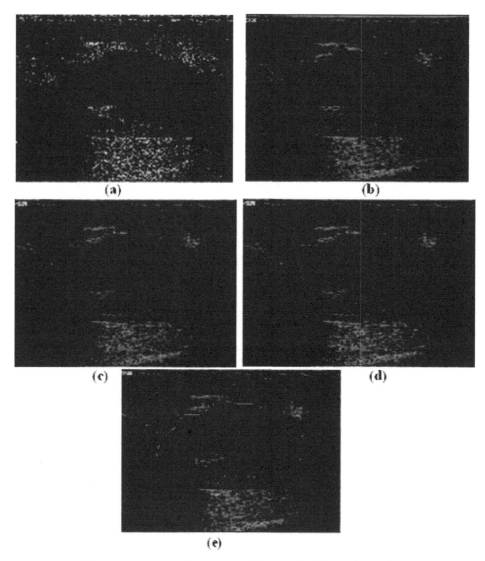

For a more accurate representation see the electronic version.

The above-mentioned algorithm is also verified on the data set from National Cancer Institute, USA. The proposed algorithm is been compared with the existing techniques: Optimal Multi component Non Local Means filter (OMNLM) and Unbiased Non Local Means filter (UNLM), which yields satisfactory result. The performance metrics in the Mean Square Error (MSE), Structural Similarity Index Measurement (SSIM), and about the Edge Preservation Index (EPI) demonstrates the ability of the proposed approach in removing noise and about preserving information. Also the individual analyses of the Rician removing noise of Breast MRI images are shown in Figure 15 and 16.

The visual image quality is enhanced for the given proposed method when compared with the existing methods in certain preserving edges and removing the certain related Rician noise.

Figure 14. Breast image (2) (a) original (b) SRAD (c) wavelet method (d) Total variation (e) adopted method

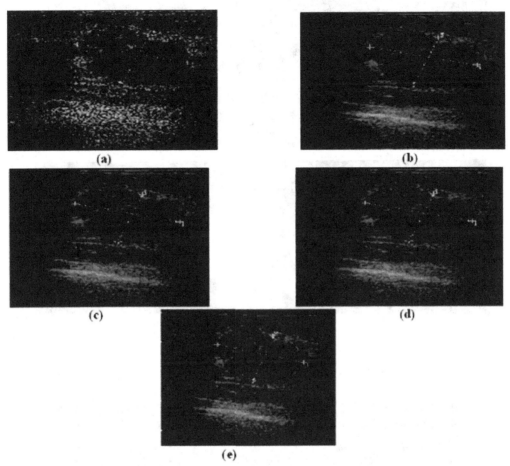

(a)

(b)

(c)

(d)

(e)

For a more accurate representation see the electronic version.

A given breast MRI image with the certain noise patches is shown in the Figure 17 (a), on which this certain patches are extracted from the image and are displayed in the next Figure 17(b). Figure 17(c), 17(d), 17(e) that demonstrates the noise removed MRI images.

Also the image quality defines the performance of removing noise which is better in the given proposed algorithm when it was been compared with the other existing algorithms, also the given proposed algorithm has preserved the certain type of edges while removing noise in which it is verified through the quality of the image.

3. CONCLUSION

The purpose of the proposed approach is to improve the image quality of breast imaging modalities which can help the radiologists to detect breast cancer precisely at the early stage and also for further analysis and treatment. The drawbacks of the existing methods are: either the image gets enhanced with loss of

Figure 15. MRI image (1) (a) original image (b) OMNLM (c) UNLM (d) proposed method

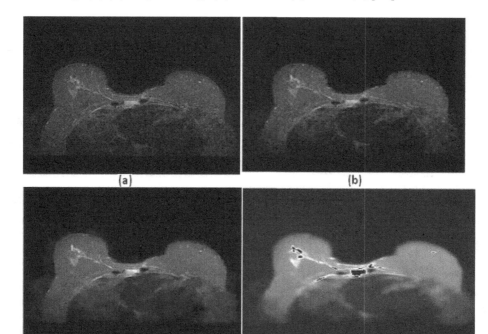

Figure 16. MRI image (2) (a) original image (b) OMNLM (c) UNLM (d) proposed method

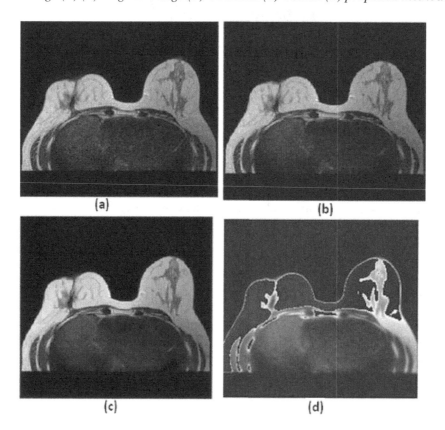

Figure 17. (a) Original image (b) Patch from the original image (c) OMNLM (d) UNLM (e) proposed method

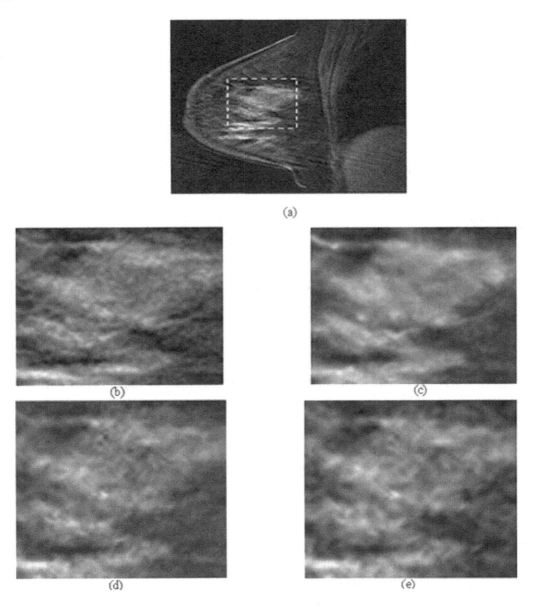

useful information or it becomes over enhanced, wherein artifacts look like calcification that may lead to misinterpretation by radiologist. To overcome the drawback the proposed approach has been implemented.

The results reveal that the proposed approach performs better than the other existing methods. The ROC curve shows that the false positives per image have been fairly reduced. The enhanced images are free from the drawbacks of excessive enhancement wherein artifacts look like calcification and masking of existing lesion. But for few images, it is showing excessive enhancement of background, this drawback has to be analyzed and rectified in the future work.

4. SCOPE OF FUTURE WORK

The future work is directed towards improving the performance of the enhancement and denoising algorithm for better detection of abnormal region in the breast. In detecting the abnormal regions, the true positives have to be increased by reducing the false positives which will improve the sensitivity of the modality. Also, the proposed approach has to be implemented into a clinical practice to test with a large number of real time data set with all classes of abnormalities. Another direction of the future work is applying image fusion algorithm on the data set of the same patient taken at the same time with multiple modalities. Each modality has its own strength in imaging and retrieving information from the image. Hence a combination of information from different modalities can yield a very informative image to aid the radiologists in finding the abnormalities.

REFERENCES

American Cancer Society. (2014). *Cancer facts & figures*. Author.

Chang, Yu, & Vetterli. (2000). Adaptive wavelet thresholding for image Denoising and compression. *Image Processing, IEEE Transactions on, 9*(9), 1532–1546.

Das, Jena, Nayak, & Naik, & Behera. (2014). A novel PSO based back propagation learning-MLP (PSO-BP-MLP) for Classification. *Computational Intelligence in Data Mining, 2*, 461–471.

Debi Acharjya. (2017). A Comparative Study of Statistical and Rough Computing Models in Predictive Data Analysis. *International Journal of Ambient Computing and Intelligence, 8*(2). doi:10.4018/IJACI.2017040103

Deka, B., & Bora, P. K. (2013). Removal of correlated speckle noise using sparse and Over complete representations. *Biomedical Signal Processing and Control, 8*(6), 520–533. doi:10.1016/j.bspc.2013.05.003

Dey, Ashour, Chakraborty, & Hassanien. (2016). Watermarking in Bio-medical Signal Processing. *Intelligent Techniques in Signal Processing For Multimedia Security.* DOI: 0.1007/978-3-319-44790-2_16

Dey, N., & Dey, G. (2014). Feature Analysis of Blind Watermarked Electromyogram Signal in Wireless Telemonitoring. Concepts and Trends in healthcare Information Systems, 205-229.

Dey, N., Nandi, B., Das, P., Das, A., & Chaudhuri, S. S. (2013). Retention of Electrocardiogram Features Insignificantly Devalorized As an Effect Of Watermarking For a Multi-Modal Biometric Authentication System. Advances in Biometrics for Secure Human Authentication and Recognition, 175–212. Doi:10.1201/b1624710

Dey, N., & Samanta, S. (2014). Optimization of Watermarking In Biomedical Signal, with 38 Reads. LAP Lambert Academic Publishing.

Dhillon, Jindal, & Girdhar. (2011). A novel threshold technique for Eliminating speckle noise in ultrasound images. *International Conference on Modelling, Simulation and Control, IPCSIT, 10.*

Fouad, K. M., Hassan, B. M., & Hassan, M. F. (2017). User Authentication based on Dynamic Keystroke Recognition. *Identity Theft: Breakthroughs in Research and Practice*. doi:10.4018/978-1-5225-0808-3. ch019

Gˮorgel, P., Sertbas, A., & Ucan, O. N. (2013). Mammographical mass detection and Classification using local seed region growing–spherical wavelet transform (lsrg–swt) hybrid Scheme. *Computers in Biology and Medicine, 43*(6), 765–774. doi:10.1016/j.compbiomed.2013.03.008 PMID:23668353

Jos'e, V. (2010). Adaptive non-local means denoising of MR images with spatially varying noise Levels. *Journal of Magnetic Resonance Imaging, 31*(1), 192–203. doi:10.1002/jmri.22003 PMID:20027588

M.D John Eng. (2014). *ROC Analysis: Web-based Calculator for ROC Curves*. Retrieved from http://www.rad.jhmi.edu/jeng/javarad/roc/JROCFITi.html

Mehdy, Ng, Shair, Md Saleh, & Gomes. (2017). *Artificial Neural Networks In Image Processing for Early Detection of Breast Cancer*. Hindawi Computational And Mathematical Methods in Medicine. 10.1155/2017/2610628\

Mhetre, N. A., Deshpande, A. V., & Mahalle, P. N. (2016). Trust Management Model based on Fuzzy Approach for Ubiquitous Computing. *International Journal of Ambient Computing and Intelligence, 7*(2). doi:10.4018/IJACI.2016070102

Sara & Kumar. (2017). Breast Cancer Detection using Image Processing Techniques. *Oriental Journal of Computer Science & Technology, 10*(2), 391-399.

Sarkar, M., Banerjee, S., & Badr, Y. (2017). Configuring a Trusted Cloud Service Model for Smart City Exploration Using Hybrid Intelligence. *International Journal of Ambient Computing and Intelligence, 8*(3). doi:10.4018/IJACI.2017070101

Tamane, S., Solanki, V. K., & Dey, N. (2017). *Privacy and Security Policies in Big Data*. doi:10.4018/978-1-5225-2486-1

Tian, Wang, Huang, Ning, Wang, Liu, & Tang. (2008). The digital database for breast ultrasound image. *Joint International Conference on Information Sciences*.

Tyagi, S., & Subhranil, Q. P. R. (2017). Trust based Dynamic multicast group routing ensuring reliability for ubiquitous environment in MANET's. *International Journal of Ambient Computing and Intelligence, 8*(1). doi:10.4018/IJACI.2017010104

Yamin, & Abdulaziz, & AbiSen. (2017). Improving Privacy and Security of User Data in Location Based Services. *International Journal of Ambient Computing and Intelligence, 9*(1).

Zhang, L., Dong, W., Zhang, D., & Shi, G. (2010). Two-stage image denoising By principal component analysis with local pixel grouping. *Pattern Recognition, 43*(4), 1531–1549. doi:10.1016/j.patcog.2009.09.023

Chapter 5
Filtration and Classification of ECG Signals

Satya Ranjan Dash
KIIT University, India

Asim Syed Sheeraz
KIIT University, India

Annapurna Samantaray
Indraprastha Institute of Information Technology Delhi (IIIT-D), India

ABSTRACT

Electrocardiogram (ECG) is a kind of process of recording the electrical activity/signals of the heart with respect to the time. ECG conveys a wide amount of information related to the structure and functions of the heart, its electrical conduction processes. ECG is a diagnostic tool that the doctors and medical professionals use to measure patients' heart activity by paying attention to the electric current flowing in the heart. Due to the presence of noises, it needs to carry out the filtration process. Filtration is the process of keeping the components of the signals of desired frequencies by setting up an "fc" value and removing the components apart from the said "fc" frequency. It is required to eliminate the noise level from the ECG signal, such that the resultant ECG signal must be free from noises. All these techniques and algorithms have their advantages and limitations which are discussed in this chapter.

1. INTRODUCTION

Electrocardiogram (ECG), is the signature of electrical movement of the heart, expressed as the summation of electrical signals originating from different regions of the heart, measured over a time interval. ECG conveys a wide amount of information related to the anatomy and the electrophysiology of the heart. It has been a diagnostic tool of choice for doctors and medical professionals to diagnose or predict cardiac abnormalities. However, due to small magnitudes of cardiac voltages observed at the skin surface, the chances of the ECG signal getting corrupted with noise are high. Understanding of the nature of the noise vital towards deciding upon the approach for its removal. Various techniques have been developed for removal of the noise, including analog filters, digital filters and feature extraction.

DOI: 10.4018/978-1-5225-5152-2.ch005

Copyright © 2018, IGI Global. Copying or distributing in print or electronic forms without written permission of IGI Global is prohibited.

Figure 1. P Q R ST Waves

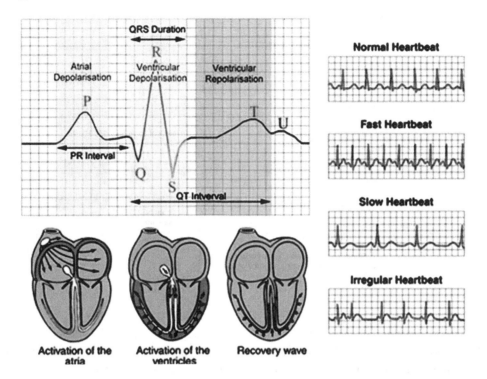

Filtration is the method of observance mechanism of the signals of required frequencies by setting up an '*fc*' value and removing the components apart from the said '*fc*' frequency. While in this process we need to eliminate the noise level from the ECG Signal, such that the resultant ECG signal must be free from noises.

Normal cardiac rhythm consists of P, QRS and T waves with parameters such as frequencies, time intervals and amplitudes well documented shown in Figure 1. However, the precise time intervals and wave shapes vary from one cardiac cycle to the other. Feature extraction mechanism determine the amplitude and intervals present in ECG signal for further analysis. Various techniques have been developed to analyze of the ECG signals. All these techniques and algorithms have their reward and restrictions which has been discussed in this chapter.

1.1 Biomedical Signals

Biomedical signals are time domain records of events such as flexing muscle or heartbeat. Any signals generated from a biological or health source can be called as Biosignals. The sources of the signal could be at molecular stage, cell level or organ level. These signals are commonly encountered in the clinic, research laboratory, sometimes even at home. Classification of biomedical signals shown in Figure 2.

Biomedical signal analysis deals with several interdisciplinary areas which helps in filtering, analysing and classifying the signals generated as a result of various physiological processes in the human body. These signals are primarily acquired for detecting specific physiological states for the purpose of diagnosis and evaluating therapy. However, these signals in raw form cannot provide much information

Figure 2. Categorization of Biomedical Signals

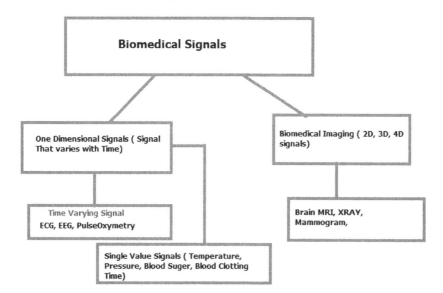

and are bound to be corrupted by noises and therefore the biomedical signal analysis techniques are used to extract the related information. This study has increasingly gained more significance with current healthcare as it helps provide cost effective aim-of care finding and personalised dealing.

Different types of Biomedical signals are:

- **Biochemical Signals e.g.:** Hormones, Neurotransmitter
- **Bioelectrical Signals e.g.:** Potentials, Currents, ECG, EEG
- **Biomechanical Signals e.g.:** Pressure, Temperature
- **Biomagnetic Signals e.g.:** Magnetocardiography (MCG)
- **Bioacoustic Signals e.g.:** Cardiac and Respiratory Sounds
- **Biooptical Signals e.g.:** Cardiac Output by dye dilution method

1.2 Biosignal Filtering

Even though surface ECG measurement is a go-to tool for doctors and medical healthcare professionals for diagnosing cardiac abnormalities, it is susceptible to noises in clinical settings. Noises and unwanted artifacts might even lead to incorrect diagnosis.

A filter circuit selectively amplifies certain set frequencies while attenuating the other frequencies. Filters can be broadly put into four categories, high pass, low pass, band pass and band stop shown in Figure 3. In case of a high pass filter, only signals with frequencies above a certain set value are amplified whereas in low pass filter signals above the set frequency value are attenuated. In case of band pass filters, all the signals between two set values of frequencies are amplified whereas in a band stop filters, the signals between two set frequency values are attenuated.

Both analog and digital filters are used for filtering ECG signals. Analog filters take in analog inputs and generates outputs in analog form, whereas the inputs and outputs in case of digital filters are in digital domain. Passive and active components such as registers, inductors, capacitors and operational amplifies

Figure 3. Different types of Filters

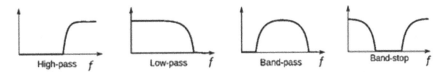

are used in construction of analog filters. In order to feed digital input to the digital filters, analog-to-digital converters (ADC) are used. Digital filters exhibit many advantages over the analog counterparts, as they are not affected by environmental conditions such as interferences, drift, and temperature while maintaining reproducibility. Most commercially available cardiac monitors choose the appropriate filter based on the noise encountered (Understanding ECG Filtering, 2014) shown in Figure 4.

The signal at the output of the filter circuit is distorted, which can be either be in amplitude or phase. As opposed to the cardiac recorders, the filters found in cardiac monitors are required to be real time. Because of this shorter-to-no delay requirement, the filter output exhibits non-linear characteristics. A phase distortion is created as the filters distort different frequencies differently. This phase distortion can be minimised by including the filters during post-processing, in cases where the real-time output of the signal is not required such as in ECG recorders (Saxena, Kumar, & Hamde, 2002).

Digital signal processing such as signal averaging, feature extraction and classification, wavelet analysis, machine learning and artificial intelligence techniques allow to the detection of abnormalities and efficient prognosis of heart disorders.

1.3 Discrete Time Signals

Discrete Time Signals (DTS) are time series that consists of sequence of functions with respect to integer domain. Discrete time signals have dependent values such as amplitude defined only at specific intervals of time (x-axis). They are usually obtained by the process of sampling of continuous time signals and each individual value is known as a sample.

Digital signals are not to be confused with the discrete time signals. Digital signals have finite levels/values of both time and amplitude (finite x-axis and y-axis) as opposed to discrete time signals which have continuous y-axis and discrete x-axis. Discrete-time signals are denoted by {x[n]} or simply x [n], where 'n' is an integer. Each element in this data sequence is called a sample. The range of samples, n is defined (wherever appropriate). The sample where n = 0 is either defined by the function x[0] or by putting an arrow under that sample as shown below,

$\{x[n]\} = \{\ldots, 0.35, 1, 1.5, -0.6, -2, \ldots\}$

The sample can either have complex or real values. We use the terms "sequences" and "discrete-time signals" interchangeably in this literature. The sampling frequency can be determined by the formula $f_s = 1/T$, where T represents the sampling interval. If the sampling interval for any sequence is not defined, it can be treated as 1 seconds. This will result in the sampling frequency of 1 Hz.

Figure 4. Noise and Noise Free ECG Signals

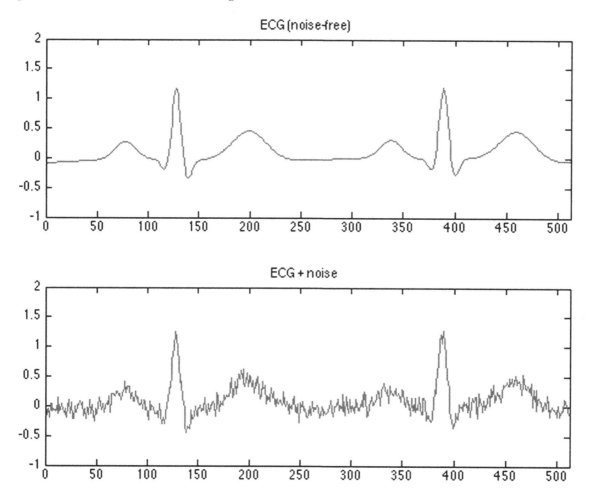

1.4 Sampling

Sampling is the process of reduction of continuous flow of signal into discrete signal. Sampling process is being carried out via different domain i.e., space, time, frequency, etc. Final results are obtained in one/two dimensional form. The sampling rate or frequency is termed as,

$f_s = 1/T$

Signals or functions varying in any dimension such as time or space can be sampled. In case of time domain signals, the continuous signal can be denoted by $s(t)$ and the intervals at which the values of dependent variable such as amplitude (y-axis) are to be measured at a fixed interval of time (T seconds) on x-axis is known as the sampling interval. The sampled function is given by the sequence:

$s(nT)$, for integer values of n.

The sampling frequency, f_s, can be define as the total number of samples found in every second. Therefore, we can mathematically define the sampling frequency as $f_s = 1/T$.

Continuous signals can be reconstructed from samples with the help of interpolation algorithms. Since interpolation, can be mathematically defined as a sequence of dirac delta functions that are modulated (multiplied) by the sample values applied to an ideal low pass filter. This is commonly referred to as Whittaker–Shannon interpolation formula. Dirac comb is the sequence of delta functions wherein the samples are at a constant time interval (T).

1.5 Discrete Fourier Transformation(DFT)

DFT is a conversion process. A continuous flow of biological signals are sampled and converted from analog to digital, the resultant obtained is given to the computer for further analysis and processes for the frequency domain (Martínez, Almeida, Olmos, Rocha, & Laguna, 2004). So it should convert the functions from time domain to frequency domain.

In DFT inputted samples are usually real number and output result is complex number. DFT is most important to perform Fourier analysis. DFT is other words we can say it is a tool that analyse and represent the discrete signals in frequency domain. It is digital form of fourier transformation in Figure 5.

The sequence of N complex numbers $x_0, x_1, ..., x_{N-1}$ is transformed into an *N*-periodic sequence of complex numbers:

$$X_k \overset{def}{=} \sum_{n=0}^{N-1} x_n . e^{-2\Pi ikn/N}, k \in Z$$

1.6 Filtering in ECG

Filtering is the process of removal of noises and unwanted artifacts. In the mechanism of ECG, Cardiac monitor plays a means to the filtering of data. Filtration process is being performed when the resultant information is ambiguous (Kania, Fereniec, & Maniewski, 2007). Most of the filtration process is been carried through bandpass filters, but it does not give appropriate result. ECG signals are very sensitive, if any small noise is interpreted then the characteristics of the signal changes. The presence of noise must be eliminated through Filtration mechanism (Li, Zheng, & Tai, 1995), removing of baseline wander shown in Figure 6.

1.6.1 Filtering Specification

Filtration is the process of retaining the components of the signals, which can be differentiated by a factor such as frequency. In case of filtration with respect to frequency, the desired frequencies are retained by setting up an '*fc*' value and removing the components apart from the said '*fc*' frequency. In order to retain the desired frequency components, their gain is set to 1 or close to 1, and the gain of the frequency components to be eliminated is set to 0 or close to 0.

In general there are four types of filters:

Figure 5. Digital and Analog Fourier Transformation

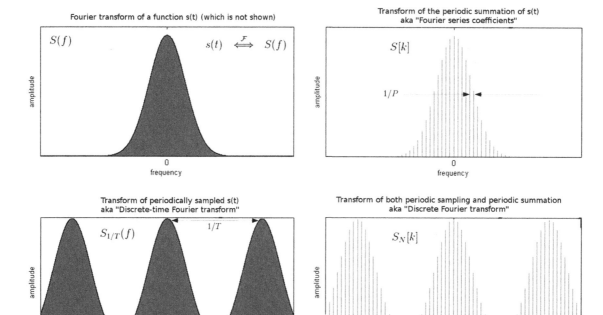

Figure 6. Remove baseline wander from ECG Signals

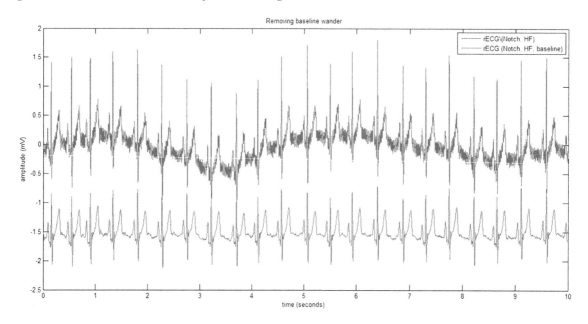

- Low-pass filter
- High-pass filter
- Band-pass filter
- Band-Stop filter

- **Passband:** The lower cut off and higher cut off for the frequency components that are endorsed to go by.
- **Stopband:** The range of frequency that are suppressed. This generally can be defined as the inverse of the passband.
- **Passband Ripples:** It is the maximum amount of attenuation in the pass band that may deviate, which is normally 1.
- **Stopband Ripples:** It is the maximum amount of attenuation in the pass band that may deviate, which is usually 0.
- **Stopband Attenuation:** It is the minimum amount of frequency components in the stopband are attenuated.
- **Transition Band:** It is the band among the pass band and stop band.
- In low pass filter, we need to set a cut off range i.e., '*fc*' such that components below the cut off range are allowed to pass through the filter. Those higher frequency above the cut off range are blocked through the filter.

The above shown in Figure 7 gives the magnitude frequency of the low pass filter. There is a must of transition band between the pass band and stop band. So, practically low pass filter will permit the frequency components under pass band '*fp*' and take away the higher components than '*fs*'.

As like LPF, In High Pass filter a certain cut off frequency '*fc*' is set such that which blocks all the frequency components lower than said '*fc*' and allows all the above frequency components w.r.t cut off frequency (Mahmoodabadi, Ahmadian, & Abolhasani, 2005).

Figure 7. Low Pass Filter

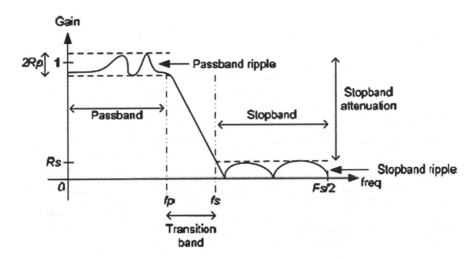

In other words, we can say it allows to pass the frequency components higher than the pass band '*fp*' and blocks the frequency components below '*fs*' shown in Figure 8.

In case of band pass filter, it allows the signals in the frequency band greater than *w*1 (omega) and less than *w*2 (omega) to pass through the filter and blocks any signal or noise apart this range of frequency shown in Figure 9.

In case of band stop Filter, it allows signals in the frequency band less than *w*1 and greater than *w*2 to pass through the filter and blocks any signal or noise apart this range of frequency shown in Figure 10.

Feature extraction of ECG mainly on multi assessment wavelet transform. ECG signals commencing tailored lead II are selected for dealing out (Kundu, Nasipuri, & Basu, 2000). Outcome applying in two wavelet filters of dissimilar time-span signals are compared (Foo, Stuart, Harvey, & Meyer-Baese, 2002). First step is to de-noise by removing the equivalent wavelet co-efficient of upper scale. QRS complex identified and every complex is use to find the peak of each waves, which include onset and

Figure 8. High Pass Filter

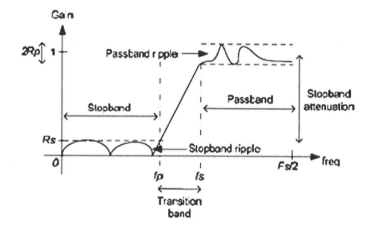

Figure 9. Band Pass Filter

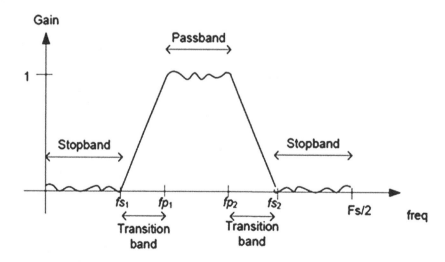

Figure 10. Band Stop Filter

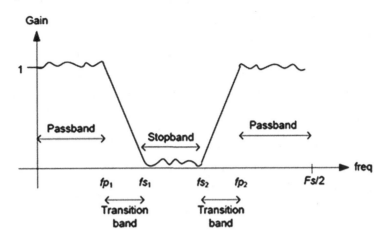

offset of the P and T waves are there during single cardiac phase. Also have different detection methods like R-detection, zero level detection, QS detection, P and T detection (Maglaveras, Stamkopoulos, Diamantaras, Pappas, & Strintzis, 1998). The dearth of especially low (< 2Hz) and very high(> 40 Hz) occurrence deliberation of ECG signals helped use to denoise the signals from association artifacts & external snooping noises easily (Mahmoodabadi, Ahmadian, & Abolhasani, 2005).

Single lead ECG delineation method based on the wavelet transformation. Every QRS is delineate through detection and identification of the peak entity waves, also the composite onset and end. Lastly the deterministic of P and T waves onset and end performed (Martínez, Almeida, Olmos, Rocha, & Laguna, 2004).

ECG Signals was denoised by MATLAB simulator and wavelet transform, by removing the corresponding wavelet of higher scale (Saritha, Sukanya, & Murthy, 2008). Other techniques are used to find characteristic points. With multi scale attribute of wavelet transform(WT) the QRS complex can be notable starting elevated P or T waves, noise, baseline drifts and artifacts. By these techniques, the recognition pace of QRS complexes is about 99.8% for MIT-BHA dataset, and P & T waves can also be identify, even with grave baseline drift and noise. A quadratic spline carry is used. It has universal linear segment. So there is a determine relation connecting ECG distinguishing points and the modulus maxima or the zero-crossing points of the WT's.

A QRS complex match to modulus maxima couple of the WT. Differing, an artifact having simply a up or down edge in firm time correspond to only single modules maximum of the WT. The algorithm can significantly trim down the consequence of the artifacts and can be distinguished not merely as QRS complex, but also as the T and P waves. Other features can be effortlessly obtained (Li, Zheng, & Tai, 1995). Classification of heart bits of normal beat, ventricular ectopic beat (VEB), supraventricular ectopic beat (SVEB), fusion of a normal and a VEB or unidentified beat type.

2. LITERATURE SURVEY

The main idea of digital ECG signal processing is to extract heart beat frequencies of any range. It is extracted heartbeat can be irregular due to lot of noise generated from environmental, breathing, physical movement. Digital signals can't be collected by the using of smart phone or wearable ECG sensors as there are many challenges like battery backup, quality of input we are going to get. By use of new improved wavelet filter, which used a circular buffer to minimize the memory across and instruction transfer value between data array. This new algorithm is very efficient for the current phone. Since it take less processing time and high battery life (Milchevski, & Gusev, 2017).

By using improved pipeline wavelet we can decrease processing time, save battery life and also this can be used in cell phone. Pre-processing of ECG and filtering or remove of the noise is the first step, through the QRS detection, we can remove the noise by giving threshold value to the high pass filter and low pass filter. Through discrete wavelet transform(DWT) also we can remove the noise of non-stationary signals which based on fourier design (Von Borries, Pierluissi, & Nazeran, 2006). Mainly noise comes from breathing and other physical activity during reading and can be removed high pass and low pass filter shown in Figure 11(a) and Figure 11(b).

Unwanted signals can be reduced by using another method known as majorization-minimization approach afterwards it can be segmented using bottom up approach, and by using this method we can have good improvement of signals to noise ratio (Yadav, & Ray, 2016), shown in Figure 12.

Due to atria depolarization / repolarization and ventricular depolarization / repolarization we get this type shown in Figure 12 of our ECG signal having any type of noise then it can be first removed properly or else it's very difficult to diagnoses the diseases. Many researcher are used infinite impulse response(IIR) filter to reduce the effect of power line interface(PLI) electrodes and electromagnetic field

Figure 11. (a) DWT Analysis; (b). DWT Synthesis

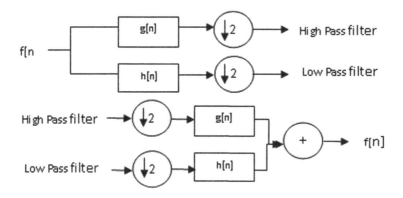

Figure 12. An ECG Signals complete Cycle

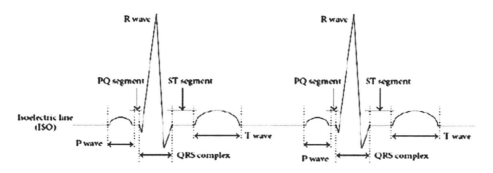

interference along with empirical mode decomposition(EMD). Non-linear bayesian filtering techniques, principal component analysis(PCA) and independent component analysis(ICA) (Barros, Mansour, & Ohnishi, 1998).

Optical mapping electrocardiogram(OM-ECG) can capture important morphology in ECG. Despite the heterogeneous wave propagation OM-ECG reproduces characteristic ECG morphology which can't be done through pseudo-ECG(Herndon, C., 2016) shown in Figure 13.

But OM-ECG leads required to be placed far from the heart. When intramural and mid- myocardial dynamics are not similar to those on the epicardial surface, the OM_ECG is unable to predict extra cardiac electric potential.

Baseline wonder artifact is one of the most common artifact of ECG. By using of morphological function and empirical mode decomposition(EMD) method morphological information can be preserved. One major limitation is introduction of ripple in the pass and stop bands leading to error of morphology. Due to use of membership function de-noising has done properly by using of the fuzzy logic (Choudhry, Puri, & Kapoor, 2016), but de-noising capability is very low in EMD.

Adaptive algorithm such as RLS and LMS (Rahman, Shaik, & Reddy, 2011), are found to not very effective for noise cancellation due to the fact the bench mark signal is not correlated very well with noise components present in the primary input (Chang, Ko, & Chang, 2010).

Thresholding techniques can also be used for de-noising of ECG signals with the help of wavelet transform. Normally ECG signals is selected randomly using data acquisition which can be expressed as shown in Figure 14.

X(m) = s(m) + b(m)

Figure 13. OM-ECG and pseudo-ECG

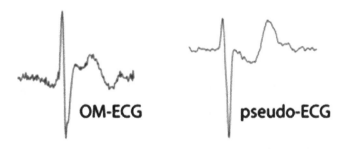

Figure 14. Basic block diagram of ECG signal processing

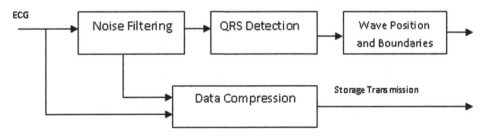

Threshholding exploits the capability of de-noising of the signals. Hard thresholding tends to have a higher variance:

$$w_{ht} = \begin{cases} w, |w| \geq t \\ 0, |w| < t \end{cases},$$

but in soft thresholding:

$$w_{st} = \begin{cases} |sign(w)||w| \geq t \\ 0, |w| < t \end{cases}$$

where w is coefficient pertaining to wavelet and t is the threshold value which is applied on the wavelet coefficient. Various other techniques like global thresholding, regressive thresholding, heursure thresholding, and minimax thresholding can also be applied (Yadav, & Mehra, 2016).

High frequency noises and enhance the QRS complexes in the signals using an EMD approach followed by an adaptive switching mean filtering (ASMF) operation is performed for further improvement of the signal quality shown in Figure 15. It is inspired by the fact that there should like a similarity in value in neighbourhood pixels. In the beginning the EMD signals is decomposed ino its intrinsic mode functions (IMFs) and a wavelet de-noising operation is performed on first through IMF.

Lastly ASMF is applied for further improvement of signal quality by reducing the noises those are spread in lowest frequency band.

It is a powerful tool to remove noises from images. In ASMF window is taken and at each iteration. Now within the window the mean and standard deviation of the samples are determined. If the difference between the centred sample value and the mean is outside the range of the threshold, then the sample is considered as a noisy sample and its value is updated with the mean value of the window. The thresholding scheme is demonstrated as:

$$\hat{S}_{i_{st}} = \begin{cases} m_i if |S_i - m_i| > \alpha \times \delta_i \\ S_i else \end{cases}$$

We can also minimize the noise and also de-noised the ECG signals by using kernel principal component analysis(KPCA) method to achieve high performance ECG signals and also giving better result than DWT, PCA method (Rakshit, & Das, 2017).

It's very difficult to get accurate ECG signals due to AC power line interference, baseline wandering, sometime gaussian or high frequency noises are there. So many methods are there to de-noising

Figure 15. Adaptive switching mean filter

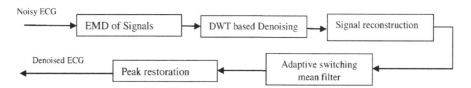

the signals among which ensemble empirical mode decomposition (EEMD) are found more effective in reducing noise from ECG signals, is a data analysis method which represent substantial improvement. Statistical characteristic of white noise, comparison has done on the basis of their higher signal noise ratio(SNR) and lower root mean square error (RSME) value (Bhardwaj, Nara, Malik, & Singh, 2016).

Gaussian low pass filter is used to remove the high frequency noise. An ECG include the P-wave, QRS- complex and T-waves. The role of T-wave and the peak point of P having the great role to approximate the baseline over certain number of cycle (Chaudhuri, Bhattacharya, & Dey, 2016).

ECG signal collection techniques is also very important as de-noising the intrusive and non-intrusive data, through iterative least square polynomial approximation method. Due to muscle contraction and interference due to power line also signals can be noise, through recursive least square filters along with modified version of linear iterative kolman filter to remove traces from ECG signals. Through fetal electrocardiogram(FEG) emerging technology. we can monitor the cardiac as well as de-nosing. Here the new online subspace inserted after removal of maternal cardiac signal removal.

A well-known multichannel technique for extraction of fECG is blind source separation (BSS) using independent component analysis (ICA), which has been shown to be more accurate and robust as compared to similar approaches (Zarzoso, & Nandi, 2001). First remove mECG than applied ICA techniques to get better result. More recently deflation subspace decomposition procedure which we call de-noising by deflation(DEFL) was proposed for signal subspace separation from full-rank noise (Sameni, 2008). Generalized Eigen value decomposition(GEVD) which is extension of online DEFL called ODEFL is introduced to remove mECG (Fatemi, & Sameni, 2017).

Manual analysis of ECG beat is very time-consuming task as it may contain hundreds of thousands beats for 24 hrs of ECG signals. Rough set theory having upper bound and lower bound concepts to keep the signal inside some boundary. This concept is very simple which can be applied to extract more accurate information from ECG dataset and we can combine rough set theory with different type of classifier techniques to generate reducts and classify ECG signals like fuzzy rough nearest neighbour, multilayer perceptron(MLP) shown in Figure 16.

Through RBF we can classify the ECG signals to normal and abnormal class by including beats of atrial fibrillation (AF) and atrial activity (AA). These beats are very important source of error as we can have these beats in normal patient or can be the patients having heart disease (Mateo, Torres, Aparicio, & Santos, 2016). Wave forms formed by different particular cardiac tissues found in the heart, feasible to identify some of its abnormalities.

Arrhythmia is a cardiac condition caused by abnormal electrical activity and it's a challenge how to detect and classify, required to detect it by using linear and non-linear experiments to characteristics the ECG signals. Mainly linear experiment recognizes the arrhythmia of noise free signals, but non-linear experiment can extract hidden information of ECG signals giving better result in noisy condition. With combination of PCA of DWT, ICA and higher order spectra(HOS), feature extraction method and different classifier, we can classify to get better result.

A new and novel method for the ECG beat classification can be done by using projected dynamic features are derived from a random projection matrix in which each column is normalized and each row is transformed by discrete cosine transform(DCT) (Elhaj, Salim, Harris, Swee, & Ahmed, 2016).

We can also extract the feature of QRS complex through Pan-Tompkins algorithm, then it is pass through LPF and HPF filters (Rao, Rao, Manikanta, & Kumar, 2016).

Figure 16. Flowchart of ECG classifier Model

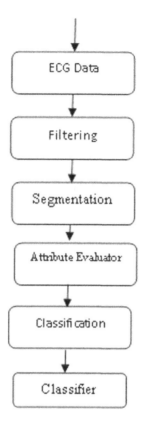

3. PROPOSED WORK

The ECG signal (MIT-BIH normal sinus rhythm) data had been retrieved from the data set, physiobank ATM having time interval of 10 seconds in MATLAB format (Welch, Ford, Teplick, & Rubsamen, 1991). ECG Signals has plotted before and after the removal of noise shown in Figure 20 and the flow of the proposed work has shown in Figure 17, and the MIT-BIH normal sinus rhythm and file details has given in Figure 18 and Figure 19.

4. RESULT ANALYSIS

The ECG data was loaded into the MATLAB using the MATLAB function load 'file name'. The val function was used to know the volume of data mentioned in Figure 21.

On the basis of those datum, we plotted the ECG signal graph using the function plot in MATLAB shown in Figure 22.

To know the artifacts present in the signal, it was verified whether the signal was in time domain or frequency domain. If found in time domain, the same were converted to frequency domain using FFT (First Four Year Transformation) which shown in Figures 23 and 24.

Figure 17. Flow chart of proposed work

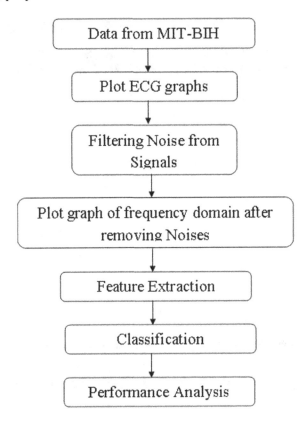

After converting/getting the signal in frequency domain, the frequency range of the ECG signal was verified to determine if the frequency range falls within the noise range, which will be filtered to remove the noise shown in Figure 25.

After removing the noise, we got the ECG signal in the form of PQRST graph representing the ECG signal, which help us to diagnosis the cardiac problem shown in Figure 26.

5. CONCLUSION

Collected the ECG signals DATA set from the online waveform database of Massachusetts General Hospital. After collection of the Data of, 'MIT-BIH Normal Sinus Rhythm Database (nsrdb)' for 10 seconds, we have got the resultant ECG signals. But, due to the presence of various noise level and disturbances, we need to undergo these signals through filtration techniques, using- "Butterworth Band stop Filter" such that, via setting a cut off limit '*fc*' we could easily filter out the ECG Signals through eliminating the Noise Level, Finally the resultant signal we found which is being free from noise. Comparative analysis has not done with other existing filtering techniques, also can't be tested with other database. Though some of the existing classification techniques has discussed, but no classification techniques has implemented in existing dataset after removing the noise.

Figure 18. MIT-BIH normal sinus rhythm

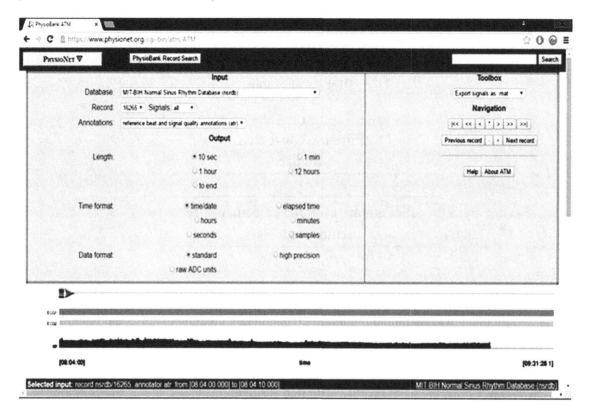

Figure 19. MIT-BIH Dataset

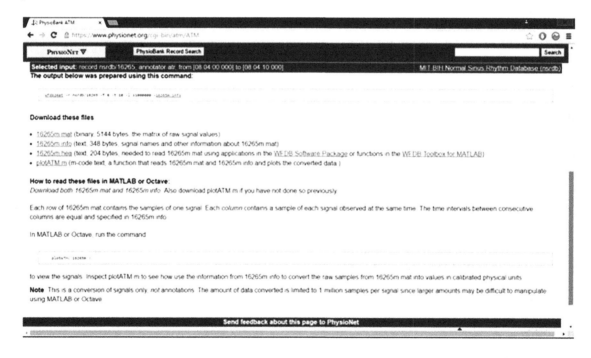

Figure 20. Filtering of noise from signals

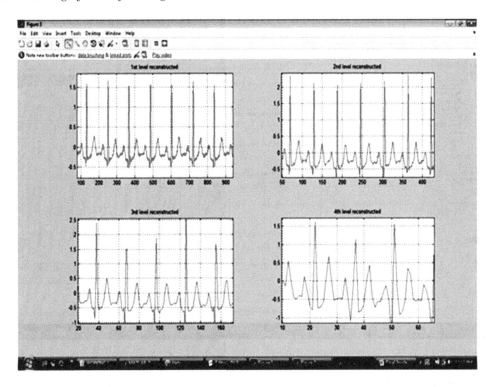

Figure 21. Result from the ECG signals

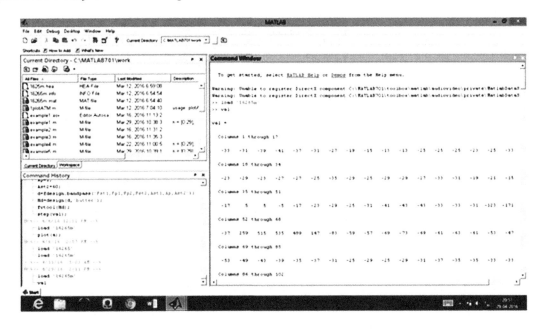

Figure 22. Plotted ECG Signals

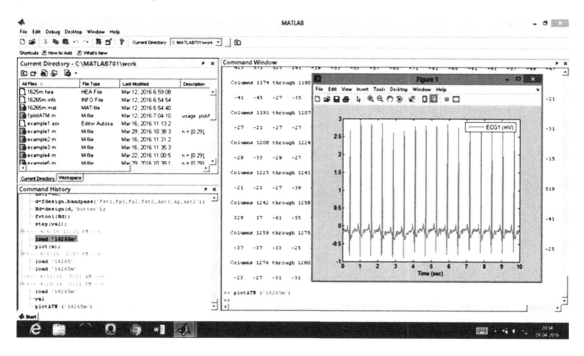

Figure 23. Domain Frequency

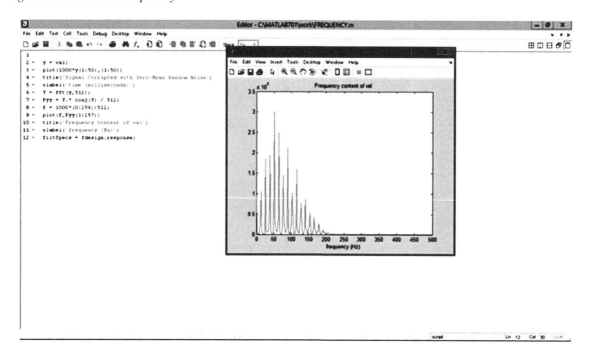

Figure 24. Converting Signals into Frequency Domain

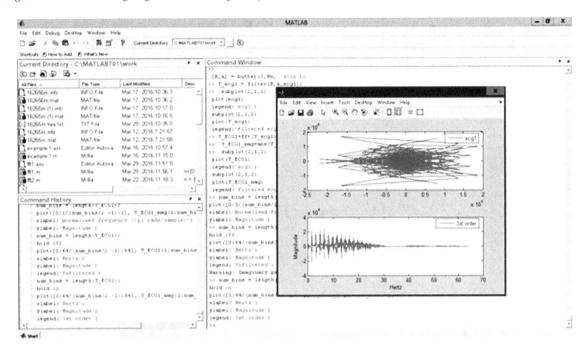

Figure 25. After removing the Noise

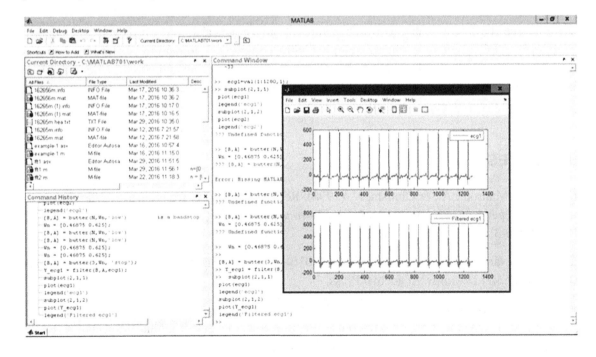

Figure 26. PQRST graph representing ECG Signals

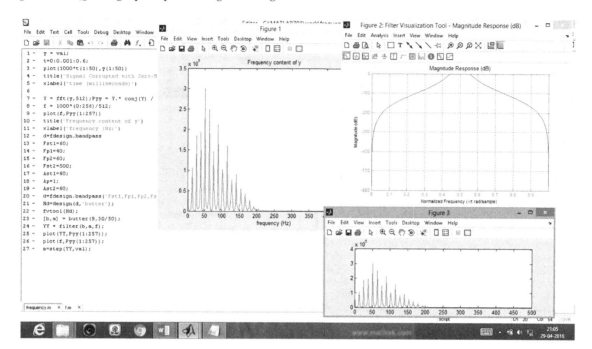

6. FUTURE WORK

Filtering also can be done after extracting the features through noises also can be removed. One important work to analyze ECG signals in other domain including compressed domain to cluster heartbeats, and minimizing the resources for the computation. The accuracy of filtering and classification can also be increased by using machine learning approach, including data reduction and feature extraction mechanism for accurate and faster diagnosis of cardiac disease.

REFERENCES

Barros, A. K., Mansour, A., & Ohnishi, N. (1998). Removing artifacts from electrocardiographic signals using independent components analysis. *Neurocomputing*, 22(1), 173–186. doi:10.1016/S0925-2312(98)00056-3

Bhardwaj, N., Nara, S., Malik, S., & Singh, G. (2016). *Analysis of ECG Signal Denoising Algorithms in DWT and EEMD Domains*. Academic Press.

Chang, C. H., Ko, H. J., & Chang, K. M. (2010). Cancellation of high-frequency noise in ECG signals using adaptive filter without external reference. In Biomedical Engineering and Informatics (BMEI), (Vol. 2, pp. 787-790). IEEE. doi:10.1109/BMEI.2010.5639953

Chaudhuri, P. N., Bhattacharya, S., & Dey, S. (2016). Baseline Drift Correction in Standard ECG Signals Using Centroid Based Approach. *International Journal of Engineering Science*, 3310.

Choudhry, M. S., Puri, A., & Kapoor, R. (2016). Removal of baseline wander from ECG signal using cascaded Empirical Mode Decomposition and morphological functions. In Signal Processing and Integrated Networks (SPIN), (pp. 769-774). IEEE. doi:10.1109/SPIN.2016.7566803

Elhaj, F. A., Salim, N., Harris, A. R., Swee, T. T., & Ahmed, T. (2016). Arrhythmia recognition and classification using combined linear and nonlinear features of ECG signals. *Computer Methods and Programs in Biomedicine*, *127*, 52–63. doi:10.1016/j.cmpb.2015.12.024 PMID:27000289

Fatemi, M., & Sameni, R. (2017). An Online Subspace Denoising Algorithm for Maternal ECG Removal from Fetal ECG Signals. *Iranian Journal of Science and Technology. Transaction of Electrical Engineering*, *41*(1), 65–79. doi:10.100740998-017-0018-4

Foo, S. Y., Stuart, G., Harvey, B., & Meyer-Baese, A. (2002). Neural network-based EKG pattern recognition. *Engineering Applications of Artificial Intelligence*, *15*(3), 253–260. doi:10.1016/S0952-1976(02)00041-6

Herndon, C., Uzelac, I., Farmer, J. T., & Fenton, F. (2016). Computational ECG reconstruction and validation from high-resolution optical mapping. In *Computing in Cardiology Conference (CinC)*, (pp. 713-716). IEEE.

Kania, M., Fereniec, M., & Maniewski, R. (2007). Wavelet denoising for multi-lead high resolution ECG signals. *Measurement Science Review*, *7*(4), 30–33.

Kundu, M., Nasipuri, M., & Basu, D. K. (2000). Knowledge-based ECG interpretation: A critical review. *Pattern Recognition*, *33*(3), 351–373. doi:10.1016/S0031-3203(99)00065-5

Li, C., Zheng, C., & Tai, C. (1995). Detection of ECG characteristic points using wavelet transforms. *IEEE Transactions on Biomedical Engineering*, *42*(1), 21–28. doi:10.1109/10.362922 PMID:7851927

Maglaveras, N., Stamkopoulos, T., Diamantaras, K., Pappas, C., & Strintzis, M. (1998). ECG pattern recognition and classification using non-linear transformations and neural networks: A review. *International Journal of Medical Informatics*, *52*(1), 191–208. doi:10.1016/S1386-5056(98)00138-5 PMID:9848416

Mahmoodabadi, S. Z., Ahmadian, A., & Abolhasani, M. D. (2005). ECG feature extraction using Daubechies wavelets. In *Proceedings of the fifth IASTED International conference on Visualization, Imaging and Image Processing* (pp. 343-348). Academic Press.

Martínez, J. P., Almeida, R., Olmos, S., Rocha, A. P., & Laguna, P. (2004). A wavelet-based ECG delineator: Evaluation on standard databases. *IEEE Transactions on Biomedical Engineering*, *51*(4), 570–581. doi:10.1109/TBME.2003.821031 PMID:15072211

Martínez, J. P., Almeida, R., Olmos, S., Rocha, A. P., & Laguna, P. (2004). A wavelet-based ECG delineator: Evaluation on standard databases. *IEEE Transactions on Biomedical Engineering*, *51*(4), 570–581. doi:10.1109/TBME.2003.821031 PMID:15072211

Mateo, J., Torres, A. M., Aparicio, A., & Santos, J. L. (2016). An efficient method for ECG beat classification and correction of ectopic beats. *Computers & Electrical Engineering*, *53*, 219–229. doi:10.1016/j.compeleceng.2015.12.015

Milchevski, A., & Gusev, M. (2017). Improved pipelined Wavelet implementation for filtering ECG signals. *Pattern Recognition Letters*, *95*, 85–90. doi:10.1016/j.patrec.2017.06.005

Rahman, M. Z. U., Shaik, R. A., & Reddy, D. R. K. (2011). Efficient sign based normalized adaptive filtering techniques for cancelation of artifacts in ECG signals: Application to wireless biotelemetry. *Signal Processing*, *91*(2), 225–239. doi:10.1016/j.sigpro.2010.07.002

Rakshit, M., & Das, S. (2017). An improved EMD based ECG denoising method using adaptive switching mean filter. In *Signal Processing and Integrated Networks (SPIN), 4th International Conference on* (pp. 251-255). Academic Press. 10.1109/SPIN.2017.8049954

Rao, P. T., Rao, S. K., Manikanta, G., & Kumar, S. R. (2016). Distinguishing normal and abnormal ECG signal. *Indian Journal of Science and Technology*, *9*(10).

Sameni, R. (2008). *Extraction of fetal cardiac signals from an array of maternal abdominal recordings* (Doctoral dissertation). Institute National Polytechnique de Grenoble-INPG, Sharif University of Technology (SUT).

Saritha, C., Sukanya, V., & Murthy, Y. N. (2008). ECG signal analysis using wavelet transforms. *Bulg. J. Phys*, *35*(1), 68–77.

Saxena, S. C., Kumar, V., & Hamde, S. T. (2002). Feature extraction from ECG signals using wavelet transforms for disease diagnostics. *International Journal of Systems Science*, *33*(13), 1073–1085. doi:10.1080/00207720210167159

Under Standing E. C. G. Filtering. (2014). Retrieved from http://www.ems12lead.com/2014/03/10/understanding-ecg-filtering/#sthash.AlhGhgBb.dpuf

Von Borries, R. F., Pierluissi, J. H., & Nazeran, H. (2006). Wavelet transform-based ECG baseline drift removal for body surface potential mapping. In Engineering in Medicine and Biology Society, (pp. 3891-3894). IEEE.

Welch, J., Ford, P., Teplick, R., & Rubsamen, R. (1991). The Massachusetts General Hospital-Marquette Foundation hemodynamic and electrocardiographic database–comprehensive collection of critical care waveforms. *Clinical Monitoring*, *7*(1), 96–97.

Yadav, O. P., & Ray, S. (2016). Smoothening and Segmentation of ECG Signals Using Total Variation Denoising–Minimization-Majorization and Bottom-Up Approach. *Procedia Computer Science*, *85*, 483–489. doi:10.1016/j.procs.2016.05.195

Yadav, T., & Mehra, R. (2016). Denoising and SNR improvement of ECG signals using wavelet based techniques. In Next Generation Computing Technologies (NGCT), (pp. 678-682). IEEE. doi:10.1109/NGCT.2016.7877498

Zarzoso, V., & Nandi, A. K. (2001). Noninvasive fetal electrocardiogram extraction: Blind separation versus adaptive noise cancellation. *IEEE Transactions on Biomedical Engineering*, *48*(1), 12–18. doi:10.1109/10.900244 PMID:11235584

Chapter 6
Wavelet and Curvelet Transforms for Biomedical Image Processing

Manas Saha
Siliguri Institute of Technology, India

Mrinal Kanti Naskar
Jadavpur University, India

B. N. Chatterji
B. P. Poddar Institute of Management and Technology, India

ABSTRACT

This chapter introduces two mathematical transforms—wavelet and curvelet—in the field of biomedical imaging. Presenting the theoretical background with relevant properties, the applications of the two transforms are presented. The biomedical applications include heart sound analysis, electrocardiography (ECG) characterization, positron emission tomography (PET) image analysis, medical image compression, mammogram enhancement, magnetic resonance imaging (MRI) and computer tomography (CT) image denoising, diabetic retinopathy detection. The applications emphasize the development of algorithms to diagnose human diseases, thereby rendering fast and reliable support to the medical personnel. The transforms—one classical (wavelet) and another contemporary (curvelet)—are selected to focus the difference in architecture, limitation, evolution, and application of individual transform. Two joint applications are addressed to compare their performance. This survey is also supplemented by a case study: mammogram denoising using wavelet and curvelet transforms with the underlying algorithms.

1. INTRODUCTION

Over the last few decades there is a sea change in biomedical signal and image processing. This is possible due to the development and integration of the system and software used in biology and medicine. This chapter introduces two mathematical transforms called wavelet and curvelet in biomedical imaging.

DOI: 10.4018/978-1-5225-5152-2.ch006

Copyright © 2018, IGI Global. Copying or distributing in print or electronic forms without written permission of IGI Global is prohibited.

It brings together some of the significant applications of both the transforms in one common plane of knowledge, understanding and implementation.

The chapter is divided into six sections - Section 1 to Section 6. Section 1 is the introductory section. Sections 2 and 3 deal with wavelet and curvelet transforms respectively. Section 4 presents the comparison of wavelet with curvelet transform using two applications. Section 5 showcases a case study on medical imaging using both the transforms. The conclusion is drawn in Section 6.

In Section 2, a theoretical background on wavelet transform is developed. The wavelet transform gained its popularity during the nineties and is still very much relevant in research and industry due to its strong underlying mathematical hypothesis. The different applications of wavelet transform are heart sound analysis, electrocardiography (ECG) characterization, electroencephalography (EEG) analysis for seizure detection, positron emission tomography (PET) image analysis, medical image compression, mammogram enhancement and detection of microcalcification and many more. Some applications are reviewed here. But at the same time, the limitations of wavelet are also projected. So "mother" wavelet becomes an active area of research. Several advanced wavelets proposed in due course of time are outlined.

One such advanced wavelet is curvelet. It is selected so that a comparison is done in between the conventional computational tool, wavelet and advanced computational tool, curvelet. The significant properties as well as architecture of curvelet are addressed in Sections 3.1 and 3.2 respectively. The important applications of curvelet like denoising of computer tomography (CT) and magnetic resonance imaging (MRI) images, retina image enhancement, optic disk detection, diabetic retinopathy detection, edge detection of light and electron microscopic images are addressed in Section 3.3. Although curvelet is recently developed, there are applications where curvelet outperforms wavelet. Such interesting applications like the classifications of human organ in CT images, breast cancer diagnosis are presented in Section 4.

Sections 5 projects a case study on the noise filtration of mammogram with the help of wavelet and curvelet transforms. It demonstrates how the transforms using the underlying shrinking techniques filter noise from a mammogram. Lastly, the noise filtration performance of wavelet and curvelet are compared to find which transform is better in filtering a particular type of noise.

2. WAVELET TRANSFORM: BACKGROUND

Wavelet is a wave of finite duration having a mean value of zero. The continuous wavelet transform (CWT) is used for signal analysis. Its partially discrete version, that is, wavelet series and its completely discrete version, that is, discrete wavelet transform are applied for signal coding, image compression and computer vision related tasks [37]. Unlike Fourier transform, its way of localizing information in time-frequency plane is unique. It has the ability to trade one type of resolution for the other. This particular feature makes it befitting for the investigation of non-stationary signals. Fortunately, majority of the biomedical images or signals are dynamic in nature. The application of wavelet in biomedical signal and image processing is very much significant.

Let, $x\left(t\right)$ be a time varying signal. Wavelet transforms engage in evaluating coefficients which are inner products of the given signal and a family of "wavelets". At a given scale a with time location b, a CWT can be written from [37] as

$$\psi_{a,b}\left(t\right) = \frac{1}{\sqrt{|a|}} \psi\left(\frac{t-b}{a}\right) \tag{1}$$

where $\psi\left(t\right)$ denotes "mother" wavelet. $\psi\left(t\right)$ is considered as a band pass function and $\dfrac{1}{\sqrt{|a|}}$ denotes energy preservation. There are different approaches to discretize time-scale parameters $\left(b,a\right)$. Individual approach generates a dissimilar kind of wavelet.

As the time t and time-scale parameters $\left(b,a\right)$ vary continuously, the CWT can be expressed from [37] as:

$$CWT\left\{x\left(t\right); a,b\right\} = \int x\left(t\right)\psi_{a,b}^{*}\left(t\right)dt \tag{2}$$

where $*$ means complex conjugate.

The wavelet series coefficients are obtained by sampling CWT coefficients. The time t remains continuous whereas time-scale parameters $\left(b,a\right)$ are sampled on what is known as "dyadic" grid located in the time-scale plane (b,a) [29]. Therefore, a general definition is:

$$C_{j,k} = CWT\left\{x\left(t\right); a = 2^{j}, b = k2^{j}\right\}, j,k \in Z. \tag{3}$$

In this case, the wavelets can be expressed as:

$$\psi_{j,k}\left(t\right) = 2^{-j/2} \psi\left(2^{-j}t - k\right). \tag{4}$$

The discrete wavelet transform (DWT) is familiar as a natural wavelet transform for discrete time signals. The important point is that both time t as well as time–scale parameters $\left(b,a\right)$ are discrete. When the structure of computation is considered, DWT resembles an octave-band filter bank as already shown in Figure 1 (Rioul, & Duhamel, 1992). The filter bank has a regular structure and is realized by repetitive application of identical cells. The DWT is computationally very efficient. Thus, when the calculation of a wavelet transform is reduced to DWT, the resulting implementation is efficient.

The remaining wavelet theory and its mathematical treatment is already available in literature. However, the properties of wavelet transform which are very much related to medical imaging are reinvestigated below.

2.1 Some Properties of Wavelet Transform

2.1.1 Wavelet Considered as a Filterbank

Let a be the scale parameter and b be the continuous shift parameter. For a fixed value of a the wavelet transform can be expressed as a convolution equation from (Unser, & Aldroubi, 1996) as:

$$T_\psi f \left(a = Const, b \right) = \left\langle f, \psi_{(a,b)} \right\rangle = \left(f * \bar{\psi}_a^{\ T} \right) (b) \tag{5}$$

where the filtering template $\bar{\psi}_a^{\ T} (x) = a^{-\frac{1}{2}} \bar{\psi} \left(-x \big/ a \right)$ corresponds to a rescaled and time-reversed version of the wavelet $\psi (x)$. The frequency response of this filter is simply $a^{\frac{1}{2}} \hat{\psi} (aw)$, where $\hat{\psi}$ is the complex conjugate of Fourier transform of ψ (Unser, & Aldroubi, 1996) .

Hence, when Equation (5) is computed for a distinct set of scales, a constant Q filterbank is obtained. This sort of investigation leads to a signal decomposition into subbands having bandwidth proportional to frequency. But in a dyadic transformation, every spectral band is almost one octave wide as shown in Figure 1(a). Under this condition, the wavelet transform is considered as a typical spectral analyzer which provides several important features like energy estimation of various subbands. Two examples extracting spectral features from the susband decomposition are: 1) turbulent heart beat analysis (Akay, Akay, Welkowitz, & Kostis, 1994) and; 2) characterization of states of fetal electrocortical activity (Akay, Akay, Welkowitz, & Lewkowicz, 1994).

If $G_1 (w)$, $G_2 (w)$,... $G_{m-1} (w)$, $H_m (w)$ represent the transfer functions of discrete filters which are related with a redundant m channel dyadic wavelet decomposition such that $G_i (w) \cong \hat{\psi} \left(2^i w \right)$ and $H_m (w)$ being a low pass filter, then a corresponding reconstruction algorithm can be obtained provided the synthesis filters shown in Figure 1 (b) are selected so that:

$$H_m (w) \tilde{H}_m (w) + \sum_{i=1}^{m-1} G_i (w) \tilde{G}_i (w) = 1 \tag{6}$$

If the wavelet $\psi (x)$ can be derived from multiresolution analysis, then its corresponding filterbank can be realized with an adaptive version of Mallat's fast algorithm without the need of subsampling (Unser, & Aldroubi, 1996). This kind of reversible wavelet decomposition is the foundation of applying noise filtration and medical image enhancement techniques.

2.1.2 Constructable Wavelet Bases

One of the big advantages of wavelet is that the *wavelet bases of L_2 (the spaces of square integrable functions)* (Unser, & Aldroubi, 1996) can be constructed. The wavelet basis is specified by the set of dilated and translated versions of the "mother" wavelet given by:

Figure 1. Wavelet considered as a filterbank. (a)"Multiband frequency response of the discrete filter-bank associated with the cubic spline Battle-Lemarié wavelets" (b) "Discrete perfect reconstruction filter-bank without subsampling"

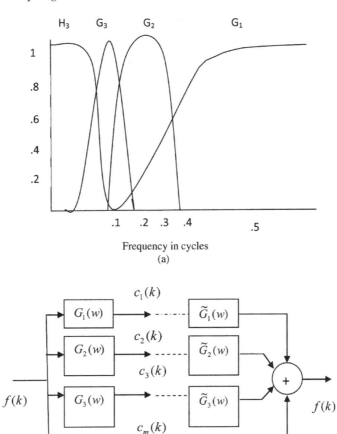

$$\left\{ \psi_{i,k} = 2^{-i/2} \psi\left(x\big/2^i - k\right) \right\}_{(i,k)\in Z^2} \tag{7}$$

where i and k are the dilation and translation indices. It is easily possible to present a signal with the help of its wavelet expansion given by:

$$f = \sum_i \sum_{k\in Z} c_{i,k} \psi_{i,k} \tag{8}$$

where the coefficients of wavelet $c_{i,k}$ are found as:

$$c_{i,k} = \left\langle f, \tilde{\psi}_{i,k} \right\rangle \tag{9}$$

The function $\tilde{\psi}$ is dual analysis wavelet. ψ and $\tilde{\psi}$ are identical in the orthogonal case. The above discussion is helpful because in the discrete domain, the decomposition Equation (7) presents a one-to-one representation of the signal in terms of its wavelet coefficients. The noise elimination, data compression, image coding of medical images are obtained by the quantization in the wavelet domain or by eliminating unimportant coefficients. This type of nearly orthogonal wavelet decomposition is advantageous to MRI images (Angelidis, 1994) and digital mammogram compression (Lucier, Kallergi, Qian, DeVore, Clark, Saff, & Clarke, 1994).

2.1.3 Wavelet as a Model of Audio and Video Signal Perception

In an auditory system, when a sound pressure $p(t)$ strikes the surface of outer ear, neuro electrical impulses are produced in the inner ear. The processing and investigation of the sound waves are carried out by linear processing stages which closely resemble wavelet transforms. It can be shown from (Unser, & Aldroubi, 1996; Yang, Wang, & Shamma, 1992) that the inner ear transforms sound pressure $p(t)$ into displacement $y(t, x_1)$ of its basilar membrane given by:

$$y(t, x_1) = \left(p(\cdot) * h(\cdot, x_1) \right)(t) \tag{10}$$

where x_1 is a curvilinear coordinate along the direction of inner ear, c is the propagation velocity, $h(t, x_1) = h(ct/x_1)$ is the inner ear bandpass filter positioned at x_1. Therefore, $y(t, x_1)$ is CWT of $p(t)$ with wavelet $h(t)$ at a time scale dependent on position x_1/c. This particular property motivates research in the coding, detection and transmission of auditory signals.

The primary visual cortex has a large number of neurons which behave like wavelets. They are commonly known as simple cells of the occipital cortex. The simple cells receive visual information from the retina and transmit it to the complex cells of the primary visual cortices. There is a remarkable

similarity between the response of the simple cells as shown in Figure 2 (a) taken from (Unser, & Aldroubi, 1996) and the cubic B-spline wavelet function shown in Figure 2 (b) which is also taken from (Unser, & Aldroubi, 1996). This type of analogy has motivated researchers to develop various multichannel neural models having group of directional Gabor wavelets (Unser, & Aldroubi, 1996; (Daugman, 1989).

2.2 Biomedical Applications of Wavelet Transform

2.2.1 Heart Sound Analysis

The pumping of heart produces heart sound. Analyzing the heart sound helps to monitor the cardiac activity. The heart sound is classified as ordinary heart sounds and murmurs. Ordinary heart sounds are generally short and impulse-like events. They represent switching of the various hemodynamic phases related to cardiac cycle. Murmurs caused due to turbulence of blood flow, characterizes cardiac diseases like defects in valves and aortic stenosis.

Khadra et al. (Khadra, Matalgah, El-Asir, & Mawagdeh, 1991) implemented wavelet transform for the time–frequency analysis and description of heart sounds. This approach of heart sound monitoring was compared with other time-frequency analyzing approaches (Obaidat, 1993). In (Obaidat, 1993), Obiadat demonstrated that certain heart sound components could only be traced by wavelet transform.

2.2.2 Electrocardiography (ECG) Characterization

The ECG is a process of recording the changes in electrical activity of the heart over a time period. The characteristic shape of the ECG signal as shown in Figure 3 is due to flow of the electric potential circulating through the heart. It reasons time bound contraction and relaxation of different cardiac muscles. In Figure 3, P wave is the first characteristic wave. It is caused due to the transmission of the cardiac excitation from the natural pacemaker, sinus node of the heart to the artia. The second characteristic wave, that is, the QRS wave is caused due to the propagation of the exciting signal from the artia to the ventricles which is commonly known as ventricular depolarization. The repolarization of the ventricles is denoted by the T wave. Now the time–frequency analysis of the waves, especially the QRS wave is very much helpful for diagnostic purpose.

Figure 2. Similarity between the receptive field of simple cortical cells and a wavelet basis function (Unser, & Aldroubi, 1996) a) Response of a simple X cell from a monkey visual cortex and its fitted Gabor elementary signal (Sugantharathnam & Manimegalai, 2011), [Figure 3, (Marĉelja, 1980)]. b) Semi-orthogonal cubic B-spline wavelet and its log log frequency response (Unser, & Aldroubi, 1996; Unser, Aldroubi, & Eden,1992)

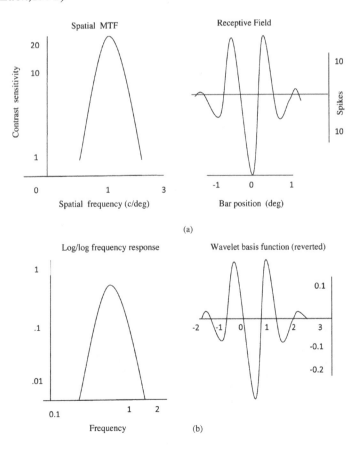

Sahambi et al. (Sahambi, Tandon, & Bhatt, 1997) demonstrates the detection of QRS and the localization of P and T waves. They employ the zero crossings of the wavelet transform to trace the exact location of QRS wave on the ECG signal. Wavelet transform is also used to detect ventricular late potentials (VLP) (Meste, Rix, Caminal, & Thakor, 1994). VLP are minute signals which have frequency content greater than 40 Hz. They are closely associated with different coronary heart diseases like ventricular arrhythmias. VLP are naturally found at the end of QRS wave or the beginning of ST segment which is shown in Figure 3. There are many techniques which detect such VLP. But Khadra et al. (Khadra, Dickhaus, & Lipp, 1993) proposed that wavelet based VLP detection outperforms other methods.

2.2.3 Electroencephalography (EEG) Analysis for Seizure Detection

Electroencephalogram is the process of monitoring the electrical activity of brain using small electrodes in the form of discs attached to the scalp. This modality of monitoring the brain functionality is particularly important to diagnose epilepsy. Epilepsy also known as seizure disorders is a neurological problem which is characterized by unpredictable and sudden seizures. A seizure is an abrupt surge of electrical impulse produced in brain. This is indicated by the presence of spikes in the EEG signal. In an advanced stage of epilepsy, the small spikes develop into high amplitude, recurrent and unpredictable oscillations. The wavelet transform is used to locate seizure and other electroencephalographic spikes (Schiff, Milton, Heller, & Weinstein, 1994). Schiff et al. (Schiff, Aldroubi, Unser, & Sato, 1994) implemented CWT to process EEG signal. Kalayci and Ozdamar (Kalayci, & Ozdamar, 1995) implemented wavelet transform for feature extraction and neural network for feature discrimination to classify abnormal EEG segments from others.

Figure 3. Waveform of one cardiac cycle of ECG signal (From Wikimedia Common [42].)

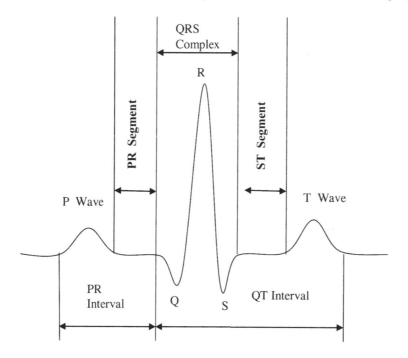

2.2.4 Positron Emission Tomography (PET) Image Analysis

PET is a nuclear medicine functional imaging modality. It helps to monitor metabolic processes occurring in body. This modality detects gamma rays radiated by a radioactive material (radio tracer). The radio tracer is either inhaled as vapor, injected into blood stream or swallowed by a patient. The radioactive emission is detected by camera to produce images which provides the molecular information. As the activity of a diseased organ is pinpointed at molecular level, PET image can detect a disease at an early stage. The image obtained from PET is very noisy and variable. Its interpretation deserves statistical investigation. The main point of PET imaging is to detect the differences in activity present between the diseased and normal subjects or with the same subject having different experimental conditions (Unser, & Aldroubi, 1996). Whatever be the case, the signal varies. As a result, multiple images or repetitive trials are required for diseased and normal subjects. Therefore, images are registered to facilitate their comparison on a pixel-by-pixel basis. This helps to compensate for inter-subject anatomical variability or intra-subject movement in the scanner. An efficient multiresolution image registration method was proposed by Unser et al. (Unser, Aldroubi, & Gerfen, 1993) to solve this problem caused due to the translational and rotational motion of a rigid body. Again, Ruttimann et al. (Ruttimann, Unser, Rio, & Rawlings,1993) used the wavelet transform to examine the difference in brain PET images. The big advantage of analyzing a PET image in the wavelet domain is that the discriminative information is reduced to a limited number of wavelet coefficients as noise is uniformly distributed throughout the coefficients (Unser, & Aldroubi, 1996).

2.2.5 Medical Image Compression

In modern health care service, the efficient compression, archival and transmission of volumetric medical images is very significant. There exist several image coding techniques (Bruylants, Munteanu, & Schelkens, 2015). Some are transform based techniques like Discrete Cosine Transform (DCT) (Pennebaker, & Mitchell, 1992), Karhunen-Loève Transform (KLT) (Blanes, Serra-Sagrista, Marcellin, & Bartrina-Rapesta, 2012) and Discrete Wavelet Transform (Boliek, 2002). Others are prediction based technique like Context-based, Adaptive, Lossless Image Coding (CALIC) (Wu, & Memon, 1997). Both the techniques have their advantages and disadvantages. The three dimension wavelet based method is superior to DCT based method in compressing large medical datasets while assuring resolution scalability, easy access and high quality.

The Digital Imaging and Communications in medicine (DICOM) is a widely accepted standard of handling, storing, transmitting data in the field of medical informatics. It has a fixed file format and a communication protocol for networks. DICOM depends on other standard image compression formats like Joint Photographic Experts Group (JPEG), Joint Photographic Experts Group- Lossless Standard (JPEG-LS) and JPEG 2000 (Bruylants, Munteanu, & Schelkens, 2015) to encode medical images. Amongst the above-mentioned coding standards, JPEG 2000 using wavelet is the best suited coding approach due to: 1) exceptional rate–distortion performance for large medical datasets; 2) supports both lossy and lossless coding; 3) allows flexible file formats; 4) resolution scalability. Bruylants et al. (Bruylants, Munteanu, & Schelkens, 2015) comprehensively examined different approaches to improve the performance of JPEG 2000 using directional wavelet transforms to compress volumetric medical images.

2.2.6 Mammogram Enhancement and Detection of Microcalcification

Sometimes an X-ray cannot be properly visualized in front of a light box. It is required to accentuate the X-ray features which are difficult to observe under normal conditions. Image enhancement refers to the image processing techniques which make the relevant image features more noticeable. Mammogram is a low voltage X-ray imaging technique of breast. It is done to examine cancer present in the breast. There is a very little difference in contrast between the small and soft tissues in a mammogram. A small change in the shape of breast can be an early indication of the breast cancer; on the contrary a relatively big lump of tissue can be non-malignant. So mammogram enhancement is very much essential prior to the detection of microcalcification.

Gorgel et al. (Gorgel, Sertbas, & Ucan, 2010) denoised and enhanced mammogram images using wavelet transform and homomorphic filtering. Laine et al. (Laine, Schuler, Fan, & Huda, 1994) implemented multiscale wavelet transform for the mammographic feature enhancement. They used 1) non-separable hexagonal wavelet transform; 2) separable dyadic wavelet transform and; 3) non-seperable, non-orthogonal wavelet transform for contrast enhancement of mammograms. The edges detected with specific resolution levels of transform domain present local support to enhance mammogram images. The mammogram images are reconstructed using wavelet coefficients which are modified locally or globally at single or multiple levels by the non-linear operators.

The microcalcifications are clusters of fine granular deposits of calcium ions in the soft tissues of the breast of women. They may be benign or malignant. Strickland and Hann (1996) proposed a double stage methodology using wavelet transform to detect and segment the microcalcifications. The first stage involves an undecimated wavelet transform (UWT) which refers to the application of normal filter bank without performing downsampling. So the four sub-bands given by: 1) low-low (LL); 2) Low-high (LH); 3) high-low (HL) and; 4) high-high (HH) continue to exist at the full size. The detection of microcalcification occurs at HH and HL+LH subbands. The second stage overcomes the drawbacks of the Gaussian assumption and offers smooth segmentation of the microcalcification edges. Mini et al. (Mini, Devassia, & Thomas, 2004) demonstrated the detection of microcalcification using multiplexed wavelet transform (MWT). The MWT was first suggested by Evangelista (Evangelista, 1994) in the year 1994 to represent pseudoperiodic signals having constant period. The MWT simplifies the investigation of pseudo-periodic signals.

For a signal $x(n)$ with period M, the MWT is defined from (Mini, Devassia, & Thomas, 2004) as a group of coefficients:

$$X_{j,k,q} = \sum_n x(n) \zeta_{j,k,q}(n) \tag{11}$$

for $j = 1, 2, ..$; k is an integer; $q = 0, 1, 2, ...M - 1$ and multiplexed wavelets denoted by $\zeta_{j,k,q}(n)$ can be expressed from (Mini, Devassia, & Thomas, 2004) as:

$$\zeta_{j,k,q}(n) = \sum_s \psi_{j,k}(s) \delta(n - sM - q). \tag{12}$$

where $\psi_{j,k}(n)$ is a set of complete and orthonormal ordinary wavelets.

The inverse MWT can be written from (Mini, Devassia, & Thomas, 2004) as:

$$x\left(n\right) = \sum_{j} \sum_{k} \sum_{q=0}^{M-1} X_{j,k,q} \zeta_{j,k,q}\left(n\right) \tag{13}$$

2.3 Limitations of Wavelet Transform and Development of Advanced Wavelet Transforms

Wavelets provide the optimal representation of 1D piecewise smooth signals like scan-lines of an image. But Do *et al.* in (Mini, Devassia, & Thomas, 2004) mentioned that practical images are not only composed of 1-D piecewise smooth scan–lines but also the discontinuity points located along the smooth curves produced due to the smooth boundaries of the objects. Although the wavelets in 2D can extract the discontinuity points but they fail to check the smoothness along the contour. This gives an impetus to explore the intrinsic geometrical structures of the images.

The limitation of the 2-D separable wavelet in representing images with smooth contours can be clearly understood by the famous example of the two painters –"wavelet" style painter and "X-let" style painter mentioned by Do *et al.* in (Mini, Devassia, & Thomas, 2004) and also M. N. Do in (Do, 2002). The "wavelet"-style painter mentioned in the above example is limited to the use of brush stroke of only square shape along a given contour as shown in Figure 4 (a). The limitation of the "wavelet"-style painter gradually becomes prominent with the increase of the resolution from coarse (big squares) to fine (medium squares) and even to finer (small squares) as illustrated in Figure 4(a). In case of very fine resolution, the wavelet style painter discussed by Do in (Do, 2002) requires more number of coefficients (small squares) than its counterpart (corresponding small rectangles) –X-let shown in Figure 4 (b) to

Figure 4. Successive refinement of a smooth contour by (a) wavelet, (b) X-let (From Do and Vetterli (Do, &Vetterli, 2005)

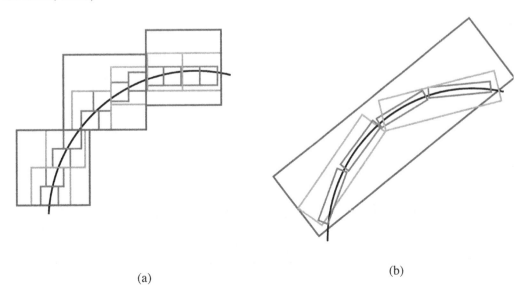

(a)   (b)

represent a given curve of an image. Therefore, it has been found that X-let transform methods are more efficient than the wavelet transform methods in representing the inherent geometrical features of images.

In this context, Do *et al.* in (Do, & Vetterli, 2005) had rightly pointed out the "wish list" for representing an image faithfully. The five features of the "wish list" are multiresolution, localization, critical sampling, directionality, anisotropy. The first three of the list are satisfied by the wavelet transform while the last two remain unsolved by the same. Thus, the example of the two painters along with the proposed wish list of Do and Vetterli (Do, & Vetterli, 2005) motivated the researchers to develop advanced wavelets like grouplet, platelet, surfacelet, contourlet, ranklet, brushlet, bandlet, curvelet and many more as presented in Figure 5.

3. CURVELET TRANSFORM: BACKGROUND

The curvelet is a two-dimensional waveform which provides a novel architecture for multiscale image analysis. It is localized in spatial and frequency domains but it is also associated with an orientation. This is a unique attribute of curvelet transform. It has emerged as one of the popular mathematical transforms for scientific computing, seismic imaging, solving differential equations and biomedical image processing.

The curvelet tiling of the frequency plane is shown in Figure 6. The Fourier plane is divided into wedges as shown in Figure 6(a). The wedge is shaped by dividing the frequency plane into radial and

Figure 5. Classification of wavelet into advanced wavelets

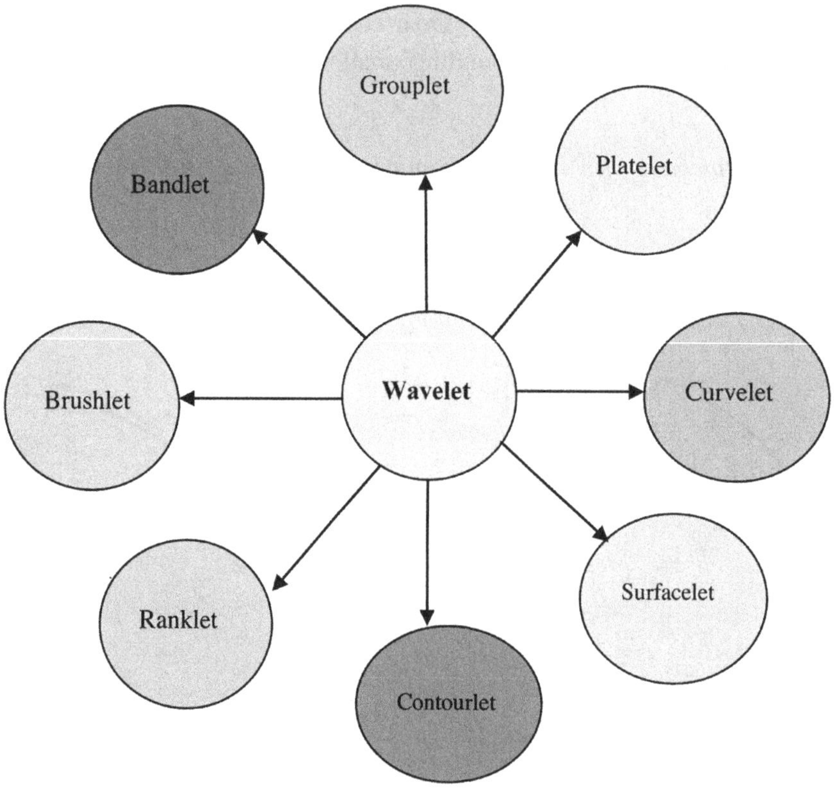

angular divisions. The radial divisions marked by concentric circles are used for band passing the image at different resolutions/scales. The angular divisions divide each bandpass image into different angles. So the consideration of a wedge as shown in the shaded region of Figure 6(a) helps us to analyze a bandpass image at a particular scale j with a particular orientation θ. The frequency support of such a wedge at scale j is given by a rectangle of 2^j by $2^{j/2}$ as shown in Figure 6(a). However, in space domain, a curvelet at scale j is an oriented "needle" whose effective support satisfying the parabolic scaling law of $width \approx length^2$ is a rectangle of 2^{-j} by $2^{-j/2}$ as shown in Figure 6(b). The needle like elements is extremely anisotropic at fine resolution.

The curvelet is considered as a function, $\psi_{a,b,\theta}(x)$ which is found by implementing parabolic dilation, rotation and translation to a specifically designed function, ψ where a is the scale parameter such that $(0\langle a\langle 1)$, b represents the location and θ denotes the orientation. So curvelet can be mathematically expressed from (Candès, 2003) as:

$$\psi_{a,b,\theta}(x) = a^{-3/4}\psi(D_a R_\theta(x-b)),$$ (14)

$$D_a = \begin{pmatrix} 1/a & 0 \\ 0 & 1/\sqrt{a} \end{pmatrix}$$ (15)

where D_a denotes parabolic scaling matrix, R_θ implies θ radians rotation, $(x_1, x_2) \in R^2$, and $\psi(x_1, x_2)$ is admissible profile.

3.1 Properties of Curvelet Transform in Comparison to Wavelet Transform

3.1.1 Fast Decay Rate for Sparse Image Representation

The curvelet transform provides nearly optimal sparse representation of objects which have curve singularities (Candes, Demanet, Donoho, & Ying, 2006). The most suitable N-term approximation $\tilde{f}$ of a smooth object f having discontinuities along twice continually differentiable C^2 curves follows $\left\| f - \tilde{f}_N \right\|_2^2 \leq CN^{-2}(\log N)^3$. But for wavelet transform, the rate of decay of wavelet coefficients is only N^{-1}. The faster decay rate of the coefficients of the curvelet transform as compared to the wavelet transform is one of the key reasons of optimal sparse image representation by the same.

3.1.2 Better Mean Square Error (MSE) for Image Reconstruction

The optimal approximation error has a direct statistical implication on the image recovery from the noisy data. The objects having curve-like singularities can be better reconstructed from noise with the help of curvelet thresholding than any other wavelet thresholding due to the better order of MSE. The change of MSE is approximately of the order $O(\varepsilon^{4/3})$ for image reconstruction by curvelet thresholding from

Figure 6. Curvelet tiling: (a) in frequency plane (b) in space domain. The Cartesian grid of the spatial plane is displayed for every scale and orientation (From Candes, Demanet, Donoho, & Ying, 2006)

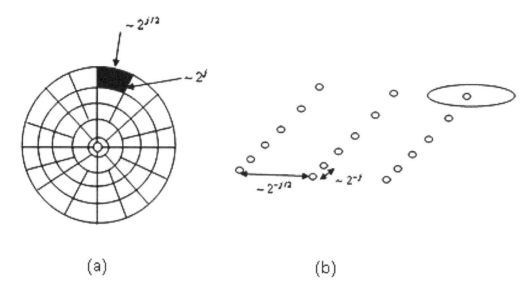

(a)   (b)

biggest $N \approx \varepsilon^{2/3}$ noisy curvelet curvelet coefficients with noise level ε; whereas wavelet thresholding provides decay of MSE no better than order $O(\varepsilon)$.

3.2 Architecture of Curvelet Transform

The digital curvelet transform called the fast discrete curvelet transform (FDCT) can be implemented in two ways: (1) FDCT via Unequispaced Fast Fourier Transform (USFFT) and; (2) FDCT via wrapping. The two implementations are conceptually the same but differ in the selection of the spatial grid which is used to translate curvelets at different resolutions and orientations. The Wrapping based FDCT is used here since it is easy to comprehend and implement. The architecture of wrapping based FDCT already discussed in (Candes, Demanet, Donoho, & Ying, 2006; Miri, & Mahloojifar, 2011) is presented in Figure 7 for easy reference. The basic concept is that the image is first decomposed into a set of frequency bands. Each band is then analyzed by curvelet transform. This approach also considers a rectangular grid to wrap the object of interest (data) to generate curvelet coefficients as shown in Figure 7.

The architecture of FDCT (Candes, Demanet, Donoho, & Ying, 2006) via wrapping is given below:

1.   The two dimensional (2D) fast Fourier transform (FFT) is applied to the given image to compute the 2D discrete Fourier transform (DFT) with Fourier samples

$$\tilde{f}[n_1, n_2]$$

where

Figure 7. Flowchart of FDCT via wrapping.(From Shah et al. [45])

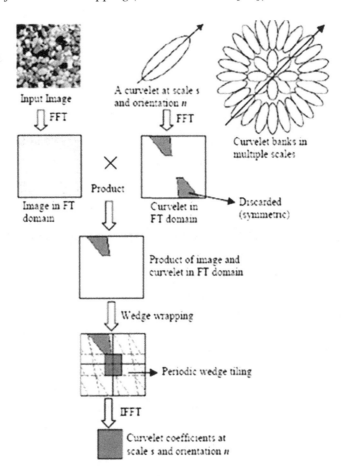

$$-\frac{n}{2} \leq n_1, n_2 \langle \frac{n}{2}.$$

2. The product of the curvelet frequency window $\tilde{U}_{j,l}[n_1, n_2]$ and the Fourier samples mentioned above is obtained as

$$\tilde{U}_{j,l}[n_1, n_2] \tilde{f}_{j,l}[n_1, n_2]$$

for every scale j and associated angle l.

3. The product is then wrapped around the origin to get

$$\tilde{f}_{j,l}[n_1, n_2] = W(\tilde{U}_{j,l}\tilde{f})[n_1, n_2].$$

4. The range of n_1 and n_2 is given by $0 \leq n_1 \langle L_{1,j}$ and $0 \leq n_2 \langle L_{2,j}$ where $\theta \in (-\pi/4, \pi/4)$, $L_{1,j}$ and $L_{2,j}$ are the sides of the data wrapping window.

5. The inverse 2D FFT is implemented to individual $\tilde{f}_{j,l}$ to obtain the discrete curvelet coefficients. The coefficients are often too many in number. The redundant coefficients are removed by the process of curvelet thresholding.

6. The curvelet thresholding [28] is given by $P_\sigma u = T^{-1} S_\sigma T(u)$ where T represents curvelet transform, T^{-1} represents inverse curvelet transform, S_σ being the thresholding function. Based on S_σ, different types of thresholding are formulated.

7. The curvelet transformed image can be reconstructed from the discrete curvelet coefficients simply by inverting each of the above steps in the sequence (4), (3), (2) and (1).

3.3 APPLICATIONS OF CURVELET TRANSFORM IN BIO-MEDICALIMAGING

3.3.1 Computed Tomography (CT) and Magnetic Resonance Imaging (MRI) Image Denoising

In modern diagnostic system, CT and MRI images are popularly used to detect several orthopedic, gastrointestinal, neural and brain diseases. Both the imaging techniques have their strength and weakness. CT imaging is often preferred due to: 1) sharp detection of bony structures, calcification and hemorrhage; 2) less imaging time; 3) economic, and; 4) accessibility. It is helpful for claustrophobic patients who cannot remain motionless during scanning. On the contrary, MRI outperforms CT scan in: 1) detecting soft tissues; 2) high contrast of images, and; 3) safety of the patient undergoing scan. The application of individual technique depends on the patient's condition.

Both the scanning techniques are affected by noise during image acquisition. The radiologists cannot properly visualize the clinically significant data. Bhadauria and Dewal (2013) demonstrated a noise reduction methodology of CT and MRI images. This methodology fuses three images: 1) denoised by curvelet transform; 2) denoised by total variation method (TVM), and; 3) edge information. The edge information is obtained by filtering the noise residual of TVM by curvelet transform. The regularization expression for TVM as suggested by Rudin et al. (Rudin, Osher, & Fatemi, 1992) can be written as:

$$\min_{f \in x} \frac{\|g - f\|^2}{2\lambda} + J(f) \qquad (16)$$

for g denotes noisy image, f denotes desired image with size $N \times N$, X denotes Euclidean space $R^{N \times N}$, $\lambda > 0$ denotes a Lagrange multiplier, $\|.\|$ denotes Euclidean norm. The discrete total variation of f given by $J(f)$ is expressed as:

$$J(f) = \sum_{1 \leq l, j \leq N} \left| (\nabla g)_{i,j} \right|. \qquad (17)$$

In (Bhadauria, & Dewal, 2013), Bhadauria and Dewal implemented projection based approach to solve Equation (16) as:

$$f = g - \lambda div \left(p^k \right) \tag{18}$$

where $\lambda div \left(p^k \right)$ is a non-linear projection with p^k being a dual variable. The iterative process for calculating the best solution of p^k can be seen in Figures 8 and 9 and

$$P_{i,j}^{K+1} = \frac{P_{ij}^k + \tau \left[\nabla \left(div \left(p^k \right) - \dfrac{g}{\lambda} \right) \right]_{i,j}}{1 + \tau \left| \left[\nabla \left(div \left(p^k \right) - \dfrac{g}{\lambda} \right) \right]_{i,j} \right|} \tag{19}$$

$$P_0 = 0$$

Figure 8. Denoising of brain CT image using curvelet transform; (a) Original image, (b) Noisy (random) image (PSNR=22.0519), (c) Soft thresholding (PSNR=26.4872), (d) Hard thresholding (PSNR=29.9437), (e) Garrote thresholding (PSNR=29.7930), (f) Partial reconstruction (PSNR=24.4251) (From Sugantharathnam, & Manimegalai, 2011)

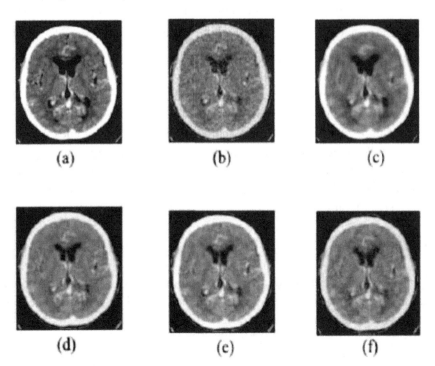

(a)   (b)   (c)

(d)   (e)   (f)

Figure 9. Denoising of brain MRI image using curvelet transform; (a) Original image, (b) Noisy (random) image (PSNR=21.6901), (c) Soft thresholding (PSNR=23.3243), (d) Hard thresholding (PSNR=25.2763), (e) Garrote thresholding (PSNR=24.7916), (f) Partial reconstruction (PSNR=22.1776) (From Sugantharathnam & Manimegalai, 2011)

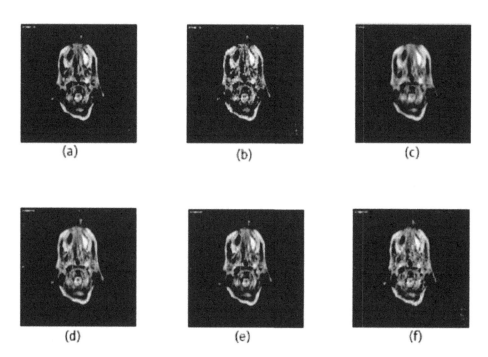

For τ is the step size. In order to assure the convergence of the algorithm, the value τ is considered as $\tau \leq \frac{1}{4}$. The performance of suggested methodology is experimented on CT and MRI scan images as demonstrated in Figures 2 and 3 of (Bhadauria, & Dewal, 2013). Sugantharathnam and Manimegalai (2011) demonstrated the use curvelet transform to denoise various image modalities using soft, hard and garrote thresholding rules and partial reconstruction methods. The experimental results shown in Figures 8 and 9 illustrate the denoising of CT and MRI images containing Random and Gaussian respectively. Rabbani et al. (Rabbani, Nezafat, & Gazor, 2009) demonstrated discrete complex wavelet based denoising of medical images. Wavelets are also used for denoising CT and MRI scan images. The denoising of brain CT scan images by wavelet is compared with curvelet (Bhadauria, Dewal, & Anand, 2011; Bhadauria, & Dewal, 2011. The curvelet outperforms wavelet in denoising brain CT images. It also preserves the edges better than wavelet.

3.3.2 Retina Image Analysis

Retina image analysis is a window to predict different human diseases like blood pressure, macular region, arteriolar narrowing, hypertension, diabetic retinopathy and many more. The following section presents three aspects of retina image analysis where curvelet transform is used.

3.3.2.1 Retina Image Enhancement

Miri and Mahloojifar (2011) suggested the use of curvelet to enhance retina image for superior vessel detection. The retina image contrast is increased by enhancing the image ridges. The mathematical morphology incorporating multistructure elements (MSEs) are implemented to obtain the image ridges, thereby enhancing retina images. The MSEs are used because the ordinary structural elements fail to detect complex edges. The concept of MSEs relies on collecting several structural elements in a single square window. So MSEs can efficiently detect different complex edges with various directionalities.

Consider a digital image $\left\{ I\left(m,n\right) \middle| m,n \in Z \right\}$. A structural element in $\left(2N+1\right) \times \left(2N+1\right)$ square window can be expressed from [33] as

$$S_i = \left\{ I\left(m + m_0, n + n_0\right), \theta_i = i \times \alpha \middle| -N \leq m_0, n_0 \leq N \right\} \tag{20}$$

where $i = 0,1,...,4N-1$, $\alpha = \dfrac{180°}{4N}$ and θ_i denotes directional angle of S_i.

The ridges which do not belong to a particular vessel tree are removed by special morphological opening by reconstruction while conserving thin vessel edges. The morphological operators by reconstruction are specially designed to emphasize on both size and shape of the features which remained unaddressed by conventional morphological operators.

3.3.2.2 Optic Disk (OD) Detection

In a healthy retina image, OD is a bright, yellowish and circular disk. The blood vessels and nerves emerge from this circular object. It is partially covered with blood vessels. The location of OD helps to detect fovea and track blood vessels in retina images. Many approaches have been demonstrated to detect OD.

Esmaeili et al. (Esmaeili, Rabbani, & Dehnavi, 2012) introduced a novel approach of OD detection using digital curvelet transform. The reason of using curvelet transform is best explained by the statistical property and sparsity of curvelet coefficients. The bright objects present in retina images, that is, OD, correspond to large curvelet coefficients. As the size of exudates area is negligible as compared to OD, the OD location can be easily outlined by curvelet coefficients. The approach of OD detection begins with the application of FDCT to the retina images to generate curvelet coefficients. Then a function, D_c that changes the values of curvelet coefficients with exponent of p is applied

$$D_c\left(x\right) = x^P \tag{21}$$

As the curvelet coefficients are sparsely distributed, there exist a limited number of large coefficients representing the main part of the images while the remaining coefficients are almost zero. Strengthening the discrete curvelet coefficients using (21), the reconstructed image is displayed with limited number of bits. The big coefficients tend to the maximum value of pixel and small coefficients (lesser than one) tend to zero. Therefore, OD which corresponds to bright region of retinal image can be approximately detected. The reconstructed retina images obtained by strengthening curvelet coefficients is shown in (Esmaeili, Rabbani, & Dehnavi, 2012).

3.3.2.3 Diabetic Retinopathy (DR) Detection

DR is one of the ophthalmic diseases caused due to the prolonged suffering of a patient from diabetes mellitus. It damages the retinal blood vessels located at the posterior part of the eye. DR, if neglected and remain untreated may lead to blindness. The different stages of DR are: 1) no DR; 2) mild nonproliferative DR (NPLDR); 3) moderate NPLDR; 4) severe NPLDR, and; 5) proliferative DR (PLDR). Alipour et al. (Alipour, Rabbani, & Akhlaghi, 2012) demonstrated automated detection of DR with the help of curvelet transform. If DR is detected, the proposed scheme detects the exact stage of DR. Using curvelet, 6 features associated with retinal vasculature: 1) area of exudates; 2) number of microaneurysm (balloon like swelling in retinal blood vessel), therein; 3) total count of microaneurysms; 4) area of blood vessels; 5) area, and; 6) regularity of foveal avascular zone are computed and provided to support vector machine (SVM) to determine exact stage of DR. SVM is a binary classifier.

Microaneurysms are known to be the initial symptom of DR. Shah et al. (Shah, Laude, Faye, & Tang, 2016) detected DR by detecting microaneurysms using curvelet transform. The flowchart of microaneurysms detection is presented in Figure 10. The blood vessels are extracted from the green band image using 2D Gabor wavelet as shown in the extreme left of Figure 10. The blood vessels are also removed from the preprocessed green band image to obtain G_{-BV} image as shown in the middle of Figure 10. The microaneurysm candidates are obtained by two parallel techniques using: 1) local thresholding and; 2) statistical features. Applying local thresholding, the microaneurysm candidates having low intensities are selected from G_{-BV} image. Using statistical features like contrast and standard deviation, microaneurysm candidates are selected from gray band image as shown in the extreme right of Figure 10. Now, microaneurysm candidates which are commonly found by both the techniques are considered as true microaneurysms. There is a disadvantage of this DR detection approach. In both the techniques, thresholds are kept low to optimize the detection of microaneurysms. As a result, hundreds of false positives (FPs) are detected. FP refers to the test result which wrongly suggests microaneurysm candidates. These FPs are caused due to low intensity blood vessels and background image.

3.3.3 Edge Detection of Light and Electron Microscopic Images

The accurate investigation of microscopic images in biomedical laboratories is a challenging and time-consuming process. It includes the examination of the presence of different types of cell or foreign bodies in bio-chemical samples like blood, sputum, urine, serum etc. The count, volume, size, color, edge of interested objects present in a given sample are thoroughly examined. So far several biomedical image analyzing tools like- NeuroLucida (Gebäck, & Koumoutsakos, 2009), Cellprofiler (Carpenter, Jones, Lamprecht, Clarke, Kang, Friman...& Golland, 2006) have been developed.

Curvelet is used here for edge detection of light and electron microscopic images. Gebäck and Koumoutsakos (Gebäck, & Koumoutsakos, 2009) proposed a novel technique using discrete curvelet transform to extract directional field from microscopic images. The directional field indicates the location as well as direction of the edges in images. The directional field is further processed by Canny edge detector to detect the edges. The two important steps of Canny edge detector are: 1) non-maximal suppression technique and; 2) thresholding technique. The non-maximal suppression technique refers to the selection of pixels *where the gradient magnitude has a local maximum in the direction of the gradient* (Gebäck, & Koumoutsakos, 2009). In thresholding technique, two thresholds – $Th1$ and $Th2$ are selected such that $Th2 > Th1$. The selected pixels whose gradient magnitude is greater than $Th2$ is denoted as 'strong' and the pixels whose gradient magnitude lies in between $Th1$ and $Th2$ is denoted as 'weak'. All the 'strong' pixels, 'weak' pixels that are connected horizontally, diagonally and vertically to the 'strong' pixels are selected by Canny edge detector to trace along the edges and mark them. Figure 11 (a) represents the electron microscopic image. The outer covering of the vesicle (a tiny fluid filled cyst or vacuole) located almost in the middle of Figure 11 (a) is intended to detect. But it a difficult task, since the image contains noise and too many small structures. The direct implementation of gradient based detector is meaningless because it detects edges everywhere. Again, smoothing the image does not yield effective result; as it equally smoothes thin and other structures. Under such a scenario, curvelet is implemented. It provides multiscale decomposition of the microscopic images. This helps to select a few scales and neglect other which contain noise and wide intensity variation. Using the desired levels of curvelet decomposition, the directional field is computed. The magnitude of the directional field is projected in Figure 11(b). Figure 11(c) which is a small part of Figure 11(b) presents direction of the directional field. Lastly, Figure 11 (d) represents the edge detected vesicle of the electron microscopic image.

4. COMPARISON OF WAVELETAND CURVELET TRANSFORMS IN BIO- MEDICALIMAGING

Earlier, the implementation of wavelet and curvelet are separately discussed in Sections 2.2 and 3.3 respectively. This section presents two biomedical applications where both wavelet and curvelet are implemented and their performance is compared. It demonstrates how curvelet outperforms wavelet from image processing perspective.

4.1 Comparison of Wavelet and Curvelet to Classify Human Organs in CT Images

The shape or gray level based classification of human organs in CT images is a difficult task. This happens due to the variation in shape of organs in a stack of slices produced during 3D imaging and the soft tissues of organ often exhibit similar gray level intensities (Dettori, & Semler, 2007). However, healthy organs have consistent texture pattern. So textural investigation of CT images is used for classifying human organs.

Dettori and Semler (2007) proposed an automated system for classifying different human organs in CT images. They emphasized on textural analysis of tissues (organs) by the multiresolution transforms namely wavelet, ridgelet and curvelet. Like curvelet, ridgelet is an advanced wavelet. The texture classification is based on three basic steps. They are: 1) segmentation of region of interest (ROI) from CT images; 2) discriminative texture feature extraction from cropped images, and; 3) design of a suitable classifier to automatically identify the images. Here, 3 wavelets – Haar, Daubechies, and Coiflet were deployed for textural analysis. The Haar wavelet performance expressed in terms of sensitivity, specificity, precision and accuracy outperforms other wavelets. So Haar wavelet is compared with curvelet. Experimental results presented in Table 1 show that curvelet is a better textural descriptor than Haar wavelet. This is due to multidirectional feature capturing capability of curvelet as compared to one dimensional feature capturing capability of wavelet.

Figure 10. Flowchart for detecting microaneurysms where BV: blood vessels, FP: False Positive, MA: Microaneurysms (From Shah, Laude, Faye, & Tang, 2016)

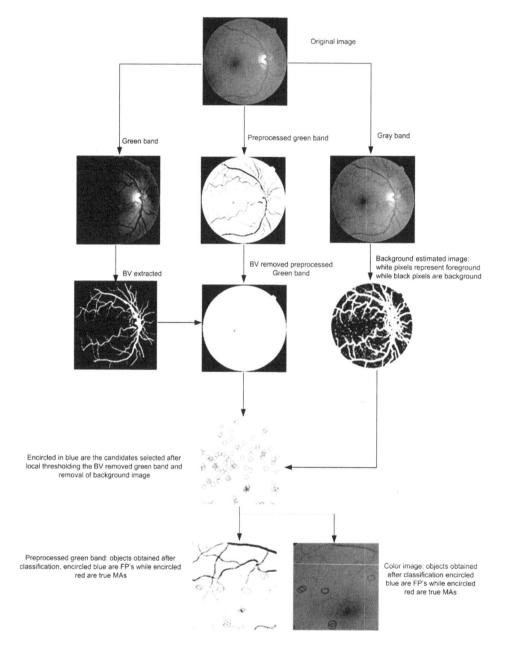

4.2 Comparison of Wavelet and Curvelet to Diagnose Breast Cancer

Breast cancer is one of the deadly cancers in women. According to the survey conducted by the International agency for Research on cancer, World Health Organization [17], more than 1 million cases of breast cancer is reported across the globe annually. So early detection of this fatal disease is very much essential to avoid extreme suffering and painful death.

Figure 11. Vesicle edge detection of an electron microscopy image; [a] Original microscopic image; [b] The magnitude of the directional field extracted from the curvelet coefficients (Gebäck, & Koumoutsakos, 2009); [c] The direction of the directional field represented by flow of arrows is shown over a small extract of [b], [d] final vesicle edge segmented microscopy image. (From Gebäck & Koumoutsakos, 2009)

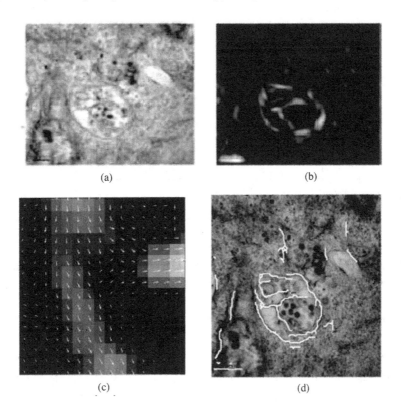

Eltoukhy et al. (2010) demonstrated a comparision between wavelet and curvelet transforms for the diagnosis of breast cancer. The objective of this study is to determine which transform is better for the representation, examination and classification of breast cancer from mammogram images. The mammograms are decomposed separately by the wavelet and curvelet transforms at desired resolution levels. A set of wavelet and curvelet coefficients are obtained from each decomposition level. The coefficients are provided to the nearest neighbor classifier. The classifier based on Euclidean distance classifies the mammogram images by computing the distances between the class core vector and feature vector as shown in Figure 12 which represents the schematic of breast cancer diagnostic system. The mammogram classification is a two-stage process. The first stage of classification is discrimination of normal tissues, benign and malignant tumors. The mean of accuracy rate obtained for classifying benign, malignant and normal tissues is presented in Figure 13. The second stage refers to the classification of different abnormalities based on geometrical properties like circumscribed mass, architectural distortion, micro-calcification clusters etc (Eltoukhy, Faye, & Samir, 2010). The average of accuracy rates obtained for classifying the above mentioned geometrical properties based abnormalities is given in Figure 14. The experimentally obtained results suggest that curvelet based features perform better than wavelet based features in diagnosing breast cancer.

Table 1. Comparison of Haar wavelet and curvelet to classify human organs (Dettori, & Semler, 2007).

Organ	Descriptor	Sensitivity	Specificity	Precision	Accuracy
Backbone	Curvelet	99.4	98.8	95.3	98.9
	Wavelet	82.6	96.1	82.6	93.7
Heart	Curvelet	89.7	99.0	95.5	97.1
	Wavelet	59.0	92.1	67.0	85.0
Kidney	Curvelet	96.0	98.1	93.5	97.6
	Wavelet	77.7	91.4	69.9	88.6
Liver	Curvelet	95.9	98.5	94.3	98.0
	Wavelet	87.3	94.4	82.6	92.8
Spleen	Curvelet	91.8	98.9	94.9	97.6
	Wavelet	65.5	94.3	69.7	89.5
Average	Curvelet	94.6	98.7	94.7	97.9
	Wavelet	74.4	93.7	74.4	89.9

5. A SHORT CASE STUDY: MAMMOGRAM DENOISING BY WAVELET AND CURVELET TRANSFORMS USING DIFFERENT THRESHOLDING TECHNIQUES

5.1 Introduction and Problem Statement

Mammogram is often corrupted by noise during the photo session. The clinically relevant data like the count, size and location of microcalcification cannot be suitably read from the mammogram. So it becomes a prime necessity to denoise mammogram before it is used for detecting microcalcifications.

5.2 Probable Solutions

There are different approaches to denoise mammogram. They are:

a. the application of linear filtering methods like Wiener filer,
b. development of new mathematical transforms,
c. innovate thresholding techniques
d. implement existing mathematical transforms - wavelet and curvelet using thresholding techniques

5.2.1 Discussion on a Particular Solution

This case study presents the fourth probable solution, that is, noise filtraion of mammogram by wavelet and curvelet transforms using different thresholding techniques as illustrated in Figure 15.

The mammogram denoising scheme is a three-step process. They are: 1) implementation of wavelet or curvelet transform to the noisy mammogram to generate discrete coefficients, some of which are unwanted and produced due to high frequency noise; 2) implementation of the thresholding technique to remove the unwanted coefficients, thereby filtering noise, and; 3) application of the inverse wavelet (curvelet)

Figure 12. Breast cancer diagnostic system using wavelet and curvelet (From Eltoukhy, Faye, & Samir, 2010)

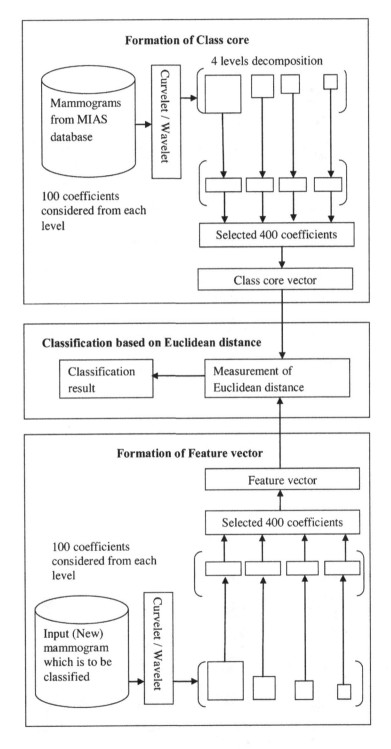

Figure 13. The mean of the accuracy rate found from the classification of normal tissues, benign and malignant tumors. Db8, Bior3.7, Sym8 are Daubechies-8, Bi-orthogonal and Symlet wavelets (From Eltoukhy, Faye, & Samir, 2010)

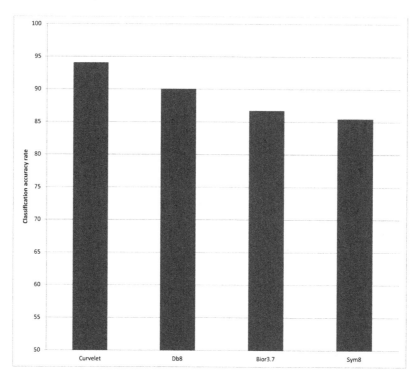

Figure 14. The mean of the accuracy rate found from the classification of different geometrical abnormalities. Db8, Bior3.7, Sym8 are Daubechies-8, Bi-orthogonal and Symlet wavelets (From Eltoukhy, Faye, & Samir, 2010)

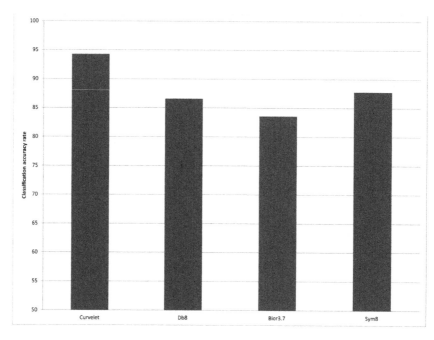

Figure 15. Mammogram denoising by the wavelet or curvelet transforms based on thresholding techniques. (From Saha, Naskar, & Chatterji, 2015)

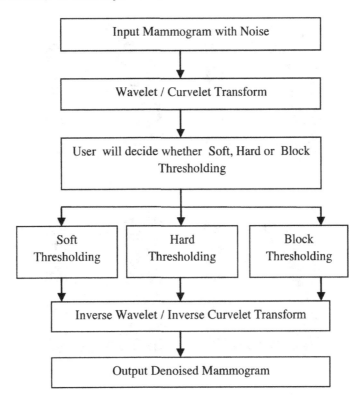

to the remaining discrete wavelet (curvelet) coefficients to reconstruct the noise free mammogram. The thresholding technique refers to the preservation or discard of a transform generated coefficient based on the threshold value set in the corresponding thresholding technique. As the thresholding technique remains same for whatever transform used, the thresholding functions mentioned below are expressed in terms of wavelet. The three thresholding techniques expressed from (Saha, Naskar, & Chatterji, 2015) are given below.

Soft thresholding function:

$$\delta_{\lambda}^{s}(d_{jk}) = \begin{cases} 0, & for \quad |d_{jk}| < \lambda \\ d_{jk} - \lambda, & for \quad d_{jk} \geq \lambda \\ d_{jk} + \lambda, & for \quad d_{jk} \leq \lambda \end{cases} \tag{22}$$

where d_{jk} denotes wavelet coefficient at the jth decomposition level, k denotes the index of the coefficient at that level and λ is the threshold level.

Hard thresholding function:

Figure 16. (a) Mammogram with Salt and Pepper noise; Noised filtered mammograms by (b) Soft Threshold Wavelet (c) Hard Threshold Wavelet (d) Block Threshold Wavelet (From Saha, Naskar, & Chatterji, 2015)

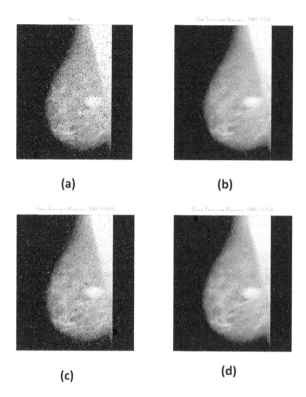

$$\delta_\lambda^H(d_{jk}) = \begin{cases} 0, & for \ \left| d_{jk} \right| < \lambda \\ d_{jk}, & for \ \left| d_{jk} \right| \geq \lambda \end{cases} \qquad (23)$$

where d_{jk} denotes wavelet coefficient at the jth decomposition level, k denotes the index of the coefficient at that level and λ is the threshold level.

Block thresholding function:

$$\hat{\theta}_{j,k} = \tilde{y}_{j,k} \cdot I \ (S_{jb}^2 > T) \ for \ (j,k) \in (j,b) \qquad (24)$$

where $S_{jb}^2 = \sum_{k \in (jb)} \tilde{y}_{j,k}^2$. (25)

S_{jb}^2 denotes the sum of the squares of wavelet coefficients given by $\tilde{y}_{j,k}$ and T is the threshold. For each resolution level j, the wavelet coefficients are divided into non-overlapping blocks having length L. The indices of the wavelet coefficients associated with b^{th} block at j^{th} resolution level is given by jb.

The different types of noise called Salt and Pepper, Poisson, Gaussian and Speckle are added to the mammograms. Then the mammograms are denoised by the wavelet and curvelet transforms using soft,

Figure 17. (a) Mammogram with Salt and Pepper noise; Noise filtered mammograms by (b) Soft Threshold Curvelet (c) Hard Threshold Curvelet (d) Block Threshold Curvelet (From Saha, Naskar, & Chatterji, 2015)

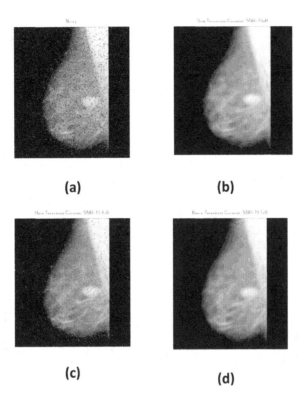

(a)   (b)

(c)   (d)

hard and block thresholding techniques. As an example, the wavelet and the curvelet transform denoised mammograms based on the three thresholding techniques for Salt and Pepper noise are presented in Figure 16(a-d) and Figure 17(a-d) respectively.

5.3 Result Analysis

Comparing three thresholding techniques using wavelet transform, as shown Figure 18, the block thresholding performs better than soft and hard thresholding techniques for Salt and Pepper, Gaussian and Speckle noises. Similarly, comparing all thresholding techniques using curvelet transform as shown in Figure 18, it is found that block thresholding gives better signal to noise (SNR) than soft and hard techniques for Salt and Pepper noise and Speckle noise too. For Poisson noise, with any transform applied, hard thresholding denoises mammogram better than the soft and block thresholding techniques. Lastly, it is observed from Figure 18, that irrespective of the selected thresholding technique selected, the curvelet is better than the wavelet in denoising mammograms subjected to Salt and Pepper, Poisson, Gaussian and Speckle noises.

Figure 18. Average SNR obtained by implementing soft, hard and block thresholding techniques based on wavelet and curvelet transform to mammograms with Salt & Pepper, Poisson, Gaussian and Speckle noises (From Saha, Naskar, & Chatterji, 2015)

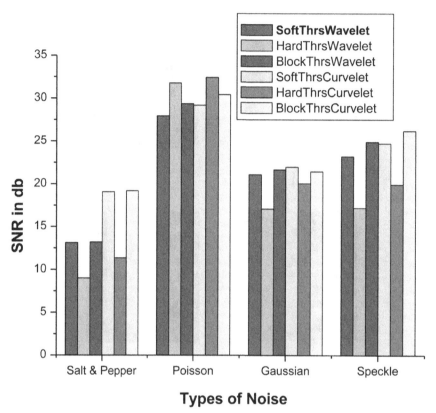

*For a more accurate representation see the electronic version.

5.4 Summary of Case Study

Evaluating the soft, hard and block thresholding techniques implemented with the wavelet and curvelet transform individually, block thresholding gives better SNR for all noises except Poisson noise. Hard thresholding when used with either wavelet or curvelet transform outperforms soft and block techniques for Poisson noise filtration from mammogram. Thus, pertiency of soft, hard and block thresholding techniques along with the associated transform is well established for mammogram noise filtration. In general, when mammogram is denoised by wavelet and curvelet using three thresholding techniques, curvelet transform is better than wavelet.

6. CONCLUSION

This chapter brings together the different applications of wavelet and curvelet transforms in the area of biomedical imaging. The applications reflect how the mathematical transforms represent, analyze, extract, utilize and interpret data for the diagnosis of human diseases. This scientific investigation abridges the gap between the medical and computer sciences.

The chapter starts with a brief introduction to wavelet transform trailed by the highlight of its selective properties related to medical imaging and applications. Out of the 6 applications – heart sound analysis, ECG characterization, EEG investigation, PET image analysis, medical image compression, mammogram enhancement and microcalcification detection, the first three are related to signal processing while remaining three are related to medical image processing. The wavelet transform performs exceptionally well in the processing of 1Dsignal; while its ability is challenged in 2D image. The limitations of wavelet transform are also discussed. The motivation of designing new advanced wavelets is presented. Curvelet, an advanced wavelet is selected in order to compare the difference in applicability of a traditional transform (wavelet) with comparatively recent transform. Like wavelet, a brief introduction of curvelet, its selective properties, architecture and different applications like denoising of CT and MR images, retina image enhancement, OD detection, DR detection, edge detection of light and electron microscopic images are presented. Medical image analysis literature suggests the superiority of curvelet transform over wavelet transform. Two joint applications -classification of human organs in CT images, diagnosis of breast cancer using wavelet and curvelet transform are provided to compare the methodology and the experimental results statistically. Lastly, a case study on mammogram denoising using soft, hard and block thresholding techniques and two transforms is presented. The case study not only focuses on the use of two transforms but also on the importance of the underlying thresholding algorithms.

Therefore, this episode would enrich the readers with the concept, approach and applicability of two generation mathematical transforms in the biomedical signal and image processing.

ACKNOWLEDGMENT

The authors acknowledge the support of Siliguri Institute of Technology, Siliguri; Jadavpur University, Kolkata and B. P. Poddar Institute of Management and Technology, Kolkata.

REFERENCES

Akay, M., Akay, Y. M., Welkowitz, W., & Lewkowicz, S. (1994). Investigating the effects of vasodilator drugs on the turbulent sound caused by femoral artery stenosis using short-term Fourier and wavelet transform methods. *IEEE Transactions on Biomedical Engineering*, *41*(10), 921–928. doi:10.1109/10.324523 PMID:7959798

Akay, Y. M., Akay, M., Welkowitz, W., & Kostis, J. (1994). Noninvasive detection of coronary artery disease. *IEEE Engineering in Medicine and Biology Magazine*, *13*(5), 761–764. doi:10.1109/51.334639

Angelidis, P. A. (1994). MR image compression using a wavelet transform coding algorithm. *Magnetic Resonance Imaging*, *12*(7), 1111–1120. doi:10.1016/0730-725X(94)91243-P PMID:7997098

Bhadauria, H. S., & Dewal, M. L. (2011, March). Performance evaluation of curvelet and wavelet based denoising methods on brain computed tomography images. In *Emerging Trends in Electrical and Computer Technology (ICETECT), 2011 International Conference on* (pp. 666-670). IEEE. 10.1109/ICETECT.2011.5760201

Bhadauria, H. S., & Dewal, M. L. (2013). Medical image denoising using adaptive fusion of curvelet transform and total variation. *Computers & Electrical Engineering*, *39*(5), 1451–1460. doi:10.1016/j.compeleceng.2012.04.003

Bhadauria, H. S., Dewal, M. L., & Anand, R. S. (2011, February). Comparative analysis of curvelet based techniques for denoising of computed tomography images. In *Devices and Communications (ICDeCom), 2011 International Conference on* (pp. 1-5). IEEE. 10.1109/ICDECOM.2011.5738492

Blanes, I., Serra-Sagrista, J., Marcellin, M. W., & Bartrina-Rapesta, J. (2012). Divide-and-conquer strategies for hyperspectral image processing: A review of their benefits and advantages. *IEEE Signal Processing Magazine*, *29*(3), 71–81. doi:10.1109/MSP.2011.2179416

Boliek, M. (2002). JPEG 2000 Image Coding System: Core Coding System. *ISO/IEC.*

Bruylants, T., Munteanu, A., & Schelkens, P. (2015). Wavelet based volumetric medical image compression. *Signal Processing Image Communication*, *31*, 112–133. doi:10.1016/j.image.2014.12.007

Candès, E. J. (2003). What is... a curvelet? *Notices of the American Mathematical Society*, *50*(11), 1402–1403.

Candes, E. J., Demanet, L., Donoho, D., & Ying, L. (2006). Fast discrete curvelet transforms. *Multiscale Modeling & Simulation*, *5*(3), 861–899. doi:10.1137/05064182X

Carpenter, A. E., Jones, T. R., Lamprecht, M. R., Clarke, C., Kang, I. H., Friman, O., ... Golland, P. (2006). CellProfiler: Image analysis software for identifying and quantifying cell phenotypes. *Genome Biology*, *7*(10), R100. doi:10.1186/gb-2006-7-10-r100 PMID:17076895

Daugman, J. G. (1989). Entropy reduction and decorrelation in visual coding by oriented neural receptive fields. *IEEE Transactions on Biomedical Engineering*, *36*(1), 107–114. doi:10.1109/10.16456 PMID:2921058

Dettori, L., & Semler, L. (2007). A comparison of wavelet, ridgelet, and curvelet-based texture classification algorithms in computed tomography. *Computers in Biology and Medicine*, *37*(4), 486–498. doi:10.1016/j.compbiomed.2006.08.002 PMID:17054933

Do, M. N. (2002). *Directional multiresolution image representations*. Academic Press.

Do, M. N., & Vetterli, M. (2005). The contourlet transform: An efficient directional multiresolution image representation. *IEEE Transactions on Image Processing*, *14*(12), 2091–2106. doi:10.1109/TIP.2005.859376 PMID:16370462

Eltoukhy, M. M., Faye, I., & Samir, B. B. (2010). A comparison of wavelet and curvelet for breast cancer diagnosis in digital mammogram. *Computers in Biology and Medicine*, *40*(4), 384–391. doi:10.1016/j.compbiomed.2010.02.002 PMID:20163793

Esmaeili, M., Rabbani, H., & Dehnavi, A. M. (2012). Automatic optic disk boundary extraction by the use of curvelet transform and deformable variational level set model. *Pattern Recognition*, *45*(7), 2832–2842. doi:10.1016/j.patcog.2012.01.002

Evangelista, G. (1994). Comb and multiplexed wavelet transforms and their applications to signal processing. *IEEE Transactions on Signal Processing*, *42*(2), 292–303. doi:10.1109/78.275603

Gebäck, T., & Koumoutsakos, P. (2009). Edge detection in microscopy images using curvelets. *BMC Bioinformatics*, *10*(1), 75. doi:10.1186/1471-2105-10-75 PMID:19257905

Gorgel, P., Sertbas, A., & Ucan, O. N. (2010). A wavelet-based mammographic image denoising and enhancement with homomorphic filtering. *Journal of Medical Systems*, *34*(6), 993–1002. doi:10.100710916-009-9316-3 PMID:20703608

Hajeb Mohammad Alipour, S., Rabbani, H., & Akhlaghi, M. R. (2012). Diabetic retinopathy grading by digital curvelet transform. *Computational and Mathematical Methods in Medicine*. PMID:23056148

Kalayci, T., & Ozdamar, O. (1995). Wavelet preprocessing for automated neural network detection of EEG spikes. *IEEE Engineering in Medicine and Biology Magazine*, *14*(2), 160–166. doi:10.1109/51.376754

Khadra, L., Dickhaus, H., & Lipp, A. (1993). Representations of ECG—late potentials in the time treauencvD-lane. *Journal of Medical Engineering & Technology*, *17*(6), 228–231. doi:10.3109/03091909309006330 PMID:8169939

Khadra, L., Matalgah, M., El-Asir, B., & Mawagdeh, S. (1991). The wavelet transform and its applications to phonocardiogram signal analysis. *Medical Informatics*, *16*(3), 271–277. doi:10.3109/14639239109025301 PMID:1758216

Laine, A. F., Schuler, S., Fan, J., & Huda, W. (1994). Mammographic feature enhancement by multiscale analysis. *IEEE Transactions on Medical Imaging*, *13*(4), 725–740. doi:10.1109/42.363095 PMID:18218551

Lucier, B. J., Kallergi, M., Qian, W., DeVore, R. A., Clark, R. A., Saff, E. B., & Clarke, L. P. (1994). Wavelet compression and segmentation of digital mammograms. *Journal of Digital Imaging*, *7*(1), 27–38. doi:10.1007/BF03168476 PMID:8172976

Ma, J., & Plonka, G. (2009). Computing with curvelets: From image processing to turbulent flows. *Computing in Science & Engineering*, *11*(2), 72–80. doi:10.1109/MCSE.2009.26

Mallat, S. G. (1989). Multifrequency channel decompositions of images and wavelet models. *IEEE Transactions on Acoustics, Speech, and Signal Processing*, *37*(12), 2091–2110. doi:10.1109/29.45554

Marĉelja, S. (1980). Mathematical description of the responses of simple cortical cells. *JOSA*, *70*(11), 1297–1300. doi:10.1364/JOSA.70.001297 PMID:7463179

Meste, O., Rix, H., Caminal, P., & Thakor, N. V. (1994). Ventricular late potentials characterization in time-frequency domain by means of a wavelet transform. *IEEE Transactions on Biomedical Engineering*, *41*(7), 625–634. doi:10.1109/10.301729 PMID:7927383

Mini, M. G., Devassia, V. P., & Thomas, T. (2004). Multiplexed wavelet transform technique for detection of microcalcification in digitized mammograms. *Journal of Digital Imaging*, *17*(4), 285–291. doi:10.100710278-004-1020-8 PMID:15692872

Miri, M. S., & Mahloojifar, A. (2011). Retinal image analysis using curvelet transform and multistructure elements morphology by reconstruction. *IEEE Transactions on Biomedical Engineering*, *58*(5), 1183–1192. doi:10.1109/TBME.2010.2097599 PMID:21147592

Obaidat, M. S. (1993). Phonocardiogram signal analysis: Techniques and performance comparison. *Journal of Medical Engineering & Technology*, *17*(6), 221–227. doi:10.3109/03091909309006329 PMID:8169938

Pennebaker, W. B., & Mitchell, J. L. (1992). *JPEG: Still image data compression standard.* Springer Science & Business Media.

Rabbani, H., Nezafat, R., & Gazor, S. (2009). Wavelet-domain medical image denoising using bivariate laplacian mixture model. *IEEE Transactions on Biomedical Engineering*, *56*(12), 2826–2837. doi:10.1109/TBME.2009.2028876 PMID:19695984

Rioul, O., & Duhamel, P. (1992). Fast algorithms for discrete and continuous wavelet transforms. *IEEE Transactions on Information Theory*, *38*(2), 569–586. doi:10.1109/18.119724

Rudin, L. I., Osher, S., & Fatemi, E. (1992). Nonlinear total variation based noise removal algorithms. *Physica D. Nonlinear Phenomena*, *60*(1-4), 259–268. doi:10.1016/0167-2789(92)90242-F

Ruttimann, U. E., Unser, M. A., Rio, D. E., & Rawlings, R. R. (1993, June). Use of the wavelet transform to investigate differences in brain PET images between patient groups. In *SPIE's 1993 International Symposium on Optics, Imaging, and Instrumentation* (pp. 192-203). International Society for Optics and Photonics. 10.1117/12.146601

Saha, M., Naskar, M. K., & Chatterji, B. N. (2015). Soft, hard and block thresholding techniques for denoising of mammogram images. *Journal of the Institution of Electronics and Telecommunication Engineers*, *61*(2), 186–191. doi:10.1080/03772063.2015.1009394

Sahambi, J. S., Tandon, S. N., & Bhatt, R. K. P. (1997). Using wavelet transforms for ECG characterization. An on-line digital signal processing system. *IEEE Engineering in Medicine and Biology Magazine*, *16*(1), 77–83. doi:10.1109/51.566158 PMID:9058586

Schematic diagram of normal sinus rhythm for a human heart as seen on ECG. (n.d.). Wikimedia Common, Public Domain. Retrieved June 15, 2017, from http://commons.wikimedia.org/wiki/File%3ASinusRhythmLabels.svg

Schiff, S. J., Aldroubi, A., Unser, M., & Sato, S. (1994). Fast wavelet transformation of EEG. *Electroencephalography and Clinical Neurophysiology*, *91*(6), 442–455. doi:10.1016/0013-4694(94)90165-1 PMID:7529683

Schiff, S. J., Milton, J. G., Heller, J., & Weinstein, S. L. (1994). Wavelet transforms and surrogate data for electroencephalographic spike and seizure localization. *Optical Engineering (Redondo Beach, Calif.)*, *33*(7), 2162–2169. doi:10.1117/12.172248

Shah, S. A. A., Laude, A., Faye, I., & Tang, T. B. (2016). Automated microaneurysm detection in diabetic retinopathy using curvelettransform. *Journal of Biomedical Optics*, *21*(10), 101404–101404. doi:10.1117/1.JBO.21.10.101404 PMID:26868326

Strickland, R. N., & Hahn, H. I. (1996). Wavelet transforms for detecting microcalcifications in mammograms. *IEEE Transactions on Medical Imaging*, *15*(2), 218–229. doi:10.1109/42.491423 PMID:18215904

Sugantharathnam, M. D., & Manimegalai, D. (2011). The curvelet approach for denoising in various imaging modalities using different shrinkage rules. *International Journal of Computers and Applications*, *29*(7), 36–42. doi:10.5120/3575-4933

Unser, M., & Aldroubi, A. (1996). A review of wavelets in biomedical applications. *Proceedings of the IEEE*, *84*(4), 626–638. doi:10.1109/5.488704

Unser, M., Aldroubi, A., & Eden, M. (1992). On the asymptotic convergence of B-spline wavelets to Gabor functions. *IEEE Transactions on Information Theory*, *38*(2), 864–872. doi:10.1109/18.119742

Unser, M. A., Aldroubi, A., & Gerfen, C. R. (1993, November). Multiresolution image registration procedure using spline pyramids. In *SPIE's 1993 International Symposium on Optics, Imaging, and Instrumentation* (pp. 160-170). International Society for Optics and Photonics.

Wu, X., & Memon, N. (1997). Context-based, adaptive, lossless image coding. *IEEE Transactions on Communications*, *45*(4), 437–444. doi:10.1109/26.585919

Yang, X., Wang, K., & Shamma, S. A. (1992). Auditory representations of acoustic signals. *IEEE Transactions on Information Theory*, *38*(2), 824–839. doi:10.1109/18.119739

Chapter 7
Pulse Oximetry:
An Introduction

Ashoka Reddy Komalla
Kakatiya Institute of Technology and Science, India

ABSTRACT

Pulse rate, body temperature, blood pressure, and respiratory rate are four vital signs indicating health status of a patient. Oxygen saturation of arterial blood (SaO2) is regarded as fifth vital sign of health status. Pulse oximeters are used in post-operative intensive care units for monitoring pulse rate and SaO2. They make non-invasive simultaneous estimation of pulse rate and SaO2 using photoplethysmogram (PPG) signals captured at red and IR wavelengths. This chapter describes the concept of oximetry, importance of non-invasive medical measurements, principle of pulse oximetry, and the block diagram approach for the design of pulse oximeters. It also presents an exhaustive review on various methods in-vogue for SaO2 estimation, identifies the problems associated with pulse oximeters. The critical limitation is that commercial pulse oximeters are as accurate as their calibration curves. Finally, it presents state-of-the-art research aimed at performance enhancement of pulse oximeters and directions for future work.

INTRODUCTION

Health of the human body can be ascertained by signals emanating from it (Bruce, 2001; Rangayyan, 2002; Sornmo & Laguna, 2005). The four traditional vital signs, normally used by medical doctors all over the globe, to obtain critical knowledge about a patient's state of health are the pulse rate, the respiratory rate, the body temperature and the blood pressure. For life, nothing is more important than oxygen supply to the body. Oxygen required for all parts of the body is carried by the arterial blood (Webster, 1997). This chapter specifically describes all the aspects of pulse oximeters. Pulse oximeter is an important medical instrument used in post-operative intensive care units for monitoring patient's pulse rate and oxygen saturation of arterial blood (SaO_2).

DOI: 10.4018/978-1-5225-5152-2.ch007

Copyright © 2018, IGI Global. Copying or distributing in print or electronic forms without written permission of IGI Global is prohibited.

BACKGROUND

Blood and Its Composition

About 55% of arterial blood is composed of a liquid called the plasma, 43% of the blood is made of red blood cells (RBCs, also known as erythrocytes), 1.5% white blood cells (leukocytes), and 0.5% platelets (thrombocytes). 90% of plasma is made of water with some proteins and other chemicals dissolved in it. On the other hand RBCs are mainly made of hemoglobin molecules. Hemoglobin is responsible for the transport of oxygen to various other cells of the body (Ganong, 1993). Typically each mm^3 of blood contains nearly six million RBCs and each RBC is made of about 280 million hemoglobin molecules. The hemoglobin concentration in blood is between 134 and 173 g/l (Kasper, 2005).

Systemic and Pulmonary Circulation

Blood is circulated throughout the body by the systemic and pulmonary circulation system (Li, 2004). The flow of arterial blood, the replenishment of oxygen and exhaling of carbondioxide are controlled by the cardio-pulmonary system, comprising the heart, lungs and the blood vessels (arteries, veins and capillaries). Arteries (except the pulmonary artery, which carries oxygen depleted blood to the lungs for replenishment of oxygen) carry oxygenated blood from the heart to all parts of the body. Arteries terminate into capillaries and the blood in the capillaries provides oxygen and nutrients to the cells and picks up the waste including carbondioxide from the cells. The capillaries terminate to small veins and the small veins lead to bigger veins. Thus oxygen depleted blood containing additional waste is brought back to the right atrium of the heart through these veins. This blood then passes to right ventricle and gets pushed through the pulmonary artery to the lungs. In the lung capillaries, the exhale of carbondioxide and infusing of oxygen takes place and the oxygen-rich blood from the lungs returns back through the pulmonary veins to the heart, thus completing one cycle.

Mechanism of Oxygen Exchange

Air inhaled during breathing enters the lungs. Oxygen in the air is trapped by the hemoglobin molecules and carbondioxide from the blood is released to the air that gets exhaled (Miller, 2005). A heterogeneous collection of gas exchange units called alveoli in the lungs surrounded by large pulmonary capillary beds aid this gas exchange through diffusion. Diffusion of a gas requires differential partial pressure. The partial pressures exerted by the two main gases added together nearly equal the atmospheric pressure. The partial pressure of oxygen (Po_2) of dry air at sea level is approximately 21 kPa but by the time air passes through the trachea and reaches the alveoli, the Po_2 falls to about 13 kPa. Blood returning to the lungs has a Po_2 of 5 kPa. A thin wall (about 0.5 µm thick) between the pulmonary capillaries and the alveoli permits diffusion of gases. Since Po_2 of air in the alveoli is 13 kPa and in the pulmonary capillaries is 5 kPa, oxygen diffuses from alveoli to the blood in the pulmonary capillaries. On the other hand, the partial pressure gradient for carbondioxide ensures the diffusion of carbondioxide from the blood to the air trapped in the alveoli. In case of nitrogen, the nitrogen in the blood and the nitrogen in alveolar air has almost same partial pressure and hence very little nitrogen is diffused in either direction.

Thus the blood returning to the left side of the heart to be pumped into the systemic circulation is replenished with oxygen. If this process is normal then the Po_2 of pulmonary venous blood would be equal to the Po_2 in the alveoli. Any malfunction would render the pulmonary vein Po_2 to be less than the Po_2 in alveoli, resulting in reduced amount of oxygen in the arterial blood. In fact, the amount of oxygen bound to the hemoglobin at any time is dictated by the Po_2 to which the hemoglobin is exposed. When the arterial blood enters body tissue through capillaries, wherein the Po_2 is lower than the arterial Po_2, oxygen is detached from the hemoglobin and enters the tissue. The total quantity of oxygen bound to hemoglobin in normal arterial blood is approximately 19 ml per 100 ml of blood at 13 kPa. On passing through tissue capillaries this amount is reduced to 14 ml per 100 ml of blood at 5 kPa. Thus nearly 5 ml of oxygen is consumed by tissues from each 100 ml of blood that passes through tissue capillaries during each cycle.

When the blood returns to the lungs, approximately 5 ml of oxygen diffuses from alveoli into each 100 ml of blood. Nearly 98.5% of the diffused oxygen gets bounded to hemoglobin molecules and the remaining 1.5% gets dissolved in plasma. Each hemoglobin molecule is capable of carrying of four oxygen molecules. When one hemoglobin molecule bounds four oxygen molecules, it becomes fully saturated with oxygen. Each gram of fully saturated hemoglobin then contains 1.3 ml of oxygen. However, not all hemoglobin molecules participate in oxygen transport.

Functional and Dysfunctional Hemoglobin

Blood contains several forms of hemoglobin, of which some are useful in oxygen transport and some are not. Functional hemoglobin are those that are capable of carrying oxygen and include hemoglobin bounded with oxygen molecules, called oxyhemoglobin (oxygenated hemoglobin, HbO_2) and hemoglobin not bounded with any other molecule called reduced hemoglobin (deoxy-hemoglobin, Hb). Hemoglobin which are incapable of carrying oxygen are called *dysfunctional hemoglobin* (dyshemoglobin). These are hemoglobin bounded with molecule(s) other than oxygen. They include carboxyhemoglobin (COHb) and methemoglobin (MetHb). COHb is formed when carbonmonoxide (CO) bonds to hemoglobin. COHb exits in varying degrees as a consequence of smoking and urban pollution. The level of COHb may become as high as 45% as a result of smoke inhalation. MetHb is oxidized hemoglobin, normally less than 1% of the total hemoglobin. MetHb is not capable of binding oxygen and hence cannot aid in oxygen transport. Under normal conditions, HbO_2 and Hb amount to 99% of the total hemoglobin present in the blood.

Oxygen Saturation

Whether a person is sleeping, resting or active, every part in the person's body requires oxygen. The amount of oxygen required for a particular part of the body depends on the degree of activity of that part but is never zero. Different organs of the body can not tolerate deprivation of oxygen even for limited periods of time and get permanently damaged. Therefore the amount of oxygen carried by the arterial blood is measured to estimate the level of functioning of various parts of the cardio-pulmonary system.

In the direct method of measurement of oxygen content, the arterial blood is completely analyzed to ascertain the various concentrations of gasses in it. Such an analysis would require drawing of blood directly from an artery and hence requires the services of a competent surgeon. Alternate methods for the determination of the gas contents of arterial blood without the need for puncturing and drawing blood from an artery have been proposed (Severinghaus & Astrup, 1986). One such method is *pulse oximetry*. In pulse oximetry, the content arterial blood oxygen is estimated in terms of a percentage (Webster, 1997; Dorsch & Dorsch, 1999).

The hemoglobin is oxygen carrying agent of blood and one molecule can carry four oxygen molecules. If in total there are N hemoglobin, then:

N Hemoglobin + N Oxygen = 25% saturated hemoglobin

N Hemoglobin + 2 N Oxygen = 50% saturated hemoglobin

N Hemoglobin + 3 N Oxygen = 75% saturated hemoglobin

N Hemoglobin + 4 N Oxygen = 100% saturated hemoglobin

Thus if each and every hemoglobin of arterial blood carries four oxygen molecules, the arterial blood is fully (100%) saturated with oxygen. Or in other words, if N_{Hb} is the number of hemoglobin molecules and N_{O_2} is the number of oxygen bounded with hemoglobin in arterial blood then we can define oxygen saturations as:

$$\text{Oxygen saturation (SaO}_2) = \frac{N_{O_2}}{4N_{Hb}} \times 100\% \times 100\% \tag{1}$$

Oxygen saturation is normally expressed as a percentage rather than as a ratio. If we represent concentration of oxyhemoglobin as $\langle HbO_2 \rangle$ and concentration of deoxyhemoglobin as $\langle Hb \rangle$ in arterial blood then Equation (1) can be rewritten as (Baura, 2002):

$$SaO_2 = \frac{\langle HbO_2 \rangle}{\langle Hb \rangle + \langle HbO_2 \rangle} \times 100\% \tag{2}$$

Rearranging Equation (2) results in:

$$SaO_2 = \frac{\dfrac{\langle HbO_2 \rangle}{\langle Hb \rangle}}{1 + \dfrac{\langle HbO_2 \rangle}{\langle Hb \rangle}} \, 100\% = \frac{Q}{1+Q} \, 100\% \tag{3}$$

where $Q = \left(\dfrac{\langle HbO_2 \rangle}{\langle Hb \rangle} \right)$ is the ratio of HbO_2 to Hb in arterial blood. Equation (2) assumes that dysfunctional hemoglobin are negligible. If both functional and dysfunctional hemoglobin are present in the arterial blood then oxygen saturation is expressed as a *fractional oxygen saturation* given by:

$$\text{Fractional } SaO_2 = \frac{\langle HbO_2 \rangle}{\langle Hb \rangle + \langle HbO_2 \rangle + \langle COHb \rangle + \langle MetHb \rangle} \times 100\% \qquad (4)$$

A healthy, nonsmoking person will have arterial oxygen saturation between 94% and 100%. Anything below 90% could quickly lead to complications. Saturations lower than 90% may be caused by chronic obstructive pulmonary disease (COPD), excessive bleeding, smoking and malfunctioning blood vessels, especially capillaries. The functional oxygen saturation of venous blood (SvO_2) is about 75% (Ahrens & Rutherford, 1993).

OXIMETRY

Oximetry deals with measurement of oxygen saturation. Three types of oximetry are now in clinical use (Pole, 2002):

1.   Invasive (*in-vitro*) CO-Oximetry and arterial blood gas analysis.
2.   Invasive fiber optic based oximetry to determine oxygen saturation in arterial flow, mixed arterial-venous flow or intra-cardiac flow.
3.   Noninvasive pulse oximetry to monitor arterial oxygen saturation at any part of the body.

Arterial Blood Gas Analyzer and CO-Oximeter

Prior to the widespread use of the present day noninvasive pulse oximeter, the arterial blood gas (ABG) analysis and CO-Oximetry were the main methods employed for the measurement of arterial oxygen saturation. As its name implies, the ABG test is conducted by taking a blood sample from an artery and performing complete gas analysis. For this purpose either the radial artery at the wrist or the brachial artery at the elbow would have to be punctured. The common practice was to draw the samples at regular intervals and analyze with *in-vitro* blood gas analyzer. The AGB analyzer gives a full picture of blood including pH, Po_2 and Pco_2, the bicarbonate concentration in addition to the SaO_2.

CO-Oximeter or haemoximeter calculates the actual concentrations of the Hb, HbO_2, COHb and MetHb but again requires a sample of blood drawn from an artery. It works on the spectrometric principles using four different wavelengths of light and measures the fractional SaO_2. The CO-Oximeter is considered as the "gold standard" (Secker & Spiers, 1997).

As both these methods are time consuming, invasive (Williams, 1998), *in-vitro* continuous and non-invasive methods are developed. One such noninvasive method is *pulse oximetry*. Pulse oximetry has now become the most popular method employed for the determination of SaO_2.

SaO$_2$ and SpO$_2$

The SaO_2 is actual saturation value in arterial blood. The SpO_2 is the saturation estimated by pulse oximetry. In the method of pulse oximetry SpO_2 is computed using a couple of photoplethysmographs.

PHOTOPLETHYSMOGRAPHY

A plethysmograph is an instrument for measuring changes in volume within an organ or whole body, usually resulting from fluctuations in the amount of blood or air it contains.

Photoplethysmography, a non-invasive electro-optic method developed by Hertzman, provides information on the blood volume flowing at a particular test site on the body close to the skin (Hertzman, 1938). A Photoplethysmogram (PPG) is obtained by illuminating a part of the body of interest and acquiring either the reflected or transmitted light. For obtaining PPG by way of detecting the transmitted light, we place a light source of wavelength λ having a constant intensity $I_{IN\lambda}$ on one side of an extremity, say fingertip, and detect the transmitted light through the finger by a suitable photo detector placed on the side opposite to that of the source as indicated in Figure 1.

A typical PPG signal, shown in Figure 2, is made of a large DC component that is due to a large part of light from the source passing through skin-muscle-bone without coming into contact with blood vessels at all and reaching the photo detector, a very small component having a very low frequency due to light from the source passing through, apart from the skin-muscle-bone, the venous blood and a much smaller component at the frequency of the heart beat due to light from the source also passing through arterial blood vessels. Just after the systole, blood volume increases in the arteries thereby reducing the received light intensity. During diastole, blood volume in the arteries decreases and hence an increase in the light transmission. Thus the part of detected signal due to the arterial blood appears pulsatile in nature at the heart rate, as shown in Figure 2. At a classical measuring site, about 99% of the detected signal comes from skin-tissue-bone, 0.9% from venous blood and about 0.1% from arterial blood volume. The pulsatile portion of the PPG arises due to the light passing through arterial blood and hence has information contained in the arterial blood flow; heart rate, heart rate variability, respiration and blood pressure to name a few (Nakajima, Tamura, & Miike, 1996). Similarly the slow varying component of a PPG is due to the venous blood. It has been shown that utilizing the slow varying component of a

Figure 1. Sensor for obtaining a PPG signal utilizing the transmitted light through finger

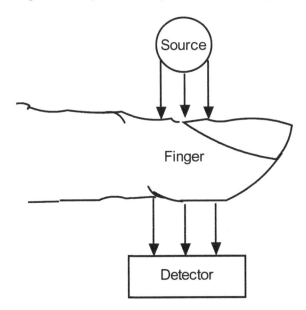

Figure 2. Components of a typical PPG signal showing individual contributions from (bone+tissue+skin), capillaries, venous blood arterial blood

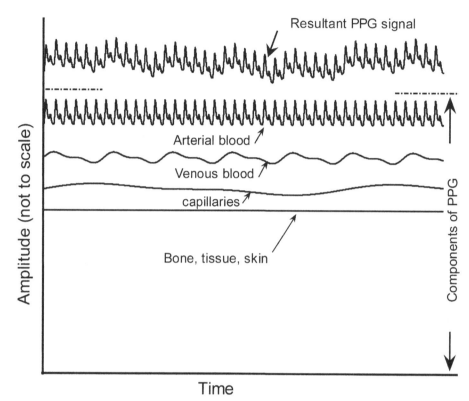

single wavelength PPG, diagnosis and monitoring of peripheral vascular hemo-dynamics and venous dysfunction (thrombosis) can be achieved (Blazek & Schultz-Ehrenburg, 1996; Sarin, Shields, Scurr, & Smith, 1992). In the method of pulse oximetry, using two PPG signals, one obtained using a light source in the red wavelength region and the other in the infrared region, the level of oxygen saturation in arterial blood is ascertained non-invasively.

To obtain a PPG, a sensor housing a suitable light source to illuminate the part of body of interest and a photo detector to detect the transmitted, as in Figure 3(b), or reflected, as in Figure 3(a), light is necessary.

The fingertip is a convenient option because a good PPG signal can be obtained with least discomfort to a patient and hence is popular with most pulse oximeter sensors (Blazek & Schultz-Ehrenburg, 1996; Reddy, George, Mohan, & Kumar, 2006; Reddy, George, Mohan, & Kumar, 2009; Reddy & Kumar, 2011).

PULSE OXIMETRY

Karl Matthes, who is regarded as the Father of oximetry, established that red light can pass through oxyhemoglobin but reduced hemoglobin absorbs it and built the first device to continuously measure blood oxygen saturation *in vivo* by transilluminating tissue. He used two wavelengths of light, one of which was sensitive to oxygen saturation and the other, which was in infrared range, was used to com-

Figure 3. Typical PPG sensors: (a) Reflectance type sensor head,(b) Transmittance type sensor head

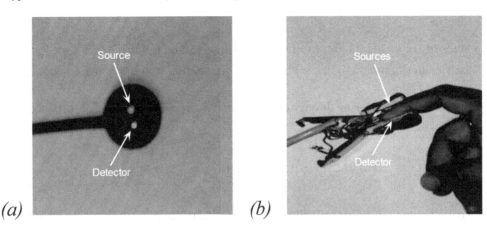

(a)   *(b)*

pensate for changes in tissue thickness and light intensity. Although useful in following the trends in saturation, difficulties with calibration made it an unwieldy device. In the early 1940s, Millikan devised an instrument and coined the term "oximeter" (Millikan, 1942), so as to regulate the oxygen delivery system to help pilots flying at high altitudes in pressurized cockpits. Most important subsequent works were performed by Goldie (Goldie, 1942), Wood and Geraci (1949), that resulted in the improvement of Millikan's ear oximeter. In 1949, Brinkman and Zijlstra (1949) were first to describe the monitoring of SaO_2 based upon skin reflectance spectroscopy from forehead, first *in-vitro*, and then *in-vivo*. Later a photoelectric method was proposed by Sekelj *et al.* (1951). In 1960, Polanyi and Hehir (1960) developed the fiber optic catheter oximeter which is the basis for the modern invasive oximeter. In 1964, Robert Shaw, built an ear oximeter, using eight wavelengths between 650 nm and 1050 nm, to identify and separate Hb species including COHb and MetHb. In early 1970s Hewlett-Packard improved his method and released the first commercial eight-wavelength ear oximeter. Meanwhile, Cohen and Wardsworth added significant advancements in noninvasive reflectance oximetry (Cohen & Wardsworth, 1972). In 1972, Takuo Aoyagi, invented the present day two-wavelength pulse oximetry (Aoyagi, Kishi, Yamaguchi, & Watanabe, 1974). However, all these early instruments suffered from one or more of the following drawbacks (Merrick & Hayes, 1976; Takatani & Ling, 1994):

1. Lack of adequate calibration procedures
2. differentiating, arterial and venous blood

Several groups started working on pulse oximetry with LEDs generated required narrowband light with controlled wavelengths (Falconer & Robinson, 1990). In course of time, pulse oximetry has become the standard technique for monitoring saturation during procedural sedation and intensive care.

Principle of Operation of a Pulse Oximeter

All the present day pulse oximeters utilize Beer-Lambert's law for their operation. The law is governed by Here, the light (I_0) is related to the light intensity of incident light (I_{IN}) by:

$$I_0 = I_{IN} e^{-\varepsilon_\lambda c L} \tag{5}$$

where I_{IN} = intensity of incident light; I_0 = intensity of transmitted light; ε_λ = the wavelength dependent extinction coefficient (l.mmol^{-1}.cm^{-1}); c = absorber concentration (mmol.l^{-1}) and L = optical path length (cm).

The light absorbed while passing through the solution is expressed in terms of absorbance (A), given by:

$$A = \ln\left(\frac{I_{IN}}{I_0}\right) = \varepsilon_\lambda c L \tag{6}$$

A is also called optical density (OD). If multiple absorbers are present in the path of light then each absorber contributes its part and the resulting total absorbance can be expressed as:

$$A = \sum_{i=1}^{k} \varepsilon_{\lambda i} c_i L_i \tag{7}$$

where, k represents the number of independent absorbers.

Since arterial blood flow is pulsatile, the absorbance due to it will also be a pulsatile signal. The pulse period is controlled by heartbeat and amplitude of pulse is proportional to the concentration of hemoglobin and optical path length. The optical attenuation characteristics of oxy and deoxy-hemoglobin (Horecker, 1943; Zijlstra, Buursma, & Meeuwsen-van der Roest, 1991; Kim, Xia, & Liu, 2005) are as given in Figure 4.

The absorption characteristics, shown in Figure 4, are important to pulse oximetry. The 600-750 nm is red (R) wavelength band and the 850-1000 nm is infrared (IR) wavelength band. Oxy-hemoglobin absorbs more IR light and deoxy-hemoglobin absorbs more red light. For best results on attenuation, the optimal wavelengths of and IR are 600 nm and 798 nm respectively. Practically, the wavelengths are chosen based on available resources. Currently available pulse oximeters use red LED at 660 nm and IR LED at 940 nm. Either the transmitted light through an extremity such as fingertip or ear lobe or the reflected light is captured to obtain two PPG signals, say red-PPG (PPG_R) and infrared-PPG (PPG_{IR}).

The PPG contains cardiac synchronous AC portion and a DC portion.

Let:

DC_R = DC value of the red PPG

DC_{IR} = DC value of the IR PPG

AC_R = AC value of the red PPG and

AC_{IR} = AC value of the IR PPG respectively.

The ratio of ratios R is calculated as:

Figure 4. Absorption spectra of Hb and HbO$_2$ [34]. An observable difference in absorption characteristics of Hb and HbO$_2$ can be seen

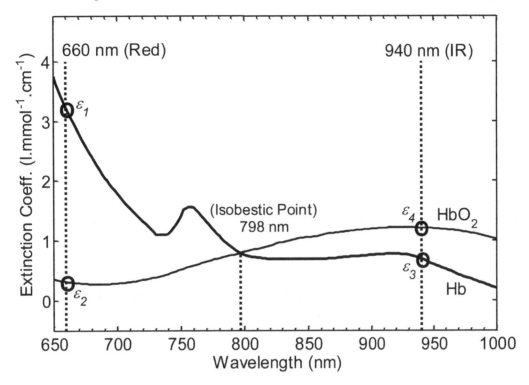

$$R = \frac{AC_R/DC_R}{AC_{IR}/DC_{IR}} \qquad\qquad (8)$$

Pulse oximeter manufacturers select a large numbers of healthy and non-smoking volunteers to capture the PPG data. The protocol followed during data capturing is as follows:

1. Volunteers are made to breathe hypoxic gases. This will change their saturations between 70% and 100% (Mendelson, 1992; Sinex, 1999).
2. Samples of their arterial blood are drawn at regular intervals.
3. The oxygen saturation (SaO_2) values are computed/measured using *in-vitro* laboratory CO-Oximeter from the samples drawn in step 2.
4. Red and IR PPGs are recorded at regular intervals, at the time of drawing their blood samples, at different saturation levels.
5. Normalized ratios (R) are calculated from those red and IR PPG signals recorded in step 4 at different intervals .
6. The SaO_2 values obtained in step 3 and normalized ratios (R) computed in step 5 are then plotted to form a calibration curve.

A typical calibration curve used by Ohmeda pulse oximeter (Wukitsch, Petterson, Tobler, & Pologe, 1988) is shown in Figure 5. An empirical linear approximation to that calibration curve (Webster, 1997; Rusch, Sankar, & Scharf, 1996), is given as:

$$SpO_2 = \left(110 - 25R\right)\%$$ (9)

Therefore, manufacturers will have unique calibration curve(s) as per the selected. In most cases, an $R = 1$ approximately indicates a saturation of 85%.

Pulse Rate

In addition to estimation of arterial oxygen saturation (SpO2), the pulse oximeter also estimates pulse rate using PPG. As PPG is a cardiac synchronous signal, it consists of one pulse or beat for every heart beat.

Commercial Pulse Oximeter

Pulse oximeters make non-invasive simultaneous estimations of pulse rate and SpO_2 using photoplethysmogram (PPG) signals captured at red and IR wavelengths. Pulse oximeter is conveniently called as "PULSE OXI" and photoplethysmogram is conveniently called as 'PLETH" among the professional anesthetists and physicians. Some forms of pulse oximeters available in the market are shown in figure 6. They are capable of estimating **BPM** in the range 30-240 bpm and **SpO_2%** in the range 70-99%.

Figure 5. A typical pulse oximeter calibration curve showing empirical relationship between actual SaO_2 and normalized ratio R

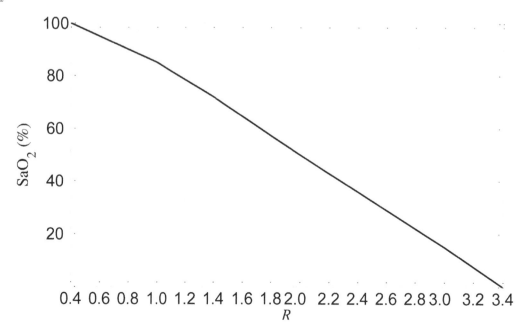

Figure 6. Some forms of the pulse oximeters available in market
(Courtesy: https://images.google.com/)

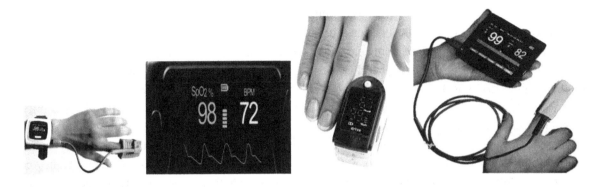

The simplest commercial pulse oximeter can be viewed as a microprocessor / microcontroller to which a PPG sensor is interfaced. Manufacturer's calibration curve equation, example Equation (9), is stored in the microprocessor / microcontroller for on-line computation of SpO_2.

SpO2: The standard pulse oximeter estimates SpO_2 in the following way:

1. The PPG sensor housing R and IR LEDs and a matching photodiode / phototransistor is attached to the patient / subject.
2. PPG sensor will acquire R and IR PPG signals of the patient.
3. The Microprocessor/microcontroller sitting inside the pulse oximeter will read the R & IR signals and calculates *R,* as per equation (8), from the acquired PPGs.
4. In the very next step, the microprocessor/microcontroller will estimate the SpO_2 by substituting R in manufacturer's unique empirically derived calibration equation, example Equation (9).

Pulse Rate: As PPG is a cardiac synchronous signal, it consists of a typical PPG pulse for every heart beat. Pulse rate is number of pulses per minute (or) number of PPG pulses in 60 seconds. It is normally expressed in terms of beats per minute (bpm).

The pulse rate is estimated in either of the following ways:

1. Pulse oximeter counts number of PPG pulses in 10 seconds.
    a. Let N = number of pulses in 10 seconds.
    b. Then, number of pulses in 60 seconds is obtained by multiplying that count N by 6
    c. Therefore, the estimated pulse rate = $N \times 6$
2. *In the second and quick method*, pulse oximeter counts number of PPG pulses in 6 seconds only.
    a. Let N =number of pulses in 6 seconds.
    b. Then, number of pulses in 60 seconds is obtained by multiplying that count N by 10
    c. Therefore, the estimated pulse rate = $N \times 10$

Issues and Problems With Pulse Oximetry

Pulse oximetry avoided discomfort of arterial puncture for saturation estimation. It has become a de facto standard for noninvasive monitoring of arterial blood and pulse rate. However, present day pulse oximeters have shortcomings and research is being carried out all over the globe in removing these shortcomings. They include probe placement, peripheral vasoconstriction (poor perfusion) (Brown, &Vender, 1988), dyshemoglobins (Bowes, Corke, & Hulka, 1989), intravascular dyes (Huch, Huch, Konig, Neuman, Parker, Yount, & Lubbers, 1988), ambient light (Amar, Neidzwski, Wald, & Finck, 1989), nail polish (Cote, Goldstein, Buschman, & Hoaglin, 1988; Chan, Chan, & Chan, 2003), skin pigmentation (Ries, Prewitt, & Johnson, 1989), and reliability problems due to movement of patient (Langton, & Hanning, 1990; Plummer, Zakaria, Ilsley, Fronsko, & Owen, 1995). As they use only two wavelengths, they can measure only two hemoglobins and thus, estimate functional saturation, not fractional saturation. Important limitation of pulse oximetry is the presence of abnormal hemoglobins. The most common and potentially most serious is carboxyhemoglobin, which the oximeter detects as oxyhemoglobin and thus overestimates the true concentration of oxyhemoglobin. Other dyshemoglobins such as methemoglobin also interfere (Barker, Tremper, & Hyatt, 1989; Bozeman, Myers, & Barish, 1997). CO-Oximetry should be employed if the presence of abnormal hemoglobin is expected.

Dyes/ pigments affect pulse oximeter measurements. The presence of methylene blue will make a pulse oximeter read erroneously (Sidi, Paulus, Rush, Gravenstein, & Davis, 1987; Scheller, Unger & Kelner, 1986). Pulse oximeters require an adequate arterial pulsation. Shock, severe hypotension, vasoconstriction or hypothermia, will produce unreliable oximeter readings (Schnapp & Cohen, 1990).

Excessive light from surgical lamps and ambient light interfere with oximetry accuracy (Trivedi, Ghouri, Shah, Lai, & Barker, 1997; Fluck, Schroeder, Frani, Kropf, & Engbertson, 2003). Interference with high intensity ambient light can be easily avoided by placing an opaque material (dark colored cloth) to surround the probe. Studies on the effect of skin pigmentation on the pulse oximetry revealed that dark skin color may influence the performance and concluded that accuracy was slightly less for subjects with dark skin color than those with lighter skin color (Cote, Goldstein, Buschman, & Hoaglin, 1989). Fingernail polish disturbed the pulse oximeter readings (Cote, Goldstein, Buschman, & Hoaglin, 1989; Chan, Chan, & Chan, 2003; White & Boyle, 1989).

MOTION ARTIFACTS

Artifact-free PPG signals are required for accurate estimation of SpO_2. In addition to arterial pulse, additional pulsations due to motion artifact lead to inaccurate estimation of SpO_2. Signal processing methods to reduce the MAs are required for reliable saturation estimations. In practice, the effect of MAs on saturation is masked by displaying previous SpO_2 reading (Rusch, Sankar & Scharf, 1996). A straight forward solution is to altogether avoid motion artifacts by securing the sensor head rigidly to the skin of the patient at a monitoring site and avoid relative motion between the sensor and the patient. However, this solution is not practical because pressure on the skin would lead to discomfort to the patient. Hence the probe in a pulse oximeter is always designed to exert bare minimum pressure on the skin, just adequate to keep the probe in place. Moreover when pressure is applied vasoconstriction occurs resulting in reduced perfusion. Sustained pressure elevates skin temperature resulting in vasodilatation leading to increased perfusion. In both cases sweating takes place resulting in deterioration of contact between the sensor and the skin. If proper compensation is not applied for these changes, then SpO_2 readings obtained will be erroneous.

Summary of Limitations of Pulse Oximetry

1. The SpO_2 estimation in vogue relies on an empirical equation realised by linear regression of the PPG data of volunteers. Therefore, the obvious limitation is that commercial pulse oximeters are as accurate as their calibration curves are. Since these curves are from 70% to 100% of SpO_2 values, manufacturers extrapolate their 70 to 100% results downward in order to display SpO_2 values below 70% (Mendelson, 1992; Hanning, & Alexander-Williams, 1995; Jurban, 1999). Light absorption is also dependent on pigmentation and thickness of test site. It was reported that as the skin pigmentation darkens, the pulse oximeter performance deteriorates (Saylor, 2003). This is mainly due to a lower signal-to-noise ratio caused by increased light absorption as the skin pigmentation darkens. It would be advantageous if the calculation of SpO_2 is made independent of skin pigmentation and intervening tissue volume. However, better accuracy is expected if the computation of SpO2 is obtained analytically without resorting to the use of "calibration curves"
2. The amplitudes of detected PPG signals depend on detector sensitivities and intensities of individual sources (red and IR LEDs). It would, indeed, be attractive if estimation of SpO_2 is made independent of LEDs intensity and detectors sensitivity of PPG sensor.
3. Patient movement will affect the reliability of pulse oximeter readings. Reduction of motion artifacts (MA) from PPG signals is an important research problem.

Challenges in Pulse Oximetry Research

The first of these challenges would be on the development of alternate SpO_2 computation strategies, which make the estimation of SpO_2 independent of patient and sensor (source and detector) dependent parameters. The whole idea is to make the SpO2 estimations independent of empirical equations drawn from calibration curves.

The second important challenge is to develop signal processing methods for MA reduction in PPG signals. This will improve reliability of SpO_2 estimation, employing pulse oximeters, to a very large extent.

Model Based Method for Estimation of Spo₂

The method presented here, not only removes the influence of patient dependent parameters, because of the well known feedback technique, in the determination of SpO_2, but also renders the pulse oximeter not to rely on calibration curves (Reddy, Bai, George, Mohan, & Kumar, 2006). A twostep procedure is followed here.

1. Normalized PPGs are to be obtained first. For this a feedback compensation based method is proposed.
2. A novel method for estimating SpO_2 from the PGs obtained in first step is proposed next.

Normalization of PPGs Using Feedback Compensation

In the transmission type PPG, the transmitted unabsorbed light to the detector gets converted into an equivalent current or voltage by the detector resulting in a PPG, a typical form of which is illustrated in figure 2. The different waveforms in figure 2 are not drawn to scale as the magnitudes of individual components differ considerably. The detected signal $v_{D\lambda}$ can be represented as:

$$v_{D\lambda} = K_{D\lambda} \left(I_{IN\lambda} \varepsilon_{ED\lambda} \langle ED \rangle \left(\langle TI \rangle \varepsilon_{TI\lambda} + \langle BO \rangle \varepsilon_{BO\lambda} + \langle BL \rangle \varepsilon_{BL\lambda} (\langle \alpha \rangle \varepsilon_{BO\lambda} + \langle \beta \rangle \varepsilon_{TI\lambda} + \langle \gamma \rangle \varepsilon_{TI\lambda} \varepsilon_{BO\lambda}) \right) \right)$$

(10)

where $I_{IN\lambda}$ = intensity of light at wavelength λ, $K_{D\lambda}$ = detector sensitivity, $\varepsilon_{ED\lambda}$ = extinction coefficient of epidermis, $\varepsilon_{BO\lambda}$, = extinction coefficient of bone, $\varepsilon_{BL\lambda}$ = extinction coefficient of blood, and $\varepsilon_{TI\lambda}$ = extinction coefficient of tissue.

$\langle ED \rangle$ = concentrations of epidermis

$\langle BO \rangle$ = concentrations of bone

$\langle TI \rangle$ = concentrations of tissue

$\langle BL \rangle$ = concentration of blood

$\langle \alpha \rangle$ = concentration of bone

$\langle \beta \rangle$ = concentration of tissue

$\langle \gamma \rangle$ = concentration of both bone and tissue

Extinction coefficient is a numeric measure of the opaqueness of a particular type of cell exposed to the light (Shao, 2016). The greater the extinction coefficient, the greater is the opaqueness. Blazek *et al.* pioneered the concept of obtaining a quantitative PPG signal by employing negative feedback compensation (Blazek & Schultz-Ehrenburg, 1996). However, in their method the feedback scheme is employed with a S&H circuit inserted in feedback loop. The feedback is enabled only for a set period just prior to a measurement. During the measurement period, the feedback is broken, albeit with the help of the sample and hold to ensure that conditions existing prior to the breaking off of the feedback are maintained during the measurement period. The feedback could not be enabled all the time in their case, since their interest is the low frequency component of a PPG signal arising due to the venous blood. In the method proposed here, a negative feedback compensation scheme without any sample and hold in the feedback path, as indicated in Figure 7, is employed. In the scheme shown in Figure 7, the intensity of light falling on the detector is first converted into an equivalent current by the photo diode detector. This current is converted into a voltage by the current-to-voltage converter (A1 in Figure 7) is filtered by the low-pass filter (LPF) to extract the DC component. The extracted DC component is compared with a preset DC reference voltage V_{ref}. The difference between the reference and the detector output is fed back to control the intensity of the source. Let the intensity of the light be initially some value. If a patient's skin is dark in color then the light falling on the detector will be low and hence the DC part of the detector output may be lower than V_{ref}, resulting in the drive to the source to be increased suitably. On the other hand, if the patient's skin is of a lighter shade, the feedback compensation scheme will reduce the drive to the source suitably so that once again the DC output is made equal to V_{ref}. The situation is the same even if the intervening volume of tissue between the source and the detector varies. The feedback will increase or decrease the drive to the source to compensate for the variations in the thickness of the finger inserted into the sensor. Mathematically speaking, the negative feedback ensures that output DC voltage $V_{DC\lambda} = K_{D\lambda}\left(I_{IN\lambda}\varepsilon_{ED\lambda}\left\langle ED\right\rangle\left(\left\langle TI\right\rangle\varepsilon_{TI\lambda} + \left\langle BO\right\rangle\varepsilon_{BO\lambda}\right)\right)$ for any patient will be equal to a pre-fixed DC reference voltage. Thus:

$$V_{DC\lambda} = K_{D\lambda}\left(I_{IN\lambda}\varepsilon_{ED\lambda}\left\langle ED\right\rangle\left(\left\langle TI\right\rangle\varepsilon_{TI\lambda} + \left\langle BO\right\rangle\varepsilon_{BO\lambda}\right)\right) = V_{ref} \tag{11}$$

Utilizing equation (2.2) and the fact that the pulsatile component of a PPG is one thousandth of its DC component, equation (2.1) can be simplified as:

$$v_{D\lambda} = V_{ref}\left(1 + \left\langle BL\right\rangle\varepsilon_{BL\lambda}\right) \tag{12}$$

So, computation of SpO_2 can be made independent by a novel method proposed below.

Model Based Method for Estimating SpO₂ From Normalized PPGs

The time varying pulsatile component $v_\lambda = V_{ref}\left(\left\langle BL\right\rangle\varepsilon_{BL\lambda}\right)$ in Equation (12) is due to the arterial blood. It contains plasma (55%), red blood cells (RBCs) (43%), white blood cells (WBCs) (1.5%) (leukocytes) and platelets (0.5%). RBCs are also known as erythrocytes. Erythrocytes are made of hemoglobin molecules. WBCs and plasma have insignificant influence on the absorption of light. At wavelength of interest, the plasma has nearly zero optical attenuation [64]. Therefore, we need to consider only the attenuation due to RBCs. Utilizing these facts, equation (12) is modified as:

$$v_\lambda \approx V_{ref}\left(\left\langle Hb\right\rangle\varepsilon_{Hb\lambda} + \varepsilon_{HbO\lambda}\left\langle HbO_2\right\rangle\right) \tag{13}$$

Here at wavelength λ

Figure 7. Schematic for obtaining normalized PPGs

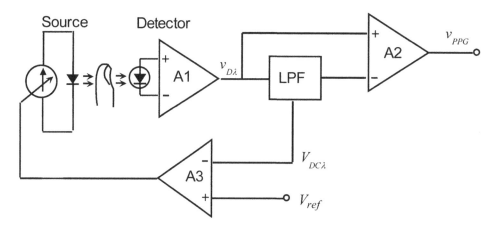

$\varepsilon_{Hb\lambda}$ = hemoglobin extinction coefficient and

$\varepsilon_{HbO\lambda}$ = oxy-hemoglobin extinction coefficient

On simplification the pulsatile portion becomes:

$$v_\lambda \approx V_{ref}\left(\varepsilon_{Hb\lambda} + \varepsilon_{HbO\lambda}\frac{\langle HbO_2\rangle}{\langle Hb\rangle}\right)\langle Hb\rangle = V_{ref}\left(\varepsilon_{Hb\lambda} + \varepsilon_{HbO\lambda}Q\right)\langle Hb\rangle \tag{14}$$

A marked difference in the absorption characteristics of Hb and HbO_2 can be seen at wavelengths 660 nm and 940 nm. The wavelength at which Hb and HbO_2 absorb to the same extent is called isobestic point. From Figure 4, it is seen that the isobestic point of Hb and HbO_2 occurs at 795±1.5 nm. These points may be used as reference points where light absorption is independent of the degree of saturation. The pulsatile signal's peak-to-peak value $V_{P\lambda}$ is given by:

$$V_{P\lambda} \approx V_{ref}\left(\varepsilon_{Hb\lambda} + \varepsilon_{HbO\lambda}Q\right) \tag{15}$$

At R and IR wavelengths, (15) becomes:

$$V_{PR} \approx V_{ref}\left(\varepsilon_1 + \varepsilon_2 Q\right) \tag{16}$$

$$V_{PIR} \approx V_{ref}\left(\varepsilon_3 + \varepsilon_4 Q\right) \tag{17}$$

Here ε_1 , ε_2 , ε_3 and ε_4 are respective extinction coefficients. Dividing equation (16) by Equation (17) results in:

$$\frac{V_{PR}}{V_{PIR}} = \frac{\left(\varepsilon_1 + \varepsilon_2 Q\right)}{\left(\varepsilon_3 + \varepsilon_4 Q\right)} \tag{18}$$

Solving for Q from Equation (2.8):

$$Q = \frac{\left(V_{PIR}\varepsilon_1 - V_{PR}\varepsilon_3\right)}{\left(V_{PR}\varepsilon_4 - V_{PIR}\varepsilon_2\right)} \tag{19}$$

From equations (2.9) and (1.3), we get:

$$SpO_2 = \frac{\left(V_{PIR}\varepsilon_1 - V_{PR}\varepsilon_3\right)}{\left(V_{PIR}\varepsilon_1 + V_{PR}\varepsilon_4\right) - \left(V_{PIR}\varepsilon_2 + V_{PR}\varepsilon_3\right)} \, 100\, \% \tag{20}$$

It is seen that none of the terms in equation (20) is patient and sensor dependent.

RESULTS

Table 1 summarizes extinction coefficients ($l.mmol^{-1}.cm^{-1}$) employed in developed prototype (Amar, Neidzwski, Wald, & Finck, 1989).

Pleths were recorded from volunteers after taking informed consent using developed proto type. At the same time PPG sensor of a commercial pulse oxi (CPO) is connected to the volunteers and noted down the saturation and bpm values indicated by CPO. The CPO used was Planet 50, manufactured by Larson and Toubro Limited. Data were collected from 31 volunteers and the SpO_2 estimation results are presented in Table 2. Terms within brackets indicate skin color and finger thickness of subject respectively.

Skin color: Fair(F), Dark(D), Normal(N);

Finger thickness: Thick(Tk), Thin(Tn), Medium(M). The SpO_2 readings from the developed instrument were compared with the ones obtained by the CPO, and the readings of the prototype were within $\pm 2\%$ of the CPO.

Table 1. Extinction coefficients employed in the prototype

Wavelength (nm)	Hb	HbO$_2$
660	$\varepsilon_1 = 3.226$	$\varepsilon_2 = 0.319$
940	$\varepsilon_3 = 0.693$	$\varepsilon_4 = 1.214$

FUTURE RESEARCH DIRECTIONS

To address the problems of pulse oximetry, several alternate SpO_2 computation strategies were developed, which make the SpO_2 independent of sensor (source and detector). Present research is directed towards SpO_2 estimation methods that do not rely on calibration curves. In this direction, another method of computation of SpO_2 using the normalized PPG signals and a model without using calibration curves was presented (Reddy, George, Mohan, & Kumar, 2008; Reddy & Kumar, 2011). This novel method based on a more detailed model that does not require feedback compensation to normalize the PPG signals is proposed. First, a model for the light propagation through test object (finger) was presented. Based on the model, an appropriate signal processing method was devised to extract patient and sensor independent

Table 2. Estimations of SpO_2 with prototype & a CPO

Subject no.	Average SpO₂ (Std. Dev)	
	Proposed method	CPO
1 (D,M)	97.26 (0.52)	98.85 (0.26)
2 (F,M)	97.74 (0.61)	98.81 (0.35)
3 (F,M)	98.58 (0.68)	99.42 (0.24)
4 (N,M)	97.80 (0.55)	98.22 (0.36)
5 (N,Tn)	98.96 (0.71)	98.57 (0.33)
6 (F,Tk)	97.32 (0.55)	98.55 (0.41)
7 (D,Tk)	96.86 (0.68)	97.93 (0.46)
8 (N,Tn)	97.59 (0.72)	98.19 (0.28)
9 (F,Tk)	97.97 (0.53)	98.83 (0.33)
10 (F,M)	97.38 (0.64)	98.76 (0.42)
11 (N,Tk)	96.96 (0.69)	98.25 (0.38)
12 (N,M)	97.44 (0.65)	98.83 (0.44)
13 (N,Tk)	98.06 (0.72)	98.99 (0.37)
14 (N,Tk)	98.72 (0.76)	99.22 (0.36)
15 (D,Tn)	97.26 (0.68)	98.47 (0.31)
16 (N,M)	97.49 (0.57)	98.66 (0.28)
17 (N,M)	98.27 (0.71)	99.14 (0.29)
18 (N,M)	98.05 (0.83)	98.29 (0.28)
19 (D,M)	97.19 (0.66)	98.55 (0.43)
20 (F,Tk)	96.99 (0.81)	97.82 (0.50)
21 (F,Tn)	97.38 (0.53)	98.61 (0.24)
22 (D,M)	97.77 (0.54)	98.59 (0.49)
23 (N,Tn)	97.32 (0.71)	98.70 (0.44)
24 (N,M)	97.91 (0.52)	99.13 (0.61)
25 (F,M)	96.53 (0.76)	97.81 (0.45)
26 (F,Tn)	96.85 (0.72)	98.22 (0.31)
27 (N,M)	98.09 (0.41)	99.18 (0.34)
28 (N,M)	96.76 (0.50)	98.33 (0.38)
29 (D,Tn)	97.89 (0.66)	98.29 (0.28)
30 (N,M)	98.36 (0.75)	99.55 (0.36)
31 (N,M)	98.22 (0.83)	99.13 (0.47)

pulsatile components from PPG signals that represent blood volume changes alone. An expression for calculation of SpO_2, utilizing the slopes and P-to-P amplitudes of PPG signals to compute SpO_2 readings directly, was derived. The method presented here dispensed with the need for feedback compensation and the necessity of calibration curves and provides stable readings. Another simpler method of measurement of SpO_2 (Reddy & Kumar, 2011) employing only the amplitudes of processed PPGs was also developed. This method also performed well with clinically acceptable estimations of SpO_2. Other methods discussed in (Shao, 2016; Verkruysse, 2017) also performed well. Hence, methods of SpO_2 estimation without resorting to ratio of ratios is the present state of the art research in pulse oximetry.

CONCLUSION

The arterial blood oxygen saturation is regarded as the fifth vital sign of health status. Pulse oximeters estimate pulse rate and oxygen saturation (SaO_2) non-invasively with the help of photoplethysmogram (PPG) signal. When SaO_2 is estimated by pulse oximeters, it is denoted by SpO_2. Commercial pulse oximeters (CPO) rely on calibration curves for SpO_2 estimation. This makes their SpO_2 estimations influenced by sensor and patient dependent parameters. Also the CPOs are as accurate as their empirical equation derived from their proprietary calibration curves. Hence current research in pulse oximetry is directed toward novel calibration free methods for SpO_2 estimations.

This chapter presented principles of photoplethysmography, pulse oximetry, detailed review of literature, and limitations of pulse oximetry. A novel model based method for calibration free estimation of SpO_2 was discussed. At the end it also discussed future trends of pulse oximetry research.

ACKNOWLEDGMENT

The author would like to thank his Ph.D supervisor Prof. V. Jagadeesh Kumar, Dept. of Electrical Engineering, IIT Madras, India for introducing him to the field of pulse oximetry.

REFERENCES

Ahrens, T., & Rutherford, K. (1993). *Essentials of Oxygenation*. Boston: Jones & Barlett.

Amar, J., Neidzwski, J., Wald, A., & Finck, A. D. (1989). Neidzwski, A. Wald and A. D. Finck, "Fluorescent light interferes with pulse oximetry. *Journal of Clinical Monitoring, 5*(2), 135–136. doi:10.1007/BF01617888 PMID:2656924

Aoyagi, T., Kishi, M., Yamaguchi, K., & Watanabe, S. (1974). Improvement of an ear-piece oximeter. Proc. Abstracts of 13th Annu. Japanese Soc. Med. Electro. Biologic Eng., 90-91.

Barker, S. J., Tremper, K. K., & Hyatt, J. (1989). Effects of methemoglobinemia on pulse oximetry and mixed venous oximetry. *Anesthesiology, 70*(1), 112–117. doi:10.1097/00000542-198901000-00021 PMID:2912291

Baura, G. D. (2002). *System theory and practical applications of biomedical signals, IEEE press series on biomedical engineering.* John Wiley & Sons.

Blazek & Schultz-Ehrenburg. (1996). Quantitative Photoplethysmography: Basic facts and examination tests for evaluating peripheral vascular functions. *VDI Verlog, 20*(192).

Bowes, W. A. III, Corke, B. C., & Hulka, J. (1989). Pulse oximetry: A review of the theory, accuracy, and clinical applications. *Obstetrics and Gynecology, 74*(3 Pt 2), 541–546. PMID:2668828

Bozeman, W. P., Myers, R. A., & Barish, R. A. (1997). Confirmation of pulse oximetry gap in carbonmonoxide poisoning. *Annals of Emergency Medicine, 30*(5), 608–611. doi:10.1016/S0196-0644(97)70077-5 PMID:9360570

Brinkman, R., & Zijlstra, W. G. (1949). Determination and continuous registration of the percentage oxygen saturation in clinical conditions. *Archivum Chirurgicum Neerlandicum, 1*, 177–183. PMID:15398660

Brown, M., & Vender, J. S. (1988). Noninvasive oxygen monitoring. *Critical Care Clinics, 4*(3), 493–509. PMID:3063350

Bruce, E. N. (2001). *Biomedical signal processing and signal modeling.* John Wiley & Sons.

Chan, M. M., Chan, M. M., & Chan, E. D. (2003). What is the effect of finger nail polish on pulse oximetry? *Chest, 123*(6), 2163–2164. doi:10.1378/chest.123.6.2163 PMID:12796214

Cheney, F. W. (1990). *The ASA closed claims study after the pulse oximeter* (Vol. 54). ASA Newsletter.

Cohen, A., & Wardsworth, N. A. (1972). Light emitting diode skin reflectance oximeter. *Medical & Biological Engineering, 10*(3), 385–391. doi:10.1007/BF02474218 PMID:5043486

Cote, J., Goldstein, E. A., Buschman, W. H., & Hoaglin, D. C. (1988). The effect of nail polish on pulse oximetry. *Anesthesia and Analgesia, 67*(7), 683–686. PMID:3382042

Dorsch, J. A., & Dorsch, S. E. (1999). *Understanding anaesthesia equipment.* Baltimore, MD: Williams & Wilkins.

Falconer, R. J., & Robinson, B. J. (1990). Comparison of pulse oximeters: Accuracy at low arterial pressure in volunteers. *BJA, 65*(4), 552–557. doi:10.1093/bja/65.4.552 PMID:2248826

Fluck, R. R. Jr, Schroeder, C., Frani, G., Kropf, B., & Engbretson, B. (2003). Does ambient light affect the accuracy of pulse oximetry? *Respiratory Care, 48*(7), 677–680. PMID:12841858

Ganong, W. F. (1993). *Review of Medical Physiology* (16th ed.). Norwalk, CT: Appleton & Lange.

Goldie, E. A. G. (1942). Device for continuous indication of oxygen saturation of circulating blood in man. *Journal of Scientific Instruments, 19*(2), 23–25. doi:10.1088/0950-7671/19/2/302

Hanning, C. D., & Alexander-Williams, J. M. (1995). Pulse oximetry: A practical review. *BMJ (Clinical Research Ed.), 311*(7001), 367–370. doi:10.1136/bmj.311.7001.367 PMID:7640545

Hertzman, B. (1938). The blood supply of various skin areas as estimated by the photoelectric plethysmograph. *The American Journal of Physiology, 124*(2), 328–340. doi:10.1152/ajplegacy.1938.124.2.328

Horecker, L. (1943). The absorption spectra of hemoglobin and its derivatives in the visible and near infra-red regions. *The Journal of Biological Chemistry, 148*(1), 173–183.

Huch, A., Huch, R., Konig, V., Neuman, M. R., Parker, D., Yount, J., & Lubbers, D. (1988). Limitations of pulse oximetry (letter). *Lancet, 1*(8581), 357–358. doi:10.1016/S0140-6736(88)91148-8 PMID:2893163

Jubran, A. (1999). Pulse oximetry. *Critical Care (London, England), 3*(2), R11–R17. doi:10.1186/cc341 PMID:11094477

Kasper, D. L. (2005). *Harrison's principles of internal medicine* (16th ed.). McGraw-Hill.

Kim, J. G., Xia, M., & Liu, H. (2005, March/April). Extinction coefficients of hemoglobin for near-infrared spectroscopy of tissue. *IEEE Engineering in Medicine and Biology Magazine, 24*(2), 118–121. doi:10.1109/MEMB.2005.1411359 PMID:15825855

Langton, J. A., & Hanning, C. D. (1990). Effect of motion artefact on pulse oximeters: Evaluation of four instruments and finger probes. *British Journal of Anaesthesia, 65*(4), 564–570. doi:10.1093/bja/65.4.564 PMID:2248828

Li. (2004). Dynamics of vascular system. World scientific publishing Co. Pte. Ltd.

Mendelson, Y. (1992). Pulse oximetry: Theory and applications for noninvasive monitoring. *Clinical Chemistry, 38*(9), 1601–1607. PMID:1525987

Merrick, E. B., & Hayes, T. J. (1976). Continuous, non-invasive measurements of arterial blood oxygen levels. *Hewlett-packard J., 28*(2), 2–9.

Miller, R. D. (2005). *Miller's anesthesia* (6th ed.). Philadelphia: Elsevier Churchill Livingstone.

Millikan, G. A. (1942). The oximeter, an instrument for measuring continuously the arterial saturation of arterial blood in man. *The Review of Scientific Instruments, 13*(10), 434–444. doi:10.1063/1.1769941

Nakajima, K., Tamura, T., & Miike, H. (1996). Monitoring of heart and respiratory rates by photoplethysmography using a digital filtering technique. *Medical Engineering & Physics, 18*(5), 365–372. doi:10.1016/1350-4533(95)00066-6 PMID:8818134

Plummer, J. L., Zakaria, A. Z., Ilsley, A. H., Fronsko, R. R. L., & Owen, H. (1995). Evaluation of the influence of movement on saturation readings from pulse oximeters. *Anaesthesia, 50*(5), 423–426. doi:10.1111/j.1365-2044.1995.tb05998.x PMID:7793549

Polanyi, M. L., & Hehir, R. M. (1960). New reflection oximeter. *The Review of Scientific Instruments, 31*(4), 401–403. doi:10.1063/1.1716990

Pole, Y. (2002). Evolution of the pulse oximeter. *International Congress Series, 1242*, 137–142. doi:10.1016/S0531-5131(02)00803-8

Rangayyan, R. M. (2002). *Biomedical signal analysis: A case study approach*. Singapore: John Wiley & Sons.

Reddy, K. A., Bai, J. R., George, B., Mohan, N. M., & Kumar, V. J. (2006). Virtual instrument for the measurement of haemo-dynamic parameters using photoplethysmograph. *Proc. 23rd Int. Conf. IEEE, IMTC-2006*, 1167-1171. 10.1109/IMTC.2006.328443

Reddy, K. A., George, B., Mohan, N. M., & Kumar, V. J. (2008, May). A Novel method of measurement of oxygen saturation in arterial blood. *Proc. 25rd IEEE International Instrumentation and Measurement Technology Conf., I2MTC-2008*, 1627-1630. 10.1109/IMTC.2008.4547304

Reddy, K. A., George, B., Mohan, N. M., & Kumar, V. J. (2009). A novel calibration–free method of measurement of oxygen saturation in arterial blood. *IEEE Transactions on Instrumentation and Measurement*, *58*(5), 1699–1705. doi:10.1109/TIM.2009.2012934

Reddy, K. A., & Kumar, V. J. (2011, May). A Novel model based method of measurement of oxygen saturation in arterial blood. *Proc. of 28th IEEE International Instrumentation and Measurement Technology Conf., I2MTC-2011*, 1-5.

Ries, A. L., Prewitt, L. M., & Johnson, J. J. (1989). Skin color and ear oximetry. *Chest, 96*(2), 287–290. doi:10.1378/chest.96.2.287 PMID:2752811

Rusch, T. L., Sankar, R., & Scharf, J. E. (1996). Signal processing methods for pulse oximetry. *Computers in Biology and Medicine, 26*(2), 143–159. doi:10.1016/0010-4825(95)00049-6 PMID:8904288

Sarin, S., Shields, D. A., Scurr, J. H., & Smith, P. D. C. (1992). Photoplethysmography: A valuable noninvasive tool in the assessment of venous dysfunction? *Journal of Vascular Surgery, 16*(2), 154–162. doi:10.1016/0741-5214(92)90103-F PMID:1495139

Saylor, J. W. (2003). Neonatal and pediatric pulse oximetry. *Respiratory Care, 48*(4), 386–398. PMID:12667266

Scheller, M. S., Unger, R. J., & Kelner, M. J. (1986). Effects of intravenously administered dyes on pulse oximetry readings. *Anesthesiology, 65*(5), 550–552. doi:10.1097/00000542-198611000-00023 PMID:3777490

Schnapp, L. M., & Cohen, N. H. (1990). Pulse oximetry: Uses and abuses. *Chest, 98*(5), 1244–1250. doi:10.1378/chest.98.5.1244 PMID:2225973

Secker, C., & Spiers, P. (1997). Accuracy of pulse oximetry in patients with low systematic vascular resistance. *Anaesthesia, 52*(2), 127–130. doi:10.1111/j.1365-2044.1997.32-az0062.x PMID:9059094

Sekelj, P., Johnson, A. L., Hoff, H. E., & Scherch, P. M. (1951). A photoelectric method for the determination of arterial oxygen saturation in man. *American Heart Journal, 42*(6), 826–848. doi:10.1016/0002-8703(51)90055-5 PMID:14885079

Severinghaus, J. W., & Astrup, P. B. (1986). History of blood gas analysis-VI. Oximetry. *Journal of Clinical Monitoring, 2*(4), 270–288. doi:10.1007/BF02851177 PMID:3537215

Shao, D. (2016). Noncontact monitoring of blood oxygen saturation using camera and dual-wavelength imaging system. *Biomedical Engineering. IEEE Transactions on, 63*, 1091–1098. PMID:26415199

Sidi, A., Paulus, D. A., Rush, W., Gravenstein, N., & Davis, R. F. (1987). Methylene blue and indocyanine green artifactually lower pulse oximetry readings of oxygen saturation: Studies in dogs. *Journal of Clinical Monitoring, 3*(4), 249–256. PMID:3681358

Sinex, J. E. (1999). Pulse oximetry: Principles and limitations. *The American Journal of Emergency Medicine, 17*(1), 59–68. doi:10.1016/S0735-6757(99)90019-0 PMID:9928703

Sornmo, L. S., & Laguna, P. (2005). *Bioelectrical signal processing in cardiac and neurological applications.* Elsevier Academic Press.

Takatani, S., & Ling, J. (1994). Optical oximetry sensors for whole blood and tissue. *IEEE Engineering in Medicine and Biology Magazine, 13*(June/July), 347–357. doi:10.1109/51.294005

Trivedi, N. S., Ghouri, A. F., Shah, N. K., Lai, E., & Barker, S. J. (1997). Effects of motion, ambient light and hypoperfusion on pulse oximeter function. *Journal of Clinical Anesthesia, 9*(3), 179–183. doi:10.1016/S0952-8180(97)00039-1 PMID:9172022

Verkruysse, W., Bartula, M., Bresch, E., Rocque, M., Meftah, M., & Kirenko, I. (2017). Calibration of contactless pulse oximetry. *Anesthesia and Analgesia, 124*(1), 136–145. doi:10.1213/ANE.0000000000001381 PMID:27258081

Webster, J. G. (1997). *Design of pulse oximeters.* Taylor & Francis Group. doi:10.1887/0750304677

White, P. F., & Boyle, W. A. (1989). Nail polish and oximetry. *Anesthesia and Analgesia, 68*(4), 546–547. doi:10.1213/00000539-198904000-00030 PMID:2929991

Williams, A. J. (1998). ABC of oxygen: Assessing and interpreting arterial blood gases and acid-base balance. *BMJ (Clinical Research Ed.), 317*(7167), 1213–1216. doi:10.1136/bmj.317.7167.1213 PMID:9794863

Wood, E. H., & Geraci, J. E. (1949). Photoelectric determination of arterial oxygen saturation in man. *The Journal of Laboratory and Clinical Medicine, 34*, 387–401. PMID:18113925

Wukitsch, M. W., Petterson, M. T., Tobler, D. R., & Pologe, J. A. (1988). Pulse oximetry: Analysis of theory, technology, and practice. *Journal of Clinical Monitoring, 4*(4), 290–301. doi:10.1007/BF01617328 PMID:3057122

Zijlstra, W. G., Buursma, A., & Meeuwsen-van der Roest, W. P. (1991). Absorption spectra of human fetal and adult oxyhemoglobin, de-oxyhemoglobin, carboxyhemoglobin and methemoglobin. *Clinical Chemistry, 37*(9), 1633–1638. PMID:1716537

Section 2

Security Over Wireless Sensor Networks and Distributed Systems

Chapter 8
Attacks and Countermeasures

Mukta Sharma
Teerthanker Mahaveer University, India

ABSTRACT

Information technology has benefitted the society enormously in all spheres of life. Medical sciences have not been left untouched, rather it is using information technology extensively for storing, retrieving, transmitting, and manipulating data. There are various simulators and software designed using virtual reality explicitly to train the medical students like computer-assisted learning (CAL). Biomedical science is a discipline that connects information science, computer science, and healthcare. Biomedical science is critically analyzing, understanding, and knowing the human body. Real-time monitoring can help studying and analyzing the chronic diseases and managing it before the adverse events. Information technology has been proven as a boon in all areas, but it has certain limitations, making it vulnerable to attacks. Information security is a matter of great concern, especially when the data is traveling through the internet, which is an insecure channel. This chapter focuses on varied attacks and their countermeasures.

INTRODUCTION

Living in 21st century with so much technological advancement in all domains is a boon. "What we used to dream is now a reality"; because of technological growth. We cannot just see a photograph of a person but we can actually do video calling with a person sitting miles apart. The technology has not just reduced the distance and speedier the task but it has actually helped the humankind to take proper decisions based on the past history (archival data) and current data. The technology if used properly can be of great help and can ensure the success. Unfortunately some people for their fun and wrong intentions misuse the technology by breaching the security. There are several attacks which eventually have taken place to fetch the information illegally. The crimes are increasing like the recent DDOS attack on Dyn's cyber security despite of all mechanisms has brought down nearly 100,000 DVRs, security cameras, thermostats, coffee makers, webcams, refrigerators, and other internet of things devices in homes across the world. WannaCry- cryptoworm; is a powerful ransom ware attack which has attacked more than 200000 systems using Microsoft windows. It encrypted the information and then seeks for ransom amount in lieu to release the key for decrypting the information.

DOI: 10.4018/978-1-5225-5152-2.ch008

Copyright © 2018, IGI Global. Copying or distributing in print or electronic forms without written permission of IGI Global is prohibited.

This chapter begins with a brief introduction about biomedical sciences, information technology, benefits of information technology in bio medical sciences. The chapter further highlights about the various attacks like Active and Passive attacks. It also shed some light on the recent crimes followed by counter measures.

MAIN FOCUS OF THE CHAPTER

Biomedical Sciences

Health informatics also called Health Information Systems; the concept was given by Gustav Wagner, 1949 in Germany. Earlier the patient and hospitals used to maintain the records or test reports even after several years. The approach has changed enormously after information technology has come into picture, the patients' records, test reports; treatment details etc. are captured, stored, analyzed, and retrieved as and when required from the database. The patients' demography and insurance details are shared conveniently to the insurance company to clear the dues. The doctors can discuss the case live with a team of expert doctors from all over the world before commencing the treatment. It has numerous advantages to use information technology in amalgamation with health care sector.

Going through the past and observing the statistics it has been assumed that a professional doctor can detect and give treatment, can assess new methods, can improve guidelines to practice, and based on the initial training received during the academic education and ongoing practice experience. According to David Eddy, a well-known quality expert, (Goldberg, 1988; Greiner, 2003) *complexity of modern medicine exceeds the inherent limitations of the unaided human mind* (Millenson, 1997). As per David (Goldberg, 1988; Greiner 2003) no practitioner needs to absorb the results of 10,000 clinical trials span over years, areas of specialty, etc. Therefore, there is a need for biomedical informatics according to (Berman, 2007) it deals with both biology and computer science. There is a need for such an intellectual fusion of biomedicine and information technology which will help to store, retrieve, analyze, and interpret the data. The Recent example of storing, retrieving, analyzing and interpreting is Google. Google has designed an Algorithm to check the status of heart by just scanning the retina of the person. Google has tried and tested on more than three lakh people and this algorithm is built using Artificial Intelligence.

Biomedical Sciences is the study of the human body, it is the way to critically analyze, understand and know the structure and function in health and disease. Biomedical science focuses on the application of medical science; the scientist is expert in biology in context with medicines and information technology. The scientists involved in the study of biomedical require an understanding of microbiology, pharmacology cell, medical biochemistry and molecular biology, anatomy, physiology, infectious diseases and neuroscience. The scientists need to know how a disease manifest in human body, understand and analyze the problem and should know how to predict and describe. For health care it is essential to improve knowledge, interventions, or technology.

Over a decade or more the bioinformatics discipline has been explored extensively to get ahead with advancements in molecular biology and genomics research. To attain thoroughness in complex biological processes researchers are using bioinformatics, for instance, studying DNA sequences or demonstrating protein structures etc.

Definition of Biomedical Science

Few popular definitions which relate to medical or biomedical science:

- (Patel, 1998) Greenes and Shortliffe (1990) shed light on medical informatics according to them it deals with the study of information science and technology to implement tasks (task and domain-based). It relates with the education, processing of information, research, and communication tasks of medical practice.
- (Shortliffe & Blois, 2006) defines it as (Concept-based), the technical domain deals with information, storing and retrieving knowledge and making optimal use for problem solving and decision making.
- According to (Van Bemmel, 1984) biomedical sciences deals with handling information based on the knowledge and expertise derived from practices in medicine and health care both theoretically and practically.
- (Musen & Van Bemmel, 1999) highlights on developing and accessing techniques and methods for acquiring, processing, and interpreting patient's data with the help of facts that is obtained in scientific research (role, task and domain-based).

Benefits of Information Technology

Information technology has benefitted the society; especially after the internet the life has revolutionized. No domain is left untouched may it be banking, hospitals, railways, airlines, schools, entertainment industry, fashion industry, hotels, etc. Everybody is appreciating and enjoying the benefits offered via information technology the fun of connecting online with somebody sitting at a distant place, shopping, transferring funds, stock trading etc.

Information technology has tremendously reduced the communication time; earlier to receive a postal mail one need to wait for several days or to make a phone call one need to book a trunk call. Now with the smart phones, IPads iPods, laptops or even desktops with internet one can do video call, conference, live chats etc. It saves a lot of time and speed up your tasks as you don't need to travel to shop, pay utility bills, book a ticket, and check account balance etc. Even for signing a contract one does not need to travel abroad for a meeting. The user can do conference call and use digital signature or digital certificate to sign in the contract/document. The doctors can discuss the real cases with other doctors in any corner of the world via conference (video call). Live discussion saves doctor's time and patient's life. The patient can share the symptoms and take online advice

It saves a lot of money of individuals and business houses. Individuals save in commuting and searching for help online they don"t need to spend much on conveyance as they can sit and transact or study online or consult online etc. and don"t need to travel physically to a certain place, don"t need to bear operation cost etc. Banks and corporate houses don"t have to spend on setting a new branch or opening a new store rather the banks are focusing on opening new ATMs.

Improves on Business Competitive Advantage: New Businesses are entering comfortably and competing with the leading brands. Business houses are not bound to invest heavily on the infrastructure as they can operate from small workplace, home etc. to do the business online. Corporates are working on cloud to save storage space and less time to share. They are *cutting cost on operations and increasing ROI* (Rate of Investment).

These days' companies are relying completely on the technology to gain the profit. The business houses are customizing the product as per the need of the customer. The most apt example for a successful online business venture is Amazon. In year 1994 a young financial analyst Jeff Bezos thought to start a venture online for which he shortlisted 20 products. Three years later he formed Amazon.com. Where he initiated with selling books, his customer-centric approach was one of the USP of Amazon. Even today Amazon's approach is to have a highly satisfied customer for which they are customizing the individual's page as per their past preference (displaying the books and other products according to the customer's last purchase or products searched). This makes Amazon the most powerful and successful company of the year in 2017.

Better CRM (Customer Relationship Management): Business houses are working hard on maintaining and managing relations with the Customers by offering them better options and giving them several choices which matches their taste. The customers have the benefit of rating and giving reviews and feedbacks about any company, product, hotel, doctor, hospital or even a movie. Based on the reviews the people make their choice/decision. Every business house is supposed to revert on any customers query within a stipulated time period, ignoring which will end-up losing their customer base.

E-Learning: Is the new way of learning and exploring things. As the student does not have to go and attend a specific lecture at some fixed time. Instead the student can learn at its self-paced speed and time without disturbing his/her schedule.

BIOMEDICAL SCIENCES AND BENEFITS OF INFORMATION TECHNOLOGY

Health is essential to all living beings rich or poor, young or old, healthy or unhealthy/unwell/ill. The present era has witnessed a tremendous metamorphosis in the medicine and healthcare sector. There have been many strides in the recent times to progress in diagnosing and treating many common diseases, yet so much is still required. In many nations millions of people die each year without getting medical treatment or due to chronic and complex diseases.

To encounter the challenges of beating these complicated diseases, the biomedical science is exploring and growing high with the technology. Besides using information technology in daily practice of healthcare and wellbeing, it can actually offer the directions for fresh grounds in the clinical sciences via tools and analyses. Tools and analyses will help in identifying subtle but noteworthy causal signals in the merging domains of clinical, behavioral, environmental, genetic, and epigenetic data (Graham, 2010).

The technology is giving (Stead & Lin, 2009) a great platform to study, analyze, evaluate and modernize not only the equipment's but even the processes which is increasing the quality of life. The focus area varies from the molecular (genomics, proteomics) to individual (clinical research, health systems management) to populations (public health) and health care delivery. To touch all domains of diagnosis, disease history, disease tracking, recovery monitoring information technology is playing a vital role.

There is plethora of other IT-based medico-applications which can truly transform the health sector scenario. At the patient level, the present era medication must use the accuracy of evidence-based diagnostic methods to provide extremely personalized cure regimen in specific and effective ways. To achieve these goals, the present era must use extensively the power of health informatics for the benefit of the large sections of society. The usage of information technology has immensely helped the doctors in managing the patient's illness history and improving the patient's health in a better way. The patients can directly take expert opinion via virtual healthcare system. Many health care Apps have been designed to help the patient to seek advice based on the symptoms. The patients now don't have to give blood sample for getting a report on their heart rather it could be just done by scanning the retina and using Google Algorithm-using Artificial Intelligence. The biomedical researchers need expertise not only biology and medicine but also information technology to use it optimally for better results.

There are numerous (Greenes, 1990) accomplishments related to medical informatics such as data mining or electronic medical records, computer graphics, artificial intelligence, virtual reality, etc. which have taken biomedical sciences to a great level. In early 1960s Ivan Sutherland and others initiated computer graphics which is a sub domain of computer science (Goldberg, 1988). Performing mathematical calculations to depict 3D graphics has made the life easier.

The list is endless, the use of biomedical sciences have benefitted the society at a large as it is helping in saving money, has improved the quality of living and probability to access and care the patient has increased tremendously (patient does not have to travel and consult face to face).

FLAWS OR LIMITATIONS OF INFORMATION TECHNOLOGY IN BIOMEDICAL SCIENCES

Biomedical research is still in its nascent years; (Goldberg, 1988) now the funds have been steadily increasing for the research which has extensively explored and given great results in clinical knowledge and technology (Georgia, 2015). The intensive care unit is the most data intensive area. Intensive care monitoring has shown major improvements in the past as compared to the rest domains of medical industry, which is still in its nascent stage. Non – compatible equipment, the absence of standard data format and proprietary limitations from industry, makes it a tough task to attain, analyze and study the patient records. Other issues like Medical Device Interoperability and Data Integration, memory requirement for capturing high resolution physiological data, complex mathematical computation in real time is a big concern.

There are several issues which have been a disaster in the history. One example of such disaster is Therac-25, a device used in medical radiation therapy. In the year 1985-87, numerous incidents were reported about massive overdoses (up to 100 times the intended dosage) of radiation due to faulty software, which led to death of more than three patients. Another case from Panama City was reported in the year 2000 in which also, many people lost their lives because of error in doses supplied based on entered data by Multidata, a US software firm. Beside this there are problems like privacy and security. The data is prone to theft, hacking, and unauthentic usage. In the recent past the entire world has suffered from ransom ware attacks, Trojans, viruses, phishing, spoofing, denial of service attacks, net extortion etc. There are various crimes some goes reported whereas some are still hidden/ not discussed. There are certain attacks which open the door for an eavesdropper/hacker and make it vulnerable for a crime. The hacker is exploiting the weaker areas/flaws not only in the operating system but also in the entire system and is making it prone to an attack.

BIOMEDICAL SIGNAL PROCESSING

There are numerous instruments to measure the health of any human body like temperature, heart rate, blood pressure, sugar level, oxygen saturation levels, brain activity, nerve condition etc. Based on these measurements taken at a specific time, doctors treat the patients. (ITIE Academy, n.a.) Biomedical signals are observations of physiological activities of organisms, ranging from gene and protein sequences, to neural and cardiac rhythms, to tissue and organ images. Biomedical signal processing will read the biomedical signals and analyze the measurement on the basis of that the clinician will take the decision. Various researches are being done to identify new ways using mathematical formulae and algorithms to process these signals. This is helpful in improvising the chronic or critical care where the practitioner will analyze the real-time patient's data. The researchers have taken biomedical signal processing to cloud computing so that the remote and rural areas should get advanced facilities. Based on complex analyses of the body signals, medical practitioners can identify or observe early indicators or symptoms for various conditions which could lead to timelier and better treatment.

INFORMATION SECURITY

Information is an asset as it has been derived after processing and analyzing the data. Information is considered useful if it is organized, correct, complete, & it reaches the authentic user timely. The information if delivered to a wrong hand or any security breach is dangerous and can damage the resources by altering the data or disclosing the information, by wasting the resources by denial of service, and fraud (Kalakota, 1997). Therefore, it is essential to secure the information may it belong to an individual, organization, corporate etc.

Computer security definition (Stallings, 2011) according to The NIST Computer Security Handbook [NIST95] is "The protection afforded to an automated information system in order to attain the applicable objectives of preserving the integrity, availability, and confidentiality of information system resources (includes hardware, software, firmware, information/data, and telecommunications)". Cyber security focuses on safeguarding not only the computer networks but also the information from penetration and from malicious damage (Craigen, 2014). CIA Triad follows few objectives as depicted below. Few factors like trust, Authentication, Non-Repudiation, Privacy, Availability has impacted the information security.

- **Confidentiality:** Focus on two important traits one is data confidentiality and the other is Privacy. Data confidentiality means information is securely shared with the authorized individual only. Whereas, Privacy ensures the rights of collecting, storing, and disclosing their personal information to only those whom they wish to share (Forouzan, 2008; Stallings, 2011).

In short, confidentiality can be defined as preserving authorized restrictions of accessing and revealing the information (it may be personal or proprietary information).

Snooping (data accessible to unauthorized user) and Traffic Analysis (Monitoring and analysis of data fetched from one transaction) are two known threats to confidentiality Symmetric key cryptography works as a security measure to safeguard this.

- **Integrity: Data Integrity:** Promises that information is consistent, trustworthy and reliable. System integrity: Should guarantee that a system is working in a proper manner, which means it should not allow unauthorized manipulation of the system (Forouzan, 2008; Stallings, 2011).

Figure 1. CIA Triad Objectives (Claessens, 2003; Lampson, 2004; Stallings, 2011)

In Brief, Integrity is protecting against improper information modification or destruction and inaccessibility by unauthorized users.

The Integrity of information is compromised through Modification (any change done to the intercepted file), Masquerading (pretending as authorized user), Replaying (replay of previously hacked message) and Repudiation (Denial of information) Integrity can be assured by data hashing using the concept of asymmetric cryptography.

- **Availability:** Is the assurance of giving the desired, correct information timely to the authentic user. Availability in brief is an agreement of accessing accurate information to the authorized user. Availability loss means disruption of access to information or an information system (Forouzan, 2008; Stallings, 2011).

In a research conducted by (Anderson, 1996) Cambridge University on security in healthcare information systems; various threats and information security problem have been examined and discussed thoroughly.

Threats and Vulnerabilities to HealthCare System: Clinical records are readily available on hospital computers. Due to computerization and connectivity there exists increased risk of security. As discussed above besides confidentiality, data integrity and availability are matter of great concern.

- **Clinical Confidentiality:** Doctors take the oath of confidentiality in which they are supposed to keep the patient's details confidential but with the use of computer the data is prone to leak.
- **Integrity Issues:** In case the information is tampered, corrupted, unreliable, or altered the doctors will tend to take incorrect decisions which may harm the patient and could even lead to the death. Therefore, many of the doctors in India even now maintain the patient history and other information on paper also, which is kept as a backup.
- **Availability Constraint:** If information from a system is unavailable as a result of any kind of reason, then this decreases its value.
- Software bugs, hardware failures or loop holes allow malicious software's, viruses, Trojans to attack the operating system and corrupt data/messages.

TYPES OF ATTACKS

The society has been benefitted by the technological growth in all areas. Recent technical advances in health care sector have transformed its capability and capacity to support and enhance patient care. At the same time the major concern area is security it is essential in all domains, but when it comes to medical sciences the security plays a pivotal role as it deals with the life of a person. According to SANS Institute report, *94% of health care organizations have been the victim of cyber-attacks*. Now days the ransom ware attacks are bothering and affecting many nations in the world. Many attackers/hackers for taking ransom are installing Ransom wares. The Operating systems are vulnerable to attack which gives a back door entry to a hacker and hackers steal the information sell it to third party, or demand ransom amount from celebrities whose data they have stolen and if amount not given they even delete the patients data. It was observed that besides data tampering with the patient records the hackers are affecting medical devices such as insulin pumps they can change dosage; defibrillators can give or prevent shocks controlled via Bluetooth, neuro-stimulators, X-Rays, and pacemakers. With the fatal dosage in pumps the patient may lend up into trouble. Similarly the medical devices with features like wireless connectivity; remote monitoring, etc. will make the device prone to attacks. The hackers are even changing the temperature of Refrigerators which contains blood, drugs, etc.

Attacks which compromises (the security) on the protection of information. There are many techniques via which invader try to invade the information. As depicted below it is Passive and Active Attacks:

Passive Attacks

Is passive in nature which means the trespasser's aim is to only read the message and know the complete information without affecting system resources like eavesdropping or monitoring the transactions. It is difficult to identify as there is no alteration done to the information or any other resources. Like the following:

- **Message Contents:** Attacker A can read all messages sent by Mr. X to Mr. Y. For instance telephone conversation, email, file transfer (sensitive information).
- **Traffic Analysis:** Attacker A observes the pattern sent by Mr. X to Mr. Y. The opponent could see and trace all the exchanged messages and can track the frequency and length of messages.

Such attacks can be barred using Cryptography as the goal of cryptography is to scramble the message so that the original message can be read by only authentic user who has the key.

Active Attacks

These attacks are simply opposite to Passive Attacks as they attempt to modify the resources and affect their operation by altering the data or creating a fake stream. They are tough to anticipate due to the vulnerabilities in hardware, network, and software. Following are the Active attacks:

- **Masquerade:** When an entity plays to be someone else or different entity. For example, Mr. X sent a message to Mr. Y, but is hacked in between & altered by the opponent A and the message is

Figure 2. Passive and Active Attacks (Stallings, 2011; Denning, 1982)

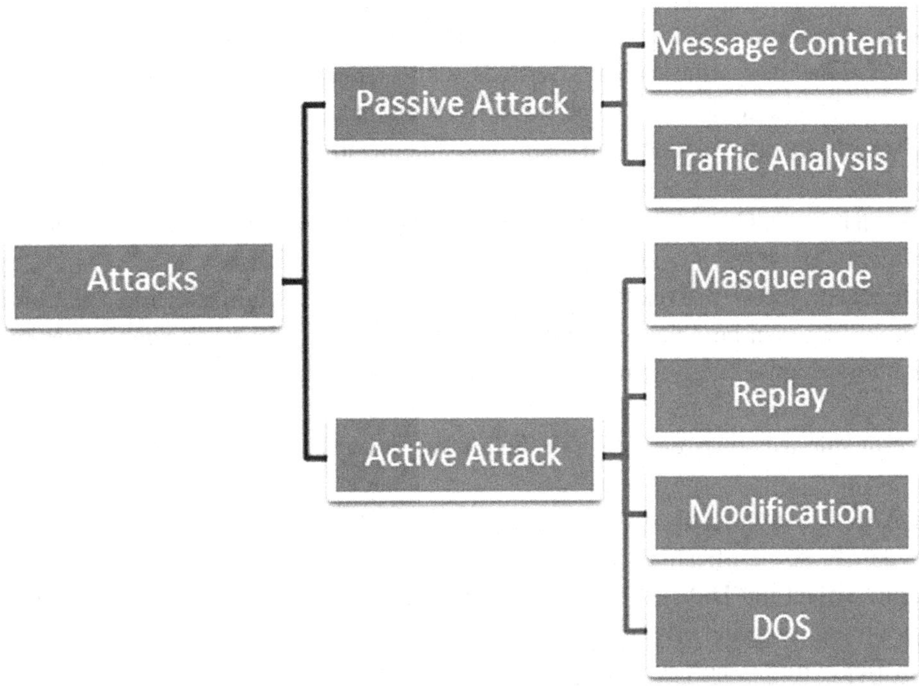

resent to Mr. Y. After receiving the message, Mr. Y will feel the message is sent by Mr. X although the word is now deceived and sent via attacker A.

- **Replay Attack:** Is acquiring the data passively and retransmitting it to produce an illicit effect. For instance, the message sent by Mr. X is transmitted to Mr. Y and simultaneously hacked by the attacker A. Later the opponent A alters and resends the message to Mr. Y portraying himself as Mr. X.
- **Denial of Service:** This attacks forbids the normal use of communications facilities. DOS might suppress or overload all messages directed to a particular destination, to degrade the performance.
- **Modification of Messages:** Any kind of modification of the original message to create an illicit effect. For instance, A message "Meet me @ KFC, 6 on coming Thursday" is modified to "Meet me @ Dominos, 5 on next Friday."

As mentioned above the different attacks in health monitoring that is modification, forging medical data, overhearing, (Appari, 2010; Moshaddique, 2011; Fatema, 2014;) denial of service, activity tracking of users, physical tampering with devices. These invade patient privacy and can be categorized broadly into two categories:

Organizational Attack: Is accessing patient's data inappropriately. This can be done either by internal employees/ agents who misuse their rights or the external ones who exploits the susceptibility of systems. According to the recent studies (NRC, 1997; Rindfleisch, 1997) organizational threats could be categorized as below:

- **Unknowingly or Accidental Disclosure:** Information leak via file sharing, or unintentionally the patient's information is sent to the wrong address by healthcare personnel.
- **Curiosity of the Internal to Know the Information:** Out of inquisitiveness an insider with data access privilege shares the patient's records with media to someone outsider. Like, an insider might be willing to know about some celebrity, politician or some acquaintance.
- **Data Breach by an Insider:** Internals who unethically mint money by sharing the patient information.
- **Data Breach by an Outsider:** Someone who enters physically in the premises to fetch the data in an unethical/ forced way to gain access to system.
- **Unauthorized Access to Health Data:** In case an outsider who has hacked the organization's network system (can be a hacker, an ex- employee, patient, insurance agent) tries to access the patient information illegally or render the system inoperable.

The above-mentioned attack can affect in the following ways:

- **Illegal Access:** Any unauthentic user tries to fetch patients' critical data might cause problems such as damaging significant data.
- **Fake Data Injection/ Data Alteration:** The intruder inserts fake results or alters the data which is very different from the original will lead to erroneous diagnosis and treatment.
- **Careful Reporting:** where an enemy freezes the report of actions by throwing authenticate packets which pass through the node.

    Systemic Threats: Arise not because of external/ outsiders but because of internals who possess the right to access patients' health details (NRC, 1997). Based on the patient's condition insurance companies may deny life insurance, an employer may deny promotion or could terminate the employment etc.

RECENT INSTANCES OF SECURITY BREACH IN BIOMEDICAL

Globally various cases have been reported for data theft and other security breach. For instance, more than 7000 patients' data has been leaked from New York Hospital (O'HARA, 2017). The patients' details along with drug used, medical issue, history, ultra sound pictures, and other details were compromised by the hacker. Another case of London, (Arndt, 2017) a health insurance company data was breached by its own employee compromising on 547000 people personal data. US Davis Health (Davis, 2017) employee responded to a Phishing email which permits hackers to view 15000 patient's details and ask for money from staff.

According to Modern Healthcare, many cases were reported like Anthem the second largest health insurer in the U.S; 78.8 million records were leaked by a cyber-attack in December 2014. In year 2011 (Conn, 2011) military health system Tricare reported that 4.9 million patients records (in tapes) were stolen. In August 2014 Tennessee-based Community Health Systems data were compromised affecting 4.5 million patients' records. Attack by a software bug named Heartbleed (Kutscher & Conn, 2014) attacked and fetched all VPN credentials by Chinese attacker. Companies like Excellues BCBS has 10.5 million affected customers and Primera has 11 million compromised records.

Ransom ware attack has actually terrified the entire world and medical institutions are no different. One such case of ransom ware is Peachtree Neurological Clinic whose systems were hacked from February 2016 till May 2017 and approximately 176925 patient's records were leaked. Another case of ransom ware was reported in England, Scotland affecting 150 other countries including India, Russia, Ukraine, etc. Wanna Decrytor is one of the most effective ransom ware variants on the web which has not attacked just the hospitals, agencies, but have also targeted the telecom sector. Similar case was reported (Jayanthi, 2016) in Keck Medicine in Los Angeles where two servers were attacked.

COUNTER MEASURES

An attacker, intruder can identify and exploit the flaws and weakness in the system and could hack and attack the system. It is essential for the organizations to ensure security. Especially when it comes to healthcare sector it is mandatory to safeguard the information as the consequences affect stakeholders, like patients, healthcare organizations, and payers (e.g. insurance). Besides the monetary loss there is a threat to life so it is necessary to provide security.

Technological advancement has tried to support, clinical methods and health services by consolidation of health records from multiple sources to a single research database. To support the interests of multiple stakeholders and agencies involved with public health, healthcare sector often share data across organizational boundaries. However, this may violate privacy as it might lead to leak of sensitive information which may cause socioeconomic repercussions for patient.

Information security plays a vital role in the smooth functioning and usage of information technology. When it comes to securing health care sector it is highly essential to safeguard credentials, servers, patient's details, and even the equipment. There are varied steps taken by health care sector to provide security against various threats and attacks. Following are the counter measures taken by healthcare sector:

SSL

SSL stands for Secure Socket Layer is a standard protocol conceptualized on the basis of cryptography by Netscape Communications Corporation. It establishes a safe link between the server and the browser (client), so that each data which traverses through that path should remain private and secure. No intruder should be able to read or tamper the data once the data is traversing via secure path using SSL. To establish a SSL connection server requires a SSL Certificate, which will be provided with a set of keys (Private and public key) and an Asymmetric key algorithm. Public Key is not kept hidden rather used by certifying Authority to issue SSL certificate. Private Key is private to the user/ recipient. A website is SSL protected if it shows https in the address bar and the address bar is green in color and proceeded with a keypad lock (see Figure 3).

In short once can say SSL makes a secure connection by handshaking and agreeing upon the set of keys and algorithm to be used for the entire session. The client and server authenticate each other before connecting; server requests the client for authentic certificate. Once the session is established neither the client nor the server has to worry about the security or numerous data can be sent securely.

Figure 3. SSL Handshake

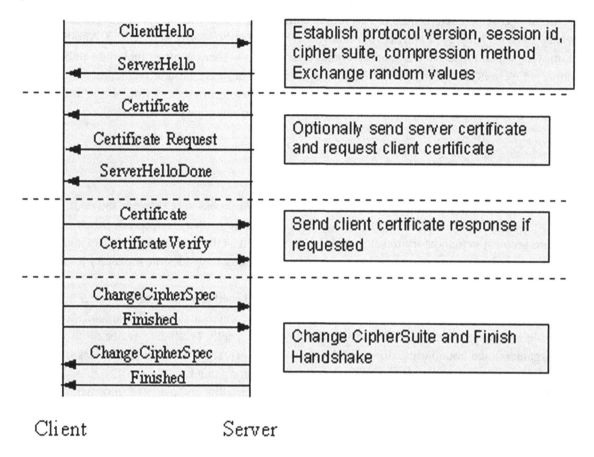

HTTPS

HTTPS is a safer version of HTTP. It is a unique protocol that combines HTTP and SSL/ TLS (transport Layer security) (HTTP + SSL/TLS). It is a popular protocol for securing the transmission of data. HTTPS is designed to transmit individual messages securely. A website specifying https:// instead of http is requesting SSL-protected documents. HTTPS (port 443) and HTTP (port 80) both protocols works on different ports and HTTPS run with SSL and HTTP works with non-SSL.

SSL complements HTTPS as SSL establishes the secure path for the entire session. HTTPS ensures the safety of every transaction making it further secure for all financial and banking transactions. The Internet Engineering Task Force (IETF) has approved these protocols as the standard for safeguarding your transactions.

Biometric

'Bios' means life and 'Metron' means to measure these two words are used to coin the term Biometric. It can be defined as a measurable physiological and behavioral characteristic as shown in Table 1. Biometric characteristics can be captured and stored for future verification. The existing biometric data is

Table 1. Physiological and Behavioral Characteristics. (Jain, 2011)

Physiological	Behavioral
Commonly Used	
Face Recognition	Signature
Fingerprint	Voice
Hand Geometry	Keystroke
Iris Recognition/ Retina	Lip motion
DNA	Body odor

compared with another instance at the time of verification (Jain, 2011). Biometrics is growing fast and is a good security solution (Fatima, 2011). In recent past biometric has gained tremendous popularity and is being used extensively to provide better security than traditional passwords, tokens, etc. (Fouad, 2016). It has been proven as a boon especially for small handy devices like laptops, mobile, tabs, IPads etc. (Belkhede, 2012). Mobile payments will be very safe and no MITM attack or any such hacking is possible with the use of biometric as to copy or steal such traits is tough.

Anti-Virus

Users should install proper anti-virus software and keep updating it to refrain from the attacks of malicious software's and they can transact easily without any fear. The users should install a good anti-virus and keep the system updated to cope with such attacks.

Anti-Phishing

Phishing is possible because of many naïve and inexperienced users (Devarakonda, 2010). Therefore, it is recommended to train the users to recognize the fake or phishing site. Many banks and third party financial companies have initiated for the training. (Alnajim & Munro, 2009) research, is on analyzing the better way to retain anti-phishing knowledge, one way is to send the training material via email and the other is to give live demo classes. According to (Pathak, 2015) more security can be provided via two factor authentications i.e. one by checking login (user id and password) and other by image verification. The system will send a mail to the email-id given by the customer. She/he has to download that the image which will be in the .png format and share it at the bank website for the authentication purpose. The image will be less than 2^{64} bits in length. The last 16 bits will be used to pass the security code for verification. This security code will be generated using a hashing algorithm MD5 (Message Digest 5).

IDS (Intrusion Detection System)

Intrusion Detection System is software designed with intent to monitor and anticipate suspicious activities on network. Anyone is trying to fetch or tamper the data by violating the policies or by using malicious software's the administrator should be informed about such cases/ issues. NIDS (Network Intrusion Detection System) is placed behind firewall to observe all inbound/outbound traffic. HIDS (Host Intrusion Detection System) runs on individual machine to check the inbound/outbound packets.

Signature based IDS monitor packets compares it with database signature like antiviruses' software's search for malicious software's (malwares). Passive IDS will detect vulnerability and report it. Reactive IDS will not only report the vulnerability but will block the traffic.

Firewall

As firewall, is the word which has been inspired from the fire-fighting or fire prevention measures. Similarly firewall is a security device which provides security to the networks. It could be both hardware and software, which will monitor the traffic both inbound and outbound and will prevent the system as it establishes a barrier between the internal and external networks. Firewall is measured as the first step in protecting private information. To safeguard the user the security solution must block the illegitimate user or intruder not only at user's end but also on kernel level. A strong firewall should provide a better security by stopping illegal network communication (Kaur, 2015). For greater security, data can be encrypted using a combination of firewalls available. Types of Firewalls are discussed below:

- **Packet Firewalls:** Also known as packet filters, as it inspects each packet in the network and accepts the packets coming from authorized IP only and drops the packets that are not specified in the list. Like Telnet is not allowed so it will block all Telnet packets. It is fairly effective and transparent, but it is challenging to configure.
- **Application Layer Firewall:** Firstly used in year 1999, to filter the packets at OSI till application layer. The benefit of using application layer firewall is to block specific content, website etc. It filters specific applications, such as FTP and Telnet servers. This is very effective, but can decrease the performance.
- **Stateful Inspection Firewall:** It classifies traffic by observing the destination port, protocol and also packet history saved in the state table. It observes all movement from the beginning to the end.
- **Proxy Firewalls:** Also called as Proxy Firewall server acts as a gateway (middle man). Proxy firewall will accept all request coming from any recipient and once it grant the access, the server will send the information to the destination computer. Here the server breaks the connection between two computers and will act as the only machine that talk to the outside world. It also examines content and make decisions accordingly.

Cryptography

Cryptography is a subset of Cryptology. Cryptology is the study of reading, writing and breaking of codes. As depicted in Figure 4 cryptology comprises of cryptography (secret writing) and cryptanalysis (breaking code). As discussed above about confidentiality, integrity, availability, and non-repudiation for securing the data. Cryptography has given a platform which can ensure the security by fulfilling all the objectives (Sharma, 2016). The concept of encryption is ancient it has begun thousands of years ago. Cryptography, the term was coined in 1658 by Thomas Browne. It is used to camouflage the plain text/ original message into some cipher/unreadable text (Sharma, 2016). It is a way of ensuring security when transmitted through an insecure channel, where unethical hacking, tampering of information is easily possible. Encryption and Decryption are two processes used to perform a cryptographic algorithm.

Figure 4. Cryptology

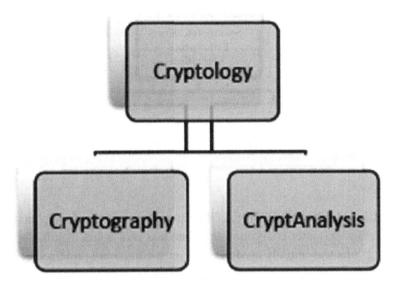

Encryption is a process which enciphers the plain/ original text into cipher text. Hackers will hack the data/ information/ message but will not be able to retrieve the original text because of encryption.

Key elements of cryptography are as follows (Forouzan, 2010; Stallings, 2011):

1. **Plain Text:** The authentic or the individual message which sender sends as an input.
2. **Key:** The secret key has an indispensable role. For the processing of an algorithm, the key is essential and given as an input. The key has to be strong; else the algorithm can be easily decrypted if the key is weak. A Key size ensures security.
3. **Encryption:** Encryption is a way of converting the original message to scrambled text.
4. **Cipher Text:** The text in a format that it is unreadable for any unintended user.
5. **Decryption:** Decryption is a way of retrieving the authentic or original text (reverse of encryption algorithm).

Cryptography can be categorized as follows:

1. **Symmetric Key or Secret Key (Sharma, 2015):** Also popular with a name conventional encryption. Symmetric encryption is known and used since long especially before 1970s prior to the development of public key. In conventional key technique sender and receiver both have same key. Sender enciphers the original message using the key while receiver deciphers the cipher using the same key (Sharma, 2015). For better security in symmetric encryption one should keep the following criteria's in mind: A strong encryption algorithm (Stallings, 2011) which is robust & resilient against a potential breach using combinations of cipher texts and key. Key should be exchanged very safely and should be kept secretly because if key is known the entire algorithm is compromised. As shown in below figure symmetric algorithms can be implemented using either stream ciphers or block ciphers.

Figure 5. Symmetric Key Encryption Algorithm

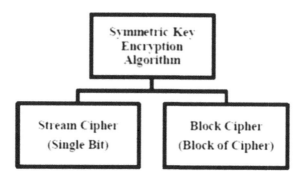

a. **A Block Cipher (Sharma, 2015):** As the name suggests breaks the plain text into blocks, the output (cipher text) after encrypting the plain text is of equal length. Typically, a block size of 64 or 128 bits was initially used. It is the most commonly preferred symmetric encryption algorithms are Block ciphers. The concept of block ciphers defines a function which takes k-bit key subset and n- bit of the plain text as parameters. The function maps the n-bit of plain text to n-bit of cipher text. Here the value 'n' defines the block length. The key is randomly generated from the key space 'K'. The function is so designed that for n-bit plain text, cipher text and a fixed key, the encryption function is a bijection. With each potential key, there is a different bijection. This whole process further allows unique decryption in invertible manner following mapping one-to-one. In short, block cipher can be defined as the function which breaks the plaintext or message into blocks, each of which is then encrypted and produces a block of Cipher text of equal size for each plaintext block.

b. **(Sharma, 2015) A Stream Cipher:** Is also known as State Cipher. A stream cipher is a symmetric cipher which operates with a time-varying transformation on individual bit of plaintext. In short, it is a method which encrypts the data one bit or one byte at a time. A sequence of plain text digits p0, p1 is encrypted into a sequence of cipher text digits c0, c1 followed by running key also called as Key-Stream. One time pad is one of the most popular examples of Stream cipher. The random key stream makes it very difficult to break. When compared with block ciphers Stream ciphers are usually faster and have a lower hardware complexity.

2. **Asymmetric Key or Public Key:** A concept originated by Diffie and Hellman, in year 1976 which involves a pair of keys called a key-pair (one public and one private Key). Public key is known to all whereas private key is private to the recipient. Anybody who has the recipient's public key can send a message but only the receiver can read the message as he has the private key (Schneier, 1996). This idea has improved the key features of networking like security, authenticity and integrity.

3. **Hash Function:** Is a way of enciphering the message into a digest which is irreversible means permanent once the data is converted to digest it cannot be converted/decrypted back to the original message. Hashing is attained with the help of mathematical transformation. It is applied to implement integrity & non-repudiation of data. Digital Signatures is based on Hashing technique. This technique extensively depends on public key or asymmetric key algorithm. Hacking is very different from encryption. Encryption involves two processes one to convert plaintext to cipher text (enciphering) and converting cipher text back to the original message (deciphering). Hacking

will convert the plain text into a fixed length; it is never converted back to the original message. Rather it is used to compare the two files for integrity and non-repudiation.

Few hashing algorithms are MD5, SHA-1, and SHA-256 etc. MD5 (*Message Digest 5)* algorithm was introduced in 1991 which produces 128 bit hash, (32 hexadecimal characters). SHA-1 (The *Secure Hashing Algorithm*) produces 160 hashes and expressed as 40 characters. SHA-256 produces 256-bit hashes and is expressed as 64 characters.

As stated above Hashing algorithms help in attaining integrity and non-repudiation of data. Hashing algorithms verifies that the file has not been corrupted, infected or tampered by any virus or attack and has been sent by authentic user only. The file size of both existing file and new file just received; hash the file and then comparing the size. If both the files size is same one can feel the integrity of data. Hashing is also used to save the password in a secure way. One way is to store the actual password as it is in the database, the better option is to hash the password and store the hashed password into database. In case database is hacked it will be difficult for the hacker to retrieve the original password.

Problem of Collision With Hashing

Some collision problem has been observed in Hashing techniques. Since hashing produces the same length according to the algorithm used, there is a high probability of two discrete files producing the same hash which leads to collision. As 256 bit hashing will produce 256 bit output and 128 bit hashing will generate 128 bit hashing value. Therefore, to reduce collision 256-bit hash (like SHA) is recommended as it produces 256 bits hash and as the length is long chances are less of collision than 128-bit hash (like MD5) in which it is more prone to collision.

Two Techniques Are Used for Cryptography Algorithm

1. **Substitution Techniques (Sharma, 2015):** Substitutes plaintext elements (characters, bits) into cipher text elements (Guttman, 1995). The rule in substitution cipher is the letter which is substituted can be used only once. A substitution cipher is one in which letters are represented by other letters; can be deciphered by the one who knows the order. Two thousand years ago Julius Caeser, roman emperor invented Caeser Cipher. Rotor machines are hardware devices that use substitution techniques. Cryptanalyst can try to break the Substitution cipher via Frequency Analysis- Word Frequency Analysis and Letter Frequency Analysis.
2. **Transposition Techniques (Sharma, 2015):** Methodically rearrange the locations of plaintext components. Mathematically the alphabets are permutated, so transposition can be said as Permutation. In short, transposition can hide the message by rearranging the letter order, without altering the actual letters used. Rail Fence is a good example of Transposition.

Real Time Usage of Cryptographic Algorithm Is Discussed Below

Cryptography is the essence of security as it focuses and covers all objectives integrity, privacy, confidentiality, authenticity, non-repudiation of data. Cryptography is used in HTTPS, SSL, TLS, etc. to make it more reliable. Every domain which is online is taking initiative to protect the credentials, important data, images, financial details, hospital documents etc. for which following steps are used and they are including cryptographic algorithms to enhance the security.

- **One Time Password:** OTP is implemented either using Mobile OTP or OTP Token (Alan, 2011). Mobile OTP is very popular and is used for e-transactions. In this an OTP is generated and SMS is sent to the user mobile, the currently generated OTP is authentic or could be used for a specific time/just one transaction. OTP Token requires a special hardware (which includes extra cost) so that OTP can be generated immediately and users don't have to wait for the SMS. This will speed up the transaction time and could be more reliable but will incur more cost. OTP is secure for replay attacks; as an intruder will not be able to guess the password as it is difficult to record the pattern. An OTP once used will be no longer valid.
- **Password Change Option:** User enters the email details along with password for logging into an email account. The password is automatically changed into a bigger password with the help of cryptographic algorithm and is then stored and compared with the hashed database.
- **Transaction-Signing Option:** After establishing an authentic channel between the sender and the receiver (Hospital, Bank etc.). It gives openness to the legal user to transact comfortably from his/her account and can share and exchange patients data, transfer funds, buy goods and services online, etc. However, complicated attacks like, manipulating transaction data are still possible on client machine. To prevent such content-manipulation attacks the user prior to sending the data to the server can mark alphanumeric transaction.
- **Certificate-Based Solution:** This has two-stage, PKI-based authentication solution characterized by open standards and a programmable, certified, secure, smart-card reader connected to a potentially exposed PC. This system is independent of user behavior. The user receives a smart card with an advanced microprocessor chip that supports RSA public-key cryptography. This acts as the secure ticket for his or her Internet banking account.

FUTURE RESEARCH DIRECTIONS

Multiple security checks and measures like firewalls, anti-virus software, filtering routers, privileges or rights to access the information, encryption and digital certification should be applied/ implemented to enhance the safety of the hospitals. Firewall restricts the unauthentic users and similarly filtering routers also confine the illegitimate Internet users to acquire the information. Symmetric key cryptography ensures privacy of data and Asymmetric key cryptography takes care of authenticity, integration and non- repudiation of data traversing between the hospitals, patients, and insurance company. Digital certificate assures the user about the authenticity of the data coming from a legitimate user. Biomedical science data should be securely transmitted to the cloud and the safety measures should be taken.

CONCLUSION

The hospitals, banks, organizations need to be more vigilant, concerned and little more conservative while sharing the users' demography/details. There are various anti-virus software's available in the market for providing security from all Malicious Software's may it be rootkit, Zombies, Worms etc. Anti-

Phishing software's for verifying Phishing attacks, Virtual Keyboard for preventing from Key-Logging issue, SSL for secure channel, HTTPS for securing every transaction, Biometric for safeguarding the data with the help of Iris, finger scan, retina, voice etc. Firewall to protect the data from unauthorized users. Cryptography for scrambling the original message into something unreadable if accessed without the knowledge of key. In case the data goes in wrong hands or hacked in between by a hacker must not be able to retrieve the original message as the hacker does not have the key.

The information should be available & retrieved by only authentic users and it should be correct and not ambiguous or tampered. Hospitals should only disseminate the patients' information to the authentic users. The employees of hospital should be refrained to share the details (health issues) and demography about patients to any external or unauthentic user. Insurance company should also follow the norms and the patient details should not be disclosed.

REFERENCES

Al Ameen & Kwak. (n.d.). Social Issues in Wireless Sensor Networks with Healthcare Perspective. *The International Arab Journal of Information Technology*, 8(1).

Alan. (2011). 5 Most Popular Two-Factor Authentication Security Devices. *Technology Bloggers*. Retrieved From http://www.technologybloggers.org/technology/5-most-popular-two-factor-authentication-security-devices/

Alnajim, A., & Munro, M. (2009). An Anti-Phishing Approach that Uses Training Intervention for Phishing Websites Detection. *6th IEEE International Conference on Information Technology - New Generations (ITNG)*.

Anderson, R. J. (1996). *Security in Clinical Information Systems*. University of Cambridge.

Appari, A., & Johnson, M. E. (2010). *Information Security and Privacy in Healthcare: Current State of Research* (Vol. 6). Int. J. Internet and Enterprise Management.

Arndt, R. Z. (2017). *Bupa breach affects more than half a million customers*. Retrieved From http://www.modernhealthcare.com/article/20170713/NEWS/170719949/bupa-breach-affects-more-than-half-a-million-customers

Belkhede, M., Gulhane, V., & Bajaj, P. (2012). Biometric Mechanism for enhanced Security of Online Transaction on Android system: A Design Approach. In *Proc* (pp. 1193–1197). ICACT.

Bemmel, J. H. V. (1984). The structure of medical informatics. *Medical Informatics*, 9(3-4), 175–180. doi:10.3109/14639238409015187 PMID:6390014

Berman, J. J. (2007). *Biomedical informatics*. Sudbury, MA: Jones and Barlett Publishers.

Castro, D. (2009). *Explaining International Health IT Leadership*. Washington, DC: Information Technology and Innovation Foundation.

Castro, D. (2009). The Role of Information Technology in Medical Research. *Atlanta Conference on Science, Technology and Innovation Policy*.

Claessens, J., Dem, V., Cock, D., Preneel, B., & Vandewalle, J. (2002). On the Security of Today's On-line Electronic Banking Systems. *Computers & Security, 21*(3), 253–265. doi:10.1016/S0167-4048(02)00312-7

Conn, J. (2011). *Tricare reports data breach affecting 4.9 million patients*. Retrieved from http://www.modernhealthcare.com/article/20110929/NEWS/110929951

Craigen, D., Diakun-Thibault, N., & Purse, R. (2014). Defining Cyber security. *Technology Innovation Management Review., 4*(10), 13–21.

Davis, J. (2017). *Phishing attack on UC Davis Health breaches data on 15,000 patients*. Retrieved From http://www.healthcareitnews.com/news/phishing-attack-uc-davis-health-breaches-data-15000-patients

Denning, D. E. R. (1982). *Cryptography and data Security*. Menlo Park, CA: Addison-Wesley Publishing Company.

Devarakonda, A. K. (2010). Security Solutions to the Phishing: Transactions Based on Security Questions and Image. In BAIP 2010, CCIS 70 (pp. 565–567). Springer-Verlag.

Fatema, N., Brad, R. (2014). Security Requirements, Counterattacks and Projects in Healthcare Applications Using WSNs - A Review. *International Journal of Computer Networking and Communication, 2*(2).

Fatima, A. (2011). E-Banking Security Issues – Is There A Solution in Biometrics? *Journal of Internet Banking and Commerce, 16*(2).

Forouzan, B. A. (2008). *Data Communications & Networking* (4th ed.). New York: Tata McGraw- Hill.

Forouzan, B. A., & Mukhopadhyay, D. (2010). *Cryptography and Network Security*. New Delhi, India: Tata McGraw-Hill.

Fouad, K. M., Hassan, M. B., & Hassan, M. F. (2016). User Authentication based on Dynamic Keystroke Recognition. International Journal of Ambient Computing and Intelligence, 7(2).

Georgia, M. A. D., Kaffashi, F., Jacono, R. J., & Loparo, K. A. (2015). Information Technology in Critical Care: Review of Monitoring and Data Acquisition Systems for Patient Care and Research. *The Scientific World Journal*. PMID:25734185

Goldberg, A. (1988). *A History of Personal Workstations*. New York: ACM Press.

Graham, S., Estrin, D., Horvitz, E., Kohane, I., Mynatt, E., & Sim, I. (2010). *Information Technology Research Challenges for Healthcare: From Discovery to Delivery:* A white paper prepared for the Computing Community Consortium committee of the Computing Research Association. Retrieved From http://cra.org/ccc/resources/ccc-led-whitepapers/

Greenes, R. A., & Shortliffe, E. H. (1990). *Medical informatics. An emerging academic discipline and institutional priority. JAMA, 263(8)*, 1114–1120. Retrieved from https://www.ncbi.nlm.nih.gov/pubmed/2405204

Greiner, A. C., & Knebel, E. (2003). *Health Professions Education: A Bridge to Quality. Institute of Medicine of the national Academice*. Washington, DC: The National Academies Press.

Guttman, B., & Roback, E. (1995). *An Introduction to Computer Security: The NIST Handbook*. Special Publication. doi:10.6028/NIST.SP.800-12

ITIE Academy. (n.d.). *Blog on Biomedical Signal & Medical Image Processing*. Retrieved From http://itieacademy.com/resources/blog/biomedical-signal-image-processing/

Jain, S., Gupta, S., & Thenua, R. K. (2011). A review on Advancements in Biometrics. *International Journal of Electronics and Computer Science Engineering.*, *1*(3), 853–859.

Jayanthi, A. (2016). *Ransomware encrypts data at Keck Medicine of USC, no ransom paid*. Retrieved From http://www.beckershospitalreview.com/healthcare-information-technology/ransomware-encrypts-data-at-keck-medicine-of-usc-no-ransom-paid.html

Kalakota, R., & Whinston, A. B. (1997). Electronic Commerce- A Manager's Guide. Addison Wesley.

Kaur, N. (2015). A survey on online banking system attacks and its countermeasures. *International Journal of Computer Science and Network Security, 15*(3).

Kutscher, B., & Conn, J. (2014). *Chinese hackers hit Community Health Systems; others vulnerable*. Retrieved From http://www.modernhealthcare.com/article/20140818/NEWS/308189946

Lampson, B. (2004). Computer Security in the Real World. *IEEE Computer*, *37*(6), 37–46. doi:10.1109/MC.2004.17

Millenson, M. L. (1997). *Demanding Medical Excellence*. Chicago: University of Chicago Press.

Musen, M. A., & Bemmel, J. H. V. (1999). *Handbook of medical informatics*. Retrieved From: http://www.mieur.nl/mihandbook/r_3_3/handbook/homepage_self.htm

National Research Council. (1997). *For the Record. Protecting electronic health information*. Washington, DC: National Academy Press.

NIH, Working Group on Biomedical Computing. (1999). *The Biomedical Information Science and Technology Initiative*. Retrieved from https://acd.od.nih.gov/documents/reports/060399_Biomed_Computing_WG_RPT.htm

O'Hara, M.E. (2017). Thousands of Patient Records Leaked in New York Hospital Data Breach. *News by NBC*. Retrieved From http://www.nbcnews.com/news/us-news/thousands-patient-records-leaked-hospital-data-breach-n756981

Patel, V. L., & Kaufman, D. R. (1998). Medical Informatics and the Science of Cognition. *Journal of the American Medical Informatics Association, 5*(6), 493–502. Retrieved From: https://www.ncbi.nlm.nih.gov/pmc/articles/PMC61330/

Pathak, G., Nishar, R., Shah, H., & Gajera, P. (2015). Study of Anti-Phishing on Internet Banking. *International Journal of Innovative and Emerging Research in Engineering, 2*(2).

Rindfleisch, T. C. (1997). Privacy, information technology, and health care. *Communications of the ACM, 40*(8), 93–100. doi:10.1145/257874.257896

Schneier, B. (1996). Applied Cryptography (2nd ed.). John Wiley & Sons, Inc.

Sharma, M., Dwivedi, S., & Garg, R.B. (2015). Let It Encrypt (LIE). *International Journal of Computer Applications, 128*(8).

Shortliffe, E. H., & Blois, M. S. (2006). The computer meets medicine and biology: the emergence of a discipline. In E. H. Shortliffe (Ed.), *Biomedical informatics: computer applications in health care and biomedicine. Springer Science* (pp. 3–45). New York, NY: Business Media, LLC. doi:10.1007/0-387-36278-9_1

Stallings, W. (2011). *Cryptography and Network Security Principles and Practices (5ᵗʰ ed.).* Pearson Education.

Stead, W. W., & Lin, S. H. (2009). *Computational Technology for Effective Health Care: Immediate Steps and Strategic Directions.* Washington, DC: The National Academies Press.

KEY TERMS AND DEFINITIONS

HTTPS: Secure Hyper Text Transfer Protocol
IDS: Intrusion Detection System
MD5: Message Digest 5
NCR: National Research Council
NIH: National Institutes of Health
OTP: One Time Password
SHA1: Secure Hashing Algorithm
SSL: Secure Socket Layer

Chapter 9
Security Risks of Biomedical Data Processing in Cloud Computing Environment

Babangida Zubairu
Jaipur National University, India

ABSTRACT

The emergence of new innovations in technology changes the rate of data generated in health-related institutions and the way data should be handled. As such, the amount of data generated is always on the increase, which demands the need of advanced, automated management systems and storage platforms for handling large biomedical data. Cloud computing has emerged as the promising technology for present and future that can handle large amount of data and enhance processing and management of the data remotely. One of the disturbance concerns of the technology is the security of the data. Data in the cloud is subject to security threats, and this has highlighted the need for exploring security measures against the threats. The chapter provides detailed analysis of cloud computing deployment strategies and risks associated with the technology and tips for biomedical data storage and processing through cloud computing services.

INTRODUCTION

Cloud computing environment enables sharing of computing resources and accessing services supported by the technology through the internet; the client of the technology can benefit from tremendous advantages offered by the technology such as boundary less accessibility of remotely stored data. The stored data can be accessed via any computing devices that can support internet connectivity such as PC and smart phone. The merits of this technology can benefit every sector of human endeavors, such as biomedical data handling, one of the challenging issues is the security of the data stored in the cloud environment, the threats can be from the malicious user behavior in the process of data accessing or other form of threat that disturb the functionality of the technology. Due to the sensitivity and concern about biomedical data in the cloud environment, a robust security measures are required for proper

DOI: 10.4018/978-1-5225-5152-2.ch009

Copyright © 2018, IGI Global. Copying or distributing in print or electronic forms without written permission of IGI Global is prohibited.

storage, delivery and processing of the data. The chapter intends to highlight and digests the security threats that can hinder the processing of biomedical data in the cloud environment and presented the countermeasures against the threats. The chapter also presents details of the merits and demerits of the services supported technologies to the organization and individual that handles data, such as biomedical one and envisaging migrating to the cloud computing. Some vital tips were presented for enhancing the technology deployment, data storage, retrieval and integration for successful delivery of biomedical data processing in the cloud environment.

BACKGROUND

Computers are used in biomedical and health related fields to support data storage, analysis, and integration of biomedical and genetic information. Now a day more advanced technologies are being evolved, the sophistication and advancement of the high throughput technologies will significantly influence more biomedical data generation. This reveals that the ability to measure, store, manage and process precise data on individuals will surpass the capabilities of traditional datacenter of organizations. Enhanced quantitative evaluation and analysis of individual data and qualities become possible due to the advancement in technologies, thereby waiving limits and increases opportunity for advanced studies and evaluation of combined factors that can predict disease and care. As more advanced technologies become available, the demands of handling volumes of increasingly detailed data and analysis may lead to potential increases for drawing erroneous conclusions about the data. This shows the need of an advanced automated system for management, retrieval, and interpretation of biomedical and health related data such as cloud computing technology. Some online database system of nucleic acid exists such as European Molecular Biology Laboratory (EMBL), Gen Bank and DNA databank of Japan, but these databases are not enough to suit the demand of most organizations in biomedical data management. For instance, EMBL is managed by the European Bioinformatics Institute in the UK to support research in molecular biology; GenBank is maintained by the National Center for Biotechnology Information (NCBI) in the US for nucleotide sequences and their protein translations. The DNA Databank is maintained by the National Institutes in Genetics in Japan for the analysis of genetic diseases and genetic fingerprinting for criminology and genetic genealogy (Francesco, Giuliana, & Luigi, 2009). The mentioned online databases may only complement the need of some organizations not all. Therefore, the need for other research institutions and organization handling biomedical data to migrate to cloud technology becomes inevitable; this will provide the avenue for data sharing with other research community around the globe. Securing data is the paramount need of most organizations, peer to peer (P2P) novel technique was presented by (Mohammad, & Adnan, 2018), the approach integrates the P2P with the caching technique and dummies from real queries, this helps in preserving privacy and security of data, Cloudlets technologies were presented by (Panigrahi, Tiwary, Pati, & Das, 2016) as the solution to big data analysis for areas that face low internet connectivity and devices disruptions, the technologies can be useful if employed to manage and process big data in the cloud computing environment. However, watermarking technique was proposed using Odd-Even Method for insertion and extraction of watermark in a bio medical image with large data hiding capacity, security as well as high watermarked quality (Kumar, Nilanjan, Sourav, Achintya, & Sheli, 2014). Similarly, Interpolation and trigonometric techniques were proposed by (Sayan, Prasenjit, Arijit, Debalina, & Nilanjan, 2014) for insertion and extraction of watermark in digital image, this accomplish by embedding secrete bits key into the gray planes of color image.

CLOUD COMPUTING AND ITS ENVIRONMENT

According (Azure, 2017), cloud computing is the delivery of computing services which includes the servers, storage, databases, networking, software, analytics and more over the Internet. Hence, the technology is a solution that provides elastic, on-demand, and scalable computing infrastructure for many application needs (Elhossiny, Nirmeen, & Fatma, 2016). The technology is supported and maintained by the companies. The companies offering the technology are called cloud service providers. The resources and services of cloud computing are used by the client on demand basis and billing is based on the usage of the services, this provides scalability of the services to the client, a client has an option of upgrading or down scaling the services based on demands, the scalability and flexibility of the technology help the client in cutting the cost of computing expenses. The technology provides substantial relieve to clients from infrastructures investment in basic hardware and software, this will enable the clients to concentrate more on innovations and creativity on new ideas to improve their services (Kar, Parida, & Das, 2016). Hence, the technology offers the following:

- Application development environment
- Data storage, back up and recover
- Host websites and blogs
- Stream audio and video services
- Deliver software based on demand
- Data Analyses

Judith Hurwitz (2016) outlined three key players in cloud technology as follows:

1. The Cloud Technology Client (CTC)
2. The Technology Service Providers (TSP) and
3. The Cloud Technology Management (CTM).

The technology defends on resources sharing such as the storage, server, software and network for optimal economy of scale through internet.

Figure 1. Cloud Technology players

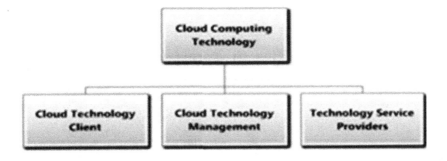

Technology Service Providers (TSP)

The infrastructure of cloud technology comprises the physical components that run applications and data storage. The physical entities enable the creation of the virtual environment for running virtual servers and virtual storage to hold application and data. Virtual abstraction is used for managing servers and storage as logical entities rather than physical. TSP is responsible for smooth running and functionality of the infrastructure as well as logical components and ensures an adequate guarantee of the services operations and security.

Cloud Technology Management (CTM)

In cloud computing, the data and application reside in the virtual environment, the virtual management and control of the data and applications are achieved through Cloud Technology Management. The goal of CTM is to ensure a smooth running of applications and services so that different applications can be used to access the same data. Accurate Information dissemination is the ultimate goal of cloud technology. For instance, a client can access stored data and run the application via the internet from far distances; the data may be stored in the US and be accessible in India. Therefore, CTM provides overall management of information dissemination, maintenance of the storage and smooth running of the cloud application services. It is the responsibility of CTM to provide 24/7 technical supports of the services to the clients, thus, CTM is the general overseer of the cloud services.

Cloud Technology Client (CTC)

This is the end-user that leases the services of cloud technology from the TSP on demand basis; the technical know-how on how the technology works, where the technology resides and how is being maintained, is of no business to the client, but only enjoy the services renders by the TSP and CTM. For example, from Figure 2, the biomedical data resides on cloud storage which is maintained by CTM, the application services for the data processing, storing and retrievals as well as application interface for accessing the data are provider responsibilities.

Figure 2. Biomedical Cloud Technology representation

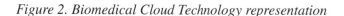

The client can access and run application services for biomedical data processing. The stored data can also be accessed and retrieved via the internet with the help of a web browser. The access of the application services and storage can be done with Personal Computer (PC), laptop, smart phone or any handheld devices that can be connected to the internet.

CLOUD TECHNOLOGY DEPLOYMENTS

Cloud computing technology has three different modes of deployments (Azure, 2017):

- Public clouds
- Private clouds
- Hybrid clouds

Public clouds are owned and operated by cloud service provider, which deliver their computing resources such as application, servers, and storage over the Internet to the public, the cloud services may be free or pay per usage, the technology is designed to use shared physical resources which are accessible over a public network. The provider owned and manages the hardware, software and supporting infrastructure. Microsoft Azure, Google and Amazon Elastic, IBM's Blue Cloud and Sun Cloud are examples of the public cloud.

Private cloud offers a separate and secure cloud based environment for only particular client, private cloud operates some advantages of the public such as scalability, on demand and self-service, but they differ in ownership, moreover, unlike public clouds, which deliver services to multiple organizations on shared basis, a private cloud is dedicated to a single organization for dedicated usage, which means the resources are exclusively dedicated for use by a single client, the services and infrastructure are maintained and manage on a private network. The private cloud can be tailored by the organization's networks since is only dedicated and accessible by a single organization. And this will make the technology to be easily managed and configured by an organization. Most private cloud is used by the financial organization, government agencies, and security organizations.

A Hybrid cloud is a cloud computing technology that employed the approaches of the public and the private cloud technology for the data and applications to be shared between the two technologies and use by a single organization. Hybrid cloud provides organizations with a better flexibility and more deployment options by allowing data and applications to be moved between private and public clouds, creating the hybrid cloud type. The hybrid cloud enables organizations to enjoy the benefits of the public cloud to store vital and protected data on public and also benefits from private cloud futures while maintaining the ability of the computational resource from the public cloud to run applications that rely on the data.

CLOUD SERVICES FOR BIOMEDICAL DATA PROCESSING

The cloud computing services provide tremendous benefits which are enjoyed by the client of the technology so as to ease and assist the client in executing task diligently and efficiently. The services can be rented by the client and use them on demand basis, that means the usage of the services can be upgraded whenever the need arises or downgraded when the client is not in-need of the services, this provides flexibility options (Hurwitz, Bloor, Kaufman, & Halper, 2016), this provide a great advantage for the client to scale-down or scale-up the services as the technology is being used.

The cloud services can be categorized into Platform as-a-Service (PaaS), Infrastructure as-a-Service (IaaS) and Software as-a-Service (SaaS), (Rani, 2014).

Platform as-a-Service (PaaS)

PaaS is the complete delivery platform that enables and provides a development environment for a software developer to develop an application or software that runs on cloud environment (Rani, 2014). The platform supports operating systems enable environment and needed services for particular software to run (Furht, & Escalante, 2010). A client need not to buzzer about the storage facility usage such as the server and the network, all these facilities are managed, control, maintain and supported by the technology providers. PaaS provides database management systems and development tools for complete web application life cycle ranging from building an application, testing, deploying, managing and updating of the application. PaaS supports the following for biomedical data processing:

- Development platform to develop and customize cloud-based applications to suit organization's need and demand.
- Platform environment to process and analyze data remotely.
- Virtual environment to store data, backup, and retrieval of data.
- Secured virtual environment for data sharing.

Advantages of PaaS in Biomedical Data Processing

- Database of biomedical data processing application can be developed for multiple platforms including mobile and PC.
- PaaS offers opportunities for organization to use sophisticated, advanced software and tools that are too expensive and costly for organization to afford.
- PaaS support distribution of biomedical data processing, since data and database are accessible remotely over the internet.

Figure 3. Cloud service

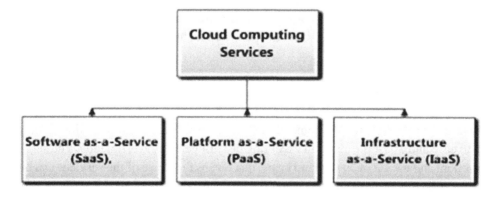

- The virtualization of storage environment supported by PaaS enhances data handling more securely.
- The PaaS capabilities enhance efficiency and easy of data management and application.

Infrastructure as-a-Service (IaaS)

IaaS offers a service to the client to rent a usage of cloud infrastructures such as the network resources, the storage facilities, the servers and other hardware resources of the cloud (Velte, Velt, & Elsenpeter, 2010), for example, a research laboratory may decide to rent a storage facility on the cloud to store biomedical data of its research or lab findings, rent a server space to host data processing applications, rent a network facility or any other cloud facility that may be needed, use them on demand basis and pay per resource usage. The basic services of IaaS as described by (Azure, 2017) are:

- IaaS offers benefits to the client of the services with the virtual development environment to develop new applications quickly; new application can be tested from the environment for ease of application deployment, the environment can be scaled up and down depends on the needs and demands of the client.
- With IaaS, organization's website can be hosted in the robust and secure platform. IaaS can handles big data Storage like biomedical data remotely; the services enable data backup and recovery for precaution against system failure and disaster.
- High-Performance Computing (HPC) for solving complex problems such as protein folding simulations and other biomedical data processing and analysis, the services enables mathematical and statistical operations on higher computing technology such as supercomputers, computer grids or computer clusters.

Advantages of IaaS in Bi-Medical Data Processing

- IaaS reduces the huge capital expense associated with establishing and managing an on-site (traditional) datacenter.
- IaaS improves availability and reliability of data processing, comparison to the traditional system of data processing. A client can access applications and data remotely even during a disaster or system outage.
- IaaS reduces cost of data processing and analysis.
- IaaS enhances the security of client applications and data than what is obtainable in traditional data center.

Software as-a-Service (SaaS)

In cloud computing, SaaS provides clients access to the applications directly for individual and enterprise users, including the content of the application, database and other infrastructure resources on demand. The accessibility of the services is via the internet, the user can use any internet based device to link to the internet and access cloud resources directly. In laboratory settings, SaaS can be rented from the service providers for storing data related to laboratory investigations, analysis, and other findings, the data stored is accessible remotely and can be accessed by multiple users concurrently from a different location. SaaS support the following services in biomedical data processing:

- Client can rent software service from service providers and tailored to suit the need and demand of an organization.
- SaaS provides web-based support so that data and database can be accessed via the internet.
- On-demand service usage metered on a pay--per usage basis.

Advantages of SaaS in Biomedical Data Processing

- The traditional system of software installation, management and debug fixing are completely eliminated compared to the on-site data center.
- SaaS service can be automatically scales up and down according to the need, demand, and level of usage.
- SaaS services provides clients with access to the advanced and sophisticated software that some organization may not afford.
- Remote service accessibility either with mobile or station PC via the internet.

BENEFITS OF BIOMEDICAL DATA PROCESSING IN CLOUD COMPUTING

- **Processing Speed:** Cloud computing facilitates provide smooth and fastest data processing since data can be processed in parallel and distributed mode regardless of location and distance.
- **Cost Effective:** To establish traditional datacenter, an organization needs to invest huge capital expenses ranging from hardware like the PCs, network facilities, servers and associated facilities. Expenses are also required for software such as OS and applications. Staffing the center with IT personnel that will take care of managing and maintenance of the center and also the provision of electricity for power and cooling of the center, all there when sum together will acquire very huge expenses to an organization. Cloud computing services can supplement the on-site data center with effective fewer expenses compare to the former.
- **Parallel Processing:** Data processing can be done from multiple terminals or systems concurrently.
- **Efficiency:** The efficiency of data processing is enhanced, for example, the rapidly increasing volume and complexity of the biomedical data from laboratories can range from hundreds of bytes to terabytes or even bigger (Anderson, 2007). The processing of such data can take a longer time with less accuracy under the traditional datacenter system, but processing of the data with cloud technology will take less time with better efficiency. However, the large size of data can be processed at a relatively less cost to the client.
- **Productivity Enhancement:** The daily task required in traditional data center consumes organization employees' time to manage the center like hardware setup and troubleshooting, cloud computing eliminates the need for these operations. The productivity of an organization can be enhanced by utilizing the time for other essential tasks.

RISKS IN BIOMEDICAL DATA PROCESSING OVER CLOUD ENVIRONMENT

Improper adequate planning when migrating to cloud computing can lead to unprecedented disappointment to the client. The client should ensure adequate security protection of the data; hence, inadequate planning when using cloud services could result in potential loss of organization's vital data and eliminating the prospective benefits of cloud computing technology. As the cloud computing popularity increases, the more serious security issues increases in deployment. In cloud technology, the facilities including the data and applications reside in the virtual environment created and maintained by the cloud services provider and the clients do not have control over the facilities but only use them as they are. The serious risk is when a provider is out of the business as a result of one reason or the other or a total failure due to natural or manmade disaster, the retrieval of the stored data and applications on the cloud may be difficult to the client. Some network devices may perform cheating during data transmission by sniffing sensitive and useful information and leak them to the malicious user (Suciu, 2013). The client must have a clear understanding of possible security risks and benefits associated with the technology when considering migration to cloud technology. The client needs to understand realistic expectations from the cloud provider, different services offered by the technology have different security requirement and approach; the client should take into consideration the security level supported by each service and capabilities of the service. However, it is important for the client to understand the regulations and the relevant obligations bounded on the provider and the client such as data retention, security provision and interoperability of client existing system with the provider's platform. These will enable the client to identify and understand the provider capabilities, legal issues and the possible legal risks before migrating data to a cloud environment. There are certain issues associated with cloud computing that an organization needs to scrutinize adequately before migration biomedical data to cloud environment, such as:

- **Reluctance of Commitment:** Migrating data to cloud environment means client's complete submission of data ownership and control, some issues that are out of service agreement may arise and the provider may be reluctant to address them in time and this will create security hitches of the data.
- **Responsibility Ambiguity:** Both the provider and client are liable to responsibilities of managing and control and security provision for data protection in the virtual cloud environment, both parties responsibilities should be clearly mentioned in the service agreement, the client and provider roles should be clearly stated to avoid ambiguities. Provider and client must understand the responsibilities and roles bounded on them and must strictly adhere to them for the successful deployment and implementation of the system.
- **Authorization:** Adequate complex authentication mechanism should be enforced since the cloud resources are accessible remotely from anywhere via the Internet, there is a need to establish a more complex verification mechanism for user identity, hence strong and adequate authentication mechanism is among the critical concern issues.
- **Failure Risk:** Client should understand that public cloud is a multi-tenancy system, the cloud resources are shared among the clients of the services and the risk of system failure is inevitable and cannot be predicted, thus adequate planning needs to be made from the client part before any happen.

- **Legal Risks:** Client should understand the legal risk carefully and must adhere to the responsibilities provided in the service agreement.
- **Apparent Maintenance**: Cloud technology provider should have proactive infrastructure maintenance capability to handle issues such as hardware failure and software updates; this will enhance reliability, availability and security of services.
- **Load Balancing:** A provider needs to support load balancing technology, this will help to reduce excess congestion by distributing incoming system's user requests across pools of instances for maximum performance of the services.

CLOUD SERVICE PROVIDER RESPONSIBILITIES

The provider of the cloud technology service should have certain obligations that are expected to be fulfilled, these include:

1. The provider is responsible for maintenance, workability, and availability of the services, the signed contract agreement between provider and client is expected to be adhered by both parties, all the agreed terms as providers responsibilities most to strictly adhere.
2. Security of the data and services must be maintained by the provider.
3. The provider is responsible for keeping transactions and system logs for system auditing.
4. Provider needs to have complete commitment for adequate delivery of the services; the services ought to remain available, operational and accessible to the client at any time.

CLOUD SERVICES CLIENT RESPONSIBILITIES

The client is expected to ensure maximum utilization of services throughout the period of the contract.

1. By agreeing to use the cloud services, the client has entered a contract and is expected to adhere to all its terms, including adherence to an upfront payment of services usage when needed.
2. It is the responsibility of the client to determine and assign who should use and access the services and data, as such, is oblige to assign the user(s) who should access and use the cloud services
3. The provider only provides space for setting and storing the data, but maintenance and updating the data is sole responsibilities of the client.

CLOUD TECHNOLOGY SECURITY TIPS

Before choosing a cloud provider an organization needs to ensure the following security guidelines are strictly abided by the service provider.

1. Confidentiality of data should be enforced to support technical and security tools such as encryption and decryption and access control, as well as data legal protections. There should be a set of very strict rules that will limit access to certain types of information except for authorized access.

This means keeping an organization's data secured and safe is the paramount and the information between the service provider and the client and should not be disclosed to an unauthorized person.

2. The service provider ought to be honest, and maintain integrity degree of confidence that the data in the cloud is what is supposed to be there and adhere to moral and ethical principles of data integrity. The data should be strictly save guided and protected against accidental, eventuality or deliberate alteration of data. The integrity should be supported by authorized and sophisticated audit system to ensure adequate adherence to rules of law.

3. Availability of data should be enforced so that the data and necessary tools and facilities subscribed by the client are available and accessible for 24x7 regardless of time and distance, theses means the client should be able to use the services as anticipated. This cannot be achieved without adequate facilities provision and capacity of the service provider.

4. The provider has clients' obligations to account for the activities and system logs of the services access and transactions for proper accountability and should be responsible for auditing the logs as well as providing secure system access control.

5. The provider has the responsibility to ensure the guarantee of the services, as well as the system workability and the system performance behaves as expected.

BIOMEDICAL DATA SCIENCE

Data science as explained by (Amos, 2017) it involves coordination and integration of disciplines such as Biomedical Informatics and Biostatistics for automated management, retrieval, and interpretation of extensive biomedical and health related information. Biomedical data science can be viewed as the scientific methods that provide conceptual integration of technologies and tools that enable the processing, retrievals, analysis, interpretation, and presentations of biomedical data in secured and understandable fashion for end-user consumption.

Figure 4. Data science in biomedical data processing

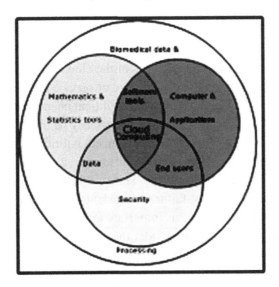

Data science as scientific method comprises fact findings and investigation for the purpose of acquiring new knowledge from the data and integrating previous knowledge from the data, this involves systematic observation, experiment, measurement, formulation, and testing of hypotheses with the aim of discovering new ideas and concepts. To achieve the success of this scientific method, techniques are required in the science of data, such as tools and theories drawn from many fields of knowledge within the broad areas of mathematics and statistics, software tools and applications, security and cloud computing from computer science (see Figure 4). The goal of biomedical data science is to turn data into actionable knowledge through vigorous analysis and interpretation of an idea from information generated based on data analysis and interpretations.

BIOMEDICAL BIG DATA IN CLOUD

Biomedical data are the type that deals with the life of a human being and such data can be generated from experiment or test carried out from collecting samples. The data may be much larger than the organization's facility's capacity to handle. Biomedical big data are data sets related to health issues that can be analyzed to discover patterns and trends associated with the facts. The advancement of new technologies and innovations has increased the rate of data generation and its complexity and these have influenced the expansion of data such as biomedical one, as such, the intensity of the data complexity cannot be handled by a traditional application designed for data processing such as relational database (Sharvari, 2017).. These have demanded new technology like cloud computing as the alternative solution for data storage and processing. Cloud Technology like all other technologies has its possible bottleneck as expressed by (Marx, 2013). With the cloud technology, a client can harness both the computing power and the facilities needed online and use them on demand to carry out data processing online with the computing services supported by the technology. The technology therefore, provides an opportunity for data to be stored in the cloud environment regardless of size for future use; such data can also be retrieved at any time regardless of distance.

Choosing cloud technology means entrusting organization's vital data to a distant service provider; the services may be subject to obstructions due to one reason or the other such as hardware failure, system outage and security threats. However, issues may arise when data are stored in several clouds and need to be merged. Several questions need to come to the client's minds for this, such as where is the data stored? Is the data stored in the client's vicinity, is the data stored in a secure form, what will happen to the data when a client no longer needs the services of the cloud service provider and can the data be transferred to a new service provider in case of a change of service provider. Many forget to think and ask them self about these critical questions. However, a political phenomenon needs to be considered in deciding cloud providers, since the provider may not necessarily be from the host country of the client. For example, making inferences from the previous and current political and power struggles among different countries across the globe, either in the same or different region, choosing a cloud provider has to be critical within the domain of future occurrences. This will helps an organization to plan adequately and avoid being a victim of circumstances; failures to make curious choices may lead an organization to be a victim of worth dilemma. Therefore, it is important for organizations and individuals envisaging migrating to cloud computing technology to consider these factors.

DATA PROTECTION IN CLOUD

Virtualization of resources is the core of cloud computing technology; the technology allows the use of abstract logical interfaces for accessing cloud resources such as the servers, network, and storage. Security is becoming a serious issue of concern in the technology, many individuals, organizations, and government establishments are becoming victims of a cyber security breach due to inadequate enforcement of security policy, data protection policy is becoming a serious problem associated with cloud storage technology, the providers of this technology are trying their best to provide and maintain the security of the technology at some level of protections but still more needs to be done. The alternate option of system backup is required as precaution mechanism. Organization's hardware and software can be utilized for a backup system to supplement cloud technology and use both as needed to complement eventualities.

Data Backup

Data backup is a system that enables a duplicate copy of vital data to be stored in another means for retrievals in a case of natural disaster or system failure; this will help to reduce the effects of a catastrophic consequence of data loss. Today, there are many data backup systems and services that will be useful for enterprises and organizations to secure data such as a biomedical one; the backup mechanism will ensure that data and information are not lost due to disaster or system failure.

Data Backup Policy

In computing technology backup process is apply to critical databases to safeguard the data against eventualities accuracy. Backup should be scheduled for at least once a week, especially during weekends or off-time hours. To supplement weekly full backups, organizations can schedule a sequence of differential or incremental data backup that backup only data that has changed since the last full backup took place (Rouse, 2016). With a backup system, an organization can keep a copy of its vital data and database system on backup storage device

SECURITY IN CLOUD TECHNOLOGY

The goal of cloud technology is to acquire the clients' data to be completely migrated to the cloud provider without considering the security risk of doing that, though some cloud providers like Google and Amazon have the infrastructure that can deflect and survive a cyber attack but not every cloud provider has such capability (Lori, 2009). Cloud computing like other related computing technologies is featured with security threats that can affect the proper performances of the technology. Adequate measures are needed to save guard the vital data stored in the cloud; the measures should include effective policy, strategy, governance and holistic approach to the security related problems. However, there is a need for a standard universal security mechanism and policy to address the challenges at the global level, and enforcement of the policy and standard for abiding by all providers should be adopted for smooth running and technology challenges handling.

TIPS FOR SELECTING CLOUD STORAGE PROVIDER

Cloud storage environment is a virtual setting that allows data to be stored and access by the client remotely; the provider of the technology needs to ensure adequate safety of the storage system. It is also vital for the client to assess the reliability and capability of a service provider before entrusting organization's vital data to the provider. Some criteria were set to be the guidelines for choosing a cloud service provider (Azure, 2017) .

- **Financial Strength:** The provider should have a good track record of financial stability with sufficient capital strength to operate successfully over the long term.
- **Truest:** The provider should have a good reputation of trust.
- **Technical Know-How:** Provider should have the technical expertise and know-how for handling technical issues, user support and capability to understand client needs.
- **Resource Monitoring:** Provider should have a provision of resource monitoring and configuration management to track and monitor services provided to clients.
- **Billing System:** There should be automated billing and accounting system to monitor resources usage and cost.
- The provider should have mechanisms for easy deployment, management and upgrades of software and applications.
- **Application Interfaces:** The provider should have provision of standard Application Interfaces (APIs) for client to easily build connections to the cloud and integration support with the client existing infrastructure
- **Service Documentation:** The provider should have adequate documentation for operating the services.
- There should be comprehensive and adequate security mechanisms, policies and procedures in place for controlling access and client systems.
- **Backup and Restore:** Provision of policies and procedures for data backup and restore of client data.

CLOUD DATA STORAGE

Data is the key component for any organization that deals with biomedical facts, the success and failure the organization depend on how the data is handling, processed and stored. Cloud data Storage is a service that enables maintenance, management, and backup of data remotely. When data is stored in the cloud, the client of the cloud service can access the data remotely. The data storage services provided by the cloud providers reduce cost of handling the data through consolidation of all the data types in one single platform of storage, organizations can achieve full capacity utilization of its strength for maximum usage of the data, and with the services supported by cloud technology, the data can be managed, processed and delivered easily either in single or distribution form. However, availability of data is assured with the services since the data can be accessed remotely provided there is internet access. The centralized online backup and control can also be achieved with the technology and this will be useful in case of disaster and system failure.

Advantages of Cloud Data Storage

- **Accessibility:** With the data stored in the cloud, the client or the user(s) can access the data from any location regardless of distance provided there is an internet connection from the access location.
- **Data Safety and Assurance:** The cloud technology offers advantage of safety since data stored on PC can be corrupt due to faulty from the storage device or other hardware failures.
- **Security:** Cloud service providers provide better and enhance security than traditional data storage
- **Data Sharing:** Data can be shared easily from one user to another in more secure manner
- **Data Recovery:** Cloud providers provide quick recovery of data in case of failure, this makes the technology safer and secure than traditional data storage system.
- **Automatic Data Backup:** Client can benefit from services supported by the provider to schedule automatic backup of data.
- **Usability of Data:** The data stored in the cloud environment can be used by more than one user at the same time. However, the data used by one user also can be reused by another user for a different purpose.
- **Disaster Recovery:** Cloud storage can be used as a backup plan in case of emergency or disaster since the data are stored at a remote location and can be accessed via the internet.
- **Cost Savings:** Organizations subscribing the services of cloud technology can reduce operational costs of data handling; storage and processing since establishing a local datacenter within an organization require the cost of staffing the datacenter, software and hardware maintenance annually. When comparing to the cost of using cloud storage; the technology offers better cost effective than traditional datacenter.

Disadvantages of Cloud Data Storage

- **Breach of Security**: To access cloud service, the user or client need to be authenticated before login, the most common login mechanism are the user-id and password, if these are not handle safely, may fall in to the wrong hands. A cyber breach like user's credentials hacking can be a serious threat to the technology and can lead to unauthorized access of the data. It is recommended to remember the login access details and keep them safely, a user should avoid using several passwords that cannot remember; it is a good idea to adopt the habit of using unique credentials for most common online accesses. However, uses of complex and sophisticated credentials are recommended to secure login and the data access.
- **Technical Hitches**: Technical failures can be a setback for the service, for example, to access the data remotely, internet connection is required. If the connection is not available at a particular access location then the user will not have access to the data. Also when an internet access goes down due to a technical problem the user will not be able to access the data. However, provider's server can fail as results of unprecedented technical issues; when any one of these happened, can be a drawback of cloud technology.
- **Provider Option**: Many cloud storage providers exist online, some are free while some are not, and an organization has the option to choose one of its choices, on which the organization can trust. It is important to take not in mind that the providers are meant for profit making due to one reason or the other, a provider may fall into a dilemma such bankruptcy which can make the

provider exit from the business, when quitting the provider may not necessarily notify its' customers. It is recommended for any organization that deals with boil-medical data to avoid free online providers and go for reputable and esteem providers, hence the security of such data is crucial to any organization.

- **Data Security:** Even though an organization has submitted its vital data to cloud providers, the risk of losing confidentiality of the data is there. Recently, there are serious concerns about the safety and privacy of data across the globe. Some security agencies were accused of accessing private data stored in the cloud without the approval of the concerned data owners. An organization migrating to cloud computing should take note of serious risks associated with the technology and make adequate plan for deployment of the technology.

- **Bandwidth Issues:** Accessing data from cloud require the use of the internet, it could be a tedious task if an organization is having a bandwidth problem, though, some cloud storage provider unlimited bandwidth and some have a specific bandwidth allowance for clients. By surpassing the allowed bandwidth, additional charges are applied to the client. These are issues that organization should take into considerations when migrating to cloud technology.

CLOUD STORAGE CLASSES

Cloud computing enables scalable data and application storage that require durability and high availability. The technology supports various categories of storage and services. Some larger organizations require processing of hundreds of terabytes of data and larger storage space such as financial and scientific organizations. Some organization requires medium processing and medium storage space. Some small organizations need small processing and small storage space. The technology providers have support for various demands with payment options of pay per service usage basis. The levels of storage support and capabilities depend on the provider operational plan; some support multi-regional, regional and low-cost storage of hot and cool access depending on data usage frequencies.

For example, Google offers four storage classes of multi-regional storage, regional storage, nearline storage, and coldline Storage. All the classes offer the same throughput, low latency, and high durability. The classes differ by their availability, minimum storage durations, and pricing for storage and access (Coldline, 2017).

- **Multi-Regional Storage:** This class is best for storing data that is frequently accessed around the world to ensure maximum availability of client's data, the provider store client data in at least two regions separated by at least 100 miles, this helps to save guard the data against an event of disruptions, such as natural disasters.

- **Regional Storage:** This class enables storing frequently accesses data in the same region and enables the client to store data at lower cost, with the data being stored in a specific regional location, instead of having data distributed over a large geographic area. The advantage of this class over multi-regional is the reduction in network charges to the client.

- **Nearline Storage:** This class is ideal for the data which is less frequently accessible on an average of once a month and is Ideal for backup, disaster recovery, and archival. A client can continuously add files to Cloud Storage and plan to access those files once a month for analysis. Hence, the plan is cost effective for less frequently uses data.

- **Coldline Storage:** This class is the ideal choice for data access at most once a year, the class offers very low cost plan compare to nearline storage and is good for data archive, online backup, and recovery.

The Microsoft azure cloud storage, on the other hand, provides four services of blob storage that support hot and cool access levels, table storage, queue storage, and file storage. The services are elastic and the client pay for the amount of data stored and the number of requests made against the data, that means client pay per usage basis (Azure, 2017).

- **Blob Storage:** Is designed for data storage of all kinds, the data can be text or binary, such as a document, media file, or application. Blob offers storage robustness, availability of data and services scalability for the client to upgrade or downgrade the services. The hot access level indicates that the data objects in the cloud storage will be more frequently accessed and this give cost benefits for the client. The Cool access level indicates that the data objects in the cloud storage will be less frequently accessed than hot access level, the plan provides lower data storage cost to the client.
- **Table Storage:** Provides support for the storage of structured datasets, the services offer storage availability at all time, the service is scalable for an upgrade and down grade, and the data from this service can be rapidly processed in a larger quantity and can be accessed easily. This type of storage class is mostly used by software developers to create agile applications since it supports fast and cost effective data access for all kinds of applications. Table storage supports flexible datasets storage, such as user data for web applications, and, biomedical data for processing via web and desktop applications.
- **Queue Storage:** Provides the client with a reliable storage facility that supports message workflow processing and asynchronous communication between various application components in the cloud services domain.
- **File Storage:** Is ideal for storing data that needs to be shared among applications, with Azure virtual machines, cloud services can share file data across application components via mounted shares, and on-premises applications can access file data in a shared mode.

Similarly, Amazon Web Services (AWS) provides on-demand cloud computing platforms such as data storage that can handle a large amount of biomedical data. AWS offers a complete range of cloud storage services to support both application and backup compliance requirements. An awesome future of AWS is support for innovations in healthcare and clinical analytics. AWS like other cloud providers provide supports for a range of storage classes (Amazon, 2017):

- **Amazon Elastic File System (Amazon EFS):** Provides scalable storage for use with Amazon EC2 instances in the AWS Cloud. EFS supports high availability and durability of the services, and provides support for storage in Big Data and analytics such as biomedical, media processing workflows, content management and web services.
- **Amazon Simple Storage Service (Amazon S3):** Is designed to support object storage and access of any type of data over the Internet. S3 is object storage built to store and retrieves any amount of data remotely; the data is accessible via web sites and mobile apps, corporate applications, and

data from IoT sensors or devices. S3 can support backup and recovery, data archive and Big Data analytics.

- **Amazon Elastic Block Storage (Amazon EBS):** Is designed to support highly available, consistent, low-latency block storage for Elastic Compute Cloud (EC2) web services by enhancing client's applications storage capacity and performances.
- **Amazon Glacier:** Is a low-cost and highly durable object storage service for long-term backup and archive of any type of object data. The service is designed to support low cost cloud storage for frequently less accessed data.
- **AWS Storage Gateway:** Is a software platform services that seamlessly links client's on-premises environment to Amazon cloud storage. The gateway connects to AWS storage services such as Amazon S3, Amazon Glacier and Amazon EBS. The technology has support for local storage with a highly optimized data transfer mechanism and connectivity to AWS Cloud storage, and helps with migration and storage bursting capabilities of the client.
- **Data Transfer Services:** Amazon supports a platform for data transfer services for data migration into and out of the AWS cloud. The services help the client to explore more cloud benefits such as accelerating data transfers quickly and securely to cloud archives and capture continuous data streaming from multiple sources.

FUTURE RESEARCH DIRECTIONS

Security is one of the main challenging issues in the cloud data storage technology as discussed in the chapter; this reveals that, there is a need for more research to be done to design and develop automatic resource and sophisticated security management system for enhancing data storage technology. This includes concrete security policy measures and standard that should be adopted by all the players in the technology.

CONCLUSION

The emergence of cloud computing technology provides many opportunities and flexibility for handling large and complex data, the services supported technologies are scalable, the client can upscale or downscale the services base on demand, similarly, the client pays the service usage based on pay as you go plan, this can provide an organization or the client opportunity to save costs and increases organization's productivity. Organizations handling biomedical data can benefit from the services support by cloud computing technology as an automated platform for handling and processing large amount of data. Despite the benefits of the technology, data in the cloud environment is subjective to security threats. The chapter provides detailed analysis of cloud computing deployment strategies, services supported by the technology for biomedical data processing and security risks associated with the services. Tips were presented in the chapter that will be useful for organization and individual considering cloud computing deployment as an alternative option for biomedical data storage and processing. The chapter also discusses the benefits that can be driven from the cloud computing technology and the demerits of the technology, the challenges associated with the technology deployment and solution to the security intimidations in the data storage were also discussed. Cloud storage classes supported by some major players in the technology were presented with different features, benefits and supported technology with related to the cloud data storage. Therefore, for organization envisaging cloud computing technology should be aware about the tremendous benefits that can be driven from the technology, which can also promote the organization's standard, but curious and serious care should taken into consideration to safeguard the integrity of the data with optimum security measures and for the organization that had embraced the technology should take extra security measures to promote the validity and integrity of the entrusted data to the cloud.

REFERENCES

Amazon. (2017). *Healthcare Providers and Insurers in the Cloud.* Retrieved 7 13, 2017, from Amazon web services: https://aws.amazon.com/health/providers-and-insurers/

Amos, C. (2017). *Biomedical data science.* Retrieved June 29, 2017, from Geisel School of Medicine: https://bmds.dartmouth.edu/biomedical-data-science

Anderson, N. R.-H., Lee, E. S., Brockenbrough, J. S., Minie, M. E., Fuller, S., Brinkley, J., & Tarczy-Hornoch, P. (2007). Issues in Biomedical Research Data Management and Analysis: Needs and Barriers. *Journal of the American Medical Informatics Association, 14*(4), 478–488. doi:10.1197/jamia.M2114 PMID:17460139

Anthony, T., & Velte, T. J. (2010). *Cloud Computing A practical Approach.* New Delhi: McGraw Hill.

Arijit Kumar, P., Nilanjan, D., & Sourav, S. (2014). A hybrid reversible watermarking technique for color biomedical images. In Computational Intelligence and Computing Research. New Delhi: IEEE.

Azure, M. (2017). *What is cloud computing?* Retrieved 7 2, 2017, from Micrososft Azure: https://azure.microsoft.com/en-in/overview/what-is-cloud-computing/

Borko Furht, A. E. (2010). *Hand Book on Cloud Computing.* London: Springer. doi:10.1007/978-1-4419-6524-0

Dimpi Rani, R. K. (2014, June). A Comparative Study of SaaS, PaaS and IaaS in Cloud Computing. *International Journal of Advanced Research in Computer Science and Software Engineering, 4*(6), 458–461.

Elhossiny, I., Nirmeen, A. E., & Fatma, A. O. (2016). *Task Scheduling Algorithm in Cloud Computing Environment Based on Cloud Pricing Models. In Computer Applications & Research.* Cairo, Egypt: IEEE.

Francesco, E., Giuliana, D., & Luigi, P. (2009). A Summary of Genomic Databases: Overview and Discussion. In Bioinformatice Data and Applications (pp. 37-59). Springer-Verlag Berlin.

George Suciu, S. H. (2013). Cloud Computing as Evolution of Distributed Computing – A Case Study. *Informações Econômicas, 7*(4), 109–122. doi:10.12948/issn14531305/17.4.2013.10

Google. (2017, June 29). *Archival Cloud Storage: Nearline & Coldline.* Retrieved July 12, 2017, from Google Cloud Platform: https://cloud.google.com/storage/archival/

Ipsita Kar, I., Parida, R. N. R., & Das, H. (2016). *Energy aware scheduling using genetic algorithm in cloud data centers. In Electrical, Electronics, and Optimization Techniques.* IEEE.

Judith Hurwitz, R. B. (2016). cloud Computing for dummies (J. Jensen, Ed.). Delhi, India: A Wiley Brand.

Lori, M. K. A. (2009). Data Security in the World of Cloud Computing. *IEEE Security & Privacy, 7*(4), 1-64.

Marx, V. (2013, June). Biology: The big challenges of big data. *Nature, 498*(7453), 255–260. doi:10.1038/498255a PMID:23765498

Mohammad, Y., & Adnan, A. A. (2018). Improving Privacy and Security of User Data in Location Based Services. *Ambient Computing and Intelligence, 9*(1), 24.

Panigrahi, C. R., Tiwary, M., Pati, B., & Das, H. (2016). Big Data and Cyber Foraging: Future Scope and Challenges. In B. Mishra, S. Dehuri, E. Kim, & G. N. Wang (Eds.), *Techniques and Environments for Big Data Analysis. Studies in Big Data* (Vol. 17). Cham: Springer. doi:10.1007/978-3-319-27520-8_5

Rouse, M. (2016, September). *What is your strategy for selectively performing data backup?* Retrieved 06 20, 2017, from TechTerget: http://searchdatabackup.techtarget.com/definition/backup

Sayan, C., Prasenjit, M., Arijit, K. P., Debalina, B., & Nilanjan, D. (2014) Reversible Color Image Watermarking Using Trigonometric Functions. Electronic Systems Signal Processing and Computing Technologies.

Sharvari, C. T., Vijender, K. S., Pati, B., & Madhuri, S. J. (2017). The Basics of Big Data and Security Concerns. In *Privacy and Security Policies in Big Data.* IGI Global.

KEY TERMS AND DEFINITIONS

Biomedical Big Data: A large and complex data related to the health status.

Biomedical Data: Row facts related to the health status that can be processed to get information.

Biomedical Data Science: A scientific method that provides conceptual integration of technologies and tools that enables processing, retrievals, analysis, interpretation, and presentations of biomedical data in secured and understandable fashion for end-user consumption.

Cloud Computing: The delivery of computing services and resources such as the servers, storage, databases, networking, software, and analytic through the internet.

Cloud Environment: An accessible virtual environment for computing resources and services that holds data and applications remotely.

Cloud Technology Client: The end-user that leases the services of cloud computing technology and uses them on demand basis.

Cloud Technology Management: The virtual management and control of the data and applications over cloud environment.

Data Processing: The act of data manipulation through integration of mathematical tools, statistics, and computer application to generate information.

Data Science: A knowledge acquisition from data through scientific method that comprises systematic observation, experiment, measurement, formulation, and hypotheses testing with the aim of discovering new ideas and concepts.

Chapter 10

Intrusion Detection System in Wireless Sensor Networks for Wormhole Attack Using Trust–Based System

Umashankar Ghugar
Berhampur University, India

Jayaram Pradhan
Berhampur University, India

ABSTRACT

Intrusion detection in wireless sensor network (WSN) has been a critical issue for the stable functioning of the networks during last decade. Wireless sensors are small and cheap devices that have a capacity to sense actions, data movement, and communicate with each other. It is a self-governing network that consists of sensor nodes deployed in a particular environment, which has wide applications in various areas such as data gathering, military surveillance, transportation, medical system, agriculture, smart building, satellite communication, and healthcare. Wormhole attack is one of the serious attacks, which is smoothly resolved in networks but difficult to observe. There are various techniques used to detect the malicious node such as LITEWORP, SAM, DelPHI, GRPW, and WRHT. This chapter focuses on detection methods for wormhole attacks using trust-based systems in WSN.

1. INTRODUCTION

WSN is a distributive, automatic governing network, which is deployed in a specific environment. Sensor nodes observe the different condition, such as compression, heat, humidity, wave direction at different areas (Tiwari, Veer, Arya, Choudhari, Sidharth, & Choudhary, 2009). A sensor node is a cheap device and has a low measurement resource. They are honestly arranged in a sensed environment (Boukerch, & Xu, 2007;Das, Nalik, Pati, & Panigrahi, 2014). WSN are broadly used in various applications such as target tracking, traffic monitoring, area observing, forest fire observing, home affirmation, health

DOI: 10.4018/978-1-5225-5152-2.ch010

Copyright © 2018, IGI Global. Copying or distributing in print or electronic forms without written permission of IGI Global is prohibited.

management devices and satellite communication. In WSN number of security issues are maintained for smooth communication and also some limitation such as less computation power, limited lifetime, less storage and low bandwidth (Du & Li, 2011; Bao, Chen, Chang, & Cho, 2012). Based on these limitations they are arranged in noisy climate. It is highly affected and sensitive to different types of attacks (Rassam, Maarof, & Zainal, 2012; Panigrahi Sarkar, Pati, & Das, 2016).

There are different types of attack namely Wormhole Attack, Hello flood Attack, Sinkhole Attack, Blackhole Attack, Sybil Attack, and Denial of Service are found. Our proposed approach considers only the Wormhole attack.

1.1. Wormhole Attack

Wormhole attack is the most destructive attacks in WSN. Generally two or more abnormal nodes create a tunnel. Here the attackers are directly connected through shortest route to each other, so that they can broadcast at a high speed over the networks with other nodes. A wormhole attack can be freely carried out against routing in the sensor networks. Thus most of routing protocols do not have any mechanism to prevent from it (Sabri & Kamoun, 2016). In other words, when the wormhole attack occurs, it drops all the packets and cause network interruption. It also acts as investigator on the packets and breaks the network security. Wormhole attack is also used in the form of merging of selective forward and Sybil attack (Singh, 2012; Yamin & Sen, 2017).

Figure 1, shows how data packets are transmitted between the two Nodes A and E, where D is a malicious node.

1.2 Types of Wormhole Attack

The wormhole attack is classified into various categories based on several techniques. Numbers of nodes are participating for fixing the path to create it wormhole into following ways (Maidamwar & Chayhan, 2012):

1. **Packet Encapsulation:** In this type, the number of data packet and node are encapsulated between two nasty nodes.

Figure 1. Wormhole Attack in WSN

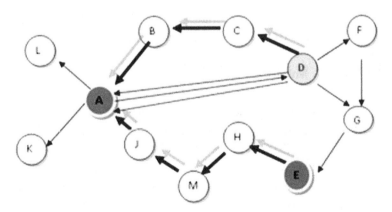

2. **Out-of-Band Channel:** In this type, only single nasty node occurs with the high speed of communication scope.

3. **Packet Relay:** In this type, the nasty node gives replays to all data packets between the source and destination nodes. Finally the duplicate node is created by nasty node.

4. **Protocol Distortion:** Here individual nasty node tries to crack the attack, which is an attack by the routing protocol.

1.3. Intrusion Detection Systems

An intrusion detection system (IDS) is a system, which is used to detect the abnormal node and defends to unauthorized access in the network. Mainly it is classified into two types: misuse IDS and anomaly IDS (Heady & Lugar, 1990). In misuse IDS, the malicious behavior of a node is calculated from the contrast of new data with the previous data. The abnormal activity in the anomaly IDS is identified from the stored normal profile (Rassam, Maarof, & Zainal, 2012). Several schemes were applied for intrusion detection in WSN. In anomaly technique that has no rules for attacks. High false positive rate is the main disadvantage of anomaly detection (Balasubramaniyan, Garcia-Fernandez, Isacoff, Spafford, & Zamboni, 1998). Another technique is also used in WSN, which is called as specification based detection, where both the anomaly and misused detection techniques is used on a single platform (Sardar, Sahoo, & Singh, 2015).

This chapter presents the intrusion detection technique by using trust based system for wormhole attacks, which uses the trust metrics. The trust value of each node is evaluated using some trust parameters. The continuity of this chapter is organized as follows: Section 2 presents the related work in wireless sensor networks. Section 3 covers proposed model for intrusion detection system in wireless sensor networks. Analytical result and discussion are presented in section 4. Finally Section 5 concludes the chapter.

2. RELATED WORK

This section focuses on the different types of intrusion detection technique for wormhole attack as well as trust-based system. The concept of trust evolved from social sciences study, where trust is evaluated between humans. In the year 2004, the trust and reputation systems were used for Wireless Sensor Networks (Chen, Wu, & Zhou, 2007; Roadknight, Parrott, Boyd, & Marshall, 2005). The recent trust calculation technique provides to increase the robustness, resource efficiency and detection performance using different methods such as fuzzy theory, statics, probability theory, graph theory and weighting method (Ishmanov, Malik, Kim, & Begalov,2013;Dey & Santhi, 2005).

2.1 Wormhole Detection Method

As per the authors adopted lightweight countermeasure for wormhole attack called LITEWORP and this result has advantages of very quick detection of wormhole attacks and the loss of fraction of packets is very less (Khalil, Bagchi, & Shroff, 2005). As per the authors describe that, wormhole attacks is found in multipath routing. In case of new root requirements source excess the network with route request (RREQ) and response is waited. The intermediate node only passes away this route request (RREQ). On the same time the receiver will wait to get route after getting route request (RREQ) and statistical analysis of multi-path (SAM) method is introduced that use Pmax and θ which is higher if wormhole attack is present. Pmax gives the probability of the route out of all possible routes and θ (theta) is the difference between top two frequently papered links. If a wormholes attack is more than PMF (probability mass function) then it gives high frequency. Here authors also analyzed the multipath routing and DSR with fine comparisons (Song, Qian, Li, 2005).

As per the authors, Delay per hop indication (DelPHI) method is used to detect wormhole attacks. It is also work on the same principle of comparison of path time distance and predicted distance. This process works in two phases, first is collection of route path by the receivers and senders include a DREQ packets similar to the concept of SAM and sign it before sending. On getting the packet the receiver has to attach with its ID and 1 hop count is increases. The minimum delay and hope count information are utilized for the minimum detection. In the next phase, "Round –Trip Travel Time" (RTT) is used for time different between sender and receiver communication history. In this process the delay per hop value (DPH) is evaluated as per the RTT/2h, where h is the hop count to the definite consecutive. In ordinary case tiny hops have tiny RTT where as in case of wormhole attack the tiny hops are giant RTT. If one delay per hop value (DPH) crosses the threshold value then all paths next to these are treated as under wormholes attacks (Chiu, & Lui, 2006)

Here the authors used a hybrid technique *Wormhole Resistant Hybrid Technique (WRHT)*. It based on watchdog and Delphi Concept. It keeps the record about the packet drop information, delay per each hop and used full phase route information in WSN. Here the authors build up method which is used for wormhole detection in every sensor devices with low costs. WHRT is an advance version AODV routing protocol. The proposed method is to allow for calculating the wormhole presence probability (WPPp) for single route in addition to hop count information in the source node over the sensor networks. At the time of route discovery process, per hop time delay probability (TDP_H) and Time delay probability (TDP_p) is calculated for detecting wormhole attacks. In the next part of the WHRT, another parameter is calculated, which is called per hop packet loss probability(PLP_p). The values of (PLP_p) and (TDP_p) are used for decision making, whether a path P is affected by wormhole attacks or not. So that the routing protocol AODV is taking correct way for the transmission over the sensors network (Singh, Singh, & Singh, 2016; Tyagi, Som, & Rana, 2017).

2.2 Trust Based Detection Technique

Trust management concept is an effective method for detecting abnormal or malicious nodes. In the recent years, the researchers have published number of articles on intrusion detection using the trust concept and its application.

As per the authors the cluster head decide the node trustworthiness, based on direct and indirect recommendation. Cluster Head is considered to be trustworthiness node because it calculated the trust. In this method trust is not calculated on each node in a network. However, the cost of extra energy consumption is high since the trust information is distributed in the network. The major disadvantage of this scheme is that, with a single compromised node the routing operation in the entire network can be paralyzed (Tanachaiwiwat, Bhindwale, & Helmy, 2004).

The authors proposed a model which is based on weighting method to detect malicious nodes by observing their data and maintaining the hierarchy of the network (Atakli, Hu, Chen, Ku, & Su, 2008).

As per the authors proposed a trust calculation algorithm (NBBTE) where each node calculates the direct and indirect trust value of its neighboring nodes using Fuzzy set theory (Feng, Xu, Zhou, & Wan,

2011; Sarkar, Banerjee, & Sangaiah, 2017). The authors proposed a trust approach for detection and prevention method for wormhole attacks in mobile ad hoc networks (MANETs), where numbers of nodes are present in a cluster. In this cluster one cluster head is present and every node is directly interacting with their neighboring node for forwarding the packets to the cluster head with unique id.

As per the authors method, when a new node is enter in the networks then it must be verified by cluster head by using trust value (Singh, Singh, & Agrawal, 2014).

The authors proposed a model, where an efficient distributed trust model for WSNs. Here, the trust of every node is evaluated using direct trust and indirect trust. During the evaluation process of direct trust, it uses some trust metrics such as communication, energy and data packet. When a monitoring node does not have the direct trust value on monitored node for communication, then the indirect trust value is computed based on the recommendations from neighboring node of the monitored node (Jiang, Han, Wang, Shu, & Guizani, 2015).

3. PROPOSED MODEL

In WSN, last few years several researchers have worked on detecting attacks. Here the authors have discussed the propose model of intrusion detection system for wormholes attack using trust based system, which is able to identify the abnormal node in the network. When the communication will take place numbers of nodes is present between the senders to destination. Each node maintains trust value of his neighboring node using Trust table. Initially some trust value is given to each node in the network, In our proposed method, trust value is calculated using some metrices, which is described in trust concept. When a node sends data to the destination, trust value is evaluated based on trust metrics. If the node trust value is larger than the predefined value, then data passes to its next neighbor node otherwise the node does not forward the data to further node i.e. the node whose trust value is less than the predefined threshold is considered as abnormal one.

In the proposed algorithm, the notations are used as follows: $G = (V, E)$ is the network where V is the set of vertices and E is the set of edges. Adjacency link is the data structure on network G. The trust of the vertex $v(i)$ on vertex $v(j)$, which is denoted by $T[i, j]$ that is numeric value. Vertex X and D are the source and destination vertex respectively of this network G. S is the trust value calculation path and here i is the loop index for increment purpose. Finally t is the threshold value which is a predefined numeric value.

3.1 Trust Concept

Now a-days, Wireless Sensor Networks (WSN) are being used for different applications, so this needs security. In this chapter, the authors have described some contribution on trust model and also introduce some technique for intrusion detection using trust concept. In WSN, trust concept plays a vital role for constructing a reliable network. Most of definition of trust in the research article mainly focus on what type of trust is used and how trust is calculated (English, & Nixon, 2002). A trust is defined as confidence level of one node to another node to get assigned work done within the specific time (Momani, 2008) and trust can be used in taking decision of several network in WSN (Lopez, & Roman, 2010).

In the trust model, the authors used several matrices for classification of trust. Here the authors have discussed the concept of Direct Trust (DT) and Indirect Trust (IT). When a trust value is evaluated on

Figure 2. Flowchart for wormhole detection

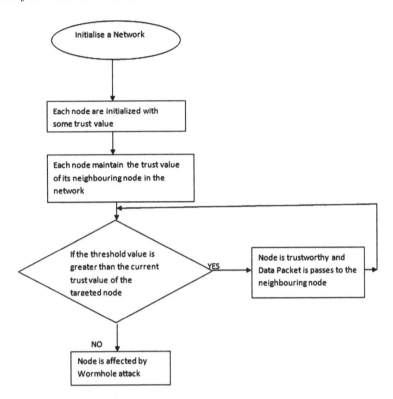

the basis of previous experience with other node is known as Direct Trust and trust value is evaluated on the basis of recommendation from the surrounding node is known as Indirect Trust (Momani, 2008).

In our proposed method, the advantages of using trust concept is used, Here the sensor node has lots of limitation such as low computing power, less memory, less energy. The trust based algorithm are good enough to meet the resource constraint nature of sensor node than other security based approach like LITEWORP, SAM, DelPHI, GRPW and WRHT etc.

3.2 Trust Calculation

Initially, the authors have assign a trust value to every node in the network is set to 05. Mathematically authors calculate the value using the following equation.

$$T\left(i, j\right)^{(t)} = \sum \frac{M_L}{K} \tag{1}$$

where $M_{L=}$ Observed value of each trust metrics, K= number of parameter in the trust metrics.

Algorithm for Wormhole Detection

```
BEGIN
    1. Create a Network G = (V, E)
    2. Construct the adjacency link of G;
    3. Assign initial trust value to each node;
    4. T[i,j]← for each node trust (v ∈ V);
    5. X ← Source Node;
    6. D ← Destination node;
    7. S ← {X};
    8. I ← 1;
       While (D ∉ S)
       For each v∈S for all other node of S as s[i].
       {
       Include v to s[i] iff
       Trust value of s[i] > T[i,j] ∈ Threshold value (t).
       }
       i← i+1;
       }
    9. D consider the first arrived node from the adjacency link of G as trust-
ed node
```

Algorithm for Trust Calculation

```
    1. Begin
    2. For i← 1 to n
    3. For j<-n to (neighbor of i)
    3. Calculate ML for each metrics.
    4. End
```

It can calculate the trust value of a node using these parameters i.e:

```
    1. Control packet
    2. Data Packet
    3. Energy
    4. False packet injection


END
```

3.3 System Model

In the Network model the nodes are deployed randomly. The nodes can broadcast with the neighboring nodes, which are in the communication range. Each node maintain a neighbor table for store the trust values. Trusted node has a trust value above a threshold value (t) in the network.

- The Network is considered to be a simple directed graph G (V, E), where V=Set of sensor nodes and E=Set of order pair (u, v), u,v € V.
- In the data Model each node (v€ S) maintains a neighbor information as Trust T[i,j]
- In the Attack model, the authors have considered wormhole attack. The attackers create a private tunnel between senders to destinations node in the network. Here two attacks connected by a high-speed channel link are placed at different ends of the network. Once the connection is set-up, the attacks collect data packet on one end of the channel and send data packet using the private tunnel and reply them at the other end (Singh, 2012).

4. ANALYTICAL RESULT AND DISCUSSION

The proposed scheme is evaluated uses Packet Delivery Ratio (PDR) and End-to-End Delay. It is analyzed in MATLAB tool. The node sends data through the trusted node. In this setup the authors assume that if the receiver is within the communication range then the node receives the data and considered transmission and propagation scheme, which are randomly selected. Table 1 shows the various parameters and their values used in the simulation of the proposed scheme.

1. **End-to-End Delay:** It is evaluated, when the data transmit between two trusted nodes from sender to receiver. The metric should be minimized for enhanced performance.

Table 1. Test bed parameters

Parameters	Values
Nodes in Network	100
Network Area	750 x750 M^2
Communication Range	50Ms
Data Rate	250kbps
Packet Size	100 bytes
Malicious Node	5-25%
No. of Runs	10
Initial Trust value	5
Trust threshold value	5

$$t_{d(i,j)} = t_{trans} + t_{prop} + t_{proc} + t_{queue} \tag{2}$$

where, t_{trans} = Transmission Delay, t_{prop} = Propagation Delay, t_{proc} = Processing Delay and t_{queue} = Queuing Delay. If 'n' numbers of nodes are taken than (n-1) links are there and the Total Delay is calculated.

$$Total\ Delay\left(T\right)_d = \left(\left(n-1\right) * T_d\,(\mathbf{i,j})\right) \tag{3}$$

2. **Packet Delivery Ratio (PDR):** To calculate the PDR, the authors assume that, if we send packets to a transmit node then PDR is between 0.75 -0.95, which is randomly generated.

$$PDR = \left(\frac{Packet\ Size}{DTR} + \frac{d}{c}\right) \tag{4}$$

The authors have injected 05-25 number of malicious node in the propose network to study the performance of the network and the result are taken from the average of 10 runs.

We compare the end-to-end delay graph of our scheme with that of the Kamini et al., (2014). As shown in Figure 3, when number of wormhole attackers is more than end to end delay is simultaneously decreased. In Kamini et al., (2014), when the wormhole attackers are 5, 10, 15, 20 and 25 than end to end delay is increased respectively, so it is not effective to detect the attacks at the network layer.

We compare the PDR graph of our scheme with that of the Kamini et al., (2014). As shown in Figure 4, when number of wormhole attackers is more than PDR is simultaneously increased. In Kamini et al., (2014), when the wormhole attackers are 5, 10, 15, 20 and 25 than PDR is decreased respectively, so it is not effective to detect the attacks at the network layer.

Figure 3. End to End Delay

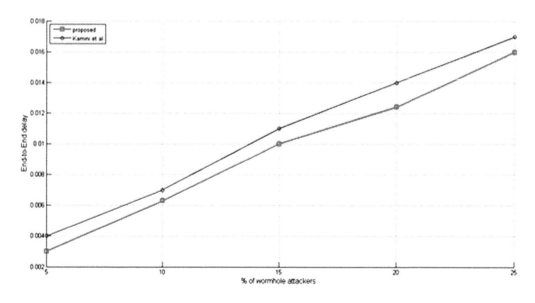

Figure 4. Packet Delivery Ratio

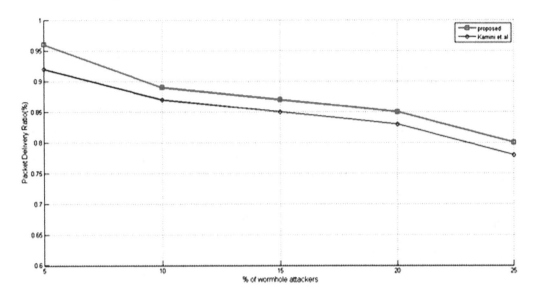

5. CONCLUSION

In this chapter number of methodologies discussed for detecting wormhole attack. Therefore, we believe that the analysis on this chapter is helping us for developing the new method to detect wormhole attacks in WSN. Finally, by evaluating the trust value of each node using different metrics and till date open research challenges studied are required for detection wormhole attacks as well as other attacks. In future we will add some different matrices for trust calculation with routing protocol at different layers in WSN.

REFERENCES

Atakli, I. M., Hu, H., Chen, Y., Ku, W.S., & Su, Z. (2008). Malicious node detection in wireless sensor networks using weighted trust evaluation. *Proceedings of the Symposium on Simulation of Systems Security.*

Bagchi & Shroff. (2005). LITEWORP: A Lightweight Countermeasure for the Wormhole Attack in Multi hop Wireless Networks. *Proceedings of the International Conference on Dependable Systems and Networks.*

Balasubramaniyan, J. S., Garcia-Fernandez, J. O., Isacoff, D., & Spafford, E. (1998). An architecture for intrusion detection using autonomous agents. In *ACSAC'98: Proceedings of the 14th Annual Computer Security Applications Conference.* IEEE Computer Society.

Bao, Chen, Chang, & Cho. (2012). Hierarchical Trust Management for Wireless Sensor Networks and its Applications to Trust-Based Routing and Intrusion Detection. *IEEE Transactions on Network and Service Management.*

Boukerch, A., Xu, L., & El-Khatib, K. (2007). Trust-based security for wireless ad hoc and sensor networks. *Computer Communications, 30*(11-12), 2413–2427. doi:10.1016/j.comcom.2007.04.022

Chen, H., Wu, H., & Zhou, X. (2007). Agent based Trust model in wireless sensor networks. In *Eight AICS International Conference on software Engineering, Artificial Intelligence, Networking and Parrallel Distributed Computing.* IEEE.

Chiu, H. S., & Lui, K. (2006). DelPHI: Wormhole Detection Mechanism for Ad Hoc Wireless Networks. *Proceedings of International Symposium on Wireless Pervasive Computing.* 10.1109/ISWPC.2006.1613586

Das, H., Naik, B., Pati, B., & Panigrahi, C. R. (2014). A Survey on Virtual Sensor Networks Framework. *International Journal of Grid and Distributed Computing, 7*(5), 121–130. doi:10.14257/ijgdc.2014.7.5.11

Dey & Santhi. (n.d.). Intelligent Techniques in Signal Processing for Multimedia Security. In *Computational Intelligence and Complexity.* Springer.

Dey, Samanta, Yang, Das, & Choudhuri. (2005). Optimization of scaling factors in electrocardiogram signal watermarking using cuckoo Search. *International Journal of Bio Inspire Computation.*

Du, J., & Li, J. (2011). A Study of Security Routing Protocol For Wireless Sensor Network. *International Conference on Instrumentation, Measurement, Computer, Communication and Control.* 10.1109/IMCCC.2011.68

English, C., & Nixon, P. (2002). Dynamic trust Models for Ubiquitous Computing Environment. Presented at *Ubicomp security workshop.*

Feng, R., Xu, X., Zhou, X., & Wan, J. (2011). A trust evaluation algorithm for wireless sensor networks based on node behaviors and d-s evidence theory. *Sensors (Basel), 11*(12), 1345–1360. doi:10.3390110201345 PMID:22319355

Heady, R., & Lugar, G. (2009). *MThe architecture of a network level intrusion detection system. Technical report.* Albuquerque, NM: University of New Mexico.

Ishmanov, F. (2013). *Trust management system in wireless sensor networks: Design considerations and research challenges.* Transaction Emerging Telecommunication Techno.

Jiang, I., Han, G., Wang, F., Shu, L., & Guizani, M. (2015). Han, G.; Wang, F.; Shu, L.; Guizani, M. "An efficient distributed trust model for wireless sensor networks. *IEEE Transactions on Parallel and Distributed Systems, 26*(5), 1228–1237. doi:10.1109/TPDS.2014.2320505

Lopez, J., & Roman, R. (2010). Trust management system for WSN: Best Practices. *Computer Communications.* doi:10.1016/j.comcom.2010.02.006

Maidamwar & Chavhan. (2012). A Survey on Security Issues to Detect wormhole Attack in Wireless Sensor network. *International Journal on Ad Hoc Networking Systems.*

Momani. (2008). *Bayesian Methods for modeling and Management of trust in WSN* (Ph.D Thesis). University of Technology, Sydney, Australia.

Panigrahi, C. R., Sarkar, J., Pati, B., & Das, H. (2016). S2S: a novel approach for source to sink node communication in wireless sensor networks. *International Conference on Mining Intelligence and Knowledge Exploration.*

Rassam, M. A., Maarof, M. A., & Zainal, A. (2012). A Survey of Intrusion Detection Schemes in Wireless Sensor Networks. *American Journal of Applied Sciences*.

Roadknight, C., Parrott, L., Boyd, N., & Marshall, I. (2005). A novel approach for real-time data management in wireless sensor networks. *International Journal of Distributed Sensor Networks*, *1*(2), 215–225. doi:10.1080/15501320590966468

Sabri & Kamoun. (2016). *GRPW-MuS-S: A Secure Enhanced Trust Aware Routing against Wormhole Attacks in Wireless Sensor Networks*. Academic Press.

Sadar, A. R., & Sahoo, R. R. (2014). Intelligent Intrusion Detection System in WSN. *Proceeding of the 3rd Int. Conf. on Front. of Intelligence Computation (FICTA)*.

Sarkar, M., Banerjee, S., & Sangaiah, A. (2017). Trust Management Model based on Fuzzy Approach for Ubiquitous Computing. *International Journal of Ambient Computing and Intelligence*.

Sing, K., & Singh, G. (2014). A trust based Approach for Detection and Prevention of Wormhole Attack in MANET. *International Journal of Computers and Applications*.

Singh. (2012). A Survey of different techniques for detection of wormhole attack in Wireless Sensor Network. *International Journal of Scientific and Engineering Research*.

Singh, M., & Das, R. (2012). *A survey of Different techniques for Detection of Wormhole attack in Wireless Sensor Network*. IJSER.

Singh, Singh, & Singh. (2016). WHRT: A Hybrid Technique For Detecting Of Wormhole Attack in Wireless Sensor Networks. In *Mobile Information Systems*. Hindawi Publishing Corporation.

Song, N., Qian, L., & Li, X. (2005). Wormhole Attacks Detection in Wireless Ad Hoc Networks: A Statistical Analysis Approach. *Proceedings of the 19th IEEE International Parallel and Distributed Processing Symposium*. 10.1109/IPDPS.2005.471

Tanachaiwiwat, S., Bhindwale, R., & Helmy, A. (2004). Location-centric isolation of misbehavior and trust routing in energy-constrained sensor networks. *IEEE International Conference on Performance, Computing, and Communications*. 10.1109/PCCC.2004.1395061

Tiwari, M., Veer Arya, K., Choudhari, R., & Sidharth Choudhary, K. (2009). Designing Intrusion Detection to Detect Black hole and Selective Forwarding Attack in WSN based on local Information. *Fourth International Conference on Computer Sciences and Convergence Information Technology*. 10.1109/ICCIT.2009.290

Tyagi, S., Som, S., & Rana, Q. (2017). Trust based Dynamic Multicast Group Routing Ensuring Reliability for Ubiquitous Environment in MANETs. *International Journal of Ambient Computing and Intelligence*, *8*(1), 70–97. doi:10.4018/IJACI.2017010104

Yamin, M., & Abi Sen, A. (2017). Improving Privacy and Security of User Data in Location Based Services. *International Journal of Ambient Computing and Intelligence*.

Chapter 11
UWDBCSN Analysis During Node Replication Attack in WSN

Harpreet Kaur
Thapar University, India

Sharad Saxena
Thapar University, India

ABSTRACT

Wireless sensor network is an emerging area in which multiple sensor nodes are present to perform many real-time applications like military application, industrialized automation, health monitoring, weather forecast, etc. Sensor nodes can be organized into a group which is led by a cluster head; this concept is known as clustering. Clustering of wireless sensor network is used when sensor nodes want to communicate simultaneously in a single network. The author organizes the sensor nodes by applying UWDBCSN (underwater density-based clustering sensor network) clustering approach in which routing of the packets is controlled by cluster head. The author also considers the security of sensor nodes which are harmful to different types of mischievous attacks like wormhole attack, denial of service attack, replication or cloning attack, blackhole attack, etc. Node replication is one of the types in which an attacker tries to capture the node and generate the replica or clone of that node in the same network. So, this chapter describes how to deal with these types of attacks. The author used the intrusion detection process to deal with this type of attack. All the detection procedure is combined with sleep/wake scheduling algorithm to increase the performance of sensor nodes in the network.

INTRODUCTION

Wireless sensor networks include the large number of multiple sensor nodes which are used for monitoring purposes such as elementary monitoring, forecast monitoring, early earthquake detection, military application etc. The sensor nodes are grouped together to perform the multiple tasks simultaneously which is monitored by a head selected by clusters of nodes in the network. The selection of cluster head is done by the sensor nodes and this overall concept of sending the data through cluster head is known as Clustering (Boyinbode, Le, Mbogho, Takizawa, & Poliah, 2010). Clustering is important when the

DOI: 10.4018/978-1-5225-5152-2.ch011

Copyright © 2018, IGI Global. Copying or distributing in print or electronic forms without written permission of IGI Global is prohibited.

multiple sensor nodes are targeted to perform the single important task. It is energy efficient and less time is used for the packet transmission because the nodes communicate through cluster head. The different clustering algorithm has been proposed like LEACH, LEACH-C, UWDBCSN, LNCA etc. are consider of having same clustering approach but routing mechanisms are different. Figure 1 below shows the clustering of various sensor nodes. The sensor nodes are organized into clusters which tend to perform similar type of tasks like in data mining.

Attacks on Wireless Sensor Networks

The author discussed about the various types of malicious attacks (Savner & Gupta, 2014) which are responsible for destroying the security of wireless sensor networks such as node replication attack, wormhole attack, jellyfish attack, Sybil attack etc. Security is major important concern because many applications directly or indirectly depend upon sensor network. They are used in everywhere in today's era. The author considered one of the dangerous types of attacks in which malicious user try to inject the attacking or malicious nodes in order to generate many insider threats. This attack is known as node replication attack. The different types of attacks on wireless sensor network are explained in Figure 2.

- **Jamming Attack (Li, Koutsopoulos, & Poovendran, 2010):** Jamming attack blocks the channel due to which the genuine nodes are unable to access the wireless communication. It is also known as denial of service attack which disrupts the normal functioning of the network and leads to many insider threats.
- **Wormhole Attack (Alajmi, 2014):** In wormhole attack, the malicious user creates the fake tunnel in the routing path of the sender and the destination nodes so that the sending node will use the fake tunnel for the immediate packet transmission and redirected them to their malicious network in order to halt the communication.
- **Sybil Attack:** In Sybil attack, the malicious attacking nodes possess the different fake identities in the same network and generate the confusion among different genuine nodes in order to increase the network delay.

Figure 1. Clustering in WSN

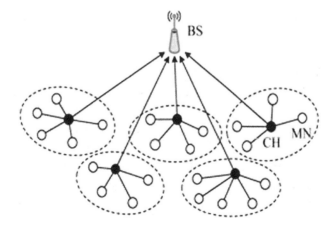

Figure 2. Different types of attacks in WSN

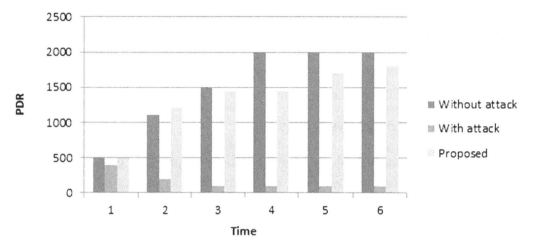

- **Jellyfish Attack (Kaur, Sarangal, & Nayyar, 2014):** In jellyfish attack, the malicious user injects the jellyfish node in the routing path and takes participation in all the communication between sender and receiver node. The jellyfish node appears as a genuine node which will steal the packet information and use in an inefficient way.

- **Routing Attack (Abdelaziz, Nafaa, & Salim, 2013):** In routing attack, the malicious adversary tries to route the packets in order to perform various attacks and mislead the normal functioning of the network. This type of attack is proved to be dangerous because they disrupt the network's activity by introducing the fake routes between the paths of the network.

- **Node Replication Attack (Mishra & Turuk, 2015):** Replication is considered to be great threat to the security of wsn. In this attack, an attacker tries to capture the sensor nodes by extracting the credentials of genuine sensor nodes, after capturing the attacker create the clone or replica of the genuine node in the same network in order to pretend that the injected clone is same as that of genuine node (Game & Raut, 2014). Replicas are very difficult to identify because they appear as legitimate node in the network. There may be case that attacker targets the multiple sensor nodes by capturing the whole cluster or cluster head and generate the clone or replica of whole cluster (Ho, 2009). Figure 3 below shows the node replication attack in sensor network.

BACKGROUND

Background study includes the concept of clustering applied to the sensor nodes using clustering algorithms like LNCA, UWDBCSN, LEACH, LEACH-C, NI-LEACH etc. Then secure communication is ensuring in these routing protocols. The previous study showed that the hierarchical clustering is used during node replication attack in sensor network using different-different clustering routing protocols that the author discussed below:

(Znaidi, Minier, & Ubeda, 2013) introduced the hierarchical node replication attack detection in sensor network and the algorithm used is LNCA (Local Negotiated Clustering Approach) (Xia & Vlajic, 2007). LNCA is a hierarchical distributed clustering routing protocol in which election mechanism is

Figure 3. Node replication attack

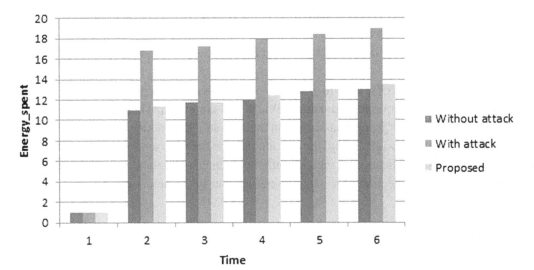

done using node degree which means the node with high number of immediate neighbor is considered as cluster head and other becomes its member. This election is done dynamically in which the node degree is calculated by each node in the network. Then the author analyses the behavior of node replication attack and detection is done using Bloom filter mechanism (Tarkoma, Rothenberg, & Lagerspetz, 2011). Each cluster head calculates the hash function and check the authenticity of each member in its circle. When the cluster head found the two different locations of same node Id, then alert is generated which indicate that there is a presence of cloning or replicated node in the network.

(Cheng, Guo, Yang, & Wang, 2015) proposed the energy efficient clustering protocol NI-LEACH which is an improvement over LEACH. The selection of cluster head is based on the energy value stored by each node and give only number of cluster head which are optimal in number. In addition, an intrusion detection process is introduced by the author who is based on the implementation of monitoring nodes. The detection rate is high in this case because multiple monitor nodes exchange the special encoder function and detect the replicated node in an efficient way.

(Tripathi & Gaur, 2013) proposed the centralized clustering detection of node replication attack in wireless sensor network. In this, the author used LEACH-C protocol which is an enhanced version of LEACH. Author used the witness node technique which has the ability to identify the replication of whole cluster if any. The witness nodes identify the replicated node ids which are generated by an attacker and alert the other sensor nodes. This approach is proved to be highly efficient in determining the replication attack.

(Saxena, Mishra, & Singh, 2013) proposed the energy efficient UWDBCSN (under-water density based clustering sensor network) which is used to perform clustering in acoustic sensor networks. The algorithm performs the selection operation of cluster head based on node density. The network model manages energy model where each node is associated with certain amount of energy and the nodes are divided into low level energy nodes and high-level energy nodes. The node which is having highest energy is selected as cluster head and its member nodes are having lowest energy and in the same way the low energy sensor nodes cover the maximum of high energy sensor nodes (Tomar, Kevre, & Shrivastava,

2015). So, in this way overall energy is maintained and hence this is appropriate method as compared to LEACH clustering. Following Figure 4 shows the UWDBCSN clustering of sensor nodes.

The author performs the UWDBCSN clustering on the randomly deployed nodes in the considered wireless sensor network. Later, the same is analyzed in the presence of node replication attack and network performance is compared.

The objective of this book chapter is to check the network performance under replication attack. The randomly deployed nodes are organized using UWDBCSN algorithm. Then node replication attack is performed in which the author made an assumption that two attacking nodes are injected which increase the packet dropping in the network and fail the communication between sender and the destination nodes. For the detection of node replication attack, the author presented the defending technique Dydog detection which is an intrusion detection process as discussed later in the next section.

MAIN FOCUS OF THE CHAPTER

The main focus of this chapter is to organize the randomly deployed nodes using energy efficient algorithm and furthermore node replication attack is detected which is found to be dangerous among sensor nodes. The author has compared the network performance on the basis of performance parameters.

Issues, Controversies, Problems

- Wireless sensor networks are found to be vulnerable to many attacks such as replication, spoofing, routing, wormhole, Sybil attack etc.
- There should be secure routing of packets which would ensure the authenticity, integrity and confidentiality of packets.

Figure 4. UWDBCSN clustering

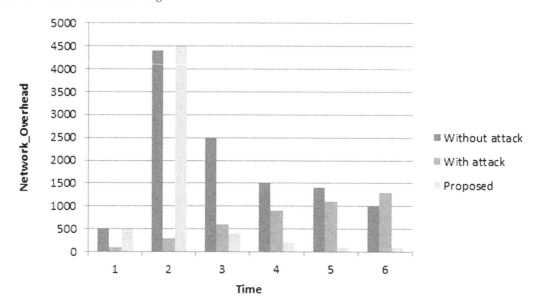

- Every node participated in the transmission procedure so there is a need to organize the node so that overall energy used is less and an efficient energy consuming process is followed by each and every sensor node.
- The replication attack after capturing the node may generate many insider threats which halt the secure communication between the sensor nodes.
- The network performance is degraded when the attacking nodes are introduced because packet drop is more. So, network performance must be a biggest concert.
- The main challenge is to maintain the energy level acquired by each sensor node in which lifetime of the network depends. If the energy is lowest then the network is no more and cannot able to perform further transmission process.
- Different node replication attack detection protocols are introduced by various researchers. But there is still need of improvement because the security of sensor network is biggest area of concern as they are used in various applications.

These are the problems and issues that should be taken into consideration. Keeping all the issues in the mind, the author proposed the solution which is proved to be efficient.

SOLUTIONS AND RECOMMENDATIONS

The author first introduces the clustering approach UWDBCSN in order to locate the multiple sensor nodes into groups which is known as cluster head, then node replication attack is performed to check the network performance, later Dydog intrusion detection process (Janakiraman, Rajasoundaran, & Narayanasamy, 2012) is applied to detect or prevent the node replication attack.

- **Network Model:** The author considered to work upon fixed number of sensor nodes which constructed a wireless sensor network. Author proposed a three-tier structure which includes sensor nodes with low energy or high energy and a base station. All the nodes are equally distributed initially with unique identification number and cluster head election mechanism is done using UWDBCSN algorithm. The structure works as follows: the sensor nodes when want to communicate send their data to the selected cluster head and cluster head then forwards the request to the sink station or base station. The author made an assumption that a malicious user is somewhere present in the network and targets the communication between the sensor nodes. The malicious user extracts all the cryptographic materials of sensor nodes and generates the replica inside the same network. In this way malicious user able to inject the replicated or attacking nodes. Our main focus is on the detection of the replicated or attacking nodes and stops the packet drop so that the sensor nodes are able to communicate securely. The author has used Dydog detection in which monitoring nodes are participating to detect the attacking or replicated nodes and tries to remove or prevent this attack. Figure 5 below represents the graphic view of hierarchical architecture in network simulator that the author considered in his implementation.

Figure 5. Network model

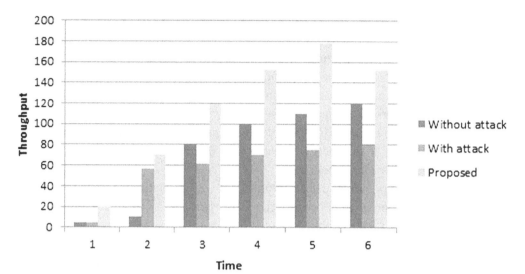

- **UWDBCSN Analysis and Detection Procedure:**
  - **UWDBCSN Analysis:** Initially, the author considers there is malicious activity between the communicating entities and the packet transmission is normal between source and the destination nodes. The randomly deployed sensor nodes are organized into clusters using UWDBCSN clustering algorithm which could be explained as follows:
    - Sensor nodes with high energy or low energy are considered.
    - The selection is based on their energy value, so energy model is main consideration while electing the cluster head.
    - The one which is having high value of energy is selected as cluster head and other sensor node start the request message in order to become the member of cluster head.
    - Cluster head checks the energy level and authenticity. Cluster head with high energy always likely to cover the more number of low energy sensors. So that the overall energy consume is less.
    - After cluster formation, the sensor nodes start the normal packet transmission through their cluster head which forward the request to the sink station or base station.

The figure below shows the graphic view of formation of 4 cluster heads using UWDBCSN algorithm. The pink color nodes are cluster head and all the green color nodes are its member. The blue color node is the sink station which can be the destination node. The Figure 6 only shows the formation of one cluster with one cluster head.

- **Node Replication Attack Detection Procedure:** The author proposed the intrusion detection process based on the clustered hierarchical structure. The algorithm is based on the implementation of monitoring nodes which are responsible for the detection of replicated node in the network. Different detection keys are maintained by these monitoring nodes. The algorithm is divided into five steps which could be explained as follows:

Figure 6. Cluster head Election

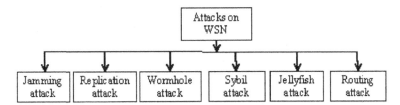

○ **Distribution Step:** The distribution step includes the unique identification key for each node in the wireless sensor network. This also include the cryptographic materials such as public and private key, digital hash signatures and hash function which is computed and verified at each step of authentication.

○ **Election of Cluster Head using UWDBCSN:** When unique identification number has been given to every node, then there is selection of cluster head using UWDBCSN as discussed in previous section. The selection is done on random basis because when the node transmits the data, energy is decreased by 1 factor. At that point the node which is having value of energy as highest is elected as cluster head. The cluster head is the one which is responsible for the overall communication between the sensor and the destination nodes.

○ **Injection of Attacking Nodes:** When the nodes are organized and there is normal transmission of data packets among the sensor nodes. This step assumes that there are two attacking nodes which are injected by the malicious users and packet drop has begun because the malicious nodes continuously tried to send the data packets and generate the flood of requests which lead to many insider threats to the important information. The following Figure 7 shows the packet drop due to the presence of attacking nodes shown in red color.

○ **Detection using Dydog Method:** Dydog method (Janakiraman, Rajasoundaran, & Narayanasamy, 2012) is a dynamic intrusion detection method which includes the multiple monitoring nodes that will also act as monitoring nodes or data forwarding nodes. Secure session key management algorithm is used for the selection of monitoring nodes which check the authenticity or verify each and every sensor nodes. This method has been proved to reduce high error rate in the wireless sensor network. The attacker is unable to create or inject the malicious or attacking nodes in the sensor network due to the presence of secure monitoring nodes. In this way the author tries to increase the security of wireless sensor network.

• **Select the Monitoring Nodes:** The nodes which are immediate neighbor of sender nodes are selected as intrusion detection nodes. They may be large in number depending upon the node degree which is the number of nodes present in their immediate area. The selection procedure follows the secure management approach. When the data forwarding nodes are not monitored by their immediate neighbor, then the two-hop neighbor node will act as intrusion detection node. In this way selection is done dynamically, as shown in Table 1.

• **Secure Routing or Management Algorithm:** Each sensor node in the network will maintain the shared secret key which is used to differentiate the genuine nodes from the attacking nodes. At every step, authentication action is performed by monitoring nodes. When the packet drop starts the neighbor, node will act as watchdog which take care of all the data communication between the sensor nodes and the sink node.

- **Deciding Module of Intrusion Detection Nodes:** Since there are multiple intrusion detection nodes but there is only one deciding node which will decide what should be the secure path followed by the data forwarding nodes in which attacking nodes are not present. The forwarding node shares its private keys with all the monitoring or intrusion detection nodes. All the intrusion detection nodes send their data bits with their TTL (time to live) value. Then forwarding node declares the deciding intrusion detection node which is having low TTL value. Then the intrusion detection node will decide which secure route should be followed in order to prevent the attack. During this process, other nodes will go into idle state to save their energy.

  ○ **Revocation Message:** After the monitoring nodes perform the detection, if they find any attacking nodes or replicated nodes, then the intrusion detection nodes will generate the alert in order to inform the other sensor nodes to stop their communication for a second until they decide which secure path should be followed for secure communication. The attacker probability to inject the replicated nodes is very less because the Dydog method (Varshney, Sharma, & Sharma, 2014) can be able to detect the multiple attacking nodes in the sensor network. Network replies are verified by each cluster head which will check the authenticity by looking at their data bits or keys associated with them.

  ○ **Sleep/Wake Scheduling Algorithm (Manirajan & SathishKumar, 2015):** The Dydog detection is combined with sleep/wake scheduling algorithm in order to increase the performance of the network. With sleep/wake approach, all those nodes who do not take part in the transmission can be able to change their state from wake state to sleep state. So, the overall energy of the network can be saved. Figure 8 shows the sleep/wake algorithm applied in addition to Dydog method in which grey nodes are in sleep state and green nodes are in wake state or participate in the transmission process.

Simulation Results

The author has compared the performance of the hierarchical network considering 500 sensor nodes on the five parameters such as throughput, packet delivery ratio, energy used, network overhead and end to end delay. the results show the efficient detection of the replication attack with Dydog intrusion detection process and the network's lifetime is increased using sleep/wake scheduling algorithm. The simulation results have been shown in the graph.

Figure 7. Injection of two attacking nodes

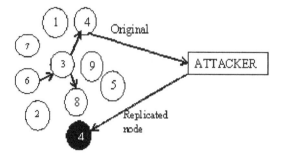

Table 1.

```
n_f :forwarding node
n_1 :one-hop neighbor node
n_2 :two-hop neighbor node
Id_s: Id of the sender node
Id_r: Id of the receiver node in n_f
data_s : data bit of sender node
data_r : data bit of receiver node in n_f
n: node taken for selection process
```

n_f $\underrightarrow{Id_s|| data_s}$ **n_1** $\underrightarrow{Id (n_1) XOR Id_s|| data_s}$ **n_2**

n_1 $\underrightarrow{Id (n_2)}$ **n_f**

n_2 $\underrightarrow{Id_s|| data_s XOR Id (n_1) XOR Id (n_2) via n_1}$ **n_f**

```
here, keys are k_1 : Id_s|| data_s XOR Id (n_1)
                k_2 : Id_s|| data_s XOR Id (n_1) XOR Id (n_2)
In k_1 → n_f or k_2 → n_f check
    If (Id_r == Id_s && data_r == data_s)
    {
        n → IDN (intrusion detection node)
    }
    Else
    {
        n → malicious node
    }
end
```

Table 2.

```
DMIDN: decision making intrusion detection node
IDNs: intrusion detection node
i: initial data packet
ack: acknowledgement
Condition applied:
DMIDN ∈ IDN (s)
```

n_f $\underrightarrow{key+ data bit+ TTL}$ IDN (s);

IDN(s) $\underrightarrow{\underset{Data bit+TTL}{Req}}$ n_f;

IDN(s) → DMIDN; iff TTL==TTL_s;

Then n_f $\underrightarrow{data_i+ ack_i}$ DMIDN ;

Figure 8. Sleep/wake Scheduling algorithm

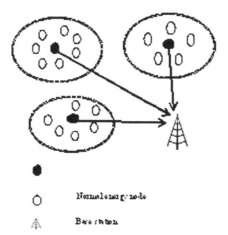

Normal energy node

Base station

- **End to End Delay:** A packet will take the total time to reach to the desired destination is called end to end delay. The figure 9 shows the delay with respect to time where the delay in the presence of attacking nodes increased as compared to the normal environment but when the author used Dydog detection integrated with sleep/wake scheduling, then the delay decreased by certain amount.
- **Packet Delivery Ratio:** It defines the ratio of the number of packets sent by the source node and the number of packets received by the destination node. The figure 10 shows the delivery of packets reduce when the attacking nodes are introduced in the network as compared to the normal environment. When the author used the intrusion detection Dydog method, then delivery of packets will be more. So delivery of packet ratio increases.
- **Energy Consumption:** It is the energy consumed during the packets transmission by each node and calculates the total energy of the whole network. The energy consumed by the attacking nodes is increased because they perform the packet dropping attack when a genuine node tries to send the packet to the base station through cluster head by duplicating their ids. When the author used Dydog method in addition to sleep/wake scheduling algorithm, the overall energy consumption will be less, and the network lifetime also increased show in Figure 11.
- **Network Overhead:** The amount of resources used by every sensor node in the network such as bandwidth, energy, memory, time etc. the overhead tends to increase in case of attacking nodes because the attacking nodes drop the large amount of packets during transmission and try to send the multiple requests to the destination node or cluster head. Figure 12 shows, when Dydog method is used the overhead is decreased by some amount because the monitoring nodes are only in the active state and other nodes go to the sleep state which decreased the certain amount of overhead in the network.
- **Throughput:** The successful complete delivery of the sent packets by the sender node to the destination node is called throughput. Throughput decreases when attacking nodes perform their attacking activity in the network and tend to harm the network security. The author increases the throughput rate by introducing the concept of Dydog detection followed by sleep/wake scheduling algorithm. Figure 13 shows the throughput with respect to time.

Figure 9. End to End delay versus time

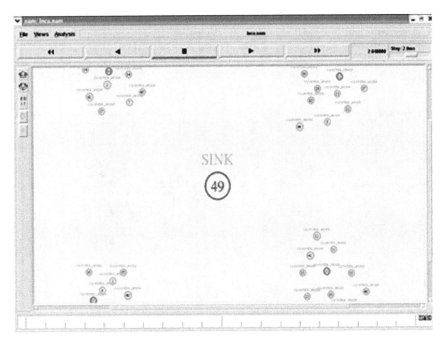

Figure 10. PDR versus time

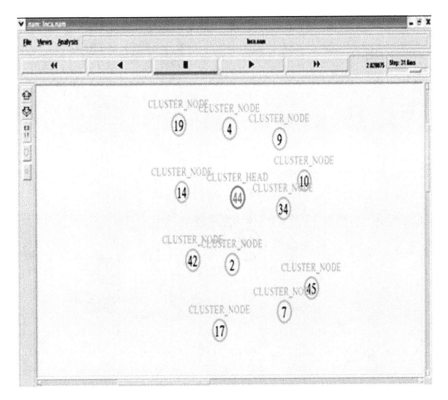

Figure 11. Energy consumption versus time

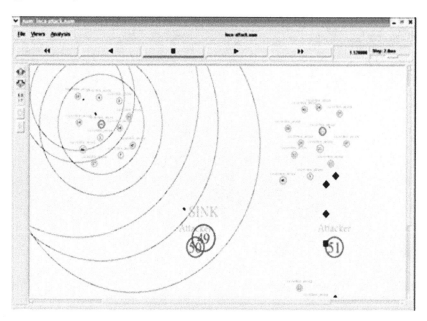

Figure 12. Network overhead versus time

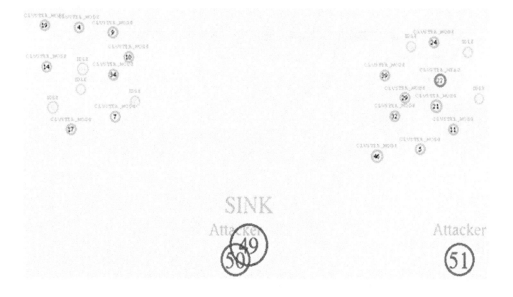

Figure 13. Throughput versus time

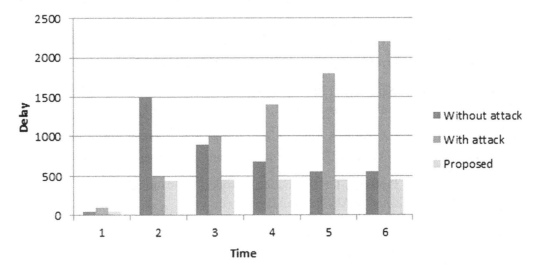

FUTURE RESEARCH DIRECTIONS

The author has proved that the introduced algorithm is efficient for the detection of attacking or replicated nodes in the network. The author suggested that the future work may include the detection of all other different types of attack like Sybil node attack, jellyfish attack, wormhole attack etc. The prevention of the attacking nodes will also be considered by using the same Dydog approach. The security of cluster head will also be considered including optimum number of sensor nodes in the network.

CONCLUSION

The security of sensor nodes should be a major or important consideration in the wireless sensor network because sensors are used everywhere in today's world. Author main focused on the concept of security in the network which can be harmed by various malicious attacks such as jellyfish attack, routing attack, wormhole attack, Sybil attack etc. There is a need to secure the senor node's activity in the network. The author has applied the UWDBCSN clustering algorithm to arrange the sensor nodes under cluster head and then analyses the network behavior under node replication attack. The intrusion detection process is used for detection which is done using monitoring nodes and proved to be efficient and the overall detection procedure is integrated with sleep/wake scheduling algorithm in order to enhance the performance of the network.

REFERENCES

Abdelaziz, A. K., Nafaa, M., & Salim, G. (2013). Survey of Routing Attacks and Countermeasures in Mobile Ad Hoc Networks. Computer Modelling Simulation (UKSim).

Alajmi,N. (2014). Wireless Sensor Networks Attacks and Solutions. *International Journal of Computer Science and Information Security.*

Boyinbode, O., Le, H., Mbogho, A., Takizawa, M., & Poliah, R. (2010). A Survey on Clustering Algorithms for Wireless Sensor Networks. Network-Based Information Systems (NBiS).

Butun, I., Morgera, S. D., & Sankar, R. (2015). A Surevy of Intrusion Detection Systems in Wireless Sensor Networks. *IEEE Communications Surveys and Tutorials*, 266–282.

Cheng, G., Guo, S., Yang, Y., & Wang, Y. (2015). *Replication attack detection with monitor nodes in clustered wireless sensor networks. In IEEE 34th International Performance.* IPCCC.

Game,S.,& Raut,C. (2014). Protocols for Detection of Node Replication Attack on Wireless sensor Network. *IOSR Journal of Computer Engineering*, 1-11.

Gupta,V., & Sangroha,D. (n.d.). Protection against packet drop attack. *Advances in Engineering and Technology Research (ICAETR).*

Ho, J. (2009). Distributed Detection Replica Cluster Attacks in Sensor Networks using Sequential Analysis. *Distributed Detection Replica Cluster Performance, Computing and Commuincations Conference (IPCCC).*

Janakiraman, S., Rajasoundaran, S., & Narayanasamy, P. (2012). *The Model- Dynamic and Flexible Intrusion Detection Protocol for high error rate Wireless Sensor Networks based on data flow. In Computing, Communication and Applications (ICCCA).* Tamilnadu, India: Dindigul.

Jin, H., & Chen, H. (2008). Lightweight session key management scheme in Sensor Networks. Future Generation Communication and Networking (FGCN 2007).

Kaur, M., Sarangal, M., & Nayyar, A. (2014). Simulation of Jelly Fish Periodic Attack in Mobile Ad hoc Networks. *International Journal of Computer Trends and Technology*, *15*(1), 20–22. doi:10.14445/22312803/IJCTT-V15P104

Li, M., Koutsopoulos, I., & Poovendran, R. (2010). Optimal Jamming attack strategies and Network Defense Policies in Wireless Senosr Networks. *IEEE Transactions on Mobile Computing*, 1119–1133.

Li, Y., Zhang, A., & Liang, Y. (2013). *Improvement of leach Protocol for Wireless Sensor Networks. In Instrumentation, Measurement, Computer, Communication and Control.* Shenyang, China: IMCCC.

Manirajan, R., & Sathishkumar, R.K. (2015). Sleep/Wake Scheduling for Target Coverage Problem in Wireless Sensor Networks. *International Journal of Advanced Research in Computer and Communication Engineering.*

Mishra, A. K., & Turuk, A. K. (2015). A Comparative Analysis of Node Replica Detection Scheme in Wireless Sensor Networks. *Journal of Network and Computer Applications*, 21–32.

Nazir, B., & Hasbullah, H. (2011). Dynamic sleep scheduling for minimizing delay in Wireless Sensor Network. *Electronics, Communications and Photonics Conference (SIECPC).*

Pelechrinis, K., Lliofotou, M., & Krishnamurthy, S. V. (2011). *Denial of Service Attacks in Wireless Networks: The Case of Jammers.* IEEE Communications Surverys & Tutorials.

Salva-Garau, F., & Stojanovic, M. (2003). Multi-Cluster Protocol for Ad-hoc Mobile Underwater Acoustic Network. *IEEE OCEANS'03 Conference.*

Savner, J., & Gupta, V. (2014). *Clustering Of Mobile Ad-hoc Networks: An approach for black hole prevention. In Issues and Challenges in Intelligent Computing Techniques.* Ghaziabad, India: ICICT.

Saxena, S., Mishra, S., & Singh, M. (2013). Clustering Based on Node Density in Hetergeneous Under-Water Sensor Networks. *Information Technology and Computer Science*, 49-55.

Tamane, S., Kumar Solanki, V., & Dey, N. (2017). Privacy and Security Policies in Big Data. *Advances in Information Security, Privacy, and Ethics*, 305.

Tarkoma,S., Rothenberg, C.E.,& Lagerspetz,E. (2011). Theory and Practice of Bloom Filters for Distributed Systems. *IEEE Communication Surveys & Tutorials*, 131-155.

Tomar,G.S., Kevre,P., & Shrivastava,L. (2015). Energy model based performance analysis of cluster based wireless sensor network. *International Journal of Reliable Information and Assurance.*

Tripathi, M., Gaur, M. S., Laxmi, V., & Battula, R. B. (2013). Energy efficient LEACH-C protocol for wireless sensor network. *Third International Conference on Computational Intelligence and Information Technology (CIIT).* 10.1049/cp.2013.2620

Varshney, T., Sharma, T., & Sharma, P. (2014). *Implementation of Watchdog Protocol with AODV in Mobile Ad Hoc Network. In Communication Systems and Network Technologies.* Bhopal, India: CSNT.

Xia, D., & Vlajic, N. (2007). *Near-Optimal Node Clustering in Wireless sensor Networks for Environment Monitoring.* Niagara Falls, Canada: Advanced Information Networking and Applications. doi:10.1109/AINA.2007.97

Znaidi, W., Minier, M., & Ubeda, S. (2013). Hierarchical Node Replication Attacks Detection in Wireless Sensor Networks. *International Journal of Distributed Sensor Networks*, 12.

KEY TERMS AND DEFINITIONS

Clustering Network: A group of sensor nodes in which multiple nodes are grouped together under cluster head which is elected by them.

Dydog Method: It is the intrusion detection process which detects the multiple attacking nodes in the network with the help of intrusion detection nodes or monitoring nodes.

End to End Delay: The time a packet will take to reach to the desired destination is called end to end delay.

Energy Consumption: It is the amount of energy consumed during the packets transmission by each node and calculates the overall energy of the whole network.

Intrusion Detection: Intrusion detection is a process of detecting any unnecessary activity in the network.

Network Overhead: The amount of resources used by every sensor node in the network such as bandwidth, energy, memory, time, etc.

Node Replication Attack: The dangerous type of attack in which an attacker can harm the functionality of the network by injecting the clone or replica in the network.

Ns2 Simulator: The network simulator which is discrete event and tcl scripts are written in OTcl and C++ language.

Packet Delivery Ratio: It defines the ratio of the number of packets sent by the source node and the number of packets received by the destination node.

Sensor: Sensor is the monitoring device which is equipped with every node in the network in order to measure the physical conditions like temperature, pressure, etc.

Sleep/Wake Scheduling: The algorithm which enhances the performance of the network by increasing the life span of the network.

Throughput: The successful complete delivery of the sent packets by the sender node to the destination node is called throughput.

APPENDIX

Table 3 represents the simulation parameters taken during implementation in network simulator.

Table 3. Simulation Parameters

Parameters	Value
Channel type	Wireless
Radio propagation model	Two ray ground
Antenna type	Omni
Link layer type	LL
Interface queue type	Droptail
Max packets in interface queue	200
MAC type	IEEE 802.11
No. of mobile nodes	50
Routing protocol	AODV
Simulation time	1000s
Speed	20

228

Chapter 12
Wireless Enhanced Security Based on Speech Recognition

S. Selva Nidhyananthan
Mepco Schlenk Engineering College, India

Joe Virgin A.
Mepco Schlenk Engineering College, India

Shantha Selva Kumari R.
Mepco Schlenk Engineering College, India

ABSTRACT

Security is the most notable fact of all computerized control gadgets. In this chapter, a voice ID computerized gadget is utilized for the security motivation using speech recognition. Mostly, the voices are trained by extracting mel frequency cepstral coefficient feature (MFCC), but it is very sensitive to noise interference and degrades the performance; hence, dynamic MFCC is used for speech and speaker recognition. The registered voices are stored in a database. When the device senses any voice, it cross checks with the registered voice. If any mismatches occur, it gives an alert to the authorized person through global system for mobile communication (GSM) to intimate the unauthorized access. GSM works at a rate of 168 Kb/s up to 40 km and it operates at different operating frequencies like 800MHz, 900MHz, etc. This proposed work is more advantageous for the security systems to trap the unauthorized persons through an efficient communication.

INTRODUCTION

1. **Digital Signal Processing Techniques:** Digital Signal Processing is a technique where digital signals are sampled and processed by many DSP techniques namely multirate processing, Fast Fourier Transform (FFT), Discrete Cosine Transform (DCT) and so on under the stream of VLSI. Each technique is processed according to its architecture.

DOI: 10.4018/978-1-5225-5152-2.ch012

Copyright © 2018, IGI Global. Copying or distributing in print or electronic forms without written permission of IGI Global is prohibited.

a. **Multirate Signal Processing:** The term Multirate is defined as the sampling of different frequencies. The process of sampling of the already sampled datum for multiple times is termed as Multirate signal processing. Due to multi-rate DSP, the processing efficiency is increased, which minimize the requirements of DSP hardware. Theories like filter bank and multi –resolution play an essential role of multiple sampling. This sampling technique is used for analysis of signals, compression, denoising etc. According to the past facts, these sorts of techniques show their hike involvement in signal processing domain and also in digital communication. In Multirate signal processing, the signal rate used in a corresponding system is expected to either increase or decrease, and some kind of signal processing is required for that. Therefore "Multi-rate DSP" is referred to the changing of the different sampling rate.

The multirate signal processing has many applications. One of its applications is speech and speaker processing and it has been explained elaborately below.

b. **Speech Processing:** Speech Recognition gives the knowledge and research in linguistics and in engineering stream. This would enrich the recognition methodologies and its technologies which recognize the spoken language to display as a text by any computerized gadget, which is categorized as the smart technologies. Hence, it is said as Speech to Text.

The production of speech produces the spoken words based on the phonemes for each and every specific word. Speech production is spontaneously generated when the words are read from a paragraph and such speech is speech repetition. Speech production differs from each language production. Language production involves embedding grammar of the language to the produced speech. Normally, during a casual conversation people tend to use four syllables, twelve phonemes etc., for each and every single second. They are also able to speak a two to three word which contains up to 100 words of vocabulary. Error occurs in case of spontaneous speech and it is about one in every 900 words during the production of speech.

The speech transmission is done through the sound waves and the principle behind in this transmission is acoustics. A sample speech transmitted signal is shown in Figure 1. The source of all sound is vibration. A source (something put into vibration) and a medium (something to transmit the vibrations) are necessary in order to make the sound. Sound waves are produced by vibrating vocal tract.

The application of speech recognition is voice user interfaces which include domestic appliance control, voice dialing, call routing, and dictation system and speech-to-text conversion.

c. **Speaker Recognition:** Speaker Recognition is the one that recognizes and identifies the voice of a person. This kind of recognition is also called as pattern recognition or voice recognition. The difference between speaker and speech is that the speech recognition identifies the person's speech but the speaker recognition denotes person's voice. Speaker verification and speaker identification are the two processes carried out through speaker recognition. Perceiving the speaker can be done by interpreting specific speaker features of the speech as part of a security procedure. The speaker identification can be done for text –independent speech and also for text -dependent speech.

Figure 1. Sample speech transmitted signal

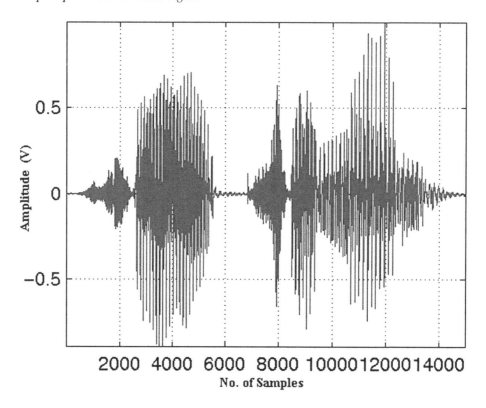

Speaker Identification involves in the determination of the specific features of the speaker utterance of the known registered speaker. The voice of the third person is analyzed and compared with the already taken samples of the speaker which is done in the identification phase. The speaker is identified as the one whose model makes a perfect match with the registered model. There are 2 models in speaker recognition: feature extraction and parameter matching. Feature extraction extracts the data from the voice signal and parameter matching identifies the unknown speaker by comparing with feature vectors extracted from the voice signal.

Identification differs from verification in decision alternatives. In verification, the alternatives are acceptance or rejection. But in case of the speaker identification, the final decision is based upon its number of speakers. There are 2 phases of identification and verification: training phase and testing phase. In training phase, a reference model for each speaker is created. In the testing phase, recognition decision is made by matching the query sample with the reference models.

The text –independent speaker identification recognize the speaker's voice and do not bother about the speech he/she spoke whereas the text –dependent will recognize both the person's voice and the speech he/she spoke. In this chapter, text –independent speaker identification is discussed and the process carried out to recognize are discussed below.

2. **Digital Signal Processing in FPGA:** The Digital Signal Processing carried out in many domains that are required a large amount of space. The signal processing techniques are carried out on FPGA which reduces the size and area and it can be done in terms of real time. The speech and speaker

Figure 2. Shows the block diagram representation of speaker identification

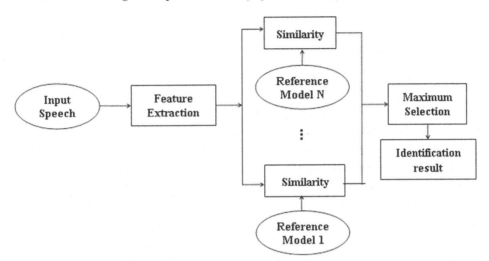

recognition techniques can be implemented in FPGA board. These designs use Block RAM for the storage of the speech signals. The speech and speaker recognition can also implement under the platforms Xilinx EDK (Embedded Development Kit) in Xilinx Platform Studio and can also be done in NIMOS II. In this chapter, the speech and speaker recognition are done under the Verilog HDL platform.

BACKGROUND

Chih Hung *et.al.,*(2015) proposed a new method called Ultra-Low Queue-Accumulator Buffering (UL-QAB) method that can be efficiently used to extract the Linear Prediction Cepstral Coefficient (LPCC) feature. In the decoding part, a template matching method is used for speech independent characteristics. The embedded ASR system use 16-bit microprocessor of memory usage 0.75KB RAMS and its recognition accuracy is 95%.

The traditional computations of the speaker recognition system matching one by one can be time-consuming. Hence, Jing Zhang *et.al.,*(2016) gave a solution for the fast recognition problem by introducing a new clustering technique called speaker model clustering method based on space position. There are three steps involved in the process of clustering based on space position. The first step is to divide the training models into multiple layers; the second step is to search the class representatives for every layer, then finally the training model are clustered by the gotten class representatives which are obtained from the second step. This method takes the Gaussian mixture model (GMM) as the speech model, the results give 0.5s per person as the recognition average speed and the correct recognition rate is less than 1% loss.

Seiichi Nakagawa *et.al.,*(2012) proposed a phase information extraction method which normalizes the phase change according to the position of the input speech and finally combines the phase information with Mel Frequency Cepstral Coefficient feature (MFCC) for identification and verification methods. The original phase information extracted gets compared to the two-phase values which create a problem and its error rate is about only 53.8% and 60.6%.

An adopted Support Vector Machine (SVM)-based method is introduced by Ta Wen Kun *et.al.*, (2012) which includes the Sequential Minimal Optimization (SMO) technique for the generation of the hyper plane. Several researchers like Tse Wei Chen, *et.al.*,(2011) adopted that generally *k*-means SMO and *k*-nearest neighbor (KNN) to develop a *k*-means-based clustering method for the speaker. The time complexity of normal *k*-means is high in hardware implementation.

Ta Wen Chen and Shao Yi Chien (2010) introduced distance metric based method for frame based speaker identification. Ta Wen Kun, Jia Ching Wang, *et.al.*, (2012) proposed realizations using hardware on SMO-based VLSI designs. This design proposed a parallel implementation of many CPUs. One problem with this proposal is that because of the presence of multiple CPU, it requires a wide chip area.

A context -dependent Hidden Markov Model (HMM) for speech recognition is proposed by Guangji He, *et.al.*, (2012) using Viterbi transition and GMM processing using 40 nm CMOS process. The memory bandwidth for a GMM computation gets minimized by using a scheme called 'variable frame look ahead'. In this proposed system, the accuracy degradation is an important limiting factor in case of Viterbi with a power consumption of 144mW and also it's not suitable for the noisy environment.

Amiya Kumar, *et.al.*, (2015) realized SMO VLSI designs for processing partitioned sets of data using parallel implementation of many CPUs. The design implemented depends on a processor of 32 power PC_POWER4 1.3 GHz. Although the multiple CPUs increase the training performance, it also increases the power consumption and cost inevitably. The new hardware architecture is proposed for an SMO training hikes its delay cost.

The first central Spectral Moment time-frequency distribution with low order Cepstral coefficients (SMAC) for an ASR is proposed by Pirros Tsiakoulis *et.al.*, (2010). SMAC appears to be proportional to the spectral derivative with respect to the filter's central frequency. SMAC incorporating low order cepstral coefficients is also considered capturing the rough spectral envelope. A standard Mel frequency scale is used for sampling the spectral moment components.

Nilanjan Dey, *et.al.*, (2012), Shubhendu Banerjee, *et.al.*, (2015), Amar, *et.al.*, (2016), Dey N, *et.al.*,(2012) *and* Debalina Biswas, *et.al.*,(2013) discussed advancements in watermarking techniques. Joy Lal Sarkar, *et.al.*, (2015), Himansu Das, *et.al.*, (2014) and Panigrahi C.R, *et.al.*, (2005) proposed new methodologies for sensor networks. Das H *et.al.*, (2015) analysed on PSO based Back Propagation Learning-MLP (PSO-BP-MLP) for Classification. Dey, *et.al.*, (2017), Nilanjan Dey, *et.al.*, (2017) and Mohammad, *et.al.*, (2017) analysed on data security. Shobha Tyagi, *et.al.*, (2017), Manash Sarkar, *et.al.*, (2017) discussed on trust based system security. Debi Acharjya, *et.al.*, (2017) discussed on predictive data analysis.

Chih Hsiang Peng, *et.al.*, (2015) discussed a Multicore and Multichannel (MCMC) and Synchronous and Forward –Backward Scheduling (SFBS) technologies in order to low the costs of the SMO trainable pattern classifier. SFBS uses synchronous and forward -backward counting for data scheduling which reduces the communication cost. Even though, it minimizes the communication cost and hardware re-quirements the memory cost gets increased associated with the hyper plane.

MAIN FOCUS OF THE CHAPTER

1. **Speech Processing in FPGA:** Speech processing includes the concept of both speech and speaker recognition. The speech recognition focuses on the recognition of text that extracted from a speech. The speaker recognition identifies the particular person. The speech and speaker recognition are

explained in detail in this chapter. The process of speech and speaker recognition is shown in Figure 3. The speech and speaker recognition are implemented in FPGA board to reduce the area and power. This kind of implementation is very useful for real- time implementation. The following processes are carried out by automatic speech and speaker recognition. They are namely:

a. Pre-processing Process
b. Speaker Identification Process
  i. Feature Extraction
  ii. Gaussian Mixture Model (GMM)
  iii. Parameter Matching

2. **Filtering in FPGA:** In signal processing, filtering is the most important process which removes the noise and the unwanted information. Filters remove some of the frequencies in order to remove unwanted information. The filter coefficients are generated by FDA tool in MATLAB.

 a. **Types of Filters:** The filters are mainly classified into two categories namely analog filter and digital filter. The digital filters are more accurate than analog filters in case of noise interference. The digital filters perform the mathematical operation on a sampled and discrete signal. The digital filters are easy to design and implement in FPGA. The digital filters are classified into the following types:

  i. **IIR Filter:** IIR filter is a recursive filter which contains an infinite set of recursive coefficients. IIR filter is based upon the property of linear time-invariant systems. IIR filter consists of a feedback loop where the previously calculated values from the output are used as the input for the next iteration. The IIR filter requires more area and there always generate an error signal at each step. Almost all the analog filters are IIR filters. IIR filters have efficiency over implementation but it is not easy to implement as Finite Impulse Response filter.

  ii. **FIR Filter:** The impulse response is finite for FIR filter. The FIR filter has no feedback and it settles at zero finite time. The input -output sequence of the FIR filter is given by,

Figure 3. Process of speech and speaker recognition

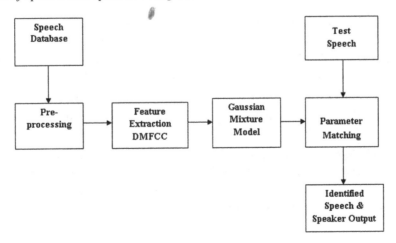

$$y(n) = \sum_{i=0}^{n} b_i x[n - i]$$

where $y(n)$ - output obtained from the filter; b_i - FIR filter coefficient; n - order of the filter; $x(n)$ - input sequence of the filter.

In most of the application, the FIR is one of the highly preferred filters than IIR filter because of its stability, no feedback requirement and easy to implement. The main disadvantage of the FIR filter is, it takes more computation power. In this chapter, the Wiener FIR adaptive filter is discussed.

    b.   **Adaptive Filters:** The transfer function of the adaptive filter with a system of the linear filter is controlled by various parameters and these parameters are adjusted by means of an optimization algorithm. The adaptive filters are digital filters because of the complexity of the optimization algorithm. This kind of filter is used in the application where the parameters are not known and keep on changing.

        i.   **Wiener FIR Filter Using Verilog HDL:** Weiner filter is one of the types of Adaptive filter. Weiner filter can solve the problems by three possibilities i.e., at first it can survive as a non-causal filter but this kind of filters are not suitable for real -time application and the second possibility is to act as a causal filter and finally, it can able to be designed in FIR filters. The Weiner FIR filter is one of the most commonly used filter type in case of any application such as voice quality by means echo cancellation, channel identification etc., furthermore it is one of the best -known filters for the removal of noise and it is the most used filter used in the pre-processing stage in speech recognition. For every N block of samples, the filter coefficients are calculated so that the filter adjusts itself to the signal's average characteristics and this makes the filter to become block-adaptive.

The output of the filter is determined by,

$$y(n) = \sum_{k=0}^{n-1} w_k x(n - k)$$

where, W_k - filter coefficient $y(n)$ - output of the Weiner FIR filter

The Wiener FIR filter coefficients are generated by FDA tool in MATLAB. The architecture of Weiner FIR filter is shown in Figure 4. The input speech text file is read by the command $readmemb ('x.txt'. mem); "b" indicates the samples that are stored in binary format. The stored data can be in hexadecimal format also that can be represented by $readmemh ('x.txt', mem). The filter coefficients W0 to Wn are parameterized in Verilog HDL. The multiplication and the addition used here is IEEE754 floating point addition and multiplication in order to reduce the size and the area power utilization.

3.   **Feature Extraction:** After the pre-processing step, feature extraction is the next section of the ASR system. This section describes the features of the enhanced speech signal. The feature extraction is much more required because the raw speech signal contains information besides the rule of the language message with high dimensionality.

Figure 4. Architecture of Weiner FIR filter

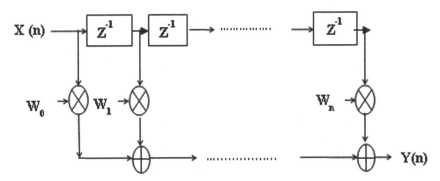

A feature vector describes the only utterance specific attributes and suppresses all irrelevant information such information about recording microphone, recording environment, and the speaker. The inclusion of nonlinguistic information in speech may create a negative effect on the classification of the phone classes. Moreover, the feature extraction must reduce the dimensionality of the speech data.

    a.   **Need for Extracting the Features:** Feature extraction converts speech data into a set of vectors which can be utilized for further process. The speech signal is not a stationary signal but if it is processed for a very short duration the speech signal appears to be stationary. By using that short period of time the framing of the speech signal is done and the windowing process is done. In this chapter, MFCC and Dynamic Mel Frequency Cepstral Coefficient (DMFCC) are given detail explanation.

    b.   **Mel Frequency Cepstral Coefficients (MFCC):** In speech processing, power spectrum and cosine transform are the representation of the Mel Frequency Cepstrum (MFC) of the Mel scale of frequency. In case of MFC, the frequency bands are spaced in Mel scale. This kind of frequency wrapping allows the better representation of the audio sound. The Mel Frequency Cepstral Coefficient (MFCC) can be carried out by the following steps:

Step 1: Pre -processing of the signal.
Step 2: Taking the Fourier transform of the signal obtained from processed sub band signal.
Step 3: Filter bank process.
Step 4: Taking Discrete Cosine Transform (DCT) for the processed signal.

        i.   **Pre-Emphasis:** Pre-emphasis is a one tap FIR filter. In the pre-processing stage of speech processing, pre-emphasis is one of the most important designs which are to hike the magnitude at higher frequencies with regard to the magnitude of low frequencies. In order to improve the overall SNR, the hostile effect is minimized for the phenomena such as attenuation distortion or saturation of recording media in subsequent parts of the system. The architecture of pre- emphasis is given in Figure 5.

The pre –emphasis is given by,

$$y\left(n\right) = x\left(n\right) - \alpha x\left(n-1\right)$$

Figure 5. The architecture of pre-emphasis

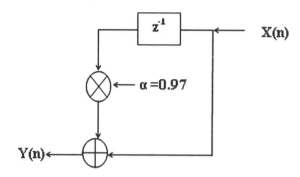

where, $x(n)$ is the speech signal; $y(n)$ output pre-emphasized speech; α - adjustable parameter and it is chosen as 0.97.

> ii. **Framing:** Speech signal appears to be stationary when looked at a short time point of view. But normally, it is not stationary. A speech signal is divided into frames of short duration so that stationery property is satisfied for the Fourier transformation. The framing model is shown in Figure 6.

The speech signal is segmented into frames of appropriate samples. While framing it is essential that the overlapping must take place between frames. No overlap leads to loss of information. The samples in a frame can be obtained as,

$$n = t_{st} f_s$$

where, t_{st} is the time period for a frame; f_s termed as input speech signal's sampling rate.

Generally, in framing first N samples are taken for each and every frame. The next frame contains M samples which are followed by N sample and overlaps it by the difference of N and M samples.

> iii. **Windowing:** Windowing is done to furnish the spectral smoothing thus reducing Gibb's phenomena of introducing discontinuities. It is done on each frame to taper the signal to the minimum value at the beginning and end. Windowing is an indispensable technique

Figure 6. Framing model

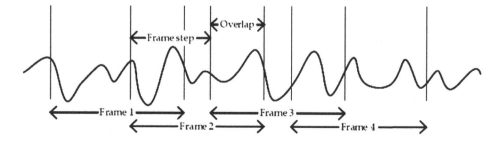

where the time -varying characteristics of vocal tract system take part in speech production mechanism are captured. The size of the window may be $10 - 20$ ms length.

Here, Hamming window function is used. Hamming Window function is given by:

$$w(n) = 0.54 - 0.46 \cos(\frac{2\pi n}{N-1}) \; 0 \leq n \leq N - 1$$

It is a combination of a rectangular window and a Hanning window. Hamming and Hanning windows have some similarities with an additional feature that Hamming window overwhelms the first side lobe. However, the side lobes falloff rate is only 20dB per decade, which is 60dB in Hanning window. The windowed signal expression is given by,

$$S_w(n) = y(n) * w(n)$$

where, $y(n)$ pre-emphasized signal and $w(n)$ - window used

iv. **Fast Fourier Transform (FFT):** FFT evaluates the Discrete Fourier Transform (DFT) efficiently. For an *N*-point transformation, the direct computation of DFT requires *N2* operations. The Cooley – Tukey algorithm reduces the number of operations (*N2*) for the DFT to (*N log2N*) for the FFT. The FFT is precisely equivalent to the DFT. FFT breaks down the arrangement of information to be changed into a progression of littler input sets of data to be changed. The term "radix" is used to determine the size of FFT decomposition. Based on the radix size the data sets are evenly decomposed into small sets. At each stage of processing, each previous stage response is combined with twiddle factor multiplication. Finally, the inputs that are split into a small set of data are undergone the FFT. Generally, FFT's can be decomposed into two types namely Decimation-In-Time (DIT) FFT and Decimation-In-Frequency (DIF) FFT using DFT's where the DIT FFT is based on the even and odd points and DIF FFT is decomposed using a first half/ second-half approach.

Let $x_0, \ldots, x_{N-1}$ are termed as complex numbers. The DFT is represented using the given formula

$$X_k = \sum_{n=0}^{N-1} x_n e^{-i2\prod kn/N} \; k = 0, \ldots \ldots N - 1$$

where, $e^{-i2\prod kn/N} = W_N$ is the twiddle factor.

v. **Mel Filter Banks:** A variety of band pass channels are utilized to isolate the input signal into different multiple components which have a solitary recurrence of a sub band of the original signal. This sort of course of action of the channel alludes to a filter bank.

One use of a filter bank is a realistic equalizer, which can lessen the parts diversely and recombine them into a changed rendition of the original signal. The filter bank in speech processing performs the analysis of a signal process which is a decomposition of the signal into its multiple components for each sub band signal. The MFCC filter bank is shown in Figure 7.

vi. **Discrete Cosine Transform (DCT):** DCT attempts to de-correlate the data. It is applied to the Mel Filter Log Energies (MFLE) to obtain the features. After de-correlation each transform coefficient can be encoded without losing compression efficiency. DCT can be shown by the sequence of finite data points which represent in terms of the sum of the cosine at various frequencies. The expression of DCT is given as follows:

$$y(k) = w(k) \sum_{n=1}^{N} x(n) \cos(\frac{\pi(2n-1(k-1)}{2N}) \ k = 1, 2, ... N$$

$$w(k) = \begin{cases} \dfrac{1}{\sqrt{N}}, & k = 1 \\ \sqrt{\dfrac{2}{N}}, & 2 \le k \le N \end{cases}$$

where $w(k)$ - transformation kernel; $x(n)$ - input; N - number of samples.

The log energies of speech and its features are affected by the noise and make it unsuitable for identification of speech. This can be overcome by applying block based transformation to DCT. The DCT is performed over the divided blocks of the filter log energies.

c. **Dynamic Mel Frequency Cepstral Coefficients (DMFCC):** MFCC is one of the frequently used extraction technique in speech processing. These coefficients represent speech based on perception and are attained from the cepstrum. However, the MFCC feature is very sensi-

Figure 7. MFCC filter bank

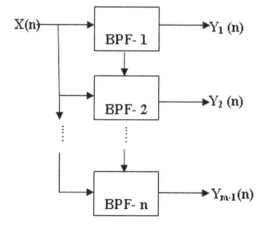

tive to noise, which drastically degrades the performance of speech processing system. To overcome this, the feature extraction is carried out through Dynamic Mel Frequency Cepstral Coefficients (DMFCC). The pitch frequency precisely represents the speakers' time varying characteristic of the vocal cords' vibration. In order to enhance the speaker identification features and to enhance the recognition accuracy Mel- filter bank is used and it also used in extracting the Dynamic MFCC feature. The steps involved in DMFCC are shown in Figure 8.

i. **Sub Band Processing:** Sub Band Processing is the process of decoding the signal into two or more frequency bands. In order to decompose the signal, the sub band processing can be done by using Discrete Wavelet Transform (DWT) and for the samples that obtained from the DWT will be converted into a frequency domain through Fast Fourier Transform (FFT).

DISCRETE WAVELET TRANSFORM

The non-stationary and time-varying speech features are able to be extracted either in time domain or frequency domain. Methods are also available to extract features in localized time- frequency domain is such as Discrete Wavelet Transform (DWT).

The DWT can be implemented as follows:

The decomposition is done by filtering the discrete signal repeatedly up to a set level N. The low pass filter gives the approximation coefficient and the detailed coefficient is given by high pass. After each level of the filter, the signal is down sampled by half the sampling frequency in the previous level. DWT decomposition process of is shown in Figure 9.

The FFT for the sub band processed signal is done as done in MFCC feature.

ii. **Pitch Detection:** By using autocorrelation method the pitch frequency for the input speech signal can be calculated and then take maximum value of the autocorrelation function. The pitch frequency is calculated by using the formula as,

$$pitchF = \frac{1}{pitchT}$$

Figure 8. DMFCC steps

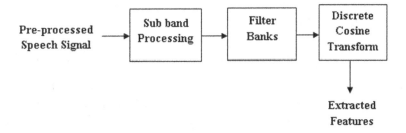

Figure 9. DWT decomposition process

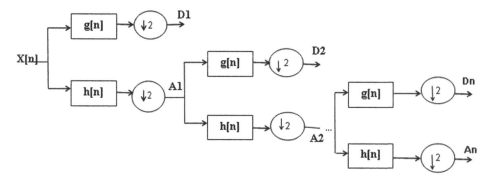

The Mel- scale refers to the mapping of linear frequencies to the log arithmetic scale for the frequencies higher than 1 KHz. This resembles human auditory perception.

The Mel scale conversions given by,

$$Mel(f_p) = 2595 \log \left(1 + f_p/700\right)$$

where, f_p is the pitch frequency.

The final two processes i.e., Filter bank and DCT are done as same done in MFCC feature extraction.

4. **Gaussian Mixture Model (GMM):** The modeling can be done by a parametric based method called Gaussian Mixture Model (GMM) and non- parametric based method called Vector Quantization (VQ). In this chapter, the parametric based GMM is used for the successive process of speaker recognition.

The datum that comes from several groups are different and is a modeled by GMM, but that data points of the same group are modeled by means of Gaussian distribution. The GMM is done by Expectation Maximization (EM) by using multi-variate Gaussian distribution function as given below,

$$N\left(x \mid \mu, \Sigma\right) = \frac{1}{\left(2\pi |\Sigma|\right)^{1/2}} \exp\left\{-\frac{1}{2}\left(x - \mu\right)^T \Sigma^{-1}\left(x - \mu\right)\right\}$$

where, x is input vector, μ is mean vector, and Σ is the covariance matrix.

The parameters of the Gaussian Mixture Model are mean, covariance matrix and mixture of weights. The parameter is estimated by Maximum Likelihood (ML) Estimation. The parameters notations are given by $\lambda = \left\{p_i, \vec{\mu}_i, \Sigma_i\right\} i = 1, \ldots\ldots, M$ where, p_i - mixture of weights; $\vec{\mu}_i$ - mean vector; Σ_i - covariance matrix.

   a. **Expectation Maximization (EM) Method**: The EM method is iterative methods which calculates at first by taking initial values and then proceed the process iteratively by updating the parameter values till it gets converged. The EM method carried out by two steps i.e.,

Expectation (E)-step and maximization (M)-step. *E- step:* The expected values are computed for the parameters. *M- step:* Parameter updating based on the ML method.

The parameters of the GMM are discussed below:

i.   **Mean Vector** ($\vec{\mu}_i$): The mean vector is estimated by the following formula,

$$\vec{\mu}_i = \frac{1}{N} \sum_{i=1}^{N} \vec{x}_i$$

where, $\vec{\mu}_i$ - mean vector; $\vec{x}_i$ - features obtained from the input speech; N is the total number of feature vector

The mean vector is estimated by using the architecture as shown in Figure 10. The implementation can be done as:

The feature vectors calculated by feature extraction are stored in a memory defined by means of a matrix. A counter is initialized, for each count each feature value is taken and processed. The feature value is added with *Reg1* which is initialized as zero. The value obtained from the adder will be stored in *Reg1*. The repetition of this process gives the overall sum of the feature and finally it is shifted by n i.e., no. of feature sample can be represented by 2^n.

ii.   **Covariance Matrix**($\sum_i$)

A covariance matrix is a matrix which defines the covariance of the adjacent elements of a random matrix. A random matrix is a random variable with multiple dimensions.

The covariance matrix can be estimated by using the formula as given below:

$$\sum_i = \frac{1}{N} \sum_{n=1}^{N} \left(x_n - \vec{\mu}_i \right) \left(x_n - \vec{\mu}_i \right)^T$$

where, $\vec{\mu}_i$ is the mean vector; $\vec{x}_n$ is the features obtained from the input speech signal; N is the total number of feature vector

The architecture of the covariance matrix is shown in Figure 11. The implementation of the covariance matrix in FPGA is as follows: The mean is estimated for the stored feature vectors. The mean and $\vec{x}_n$ are undergone a subtractor and stored in a matrix. The matrix is transposed and matrix multiplication is done. Finally, the matrix is averaged by the number of samples of a feature vector.

iii.   **Mixture of Weights**(p_i): The final parameter of the GMM is a mixture of weights. The mixture of weights can be estimated by dividing the multi- variate Gaussian distribution with the total sample of the feature vector.

The mixture of weights is given by,

Figure 10. Architecture used for the mean vector

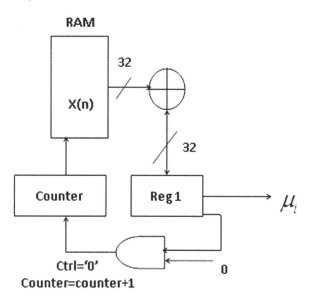

Figure 11. Architecture of convariance matrix

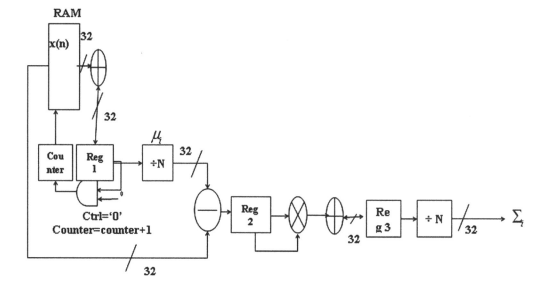

$$p_i = \frac{1}{T} \sum_{i=1}^{T} p\left(i \middle| \vec{x}_i, \lambda\right)$$

The mixture of weights determined by using Multivariate Gaussian distribution function i.e., $p\left(i \middle| \vec{x}_i, \lambda\right)$. The Gaussian distribution can be calculated by,

$$p\left(x\,\middle|\,\mu,\sigma^2\right) = \frac{1}{\sqrt{2\pi\sigma^2}}\,e^{-\frac{(x-\mu)^2}{2\sigma^2}}$$

The mixture of weights can be implemented in FPGA by using the architecture as shown in Figure 12. The variance and the constant values are multiplied and taken square root by using square root architecture as shown in Figure 13. The square root is estimated by Control Adder Subtractor (CAS) block. The CAS block start is operation after getting the enable signal the first bit get to start doing the square root operation.

The parameters mean vector, covariance matrix and mixture of weights are used to calculate the Gaussian mixture density which is given by,

$$p\left(\vec{x}\,\middle|\,\lambda\right) = \sum_{i=0}^{M} p_i b_i\left(\vec{x}\right)$$

where, p_i is the mixture of weight; M is the Gaussian density of M component densities; $b_i\left(\vec{x}\right)$ is the D-variate Gaussian function.

The determined GMM values are used for the identification of the speaker by using clustering technique.

5.   **Clustering Technique Using FPGA:** In the clustering process, a set of objects is partitioned into subsets, also known as clusters. The objects present within the cluster are similar, but the data are dissimilar when the objects present in different subsets. The cluster is considered to be more distinct from the objects of the same cluster which are very similar (or having more homogeneity) and very dissimilar between the other group of a cluster. A data represented by few clusters will inevitably lose the finer details, but at the same time, achieve simplification. The analysis of gene expression data, data compression, anomaly detection, and statistical data analysis, recognition of patterns,

Figure 12. Architecture implemented by FPGA

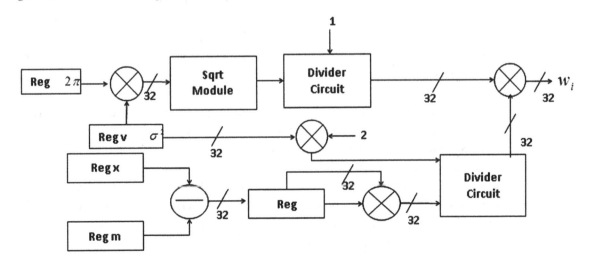

Figure 13. Square root architecture

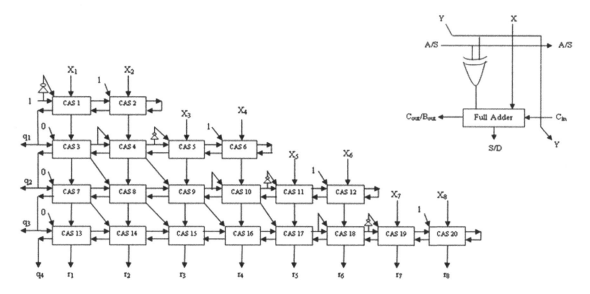

machine language, image information, bio-informatics, information retrieval and structuring results of search engines are done by clustering techniques.

The most common concept of clusters involves groups that have a short distance between the subsets, dense areas of the data space with specific statistical distributions. Thus, a multi-objective optimization problem is solved by clustering. The chapter clearly explains the *K*- Medoids Clustering Algorithm and Partition Around Medoids (PAM) Clustering Algorithm.

The clustering techniques are implemented by cluster the datum in the RAM of the corresponding FPGA board by performing the operation which is discussed below for the two types of clustering.

    a.   **Types of Clustering Technique:** Clustering can be done by many methods the types of clustering are discussed as follows:

        i.   **Exclusive Clustering:** The datum are clustered in a way, where the datum belongs to a distinct cluster then the data will be not get included to any other group or cluster. A bi-dimensional plane gives the separation line for each cluster.

        ii.   **Overlapping Clustering:** The overlapping clustering uses fuzzy sets for clustering the data from the memory. Each data from the memory is present in two or more different cluster which is having different degrees of membership. In this type of clustering, all data are associated with specific member value.

        iii.   **Hierarchical Clustering:** The Hierarchical clustering algorithm is determined between any two nearest clusters based on its union between those clusters. At first, itself all data are assigned to each cluster. The final clusters are formed after few iterations which undergoes by hierarchical.

        iv.   ***k*-means Clustering:** *k*- means is an unsupervised learning algorithm and one of the best simplest algorithm among the notable of all clustering algorithm. The number of iterations is assumed by means of *k* values. The procedure to classify a given datum through a certain number of clusters (assume k clusters) fixed a priority.

In the proposed system K-Medoids clustering and PAM clustering is used for speaker identification.

b.   ***K*-Medoids Clustering Algorithm using Verilog HDL:** K- Medoids Clustering Algorithm is one of the simplest clusterings among all other clustering algorithms. The main idea is to define centroids i.e., each cluster consists of a cluster head. These centroids should be placed in a way that the cluster head present in different location causes a different result. So, the better choice is to place the centroids of the cluster as much as far away from each other different clusters. Secondly from the given data set, the datum belongs to the distinct cluster are taken which associate it to the nearest centroid. When there is no pending data in the data set, the first step is completed and an early cluster age is done. Hence, there occurs a re-calculation of k new centroids as barycenter of the clusters which obtain from the previous step. After the first iteration, new centers are determined and new clusters have created between the same data set points and the nearest new centroid. This process is recursive and the datum is generated as a loop format. As a result of this loop k times, the centroids change its location step by step until no more changes are done. K- Medoids is more robust than k-means in the presence of noise and outliers. The flow of K- Medoids Clustering is shown in Figure 14. The steps of K- Medoids Clustering are summarized as follows:

Step 1: Randomly select the cluster head from the set.
Step 2: Find the minimum distance by means of Manhattan distance of each data point in the set.
Step 3: Take arithmetic mean of the data in each cluster and declare it as the next cluster head.
Step 4: Repeat Step 2 and 3 till the cluster remains same.

The K-Medoids Clustering can be implemented as follows:

The input vector of n bit each gets stored in a RAM of N x 1. The cluster head was assumed for the first iteration. Three registers is used out of which two to store cluster heads and other to hold the value. The comparator is used to find the minimum difference between the cluster head and the values. The value gets stored in a memory with the corresponding minimum difference cluster head. The iteration will repeat till the cluster has no change.

The Verilog HDL code for the K-Medoids Clustering can be written for each and every small module for the read and write operation that performs using memory. By using, address i.e., *addr* the RAM can be accessed. A comparator is designed for the condition $A<B$. If this condition is true it provides enable signal then the data is stored in the corresponding memory when the condition becomes false a disable signal produce also store the data in its respective RAM. Then after the first iteration, the new center is calculated through mean and this is stored in a dummy register.

c.   **Partition Around Medoids (PAM) Clustering using Verilog HDL:** The calculation of Partition Around Medoids clustering algorithm is planned to discover a grouping of articles called medoids that are midway situated in clusters. Objects that are likely characterized as medoids are set into a set S of chose articles.

The main objective of Partition around Medoids algorithm is to reduce the total dissimilarity of objects to their nearby cluster selected object. This automatically minimizes the sum of the dissimilarities between an object and to their nearby selected object. The flow of PAM Clustering is shown in Figure 15.

Figure 14. Flow of K-Medoids Clustering

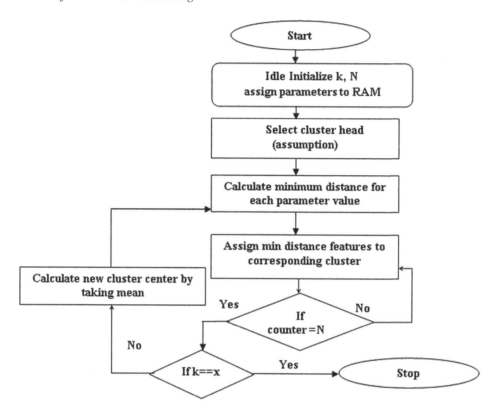

The steps of PAM clustering algorithm are summarized as follows:

Step 1: The Build phase, collects the k objects from the total data sample set.

Step 2: The Swap phase, the center data are exchanged for the next iteration from the set of data. This phase will improve the clustering quality.

The PAM Clustering can be implemented as follows:

The input vector of *n* bit each gets stored in a RAM of *N* x 1. The cluster head was assumed for the first iteration. Three registers is used out of which two to store cluster heads and other to hold the value. The comparator is used to find the minimum difference between the cluster head and the values. The values get stored in a memory with the corresponding minimum difference cluster head. The iteration will repeat till the cluster has no change and it takes cluster head as an assumption for the next iteration.

The Verilog HDL design for the PAM clustering algorithm is same as the *K-* Medoids Clustering algorithm but the difference is there is no need for taking mean of the clusters for the next iteration. The cluster head is taken randomly for the next iteration.

The Recognition Accuracy of Speech and Speaker Recognition are shown in Figure 16 and 17.

6. **Wireless Technology:** Remote innovation utilizes radio waves to transmit data without connections or wiring. Albeit remote interchanges have been used since 1876, the modernization is currently being used broadly to make remote PC systems. There are numerous models for remote interchanges, including Bluetooth, DECT and WiMax.

Figure 15. Flow of PAM Clustering

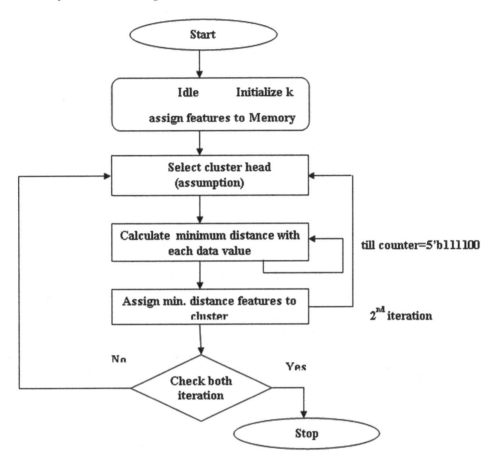

a. **Wireless Modules:** Wireless modules are used as gadgets which transmit and receive information from the source and the medium used for the transmission is air or other waves. The various wireless modules are discussed as follows:

    i. **Bluetooth:** Bluetooth is a module used in wireless technology standard which is meant for exchanging data over a short distance. Bluetooth use UHF radio waves of shorter wavelength in a band called Industrial, Scientific and Medical (ISM) band at a distance of 2.4 to 2.485 GHz from fixed to a mobile. IEEE 802.15.1 is defined as the IEEE standard for the wireless module Bluetooth.

In HC-05 Bluetooth module is very easy to use Bluetooth SPP (Serial Port Protocol), which is designed for connection setup of the transparent wireless serial. Serial port Bluetooth module has a proficient Bluetooth V2.0+EDR (Enhanced Data Rate) of 3Mbps Modulation for a range of 2.4GHz radio transceiver and baseband. This module has an external single chip Bluetooth with CMOS technology. It has the footprint as small as 12.7mm of length and 27mm of breadth hence because of this kind of dimensions the design/development cycle gets reduced.

Figure 16. (a) shows the accuracy for a set of 10 speeches for MFCC and DMFCC features. It is proved from the Figure 16(b) the recognition done through DMFCC is more accurate and efficient than MFCC feature

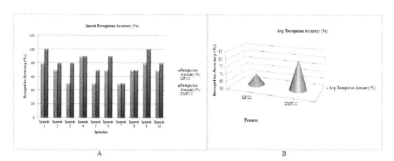

SPECIFICATION

The hardware features of Bluetooth are as follows. It has the sensitivity of Typical -80dBm.IT has transmitting power Up to +4dBm RF transmit power. For operating it requires a Low Power of 1.8V for Operation and 1.8 to 3.6V for I/O. It has PIO control. It has UART interface with programmable baud rate. It is also available with an integrated antenna.

The software features of Bluetooth has the Default Baud rate of 38400, it has 8bit data of 1 bit as stop bit and no parity. Baud rate such as 9600, 19200 etc., are allowed to access by this module. It gave a rising pulse in PIO0, then the device will be disconnected. It has a Status instruction port PIO1: low to disconnect and high to connect the port.

ii. **Zigbee:** The wireless module Zigbee has low power and long life battery advancement and also it is easy to implement in remote control and checking applications. The average current of zigbee gets reduced because of down in latency. Zigbee chips are typically integrated to a flash memory between 60-256 KB with radios and with microcontrollers. The operating frequency of the zigbee is about ISM 2.4 – 2.4835 GHz frequency band. The zigbee has the standardization of IEEE 802.15.4 base band. Zigbee has a characterized rate of 250 Kbit/s which is more appropriate for irregular information transmissions from a sensor or into the device.

Figure 17. (a) shows the recognition accuracy of speaker for Gaussian Mixtures 8 and 16. It is inferred from Figure 17(b) that the speaker recognition accuracy using GMM gives more accurate result when the Gaussian Mixture is 16 when compared to 8. Thus, by increasing the Gaussian mixture accurate recognition of speaker can be done

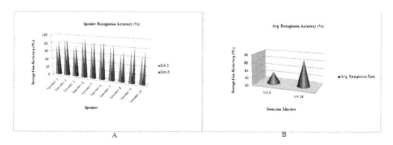

iii. **Global System for Mobile Communication(GSM):** GSM is considered as exceptionally productive correspondence through the versatile which will be helpful in mechanical controls, vehicles and apparatuses which would be controlled from anyplace else. It is likewise exceedingly monetary and more affordable. Worldwide System for Mobile communication (GSM) is a moment era cell standard created to cook voice administrations and information delivery using computerized modulation. GSM is an advanced versatile communication framework.

It utilizes a variety of time domain modulation access (TDMA) and is the most generally utilized of the three advanced remote communication technologies (TDMA, GSM and CDMA). GSM digitizes and packs the information, at that point GSM sends the information to down a channel with two different surges of client information each has its own circumstances opening. It works at either 900MHz or 1800MHz recurrence band.

SPECIFICATION

GSM900

- Mobile to BTS (uplink): 890-915 MHz
- BTS to Mobile (downlink): 935-960MHz Bandwidth: 2*25 MHz

GSM 1800

- Mobile to BTS: 1710-1785 MHz (i.e., for uplink)
- BTS to Mobile 1805-1880 MHz (i.e., for downlink) Bandwidth: 2*75MHz

SIM900 can fit almost all the space requirements in M2M applications, especially for the slim and compact demand of design. The Single-chip processor is one of the powerful processors which is used to design SIM900. It uses theAMR926EJ-S core. It is a Quad - band GSM/GPRS module with a size of length 24mm, breath 24mm and height 3mm. It supports an embedded Powerful TCP/IP protocol stack.

iv. **General Packet Radio Service (GPRS):** General Packet Radio Service has a mobile data service over 2G and 3G of cellular worldwide communication for versatile interchange i.e., GSM. The GPRS is standardized by European Telecommunication Standard Institute (ETSI). GPRS is one of the best effort service device and its throughput and latency purely depend on the number of users are using in the network. In case of a 2G cellular communication system, the data rate of GPRS is about 56 -114 Kbit/second.

b. **Why Global System for Mobile Communication?** Based upon the wireless device modules GSM is considered as the best for this kind of security purpose application. Because, while considering Zigbee even though it is cost effective and easy to implement it can only operate well within a shot range, but for far distance all its criteria become critical. However, Bluetooth can operate in a relatively short distance Radio Frequency (RF) communication which operates only at 2.4 GHz about 12.5 cm of the Industrial, Scientific and Medical (ISM) band. In case of GPRS wireless module, it is a routing concept but GSM is a location area concept. In

GPRS, the time slot is asymmetric for both uplink and downlink and has multiple time slots whereas for GSM it is symmetric and one time slot. The main fact that GSM used in security application is the distance because the person must get his/her alert information at any cost of where he/she is about.

c. **FPGA of a Security System Module:** GSM is a digital mobile communication system. Each data is digitized and compressed and then using GSM it sends through a channel with two streams of data where each stream of data has its individual slot. It can operate at any one band 900 MHz or 1800 MHz respectively. The GSM module communicates the microcontroller with mobile phones through UART. Three signals namely RXD signal to receive, TXD signal to transmit, and GND for common ground are needed for the Universal Asynchronous Receiver/Transmitter (UART) or Universal Synchronous/Asynchronous Receiver/Transmitter (USART). The flow of GSM with FPGA is shown in Figure 18.

To transfer the data via GSM, the baud rate of the serial port has to be set initially. The baud rate of GSM is set as same as that of the serial port. Then the data availability of serial port has to be check. If the data is available at serial port, the data is read from the serial port and the data is sent via GSM. If the serial port data is not available, the baud rate of the GSM has to be reset. After sending the data or information via GSM to the base station, the sender has to wait for the acknowledgment that generated

Figure 18. The flow of GSM with FPGA

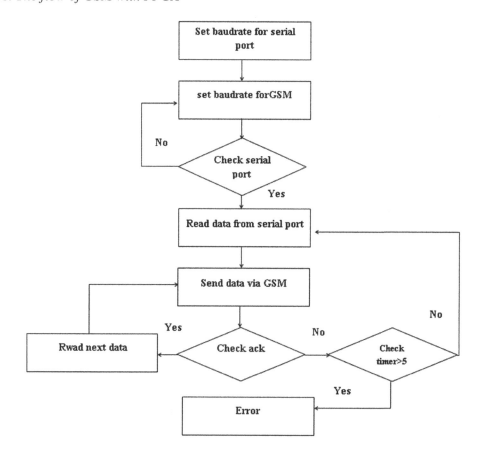

Figure 19. Implementation of the security system

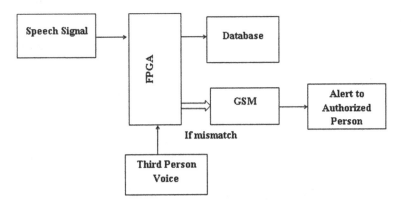

for the transmitted data. At once when the acknowledgment is received then the next data is transmitted via GSM else sender has to wait for the time to exceed. If the time exceeds, the data transmission process will be terminated else the previously transmitted data will be resent via GSM.

The implementation of the security system is shown in Figure 19. The speaker that recognized is stored in a database for further use. The GSM module is attached to the FPGA serial port. When any voice is sensed by the FPGA through audio codec the voice of the person is in the speaker recognition process. After the process is complete the voice pattern is compared with the other voice pattern in the database. If the comparing voice is proved as an unauthorized person's voice then the FPGA will transmit the enable or the indicating signal to the GSM connected via the serial port of FPGA. Once the GSM get the message or the signal the GSM will transmit the signal to respective person's phone through a message from the SIM in GSM to the recipient's SIM. Thus the person gets aware of the condition taken around his/her home or any other place that is needed to be the guard.

CONCLUSION

This chapter gives the knowledge about the pre-processed signal of speech and the feature extraction is carried out by taking DMFCC feature through pitch frequency. It also explains the usage of Mel filter bank which improves the accuracy of recognition. It is also inferred that the DMFCC feature shows accuracy about 80%. The feature vectors are classified by means of Gaussian Mixture Model classifier and the parameters obtained are grouped into clusters by k-Medoids Clustering and PAM Clustering. As by increasing the Gaussian Mixture (M) in GMM classifier it gives the best recognition accuracy rate in speaker recognition. The ASSR system is designed and coded in Verilog HDL. The module GSM interfacing with the FPGA board is also studied and designed.

REFERENCES

Amar, Y. B., Trabelsi, I., Dey, N., & Bouhlel, S. (2016). Euclidean Distance Distortion Based Robust and Blind Mesh Watermarking. *International Journal of Interactive Multimedia and Artificial Intelligence*, *4*(2), 46. doi:10.9781/ijimai.2016.428

Banerjee, Chakraborty, Dey, Pal, & Ray. (2015, February). High Payload Watermarking using Residue Number System. *I.J. Image, Graphics and Signal Processing*, 1-8.

Biswas, D., Das, P., Maji, P., Dey, N., & Chaudhuri, S. S. (2013). Visible watermarking within the region of non-interest of medical images based on fuzzy c-means nd harris corner detection. ICCSEA, SPPR, CSIA, WimoA, 161–168.

Chen & Chien. (2011). Flexible Hardware Architecture of Hierarchical K-Means Clustering for Large Cluster Number. *IEEE Transactions on Very Large Scale Integration (VLSI) Systems, 19*(8).

Chen, B.-W., Lin, P.-C., Wang, J.-F., Kuan, T.-W., & Chou, C.-H. (2015). Memory-efficient buffering method and enhanced reference template for embedded automatic speech recognition system. *IET Computers & Digital Techniques, 9*(3), 153–164. doi:10.1049/iet-cdt.2014.0008

Das, H., Jena, A. K., Nayak, J., Naik, B., & Behera, H. S. (2015). A Novel PSO Based Back Propagation Learning-MLP (PSO-BP-MLP) for Classification. In Computational Intelligence in Data Mining: Vol. 2. Smart Innovation, Systems and Technologies. Springer. doi:10.1007/978-81-322-2208-8_42

Das, H., Naik, B., Pati, B., & Panigrahi, C. R. (2014). A Survey on Virtual Sensor Networks Framework. *International Journal of Grid and Distributed Computing, 7*(5), 121–130. doi:10.14257/ijgdc.2014.7.5.11

Debi Acharjya & Anitha. (2017). A Comparative Study of Statistical and Rough Computing Models in Predictive Data Analysis. *International Journal of Ambient Computing and Intelligence Archive, 8*(2), 32-51.

Dey, Solanki, & Tamane. (2017). *Privacy and Security Policies in Big Data.* IGI Global.

Dey, N. (2017). *Intelligent Techniques in Signal Processing for Multimedia Security, book* (V. Santhi, Ed.). Springer International Publishing. doi:10.1007/978-3-319-44790-2

Dey, N., Acharjee, S., Biswas, D., & Das, A. (2012). Medical Information Embedding in Compressed Watermarked Intravascular Ultrasound Video. *Scientific Bulletin of the Politehnica University of Timisoara - Transactions on Electronics and Communications, 57*(71).

Dey, N., Mukhopadhyay, S., Das, A., & Chaudhuri, S. S. (2012, July). Analysis of P-QRS-T Components Modified by Blind Watermarking Technique Within the Electrocardiogram Signal for Authentication in Wireless Telecardiology Using DWT. *I.J. Image. Graphics and Signal Processing, 2012*(7), 33–46. doi:10.5815/ijigsp.2012.07.04

Dey, N., Pal, M., & Das, A. (2012, May-June). A Session Based Blind Watermarking Technique within the NROI of Retinal Fundus Images for Authentication Using DWT, Spread Spectrum and Harris Corner Detection. *International Journal of Modern Engineering Research, 2*(3), 749–757.

Dey, N., Roy, A. B., Das, A., & Chaudhuri, S. S. (2012). Stationary Wavelet Transformation Based Self-recovery of Blind-Watermark from Electrocardiogram Signal in Wireless Telecardiology. In S. M. Thampi, A. Y. Zomaya, T. Strufe, J. M. Alcaraz Calero, & T. Thomas (Eds.), *Recent Trends in Computer Networks and Distributed Systems Security. SNDS 2012. Communications in Computer and Information Science* (Vol. 335). Berlin: Springer. doi:10.1007/978-3-642-34135-9_35

He, G., Sugahara, T., Miyamoto, Y., Fujinaga, T., Noguchi, H., Izumi, S., ... Yoshimoto, M. (2012, August). A 40 nm 144 mW VLSI Processor for Real-Time 60-kWord Continuous Speech Recognition. *IEEE Transactions on Circuits and Systems. I, Regular Papers, 59*(8).

Kuan, Wang, Wang, Lin, & Gu. (2012). VLSI Design of an SVM Learning Core on Sequential Minimal Optimization Algorithm. *IEEE Transactions on Very Large Scale Integration (VLSI) Systems, 20*(4).

Kumar, A., Mahapatra, K., Kabi, B., & Routray, A. (2015). A novel approach of Speech Emotion Recognition with prosody, quality and derived features using SVM classifier for a class of North-Eastern Languages. *IEEE 2nd International Conference on Recent Trends in Information Systems.*

Mohammad & Abi. (2017). Improving Privacy and Security of User Data in Location Based Services. *International Journal of Ambient Computing and Intelligence, 9*(1).

Nakagawa, S., Wang, L., & Ohtsuka, S. (2012, May). Speaker Identification and Verification by Combining MFCC and Phase Information. *IEEE Transactions on Audio, Speech, and Language Processing, 20*(4), 1085–1095. doi:10.1109/TASL.2011.2172422

Panigrahi, C. R., Sarkar, J. L., Pati, B., & Das, H. (2005). S2S: A Novel Approach for Source to Sink Node Communication in Wireless Sensor Networks. In R. Prasath, A. Vuppala, & T. Kathirvalavakumar (Eds.), Lecture Notes in Computer Science: Vol. 9468. *Mining Intelligence and Knowledge Exploration.* Cham: Springer.

Peng, Kuan, Lin, Wang, & Wu. (2015). Trainable and Low-Cost SMO Pattern Classifier Implemented via MCMC and SFBS Technologies. *IEEE Transactions on Very Large Scale Integration (VLSI) Systems, 23*(10).

Sarkar, Soumya, & Sangaiah. (2017). Configuring a Trusted Cloud Service Model for Smart City Exploration Using Hybrid Intelligence. *International Journal of Ambient Computing and Intelligence, 8*(3).

Sarkar, G., & Saha, G. (2010). Real Time Implementation of Speaker Identification System with Frame Picking Algorithm. *Elsevier, Procedia Computer Science, 2*, 173–180. doi:10.1016/j.procs.2010.11.022

Sarkar, J. L. (2015). A Novel Approach for Real-Time Data Management in Wireless Sensor Networks. *Proceedings of 3rd International Conference on Advanced Computing, Networking and Informatics,* 599-607.

Tsiakoulis, P., Potamianos, A., & Dimitriadis, D. (2010, June). Spectral Moment Features Augmented by Low Order Cepstral Coefficients for Robust ASR. *IEEE Signal Processing Letters, 17*(6), 551–554. doi:10.1109/LSP.2010.2046349

Tyagi, S., Som, S., & Rana, Q. P. (2017). Trust based Dynamic Multicast Group Routing Ensuring Reliability for Ubiquitous Environment in MANETs. *International Journal of Ambient Computing and Intelligence, 8*(1), 70–97. doi:10.4018/IJACI.2017010104

Zhang & Chen. (2016). A speaker model clustering method based on space position. *International Journal of Advanced Computer Research, 6.*

Section 3
Security Through Machine Learning Techniques and Watermarking Techniques

Chapter 13

Algorithms for Detection and Classification of Abnormality in Mammograms:
An Overview

Anuradha Chetan Phadke
Maharashtra Institute of Technology, India

Priti P. Rege
College of Engineering Pune, India

ABSTRACT

Mammography is a popular imaging modality currently in use for routine screening of breast. Radiologists look for some of the significant signs of breast cancer while examining the mammogram visually. These signs are bounded masses, clusters of micro-calcifications, spiculations, and architectural distortions. Developing computer-aided algorithms for the detection and classification of abnormalities in mammograms is an extremely challenging task because of significant variableness in the type, size, shape, texture variation of abnormal region, and variability in the structure of surrounding tissues of the breast. The main objective of this chapter is to introduce dominant features of various signs of abnormalities and to discuss techniques to detect various abnormalities in mammograms. This knowledge will help to develop a system that is useful for the early detection and classification of breast cancer.

INTRODUCTION

Breast Cancer is women's foremost health issue in developed as well as developing countries. According to American Cancer Society statistics, 252,710 invasive breast cancer cases in women are estimated to be diagnosed in 2017 and 40,610 breast cancer deaths of women are estimated in 2017. There are 89% of breast cancer deaths in women with ages 50 years or above (American Cancer Society, 2017). Breast cancer incidence and mortality rates vary considerably by race or ethnicity. There is requirement of

DOI: 10.4018/978-1-5225-5152-2.ch013

Copyright © 2018, IGI Global. Copying or distributing in print or electronic forms without written permission of IGI Global is prohibited.

taking effective actions in order to control this deadly disease in future. Cancer is extremely dangerous and potentially challenging issue.

It is possible to reduce death rate due to breast cancer, by using mammographic screening to detect it at early stage. Mammography is a noninvasive test where a low dose X-ray image of breast is captured in the form of digital or digitized mammogram. Mammography is a promising technique which aids medical doctors to examine breast for the early detection and diagnosis of breast cancer. It captures two projections of each breast, a top-to-bottom view named Cranio-Caudal (CC) view and a side view taken at an angle named Mediolateral Oblique (MLO) view. If detected, proper treatment can be given at the initial stages and a patient's life can be saved.

Some of the significant signs of breast cancer such as masses, clusters of micro-calcifications, spiculated masses and architectural distortions are checked by radiologists and breast surgeons during visual examination of mammogram. Examples of mammograms for each type of abnormality are shown in Figure 1. The breast imaging reporting and data system (BI-RADS), is a standard for reporting and classification of mammogram studies. BI-RADS is defined by the American College of Radiology, (American College of Radiology [ACR], 1998).

As the number of mammograms to be analyzed by the radiologists and breast surgeons is enormous, there is possibility that they may miss some subtle abnormalities. Computer based system which is designed using the expert knowledge of radiologists and oncologists to detect abnormalities can act as second opinion and assists the radiologists to increase performance of diagnosis.

The main goal of the proposed chapter is to introduce dominant features of various signs of abnormalities in breast and to discuss existing algorithms for detection and classification of abnormalities in mammograms. The chapter also presents recent progress in the field of development of algorithms for computer assisted detection of breast cancer. This knowledge will help to develop a system which is useful for the early detection and classification of abnormalities in breast using mammogram image analysis. Some of the techniques implemented by authors to detect various types of abnormalities in mammograms are explained in detail.

Figure 1. Examples of Mammograms with (a) circumscribed mass (b) micro-calcifications (c) architectural distortion (d) speculated lesions Source: MIAS Database

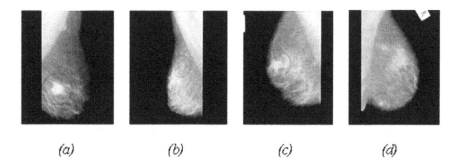

(a)   (b)   (c)   (d)

BACKGROUND

This section describes existing computer based algorithms for the detection of cancerous tissues in breast by processing and analyzing digital mammograms. The literature reviewed is divided into five groups namely, Pre-processing techniques, Techniques for detection and classification of masses, Techniques for detection and classification of micro-calcifications, Techniques for detection of architectural distortion - spicules and Techniques for overall abnormality detection.

Pre-Processing of Mammograms

The preprocessing of mammograms is needed, firstly to remove the artifacts and secondly to enhance the mammogram quality. If tiny abnormalities are clearly visible in the dense breast background then the accuracy of diagnosis of breast cancer can be improved. Visibility of abnormal tissue can be improved by enhancing the contrast of the mammogram.

Ayman et al. (2006) introduced pre-processing techniques for reducing the size using image shrinking and pixel depth conversion. Image is resized to reduce the size by 87% and then enhanced to improve the quality. In the work by Saltanat at al. (2010), an exponential mapping is applied to each pixel in the mammogram. Then the morphological operations like opening and closing are used to clear the unwanted small regions and to sharpen the boundary of the regions. Then a threshold is set using region growing technique and binary image is derived which is used to segment the pectoral muscle. In spite of changes in dimensions and location of pectoral muscle and presence of artifacts, the algorithm accurately marks the boundary of pectoral muscle. Wang et al. (2010) proposed a new method to detect the pectoral muscle edge using a Discrete Time Markov Chain (DTMC) and an active contour method. DTMC algorithm has the chance to obtain the false pectoral muscle boundary at the lower part of the mammogram if the pectoral muscle mixes with the glandular tissues. To improve the detection precision, validation is done and correction is applied by replacing the false part of the rough muscle boundary by a straight line. Next step is application of an active contour model in order to refine the boundary. The experimental results indicated that the percentages of false positive (FP) and false negative (FN) pixels are less than 5% in 77.5% mammograms. Maitra et al. (2011) used three step processes to pre-process the mammograms. In this method, contrast of image is improved using contrast limited adaptive histogram equalization (CLAHE). The CLAHE method seeks to reduce the noise and edge- blurring effect in homogeneous areas. In order to get uniform distribution or specified distribution, CLAHE is applied on each tile. Then a rectangle is initialized so that pectoral muscle can be removed using seeded region growing algorithm.

From the surveyed papers it can be concluded that contrast enhancement and removal of pectoral muscle are two important pre-processing techniques. Because of contrast enhancement, abnormal lesions become visible in complex background of mammogram. As abnormal lesions and pectoral region may have similar intensity and texture, removal of pectoral muscle reduces number of wrong detections during abnormality detection.

Detection and Classification of Masses

A mass in a breast is a 3D lesion that appears more prominent from the surrounding breast tissues. A benign mass abnormality in a mammogram is characterized by its smooth border and malignancy is characterized by irregular borders. In complete mass detection system, first phase is to check presence of suspicious lesion and second phase is classification of mass into benign or malignant class.

Kekre et al. (2010) demonstrated segmentation and detection of cancerous lesions in breast by using vector quantization (VQ) technique. A feature vector is obtained by first dividing the image into sub-blocks and then converting each sub-block into one dimensional array. Then image is divided into clusters by using Kekare's median fast codebook generation algorithm. After VQ segmentation, object with largest area is selected and its boundary is superimposed on the original mammogram. Mass identification rate of the proposed method is 68.5%. Mencattini et al. (2008) used a region-based segmentation procedure to segment masses in mammograms. The algorithm starts by removing artifacts from the selected region of interest (ROI). Then the ROI contrast is enhanced using nonlinear operator. For faster implementation of region growing algorithm, it is applied on decimated image instead of original image. In mammograms, there is a chance that the fibrous normal tissues are connected to the mass and is detected as part of mass boundary. These connected parts are removed by applying certain morphological operations. The algorithm is found to be efficient in computation time, adaptable and robust one.

Megalan et al. (2012) compared the performance of region based active contour models & level set methods in detecting masses from mammogram images. In region based segmentation, the initial mask based on the region of interest is specified. In order to improve speed of computation, size of image is reduced. External and internal energies are analyzed iteratively to detect the abnormalities. Abnormality region is identified as a line evolving curve. The second method implemented to detect the mass is partial differential equation based level set method. The given image is applied to the deformable based level set methods. During each iteration, the initial curve moves closer to the actual object boundary. Region based segmentation method has indicated advantages such as high-speed operation, not susceptible to the over segmentation. Boujelben et al. (2012), worked on semi- automation detection of breast mass using implicit deformable model i.e. level set method. To minimize the temporal complexity, narrow band fast marching method is used in the level set algorithm. To solve the problem of over segmentation (also addressed by Megalan, Ranjith, & Thandaiah, 2012), adaption of level set is done using edge and region criteria. After detection of mass boundary, various features for boundary description, texture description and region description are extracted and used by KNN classifier and MLP classifier to perform classification of masses into benign and malignant. Experimentation indicates that the results are accurate because of the cooperation of boundary, region and texture features. The sensitivity and specificity of the system is up to 90%.

Mencattini et al. (2011) developed a novel system for the mass border extraction, using Spatial Fuzzy C-Means (SFCM) segmentation. In the second step the boundary is refined by active contours model without edge. SFCM is applied on the selected ROI to form four classes of pixels. The pixels near the center are used to initialize the mask. The initial contour is obtained by applying morphological operations on the initial mask. Using an active contour method final boundary is identified. The method gives good performance for both types of databases i.e. direct digital mammograms and digitized mammograms. A pattern classification step is used to test malignancy of detected mass. Rangayyan et al. (2010) demonstrated a novel method based on frequency domain technique to determine the fractal dimension. In this work, the 2D contour is transformed into 1D signature. The 1D signature is then normalized along both axes. The fractal dimension using 1/f model is computed using the power spectral analysis (PSA) method applied to the 1D signature of the contours of the masses. The FD is computed using box-counting method to analyze masses in mammograms by Guo et al. (2005). Here, classification of breast masses and abnormal regions is performed using fractal dimension and support vector machine classifier. In the system proposed by Nandi et al. (2006), combination of edge sharpness features, shape features and statistical texture features is used. Out of total twenty-two features, only nine features are selected at a time by using one of the various feature selection methods. According to the results of feature selection tests, two feature sets with significant features are formed. Genetic programming classifier is designed using these two feature sets. The most important feature found is the shape measure of fractional concavity. The performance of classification is observed to be varying from 90% to 100% depending on the selected combination of sharpness, shape and texture features.

Timp and Karssemeijer (2004) presented an automatic technique using segmentation by dynamic programming to detect abnormalities. First the ROI is transformed to polar space. Then dynamic programming is applied to find the best possible path from one of the point in the initial column to one of the point in the last column of the image. The best possible path is given by that path for which cumulative cost is at its minimum value. Summation of the local costs of all the points in the path gives the cumulative cost of a path. After detection of optimal path, the image is transformed back to rectangular space which indicates the segmented mass. This segmentation algorithm is robust and has shown average overlap percentage of 69% for dynamic programming, 60% for discrete contour model and 58% for region growing.

In the framework by Wang et al. (2007) pyramidal approach is used for mass detection in mammograms. Preprocessing with exponential transformation is done in order to enhance the contrast between the mass and the surrounding tissues. First step in the pyramidal linking algorithm is to build the pyramid. This is followed by pyramidal linking and averaging of linked pixels. The pyramid linking generates smooth regions with definite boundaries. Using grey-plane slicing algorithm suspicious regions are extracted. Very small and very large connected components are rejected. From each isolated region, six features are extracted and using binary tree classification suspicious regions are discriminated from normal regions. The proposed pyramidal segmentation method gives sensitivity rate of 86.5% at 0.6 FP per image.

To summarize, various mass detection methods can be broadly classified into vector quantization segmentation, region growing, dynamic programming in polar domain and active contours. Comparison of various methods is a bit difficult task as there is no uniformity in the database used for experimentation and secondly, different works use different performance measures. Though the VQ approach is easy to implement and faster in response, mass identification rate by vector quantization method claimed by Kekare et al. (2010) is comparatively low i.e. 68.5%. Advantage of Spatial Fuzzy C-Means (SFCM) segmentation by Mencattini et al. (2011) is that it can initialize the mask close to the actual mass boundary and hence needs less number of iterations for refining the boundary by active contour method. As concluded by Megalan et al. (2012) the region based active contour model is the promising model for the mammogram images than level set method. Over segmentation problem of level set method is solved by Boujelben et al. (2012), with adaption of level set using edge and region criteria. Timp et al. (2004) introduced a robust technique using dynamic programming for automatic segmentation of masses. A benign mass usually has well defined margins and homogeneous texture near boundary and malignant mass has a speculated and irregular boundary and heterogeneous texture. Hence various shape, boundary and texture features are reported in the previous work for classification of masses. As mentioned by

Rangayyan et al. (2010), use of FD of 1D signature of 2D mass contour by PSA method is very effective in classifying malignant and benign masses.

Detection and Classification of Micro-Calcifications

Micro-calcification clusters are key indicators of cancerous abnormality in breast. Because of complex background, tiny micro-calcifications are not easily visible in mammograms. Thus there is need of pre-processing steps like enhancing the contrast and enhancing fine details. Usually micro-calcification detection step is followed by classification of micro-calcifications into benign and malignant classes.

The study by Karahaliou et al. (2007) demonstrated use of texture properties of the tissue in the neighborhood of micro-calcification clusters (MCs) to analyze mammograms. Texture analysis is applied on ROIs of size 128 x 128, containing the MCs. A wavelet transform based contrast enhancement technique is used to pre-process the ROI. A threshold is applied to separate MCs from the surroundings. First and second order statistical features and Laws' texture measures are captured from the surrounding area. Classification into malignant and benign MCs is done using K-nearest neighbor classifier. Training and testing is done by using "leaving-one-out method". The highest performance in terms of overall accuracy of 89%, sensitivity 90.74% and specificity 86.96% is obtained with the Laws' texture energy measures. Oliver et al. (2012) designed a high accuracy system for detection of micro-calcification clusters using knowledge-based approach. Bank of filters are used to capture local structure of the micro-calcifications. The work is divided into three parts. In first part, the small regions containing a micro-calcification from known mammogram samples are convolved with a bank of filters to form the word dictionary. These words of the dictionary are then convolved with regions containing a micro-calcification and regions without a micro-calcification and thus training database is ready. Afterwards the gentle boost classifier is trained using the training data. Lastly, new mammograms are given as input to the trained classifier pixel by pixel and each pixel is classified and a probability image is generated. Algorithm developed by Balakumaran and Vennila (2011) uses foveal method for detecting micro-calcification in mammogram. In this work, selected ROI using skewness and kurtosis is decomposed to n levels using dyadic wavelet transform. Foveal method marks an area as micro-calcification if its perceivable contrast is greater than the adaptively selected threshold. The foveal method is applied to LL band at each level. If the approximation coefficients are marked by foveal algorithm, corresponding detail planes are retained otherwise they are assigned zero value. Then the image is reconstructed from the retained significant coefficients. To detect micro-calcification, image is reconstructed by suppressing lowest frequency sub-band. With the proposed method true positive ratio of 91.1% at 1.5 false positive per image is achieved.

Wang and Karayiannis (1998) used discrete wavelet transform to represent different frequency sub-bands in a mammogram. The micro-calcifications represent high frequency contents in an image. Therefore, in order to detect micro-calcifications, low frequency sub-band is discarded and the mammogram is reconstructed using only high frequency sub-bands. Preliminary experiments proved that wavelet based sub-band image decomposition has potential of detecting micro-calcifications but further investigations are needed to improve the performance. Similar approach using wavelet transform is also presented by José and Bruno (2005).

Algorithm developed by Carmen et al., (2001) uses region growing technique with linear prediction error for seed selection. Gaussian low pass filtered image is subtracted from original image to get high pass filtered image where micro-calcifications are enhanced. The seed selection step uses 2D linear prediction error to detect potential micro-calcifications. It is very difficult to predict a micro-calcification pixel which is a point of non-stationarity in a homogeneous neighborhood. Thus it gives large amount of error. If the prediction error is greater than predetermined threshold, the pixel is selected as seed for the region growing algorithm. The proposed method shows a significant reduction in the computational time and false positives. Ghada Saad et al., (2016) implemented a two-stage method for detecting micro-calcifications in breast. In the first phase, after background noise removal by Wiener filter, probable micro-calcification regions are identified using Law's filters. In the second phase the probable suspicious region is selected by manual cropping and its texture features are given as input to the ANN or Adaboost classifier to classify it as normal, benign or malignant. The algorithm has shown overall accuracy of 98%.

To conclude, as micro-calcifications represent high frequencies, multi-scale decomposition methods are widely used. The main aim of these methods is to take advantage of the dissimilarity in frequency content between MCs and the adjacent background for the detection of MCs. Use of statistical features, GLCM texture features and Laws' texture energy measures is presented for classification of MCs into benign and malignant.

Detection of Architectural Distortion and Spicules

Architectural distortion is distortion to the normal radial pattern of breast and it show signs of a node-like pattern with spiculations that appear to radiate from a point (American College of Radiology [ACR], 1998). Detection of architectural distortion with high accuracy plays an important role in early detection of breast cancer.

Matsubaraa et al. (2003) developed a technique to detect architectural distortions that are present near skin-line and within mammary tissues. In this method, the mammary gland region is detected by binarization and distortion is determined by top hat filtering. Then information about size and position of distortions is used to eliminate the false positives. Sensitivities of 94% and 84% were demonstrated for the above two cases respectively by the proposed method. Ayres and Rangayyan (2003) presented a technique based on oriented features to detect architectural distortion in mammograms. Gabor magnitude response is used to determine local orientation information of all pixels in the ROI. The type of phase representation is decided by sliding the analysis window through the orientation field. Six features captured from the phase representations are given to quadratic discriminant classifier to decide whether the given ROI is present with architectural distortion or with normal pattern. Sensitivity of 80% and specificity of 80% is achieved with this method.

In the first phase of method proposed by Biswas and Mukherjee (2011), oriented filter banks at various scales are used to analyze mammograms and to form texture descriptors. In the next phase it is trained for latent textural primitives from the collected features based on Gaussian mixture model. The results indicate that the proposed approach performs better than other competing approaches. Sheng et al. (2001) represented the original mammogram at multiple resolutions using Quincunx transform which is a linear phase non-separable two-dimensional (2-D) wavelet transform. For every pixel at each resolution two sets of features are derived. First set of features based on gradient orientation histogram is useful for detecting spicules surrounding the central mass portion. Another set of features based on pixel intensity helps to detect the central mass portion. Multi-resolution approach resolves the difficulty of determining the neighborhood size in advance and improves processing speed. Classification is performed by using binary tree technique. Experimental results have indicated that this technique can detect spicules of various sizes at low false positive rates and with high speed. The technique developed by Sampat and Bovik (2003) operates in two phases. First the spicules are enhanced and then the point of convergence of spicules is determined. For the enhancement of mammogram, radon transformed image is filtered by column filter, a threshold is applied and then inverse radon transformation is done. For the detection stage, sine and cosine radial speculation filter banks are used. Output of each bank is added point wise to get the final output and its maxima indicates the location of spicule. With slight modifications in the algorithm it can be used for the detection of architectural distortions.

To summarize, most of the reported work, used oriented features to detect architectural distortion and speculated lesions in mammograms. Linear structures are enhanced by Radon transform. Active contour models are also tested for the detection of spicules.

Overall Abnormality Detection and Classification

Ultimate aim of CAD system is to detect all types of abnormalities in breast by using digital mammogram analysis and to further classify them into benign and malignant types. Review of various techniques for detection of more than one abnormality or all types of abnormalities is presented here.

In the work proposed by Mudigonda et al. (2001) detection of circumscribed and speculated masses in mammographic images is done using segmentation of mass regions. Mammogram image is first enhanced by Gaussian filter and then sub-sampled. Segmentation algorithm starts from the center of mass and develops intensity links into the neighboring regions in the image. Accuracy of 74% is achieved with this method of mass detection. Further the regions segmented were classified as benign masses or malignant tumors by computing texture measures in adaptive ribbons of pixels surrounding the mass regions. The measures achieved an area of 0.79 under the ROC curve. In the work proposed by Vibha and Rege (2007), use of Chebyshev moments (CMs) is tested for detection of type of abnormality and malignancy. To achieve rotation and scale invariance, combination of Chebyshev moment and Log-polar coordinate system is proposed. For every ROI, 10 CMs are computed and by analyzing these values it is found that two second order moments are useful for classifying malignancy into different types and T03 and T23 can distinguish between normal, benign and malignant samples.

Rashed et al. (2007) interpreted mammograms using multi-resolution analysis. The given mammogram image is decomposed using Daubechies (Db) wavelet up to four levels. Feature vector is constructed by using fraction of wavelet coefficients at every level and Euclidian distance based classifier is used. Db4, Db8 and Db16 wavelets were tested for first level classification where ROIs were classified according to the type of abnormality and for second level classification where ROIs were classified according to malignancy. Experimentation is also done using varying percentage of selected coefficients. Highest correct classification rate is achieved with DB8 wavelet. Nithya and Santhi (2011) demonstrated use of maximum difference method for selecting important Haralick texture features based on GLCM with neural network classifier. The proposed method of feature selection leads to classification with greater accuracy.

In the framework by Phadke and Rege (2014), principal component analysis is used to transform the initial data set into a new set of vector samples where desired dimension can be selected. Data size is reduced by selecting first few important components. It is followed by independent component analysis (ICA) to capture maximum independent features. Two types of classifiers: support vector machine and artificial neural network are tested for classifying ROI as normal or malignant. Results of experimentation by varying number of principal components (PCs) reveals, 6 to 10 PCs give good results for both the classifiers. SVMs-based classification with different kernel functions is applied for mammograms classification. The results show that SVM classifier with linear kernel achieves highest accuracy of 70.83% for the testing set. Comparison of results by SVM and ANN classifiers indicates that ANN classifier gives better accuracy of classification than SVM classifier which is 87.81%. Phadke and Rege (2015) demonstrated combined use of local and global features for classifying abnormal ROI from normal ROI. Abnormal ROIs includes both benign and malignant samples. A total of 34 features are used comprised of two Chebyshev moments and nineteen GLCM features determined over the local neighborhood and thirteen features based on Laws' energy and Gabor transform computed for the complete ROI of size 128 x 128. Proposed system has shown encouraging performance in terms of classification accuracy of 93.17% with the SVM classification technique.

Kriti et al. (2016) predicted type of breast density by using textural features derived from Law's texture energy images. Direct relation between breast density and risk of cancer development makes prediction of breast density clinically important. Bhattacherjee et al. (2016) used back propagation neural network for classification of breast cancer with Wisconsin breast cancer dataset and achieved very high accuracy of 99.27%. Cheriguene et al. (2016) proposed a novel computer aided system for classification of breast tumor based on feature selection and static classifier selection scheme. Zemmal et al. (2016) experimented use of semi supervised support vector machine technique for the diagnosis of breast cancer and obtained encouraging results.

In the reported work, various features like GLCM texture features, Chebyshev moments, Multi-resolution features, PCA-ICA features are used for classification of breast tissues in normal and abnormal classes. There is still scope for improvement in the accuracy of classification. Hence new features, other types of classifiers can be tested.

Summary of Literature Review

From the literature review, it is proven that CAD tools can be used as second opinion and can definitely improve the performance of the radiologists. From the literature survey it is concluded that, micro-calcifications can be detected efficiently using multi-resolution analysis of mammograms by wavelet transform. Radial pattern converging outward from the center is unique feature of architectural distortion and spicules. Thus, features based on orientation information are useful for detecting these abnormalities. Gabor filters, gradient based phase analysis and oriented texture analysis can be used to acquire directional features of architectural distortion and spicules. Vector quantization (VQ) technique, region based active contour models & level set methods, Spatial Fuzzy C-Means (SFCM) segmentation are useful techniques to delineate the mammographic masses but these techniques are not useful for detection of other types of abnormalities like micro-calcifications or architectural distortions. The features useful for categorization of masses into benign and malignant types are moments, GLCM texture features, laws texture energy measures, fractal dimension etc. Principal features and or methods with respect to the type of abnormality and or malignancy are indicated in Table 1.

METHODS FOR DETECTION OF ABNORMALITY

Various image processing methods to detect abnormality in breast by analyzing digitized mammograms are discussed in detail in this section. These methods are divided into five groups namely, Pre-processing of mammograms, Detection and classification of masses, Detection and classification of micro-calcifications, Detection and classification of architectural distortions - spiculated masses and Detection and classification of all types of abnormalities.

Table 1. Dominant Features

Type of Abnormality	Features
Circumscribed Masses	Chebyshev Moments, Haralick's texture features, Fractal Dimension
Micro-Calcification	Features based on Wavelet Transform
Architectural Distortion	Directional features like Gabor transform based features, Laws' texture energy measures
Spiculated Lesion	Quincunx Wavelet Transform and orientation based features
Noraml / Malignant Classification of All Abnormalities	PCA-ICA Features
Normal / Abnormal Classification	GLCM, Chebyshev moments, Fractal Dimension, Gabor transform, Laws' texture energy measures

Database Used and Scope of the Work

Authors implemented and tested the algorithms on database provided by Mammogram Image Analysis Society (MIAS) (Suckling, Astley, Betal, Cerneaz, Dance, & Kok, 1994). MIAS provides database of only medio-lateral oblique (MLO) view of mammograms. The size of each image is 1024 pixels x 1024 pixels. MIAS database consist of 322 mammograms which are distributed among 208 normal, 66 benign, and 48 malignant cases. There are 10 architectural distortions, 8 spiculations, 9 micro-calcifications, 4 circumscribed masses, 8 miscellaneous masses and 9 asymmetries in the total 48 malignant cases. Total 66 benign cases include 9 architectural distortions, 11 spiculations, 15 micro-calcifications, 18 circumscribed masses, 7 miscellaneous masses and 6 asymmetries. For each image in the database, background tissue type, type of abnormality, center and radius of the abnormality are provided.

Cranio-caudal (CC) views of left and right breast are not provided. Therefore, authors restricted the survey to single view mammogram analysis. Secondly authors restricted the study to two-dimensional mammogram analyses. Authors have not considered three-dimensional breast digital tomo-synthesis data (DBT) because of unavailability of enough amounts of DBT data from non-public source for all types of abnormal tissues in breast.

Preprocessing of Mammograms

1. Key Features of the Implemented Method
   a. It mainly performs two tasks:
      i. To remove unwanted labels and tape marks
      ii. To remove the pectoral muscle if the mammogram is in MLO view.
   b. Use of Canny edge detection and Hough transform for removal of pectoral muscle.
2. Description of the Method

Detailed methodology used to pre-process the mammogram while detecting masses is given by Algorithm 1. The first phase of algorithm is removal of undesired data like tape marks, labels from the background by using region growing technique followed by enhancement of breast boundary using global histogram processing. The second phase is pectoral muscle removal. Pectoral muscle has intensities similar to masses and hence causes incorrect detection of suspicious masses. Thus pectoral muscle removal prior

Algorithm 1. Pre-Processing of Mammogram

```
Input: Mammogram image
Output: Pre-processed image
Begin
    1. Read the input mammogram.
    2. Determine a binary mask representing breast portion of the mammogram by
applying region growing algorithm.
    3. Remove the unwanted data from the mammogram by application of the binary
mask on the original mammogram.
    4. Remove the black strip behind the mammogram which doesn't have any use-
ful information. This will reduce the amount of data to be processed by next
stages.
    5. Apply global histogram processing to enhance the breast boundary.
    6. Apply Canny edge detector to detect edges at the top right corner of the
mammogram where pectoral muscle is positioned.
    7. Apply Hough transform to detect all the line segments in this region.
The longest line segment represents edge of pectoral muscle.
    8. Remove pectoral muscle by assigning black level to all the pixels above
the edge of pectoral muscle.
    9. Detect the approximate location of mass by applying pseudo coloring to
the image.
End
```

to the mass detection reduces the number of false positives and leads to improvement in the accuracy of mass detection.

3. Results and Discussion

The original mammogram and the results of pre-processing of mammogram at various stages are demonstrated by Figure 2 (a) to Figure 2 (e) respectively. A different scale is used while displaying all these mammograms.

Detection and Classification of Masses

1. **Key Features of the Method:** Important features of the proposed method are:
   a. Detection of mass boundary by Active contour based segmentation.
   b. Use of fractal dimension of the signature of the mass boundary for classifying masses into benign and malignant classes.
   c. Use of a total of 22 mammograms comprising of 18 benign masses and 4 malignant masses from MIAS database for the experimentation.
2. Description of the Method

Figure 2. (a) Original Image (b) Image obtained after background removal (c) Output of Canny edge detector (d) Pectoral muscle removed image (e) Pseudo colored image

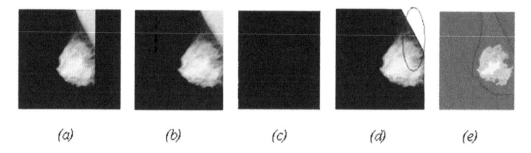

     (a)   (b)   (c)   (d)   (e)

a.   **Detection of Mass Boundary:** Level-set method based deformable contour model is used to trace the boundary of the mass. The algorithm starts with an initial curve. The approximate location of mass obtained by the pre-processing algorithm is used to initialize the starting contour. The contour is represented by the zero-level set of a smooth function. It is propagated to acquire the shape of the object by using a time-dependent partial differential equation. In every iteration, the contour moves closer to the desired object boundary based on internal and external energies. Active contour technique is based on energy minimization principle given by the sum of an internal energy and external energy. When the active contour aligns itself with the object boundary, the external energy is supposed to be minimal.

b.   **Classification of Masses:** The delineated boundary of the mass is converted to the one-dimensional signature by plotting the radial distance of each point on the contour to the centroid of the contour with respect to the index of the contour point. If the signature is smooth it represents benign mass and if it is uneven and jagged it represents a malignant mass. Smoothness or roughness of the boundary can be measured in terms of the fractal dimension (FD) of 1D signature and thus FD can be used to identify malignant and benign masses.

In the present work, fractal dimension of the 1D signature of the mass boundary delineated by the deformable contour method is computed via Power Spectral Analysis (PSA) and a threshold based classifier is designed to differentiate between benign and malignant masses (Dhanelekshmi & Phadke, 2013). The detailed process for the detection and classification of masses is given by Algorithm 2.

3.   Results and Discussion

Performance measures of the implemented system of mass detection using deformable contours and classification using fractal dimension by PSA method are specificity of 83%, sensitivity of 75% and accuracy of 82%. Deformable contours act as a best means to mark the boundary of the circumscribed masses in mammograms as it is capable of integrating pixel by pixel image information into smooth and linked curves. Fractal analysis acts as a promising method to differentiate between the benign masses and the malignant tumors.

Algorithm 2. Detection and Classification of Circumscribed Masses

```
Input: Pre-processed image
Output: Decision = Benign / Malignant mass
Begin
   1. Initialize the number of iterations, value of the smoothing term α and
the starting contour for the pre-processed mammogram.
   3. Represent the initial contour using a signed distance map 'Φ'.
   4. Use the mask B(x,y) to set the local region near the contour.
```

$$B\left(x,y\right) = \begin{cases} 1, x - y < r \\ 0, \ otherwise \end{cases}$$

```
   5. Compute the localized means uₓ and vₓ of interior and exterior of the
curve respectively for the selected local region using the following equa-
tions.
```

$$u_x = \frac{\int B\left(x,y\right).H\phi\left(y\right).I\left(y\right)dy}{\int B\left(x,y\right).H\phi\left(y\right).dy}$$

$$v_x = \frac{\int B\left(x,y\right).(1 - H\phi\left(y\right)).I\left(y\right)dy}{\int B\left(x,y\right).(1 - H\phi\left(y\right)).dy}$$

```
   where interior of the curve C is represented by HΦ(x) and exterior is rep-
resented by (1- HΦ(x)). The area just around the curve is given by δΦ(x).
   6. Determine image based forces f using
```

$$f = -\left(\left(u_x - v_x\right)\left(\left(B\left(x,y\right)H\phi\left(y\right)I\left(y\right) - u_x\right)/A_{in} + \left(B\left(x,y\right)\left(1 - H\phi\left(y\right)\right)I\left(y\right) - v_x\right)/A_{out}\right)\right)$$

```
   where, A_in and A_out represent the areas of inside and outside local regions
near the contour.
   7. Determine curvature 'kappa' (k) by the following equation.
```

$$k = \frac{\varnothing_{xx}\varnothing_y^2 - 2\varnothing_x\varnothing_y\varnothing_{xy} + \varnothing_{yy}\varnothing_x^2}{\left(\varnothing_x^2 + \varnothing_y^2\right)^{3/2}}$$

```
   where Φ_x, Φ_y and Φ_xy are central derivatives of Φ in horizontal, vertical
and diagonal directions respectively.
   8. Minimize the energy by applying gradient descent using following equa-
tions.
```

$$\frac{d\varnothing}{dt} = \frac{f}{\max\left(\left|f\right|\right)} + \propto k$$

```
   and
```

$$dt = 0.45 / \left(\max\left(\frac{d\varnothing}{dt}\right) + \varepsilon\right)$$

```
   9. Evolve the curve using,
```

continued on following page

Algorithm 2. Continued

$$\varnothing = \varnothing + dt\frac{d\varnothing}{dt}$$

```
   10. If current iteration is less than the total number of iterations go to
step 5 else mark the current position of the curve as mass boundary.
   11. Determine 1D signature of the detected mass boundary.
   12. Determine fractal dimension F_d of the mass using PSA method.
   13. Compare F_d with the predetermined threshold. If F_d is less than the
threshold then it is a benign mass else it is malignant mass.
End
```

Detection and Classification of Microcalcifications

1. **Key Features of the Method:** Important features of the proposed method are:
    a. Use of wavelet transform to decompose the image into frequency sub-bands and to detect micro-calcifications by enhancing high frequency sub-band.
    b. Classification of micro-calcifications into benign and malignant classes by using Artificial Neural Network (ANN) classifier.
    c. Use of a total of 52 ROIs of size of 256 x 256 comprised of 26 normal ROIs, 15 ROIs with benign micro-calcifications and 11 ROIs with malignant micro-calcifications from MIAS database.
2. Description of the Method

Detection of micro-calcifications is an extremely difficult task, as the abnormality is almost invisible in the surrounded dense breast tissues. Micro-calcifications are tiny bright spots and hence represent high frequency components. As micro-calcifications represent high frequency information, the high frequency sub-band of the image decomposed using wavelet-transform is used as feature to detect and classify mammograms into micro-calcifications and normal mammograms.

The digitized mammogram image can be decomposed up to the desired number of levels by applying wavelet transform with a decimation factor of 2. Wavelet analysis decomposes the image at multiple resolutions. At each level of decomposition, four sub-bands are generated: LL sub-band containing low frequency coefficients (approximation data) and LH, HL, HH sub-bands containing high frequency co-efficients (detailed data). Micro-calcifications appear as a cluster of minute intense spots on a complex dense background of breast tissues and thus represent high frequencies of the image data. Hence amplification of high frequency sub-bands by some gain factor leads to enhancement of micro-calcifications and thus improves visibility of micro-calcifications in the reconstructed image. Algorithm 3 explains in detail the process for the detection of micro-calcifications in the given ROI (Phadke & Rege, 2013b).

Wavelet coefficients from the LH, HL and HH sub-bands are used as feature vector to classify the given ROI into normal or micro-calcified ROI. An artificial neural network (ANN) is trained to classify the samples into two classes i.e. normal or micro-calcification using the feature vectors of the samples from the training set. If the sample is detected as micro-calcified it is further classified into benign or malignant class using another trained ANN classifier.

Algorithm 3. Detection of Micro-Calcifications

```
Input: Mammogram ROI
Output: ROI with enhanced micro-calcifications
Begin
   1. Read Mammogram ROI.
   2. Decompose the ROI using Wavelet transform with Dubache-4 wavelet up to
seventh level.
   3. If the detail wavelet coefficient value (coefficients from LH, HL and HH
sub-bands) is greater than the pre-determined threshold, multiply it by a gain
factor.
   4. Apply inverse wavelet transform on the modified wavelet coefficients and
reconstruct the ROI.
   5. Detect the location of micro-calcifications by applying threshold on the
reconstructed ROI.
End
```

3.   Results and Discussion

Figure 3 demonstrates results of the proposed method to detect micro-calcifications for two sample mammograms from MIAS database.

At first level of classification i.e. classification of abnormal ROIs (micro-calcified) from normal ROIs, an accuracy of 99% is achieved with the ANN classifier. An accuracy of 96% is obtained for the further classification of micro-calcifications into benign and malignant classes.

Enhancement of detailed coefficients is an effective technique to enhance and detect micro-calcifications in a mammogram. These features are also useful to classify micro-calcifications as benign or malignant.

Figure 3. (a) Original ROI (b) Enhanced ROI

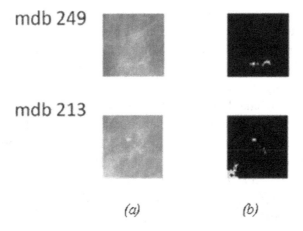

Detection and Classification of Architectural Distortions, Spiculated Masses

Architectural distortion show signs of a node-like pattern with spiculations that appear to radiate from a point (ACR, 1998). Spiculated masses have a central portion similar to circumscribed masses surrounded by radiating spicules. Thus, oriented features are useful to detect potential sites of architectural distortions and speculated lesions. Phadke and Rege (2013a) implemented a technique to detect architectural distortions using oriented features based on Gabor filters and Laws' texture measures and has demonstrated accuracy of 85.00%. In this section a methodology to detect spiculated lesions using multi-resolution analysis is explained.

1. **Key Features of the Method:** Important features of the proposed method are:
   a. Uses a multi-resolution representation of mammogram using Quincunx wavelet transform.
   b. No need to decide the neighborhood size in advance, to capture the features of spicules of varying sizes, because of multi-resolution representation.
   c. Use of features based on the histogram of gradient orientations.
   d. Use of a total of 45 normal ROIs and eight spiculated ROIs of size of 128 x 128 from MIAS database for the experimentation.
2. Description of the Method

In the proposed work, mammogram is decomposed into multiple spatial resolutions using Quincunx wavelet transform which is a linear phase non-separable 2D perfect reconstruction transform. Non-separable transform avoids phase distortion and addition of bias in the horizontal and vertical directions.

If the original mammogram has the finest spatial resolution of N x N pixels, then at every level of decomposition, the image resolution is decreased by a factor of $1/\sqrt{2}$ and the image at the second level has resolution of $N/\sqrt{2}$ x $N/\sqrt{2}$ pixels. The images of (N x N), (N/2 x N/2), . . . spatial resolutions are used for feature extraction. Same set of features extracted at a coarser resolution with the same window size can detect larger lesions than that at the finer resolution. Thus, it resolves the problem of deciding window size a priori. Detection of the smallest possible spiculated lesions is possible by selecting very small neighborhood at the finest resolution for feature extraction. Flowchart of the proposed system is shown in Figure 4.

An ROI with speculated lesions shows almost uniform histogram of gradient orientations as spicules are spread in almost all directions where as a normal ROI shows peaked histogram as normal patterns are oriented only in the direction towards the breast nipple. Therefore the standard deviation of gradient orientation in the speculated ROI will be larger than that in the normal ROI. Thus the features based on histogram of gradient orientations are useful to differentiate between normal and speculated lesion. A total of four features are captured from the low frequency wavelet coefficient at the finest resolution to detect smallest possible speculated lesions. These four features are namely mean pixel brightness, standard deviation of pixels, standard deviation of gradient orientation histogram (σ_{hist}) and standard deviation of folded gradient orientation (σ_θ') in the predefined neighborhood. As the features behave equally in all directions, a circular neighborhood is used. A larger neighborhood radius is used for last two features as they respond stronger to a spiculated lesion if the entire halo of spicules is included in the feature extraction window, while a smaller neighborhood radius is used for the first two features as they respond better to the central mass of the lesion (Liu, Babbs, & Delp, 2001). The detailed algorithm for extracting features of the ROI is given by Algorithm 4. A decision based classifier is implemented

Figure 4. Flowchart of proposed technique for detection of spiculated lesion

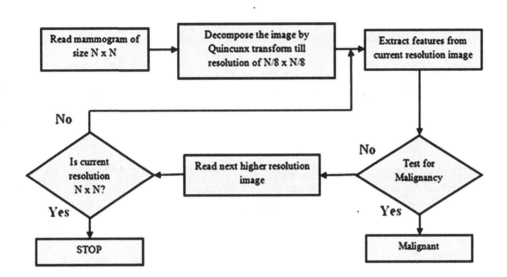

to classify the given ROI as normal or malignant. For an unknown sample, a feature vector containing four features is determined using Algorithm 4 and then it is applied as input to the classifier explained by Algorithm 5. The thresholds were obtained by analyzing the features extracted at every resolution for every image in the training database.

3.   Results and Discussion

Table 2 demonstrates the performance measures obtained with the proposed system for the spiculated lesion detection.

The Quincunx wavelet transform acts as a promising tool to represent mammogram at multiple spatial resolutions. Detection of abnormality starts at coarser resolution before proceeding to finer resolutions. If there is a positive detection at a coarser resolution, no feature extraction and detection are needed at all finer resolutions. Extracting features at coarser resolutions for relatively large regions significantly reduces the amount of computation. The proposed multi-resolution technique can detect spiculated lesions of various sizes with high value of both performance measures: the sensitivity and the specificity.

Detection and Classification of All Types of Abnormalities

This section briefly explains classification of all types of abnormalities from normal ROI by fusion of local and global features. A technique to classify malignant ROI from normal or benign ROI using PCA-ICA futures is also explained.

1.   Classification using Fusion of Local and Global Features

Proposed method (Phadke & Rege, 2015) uses local as well as global features for classifying abnormal ROI from normal ROI. Abnormal ROIs includes both benign and malignant samples. The local features

Algorithm 4. Feature Extraction for Spiculated Lesion

```
Input: Decomposed ROI using Quincunx wavelet transform
Output: Features mean, standard deviation, σ_hist and σ_θ'
Begin
    1. Create circular mask of radius 30 for determining σ_hist and σ_θ'.
    2. Create circular mask of radius 20 for determining mean and standard de-
viation.
    3. Multiply the ROI with the circular mask to select the circular neighbor-
hood.
    4. Determine the mean pixel brightness and the standard deviation of pixel
brightness in the circular neighborhood of radius 20.
    5. Apply Prewitt operator to obtain gradient orientations.
    6. Plot the histogram of gradient orientations within the neighborhood of
30 using 256 bins.
    7. Calculate the average bin height of the histogram of gradient orienta-
tions.
    8. Determine σ_hist and σ_θ' from the histogram.
    9. Determine the number of positive as well as negative gradient orienta-
tions.
    10. Estimate the folded gradient orientation by computing average of all
gradient orientations.
    11. Determine the mean of folded gradient orientation.
    12. Determine σ_θ' i.e. standard deviation of the folded gradient orienta-
tion.
End
```

Algorithm 5. Decision Based Classification

```
Input: Four features for the given ROI
Output: Decision = Normal / Spiculated ROI
Begin
    1. Declare variable flag and initialize it to zero.
    2. If mean is less than the threshold then increment the flag.
    3. If standard deviation is less than the threshold then increment the
flag.
    4. If σ_hist is less than the threshold then increment the flag.
    5. If σ_θ' is less than the threshold then increment the flag.
    6. If flag is greater than or equal to 3, then the ROI is classified as
normal else it is classified as spiculated lesion.
End
```

Table 2. Performance Measures of Spiculated lesion detection

Sensitivity (%)	Specificity (%)	Accuracy (%)
87.50	91.11	90.56

used are, nineteen Haralick's texture measures derived from GLCM of a small block of size 32 x 32 around the center of the ROI and discrete Chebyshev moments over a small block of size 8 x 8 and 16 x 16. Before determining the Chebyshev moments, Median filter is applied on the ROI to remove the unwanted high frequency data. Contrast of selected sub-block is improved by application of CLAHE prior to the computation of Haralick's features. Before capturing the global features, un-sharp masking is applied on the mammogram in order to sharpen the features of interest like radiating patterns in architectural distortions and spiculations, and bright spots in micro-calcifications. A total of thirteen features based on fractal dimension, Laws' energy and Gabor transform are computed for the complete ROI of size 128 x 128 and are used as global features. Thus a total of 34 features comprised of a total of 21 local features and a total of 13 global features are determined for each ROI. Concatenation of local and global features has resulted in the improved classification accuracy of 93.17% with the SVM classification technique.

2. PCA and ICA Based Classification

In the proposed method principal component analysis (PCA) is used as pre-processing step for independent component analysis (Phadke & Rege, 2014). Main aim of using PCA is to reduce the dimensionality. Independent components are used as features to differentiate between malignant and normal or benign samples. Performance of classification is compared for the two classifiers namely support vector machine (SVM) and artificial neural network (ANN). Results of experimentation by varying number of principal components (PCs) reveals that 6 to 10 PCs give good results for both the classifiers. SVMs-based classification with different kernel functions is applied for mammograms classification. The results show that SVM classifier with linear kernel achieves highest accuracy of 70.83% for the testing set. Comparison of results by SVM and ANN classifiers indicates that ANN classifier gives better accuracy of classification than SVM classifier which is 87.81%.

FUTURE RESEARCH DIRECTIONS

In this chapter, image processing techniques to detect various types of abnormalities in mammograms are discussed. Most of these methods work on a small ROI instead of complete mammogram. For example, fusion of local and global features technique uses ROI of size of 128 x 128. This technique can be extended for the detection of location of abnormality in the mammogram. Here, a window of size of 128 x 128 can be scrolled around each and every pixel and various local and global features are determined for each pixel. Using the features and SVM classifier a decision can be taken for each pixel, regarding whether it is normal or abnormal. All the pixels labeled as abnormal can be highlighted to indicate the spatial location of abnormality.

In order to detect spatial location of abnormality, it is necessary to determine features in the neighbourhood of each pixel in the given mammogram. This needs tremendous amount of computations. Thus time required to process the complete mammogram is very large. In order to improve speed, all these abnormality detection algorithms can be implemented on parallel computing platform like CUDA: Compute Unified Device Architecture.

The algorithms discussed in the chapter use single mammogram view. These algorithms can be applied on multiple projection views of the same breast and information from different views can be combined for better interpretation of mammograms and improvement in performance.

In the proposed work two types of classifiers are used namely ANN and SVM. New classification techniques like genetic algorithms, deep learning can be tested for improvement of accuracy. Kausar et al. (2016) used combination of support vector machines and K-means clustering for the classification of clinical data for early diagnosis of coronary artery disease. Similar techniques based on combination of supervised and unsupervised learning can be tested for the early detection of breast cancer. New features can be added to the proposed system in order to further improve the overall performance of the system.

CONCLUSION

The research avenues in the field of mammogram image analysis are explored in this chapter. Various methods for the classification of individual abnormality and all types of abnormalities from normal ROI of digitized mammogram are explained. As evident from the literature survey, there are four types of abnormalities namely masses, clusters of micro-calcifications, spiculated masses and architectural distortions. Dominant features specific to the type of abnormality are combined to develop an algorithm for the detection of all types of abnormalities.

Megalan et al. (2012) demonstrated the effectiveness of active contour models to detect masses in the mammogram images. Rangayyan et al. (2010) demonstrated the usefulness of fractal analysis via frequency domain approach for classification of masses. In the proposed work these two methods are combined to form a complete system to detect and classify circumscribed masses. Fractal analysis by PSA method has shown potential to differentiate between benign and malignant masses. Features based on histogram of gradient orientations are proved effective in detection of speculated lesions in digitized mammograms. The method based on combined use of dominant local and global features for classification of ROI into normal and abnormal classes has shown highest classification accuracy. PCA and ICA features along with the ANN classifier have shown accuracy of 87.81% for the classification of malignant ROIs from other ROIs.

ACKNOWLEDGMENT

The authors would like to express their sincere thanks to Board of College and University Development, Savitribai Phule Pune University for supporting the research work (Grant Number OSD/BCUD/230/61) and to Dr. Shekhar Kulkarni of Aastha, Breast cancer support group, India for guiding on medical aspects of breast cancer and mammograms.

REFERENCES

American Cancer Society. (2017). *Breast Cancer Statistics*. Retrieved from http://pressroom.cancer.org/BreastCancerStats2017

American College of Radiology (ACR). (1998). *Illustrated breast imaging reporting and data system* (3rd ed.). Reston, VA: BI-RADS.

Ayman, A., Qahwaji, R. S., Aqel, M. J., Hussam, A., & Salehand, M. H. (2006). Efficient Pre-processing of USF and MIAS Mammogram Images. *Journal of Computational Science, 3*(2), 67–75.

Ayres, F. J., & Rangayyan, R. M. (2003). Characterization of Architectural Distortion in Mammograms. In *Proceedings of the 25" Annual International Conference of the IEEE EMB* (Vol 1, pp. 886-889). Cancun, Mexico: IEEE. 10.1109/IEMBS.2003.1279907

Balakumaran, T., & Vennila, I. (2011). *Detection of Microcalcification Clusters in Digital Mammograms using Multiresolution based Foveal Algorithm*. Paper presented at IEEE International 2011 World Congress on Information and Communication Technologies. 10.1109/WICT.2011.6141323

Bhattacherjee, A., Roy, S., Paul, S., Roy, P., Kausar, N., & Dey, N. (2016). Classification Approach for Breast Cancer Detection Using Back Propagation Neural Network: A Study. In W. B. A. Karaa & N. Dey (Eds.), Biomedical Image Analysis and Mining Techniques for Improved Health Outcomes. Academic Press. doi:10.4018/978-1-4666-8811-7.ch010

Biswas, S. K., & Mukherjee, D. P. (2011). Recognizing Architectural Distortion in Mammogram: A Multiscale Texture Modeling Approach with GMM. *IEEE Transactions on Biomedical Engineering, 58*(7), 2023–2030. doi:10.1109/TBME.2011.2128870 PMID:21421429

Boujelben, A., Tmar, H., Abid, M., & Mnif, J. (2012). Automatic Diagnosis of Breast Tissue. *Advances in Cancer Management*. Retrieved from: http://www.intechopen.com

Carmen, S., Javier, D., Begoña, A., & Rangayyan, R. M. (2001). *Use Of 2d Linear Prediction Error to Detect Microcalcifications In Mammograms*. Retrieved from: citeseerx.ist.psu.edu/viewdoc/download

Cheriguene, S., Azizi, N., Zemmal, N., Dey, N., Djellali, H., & Farah, N. (2016). Optimized Tumor Breast Cancer Classification Using Combining Random Subspace and Static Classifiers Selection Paradigms. In A. E. Hassanien, C. Grosan, & T. M. Fahmy (Eds.), *Applications of Intelligent Optimization in Biology and Medicine. Intelligent Systems Reference Library* (Vol. 96). Cham: Springer; doi:10.1007/978-3-319-21212-8_13

Dhanelekshmi, M., & Phadke, A. C. (2013). Classification Using Fractal Features of Well-Defined Mammographic Masses Using Power Spectral Analysis and Differential Box Counting Approaches. In L. Suresh, S. Dash, & B. Panigrahi (Eds.), *Artificial Intelligence and Evolutionary Algorithms in Engineering Systems, Advances in Intelligent Systems and Computing* (pp. 495–501). New Delhi: Springer. doi:10.1007/978-81-322-2135-7_53

Ghada, S., Ahmad, K., & Qosai, K. (2016). ANN and Adaboost application for automatic detection of microcalcifications in breast cancer. *The Egyptian Journal of Radiology and Nuclear Medicine, 47*(4), 1803–1814. doi:10.1016/j.ejrnm.2016.08.020

Guo, Q., Ruiz, V., Shao, J., & Guo, F. (2005). A novel approach to mass abnormality detection in mammographic images. In *Proceedings of the IASTED International Conference on Biomedical Engineering*, (pp. 180-185). Innsbruck, Austria: IASTED.

José, S., & Bruno, R. (2005). *Detection of Calcifications in Digital Mammograms using Wavelet Analysis and Contrast Enhancement*. Paper presented at IEEE conference, Faro, Portugal.

Karahaliou, A., Skiadopoulos, S., Boniatis, I., Sakellaropoulos, P., Likaki, E., Panayiotakis, G., & Costaridou, L. (2007). Texture analysis of tissue surrounding microcalcifications on mammograms for breast cancer diagnosis. *The British Journal of Radiology*, 80(956), 648–656. doi:10.1259/bjr/30415751 PMID:17621604

Kausar, N., Abdullah, A., Samir, B. B., Palaniappan, S., AlGhamdi, B. S., & Dey, N. (2016). Ensemble Clustering Algorithm with Supervised Classification of Clinical Data for Early Diagnosis of Coronary Artery Disease. *Journal of Medical Imaging and Health Informatics*, 6(1), 78–87. doi:10.1166/jmihi.2016.1593

Kekre, H. B., Sarode, T., Gharge, S., & Raut, K. (2010). Detection of Cancer Using Vector Quantization for Segmentation. *International Journal of Computers and Applications*, 4(9), 14–19. doi:10.5120/856-1199

Kriti, V. J., Dey, N., & Kumar, V. (2016). PCA-PNN and PCA-SVM Based CAD Systems for Breast Density Classification. In Applications of Intelligent Optimization in Biology and Medicine. Springer.

Liu, S., Babbs, C. F., & Delp, E. J. (2001). Multiresolution Detection of Spiculated Lesions in Digital Mammograms. *IEEE Transactions on Image Processing*, 10(6), 874–884. doi:10.1109/83.923284

Maitra, I. K., Nag, S., & Bandopadhyay, S. (2011). *Techniques for preprocessing of digital mammogram*. Elsevier Computer Methods and Programs in Biomedicine; doi:10.1016/j.cmpb.2011.05.007

Matsubaraa, T., Ichikawa, T., Hara, T., Fujita, H., Kasai, S., Endo, T., & Iwase, T. (2003). Automated detection methods for architectural distortions around skinline and within mammary gland on mammograms. *International Congress Series*, 1256, 950–955. doi:10.1016/S0531-5131(03)00496-5

Megalan, L. L., Ranjith, A., & Thandaiah, R. P. (2012). Analysis of Mammogram Images using Active Contour Segmentation process and Level Set Method. *International Journal of Emerging Technology and Advanced Engineering*, 2(2), 204–207.

Mencattini, A., Rabottino, G., Salmeri, M., Lojacono, R., & Colini, E. (2008). Breast Mass Segmentation in Mammographic Images by an Effective Region Growing Algorithm. In J. Blanc-Talon, S. Bourennane, W. Philips, D. Popescu, & P. Scheunders (Eds.), Lecture Notes in Computer Science: Vol. 5259. *Advanced Concepts for Intelligent Vision Systems* (pp. 948–957). Berlin: Springer. doi:10.1007/978-3-540-88458-3_86

Mencattini, A., Salmeri, M., Casti, P., & Pepe, M. L. (2011). Automatic breast masses boundary extraction in digital mammography using spatial fuzzy c-means clustering and active contour models. In *Proceedings of Conference on Medical Measurement and Applications, on Medical Imaging* (pp. 632-637). Academic Press. 10.1109/MeMeA.2011.5966747

Mudigonda, N. R., Rangayyan, R. M., & Leo, D. J. E. (2001). Detection of Breast Masses in Mammograms by Density Slicing and Texture Flow-Field Analysis. *IEEE Transactions on Medical Imaging*, *20*(12), 1225–1227. doi:10.1109/42.974917 PMID:11811822

Nandi, R. J., Nandi, A. K., Rangayyan, R. M., & Scutt, D. (2006). Classification of breast masses in mammograms using genetic programming and feature selection. *Medical & Biological Engineering & Computing*, *44*(8), 683–694. doi:10.100711517-006-0077-6 PMID:16937210

Nithya, R., & Santhi, B. (2011). Mammogram classification using maximum difference feature selection method. *Journal of Theoretical and Applied Information Technology*, *33*(2), 197–204.

Oliver, A., Torrent, A., Xavier, L., Meritxell, T., Lidia, T., Melcior, S., ... Reyer, Z. (2012). Automatic microcalcification and cluster detection for digital and digitized mammograms. *Elsevier Knowledge Based System*, *28*, 68–75. doi:10.1016/j.knosys.2011.11.021

Phadke, A. C., & Rege, P. P. (2013a). Classification of Architectural Distortion from Other Abnormalities in Mammograms. *International Journal of Application or Innovation in Engineering & Management*, *2*(2), 42-48.

Phadke, A. C., & Rege, P. P. (2013b). Detection and Classification of microcalcifications using Discrete Wavelet Transform. *International Journal of Emerging Trends and Technologies in Computer Science*, *2*(4), 130–134.

Phadke, A. C., & Rege, P. P. (2014). Comparison of SVM & ANN Classifier for Mammogram classification Using ICA features. *WIT Transaction on Information and Communication Technologies*, *49*, 499-506. doi: 10.2495/ ICIE20130581

Phadke, A. C., & Rege, P. P. (2015). Fusion of Local and Global Features for Classification of Abnormality in Mammograms. *Sadhana - Academy Proceedings in Engineering Science*, *41*(4), 385-395. doi: 10.1007/s12046-016-0482-y

Rangayyan, R. M., Oloumi, F., & Nguyen, T. M. (2010). Fractal Analysis of Contours of Breast Masses in Mammograms via the Power Spectra of their Signatures. In *Proceedings of the 32nd Annual International Conference of the IEEE EMBS* (pp. 6737-6740). Buenos Aires, Argentina: IEEE. 10.1109/IEMBS.2010.5626017

Rashed, E. A., Ismail, A. I., & Zaki, S. I. (2007). Multiresolution mammogram analysis in multilevel decomposition. *Elsevier Pattern Recognition Letters*, *28*(2), 286–292. doi:10.1016/j.patrec.2006.07.010

Saltanat, N., Hossain, M. A., & Alam, M. S. (2010). An Efficient Pixel Value based Mapping Scheme to Delineate Pectoral Muscle from Mammograms. In *Proceedings of the IEEE 2010 conference on Bio-inspired Computing: Theories and Applications (BIC-TA)* (pp. 1510-1517). IEEE. 10.1109/BICTA.2010.5645272

Sampat, M. P., & Bovik, A. C. (2003). Detection of Spiculated Lesions in mammograms. In *Proceedings of the 25th Annual International Conference of the IEEE Engineering in Medicine and Biology Society* (Vol. 1, pp. 810-813). IEEE.

Sheng, L., Charles, F. B., & Edward, J. D. (2001). Multiresolution Detection of Spiculated Lesions in Digital Mammograms. *IEEE Transactions on Image Processing*, *10*(6), 874–884. doi:10.1109/83.923284

Suckling, J., Astley, S., Betal, D., Cerneaz, N., Dance, D. R., & Kok, S. L. (1994). International Congress Series: Vol. 1069. *The Mammographic Image Analysis Society Digital Mammogram Database*. Excerpta Medica. Available at http://peipa.essex.ac.uk/info/mias.html

Timp, S., & Karssemeijer, N. (2004). A new 2D segmentation method based on dynamic programming applied to computer aided detection in mammography. *Medical Physics*, *31*(5), 958–971. doi:10.1118/1.1688039 PMID:15191279

Vibha, S. V., & Rege, P. P. (2007). Malignancy texture classification in digital mammograms based on Chebyshev moments and log polar transformation. *ICGST-BIME Journal*, *7*(1), 29–35.

Wang, H., Huang, L., & Zhao, X. (2007). Automated detection of masses in digital mammograms based on pyramid. In *Proceedings of the 2007 International Conference on Wavelet Analysis and Pattern Recognition* (pp. 2-4). Beijing, China: Academic Press. 10.1109/ICWAPR.2007.4420660

Wang, L., Zhu, M., Deng, L., & Yuan, X. (2010). Automatic pectoral muscle boundary detection in mammograms based on Markov chain and active contour model. *Journal of Zhejiang University-Science C (Computers & Electronics)*, *11*(2), 111-118.

Wang, T. C., & Karayiannis, N. B. (1998). Detection of Microcalcifications in Digital Mammograms Using Wavelets. *IEEE Transactions on Medical Imaging*, *17*(4), 498–509. doi:10.1109/42.730395 PMID:9845306

Zemmal, N., Azizi, N., Dey, N., & Sellami, M. (2016). Adaptive Semi Supervised Support Vector Machine Semi Supervised Learning with Features Cooperation for Breast Cancer Classification. *Journal of Medical Imaging and Health Informatics*, *6*(1), 53–62. doi:10.1166/jmihi.2016.1591

ADDITIONAL READING

Ayres, F. J., Rangayyan, R. M., & Leo Desautels, J. E. (2011). *Analysis of Oriented Texture with applications to the Detection of Architectural Distortion in Mammograms, Synthesis lectures on Biomedical Engineering* (J. D. Enderle, Ed.). Morgan and Claypool Publishers.

Cabral, T. M., & Rangayyan, R. M. (2012). *Fractal Analysis of Breast Masses in Mammograms, Synthesis lectures on Biomedical Engineering* (J. D. Enderle, Ed.). Morgan and Claypool Publishers.

Dey, N., & Ashour, A. (2016). *Classification and Clustering in Biomedical Signal Processing*. IGI Global; doi:10.4018/978-1-5225-0140-4

Oliver, A., Torrent, A., Xavier, L., Meritxell, T., Lidia, T., Melcior, S., ... Reyer, Z. (2012). Automatic microcalcification and cluster detection for digital and digitized mammograms. *Elsevier Knowledge Based System*, *28*, 68–75. doi:10.1016/j.knosys.2011.11.021

Phadke, A. C., & Rege, P. P. (2014). Comparison of SVM & ANN Classifier for Mammogram classification Using ICA features. *WIT Transaction on Information and Communication Technologies, WIT press,* 49, 499-506. doi: 10.2495/ ICIE20130581

Phadke, A. C., & Rege, P. P. (2015). Fusion of Local and Global Features for Classification of Abnormality in Mammograms. *Sadhana - Academy Proceedings in Engineering Science, Springer,* 41(4), 385-395. doi: 10.1007/s12046-016-0482-y

Rangayyan, R. M. (2005). *Biomedical Image Analysis, The Biomedical Engineering Series* (M. R. Neuman, Ed.). Boca Raton, Florida: CRC Press.

Timp, S., & Karssemeijer, N. (2004). A new 2D segmentation method based on dynamic programming applied to computer aided detection in mammography. *Medical Physics*, 31(5), 958–971. doi:10.1118/1.1688039 PMID:15191279

KEY TERMS AND DEFINITIONS

Accuracy: Accuracy is percentage of correctly classified normal as well as abnormal samples out of total samples, and it is given by the ratio of addition of true positive and true negative samples to the total number of samples under test.

False Negative (FN): It is the number of abnormal samples detected as normal samples by the classifier algorithm.

False Positive (FP): It is the number of normal samples detected as abnormal samples by the classifier algorithm.

Sensitivity: Sensitivity is percentage of correctly classified abnormal samples and it is given by the ratio of true positive to the addition of true positive and false negative samples.

Specificity: Specificity is percentage of correctly classified normal samples and it is given by the ratio of true negative to the addition of true negative and false positive samples.

True Negative (TN): It is the number of normal samples detected as normal samples by the classifier algorithm.

True Positive (TP): It is the number of abnormal samples detected as abnormal samples by the classifier algorithm.

APPENDIX

Mammogram diagnosis is described by radiologists using a standard developed by the American College of Radiology (ACR), named Breast Imaging Reporting and Database System (BI-RADS). Table 3 shows the category, assessment and required action of BI-RADS (ACR, 1998). The radiologist assigns one of the seven levels of BI-RADS when a mammogram statement is generated and recommends respective follow up plan to the patient.

Table 3. BI-RADS Categories and Assessment

BI-RADS Category	Assessment	Recommendations
0	Incomplete	Other mammographic views and techniques or ultrasound needed
1	Negative, no findings	Routine screening
2	Benign	Routine screening
3	Probably benign	Short-term follow-up to establish stability
4	Suspicious abnormality	Biopsy should be advised
5	High indication of malignancy	Apt treatment should be advised
6	Already recognized biopsy confirmed malignancy	Apt treatment should be advised

(Data Source: ACR, 1998)

Chapter 14

A Novel Approach for Computer-Aided Diagnosis for Distinction Between Benign and Malignant of Lung Nodules Based on Machine Learning Techniques

Shashidhara Bola
Dayananda Sagar College of Engineering, India

ABSTRACT

A new method is proposed to classify the lung nodules as benign and malignant. The method is based on analysis of lung nodule shape, contour, and texture for better classification. The data set consists of 39 lung nodules of 39 patients which contain 19 benign and 20 malignant nodules. Lung regions are segmented based on morphological operators and lung nodules are detected based on shape and area features. The proposed algorithm was tested on LIDC (lung image database consortium) datasets and the results were found to be satisfactory. The performance of the method for distinction between benign and malignant was evaluated by the use of receiver operating characteristic (ROC) analysis. The method achieved area under the ROC curve was 0.903 which reduces the false positive rate.

1. INTRODUCTION

Automated segmentation and classification of lung tumors into harmless or harmful is a challenging task and is of vital interest for medical applications like diagnosis and surgical planning. It improves the accuracy and assist radiologist for better diagnosis.

The difficult task in Computer-Aided Diagnosis (CAD) system is to improve the accuracy in grouping lung nodules as benign (harmless tumor) and malignant (harmful tumor). Classification process is useful

DOI: 10.4018/978-1-5225-5152-2.ch014

Copyright © 2018, IGI Global. Copying or distributing in print or electronic forms without written permission of IGI Global is prohibited.

for the early diagnosis of lung cancer which in turn increases the survival rate of patient. The proposed method addresses the grouping of lung nodules as harmless or harmful with less number of false positives by extracting shape, margin and textural features based on ANN. ANN has several advantages such as the generalization and the capabilities of learning from training data without knowing the rules in priori.

Al-Kadi and Watson (2008) have discussed the fractal analysis of time sequenced contrast enhanced CT images to discriminate harmful or harmless tumors. The accuracy of their proposed system showed up to 83% in differentiating benign and malignant. Xiaoguang (Lu, Wei, Qian, & Jain, 2001) tried with Support Vector Machine (SVM) to divide the type of the lung cancer.

Wei-Chih Shen et al (2011) have used Tumor Disappearance Ratio (TDR) and density features to design a computer-aided diagnosis system to assist radiologist. The accuracy of designed classification model is 70.97%. Iwano et al (2005) proposed a system to automatically divide nodules identified on High Resolution CT (HRCT) and compared the accuracy with the radiologists.

Lee et al (2010) proposed a two-step supervised learning scheme based on image based gray level, texture and shape features with random space method and genetic algorithm. El-Baz et al (2012; 2010) used 2D approach for early evaluation of harmful tumors based on the intensity in HU with a 2D rotationally invariant second-order Markov Gibbs Random Field(MGRF). S.K. vijay Anand (Anand, 2010) has used features like area, solidity, eccentricity, energy, contrast, homogeneity with Artificial neural network.

Suzuki et al (2005) have proposed a multiple Massive-Training Artificial Neural Networks (MTANN) for the classification of nodules as harmless or harmful. C Henschke et al (2005) have used (ANN) to differentiate harmless or harmful tumors.

As per the survey, the accuracy of grouping the nodules as harmless or harmful is approximately 83 to 87%. In this direction an attempt is made to improve the accuracy rate for the classification.

The rest of the paper is organized as follows: In Section 2, theory is discussed. Section 3 gives the methods. Results and Discussion is given by Section 4. Conclusion is given in Section 5.

2. BACKGROUND

The datasets were taken from LIDC database which contains benign and malignant lung nodules. 39 CT images were used to classify the lung nodules. The CT images are in Digital Imaging and Communications in Medicine (DICOM) format and is measured in Hounsfield Units (HU). To convert HU to gray level, 1024 value to be added to HU. 17 CT images were taken for training the Artificial Neural Network and 22 images used for testing of the Artificial Neural Networks.

The lung nodules are classified based on the features like shape, margin and texture (calcification pattern) as shown in the Figures 1, 2 and 3.

3. METHODS

The steps involved in segmentation and classification of lung nodule as benign and malignant are depicted in Figure 4. Chest CT image is taken as input and lung regions are segmented based on thresholding and morphological operations. Lung nodules are extracted from lung region and features like shape, margin and texture features are extracted from lung nodules. Artificial Neural network is used to classify lung nodules as benign and malignant based on the features extracted from the training data.

Figure 1. Morphological characterization of lung nodules (Moulay & Mexiane, 2009)

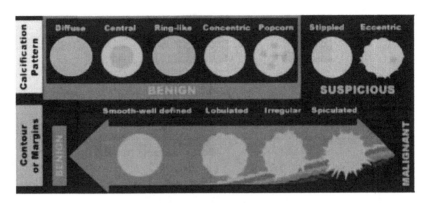

Figure 2. Benign pattern

Figure 3. Malignant pattern

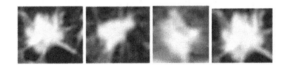

3.1 Extraction of Lungs Using Thresholding and Morphological Operators

The extraction of lungs acts as a vital role to accelerate the procedure of detection and analysis of tumors. In our previous work, an algorithm was designed to segment lung regions based on morphological operators which is presented in (Sasidhar, Babu, Ravishankar, & Rao, 2013).

3.2 Extraction of Lung Nodule Based on Intensity, Shape and Area Features

After segmenting lung areas, identification of tumors could be done as shown in algorithm 1. Lung areas is the input for the proposed algorithm. Threshold is applied to get different components (nodules and non-nodules).

Roundness (Samir Labib Habib, 2009) is applied to examine shape of the tumor which is given by:

$$Roundness = 4*pi*Area/perimeter^2 \qquad (1)$$

Figure 4. Classification of lung nodules process

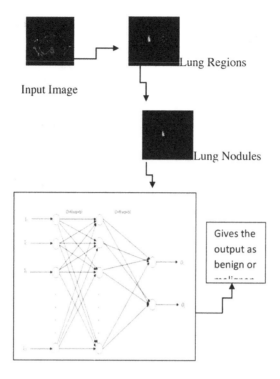

where Area is the area of the object and perimeter is the perimeter object. This metric is equal to one for circle and it is less than one for other objects. Area feature is applied to obtain the mask for extraction of tumors. The mask is superimposed with the lungs to extract tumor.

3.3 Feature Extraction of Lung Nodules

Lung nodules are classified into benign or malignant based on their appearance, texture and margin variation features.

- **Appearance Features:** Area, Perimeter, Convex Area, EquivDiameter, Eccentricity, Extent, Circularity.

Algorithm 1. Pseudo Code to Detect and Segment Lung Nodules

```
Require: Lung Regions
Step 1: Apply intensity threshold, shape feature is given by the equation (1)
and area features to get nodule mask.
Step 2: Superimpose the mask with the input image to obtain tumors
Step 3: End
```

- **Texture Features:** Energy, Contrast, Correlation, Solidity, Homogeneity.
- **Margin Variation:** It is a margin feature which specifies whether border is smooth or speculated. If the margin of the nodule is smooth then the nodule is benign otherwise it is malignant. The following steps are given in Algorithm 2.

The input for the margin variation is the lung nodule, erode the lung nodule by one pixel and subtract it with original lung nodule to get the border points. Find the centriod (x_c, y_c) of lung nodule and the Euclidean Distance (D) between centriod and the border points (x_i, y_i) i varies from 1 to n and n is total number of border points Euclidean distance is given by Equation (2):

$$D = \left[\left(x_i - x_c \right)^2 + \left(y_i - y_c \right)^2 \right]^{1/2} \tag{2}$$

Find the average distance (meand) between centriod and the border points, which gives the radius of corresponding circle is given by (3):

$$meand = mean\left(D\right) \tag{3}$$

Find the difference in distances (diff) calculated in Equation (4) along the consecutive points of nodule border is given by Equation (4):

$$diff = \left| D_i - D_{i+1} \right| \forall_{i=1 \text{ to } n-1} \tag{4}$$

Find the maximum of differences (maxd) computed in Equation (4) is given by Equation (5):

$$maxd = \max\left(diff\right) \tag{5}$$

Algorithm 2. Pseudo Code to Find Counter Variation of Lung Nodule

```
Require: Lung Nodules
Step 1: Get border points of the lung nodule.
Step 2: Find Euclidean distance between centriod and the border points is giv-
en by the Equation (2).
Step 3: Find the radius of the circle is given in Equation (3).
Step 4: Find the difference in distances (diff) calculated in Equation (2)
which is given by the Equation(4).
Step 5: Find the maximum of differences of Step 4 which is given by Equation
(5).
Step 6: Margin variation is calculated by Equation (6).
Step 7: End.
```

Margin variation (in %) is calculated by the in the Equation (6):

$$Variation = \left(maxd \ / \ meand \right) * 100 \qquad (6)$$

3.4 Classification of Lung Nodules Using Artificial Neural Network

Before the actual classification process, neural network is first trained with training data consisting of the 13 features extracted from different nodules (17 images are used for training purpose).

For evaluation, the proposed method used 22 images of 22 patients which contain 9 benign and 13 malignant nodules. The output values lie in the range 0 to 1. The target values are assumed to be [1 0] for malignant nodules, and [0 1] for benign nodules.

4. RESULTS AND DISCUSSION

Input image for the classification is as shown in the Figure 5(a). Lung regions separation is done by using intensity threshold and morphological operations as shown in the Figure 5(b). The extraction of lung nodules are based on intensity threshold and appearance features which is depicted in the Figure 5(c). In Table 1, the features from the lung nodule are extracted.

From the segmented nodule, 13 major features mentioned in section 2 (C) were extracted from 22 test nodules and given as input to artificial neural network with 10 neurons in hidden layer. The output of artificial neural network is either 1(malignant) or 0(benign). The performance of proposed approach is tested based on four performance metrics such as accuracy, sensitivity, specificity and precision as shown in Table 2.

Calculation of performance metrics is based on four parameters viz, True positive (TP), False positive (FP), False negative (FN) and True negative (TN).

Figure 5. (a) Input image; (b) Segmentation of lung regions; (c) Extraction of Lung Nodule

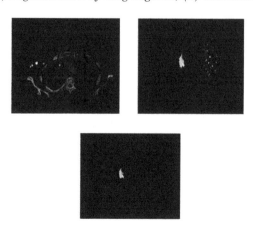

Table 1. Feature extraction from lung nodule

CT Image	Nodule	Area	Margin Variation	Eccentricity
		344	48	0.772
		4632	22	0.180
		1069	33	0.511
		967	53	0.773

- **True Positive (TP):** Tumors classified by the algorithm and the radiologist as malignant are known as True positive.
- **False Positive (FP):** Tumors classified as malignant by the algorithm and benign by the radiologist are known as false positive.
- **False Negative (FN):** Tumors classified as benign by the algorithm and malignant by the radiologist are known as false positive.
- **True Negative (TN):** Tumors classified by the algorithm and the radiologist as benign are known as True positive.

Specificity is the number of correctly classified negative (Benign) nodules out of actual negative nodules.

$$Specificity = \left(TN \right) / \left(TN + FP \right) \tag{7}$$

Accuracy is the number of correctly classified nodules (Benign and Malignant) out of all nodules.

$$Accuracy = \left(TP + TN \right) / \left(TP + FP + TN + FN \right) \tag{8}$$

Precision is the number of correctly classified positive nodules (Malignant) out of all positive nodules.

Table 2. Performance Measures and comparative study

Performance Measures	Vijai Anand (Anand, 2010)	Proposed Method
Specificity	77.7%	88.8%
Accuracy	81.8%	90.9%
Precision	84.6%	92.3%
Recall	84.6%	92.3%

Figure 6. Receiver Operating Characteristic Curve for the proposed method

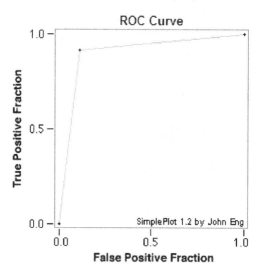

Figure 7. Receiver Operating Characteristic Curve in (Anand, 2010)

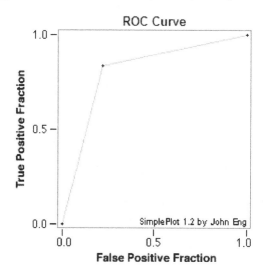

$$Precision = \left(TP \right) / \left(TP + FP \right) \tag{9}$$

Recall is the number of correctly classified nodules (Malignant) out of actual positive nodules.

$$Recall = \left(TP \right) / \left(TP + FN \right) \tag{10}$$

The performance of the classifier model is determined with the help of Receiver Operating Characteristics (ROC) curve. ROC curve is a plot of the true positive rate versus the false positive rate as shown in the Figures 6 and 7. Area under the curve for proposed method was found out to be 0.903.

Existing System (Anand, 2010) used the classifier model (Artificial neural network) with 9 features. The performance of this approach is evaluated based on four performance metrics such as accuracy, sensitivity, specificity and precision as shown in Table 2.

Area under the curve for existing method was found out to be 0.806 which indicates the false positive rate is high compared to proposed method.

After comparing the performances in table and ROC curves of both approaches, proposed method gives better results with respect to all four metrics.

5. CONCLUSION

The proposed method is able to tell whether the tumor is harmless or harmful in nature with an accuracy of 90.9%. The plot of ROC curve depicts a significant reduction in false positive rate (Area under curve 0.903) compared to existing approach (Area under curve 0.806), hence reducing the misclassification probability.

REFERENCES

Al-Kadi & Watson. (2008). Texture analysis of aggressive and nonaggressive lung tumor CE CT images. IEEE Transactions on Biomedical Engineering, 55(7), 1822-1830.

American cancer society, cancer facts and figures. (2013). New York, NY: American Cancer Society.

El-Baz. (2010). Appearance analysis for diagnosing malignant lung nodules. *Proceedings of the International Symposium on Biomedical Imaging*.

El-Baz, A. (2012). Appearance based diagnostic system for early assessment of malignant lung nodules. Proceedings of the IEEE International Conference on Image Processing, 533-536.

Habib. (2009). *A Computer aided diagnosis system (CAD) for the detection of pulmonary nodules on CT scans.* Systems and Biomedical Engineering Department, Faculty of Engineering, Cairo University.

Henschke, C., Sone, S., Markowitz, S., Tockman, M., Shaham, D., Zulueta, J., ... Klippenstein, D. (2005). *CT screening for lung cancer: The relationship of disease stage to tumor size Lung Cancer*. Elsevier.

Iwano, S., Nakamura, T., Kamioka, Y., Ikeda, M., & Ishigaki, T. (2008). Computer-aided differentiation of malignant from benign solitary pulmonary nodules imaged by high-resolution CT. *Computerized Medical Imaging and Graphics*, *32*(5), 416–422. doi:10.1016/j.compmedimag.2008.04.001 PMID:18501556

Iwano, S., Nakamura, T., Kamioka, Y., & Ishigaki, T. (2005). Computer-aided diagnosis: a shape classification of pulmonary nodules imaged by high-resolution CT. Computerized Medical Imaging and Graphics, 29(7), 565-570.

Lee, M. C., Wiemker, R., & Boroczky, L. (2010). Computer aided diagnosis of pulmonary nodules using a two-step approach for feature selection and classifier ensemble construction. *Artificial Intelligence in Medicine*, *50*(1), 43–53. doi:10.1016/j.artmed.2010.04.011 PMID:20570118

Lu, Wei, Qian, & Jain. (2001). Learning-based pulmonary nodule detection from mutliscale CT data. *IEEE Transactions on Medical Image.*

Mexiane, M. A. (2009). Current Concepts in imaging and management of the solitary pulmonary nodule. *Le Journal Medical Libanais.*

Sasidhar, B., Ramesh Babu, D. R., Ravishankar, M., & Bhaskar Rao, N. (2013). Automated Segmentation of Lung Regions using Morphological Operators in CT Scan. *International Journal of Scientific and Engineering Research, 4*(9).

Shen, Yu, & Chuang. (2011). Computer Aided Diagnosis for Pulmonary Nodule on Low-Dose Computed Tomography (LDCT) using Density Features. In *Eighth International Conference Computer Graphics, Imaging and Visualization*. IEEE.

Suzuki, K., Li, F., Sone, S., & Doi, K. (2005). Computer-aided diagnostic scheme for distinction between benign and malignant nodules in thoracic low-dose CT by use of massive training artificial neural network. IEEE Transactions on Medical Imaging, 24(9), 1138-1150.

Vijai Anand, S. K. (2010). *Segmentation coupled textural feature classification for lung tumor prediction.* ICCCCT. doi:10.1109/ICCCCT.2010.5670607

Chapter 15
Automatic Detection of Tumor and Bleed in Magnetic Resonance Brain Images

Jayanthi V. E.
PSNA College of Engineering and Technology, India

Jagannath Mohan
VIT University, India

Adalarasu K.
Sastra University, India

ABSTRACT

Brain tumor and intracerebral hemorrhage are major causes for death among the people. Brain tumor is the growth of abnormal cells multiplied in an uncontrolled manner in brain. Magnetic resonance imaging (MRI) technique plays a major role for analysis, diagnosis, and treatment planning of abnormalities in the brain. Bleed is detected manually by radiologists, but it is laborious, time-consuming, and error prone. The automatic detection method was performed to detect the tumor as well as bleed in brain under a single system. The proposed method includes image acquisition, pre-processing, patch extraction, feature extraction, convolutional neural network (CNN) classification, and fuzzy inference system (FIS) to detect the abnormality with reduced classification loss percentage. This chapter is compared with the existing system of tumor detection using convolution neural network based on certain features such as skewness, kurtosis, homogeneity, smoothness, and correlation.

INTRODUCTION

Major abnormality in the brain is brain tumour, stroke, brain swelling and hydrocephalus. Brain tumour and brain stroke are one of the major causes for increasing mortality rate among the people. If tumour and stroke is detected correctly at in the early stage then the chance of survival is increased. This kind of abnormality is detected by various image processing techniques in MRI image. Cerebrovascular disease

DOI: 10.4018/978-1-5225-5152-2.ch015

Copyright © 2018, IGI Global. Copying or distributing in print or electronic forms without written permission of IGI Global is prohibited.

is commonly known as brain stroke or haemorrhage and it is caused by blood vessel blocks or leakage of blood. Benign tumour and malignant tumour are the type of brain tumour. People are affected by tumour in India are near about 80271 in 2007. The American Brain Tumour Association (ABTA) estimated that 62930 new cases of primary tumourare diagnosed in 2010. According to National Brain Tumour Society, people having primary tumour are about 688,000 and according to Central Nervous System (CNS) in the United States, 138,000 people with malignant tumour and 550,000 with non-malignant tumours. Primary tumour is originated in the brain. They can be cancerous or noncancerous. Slow-growing and rarely spread type of noncancerous brain tumour is benign. It has well-defined borders and it is removed completely by surgery and less chances to come back. Cancerous type of malignant brain tumour is fast-growing and it is spread the nearby healthy brain cells. This type of tumour may come back even if completely removed by surgery. Secondary type of tumour originates in other than brain part of the body such as breast and kidney and then spreads into the brain.

The abnormal cells are accumulated in brain it causes the brain tumour or intracranial neoplasm. These cells are growing faster and produce the damage in brain tissues. To diagnose the brain tumour the magnetic resonance imaging (MRI) scans are usually utilized (Galldiks, Law, Pope, Arbizu, & Langen, 2017; Franciszek, Bram, Chirstian, Michael, Klaus, Hans-peter, Barbara, Rafal, & Joanna, 2017; Dey, Das, Chaudhuri, & Das, 2012). Even though, the brain tumour segmentation and detection technique seem to be a tedious task for the radiologists. So, automatic systems which yield the accurate results are needed (Ivan, & Iker, 2017).

BACKGROUND

Many of the researchers proposed many methods to find brain tumour, stroke and other kinds of abnormalities in human brain using MR imaging (Isin, Direkoglu, & Sah, 2016). T2 weighted MR images were used for detection of tumour (Nidhi, & Pritee, 2017). The MR image segmentation utilizing pattern recognition method has been analysed (Bezdek, Hall, & Clarke, 1993). Method like Artificial Neural Network (ANN) can be used for brain segmentation and pattern recognition in order to detect the brain tumour (Parra, Iftekharuddin, & Kozma, 2003; Sayed, Zaghloul, & Nassef, 2016). Tissue probability mapping is used to measure the similarity to detect the brain tumour is proposed (Schwarz, Kasparek, Provaznik, & Jarkovsky, 2007) and it gives the best result in case of large initial miss-registration.Atlas based fuzzy connectedness segmentation technique used for automatic segmentation of brain MRI image is explained (Zhou & Bai, 2007). The result gives important data by measuring the difference between abnormal and normal brain. In atlas registration, PABLIC correction and Re-FC segmentation are applied to detect the brain tumour automatically in MRI scanned image. To remove the overall position and scale differences between the atlas and MRI, atlas registration concept is used. This is based on four concepts, i.e., normalized mutual information as the similarity measure, nearest neighbour interpolation, similarity transform and power optimization. HSOM based segmentation and wavelet packet features are used to detect and characterize the brain tumour is discussed (Gladis Pushpa Rathi & Palani, 2010).

Support Vector Machines (SVM) classifier is used to detect the tumour in MRI image by applying morphological functions to remove speckles (Guo, Zhao, Wu, Li, Xu, & Yan, 2011). The system is designed only for the detection of braintumour not for other kind of abnormalities in brain by using segmentation and histogram threshold technique is described (Kowear & Yadev, 2012) Solmaz et al. (2017) presented the automatic detection of brain tumour in 3D images. Histogram matching is used for the pre processing. From the background of the flair image, the region of interest is separated. Local binary patterns were used to extent the orientation gradients for 3D images. Texture based tumour detection and automated segmented system is developed (Mukesh & Mehta, 2011) and the problem of this system is a small amount of pixels which are misclassified and the execution time is not sufficient. Most of the researcher proposed a system to find any one of the abnormality in the brain such as brain tumour and stroke. So, an intelligent diagnosis system is needs to classify all kinds of abnormalities under a single system. This is the key factor to develop a system to find abnormalities using MRI scanned images under single system. Another method was developed to segment and the brain tumour in MR images that is called Meyer's flooding watershed Algorithm (Patil & Bhalchandra, 2012). The drawback of this system is used for only detecting the tumour area not for classification of tumour types and shapes. Automated brain tumour detection and identification using probabilistic neural network techniques approach is introduced (Dahab, Ghoniemy, & Selim, 2012).

In brain tumour identification, MRI scan images are most referred by many authors for detection of tumour. These MRI scan images are gray level images whose gray scale varies from 0 to 255. Brain tumour segmentation using Improved Fuzzy c-Means Clustering (IFCM) for MRI scan images is presented (Shen, Sandhom, Gramat, Dempsey, & Patterson, 2003; Biswas, Das, Maji, Dey, & Chaudhuri, 2013). This proposed method has been used to determine the similarity measurement. It is depending on pixel intensity or feature attraction and spatial position of neighbourhood. Bauer et al. (2012) proposed anapproach that is for tumour growth modelling it integrates the different approaches for simulation namely discrete and continuous. Here, intensity normalization, edge- preserving, smoothing and bias field corrections are carried out in between the atlas and the patient image. Different edge detection techniques are explained to identify the edges for detecting brain tumour in MRI scan image (Sharma, Diwakar, & Choudhary, 2012). The brain tumour detection is done by using watershed segmentation techniques along with the morphological operators to detect tumour in MRI scan images is described (Mustaqeem, Javed, & Fatima, 2012). Classification of tumour in Human brain MRI scan images using wavelet and support vector machine technique is introduced (Ahmed, ul-Hassan, Shafi, & Osman, 2012). Iterative Fuzzy LDA algorithm is used to find a stroke in CT image is clearly explained (Ming-Sian, Chong-Guang, Chiun-Li, & Shih-Hua, 2013). To assess the brain tumour different techniques were used called Mass Spectrometry (MS) and machine learning technique (Gholami, Norton, Eberlin, & Nathalie, 2013). Neuro-fuzzy classifier technique is used in automatic detection of brain tumour is proposed for detecting brain tumour (Karuna and Joshi, 2013). The problem of this system is many input images needed to train a neuro-fuzzy classifier. To evaluate tumour tissues, MS imaging tool is used. Huang et al. (2014) suggested an algorithm for segmenting of Brain tumour using Local independent Projection based Classification (LIPC) method. The LIPC implementation is done by considering dictionary construction, locally linear representation and classification steps. High Resolution (HR) with different contrast image is used for detecting brain tumour by applying patch approach is described (Jafari-Khouzani, 2014). A method is introduced that is fully automatic used to detect brain tumour (Sehgal, Goel, Mangipudi, Mehra, & Tyagi, 2016).

DETECTION OF BRAIN TUMOUR AND BLOOD BLEED

MR imaging modality is a visualization technique that allows the images of internal anatomy to be acquired in a safe and non-invasive approach. It has the ability to distinguish between different soft tissues such as gray and white matter. Using this technique, ailments of brain like brain tumour, cerebral bleed, hydrocephalus (fluid accumulation in brain) can be diagnosed.

The method for the detection of tumour and cerebral bleed in MRI brain image involves the following steps. The block diagram of tumour and bleed detection in MRI brain image using Matlab tool is shown in the Figure 1.

The modules include,

- Pre-processing
- Patch and Feature Extraction
- Convolution Neural Network (CNN)
- Fuzzy Inference

Pre-Processing

The most affected region in MRI brain tumour image is identified in pre-processing step by applying Otsu Binarization method, which find out the optimum threshold classifying value of foreground pixels and background pixels and their intra-class variance is minimal.

Patch and Feature Extraction

The pre-processed image is further converted into grid image consisting of number of small patches using patch extraction process. Feature extraction is a major part of pattern recognition and in image processing that is used for dimensionality reduction. If a large data is applied as input in an algorithm, then the processing will take long time. This is seemed to be redundant. So the reduced set of features (features vector) will be used in input data. Feature Extraction is helpful to identify the exact location of brain tumour in an image. Feature extraction is a process that transforming the input data into the set of features. GLCM and Gabor were used for extracting some features, i.e., contrast, shape, correlation, homogeneity, entropy, energy, colour, texture, intensity, skewness, kurtosis and smoothness.

The purpose of feature extraction is fabricating the raw data as important for next processing step. Among the different textures, the features are extracted and it is maximized within class similarity and minimized in between class similarity. The various types of tumours are very different with different grades. The different type and grade of the tumours used to separate the features for brain tumour segmentation. The feature extraction seems to be a very useful challenging task for the different complexity texture structures such as white material (WM), gray material (GM), and Cerebro Spinal Fluid (CSF) in brain images (Solmaz & Farshad, 2017). Image intensity is the major segmentation process in brain tumour because of the different textures that having the different gray levels.

Convolutional Neural Network

Height, width and depth of an image are considered as the three layers of feed forward Convolutional Neural Networks (CNN). Locally connected and parameters sharing are the two important concept used for developing a CNN to reduce the amount of parameters needs to train the network. Three different convolutional, pooling, and fully-connected layers are used to construct the full CNN architecture. Convolutional layer considered as performing convolution many times on the previous layer. Pooling layer is

Figure 1. Block diagram of tumor and bleed detection in MRI brain image

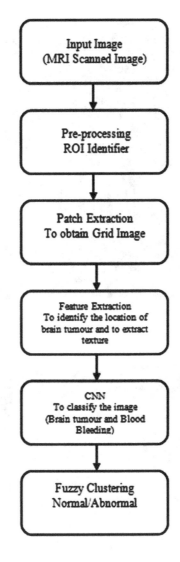

inserted in between convolutional and fully connected layer to reduce the amount of parameters by down sampling the previous layer and hence the computation time of the network is less but in small dataset, it might cause over fitting. Fully connected layer is the final layer which connects all the neurons in the previous layer to the neuron in next layer.

Fuzzy Clustering

Fuzzy cluster is a method that focuses on the enhanced association for the maintenance and recovery of multidimensional data. It uses the basic property, i.e., nearest neighbour search algorithm to cluster a dataset into different clusters. In this, the element belongs to more than one cluster are associated with membership function. In fuzzy clustering, each element membership value belongs to a specific class. Using the segmented image, the PSNR value is calculated by the use of fuzzy clustering. Each

Figure 2. Input and pre-processed image of brain tumor

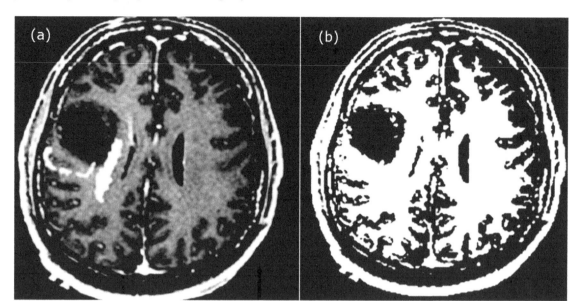

Figure 3. Patch Extracted Image

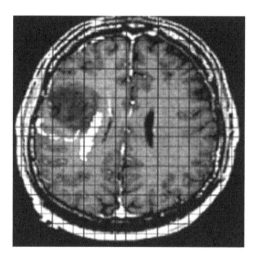

PSNR value corresponds to a fuzzy class and represents by a set of membership levels. The membership levels for each PSNR value is interpreted by five natural language terminology: (i) Very low; (ii) low; (iii) medium; (iv) high, and; (v) very high. PSNR values are the five different member ship function used for fuzzy clustering technique. The input data sequence of fuzzy clustering is $S_1, S_2, \ldots S_n$. Where, S_i indicates the PSNR value of every segment and n is the number of segments. PSNR values represent the membership function of fuzzy clustering in original and blurred image. Fuzzy clustering algorithm includes the following steps:

Step 1: First calculate the minimum and maximum values of PSNR in the segmented image

Figure 4. CNN classifier image of brain tumour and blood bleedTable 1. Features extracted from the MR brain images using Gabor filter values

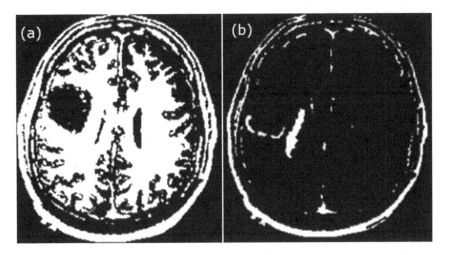

$C_{min} = \min\{S_1, S_2, \ldots \ldots S_n\}$, $C_{max} = \max\{ S_1, S_2, \ldots \ldots S_n\}$

Step 2: Calculate the value of different classes

$C_i = C_0 + i/6 \times (C_{max} - C_{min})$

Step 3: Set U=0. Using following predefined conditions update the value of μ_{ij}.

Condition 1: If $S_i \leq C_1$ then $\mu_{ij} = 1$ and $\mu_{i,j} \neq 1 = 0$

Condition 2: If $C_j < S_i \leq C_{j+1}$ then compute,

where $\mu_{ij} = \dfrac{C_{j+1} - S_i}{C_{j+1} - C_j}$; $\mu_{i,j+1} = 1 - \mu_{ij}$ and $\mu_{i, Kj \neq j, j+1} = 0$

Condition 3: If $S_i < C_5$, $\mu_{i, k \neq 5} = 0$ and $\mu_{i,5} = 1$.

Step 4: Shift the classes $C_j = \dfrac{\sum_{j=1}^{n} \mu_{ij} x_j}{\sum_{j=1}^{n} \mu_{ij}}$

Step 5: If the value of C_j remain unchanged then algorithm stops, otherwise it goes to Step3.

Table 1.

Feature	Contrast	Correlation	Energy	Homogeneity	Mean	SD	Entropy	RMS	Variance	Smoothness	Kurtosis	Skewness	IDM
Benign	0.2333	0.1284	0.7491	0.9308	0.0019	0.0898	2.6632	0.0898	0.0081	0.8778	7.2707	0.6117	-0.0366
Benign	0.2717	0.0931	0.7686	0.9338	0.0024	0.0898	3.2698	0.0898	0.0081	0.8974	7.9567	0.8862	0.4926
Benign	0.2272	0.1326	0.7439	0.929	0.0043	0.0897	3.6046	0.0898	0.008	0.9406	5.9972	0.5218	0.37
Benign	0.2442	0.1007	0.7409	0.9263	0.0032	0.0898	3.5797	0.0898	0.008	0.9234	6.2735	0.6332	0.5257
Benign	0.2033	0.1126	0.7554	0.9331	0.0019	0.0898	3.6549	0.0898	0.008	0.8783	5.8117	0.3408	1.001
Benign	0.2558	0.0895	0.7557	0.9314	0.0025	0.0898	3.0756	0.0898	0.0081	0.904	7.7971	0.5774	-0.2601
Benign	0.2155	0.0951	0.7378	0.9274	0.0028	0.0898	3.6283	0.0898	0.008	0.9132	5.3238	0.323	1.0419
Benign	0.2925	0.1584	0.7588	0.933	0.0057	0.0896	2.6622	0.0898	0.008	0.9551	13.0402	1.3124	1.2778
Benign	0.2341	0.1321	0.753	0.9315	0.0035	0.0897	3.1562	0.0898	0.008	0.9291	7.4848	0.5212	-1.0392
Benign	0.2689	0.0977	0.7861	0.941	0.000687	0.0898	2.7465	0.0898	0.0081	0.7186	10.9703	0.7365	0.119
Malignant	0.2433	0.1294	0.7606	0.9344	0.0034	0.0897	2.9949	0.0898	0.0081	0.927	7.6801	0.6318	0.3816
Malignant	0.2272	0.1326	0.7439	0.929	0.0043	0.0897	3.6046	0.0898	0.008	0.9406	5.9972	0.5218	0.37
Malignant	0.275	0.118	0.7688	0.9346	0.0046	0.0897	3.029	0.0898	0.0081	0.9453	13.1839	1.0085	0.2863
Malignant	0.2272	0.0908	0.7522	0.9308	0.0034	0.0897	3.6783	0.0898	0.008	0.927	5.5966	0.4004	1.0469
Malignant	0.2517	0.0734	0.7402	0.9267	0.0035	0.0897	3.5239	0.0898	0.008	0.9284	6.522	0.4979	1.6524
Malignant	0.2439	0.1072	0.731	0.9246	0.0046	0.0897	3.5484	0.0898	0.0081	0.9446	6.5235	0.6204	0.503
Malignant	0.2925	0.1584	0.7588	0.933	0.0057	0.0896	2.6622	0.0898	0.008	0.9551	13.0402	1.3124	1.2778
Malignant	0.2745	0.1095	0.7549	0.9308	0.0054	0.0897	3.1085	0.0898	0.008	0.9523	11.1148	1.0231	-0.6151
Malignant	0.2161	0.1382	0.7548	0.9325	0.0025	0.0898	3.3156	0.0898	0.0081	0.9032	6.232	0.3121	0.5631
Malignant	0.2786	0.1427	0.7604	0.9321	0.0053	0.0897	3.1943	0.0898	0.0081	0.9516	9.7318	0.9914	1.8546

Figure 5. CNN classifier and fuzzy inference system output images for tumour and blood bleed

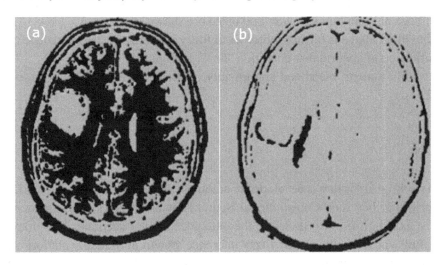

Table 2. Performance metrics obtained from the proposed algorithm. CNN – Convolutional Neural Network; FIS – Fuzzy Inference System

Bleed and Tumour Detected in Brain Pattern	
Classification Loss (CNN) in %	4.8720
Classification Loss (CNN + FIS) in %	4.4124
Classification Accuracy (CNN) in %	95.1280
Classification Accuracy (CNN + FIS) in %	95.5876
No Bleed Detected in Abnormal Brain Pattern	
Classification Loss (CNN) in %	6.3415
Classification Loss (CNN + FIS) in %	4.8286
Classification Accuracy (CNN) in %	93.6585
Classification Accuracy (CNN + FIS) in %	95.1714

RESULT AND DISCUSSION

Harvard Medical School, OASIS and ADNI dataset MR brain images are used to test the performance of the system. The testing and training set holds the T2-weighted MR brain images in axial plane with 256×256 in-plane resolution. MRI scanned brain image is subjected to pre-processing step for converting gray scale image into binary image using Otsu's Binarization method and the resultant images are shown in Figure 2.

The pre-processed image is further converted into grid image consisting of number of small patches using patch extraction process to reduce the large size of an image (Figure 3).

After patch extraction, features are extracted using Gabor filter. The extracted features include entropy, standard deviation, mean, homogeneity, smoothness, skewness and kurtosis. These extracted features are used to classify the condition for normal or abnormal of brain pattern and they are listed in Table 1. CNN classifier image of brain tumour and blood bleed are shown in Figure 4.

Then CNN classified image is further subjected to fuzzy inference system to reduce the loss of percentage in classification of abnormality condition shown in Figure 5.

The result of brain tumour, bleed and abnormality of image detection CNN classifier results are listed in Table 2.

CONCLUSION

In this proposed work, an algorithm is developed to automatically detect tumour and blood bleed in MRI brain image is primarily based on Convolutional Neural Network (CNN). Classification loss percentage is high in the existing methods; therefore the outcomes are not accurate. This drawback leads to the need of adopting a novel method using fuzzy inference system in Matlab® platform. The extracted features add a core to the possible right outcome and also it shows color variation in the output image. This method helps to save the computational time for pathologist and provide better outcomes to detect the abnormalities and also it reduces the loss percentage in the classification. The future work of this proposed method is to classify the stages of brain tumour with grades of severity.

REFERENCES

Ahmad, M., ul-Hassan, M., Shafi, I., & Osman, F. (2012). Classification of tumours in human brain MRI using wavelet and support vector machine. *IOSR Journal of Computer Engineering, 8*(2), 25-31.

Bauer, S., May, C., Dionysiou, D., Stamatakos, G., Buchler, P., & Reyes, M. (2012). Multiscale modeling for image analysis of brain tumour studies. *IEEE Transactions on Biomedical Engineering, 59*(1), 25–29. doi:10.1109/TBME.2011.2163406 PMID:21813362

Bezdek, J. C., Hall, L. O., & Clarke, L. P. (1993). Review of MR image segmentation techniques using pattern recognition. *Medical Physics, 20*(4), 1033–1048. doi:10.1118/1.597000 PMID:8413011

Biswas, D., Das, P., Maji, P., Dey, N., & Chaudhuri, S. S. (2013). Visible watermarking within the region of non-interest of medical images based on fuzzy c-means and Harris corner detection. *Proceedings of the Third International Conference on Computer Science, Engineering & Applications*, 161-168. 10.5121/csit.2013.3517

Dahab, D. A., Ghoniemy, D. S. A., & Selim, G. A. (2012). Automated brain tumour detection and identification using image processing and probabilistic neural network techniques. *International Journal of Image Processing and Visual Communication, 1*(2), 1–8.

Dey, N., Das, P., Chaudhuri, S. S., & Das, A. (2012). Feature analysis for the blind-watermarked electroencephalogram signal in wireless telemonitoring using Alattar's method. *Proceedings of the Fifth International Conference on Security of Information and Networks*, 87-94. 10.1145/2388576.2388588

Franciszek, B., Bram, S., Chirstian, W., Michael, G., Klaus, M.-H., Hans-peter, M., ... Joanna, P. (2017). MiMSeg - an algorithm for automated detection of tumor tissue on NMR apparent diffusion coefficient maps. *Information Sciences, 384*, 235–248. doi:10.1016/j.ins.2016.07.052

Galldiks, N., Law, I., Pope, W. B., Arbizu, J., & Langen, K.-J. (2017). The use of amino acid PET and conventional MRI for monitoring of brain tumor therapy. *NeuroImage. Clinical, 13*, 386–394. doi:10.1016/j.nicl.2016.12.020 PMID:28116231

Gholami, B., Norton, I., Eberlin, L. S., & Nathalie, Y. R. A. (2013). A statistical modeling approach for tumour-type identification in surgical neuropathology using tissue mass spectrometry imaging. *IEEE Journal of Biomedical and Health Informatics, 17*(3), 734–744. doi:10.1109/JBHI.2013.2250983 PMID:24592474

Gladis PushpaRathi, V.P., & Palani, S. (2011). Detection and characterization of brain tumour using segmentation based on HSOM Wavelet packet feature spaces and ANN. *Proceedings of the Third International Conference on Electronics Computer Technology.*

Guo, L., Zhao, L., Wu, Y., Li, Y., Xu, G., & Yan, Q. (2011). Tumour detection in MR images using one-class immune feature weighted SVMs. *IEEE Transactions on Magnetics, 47*(10), 3849–3852. doi:10.1109/TMAG.2011.2158520

Huang, M., Yang, W., Wu, Y., Jiang, J., Chen, W., & Feng, Q. (2014). Brain tumour segmentation based on local independent projection-based classification. *IEEE Transactions on Biomedical Engineering, 61*(10), 2633–2645. doi:10.1109/TBME.2014.2325410 PMID:24860022

Isin, A., Direkoglu, C., & Sah, M. (2016). Review of MRI-based brain tumour image segmentation using deep learning methods. *Procedia Computer Science, 102*, 317–324. doi:10.1016/j.procs.2016.09.407

Ivan, C., & Iker, G. (2017). MRI segmentation fusion for brain tumor detection. *Information Fusion, 36*, 1–9. doi:10.1016/j.inffus.2016.10.003

Jafari-Khouzani, K. (2014). MRI upsampling using feature-based nonlocal means approach. *IEEE Transactions on Medical Imaging, 33*(10), 1969–1985. doi:10.1109/TMI.2014.2329271 PMID:24951680

Karuna, K., & Joshi, A. (2013). Automatic detection and severity analysis of brain tumours using GUI in MATLAB. *International Journal of Research in Engineering and Technology, 2*(10), 586–594. doi:10.15623/ijret.2013.0210092

Kowear, M. K., & Yadev, S. (2012). Brain tumour detection and segmentation using histogram thresholding. *International Journal of Engineering and Advanced Technology, 1*(4), 16–20.

Ming-Sian, L., Chong-Guang, C., Chiun-Li, C., & Shih-Hua, L. (2013). Stroke area detection using texture feature and iFuzzyLDA algorithm. *International Journal of Electronics and Electrical Engineering, 1*(2), 1–4.

Mukesh, K., & Mehta, K. K. (2011). A texture based tumour detection and automated segmentation of MRI brain tumour images. *International Journal of Computer Technology and Applications, 2*(4), 855–859.

Mustaqeem, A., Javed, A., & Fatima, T. (2012). An efficient brain tumour detection algorithm using watershed and thresholding based segmentation. *International Journal of Image. Graphics and Signal Processing, 10*, 34–39. doi:10.5815/ijigsp.2012.10.05

Nidhi, G., & Pritee, K. (2017). A non-invasive and adaptive CAD system to detect *brain tumor* from T2-weighted MRIs using customized Otsu's thresholding with prominent features and supervised learning. *Signal Processing Image Communication, 59*, 18–26. doi:10.1016/j.image.2017.05.013

Parra, C., Iftekharuddin, K. M., & Kozma, R. (2003). Automated brain data segmentation and pattern recognition using ANN. *Proceedings of the Second International Conference on Computational Intelligence, Robotics and Autonomous Systems (CIRAS)*.

Patil, R. C., & Bhalchandra, A. S. (2012). Brain tumour extraction from MRI images using MATLAB. *International Journal of Electronics, Communication & Soft Computing in Science & Engineering, 2*(1), 1–4.

Sayed, A. M., Zaghloul, E., & Nassef, T. M. (2016). Automatic classification of breast tumours using features extracted from magnetic resonance images. *Procedia Computer Science, 95*, 392–398. doi:10.1016/j.procs.2016.09.350

Schwarz, D., Kasparek, T., Provaznik, I., & Jarkovsky, J. (2007). A deformable registration method for automated morphometry of MRI brain images in neuropsychiatric research. *IEEE Transactions on Medical Imaging, 26*(4), 452–461. doi:10.1109/TMI.2007.892512 PMID:17427732

Sehgal, A., Goel, S., Mangipudi, P., Mehra, A., & Tyagi, D. (2016). Automatic brain tumour segmentation and extraction in MR images. *Proceedings of the IEEE Conference on Advances in Signal Processing (CASP)*.

Sharma, P., Diwakar, M., & Choudhary, S. (2012). Application of edge detector for brain tumour detection. *International Journal of Computers and Applications, 58*(16), 21–25. doi:10.5120/9366-3820

Shen, S., Sandham, W., Granat, M., & Sterr, A. (2005). MRI fuzzy segmentation of brain tissue using neighborhood attraction with neural network optimization. *IEEE Transactions on Information Technology in Biomedicine, 9*(3), 459–467. doi:10.1109/TITB.2005.847500 PMID:16167700

Shen, S., Sandhom, W. A., Gramat, M. H., Dempsey, M. F., & Patterson, J. (2003). A new approach to brain tumour diagnosis using fuzzy logic based genetic programming. *Proceedings of the 25th Annual International Conference of the IEEE Engineering in Medicine and Biology Society*. 10.1109/IEMBS.2003.1279903

Solmaz, A., & Farshad, T. (2017). Detection of Brain Tumor in 3D MRI Images using Local Binary Patterns and Histogram Orientation Gradient. *Neurocomputing, 219*, 526–535. doi:10.1016/j.neucom.2016.09.051

Zhou, Y., & Bai, J. (2007). Atlas-based fuzzy connectedness segmentation and intensity non-uniformity correction applied to brain MRI. *IEEE Transactions on Biomedical Engineering, 54*(1), 122–129. doi:10.1109/TBME.2006.884645 PMID:17260863

KEY TERMS AND DEFINITIONS

Brain: The human brain is the central organ of the human nervous system and with the spinal cord makes up the central nervous system. The brain consists of the cerebrum, the brainstem, and the cerebellum. It controls most of the activities of the body, processing, integrating, and coordinating the information it receives from the sense organs, and making decisions as to the instructions sent to the rest of the body. The brain is contained in, and protected by, the skull bones of the head. The cerebrum is the largest part of the human brain.

Brain Tumor: The brain is the body organ composed of nerve cells and supportive tissues like glial cells and meninges. There are three major parts; they control people activity like breathing (brain stem), activity like moving muscles to walk (cerebellum), and senses like sight and our memory, emotions, thinking, and personality (cerebrum). Primary brain tumors can be either malignant (contain cancer cells) or benign (do not contain cancer cells). A primary brain tumor is a tumor which begins in the brain tissue. If a cancerous tumor starts elsewhere in the body, it can spread cancer cells, which grow in the brain. These type of tumors are called secondary or metastatic brain tumors.

Convolutional Neural Network (CNN): In machine learning, a convolutional neural network is a class of deep, feed-forward artificial neural networks that has successfully been applied to analyzing visual imagery. CNNs use a variation of multilayer perceptrons designed to require minimal preprocessing. They are also known as shift invariant or space invariant artificial neural networks (SIANN), based on their shared-weights architecture and translation invariance characteristics.

Fuzzy Inference System (FIS): Fuzzy inference systems have been successfully applied in fields such as automatic control, data classification, decision analysis, expert systems, and computer vision. Because of its multidisciplinary nature, the fuzzy inference system is known by a number of names, such as fuzzy rule-based system.

Magnetic Resonance Imaging (MRI): Clinical magnetic resonance imaging is an imaging technique used in radiology to form pictures of the anatomy and the physiological processes of the body in both health and disease. MRI scanners use strong magnetic fields, radio waves, and field gradients to generate images of the organs in the body. MRI does not involve x-rays, which distinguishes it from computed tomography.

Chapter 16

Mutual Correlation–Based Anonymization for Privacy Preserving Medical Data Publishing

Ashoka Kukkuvada
Bapuji Institute of Engineering and Technology, India

Poornima Basavaraju
Bapuji Institute of Engineering and Technology, India

ABSTRACT

Currently the industry is focused on managing, retrieving, and securing massive amounts of data. Hence, privacy preservation is a significant concern for those organizations that publish/share personal data for vernacular analysis. In this chapter, the authors presented an innovative approach that makes use of information gain of the quasi attributes with respect to sensitive attributes for anonymizing the data, which gives the fruitfulness of an attribute in classifying the data elements, which is a two-way correlation among attributes. The authors show that the proposed approach preserves better data utility and has lesser complexity than former methods.

1. INTRODUCTION

The advancements in the field of information technology has improved our standard of living. With the lightening growth in computing, networking and database technologies results into collection and integration of tremendous amount of digital data. Data Mining involves the process of deriving functional, interesting and previously concealed information from the collection of large data bases. Present industry is focused on retrieving, managing and securing huge amount of data. For the purpose of business analytics or because of government policies, this data need to be shared/published among various organizations. For example, The US government open data and the data of 105 departments of government of India is published in the open data portals (U.S. Government's open data, (n.d.); Open

DOI: 10.4018/978-1-5225-5152-2.ch016

Copyright © 2018, IGI Global. Copying or distributing in print or electronic forms without written permission of IGI Global is prohibited.

Government Data, (n.d.). Also, sharing of healthcare data helps in computer assisted clinical decision support. For example, Red Cross Blood Transfusion Service (BTS) is an organization that provides services that includes collecting and examine the blood from the donors and dispense the blood to various public hospitals. Government Health Agency in United States of America systematically collects patient's information from public hospitals that contains patient specific healthcare data. This patient specific healthcare data is shared with Red Cross Blood Transfusion Service (BTS) for the purpose of auditing and data analysis which can improve the estimated future blood consumption at different hospitals and also makes recommendations on the blood usage medical cases. Here the patient's privacy must be protected while sharing data between Government Health Agency and the Red Cross BTS. Figure-1 depicts the various stakeholders in the Red Cross BTS system. The blood is collected from the donors and after examination it will be distributed to various public hospitals. The hospitals transfuse the blood to the needed patients, also the hospitals are responsible for maintaining the patient health records and the blood transfusion information like name of the doctor in charge, type of illness, reason and amount of blood transfusion etc. Periodically public hospitals have to put forward, blood usage data along with individual patient's surgery data to Government Health Agency. The Government Health Agencies in turn submit this data to the Red Cross BTS for the purpose of auditing and analysis. The intention of this auditing and analysis is to enhance the subsequent blood consumption in several hospitals and to make suggestions on the imminent medical cases. Here, patient's privacy must be protected while sharing the data between hospitals and the Red Cross BTS.

Data publishing exists in other domains also. For example, the popular online movies rental service provider-Netflix, published a data set that consists of movie ratings of 500,000 members, to enhance the perfection of movie recommendations depending on personal preferences (Bennett & Lanning, 2007); AOL-a web portal and online service provider based in New York, published the query logs of 650,000 users, but deleted immediately for privacy matters.

Typically the data will be gathered from different locations in different format, and compiled into the format that is suitable to store in Data Warehouse. In this scenario the Data Warehouse is the data receiver who collect data from multiple data publishers. The data publisher, generally an independent

Figure 1. Scenario of Red Cross BTS system

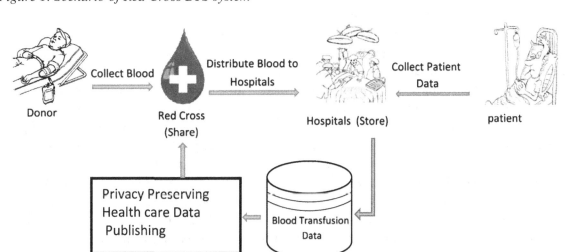

organization collects data from the actual data owners/holders. Data publisher share data for research purpose or for mutual benefit or due to policy decisions by the government. When this data consists of personal sensitive values, privacy of an individual will become an important concern. So, the task of sheer importance is, to develop methods and tools for publishing data in an adverse environment, so that the released data remains practically useful without disclosing individual's privacy. This undertaking is called as Privacy Preserving Data Mining (PPDM). In the past few years the research community has contributed several methods and techniques for Preserving Data Mining. Significant number of research in this area also come from statistics, Big Data Analytics, economics and Cryptography. An initial survey on different methods of PPDM can be found in (Benjamin, Fung, Wang, Chen, & Yu, 2010). There are various directions to enforce PPDM; they are, Randomization, Cryptographic Techniques and PPDP. In the past research there is no clear distinction between PPDM and PPDP, but in recent research PPDP is different from PPDM in several ways.

1. PPDP deals with techniques for publishing data, not techniques for mining the data. In deed it is expected that conventional data mining methods are applied on the published data.
2. The truthfulness of the data is not cultivated in PPDM as it uses randomization or the Cryptographic techniques. The truthfulness is maintained in PPDP.
3. PPDM targeted in performing some data mining operations on the data where as PPDP doesn't perform the actual data mining tasks, but concentrates on how to publish the data so that the anonymous data is useful for data mining.

1.1 PPDP Model

PPDP model can be expressed as shown in Figure 2. In the lower layer there is the data publisher and the upper layer has the data recipient.

The overall model is clefted into data assortment phase and data publishing phase. In data assortment phase the publisher collects data in its original form from the record holders. In the data publishing phase the data publisher releases the data to the data recipients by ensuring privacy. In this model we assume that the data publisher is devoted loyal person with whom the record owners exchange their sensitive information. The data recipients are untrusted ones, so that sensitive data must be safeguarded.

As a solution to these privacy issues, diverse number of PPDP techniques have been developed. Few compelling works for this research are, Randomization method (Agrawal & Aggarwal, 2001), Data swapping (Dalenius & Reiss, 1982), Cryptographic approach (Pinkas, 2002) and Anonymization techniques. Accuracy of randomization depends on how large the distribution of the data is, and the amount of randomization applied, but it suffers from huge information loss. Data swapping suffers from skewness attack (Domingo-Ferrer & Torra, 2008), cryptographic techniques are computationally very expensive for large and high dimensional data sets. Most popular PPDP techniques are Anonymization techniques, because they have lesser information loss and high data utilitymany. Some of the well-received anonymization techniques are, k-anonymity (Sweeney, 2002; Samarati, 2001; LeFevre, DeWitt, & Raghu Ramakrishnan, 2005; LeFevre, DeWitt, & Ramakrishnan, 2006), ℓ-diversity (Machanavajjhala, Gehrke, Kifer, & Venkitasubramaniam, 2006; Domingo-Ferrer & Torra, 2008), t-closeness (Ninghui, Tiancheng, & Venkatasubramanian, 2007), m-invariance (Xiao & Yufei Tao, 2007), Personalized Privacy (Xiao & Tao, 2006), Slicing (Li, Li, Jian Zhang, & Molloy, 2012) etc. It has been shown in (Aggarwal, 2005; Kifer & Gehrke, 2006) that k-anonymity losses significant information loss and suffers from homogene-

Figure 2. PPDP architecture

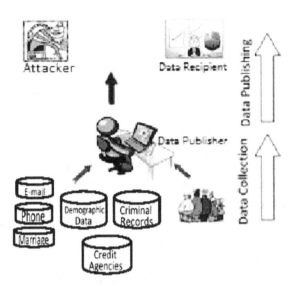

ity and background knowledge attack. ℓ-diversity has better data utility than k-anonymity, but it suffers from skewness attack (Domingo-Ferrer & Torra, 2008). As the Quasi-Identifiers are published as it is, this technique can't avoid membership disclosure (Nergiz, Atzori, & Clifton, 2007). t-closeness requires the distribution of sensitive attribute in each bucket to be close to the distribution of the attribute in the original table. This condition significantly damages data utility as well as the correlation between QID and SAs. m-invariance (Xiaokui Xiao & Yufei Tao, 2007) is a dynamic data re-publishing model as it allows both record insertions and deletions with multiple release of data. But m-invariance doesn't guarantee privacy if the life span is broken. That is, it happens if a record reappears after its first life span.

These limitations are eliminated in personalized privacy (Xiao & Tao, 2006), but it suffers from 'play safe problem' where The record owner may play safe by fixing his/her guarding node as "Any disease" which will keep him/her in safer privacy zone. But this play safe will result in inaccurate results in many data mining tasks. Slicing (Li, Li, Jian Zhang, & Molloy, 2012) is more powerful technique when privacy protection and information loss is concerned, it partitions the data table both vertically and horizontally. Vertical partitioning is done by grouping the attributes based on correlation among the attributes. They use mean square contingency coefficient to measure the correlation among the attributes and based on these correlation values, attribute clustering will be done using k-medoid method, to partition attributes into columns. Which will be computationally very expensive. Horizontal partitioning is done by grouping tuples into buckets, for which they use 'Mondrian' algorithm (LeFevre, DeWitt, & Ramakrishnan, 2006), which is not an optimal algorithm for tuple partitioning.

An improvement of the k-anonymity/ℓ-diversity was suggested in (Md. Enamul Kabir, 2011), (Bhaladhare & Jinwala, 2016), where the researchers presented a systematic clustering technique for k-anonymization. In this method grouping of the tuples will be done systematically to satisfy k-anonymity/ ℓ-diversity, which has better data utility and execution time. An independent ℓ-diversity principle to avoid corruption attack (Tao, Xiao, Li, & Zhang, 2008) was proposed in (Zhu, Tian, & Lü, 2015) that integrates perturbation and generalization to conserve more data utility. Preserving privacy for unstructured textual medical data was discussed in (Fengli, Zhang, Yijing, & Ba, 2015; Sánchez, Batet, & Viejo, 2014) where, sensitive association rules are sanitized by altering the support and confidence of related items.

Big data analytics is a trending area that makes remarkable revolution in traffic control, disease outbreak perception, smart grids, product recommendation etc. Latest research and innovations in the field of Privacy and Security Policies in Big Data are discussed in (Tamane, Solanki, & Dey, 2017). Privacy preserving for big data analytics to safeguard differential privacy for individual data contributors was done in (Fan & Jin, 2015). The authors propose a generic framework to generate analysis results on a sampled data bases. The researchers in (Huafeng Ba, Xiaoming Gao, Xiaofeng Zhang, & Zhenyu He, 2014) proposes the methods to ensure the data privacy for high-dimensional co-related data. In their work they implemented a novel technique that protects user privacy by instinctually determining the suitable set of semi-id features in preference to manually designating them by tuning the privacy level control parameter. A differential privacy approach for enhanced classification accuracy was proposed in (Zaman, Obimbo, & Dara, 2016), in which the authors present a non-interactive algorithm to satisfy ε-differential privacy. Preserving privacy for outsourced multimedia material is proposed in (Weng, Amsaleg, & Furon, 2016). The authors use privacy preserving framework based on robust hashing and partial encryption techniques. Hiding personalizes anonymity of attributes was presented in (Rajesh, & Selvakumar, 2015). Here in order to maintain privacy, the authors developed a method that enumerates and concatenates the attributes using multi-level encryption. Preserving privacy for Location Based Services (LBS) data was done by (Yamin, & Sen, 2018). Here authors propose a technique that integrates dummies from actual queries and peer to peer (P2P) with caching techniques to improve privacy and performance.

All these approaches for PPDP assume that the attributes of the input Microdata are categorized into three classes: (1) Identifying Attributes: that distinctively identify an individual, for example, Social Security Number or Name; they are wiped out from the published table; (2) Quasi Identifiers (QID): which can be used by the opponent to link these values to a publicly accessible external database (voter list) to identify an individual, for example, Gender, Zipcode and Birthdate. Sometimes it may also contain attacker's auxiliary information about input micro data, and; (3) Sensitive attributes (SA): which are unknown to the adversaries and are used in data mining and statistical analysis, for example, Disease, Income, etc. An illustrative original Microdata table is shown in Table 1.

1.2 Motivation and Paper Outline

To overcome the limitations deliberated above, we are motivated to propose a novel approach for PPDP. We used the concept of entropy of the data set to find the effectiveness of an attribute to classify the data, which in turn gives us the mutual correlation among QIDs and SAs. By using this correlation the input microdata table is sliced vertically. For horizontal partitioning the optimum partitioning algorithm for ℓ-diversity is used.

At first, it start with the care full analysis of entropy and formalize the concepts that motivated the new technique that gives the efficacy of the attributes to classify data. We concentrate on the accuracy of classification application that provide a simple framework that partitions the data table, vertically by correlation in terms of information gain from the entropy and horizontally by optimal partitioning for ℓ-diversity.

We developed an entropy based partitioning algorithm for slicing the table that preserve considerable amount of information in the microdata. Our preliminary result specifies that the proposed method can improve data utility, which in turn increases the precision of several data mining tasks. To the best

Table 1. Input microdata table

Name	Gender	Education	Race	Occupation	Salary
Arun	M	Bachelor	White	Tech-support	≤ 50k
Basu	F	Bachelor	White	Tech-support	≤ 50k
Chandan	M	Bachelor	White	Sales	>50k
David	M	Bachelor	Asian	Professional	>50k
Edwin	M	Masters	Black	Professional	>50k
Fatima	F	Masters	Black	Professional	≤ 50k
Greeshma	F	Masters	Black	Sales	>50k
Henry	M	Bachelor	Asian	Tech-support	≤ 50k
Imthiyaz	M	Masters	Black	Tech-support	>50k
Johnson	M	Masters	Asian	Professional	>50k
Kate	F	Masters	Asian	Tech-support	>50k
Latha	F	Bachelor	Asian	Sales	>50k
Manju	M	Masters	White	Sales	>50k
Nikhil	F	Bachelor	Asian	Professional	≤ 50k

of our knowledge this is the first of its kind which take account of entropy based information gain for correlation in slicing the table.

The rest of the paper is organized as follows. In Section 2 we formalize the concept of Mutual correlation based on Information Gain. Section 3 gives the entropy based slicing Algorithm. Experimental evaluation of our approach is given in Section 4 and Section 5 concludes the paper with future research directions.

2. INFORMATION GAIN

In the field of machine learning, Information Gain (IG) is usually utilized as a term-goodness criterion. It is calculated through the entropy of a system, i. e. of the amount of disorder in the system. In other words, Entropy is a measure of (im)purity of an arbitrary collection of examples. Therefore, the entropy of a dataset is the elementary calculation to compute IG. If the target attribute in the input microdata which can take on c different values, then entropy of data S relative to this c-wise classification is given by

$$Entropy(S) = \sum_{i=1}^{c} -p_i \log_2(p_i)$$

(1)

where p_i is the proportion of S belonging to class i.

The effectiveness of an attribute in classifying the data is measured by 'Information Gain' (IG). That is, Information Gain measures the quantity of information about target class prediction, if the only information accessible is the presence of a feature and its corresponding class distribution. Precisely it measures the expected decrement in entropy. For a data set S and attribute A the Information Gain is given by:

$$IG(S, A) = Entropy(S) - \sum_{v \in values(A)} \frac{|S_v|}{|S|} Entropy(S_v) \qquad (2)$$

where Values (A) is the set of all possible values for attribute A, and $S_v \subseteq S$ for which attribute A has value v. Hence from equation (2) IG(S, A) is the information provided about the target function value, given the value of some attribute A.

IG looks discretely at each feature, calculate its information gain and quantify how relevant and important it is to the class label. Calculating the information gain for a feature includes computing the entropy of the class label for the complete data set and deducting the conditional entropies for all possible values of that feature. The calculation of entropy needs a frequency count of the class label by feature value. That is; all instances are chosen with some feature value v, after that the number of occurrences of each class within these instances are counted, and then the entropy of v is computed. For each possible values of v of the feature, this step is repeated. The algorithm for Information Gain calculation is given below.

```
Algorithm InfoGain(S, A)
Input: Input Microdata table T, with A attributes.
Output: IG(S, A) for each attribute a_i ∈ A.
Begin
    1. Sum = 0;
    2. C ← domain of class label;
    3. A ← domain of an attribute values;
    4. For each c_i ∈ C
        a. Calculate p(c[i]);
        b. H_c = Sum + p(c[i]) * log_2 p(c[i]);
        c. Sum ← H_c
    5. For each a_j ∈ A;
        a. Calculate p(a[j]);
        b. Sum1= Sum + p(a[j]) * log_2(p(a[j]));
        c. Sum ← Sum1;
    6. For each c_i do
        a. For each a_j do
                i. Calculate p(c[i]a[j]);
                ii. M = Sum + p(c[i]) a[j]) *log_2 p(c[i]a[j]);
                iii. Sum ← M;
    7. H(C/A) = (-1)*Sum1*(-1)*M;
    8. IG = H_c - H(C/A)
    9. Return IG.
End
```

For illustration consider the microdata in Table 1, for the attribute Gender which have the values *male* and *female*, there are 14 examples (tuples). For salary value greater than 50k, out of 14 examples, there are 9 positive (tuples 3, 4, 5, 7, 9, 10, 11, 12 and 13) examples and 5 negative (tuples 1, 2, 6, 8 and 14) examples. Therefore Information Gain is given by:

$$IG(S, Gender) = Entropy(S) - \sum_{v \in \{Male, Female\}} \frac{|S_v|}{|S|} Entropy(S_v)$$

Entropy (s) = $-(9/14)\log_2(9/14) - (5/14)\log_2(5/14) = 0.940$

and

$S_{male} \leftarrow \{$ 6 positive, 2 negative $\}$ (out of 8 male examples)

$S_{female} \leftarrow \{3$ positive, 3 negative$\}$ (out of 3 female examples)

Therefore:

IG(S, Gender) = $0.940 - (8/14)$ Entropy $(S_{male}) - (6/14)$ Entropy (S_{female})

If the entropy of male and female examples are calculated as above, we get

IG(S, Gender) = $0.940 - (8/14) \, 0.811 - (6/14) \, 1.00 = 0.048$

Similarly for the other attributes Education, Race and Occupation the IG values are calculated, as given below.

IG(S, Education) = 0.151

IG(S, Race) = 0.029

IG(S, Occupation) = 0.246

According to Information Gain measure the attribute occupation has highest value hence it has highest prediction accuracy (so the correlation) of target attribute. Therefore while dividing the table vertically the attributes Occupation and Salary are kept in same column and others in other columns. We may also add another attribute for the above column by calculating second level Information gain of the remaining attributes for various values of occupation, that is, for Tech-support, Sales and Professional. The horizontal partitioning was done using optimal partitioning method to satisfy ℓ-diversity. For example when Table 1 is sliced by this technique, the output table is shown in Table 2. This sliced table is completely privacy protected in the sense that it is not possible predict/identify an individual from this table.

3. ENTROPY-SLICING ALGORITHM

The Information Gain based Slicing Algorithm has two parts. In the first part the efficacy of an attribute in the form of Information Gain based on entropy to classify the data is calculated for each QIDs. That will be used to determine the attribute partitioning (column partitioning) criteria. Next, the second part

Table 2. The sliced table

(Gender, Education, Race)	(Occupation, Salary)
F, Masters, Black M, Bachelor, Asian M, Bachelor, White M, Bachelor, White M, Masters, Black F, Masters, Black F, Bachelor, White	Tech-support, ≤ 50k Tech-support, ≤ 50k Sales, >50k Professional, >50k Professional, >50k Professional, ≤ 50k Sales, >50k
F, Bachelor, Asian M, Masters, Black F, Bachelor, Asian F, Masters, Asian M, Masters, Asian M, Bachelor, Asian M, Masters, White	Sales, >50k Professional, >50k Tech-support, ≤ 50k Professional, ≤ 50k Sales, >50k Tech-support, >50k Tech-support, >50k

is the optimal tuple partitioning for ℓ-diversity slicing. The complexity of the Step 2 (calculation of IG values for each QIDs) is O(m), where m is the number of QID attributes. The tuple partition (Steps 5 to 8) takes O(n log n). The generalization in Step 9 take O(n log n). Therefore the overall complexity of the algorithm is O(n log n) which is efficient than slicing (Li, Li, Jian Zhang, & Molloy, 2012).

Algorithm Entropy-Slicing
Input: Private Microdata table T, Number of attributes per column k, l .
Output: The publishable table T*.
    1. If (n < TH_min) then return with warning message // T should contain minimum TH_min records
    2. Calculate IG_i (Information Gain) for all QIDs. 1≤ i ≤ m.
    3. Vertically partition T, with k no. of attributes based on IG.
    4. Initialize T*=Φ
    5. For each tuple t_i ∈ T (1 ≤ i ≤ n)
    6. Search t_i.QID for matching bucket.
    7. If found Put t_i in the Bucket
    8. Else initialize new bucket with t_i in T*
    9. Perform generalization, if tuple insertion violates ℓ-diversity.
    10. Randomly permute tuples within each bucket.

3.1 Privacy Protection

The proposed algorithm guarantees protection against different types of attacks. Record linkage attack occurs when the published data is linked/compared with publicly available open data like voter registration list. When the entire bucket has same sensitive attribute value, it results in homogeneity attack. If the attacker has some background knowledge of the sensitive values, it may results in background knowledge attack. In Attribute Linkage attack the adversary may not precisely identify the record of the victim, but can identify his/her sensitive values from the published data, based on the set of sensitive values related to the group that the victim belongs to. If some sensitive values predominates in a group, it is relatively easy to identify the victim. Record linkage, table linkage and attribute linkage attacks are effectively thwarted because of the random permutation of tuples in each buckets. In the proposed algorithm as each of the buckets conforms ℓ-diversity, it avoids homogeneity attack, background knowledge attack and probabilistic attack.

4. EXPERIMENTS

In this section, the experimental estimation of the efficacy of the proposed approach as related to k-anonymity, ℓ-diversity and Slicing was done. This research is carried out on an Intel i5 processor with 4GB memory on Gnu C++ compiler. For experimental analysis, the adult dataset from UCI machine learning repository (Lichman, 2013) and the CUPS data set (http://kdd.ics.uci.edu/databases/kddcup98/kddcup98.html) are used. The UCI adult data set contains fifteen attributes. After removing tuples with missing and null values, there are around 45k effective tuples in total. In our experiments we have used Age, Education, Marital status, Race, Sex and Country as Quasi Identifiers. The attribute Occupation is treated as sensitive attribute. There are 96367 records in CUPS data set that has 479 attributes. We have taken Age, Gender, T_code, Cluster and Domain as Quasi Identifiers. The attribute Income is considered as sensitive attribute. The remaining attributes in CUPS data set have very poor data quality, so our endeavor to add more quasi identifiers was limited to these six attributes. The value of ℓ is set to 4. We did the experiments for classification accuracy and computational efficiency. We used weka tool for evaluation of classification accuracy for Decision Tree and Naïve Bayes method. Learning the classifier was done with 10-fold cross validation.

Figure 3 gives the accuracy of classification for Naïve Bayes and Decision Tree (J48) classifiers. We observe from the results that mutual correlation based entropy slicing is at par with normal slicing and its performance is better compared to k-anonymity and ℓ-diversity.

We also investigated the computational cost of our technique with k-anonymity, ℓ-diversity and Slicing on both data sets. Figure 4 shows the experimental results for execution time in seconds with the work load of 10k, 20k and 40k records of the UCI adult data set. The figure unveils that our entropy based slicing algorithm shows better performance than normal slicing with respect to computational cost. In Figure 5 the computational cost for CUPS data set reveals that, the proposed algorithm scales well for high dimensional data sets.

4.1. EVALUATION METRICS

The critical element in data sharing/publishing is to protect individual's privacy, meanwhile it is also essential that, utility of the data needs the same extent of preservation. In order to balance these two contradicting goals 'privacy/utility', there is no universally accepted evaluation metric by the research fraternity. A few of the prominent metrics are Hiding Failure (HF), Information Loss (IL), Minimal distortion (MD), Discernibility Metric (DM), Weighted Hierarchical Distance (WHD), Information Gain/Privacy Loss (IGPL) trade off, Misclassification error (ME) etc. Out of which, Information Loss metric can be used as a performance metric for majority of the Privacy Preserving techniques, which is computed as follows:

Figure 3. Classification accuracy for UCI-adult data set

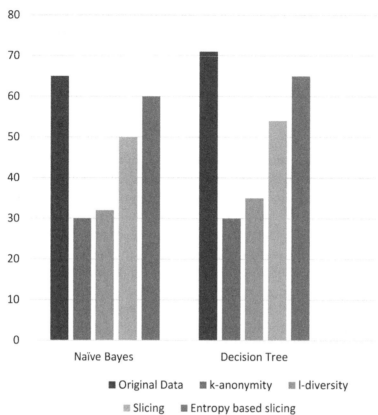

■ Original Data   ■ k-anonymity   ▩ l-diversity

▩ Slicing   ■ Entropy based slicing

*For a more accurate representation see the electronic version.

$$I\_Loss(T^*) = \sum_{j=1}^{f} ws \frac{(The\ no.\ of\ values\ int^*.SA(j)) - 1}{The\ no.\ of\ values\ in\ the\ domain\ of\ SA}$$

$$+$$

$$\sum_{i=1}^{d} wq \frac{(The\ no.\ of\ values\ int^*.QI(i)) - 1}{The\ no.\ of\ values\ in\ the\ domain\ of\ A(i)}$$

For each tuples t* ∈ T*.

Here f is the number of sensitive arrtibutes, d is the number of QIDs, *ws* and *wq* are the positive penalty costs for loosing precision after generalization. In our research these values are set to 1. We evaluated the Information Loss for UCI adult data as well as CUPS data set. Figure 6 and Figure 7 compares the information Loss for varying number of input records. We can observe that mutual correlation based entropy slicing has very less information loss compared to k-anonymity and ℓ–diversity, and is at par with slicing technique.

Figure 4. Computational cost (for UCI-adult data set)- no. of records vs execution time (sec)

10
9
8
7
6
5
4
3
2
1
0
10000
20000
40000
k-anonymity
l-diversity
Slicing
entropy based slicing

**For a more accurate representation see the electronic version.*

Figure 5. Computational cost (for CUPS data set)- no. of records vs execution time (sec)

14
12
10
8
6
4
2
0
20000
40000
60000
80000
k-anonymity
l-diversity
Slicing
entropy based slicing

**For a more accurate representation see the electronic version.*

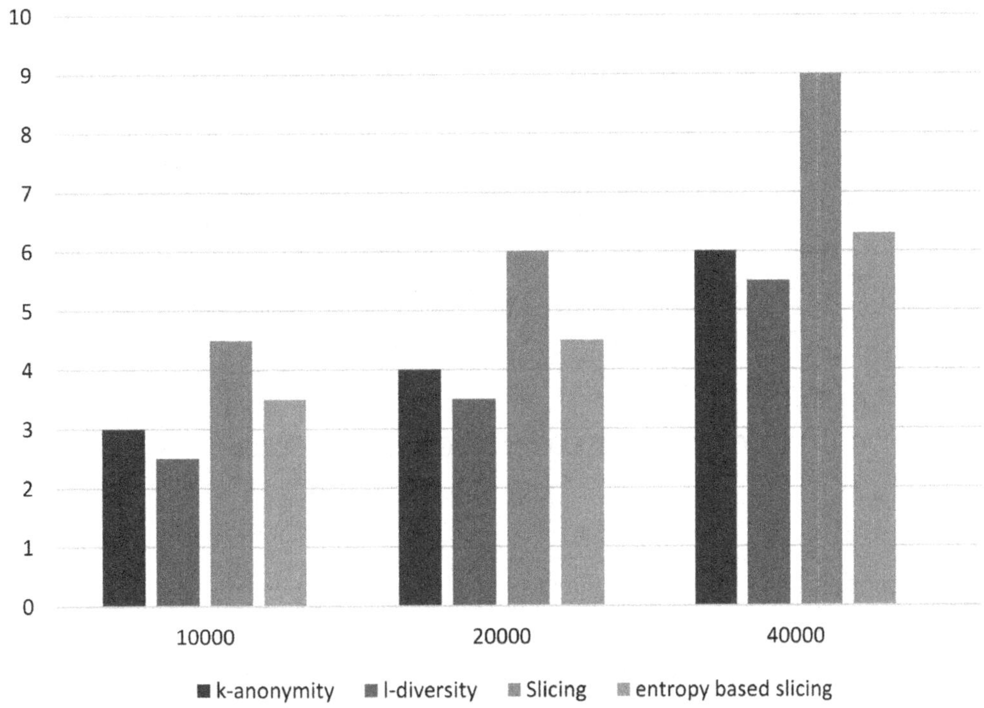

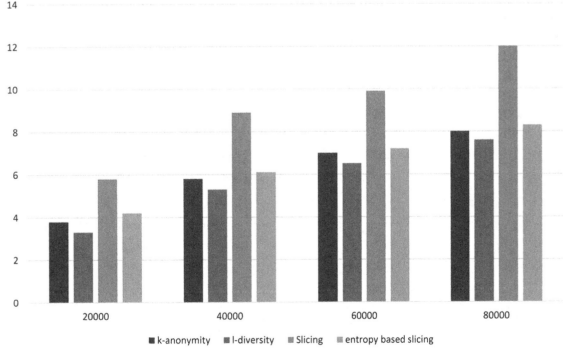

Figure 6. Information Loss (for UCI-adult data set)

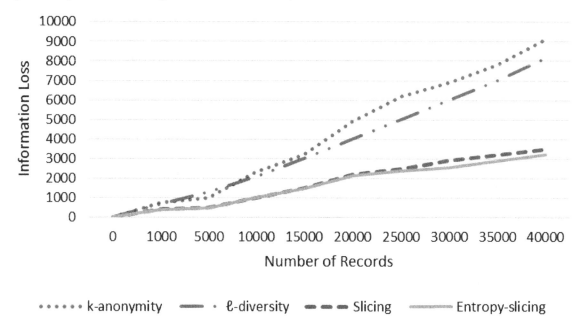

Figure 7. Information Loss (for CUPS data set)

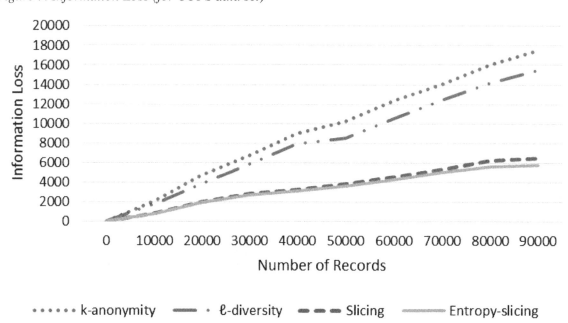

5. CONCLUSION AND FUTURE WORK

Sharing of data/knowledge is indispensable part of many individuals and establishments. As the data is scattered across diverse locations in different format, Privacy Preserving Data Publishing is a sanguine methodology for preserving individual's privacy and defending sensitive information. In this paper we presented a new technique 'Mutual correlation based anonymization' for preserving privacy in Medical data publishing, which can preserve the privacy of multiple heterogeneous sensitive attributes. The general method proposed by our work is that; by considering the effectiveness of an attribute in terms of information gain from entropy for partitioning the attributes, slicing was done. The experiments shows that Information Gain based slicing has excellent classification accuracy and computational cost when scrutinized with normal slicing.

The work motivates several directions for upcoming research. The experiment was done for single release data, whereas sequential release and multiple release data privacy is still in its infant stage. Research on hybrid technique that combines the plus points of anonymization, slicing, perturbation etc. can be considered.

Finally, while there exists abundant anonymization algorithms, providing privacy for unstructured data is still in its suckling stage. Therefore more stress need to be given in designing effective algorithms for privacy preserving in an unstructured data.

The privacy preserving mechanism clear up only the technical side of the issue but, the nontechnical difficulties of the problem can be effectively solved with versatile research in collaboration with social scientists, psychologists and public policy makers.

REFERENCES

Aggarwal, C. (2005). On k-Anonymity and the Curse of Dimensionality. *Proc. Int'l Conf. Very Large Data Bases (VLDB)*, 901-909.

Agrawal, D., & Aggarwal, C. C. (2001). On the design and quantification of privacy preserving data mining algorithms. *Proc. of the 20th ACM Symposium on Principles of Database Systems (PODS)*, 247–255. 10.1145/375551.375602

Ba, H., Gao, X., Zhang, X., & He, Z. (2014). Protecting Data Privacy from Being Inferred from High Dimensional Correlated Data. In *Proceedings of the 2014 IEEE/WIC/ACM International Joint Conferences on Web Intelligence (WI) and Intelligent Agent Technologies (IAT)* . IEEE Computer Society. 10.1109/WI-IAT.2014.139

Bennett & Lanning. (2007). The Netflix Prize. *Proceedings of KDD Cup and Workshop 2007*.

Dalenius, T., & Reiss, S. P. (1982). Data-Swapping: A Technique for Disclosure Control. *Journal of Statistical Planning and Inference*, 6(1), 73–85. doi:10.1016/0378-3758(82)90058-1

Domingo-Ferrer, J., & Torra, V. (2008). A critique of k-anonymity and some of its enhancements, *Proc. of the 3rd International Conference on Availability, Reliability and Security (ARES)*, 990–993. 10.1109/ARES.2008.97

Fan, L., & Jin, H. (2015). A Practical Framework for Privacy-Preserving Data Analytics. In *Proceedings of the 24th International Conference on World Wide Web (WWW '15)*. ACM. 10.1145/2736277.2741122

Fengli, Z., & Yijing, B. (2015). ARM-Based Privacy Preserving for Medical Data Publishing. *Cloud Computing and Security: First International Conference, ICCCS 2015*. 10.1007/978-3-319-27051-7_6

Fung, Wang, Chen, & Yu. (2010). Privacy-preserving data publishing: A survey of recent developments. *ACM Comput. Surv., 42*(4). DOI:10.1145/1749603.1749605

Kabir, M. E., Wang, H., & Bertino, E. (2011, February). Md. Enamul Kabir, Hua Wang, and Elisa Bertino: (2011). Efficient systematic clustering method for *k*-anonymization. *Acta Informatica, 48*(1), 51–66. doi:10.100700236-010-0131-6

Kifer, D., & Gehrke, J. (2006). Injecting Utility into Anonymized Data Sets. *Proc. ACM SIGMOD Int'l Conf. Management of Data (SIGMOD)*, 217-228.

LeFevre, K., DeWitt, D. J., & Ramakrishnan, R. (2005). Incognito: efficient full-domain K-anonymity. In *Proceedings of the 2005 ACM SIGMOD international conference on Management of data (SIGMOD '05)*. ACM. 10.1145/1066157.1066164

LeFevre, K., DeWitt, D. J., & Ramakrishnan, R. (2006). Mondrian Multidimensional K-Anonymity. *22nd International Conference on Data Engineering (ICDE'06)*, 25-25. 10.1109/ICDE.2006.101

Li, T., Li, N., Zhang, J., & Molloy, I. (2012). Slicing: A New Approach for Privacy Preserving Data Publishing. *IEEE Transactions on Knowledge and Data Engineering, 24*(3), 561–574. doi:10.1109/TKDE.2010.236

Lichman, M. (2013). *UCI Machine Learning Repository*. Irvine, CA: University of California, School of Information and Computer Science.

Machanavajjhala, A., Gehrke, J., Kifer, D., & Venkitasubramaniam, M. (2006). *ℓ*-Diversity: Privacy Beyond k-Anonymity. *Proc. Int'l Conf. Data Eng. (ICDE)*, 24.

Nergiz, M. E., Atzori, M., & Clifton, C. (2007). Hiding the Presence of Individuals from Shared Databases. *Proc. ACM SIGMOD Int'l Conf. Management of Data (SIGMOD)*, 665-676. 10.1145/1247480.1247554

Ninghui, L., Tiancheng, L., & Venkatasubramanian, S. (2007). t-Closeness: Privacy beyond k-anonymity and *ℓ*-diversity. *Proceedings - International Conference on Data Engineering*, 106-115.

Bhaladhare & Jinwala. (2016). Novel Approaches for Privacy Preserving Data Mining in *k*-Anonymity Model. *Journal of Information Science and Engineering, 32*(1), 63–78.

Open Government Data (OGD) of India. (n.d.). Retrieved from https://data.gov.in/

Pinkas, B. (2002). Cryptographic techniques for privacy-preserving data mining. *ACM SIGKDD Explorations Newsletter, 4*(2), 12–19. doi:10.1145/772862.772865

Rajesh, N., & Selvakumar, A. L. (2015). Hiding personalised anonymity of attributes using privacy preserving data mining. *Int. J. Advanced Intelligence Paradigms, 7*(3/4), 394–402. doi:10.1504/IJAIP.2015.073717

Samarati, P. (2001). Protecting Respondents' Identities in Microdata Release. *IEEE Transactions on Knowledge and Data Engineering, 13*(6), 1010–1027. doi:10.1109/69.971193

Sánchez, D., Batet, M., & Viejo, A. (2014, December). Utility-preserving privacy protection of textual healthcare documents. *Journal of Biomedical Informatics, 52*(C), 189–198. doi:10.1016/j.jbi.2014.06.008 PMID:24998814

Sweeney, L. (2002). k-Anonymity: A Model for Protecting Privacy. *Int'l J. Uncertainty Fuzziness and Knowledge-Based Systems, 10*(5), 557–570. doi:10.1142/S0218488502001648

Tamane, S., Solanki, V. K., & Dey, N. (2017). *Privacy and Security Policies in Big Data.* Hershey, PA: IGI Global; doi:10.4018/978-1-5225-2486-1

Tao, Y., Xiao, X., Li, J., & Zhang, D. (2008). On Anti-Corruption Privacy-Preserving Publication. In *Proc. ICDE 08* (pp. 725–734). IEEE Computer Society.

The home of the U.S. Government's open data. (n.d.). Retrieved from https://www.data.gov/

Weng, L., Amsaleg, L., & Furon, T. (2016). Privacy-Preserving Outsourced Media Search. *IEEE Transactions on Knowledge and Data Engineering, 28*(10), 2738–2751. doi:10.1109/TKDE.2016.2587258

Xiao, X., & Tao, Y. (2006). Personalized privacy preservation. *Proc. Of ACM International Conference on Management of Data (SIGMOD).*

Xiao, X., & Tao, Y. (2007). m-invariance: Towards privacy preserving re-publication of dynamic datasets. *ACM SIGMOD International Conference on Management of Data,* 689–700. 10.1145/1247480.1247556

Yamin, M., & Sen, A. A. A. (2018). Improving Privacy and Security of User Data in Location Based Services. *International Journal of Ambient Computing and Intelligence, 9*(1), 19–42. doi:10.4018/IJACI.2018010102

Zaman, Obimbo, & Dara. (2016). A Novel Differential Privacy Approach that Enhances Classification Accuracy. In *Proceedings of the Ninth International C* Conference on Computer Science & Software Engineering (C3S2E '16).* ACM. DOI: 10.1145/2948992.2949027

Zhu, H., Tian, S., & Lü, K. (2015). Privacy-Preserving Data Publication with Features of Independent -Diversity. *The Computer Journal, 58*(4), 549–571. doi:10.1093/comjnl/bxu102

Chapter 17
A Hybrid Watermarking Technique for Copyright Protection of Medical Signals in Teleradiology

Rohit M. Thanki
C. U. Shah University, India

Surekha Borra
K. S. Institute of Technology, India

Komal Borisagar
Atmiya Institute of Technology and Science, India

ABSTRACT

Today, an individual's health is being monitored for diagnosis and treatment of diseases upon analyzing various medical data such as images and signals. Modifications of this medical data when it is transferred over an open communication channel or network leads to deviations in diagnosis and creates a serious health issue for any individual. Digital watermarking techniques are one of the solutions for providing protection to multimedia contents. This chapter gives requirements and various techniques for the security of medical data using watermarking. This chapter also demonstrates a novel hybrid watermarking technique based on fast discrete curvelet transform (FDCuT), redundant discrete wavelet transform (RDWT), and discrete cosine transform (DCT). This watermarking technique can be used for securing medical various types of medical images and ECG signals over an open communication channel.

1. INTRODUCTION

In recent days, treatment and diagnosis of the patient are being solved by various types of medical data which is in the form of images or signals such as Magnetic Resonance Imaging (MRI), X-RAY, Computerized Tomography (CT) and Ultrasound (US), ECG signals and EEG signals. This medical data

DOI: 10.4018/978-1-5225-5152-2.ch017

Copyright © 2018, IGI Global. Copying or distributing in print or electronic forms without written permission of IGI Global is prohibited.

of the patient is transferred from one doctor to another doctor for better health solution and treatment. Transferring medical data over a transmission medium is known as telemedicine and is defined by The American Hospital Association (AHA) as:

the use of medical data exchanged from one site to another via electronic communications to improve a patient's clinical health status, including an increasing variety of applications and services using two-way video, email, smart phones, wireless tools and other forms of telecommunications technology (American Hospital Association, 2015; Yassin, 2015).

The telemedicine or Teleradiology application includes emergency treatment, home monitor, military applications and medical education (Yassin, 2015) and ehealth, where the security and privacy of medical data are always associated with them. Hence, there is a need for development of methodologies or techniques that can fulfill the security requirement of the application.

Since last decade, various researchers and different agencies are working on to design of various techniques, rules, and standards for security and privacy requirements of medical information in teleradiology application. The first international standard for security of medical data is developed by International Standard Organization in 2008 and whose name is ISO 27799:2008 (ISO 27799:2016, 2016). In 2016, this standard is revised and is used for security management of medical data. This standard defined different security and quality parameters for various types of medical data like medical images, medical videos, and medical signals. Also, some countries defined their own standard for security of medical data. For example, USA has used the standard Health Insurance Portability and Accountability (HIPAA) (HIPAA, 1996) and Code of Federal Regulations numbers 45 (CFR 45) (CFR 45, 2010). Also, in 1983, American College of Radiology (ACR) and the National Electrical Manufacturers Association (NEMA) has made one agency by name Digital Imaging and Communication in Medicine (DICOM) (DICOM, 2009) for developing a standard database for medical data and rules for security of medical data.

To design and implement security mechanisms based on available standards for privacy and security of medical data, various teleradiology models are designed by the researchers. Ruotsalainen (Ruotsalainen, 2010) developed a standard model for online transmission and for offline transmission. The online transmission of medical data is done via the internet and offline transmission of medical data is done via hard copy, hard disk or floppy. He also pointed out various security requirements for models used in teleradiology applications. In any standard teleradiology model, privacy and security of medical data are affected at mainly three points which are indicated in Figure 1.

Security is needed in the following cases: 1. When medical data is stored at system database of hospital or data is transferred from one doctor to another doctor within a hospital. 2. When medical data is transferred from one hospital to another hospital or remote treatment house via online transmission or offline transmission. 3. The security of medical data at the remote treatment house. In all these cases, the corruption or modification of medical data is possible, which may lead to wrong diagnosis and treatment of the patient. When designing any model for teleradiology applications, the model must fulfill the various security requirements which are mentioned below (Ruotsalainen, 2010; Baur, Engelmann, Saurbier, Schroter, Baur, & Menizer, 1997):

1. All concerned points or hardware used in the model must have the same security level.
2. At all points, authorization of doctors or users must be performed through various authenticate process and controls.

Figure 1. Standard teleradiology model

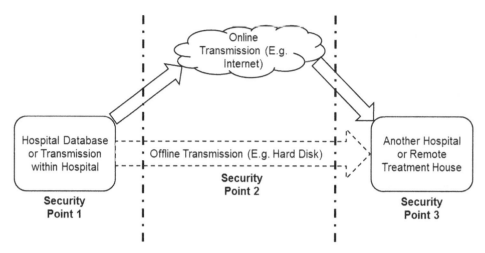

3. Authenticity, confidentiality, and integrity of all medical data have to be secured during various medical sessions such as consultation, processing, management, and storage.

Based on the basic requirements of models, any teleradiology model must have three characteristics such as confidentiality, reliability, and availability (Ruotsalainen, 2010; Baur, Engelmann, Saurbier, Schroter, Baur, & Menizer, 1997; Epstein, 1998). The confidentiality characteristic of the model is ensures that only authenticated user can access medical data. The reliability characteristic of the model depends on integrity (modification data cannot be performed by the unauthenticated user) and authenticity (authentication of medical data provides to authenticated user). The availability characteristic of the model has ensured that system access is available for all authenticated users in normal condition. The security requirements of models based on these requirements against various threats are summarized in Table 1.

In last decade, researchers developed and implemented various security techniques for the security of medical data using concepts of computer and network security (Dey, Ashour, Chakraborty, Banerjee, Gospodinova, Gospodinov, & Hassanien, 2017; . These techniques such as firewall, Virtual Private Network (VPN), encryption, cryptographic hashing (Machine Authentication Code (MAC), Machine Detection

Table 1. Security requirements of teleradiology model

Security Requirement	Threats	Security Measures
Confidentiality	Modification of data at system storage; During communication between two checkpoints;	Data encryption; Time duration of Data storage; Access control services and User control services; Checking of unauthorized access of data
Reliability	Illegal creation, duplication, and modification of data which is stored or transmitted through medium	Data encryption; Checking of authentication of data; Access control services
Availability	Modification on storage system; Corrupted hard drive; Alternation of data in storage system	Access control services for data related operation such as writing, reading; use some software such as antivirus software and firewall for security against virus

Code (MDC), and Digital Signature) and image hashing are currently used for security of medical data (Nyeem, Boles, & Boyd, 2013). The limitation of these existing security techniques are summarized in Table 2 (Nyeem, Boles, & Boyd, 2013; Paar & Pelzl, 2010; Voloshynovskiy, Koval, Beekhof, & Pun, 2009; Goldwasser & Bellare, 2008; Xiaoyun, Xuejia, & Hongbo, 2004; Preneel, 2003; Kalker, 2001; Coatrieux, Maitre, Sankur, Rolland, & Collorec, 2000; Zhou, Huang, & Lou, 2000).

Currently, research on the application of digital watermarking for security of medical data became a very hot topic. Digital watermarking has various properties which overcome the limitations of existing security techniques, and are used in the security of multimedia data in various multimedia applications (Cox, Miller, Bloom, Fridrich, & Kalker, 2007). Coatrieux (2000) and his research team gave applications of watermarking in medical imaging, and the related the security requirements to be satisfied for Teleradiology applications. The basic comparison of watermarking technique with various existing security techniques are summarized in Table 3 (Nyeem, Boles, & Boyd, 2013). The comparison in Table 3 shows that digital watermarking techniques are used for any type of medical data, provides copyright protection, authentication, using various types of embedding and extraction procedures. The comparison also shows that digital watermarking is provides good option for the security of medical data in Teleradiology application.

The rest of the chapter is organized as follows: Digital watermarking in teleradiology application, requirements of digital watermarking for the security of medical data and applications of digital watermarking for medical images are discussed in section 2. Section 3 gives complete literature review of recent and existing watermarking techniques for the security of medical data. Section 4 gives methodology, results, and discussion of proposed watermarking technique for the security of medical data. Finally, section 5 gives the conclusion of the chapter.

2. DIGITAL WATERMARKING FOR TELERADIOLOGY APPLICATION

Digital watermarking is used for copyright protection of multimedia data in various applications including the teleradiology (Que, 2010; Liew & Zain, 2009). The digital watermarking is a process that adds secure watermark data (e.g. text, logo or binary image) into the host data (e.g. digital image, digital video, etc.) to generate watermarked data. Generally, digital watermarking has two blocks: watermark embedder and watermark extractor as shown in Figure 2. The watermark data is inserted into the host

Table 2. Limitations of existing security techniques for security of medical data

Existing Security Techniques	Limitations
Firewall and Virtual Private Network (VPN)	These techniques provide security to data within internal system of the network. These techniques can be easily bypassed by imposter or attacker.
Encryption Technique	This technique is used for security of data at system database and over the communication channel. The limitation of this technique is that if once secret key is decrypted, then data is not secured anymore. The decryption of secret key is easier nowadays due to many encryption techniques available in the literature.
Hash Technique (Cryptographic and Image Hashing)	This technique is not identified where data is corrupted or modified. The security of technique depends on strength of hash functions but once the hash function is decrypted then data is not secured anymore. This technique is also data sensitive technique and only applicable to one type of data at a time.

Table 3. Comparison of watermarking techniques with existing security techniques

Features	Encryption Technique	Hash Technique	Watermarking Technique
Application	Copyright Protection	Copyright Protection	Copyright Protection and Authentication
Host Data	Text message (Also applicable for Image and audio data but this data is converted into text data)	Text message and Image Data	Mostly Image Data, Video Data or Audio Data
Secure Data	Text Data	-	Watermark Data (Mostly text data, logo or binary image)
Secret Key	Required	Optional	Optional
Input of Technique	Temporary Block of Host Data	Temporary Block of Host Data	Host Data and Watermark Data
Output of Technique	Secure Text Data	Secure Hash Values	Watermarked Data
Extraction Method	Blind	Non-blind	Blind, Semi-blind and Non-blind
Effect on Quality of Data	No	No	Yes (some degradation took place on host data)
Robustness	Yes	Yes	Yes (also designed as semi-fragile and fragile)
Authentication Check	Possible	Possible	Possible
Tamper Identification	No	No	Yes
Data Independent	No	No	Yes

data by watermark embedder based on some embedding key (which is optional in some cases), whereas a watermark extractor is responsible for extraction of watermark from the watermarked data. The output of watermark embedder is watermarked data and output of watermark extractor is extracted watermark.

When any watermarking technique is designed for medical data, it must meet two issues: security (e.g., copyright protection and authentication, security of watermark data, etc.) and system considerations (e.g., memory size, bandwidth requirement, etc.) (Nyeem, Boles, & Boyd, 2013). The watermarking

Figure 2. Basic blocks of watermarking (a) watermark embedder (b) watermark extractor

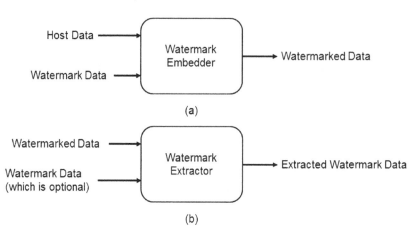

techniques are divided into two types: spatial domain technique and transform domain technique based on the processing domain (Langelaar, Setyawan, & Lagendijk, 2000). The spatial domain watermarking techniques are easy to implement but less robust against various manipulations or attacks ((Langelaar, Setyawan, & Lagendijk, 2000; Thanki & Kothari, 2016). The transform domain watermarking techniques are more robust compared to spatial domain watermarking techniques. The examples of spatial domain watermarking techniques are LSB substitution, spread spectrum method, etc., The transform domain watermarking techniques are based on Fast Fourier Transform (FFT), Discrete Cosine Transform (DCT), Discrete Wavelet Transform (DWT) and advanced transforms such as Singular Value Decomposition (SVD), Fast Digital Curvelet Transform (FDCuT) etc., The advantages, requirements, and applications of watermarking techniques for the security of medical data are given in next subsections.

2.1. Advantages of Digital Watermarking

Due to some advantages of digital watermarking, nowadays digital watermarking has been used for security of medical data (Nyeem, Boles, & Boyd, 2013). Some advantages of digital watermarking are mentioned below:

- **Security and Privacy:** The basic and most important property of digital watermarking is data embedding capability. The digital watermarking can confidentiality embeds the secure data into the host data. For the security of medical data (Electronic Patient Record (EPR), the diagnostic analysis such as treatment procedure etc. can be embedded in the host data to provide security against impostor or invalid manipulations (Chao, Hsu, & Miaou, 2002; Fallahpour, Megias, & Ghanbari, 2009).
- **Indexing:** Some embedding keys or secret indexing values can be embedded into the medical data and are used for authenticity check of extracted image (Das & Kundu, 2012).
- **Non-Repudiation:** Watermarked data is transmitted between hospitals in teleradiology applications. There is a possibility of repudiation of data when doctors or another person in the hospital says that they did not send this data. The secret key based watermarking techniques can solve the non-repudiation problem in multimedia applications (Cheung, Chiu, & Ho, 2008; Zhou, Rockwood, & Sagetong, 2002). So some key or logos can be inserted into medical data for safer and secure transmission of medical data.

2.2. Requirements of Digital Watermarking

The requirements of digital watermarking are mainly associated with watermark embedder and watermark extractor. The watermarking requirement for medical images is mainly security and privacy, fidelity and computational complexity. The typical requirements for watermark embedder include imperceptibility, embedding capacity, invertibility, etc. Similarity, blindness, robustness, and error probability are associated with watermark extractor. The more details on requirements are given below:

- **Imperceptibility:** The imperceptibility determines the similarity between the original host data and its watermarked version. Various metrics like Peak Signal to Noise Ratio (PSNR), Signal to Noise Ratio (SNR) and Weighted PSNR (WPSNR) are used for finding imperceptibility of host data.

- **Embedding Capacity:** The embedding capacity determines how many numbers of bits can be embedded by watermark embedder. The high embedding capacity is an important requirement for designing of watermarking technique. But at the same time, large watermarks may introduce more degradation of watermarked data leading to less imperceptibility. Robust watermarking techniques are normally used for copyright protection and authentication. But have low embedding capacity compared to fragile/semi fragile technique (Fan & Hongbin, 2004; Yu, Cao, Fang, & Li, 2003).

- **Invertibility:** This indicates if the extraction process is the inverse of the embedding process. This type of watermarking technique is referred to as reversible watermarking which can recover original data from distorted watermarked host data. In this technique, original data is required for extraction of watermark data from the watermarked data.

- **Robustness:** This is a very important requirement for a watermarking extractor. Robustness is defined as resistance capacity of a technique against any manipulations or modification of the host data due to various signal processing operations for undetectability of watermark data. This requirement is divided into three types such as robust, semi-fragile and fragile. In a robust watermarking, watermark data can be extracted from corrupted or modified watermarked data. In a semi-fragile and fragile watermarking, the watermark cannot be extracted from corrupted or modified watermarked data.

- **Blindness:** Blindness in watermarking refers to the ability of watermark extractor to extract watermark data without knowledge of original watermark data.

- **Similarity:** It determines the similarity between the original watermark data and its extracted version. Various metrics like Normalized Cross Correlation (NCC) and Structural Similarity Index Measure (SSIM) are used for finding the similarity of watermark data.

- **Error Probability:** This is another important requirement for extraction performance of a watermarking technique. For any application, zero error probability is always ideal but practically it is difficult to achieve higher robustness. Some error probability rates such as Bit Error Rate (BER), False Positive Rate and False Negative Rate, etc., are commonly used for any watermarking technique.

2.3. Applications of Digital Watermarking for Medical Images

The robust watermarking and fragile watermarking can be used for authentication and protection of medical data in teleradiology application (Amar, Trabelsi, Dey, Shi, Satapathy, & Bouhlel, 2017; Acharjee, Ray, Chakraborty, Nath, & Dey, 2014; Nandi, Roy, Dansana, Karaa, Ray, Chowdhury, & Dey, 2017). Some important applications of watermarking techniques for medical images are mentioned below.

- **Copyright Protection and Authentication:** Watermarking is particularly used for copyright protection and authentication of medical images. The important details of medical images can be stored such ways that no manipulation can be done on images. This can be achieved by watermarking the medical data after acquisition.

- **Tamper Identification and Reconstruction:** Medical data such as X-Ray images, CT images, and MRI images can be easily tampered by using image processing operation. Thus, the protection and authentication of these medical data are required in teleradiology application (Fotopoulos, Stavrinou, & Skodras, 2008). A fragile watermarking technique can be used for tamper identification of medical data. Tamper reconstruction of the medical image can be achieved by three levels

(Chiu, Hung, Cheng, & Kafeza, 2007): tamper identification, tamper localization and possible reconstruction of approximate tamper region.

After discussion on advantages, requirements, and applications of digital watermarking, the observation suggests that the watermarking technique designed for medical data should satisfy some requirements: (a) the technique should be invisible, robust and blind; (b) watermark data should have minimum information which can provide authentication; (c) embedding process should be done such that less degradation takes place on medical data.

3. BRIEF LITERATURE OF WATERMARKING TECHNIQUES FOR MEDICAL DATA

Many researchers designed efficient watermarking techniques in various domains in last decade. These techniques are designed in spatial, transform and hybrid domain. The research on watermarking techniques shows that spatial domain techniques have limitations: less robust and less imperceptibility. The transform domain techniques have more imperceptibility compared to spatial domain techniques but have less embedding capacity. Hybrid watermarking techniques proved better imperceptibility compared to spatial and transform domain techniques with high robustness against attacks. The various hybrid watermarking techniques which are related to proposed techniques are given below.

Singh (Singh, Singh, Singh, & Siddiqui, 2018) and his research team designed Non-subsampled Contourlet Transform (NSCT), Singular Value Decomposition (SVD) and Discrete Cosine Transform (DCT) based non-blind hybrid watermarking technique for the security of medical data. In this technique, the watermark information is inserted into the mid band hybrid frequency coefficients of the medical images to generate watermarked medical image. Chakraborty (2017) and his research team given comparative analysis of SVD based watermarking technique for security of medical data. Rohit (2017) and his research team designed Fast Discrete Curvelet transform (FDCuT) and Discrete Cosine Transform (DCT) based blind hybrid watermarking technique for the security of medical data. In this technique, watermark information is inserted into the high frequency hybrid coefficients of medical images to generate watermarked medical image. Parah (2017) and his research team given DCT based watermarking technique with chaotic encryption for security of medical data.

Roy (Roy & Pal, 2017) and his designed Redundant Discrete Wavelet Transform (RDWT) and DCT based blind hybrid watermarking technique. In this technique, mid band DCT coefficients of LH wavelet subband of the image are modified by PN sequences according to watermark bit. The Arnold scrambling is applied on watermark to generate secure watermark before embedding it into host medical image. Thakkar (Thakkar and Srivastava, 2017) and his research team have designed blind hybrid watermarking technique based on DWT and SVD for medical data. In this technique, first ROI of the medical image is defined and then the singular value of wavelet subbands of ROI of the medical image is extracted. The logo and EPR data are embedded into these singular values to get modified ROI of the medical image. The fusion is applied on modified image with unmodified RONI of the medical image to generate watermarked medical image. The limitation of this technique is that it is only applicable on ROI of the medical image.

Nagpal (2016) and his research team have designed hybrid technique using DWT, Artificial Neural Network (ANN) and encryption for medical data. In this technique, Riverst Shamir Adleman (RSA) type encryption is applied on watermark data to improve security, which can be further be inserted into wavelet coefficients of medical data using ANN approach. Kishore (2016) and his research team have given a review and comparison of three various hybridwatermarking approaches for medical data. Their comparison shows that the DWT-SVD based medical image watermarking technique is performed better than other two reviewed techniques.

Mahmood (Mahmood, 2015) designed non-reversible hybrid technique for medical data. In this technique, Region of Background (ROB) of host medical image is found using segmentation map approach after diving into blocks. Then entropy is found for each block and DCT is applied on low entropy valued blocks which are chosen for embedding. The watermark data is embedded into DCT coefficients using various approaches like LSB or difference expansion approach. Singh (Singh, 2015) have proposed various hybrid watermarking techniques for protection of medical data. In these techniques, the author used different encoding methods like Hamming code, Bose-Chaudhuri-Hocquenghem (BCH) code and Reed -Solomon code for thesecurity of EPR and watermark logo. Then this secure watermark information is embedded into various subbands of host medical image using various approaches to generate a secure medical image.

Venkartam (2014) designed hybrid watermarking technique using Lifting Wavelet Transform (LWT) and SVD for medical data protection. Here, the singular values of all wavelet subbands is modified according to bits of the watermark to get watermarked medical image. The limitation of this technique is that it does not use any security approach for amedical image. Pal (2013) have designed a hybrid watermarking technique for color medical image protection using approaches like even-odd shifting and difference approach. In this technique, watermark data is inserted into R channel of medical image using even-odd shifting approach, while watermark data is inserted into B channel is modified using a different approach.

Dey (2012a, 2012b) designed a hybrid watermarking technique using DCT, DWT, and SVD for the protection of ECG signal and Ultrasound video. This technique has not used any security mechanism for encrypting the medical data. Rathi (Rathi & Inamdar, 2012) designed hybrid watermarking technique using Region of Non-Interest (RONI) and LWT for medical data protection. In this technique, LWT is applied on RONI of the medical image to get wavelet coefficients. Then watermarked medical image with multiple watermarks is generated by modifying wavelet coefficients according to watermark data and a secret key. Mostafa (2010) designed hybrid watermarking technique using DCT and cryptography. In this technique, EPR data is encrypted using BCH code. Then two wavelet subbands of host medical image are divided into blocks where they are modified by watermark bits.

After reviewing papers on hybrid watermarking techniques for the security of medical data, it is observed that most of the existing watermarking techniques have less imperceptibility, nonblind approach and uses the correlation of PN sequences for blind extraction of the watermark. Also, the robustness test of many existing schemes is missing against various watermarking attacks. In this chapter, a technique is proposed to overcome the limitations of two recently existing technique like Roy (Roy & Pal, 2017) technique and Thakkar (Thakkar & Sirvastava, 2017) technique. The Roy technique used RDWT, DCT, two PN sequences and used correlation property of PN sequences for extraction of watermark data. These two techniques are less robust and imperceptible for different types of medical images. Thakkar scheme has a limitation that it is only applicable on Region of Interest (ROI) of the medical image. Thus, there is a requirement for the design of new hybrid watermarking techniques which overcomes the above mentioned issues in medical data protection.

In this chapter, a blind watermarking technique is proposed for securing medical data like Computerized Tomography (CT) image, Magnetic Resonance Imaging (MRI) image, Ultrasound (US) image, X-Ray image and ECG signal. The technique is extended version of the technique proposed by Rohit (2017) and his research team. In that technique, the Redundant Discrete Wavelet transform is added to achieve high imperceptibility to watermarked medical image, better robustness and also applied on ECG signal protection. The technique is designed using Fast Discrete Curvelet Transform (FDCuT), Redundant Discrete Wavelet Transform (RDWT), Discrete Cosine Transform (DCT) and White Gaussian Noise (WGN) sequences. For the teleradiology applications, a different copyright information in terms of binary logo and binary symbol is inserted into the medical data. To implement this technique, first FDCuT is applied on the host medical data. Then RDWT is applied on the high frequency curvelet coefficients to get different wavelet subbands like LL, LH, HL, and HH. The DCT is applied on the blocks of LL subbands of high frequency (HF) curvelet subband with the size of 8×8. The watermark bits are inserted into the mid band DCT coefficients of each DCT block of host medical data. Extraction of watermark bits can be performed using the correlation of WGN sequences. The next section gives complete implementation details and results of proposed techniques.

4. PROPOSED WATERMARKING TECHNIQUE FOR MEDICAL DATA

In this chapter, a blind medical watermarking technique based on FDCuT-RDWT-DCT is proposed, to be more imperceptible and more robust against various attacks. The basic mathematics of FDCuT, DCT and White Gaussian Noise (WGN) sequences are presented by Rohit (2017). The basic mathematics of RDWT is given by Roy (Roy & Pal, 2017).

In this technique, FDCuT is applied on host medical data to get various frequency bands such as Low Frequency (LF), Mid Frequency (MF) and High Frequency (HF). The reason behind choosing FDCuT in proposed technique is that it presents data in term of edges and provides better imperceptibility compared to another transforms. For FDCuT decomposition of medical data, 7 scale parameter and 16 orientation parameter are used. Then RDWT is applied on HF subbands of curvelet to get wavelet subbands like LL, LH, HL, and HH. The reason behind choosing RDWT in proposed technique is that it provides shift invariance for better extraction of watermark data at extraction side. It eliminates downsampling and upsampling process of DWT. It provides more robust process compared to DWT. A block-wise DCT is applied on LL subband of HF curvelet transform of the host medical data. Then two WGN sequences are inserted into mid band frequency DCT coefficients based on the watermark bits to generate watermarked medical data. The blind extraction of watermark data is done in proposed technique using the correlation between WGN sequences and watermarked data. The steps for watermark embedding and watermark extraction are given in the following subsections 4.1 and 4.2. The results of proposed watermarking technique are given in subsection 4.3. The application of proposed watermarking technique for ECG signal protection is given in subsection 4.4. The comparison of proposed watermarking technique with existing watermarking techniques is given in subsection 4.5.

4.1 Proposed Watermark Embedding

In this technique, a watermark data is embedded into FDCuT-RDWT-DCT of host medical data using WGN sequences. The block diagram of a proposed embedding process is given in Figure 3. The steps for watermark embedding process are given below.

Step 1: The watermark data is represented in term watermark vector.
Step 2: Calculate the size of the host medical data and apply frequency wrapping based FDCuT to get LF, MF and HF subband of host medical data.
Step 3: Apply RDWT on HF curvelet subband to get wavelet subbands like LL, LH, HL, and HH. Convert LL wavelet subband into non-overlapped blocks.
Step 4: Apply block-wise DCT on non-overlapped blocks to get different frequency coefficients. Chose Mid Band Frequency (MBF) for watermark bit embedding.
Step 5: Generate two high uncorrelated White Gaussian Noise (WGN) sequences using noise generator, each of size equal to the size of MBF.
Step 6: Embed each watermark bit in MBF DCT coefficients of the block based on following conditions.

- If watermark bit is zero then:

$$Modified\_DCTCoefficients = DCTCoefficients + k * WGN\_Sequence\_0 \qquad (1)$$

where, Modified_DCTCoefficients corresponds to the modified MBF DCT coefficients of the block, DCTCoefficients is original MBF DCT coefficients of the block, k is the gain factor, and *WGN_Sequence_0* is WGN sequence for watermark bit 0.

- If watermark bit is one then:

$$Modified\_DCTCoefficients = DCTCoefficients + k * WGN\_Sequence\_1 \qquad (2)$$

where, Modified_DCT Coefficients corresponds to the modified MBF DCT coefficients of the block, DCT Coefficients is original MBF DCT coefficients of the block, k is the gain factor, and *WGN_Sequence_1* is WGN sequence for watermark bit 1.

- This process is repeated for all the MBF DCT coefficients of each block of host medical image.

Step 7: Apply inverse block-wise DCT on modified MBF coefficients keeping with other DCT coefficients as it is so as to get modified LL wavelet subband of host medical data.
Step 8: Apply inverse RDWT on modified wavelet subband with other wavelet coefficients as to get modified HF curvelet subband of host medical data.
Step 9: Apply Inverse frequency wrapping based FDCuT on modified HF curvelet subband to get watermarked medical data.

Figure 3. Block diagram of proposed watermark embedding

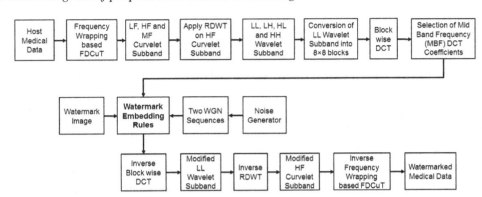

4.2 Proposed Watermark Extraction

In this scheme, a watermark bit is extracted blindly using the correlation between watermarked medical data and two WGN sequences. The block diagram of the proposed extraction process is given in Figure 4. The steps for watermark extraction are given below.

Step 1: Take the watermarked medical data. Apply frequency wrapping based FDCuT to get LF, MF and HF subband of watermarked medical image.

Step 2: Apply RDWT on HF curvelet subband to get wavelet subbands like LL, LH, HL, and HH. Convert LL wavelet subband into non-overlapped blocks.

Step 3: Apply block-wise DCT on non-overlapped blocks to get different frequency coefficients. Choose Mid Band Frequency (MBF) coefficients for watermark bit extraction.

Step 4: Take the two highly uncorrelated White Gaussian Noise (WGN) sequences which are generated during Watermark embedding process.

Step 5: Extract the watermark bit from MBF DCT coefficients based on the following procedure.

$$Correlation\_Sequence\_0 = corr2(MBF\_DCTCoefficients, WGN\_Sequence\_0) \tag{3}$$

$$Correlation\_Sequence\_1 = corr2(MBF\_DCTCoefficients, WGN\_Sequence\_1) \tag{4}$$

Figure 4. Block diagram of proposed watermark extraction

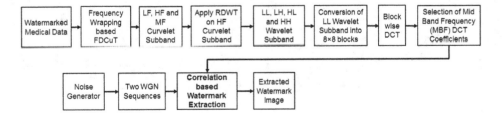

Step 6: If *Correlation_Sequence_1>Correlation_Sequence_0* then watermark bit is set as bit 1. Otherwise, a watermark bit is set as bit 0.

Step 7: Apply reshape on bits vector to get extracted watermark data.

4.3 Results of Proposed Watermarking Technique

The performance of any watermarking technique varies with different types of medical data. The proposed technique is tested and analyzed using various medical images such as X-Ray, US, MRI, and CT. The size of these images is 1024×1024 pixels with 8 bit gray scale. The test host medical image is taken from the MedPix™ medical image Database and is shown in Figure 5. A set of two watermark monochrome images are chosen as logos: one with smooth details and another with sharp details are used for implementation and testing of proposed technique. The size of watermark logos is 128×128 pixels with 8 bit monochrome images (shown in Figure 6). The implementation of the proposed technique is done on the laptop 2 GHz core two Duo processor with 2 GB RAM using MATLAB 2013a software.

In the proposed technique, a medical image with a size of 1024×1024 pixels is taken as host image and FDCuT is applied to it to get its curvelet coefficients. Then db1 RDWT is applied to HF curvelet coefficients to get its wavelet subbands: LL, LH, HL, and HH. The LL wavelet coefficients with size 1024×1024 are chosen for watermark logo embedding. Then LL wavelet coefficients are converted into 16384 non-overlapping blocks with 8×8. The MBF DCT coefficients of each block are obtained by application of block-wise DCT on it. The watermark logo is converted into a vector of size 16384. Then according to each bit value of watermark bit, MBF DCT coefficients of each block of host medical image are modified by two WGN sequences. The modified 16384 blocks of the medical image are obtained after watermark embedding process. The inverse block-wise DCT is applied to modify DCT to get modified LL wavelet subbands coefficients with the size of 1024×1024. Then inverse RDWT is applied to modified LL subbands with unmodified wavelet subbands to get modified HF curvelet subband of the medical image. Then inverse FDCuT is applied to modified HF curvelet subband with unmodified curvelet subband to get watermarked medical image. Hence, one watermark bit is inserted into each block of the host medical image.

A Peak Signal to Noise Ratio (PSNR) is used to measure imperceptibility between original host medical image and watermarked medical image. The equation for PSNR calculation is given by Kutter (Kutter & Petitcolas, 1999). The robustness of proposed technique can be measured by normalized cross correlation (NCC). The equation for NCC calculation is also given by Kutter (Kutter and Petitcolas,

Figure 5. Test host medical images (a) x-ray (b) US (c) MRI (d) CT

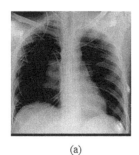 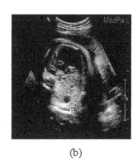 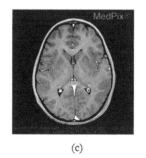 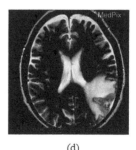

(a) (b) (c) (d)

Figure 6. Test watermark logos

(a) Watermark 1 (WM1)   (b) Watermark 2 (WM2)

1999). The robustness of any watermarking technique is high if NCC value is close to one. These two measures, imperceptibility test and robustness test of proposed techniques are performed and analyzed for various medical images.

4.3.1 Imperceptibility Test

An imperceptibility test of proposed technique is analyzed by various types of medical images. This test is performed to analyze how medical image is degraded after insertion of watermark data into it. Higher imperceptibility is achieved if the watermarked medical image appears close to the original medical image. For analysis of imperceptibility test, PSNR is calculated between watermarked medical image and original medical image, and NCC is calculated between original watermark logo and its extracted version. The PSNR and NCC values of proposed technique are compared with two existing techniques: Roy technique (2017) and Thakkar technique (2017). Figure 7 shows quantitative results of proposed technique when tested on different medical images and watermark logos. Results include watermarked medical images and extracted watermark images. The proposed watermark embedding process is performed by a constant gain factor k with value 3.

In the proposed technique, the performance depends on the WGN sequences and gain factor. In this technique, the gain factor value is variable while the value of WGN sequences is fixed. So the gain factor affects the quality of watermarked medical images. Here, the range of gain factor k varies from 3 to 15, as per HVS property of watermarking requirements. The results in Figure 7 show the extracted watermark logo with some noise without the effect of any attacks. This happens because WGN sequences are used in proposed technique and these sequences have an influence on watermarked medical images. At watermark extraction, the correlation between these sequences and watermarked medical image is performed. The resultant correlation values are less for small gain factors which cause low quality extracted watermark images. As the value of gain factor increases, the correlation values also increases. Figure 7 shows the extracted watermark logo using different gain factor (k) values. The corresponding PSNR and NC values are tabulated in Table 4. The results show that when the gain factor is high, the quality of extracted watermark images is also high.

The corresponding PSNR values and NC values of proposed technique are compared with Roy technique (Roy & Pal, 2017) and Thakkar technique (Thakkar & Srivastava, 2017) and are tabulated in Table 5. The comparison of techniques is performed using US and CT medical images, watermark logo as watermark 2 and gain factor k as 3, and without application of any attacks. The average value of PSNR of watermarked medical images of proposed technique is around 55.28 dB, while the average

Figure 7. Watermarked medical images and extracted watermark logos using proposed technique with gain factor k = 3

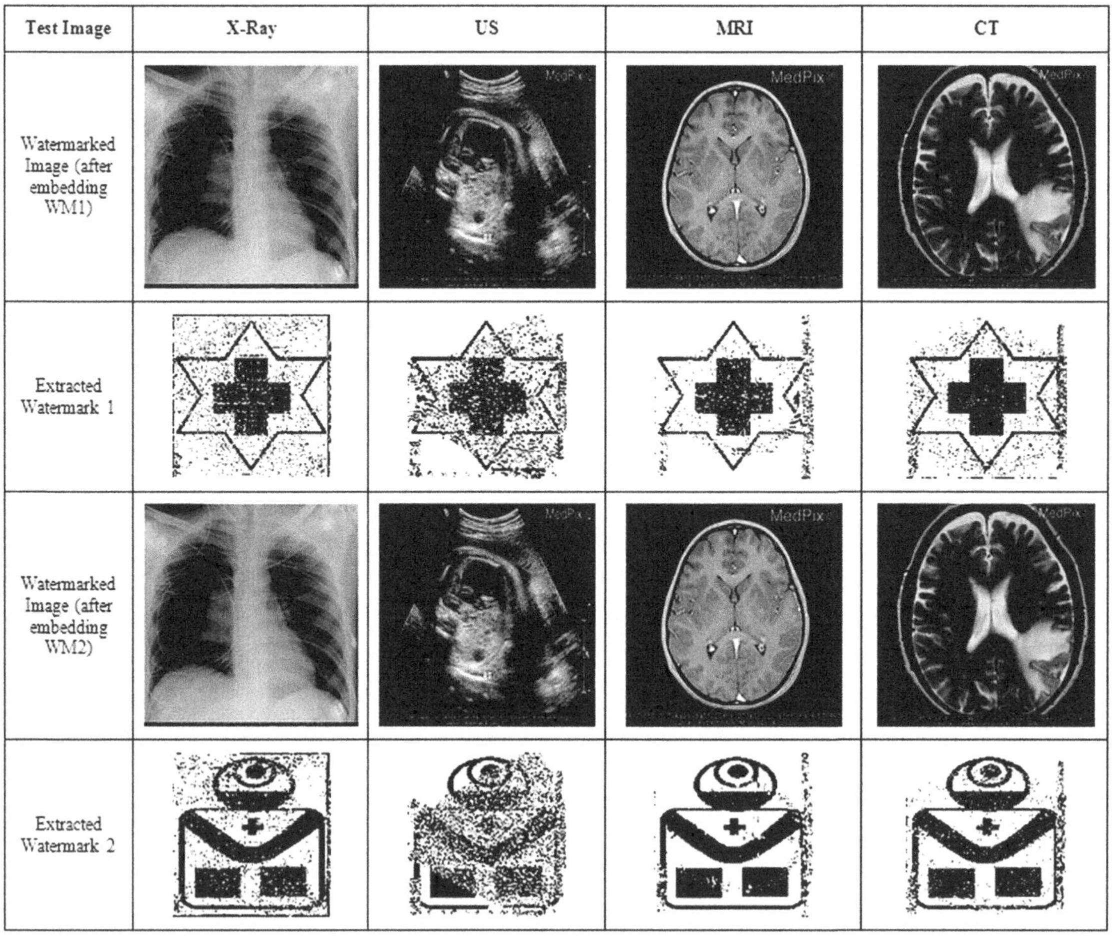

value of PSNR of Roy technique is around 52 dB, and that of Thakkar technique is around 26.87 dB. Thus, it indicates that the watermarking medical image is not much affected by embedding watermark logo bits. The proposed technique provides better imperceptibility compared to the other two techniques.

Note that the average value of NCC of extracted watermark logos of proposed technique is around 0.8715, while the average value of NCC of extracted watermark logos of Roy technique is around 0.7802 and Thakkar technique is around 0.8358. Thus, it indicates that the extraction of watermark logos in the proposed technique is better than the recent existing techniques: Roy technique (2017) and Thakkar technique (2017).

4.3.2 Robustness Test

For robustness test of proposed technique, various image processing attacks such as JPEG compression, filtering such as median, mean, Gaussian low pass filter, blurring, sharpening, different noise additions such as Gaussian noise, salt and pepper noise, speckle noise, and geometric attacks such as rotation,

Figure 8. Extracted watermark logos using various different gain factors

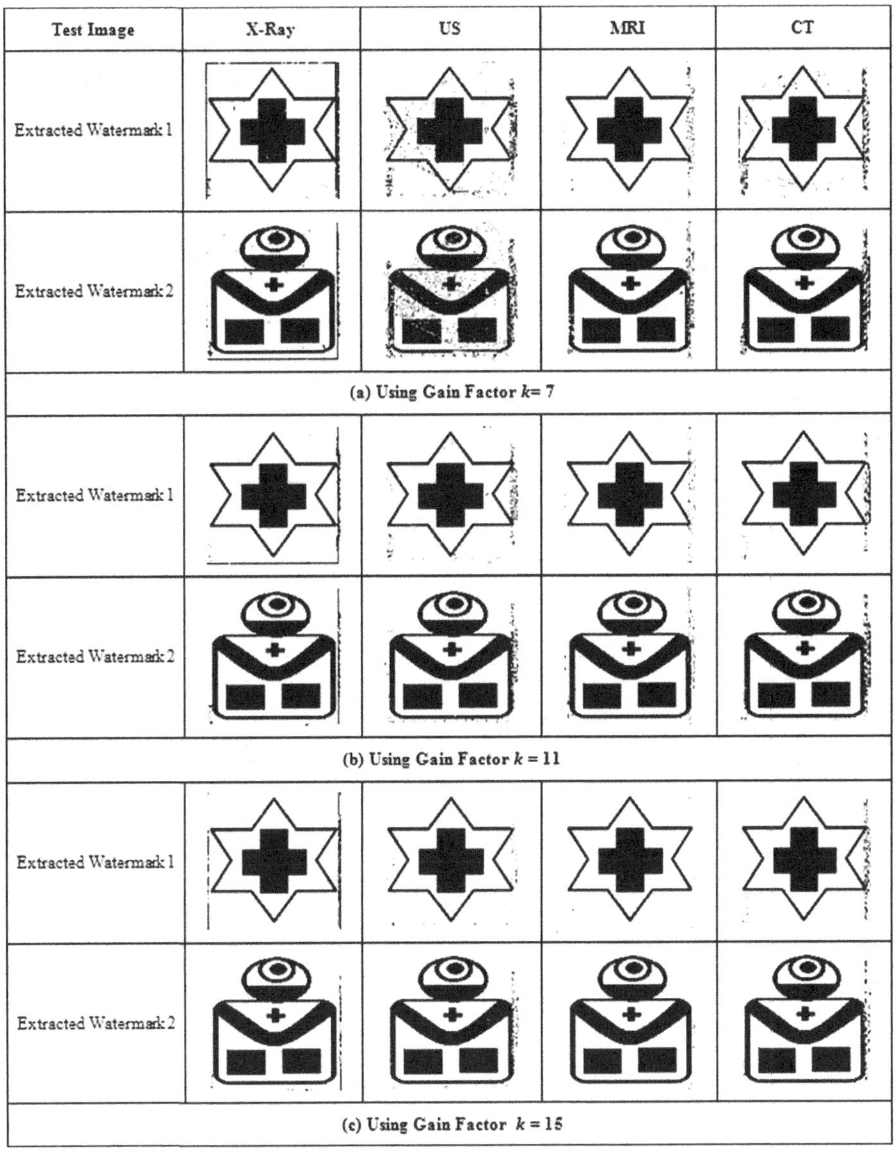

cropping and flipping are applied on watermarked medical images. At extraction side, if the extraction of watermark image is possible from corrupted watermarked medical image, then the technique is robust and secure. The robustness of proposed technique against various image processing attacks is measured by NCC. In addition, NCC value of proposed technique is compared with NC value of Roy Technique (2017) and Thakkar Technique (2017) for the same set of medical images. The NC values obtained for various image processing attacks for watermarked CT medical image (which is watermarked by WM2 image) are given below.

A Hybrid Watermarking Technique for Copyright Protection of Medical Signals in Teleradiology

Table 4. Values of PSNR (dB) and NCC for proposed technique using various gain factor k values

Test Image	PSNR (dB)		NCC	
	Watermark 1	Watermark 2	Watermark 1	Watermark 2
(a) For Gain Factor $k = 3$				
X-Ray	58.72	57.89	0.8710	0.8409
US	55.52	57.30	0.8232	0.7996
MRI	53.30	52.40	0.9423	0.9636
CT	54.72	53.25	0.8932	0.9434
(b) For Gain Factor $k = 7$				
X-Ray	46.44	47.05	0.9462	0.9617
US	43.79	46.29	0.9582	0.9432
MRI	41.51	42.43	0.9902	0.9839
CT	48.36	42.11	0.9633	0.9665
(c) For Gain Factor $k = 11$				
X-Ray	41.41	39.15	0.9703	0.9807
US	36.99	36.79	0.9839	0.9838
MRI	35.17	36.80	0.9945	0.9912
CT	32.97	34.92	0.9841	0.9759
(d) For Gain Factor $k = 15$				
X-Ray	33.28	34.27	0.9737	0.9886
US	28.82	29.46	0.9969	0.9917
MRI	29.43	27.06	0.9996	0.9991
CT	28.21	29.64	0.9850	0.9893

Table 5. Comparison of PSNR (dB) and NCC of proposed technique with Roy technique (2017) and Thakkar technique (2017) without application of watermarking attacks

Test Image	Thakkar Technique (2017)		Roy Technique (2017)		Proposed Technique	
	PSNR (dB)	NCC	PSNR (dB)	NCC	PSNR (dB)	NCC
US	26.20	0.7823	54.19	0.7418	57.30	0.7996
CT	27.54	0.8892	49.81	0.8185	53.25	0.9434

4.3.2.1. JPEG Compression Attack

The JPEG compression compresses any image without much affecting the visual information of the image. The JPEG compression with different quality factors are applied on watermarked CT medical images and then theWM2 image is extracted using proposed technique. Figure 9 shows the extracted watermark logos with the NCC values for the compression attack of a watermarked CT medical image. The results show that proposed technique performed better than Roy Technique (2017) and Thakkar Technique (2017) under this attack.

4.3.2.2. Noise Addition Attack

The different noises such as Gaussian noise, salt & pepper noise, and speckle noise are applied on the watermarked CT medical image and then the watermark WM2 is extracted using proposed technique.

Figure 10 shows the extracted watermark logos with the NCC values for the noise addition attacks after applying on a watermarked CT medical image. The results show that proposed technique performed better than Roy Technique (2017) and Thakkar Technique (2017) under this attack.

4.3.2.3. Filtering Attack

Different image processing filters such as median filter, mean filter and Gaussian low pass filter are applied on the watermarked CT medical image and then the watermark WM2 is extracted using proposed technique. The size of filter mask is 3×3. Figure 11 shows the extracted watermark logo with the NCC values after application of filtering attacks on a watermarked CT medical image. The results show that the proposed technique performed better than Roy Technique (2017) and Thakkar Technique (2017) under this attack.

4.3.2.4. Blurring Attack, Sharpening Attack, and Histogram Equalization Attack

The advanced image processing operation like blurring, sharpening, and histogram equalization are also applied on the watermarked CT medical image. Figure 12 shows the extracted watermark logos with the NCC values for the corresponding attacks. The results show that proposed technique performed better than Roy Technique (2017) and Thakkar Technique (2017) under these attacks.

Figure 9. Extracted watermark logos and NCC value of proposed technique, Roy technique (2017) and Thakkar technique (2017) under JPEG compression attack

JPEG Compression Attack	Roy Technique (2016)	Thakkar Technique (2016)	Proposed Technique
Q = 90	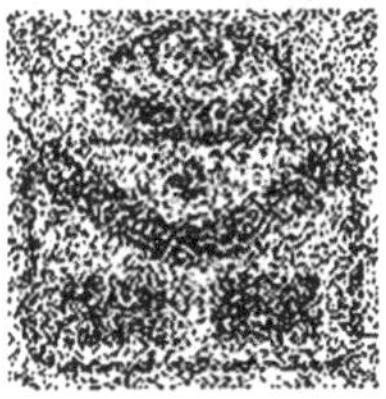 NCC = 0.6920	 NCC = 0.8817	 NCC = 0.9302
Q = 70	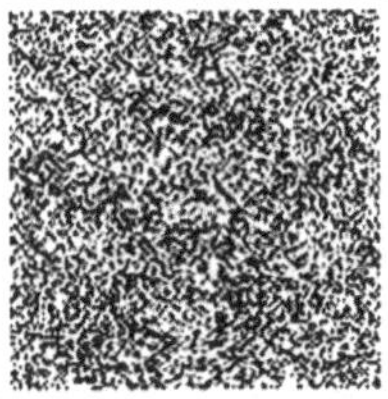 NCC = 0.5936	 NCC = 0.8655	 NCC = 0.7705

Figure 10. Extracted watermark logos and NCC value of proposed technique, Roy technique (2017) and Thakkar technique (2017) under JPEG compression attack

Noise Addition Attack	Roy Technique (2016)	Thakkar Technique (2016)	Proposed Technique
Gaussian Noise (Mean = 0, Variance = 0.001)	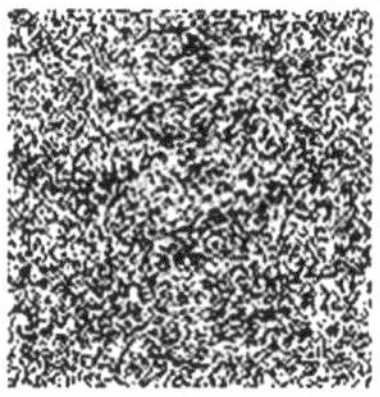 NCC = 0.5706	 NCC = 0.7611	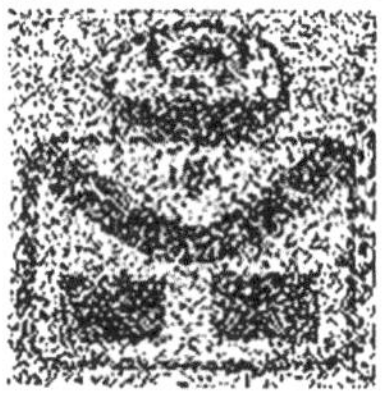 NCC = 0.7124
Salt & Pepper Noise (Variance = 0.005)	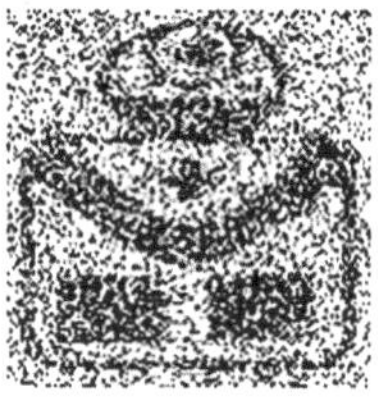 NCC = 0.7328	 NCC = 0.8225	 NCC = 0.8667
Speckle Noise (Variance = 0.004)	 NCC = 0.6506	 NCC = 0.8581	 NCC = 0.8746

4.3.2.5. Geometric Attack

Different Geometric Attack: Flipping and cropping are applied on the watermarked CT medical image. Figure 13 shows the extracted watermark logos with the NCC values for this attack after applying on a watermarked CT medical image. The results show that proposed technique performed better than Roy Technique (2017) and Thakkar Technique (2017) under this attack.

4.3.3 False Positive Rate Test

The results of this test are used for evaluation of security requirements of the proposed watermarking technique. This rate gives how many watermark logos are extracted from an unauthorized host image, which doesn't actually belong to the right owner. The false positive results for 5 non-watermarked images are shown in Figure 14. This rate is said to occur if an extracted watermark logo shows visual information of owner's watermark logo. For false positive test, the proposed technique is tested on a large data set by assuming that a visual trace may appear if the NCC value of extracted logo is high (exceeds 0.55); a false positive rate of zero is obtained for the proposed technique, when tested on 100 test medical images which are taken from the MedPix™ medical image database. According to I. J. Cox (2000): *A false positive rate of 10^{-6} can meet the security requirements* and hence our proposed technique can meet the security requirements of watermarking.

Figure 11. Extracted watermark logos and NCC value of proposed technique, Roy technique (2017) and Thakkar technique (2017) under filtering attack

Filtering Attack	Roy Technique (2016)	Thakkar Technique (2016)	Proposed Technique
Mean Filter (3×3)	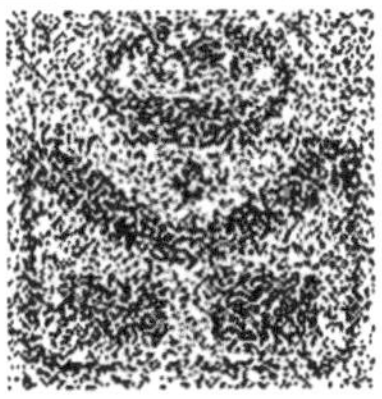 NCC = 0.7102	 NCC = 0.8110	 NCC = 0.8889
Median Filter (3×3)	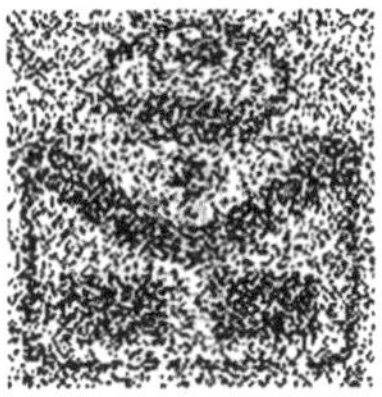 NCC = 0.7042	 NCC = 0.8262	 NCC = 0.9072
Gaussian Low Pass Filter (3×3)	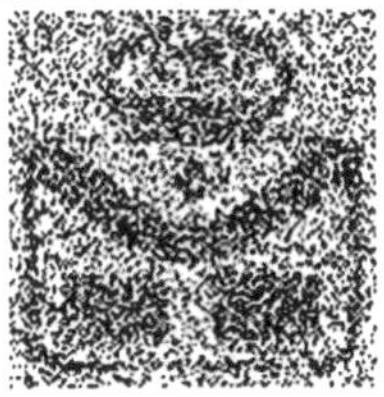 NCC = 0.7102	 NCC = 0.8110	 NCC = 0.8325

4.4 Application of Proposed Watermarking Technique for ECG Signal Protection

This proposed watermarking technique is also applicable for the security of medical signal. For testing of proposed watermarking technique for medical signal, ECG signal with 25600 samples is taken as host medical data and watermark logos with the size of 20×20 pixels are taken. The ECG signal is taken from the Physionet ECG Database (Physionet, 1995 – 2017). When this proposed technique is applied to themedical signal, the signal is converted into a 2D matrix. This step is performed because of proper operation of watermark embedding and watermark extraction. Figure 15 shows the sample ECG signal and watermark logo. Figure 16 and 17 shows the watermarked ECG signal and extracted watermark logos, respectively. The results for ECG signal are generated using gain factor $k = 30$. A Signal to Noise Ratio (SNR) is used to measure imperceptibility between original ECG signal and watermarked ECG signal. The equation for SNR calculation is given by Kutter (Kutter & Petitcolas, 1999). Table 6 shows the value of SNR and NCC of proposed watermarking technique for ECG signal. The results show that this proposed watermarking technique is equally performed for the security of ECG signal (Figure 18).

Figure 12. Extracted watermark logos and NCC value of proposed technique, Roy technique (2017) and Thakkar technique (2017) under blurring attack, sharpening attack and histogram equalization attack

Different Attacks	Roy Technique (2016)	Thakkar Technique (2016)	Proposed Technique
Blurring	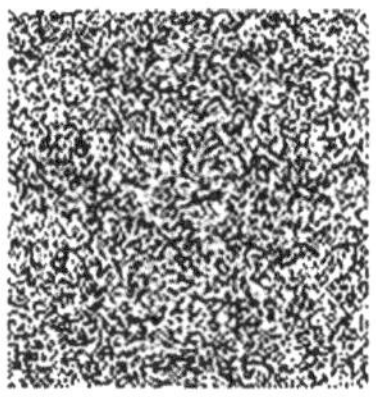 NCC = 0.5550	 NCC = 0.0923	 NCC = 0.8281
Sharpening	 NCC = 0.8185	 NCC = 0.8823	 NCC = 0.9420
Histogram Equalization	 NCC = 0.7791	 NCC = 0.8705	 NCC = 0.9110

Figure 13. Extracted watermark logos and NCC value of proposed technique, Roy technique (2017) and Thakkar technique (2017) under geometric attack

Geometric Attack	Roy Technique (2016)	Thakkar Technique (2016)	Proposed Technique
Flipping	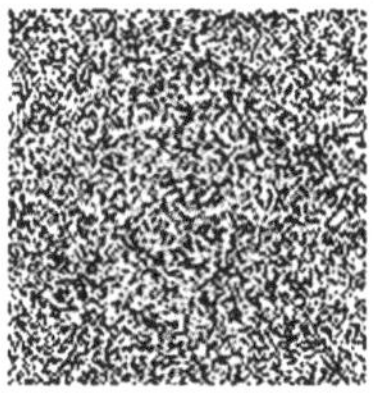 NCC = 0.5494	 NCC = 0.0503	 NCC = 0.7533
Cropping	 NCC = 0.8192	 NCC = 0.8528	 NCC = 0.8945

Figure 14. False positive test results of proposed watermarking technique

Sl. No	Non-watermarked Image	Extracted watermark logo 1 using the proposed technique	NCC1	Extracted watermark logo 2 using the proposed technique	NCC2
1	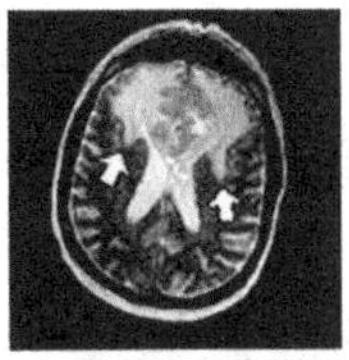	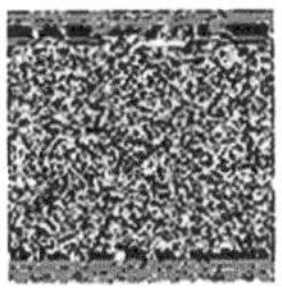	0.4772	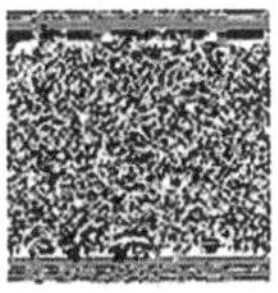	0.4954
2	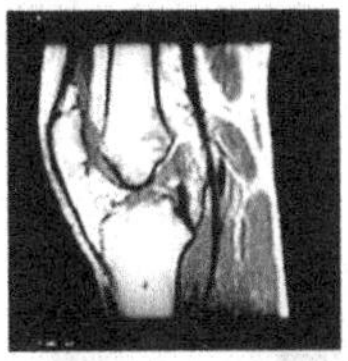		0.4952		0.5001
3	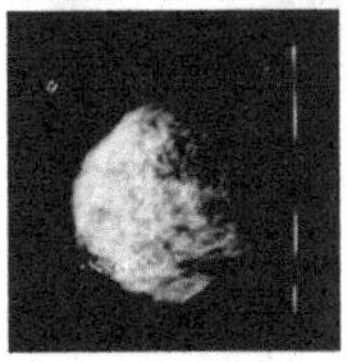		0.4987	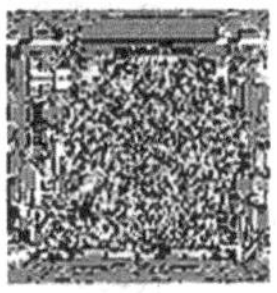	0.5019
4	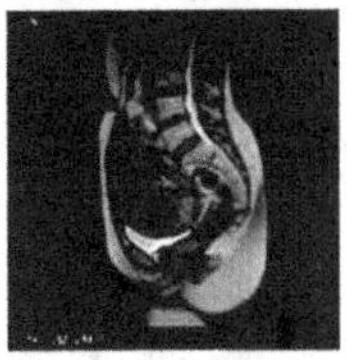		0.4949	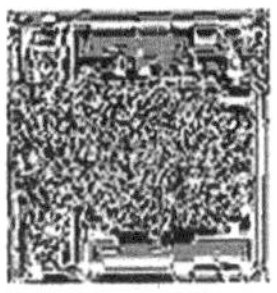	0.5138
5	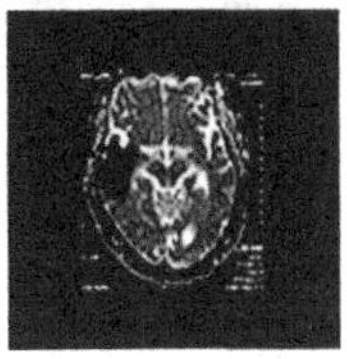	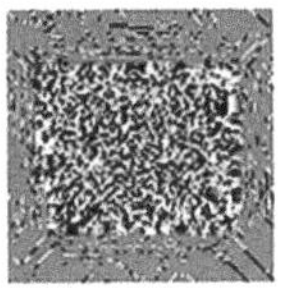	0.5070	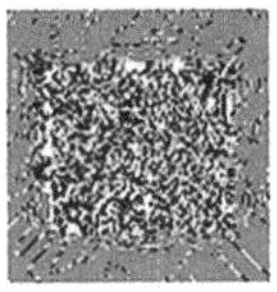	0.5052

4.5 Comparison of Proposed Watermarking Technique With Existing Watermarking Techniques

In Table 7, the performance of proposed technique is compared with two recently developed watermarking techniques for the security of medical image. The proposed technique performs well compared to two recently existing watermarking techniques: Roy technique (2017) and Thakkar technique (2017) against all types of image processing attacks except for JPEG compression attack with Q = 70 and Gaussian noise attack with $\mu = 0$, $\sigma = 0.001$. The comparison of the techniques is performed by same medical images which are used in proposed technique.

Figure 15. Test ECG signal and watermark logos; (a) Original ECG signal; (b) watermark logo 1 (WL1); (c) watermark logo 2 (WL2)

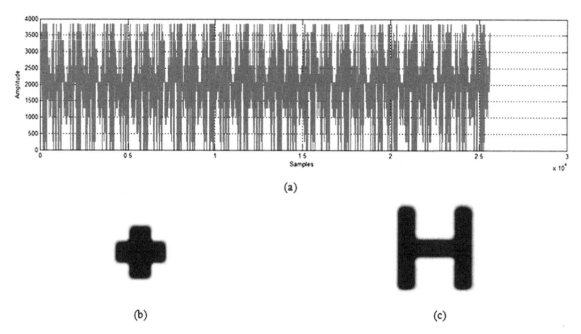

Figure 16. Watermarked ECG signal; (a) watermarked ECG signal (after embedding WL1); (b) watermarked ECG signal (after embedding WL2)

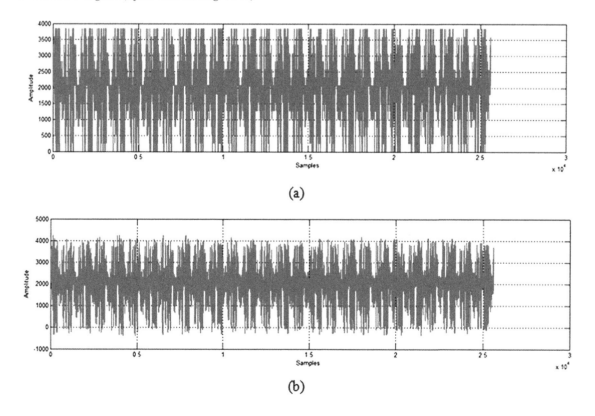

342

Figure 17. Extracted watermarked logos; (a) extracted watermark logo 1; (b) extracted watermark logo 2

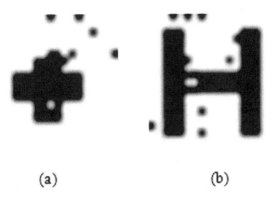

(a)   (b)

Figure 18. Section of ECG signal; (a) original ECG signal; (b) watermarked ECG signal

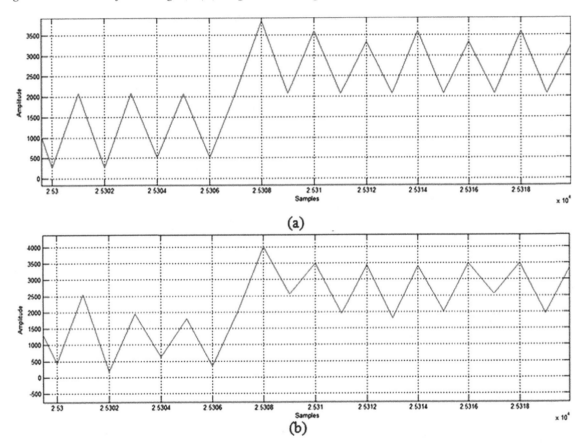

The proposed technique is also compared with Roy Technique (2017), Thakkar Technique (2017), and Singh Technique (2018) by various features in Table 8. While the watermarking in the proposed technique is performed in the FDCuT+RDWT+DCT domain, the watermarking in the Roy technique (2017) is in RDWT+DCT domain, Thakkar technique (2017) in the DWT+SVD domain, and Singh Technique (2018) in the NSCT+DCT+SVD domain. The maximum PSNR value in the Roy technique (2017) is

Table 6. Values of SNR (dB) and NCC for proposed technique for ECG Signal

Quality Measure	Watermark 1	Watermark 2
SNR (dB)	20.96	21.55
NCC	0.9821	0.9685

Table 7. Performance comparison of proposed technique with Roy technique (2017), Thakkar technique (2017) for CT medical image under various watermarking attacks

Attacks	NCC for Watermark Logo		
	Roy Technique (2017)	Thakkar Technique (2017)	Proposed Technique
JPEG Compression (Q=90)	0.6920	0.8817	0.9302
JPEG Compression (Q=70)	0.5936	0.8655	0.7705
Gaussian Noise ($\mu = 0$, $\sigma = 0.001$)	0.5706	0.7611	0.7124
Salt & Pepper Noise (($\mu = 0.005$)	0.7328	0.8225	0.8667
Speckle Noise (($\mu = 0.004$)	0.6506	0.8581	0.8746
Mean (2×2)	0.7102	0.8110	0.8889
Median (2×2)	0.7042	0.8262	0.9072
Gaussian LPF(2×2)	0.7102	0.8110	0.8325
Blurring	0.5550	0.0923	0.8281
Sharpening	0.8185	0.8823	0.9420
Histogram Equalization	0.7791	0.8705	0.9110
Flipping	0.5494	0.0503	0.7533
Cropping	0.8192	0.8528	0.8945

56.03 dB, in the Thakkar technique (2017) it is 28.54 dB, in the Singh technique (2018) it is 36.8402 dB, and in the proposed scheme it is 58.86 dB. The maximum NCC value in Roy technique (2017) is 0.8516, in the Thakkar technique (2017) it is 0.9836, in the Singh technique (2018) it is 0.9990, and in the proposed technique it is 0.9636. The average results indicate that the performance of the proposed technique is better in terms of imperceptibility and security.

5. CONCLUSION

The security of medical data in teleradiology application became necessary nowadays. In this chapter, the role of the watermarking technique in providing the security of medical data in teleradiology application is discussed: advantages, requirements, and applications of watermarking for medical data protection along with a review of existing watermarking techniques and their limitations for the security of medical data for teleradiology. A novel blind and hybrid watermarking technique for medical data using Fast Discrete Curvelet Transform (FDCuT), Redundant Discrete Wavelet Transform (RDWT), Discrete Cosine Transform (DCT) and two WGN sequences is also presented in this chapter. For blind

Table 8. Comparison of proposed technique with Roy technique (2017), Thakkar technique (2017) and Singh technique (2018) with various features

Features	Roy Technique (2017)	Thakkar Technique (2017)	Singh Technique (2018)	Proposed Technique
Types of Watermarking	Robust	Robust	Robust	Robust
No. of Image Processing Transforms	2	2	3	3
Used Transform for Watermark Embedding	Redundant Discrete Wavelet Transform (RDWT) and Discrete Cosine Transform (DCT)	Discrete Wavelet Transform (DWT) and Singular Value Decomposition (SVD)	Nonsubsampled Contourlet Transform (NSCT), Singular Value Decomposition (SVD) and Discrete Cosine Transform (DCT)	Fast Discrete Curvelet Transform (FDCuT), Redundant Discrete Wavelet Transform (RDWT) and Discrete Cosine Transform (DCT)
Other Method Used	Arnold Scrambling	Error Correcting Code	Not used	Not used
Limitation of technique	Not any	Applicable only ROI of Medical Data	Not any	Not any
Maximum PSNR (dB)	56.03	28.54	36.8402	58.86
Maximum NCC	0.8516	0.9836	0.9990	0.9636

extraction of watermark logo, MBF DCT coefficients of LL subband of HF curvelet subband of the medical image is modified by two WGN sequences in such a way that blind extraction of watermark logo bits are possible at extraction side. The proposed technique is implemented and tested for different medical data such as X-Ray image, US image, CT image, MRI image and ECG signal. The performance of proposed technique is compared with the performance of two existing techniques: Roy technique (2017) and Thakkar technique (2017) and is found that the proposed technique performed better in terms of imperceptibility and security. The average PSNR value is around 42.59 dB, and average NC value is around 0.9535 for all types of watermarked medical images in the proposed technique. This scheme may be used for security of medical data in teleradiology application. The limitations of this technique are that it is unable to embed text format data and some noise is always visible in the extracted watermark logos.

ACKNOWLEDGMENT

This research received no specific grant from any funding agency in the public, commercial, or not-for-profit sectors.

REFERENCES

Acharjee, S., Ray, R., Chakraborty, S., Nath, S., & Dey, N. (2014, July). Watermarking in motion vector for security enhancement of medical videos. In *Control, Instrumentation, Communication and Computational Technologies (ICCICCT), 2014 International Conference on* (pp. 532-537). IEEE. 10.1109/ICCICCT.2014.6993019

Amar, Y. B., Trabelsi, I., Dey, N., Shi, F., Satapathy, S. C., & Bouhlel, M. S. (2017). Robust Watermarking of Polygonal Meshes Based on Vertex Norms Variance Distortion. *Journal of Global Information Management*, *25*(4), 46–60. doi:10.4018/JGIM.2017100104

American Hospital Association. (2015, January). The Promise of Telehealth for Hospitals, Health Systems, and Their Communities. *Trend Watch.*

Baur, H., Engelmann, U., Saurbier, F., Schroter, A., Baur, U., & Menizer, H. (1997). How to Deal with Security Issues in Teleradiology. *Computer Methods and Programs in Biomedicine*, *53*(1), 1–8. doi:10.1016/S0169-2607(96)01798-1 PMID:9113462

Chakraborty, S., Chatterjee, S., Dey, N., Ashour, A. S., & Hassanien, A. E. (2017). Comparative approach between singular value decomposition and randomized singular value decomposition-based watermarking. In *Intelligent Techniques in Signal Processing for Multimedia Security* (pp. 133–149). Springer International Publishing. doi:10.1007/978-3-319-44790-2_7   .

Chao, H., Hsu, C., & Miaou, S. (2002). A Data Hiding Technique with Authentication, Integration, and Confidentiality for Electronic Patient Records. *IEEE Transactions on Information Technology in Biomedicine*, *6*(1), 46–53. doi:10.1109/4233.992161 PMID:11936596

Cheung, S., Chiu, D., & Ho, C. (2008). The Use of Digital Watermarking for Intelligence Multimedia Document Distribution. *Journal of Theoretical and Applied Electronic Commerce Research*, *3*(3), 103–118. doi:10.4067/S0718-18762008000200008

Chiu, D., Hung, P., Cheng, V., & Kafeza, E. (2007, January). Protecting the Exchange of Medical Images in Healthcare Process Integration with Web Services. In *System Sciences, 2007. HICSS 2007. 40*th *Annual Hawaii International Conference on* (pp. 131 – 131). IEEE. 10.1109/HICSS.2007.451

Coatrieux, G., Maitre, H., Sankur, B., Rolland, Y. & Collorec, R. (2000). Relevance of Watermarking in Medical Imaging. *Proceedings of Information Technology Applications in Biomedicine*, 250 – 255.

Cox, I., Miller, M., & Bloom, J. (2000). Watermarking Applications and Their Properties. *Proceedings of the International Conference on Information Technology: Coding and Computing – ITCC 2000*, 6 – 10.

Cox, I., Miller, M., Bloom, J., Fridrich, J., & Kalker, T. (2007). *Digital Watermarking and Steganography*. Burlington: Elsevier.

Das, S., & Kundu, M. (2012, January). Effective Management of Medical Information through a Novel Blind Watermarking Technique. *Journal of Medical Systems*, *36*(5), 3339–3351. doi:10.100710916-012-9827-1 PMID:22327385

Dey, N., Ashour, A. S., Chakraborty, S., Banerjee, S., Gospodinova, E., Gospodinov, M., & Hassanien, A. E. (2017). Watermarking in Biomedical Signal Processing. In *Intelligent Techniques in Signal Processing for Multimedia Security* (pp. 345–369). Springer International Publishing. doi:10.1007/978-3-319-44790-2_16

Dey, N., Biswas, D., Roy, A., Das, A., & Chaudhuri, S. (2012, November). DWT-DCT-SVD based Blind Watermarking Technique of Gray Image in Electrooculogram Signal. *2012 12*th *International Conference on Intelligent Systems Design and Applications (ISDA)*, 680 – 685.

Dey, N., Das, P., Roy, A., Das, A., & Chaudhuri, S. (2012, October). DWT-DCT-SVD based Intravascular Ultrasound Video Watermarking. *2012 World Congress on Information and Communication Technologies (WICT)*, 224 – 229. 10.1109/WICT.2012.6409079

DICOM. (2009). *DICOM, Part 15: Security and System Management Profiles, PS 3.15 – 2009*. Available: ftp://medical.nema.org/medical/dicom/2009/

ECG Signal. (n.d.). Available at https://physionet.org/physiobank/database/#ecg

Epstein, M., Pasieka, M., Lord, W., Wong, S., & Mankovich, N. (1998). Security for the Digital Information Age of Medicine: Issues, Applications, and Implementation. *Journal of Digital Imaging*, *11*(1), 33–44. doi:10.1007/BF03168723 PMID:9502324

Fallahpour, M., Megias, D., & Ghanbari, M. (2009). High Capacity, Reversible Data Hiding in Medical Images. *16th IEEE International Conference on Image Processing (ICIP)*, 4241 – 4244. 10.1109/ICIP.2009.5413711

Fan, Z., & Hongbin, Z. (2004). Digital Watermarking Capacity and Reliability. *Proceedings of IEEE International Conference on e-Commerce Technology*, 295 – 298.

Fotopoulos, V., Stavrinou, M., & Skodras, A. (2008). Medical Image Authentication and Self-Correction through an Adaptive Reversible Watermarking Technique. *8th IEEE International Conference on Bioinformatics and Bioengineering*, 1 – 5. 10.1109/BIBE.2008.4696803

Goldwasser, S., & Bellare, M. (2008, July). *Lecture Notes on Cryptography*. Available: http://cseweb.ucsd.edu/~mihir/papers/gb.html

2016. ISO 27799:2016. (n.d.). *Health Informatics – Information Security Management in Health using ISO/IEC 27002*. Available: https://www.iso.org/standard/62777.html

Kalker, T., Haitsma, J., & Oostveen, J. C. (2001). Issues with Digital Watermarking and Perceptual Hashing. *Proceedings of the Society for Photo-Instrumentation Engineers*, *4518*, 189–197. doi:10.1117/12.448203

Kishore, P., Rao, M., Prasad, C., & Kumar, D. (2016, March). Medical Image Watermarking: Run through Review. *Journal of Engineering and Applied Sciences (Asian Research Publishing Network)*, *11*(5), 2882–2899.

Kutter, M., & Petitcolas, F. (1999, January). A Fair Benchmark for Image Watermarking Systems. *Electronics Imaging'99. Security, and Watermarking of Multimedia Contents*, *3657*, 1–14.

Langelaar, G., Setyawan, I., & Lagendijk, R. (2000, September). Watermarking of Digital Image and Video Data – A State of Art Review. *IEEE Signal Processing Magazine*, *17*(5), 20–46. doi:10.1109/79.879337

Liew, S., & Zain, J. (2010). Experiment of Tamper Detection and Recovery Watermarking in PACS. *Second International Conference on Computer Research and Development*, 387 – 390. 10.1109/ICCRD.2010.37

Mahmood, A. (2015, July). *Adaptive Approaches for Medical Imaging Security* (Ph.D. Thesis). University of Guelph, Canada.

MedPix™ Medical Image Database. (n.d.). Available at http://rad.usuhs.mil/medpix/medpix.html, https://medpix.nlm.nih.gov/home

Mostafa, S., El-Sheimy, N., Tolba, A., Abdelkader, F., & Elhindy, H. (2010). Wavelet packets based blind watermarking for Medical Image Management. *The Open Biomedical Engineering Journal*, *4*(1), 93–98. doi:10.2174/1874120701004010093 PMID:20700520

Nagpal, S., Bhushan, S., & Mahajan, M. (2016, April). An Enhanced Digital Image Watermarking Scheme for Medical Images using Neural Network, DWT, and RSA. *International Journal of Modern Education and Computer Science*, *4*(4), 46–56. doi:10.5815/ijmecs.2016.04.06

Nandi, S., Roy, S., Dansana, J., Karaa, W. B. A., Ray, R., Chowdhury, S. R., ... Dey, N. (2014). Cellular automata based encrypted ECG-hash code generation: An application in inter human biometric authentication system. *International Journal of Computer Network and Information Security*, *6*(11), 1–12. doi:10.5815/ijcnis.2014.11.01

Nyeem, H., Boles, W., & Boyd, C. (2013). A Review of Medical Image Watermarking Requirements for Teleradiology. *Journal of Digital Imaging*, *26*(2), 326–343. doi:10.100710278-012-9527-x PMID:22975883

Paar, C., & Pelzl, J. (2010). Hash Functions: Understanding Cryptography. Springer Berlin Heidelberg.

Pal, A., Dey, N., Samanta, S., Das, A., & Chaudhuri, S. (2013, December). A Hybrid Reversible Watermarking Technique for Color Biomedical Images. *IEEE International Conference on Computational Intelligence and Computing Research (ICCIC)*, 1 – 6. 10.1109/ICCIC.2013.6724177

Parah, S. A., Sheikh, J. A., Dey, N., & Bhat, G. M. (2017). Realization of a New Robust and Secure Watermarking Technique Using DC Coefficient Modification in Pixel Domain and Chaotic Encryption. *Journal of Global Information Management*, *25*(4), 80–102. doi:10.4018/JGIM.2017100106

Preneel, B. (2003, February). *Analysis and Design of Cryptographic Hash Functions*. Ph.D. Thesis. Available: http://homes.esat.kuleuven.be/~preneel/phd_preneel_feb1993.pdf

Que, D., Wen, X., & Chen, B. (2009). PACS Model based on Digital Watermarking and its Core Algorithms. *MIPPR 2009 – Medical Imaging, Parallel Processing of Images, and Optimization Techniques: 6th International Symposium on Multispectral Image Processing and Pattern Recognition*.

Rathi, S., & Inamdar, V. (2012, August). Medical Images Authentication through Watermarking preserving ROI. *Health Informatics – International Journal (Toronto, Ont.)*, *1*(1), 27–42.

Roy, S., & Pal, A. (2017, February). A Robust Blind Hybrid Image Watermarking Scheme in RDWT-DCT domain using Arnold Scrambling. *Multimedia Tools and Applications*, *76*(3), 3577–3616. doi:10.100711042-016-3902-4

Ruotsalainen, P. (2010). Privacy and Security in Teleradiology. *European Journal of Radiology*, *73*(1), 31–35. doi:10.1016/j.ejrad.2009.10.018 PMID:19914020

Singh, A. (2015, May). *Some New Techniques of Improved Wavelet Domain Watermarking for Medical Images* (Ph.D. Thesis). NIT Kurukshetra.

Singh, S., Singh, R., Singh, A., & Siddiqui, T. (2018). SVD-DCT based Medical Image Watermarking in NSCT Domain. In *Quantum Computing: An Environment for Intelligent Large Scale Real Application* (pp. 467–488). Cham: Springer. doi:10.1007/978-3-319-63639-9_20

Thakkar, F., & Srivastava, V. (2017, February). A Blind Medical Image Watermarking: DWT-SVD based Robust and Secure Approach for Telemedicine Applications. *Multimedia Tools and Applications, Springer, 76*(3), 3669–3697. doi:10.100711042-016-3928-7

Thanki, R., Borra, S., Dwivedi, V. & Borisagar, K. (2017). An Efficient Medical Image Watermarking Scheme based on FDCuT – DCT. *Engineering Science and Technology, an International Journal, 20*(4), 1366 – 1379.

Thanki, R. & Kothari, A. (2016, July). Digital Watermarking – Technical Art of Hiding a Message. *Intelligent Analysis of Multimedia Information*, 426 – 460.

US Government. (1996, July). *The Health Insurance Portability and Accountability Act (HIPAA)*. Available: https://www.hhs.gov/hipaa/index.html

US Government. (2010, October). *Code of Federal Regulations – Title 45, subtitle A – Department of Health and Human Services, part 164 – Security and Privacy*. Available: https://www.gpo.gov/fdsys/pkg/CFR-2010-title45-vol1/pdf/CFR-2010-title45-vol1.pdf

Venkatram, N., Reddy, L., & Kishore, P. (2014, August). Blind Medical Image Watermarking with LWT-SVD for Telemedicine Applications. *WSEAS Transactions on Signal Processing, 10*, 288–300.

Voloshynovskiy, S., Koval, O., Beekhof, F., & Pun, T. (2009, January). Conception and Limits of Robust Perceptual Hashing: towards Side Information assisted Hash Functions. Media Forensics and Security. doi:10.1117/12.805919

Xiaoyun, D., Xuejia, L., & Hongbo, Y. (2004). *Collisions for Hash Functions MD4, MD5, HAVAL-128, and RIPEMD*. Academic Press.

Yassin, N. (2015, November). Digital Watermarking for Telemedicine Applications: A Review. *International Journal of Computers and Applications, 129*(17), 30–37. doi:10.5120/ijca2015907183

Yu, N., Cao, L., Fang, W., & Li, X., (2003). Practical Analysis of Watermarking Capacity. *International Conference on Communication Technology, 2*, 1872 – 1877.

Zhou, W., Rockwood, T., & Sagetong, P. (2002). Non-repudiation Oblivious Watermarking Scheme for Secure Digital Video Distribution. *IEEE Workshop on Multimedia Signal Processing*, 343 – 346.

Zhou, X. Q., Huang, H. K., & Lou, S. L. (2000, February). Secure Method for Sectional Image Archiving and Transmission. Medical Imaging 2000: PACS Design and Evaluation: Engineering and Clinical Issues, 390 – 399.

Chapter 18
Medical Signal Security Enhancement Using Chaotic Map and Watermarking Technique

Ajita Sahay
KIIT University, India

Chittaranjan Pradhan
KIIT University, India

Amandip Sinha
West Bengal University of Technology, India

ABSTRACT

This chapter explores medical signal security enhancement using chaotic map and watermarking techniques. This new approach provides security to both the medical image and also maintains the confidentially of both the patient and doctor. Medical image encryption is done by using 2D Gaussian iterated map and BARCODE ECC200. Personal data is encoded in barcode. The encrypted image and barcode are embedded using DCT and DWT, which provides high PSNR values and higher NC value, which help to provide more security.

INTRODUCTION

As a fast growing world, everyone uses internet for their communication where they exchange personal information, text, audio, still images, animation video etc. The transmission has been done through channel which arises the word security because it may be possible while image transferred through channel some hacker try to interrupt the channel and get the image or he can even modify the image. Hence, everyone wants security in every field. Thus, many new approaches have been developed to ensure the security proof of originality and authentication. Image encryption is one of the method which has been

DOI: 10.4018/978-1-5225-5152-2.ch018

Copyright © 2018, IGI Global. Copying or distributing in print or electronic forms without written permission of IGI Global is prohibited.

proposed last few decades which deals with the modification of pixels of digital image (Wang, Ding, Zhang, & Ding, 2008).

In medical field, hospital – treatment – patient – doctors – disease are very common terms which are being used in this field but besides this, there is one more term which is called security in parallel moving in every one's mind whether he/she is a patient or doctor, because in any treatment hospital updates their database with patient full information like phone number, photo, age, identity proof, mail id, and the disease from which patient suffer, his/her diagnosis etc. Hospital also maintains their database for doctors which contains all information about doctors and also their patient names, their prescriptions to the patients. All these things are updated in their database. All these things are stored on a computer, which may be accessed illegally and someone may misuse the information to make fake identity etc. So, healthcare providers must take proper measures for patient data safety (Agrawal, & Sharma, 2016). PHI i.e. Patient health information referred as from an unofficial access and breaking of privacy and confidentiality. Hence, encryption is the best form of protection of such issues and to preserve the privacy confidentiality. So many different techniques are already introduced for the encryption. The federal government requires the secure handling of electronic media and PHI with standards put forth by the Health Insurance Portability and Accountability Act i. e. called HIPAA of 1996.

On the other hand, when patient visit first time for checkup to the consultant doctor, then that doctor first go through the previous record and documents of that patient before starting the treatment. One possible way is to send medical images along with a specialist report, over a computer network. Computer networks are complex and may be spying by the third party. That time the security problem may arise when patient data is sent over the network. Since security is our first concern and the security issues arise here, the medical imagery cannot be sent. Hence, to avoid such issues, the encryption technique is preferable for the protection of these data. So many different techniques are already introduced for the encryption because it is the best form of protection. Thus, in this chapter we try to provide security to both personnel as well as medical image.

Images are categorized as raster images and vector images. Raster images are defined as bitmap images, which are made up of bits, pixels. Each bit can be visualized as a dot which is defined by number of pixels per unit of measurement and it determines the resolution of the image, which is represented by ppi (pixel per inch) or dpi (dots per inch). Vector images are mathematical arrangements of points, where each point is connected by mathematical formulae. Most of the images are connected by straight lines.

Chittaranjan Pradhan et. al. (2014) explains digital watermarking is the technique which protects the data from being compromised or redistribution. It preserves the integrity and authenticity of the digital data. Digital watermarking technique is divided into two groups on the basis of feature set the watermark is embedded in; i.e. Spatial domain watermarking or Frequency domain (or Transform domain) watermarking. Spatial domain type deals with the image Matrix; whereas transform domain deals with the rate of which pixels value are changing in spatial domain.

BACKGROUND

Different approaches have been proposed for providing security to medical images. Like medical image encryption, authors generate pseudo random numbers by using chaotic maps and applying XOR operation with each bit of image pixels. Some approaches provide security to both personnel and medical image at the same time. The following section deals with the work done by different researchers in this area.

A. Giakoumaki et. al. (2003) proposed a medical image watermarking scheme based on wavelet transform. This paper addressed the problems of medical confidentiality protection and both origin and data authentication. William Puech et. al. (2005) proposed a crypto-compression of medical images by selective encryption of DCT. This paper presented a method of partial or selective encryption for JPEG images. Yin Dai et. al. (2012) proposed a medical image encryption technique based on a composition of logistic maps and Chebyshev maps.

Amarit Nambutdee et. el. (2015) proposed a medical image encryption based on DCT-DWT domain combining 2D- Data matrix barcode. They used scrambling algorithm to hide the patient information and required unique patient password to access a real image. Muath AlShaikh et. al. (2016) proposed a novel CT scan image watermarking scheme in DWT transform coefficients. Ritu Agrawal et. al. (2016) proposed a medical image watermarking technique in the application of e-diagnosis using M-ary modulation. The proposed model was robust and lossless in nature. Amit Kumar Singh et. al. (2017) presented a comprehensive review of medical image watermarking techniques in both spatial and transform domain.

IMAGE WATERMARKING

Digital watermarking is the process where information is inserted into digital signal, where signal may be video, audio, images etc. Digital watermarking is of four types (Pradhan, Rath, & Bisoi, 2012):

1. Perceptible Digital Watermarking
2. Imperceptible Digital watermarking
3. Blind Digital watermarking
4. Non-Blind Digital watermarking

Image watermarking technique is defined as some information in the form of image is embedded into original image. The embedded information may be visible or invisible. This hidden information is used to provide security to original image and also protect from illegal copying or misuse the information. The watermarking can be done in two ways as:

1. Spatial domain watermarking
2. Transform domain watermarking

1. Spatial Domain Technique

It deals with the pixels values of image by modifying it and generally analyze it with respect to time. This is one of the simplest way to embed the watermark. In spatial domain watermarking, the authors choose a pseudo random of pixel set and to modify the least significant bit. The major disadvantage of this technique is that it is very sensitive to noise and common signal. Hence it cannot be used in practical application generally (Abraham & Paul, 2014). One example of spatial domain are:

$$g(x,y) = \sum_{s=-a}^{a}\sum_{t=-b}^{b}\omega(s,t)f(x-s,y-t) \tag{1}$$

where, f (x, y) and g (x, y) are the input and output images respectively. The convolution kernel is w (s, t). The output image be generated by using the following equation.

$$g = \omega * f \tag{2}$$

2. Transform Domain Technique

In Transform domain watermarking technique, digital image is processed by using specific transformation. This technique can be applied to either the whole image or the smaller blocks of it. The block size can be of 8 x 8 or 16 x 16 size. This technique (also known as frequency domain technique) analyzes with respect to frequency. In terms of transform domain, the image is split into various frequency bands. Frequency domain transform uses the techniques like DCT (Discrete Cosine Transform), DWT (Discrete Wavelet Transform) etc. to transfer an image to its frequency representation.

a. DCT (Discrete Cosine Transform)

It helps to divide the image into two parts with respect to image's optical quality. It transforms the image from spatial domain to frequency domain (Abraham & Paul, 2014) as shown in Figure 5.

The general equation of DCT for one dimension is:

$$F\left(U\right) = \left(\frac{2}{N}\right)^{\frac{1}{2}} \sum_{i=0}^{N-1} \Delta\left(i\right).\cos\left[\frac{\pi.\mu}{2.N}\left(2i+1\right)\right] f\left(i\right) \tag{3}$$

The respective inverse 1D DCT transform is simple $F^{-1}\left(U\right)$ i.e.

$$\Delta\left(i\right) = \begin{cases} \dfrac{1}{\sqrt{2}}, \varepsilon = 0 \\ 1, otherwise \end{cases} \tag{4}$$

Figure 1. First level

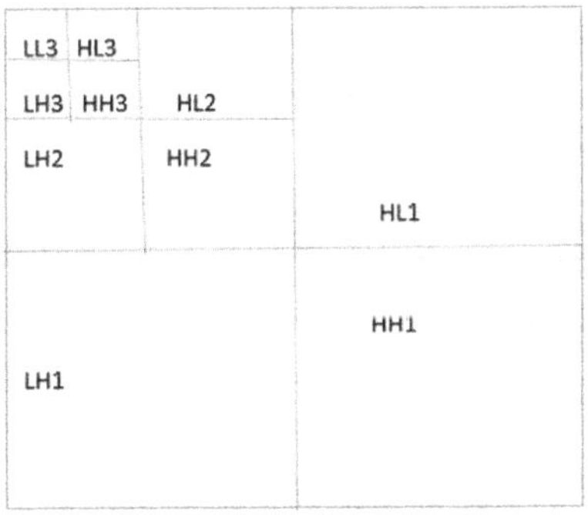

Figure 2. Second level

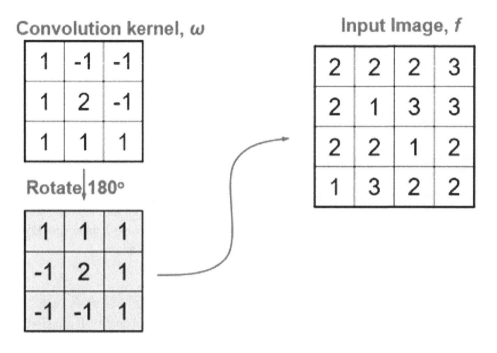

Figure 3. Third level

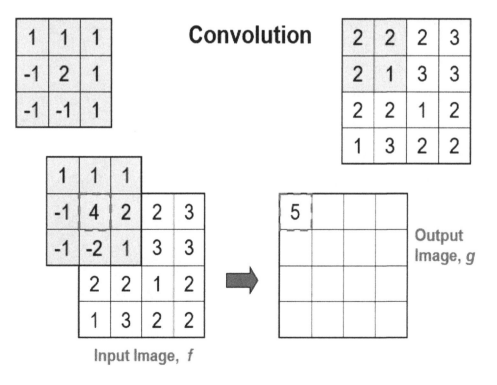

Figure 4. Fourth level

Convolution
1 1 1
-1 2 1
-1 -1 1
2 2 2 3
2 1 3 3
2 2 1 2
1 3 2 2
1 1 1
-2 4 2 3
-2 -1 3 3
2 2 1 2
1 3 2 2
Input Image, f
5 4
Output Image, g

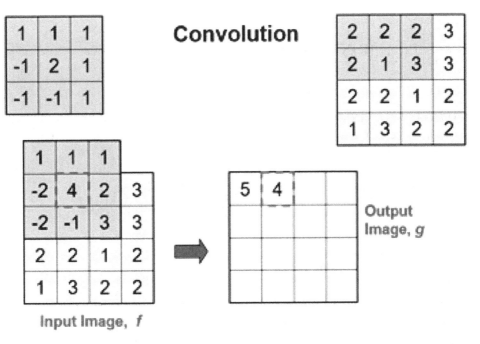

Figure 5. DCT in block

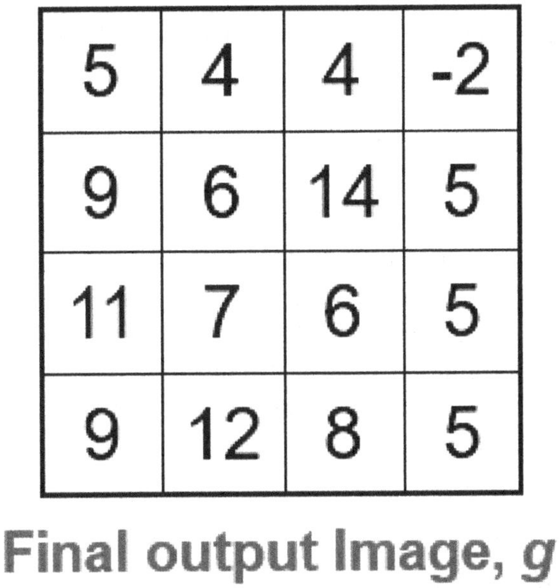

5 4 4 -2
9 6 14 5
11 7 6 5
9 12 8 5
Final output Image, g

The two dimension version of DCT is:

$$F\left(u,v\right)=\left(\frac{2}{\sqrt{UV}}\right)T\left(U\right)T\left(V\right)\sum_{X=0}^{U-1}\sum_{Y=0}^{V-1}f\left(x,y\right)x\cos\left(\frac{2x+1}{2U}\right)\pi u\cos\left(\frac{2y+1}{2V}\right)\pi v \tag{5}$$

where T(u), T(v) =1/ $\sqrt{2}$, F(u, v) and F(x, y) represent the pixel value in DCT domain and spatial domain. M x N is the image's size. In many researches transform image by DCT then divided into non-overlapped M x M block. The inverse DCT equation is represented as:

$$F\left(x,y\right)=\left(\frac{2}{\sqrt{UV}}\right)\sum_{X=0}^{U-1}\sum_{Y=0}^{V-1}F\left(u,v\right)T\left(u\right)T\left(v\right)x\cos\left(\frac{2x+1}{2U}\right)\pi u\cos\left(\frac{2y+1}{2V}\right)\pi v \tag{6}$$

Following are the features of using DCT:

- It helps us to see what sine waves makeup our underlying signal. The more complex sine wave will more complex graph.
- Filtering involves like attenuating or removing certain frequencies.
- It is very efficient for multimedia compression.

Figure 6 represents the original cameraman image. After applying DCT to this image, the transformed image is represented by Figure 7. When inverse DCT is applied to this, the reconstructed image is generated as shown in Figure 8.

b. DWT (Discrete Wavelet Transform)

According to the Fourier transformation concept, the signal is defined as sum of the information series of cosines and sines. This summation is also called Fourier expansion. This expansion is based on only frequency resolution and there is no time resolution involved. That means we are able to determine all the present frequency in the signal but we are unable to detect when they are present. To overcome this disadvantage of Fourier transform, discrete wavelet transform comes to the picture. DWT is able to represent a signal in time and frequency domain at the same time (Liu & Li, 2010; Pradhan, Rath, & Kumar Bisoi, 2012).

Figure 6. Cameraman image

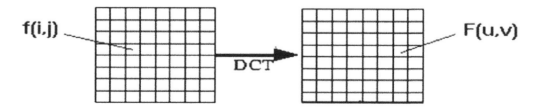

Figure 7. DCT converted image

Figure 8. Reconstructed image

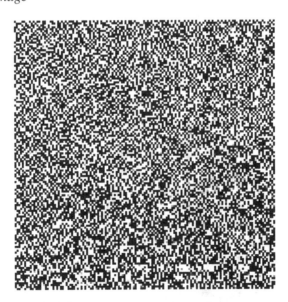

According to the Mallat-tree decomposition or Mallat algorithm, DWT is decomposed into successively by low pass filter and high pass filter (as shown in Figure 9).

Where, f is the signal, G denotes the low pass filter and H denotes the high pass filter. At each level of decomposition, the low pass filter gives coarse approximation and the high level gives detailed information.

The wavelet decomposition is always split into four parts i.e. horizontal direction, vertical direction, diagonal direction and low frequency part, and it can be decomposed on and on. The wavelet transformed image has a low frequency band LL3 and high frequency bands LHi, HLi, HHi where i=1 .. 3 (as shown in Figure 10). By taking Baboon image as the input, Figure 10 represents the three level DWT decomposition of it. The low frequency part with a few in horizontal, vertical and diagonal parts [G, H] concentrated the main energy.

Data Matrix

Data matrix is also called as Two-Dimensional Barcode. Data matrix is mainly used for encoding large amount of data. Data may be in text format or in numeric format. Usually data size ranges from few bytes to 1556 bytes and the barcode size depends on the encoded message. In two dimensional barcode, it consist of only combination of two colors i.e. white and black. The shape of barcode is generally square or rectangle which represents the bits. The cells are categorized into two types: light or dark. Light cell is expressed as 0 and dark cell is expressed as 1 or vice versa.

Figure 9. Mallat tree decomposition

Figure 10. Three levels of decomposition

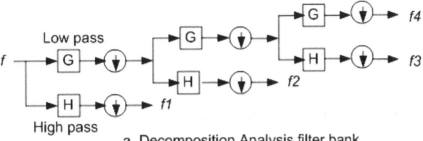

a. Decomposition Analysis filter bank

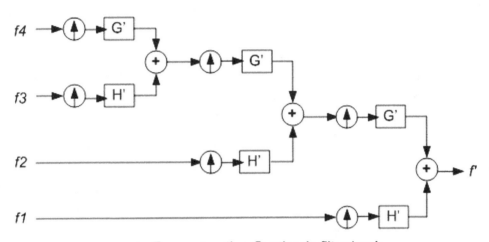

b. Reconstruction Synthesis filter bank

Data matrix is made up of two solid adjacent boundaries borders in an L shape which is called finder path and other two borders consisting alternative light and dark cells which is called timing pattern. The encoded information are stored between these two boundaries of rows and column. Both the boundaries have their own responsibilities. For location and orient the symbols, finder path is used; whereas timing pattern is used to count the number of rows and columns in the symbol. Each code is unique which makes the barcode more secure. Error correction helps to increase the reliability of the barcode by making it readable even after damage of one or more cells because error correction enables reconstruction of the original data using different ways. Data matrix barcode are used in various purpose to prove originality, confidentiality, and authentication (Nambutdee & Airphaiboon, 2015). It is used in various fields like Paytm to accept payment, post office when parcel has been dispatched, industrial engineering, food industry etc.

New version of Data matrix of two dimensional barcode ECC 200 used in Reed-Solomon codes for error and recovery. ECC added some more extra features as compare to data matrix like:

- It provides light images on a dark background which is called inverse reading symbols.
- It extended channel interpretation i.e. specification of the character set.
- It uses rectangular symbols; whereas data matrix generally used square symbols.

- It provides the structure which can link up to 16 different symbols for encoding large amount of data.

Gauss Iterated Map

Chaotic map is very useful to ensure security. It has the properties like deterministic in nature, easy to generate and difficult to estimate. Gauss iterated map is one type of chaotic map which also generate a pseudo random number (Zhou, Shi, Bao, & Yang, 2010; Zhou, Bao, & Chen, 2014). It is a nonlinear iterated map of the reals into real interval as provided by Gaussian function:

$$X_{N+1} = \exp\left(-\alpha X_N^2\right) + \beta \tag{7}$$

where, α $and\beta$ are real parameters. Gauss iterated map shows best result when the value of α has some positive value lies between +1 to +6 and β value lies between -1 to +1 (Zhou, Shi, Bao, & Yang, 2010). The bell shaped Gaussian function map is similar to logistic map. Figure 11 shows the Gaussian map with $\alpha = 4.9$ and $\beta = -1 to +1$ which resembles like mouse, that's why it is also called as mouse map.

The basic feature of Gauss map which makes it different from logistic map are:

- Reverse period
- Coexisting Attractor
- Doubling
- **Two parameters, i.e.** α $and\beta$

Figure 11. 1D Gauss iterated map

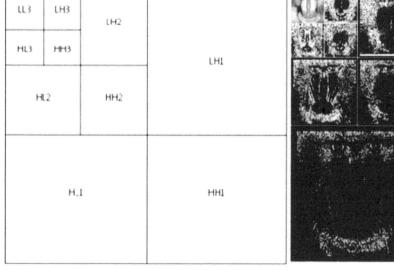

a. 3-level DWT decomposition

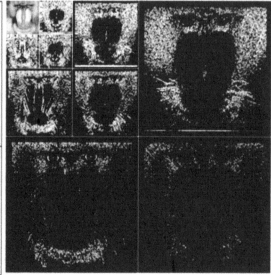

b. 3-level DWT decomposition of Image

The analysis of its behavior of long term iterators and becomes more complicated than the logistic map. Let's consider an image with size M × M and generate a sequence up to image size, i.e. M x M iteration using Equation 7 and then quantized to binary format by using Equation 8.

$$S(i) = \begin{cases} 0, 0 < X(n) \leq 0.5 \\ 1, 0.5 < X(n) \leq 1 \end{cases} \tag{8}$$

Where, X(n) is a random number in sequence and S(i) is quantized sequence. Then S (i) is XOR with each bit of M x M image to produce the encrypted image. The initial value lies between 0 and 1.

2D Gauss Iterated Map

2D Gauss iterated map has come to overcome the disadvantage of 1D Gauss iterated map as well as 2D Logistic map. It has been developed by using more number of parameters and key spaces to make it more complex, robust and secure in nature (Pisarchik & Zanin, 2012; Sahay & Pradhan, 2017).

$$A[X, Y] = \begin{matrix} X_{N+1} = \exp(-\alpha_1 X_N^2) + \beta_1 + \gamma_1 X_N^2 \\ Y_{N+1} = \exp(-\alpha_2 Y_N^2 + \beta_2 + \gamma_2 X_N^2 Y_N^2 \end{matrix} \tag{9}$$

where, N=1, 2, 3……. $\alpha_1, \beta_1, \gamma_1, \alpha_2, \beta_2, \gamma_2$ α are the system control parameter. X_0, Y_0 are the initial conditions. The values of parameters range are

$$0 < X_N, Y_N \leq 1; 1.75 \leq \alpha_1 \leq 4.5; -1 \leq \beta_1 \leq 1; 3 \leq \gamma_1 \leq 5.5; 2 \leq \alpha_2 \leq 4.5; -1 \leq \beta_2 \leq 1; 3 \leq \gamma_2 \leq 4$$

Figure 12 shows the graph by taking

$$\alpha_1 = 2.9, \beta_1 = -0.56, \gamma_1 = 4.75, \alpha_2 = 3.53, \beta_2 = -0.81, \gamma_2 = 3.45, X_0 = 0.12, Y_0 = 0.34$$

As we can see the above graph has very complex structure which helps to provide more security during encryption process. The quantization function used to convert the decimal points to binary bits is:

$$S(t) = \begin{cases} 0, 0 < 2K(i, j) \leq 0.5 \\ 1, 0.5 < 2K(i, j) \leq 1 \end{cases} \tag{10}$$

where, 2K(i, j) is a random number in sequence and S(t) is quantized sequence. In 2D Gauss iterated map, 1D matrix multiplied with Y transposed matrix to generate 2D Matrix. Which is called 2K Matrix (Kumar Kabi, Saha, Pradhan, & Bisoi, 2014).

Figure 12. 2D Gauss iterated map

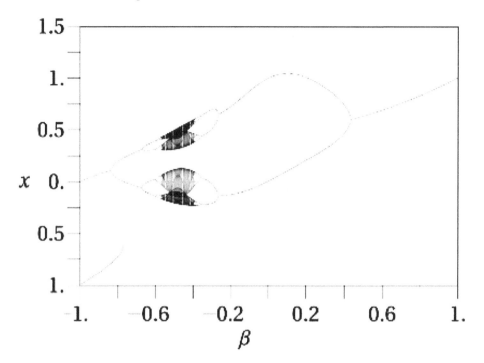

PROPOSED METHOD

In this proposed approach, we are embedding the information and provide security to personal information as well as medical image. The steps for embedding are:

- First patient updates his/her information in hospital database. The information is encoded using barcode ECC200. Then encode the information into data matrix.

1. Take the patient medical image and embed the barcode into that medical image by generating pseudo random sequence Gauss 2D iterated map (Liu, & Miao, 2016). The final embedding process has been done by using image watermarking.

Watermark Embedding Process

The steps for watermark embedding are:

- First convert the personal data of patient in encrypted form by using two dimensional barcode i.e. ECC200 which helps to improve the high capacity of watermark W1.
- Then scrambling of pixels is done by using 2D Gauss iterated map on the original watermark image using Equation 9.

- Then second scrambling is performed by using 1D Gauss iterated map which is given in Equation 7. By the second scrambling we will make it more complex and follow the new sequence of sorting in ascending order defined in Equation 11 and Equation 12.

$$NewSequence = Sort_{Ascending}\left(X_i\right) \tag{11}$$

$$W_{s2} = W_{s1}\left(NewSequence\right) \tag{12}$$

- Apply DCT technique in the original cover image into 8 x 8 non overlapping blocks with N x N size of an original image, we get A_{DCT} by using Equation 13.

$$A_{DCT}\left(P\right) = DCT\left(A_{D(i,j)}\right) \tag{13}$$

where, P=1, 2… N/8.

- Separate the original cover image into non overlapping block size 8 x 8. After that we apply DWT to the original image up to two level of decomposition to get the coefficient $DWT_{cff.}$
- By using the Equation 13, we store the value of the position (1, 2) in position (1, 1). DCT will use for comparison the position (1, 2) in next position which decide the considerable area for embed the information.
- $DWT_{cff\ (index)}$ is the matrix size N/8 x 1. Z is the matrix size of N/8 x N/8 as given in Equation 14.

$$T\left(index\right) = DWT_{cff(1,2)} \tag{14}$$

$$C\left(i\right) = \begin{cases} 0, if\ I_{DCT}\left(i\right) > T\left(i\right) \\ 1, if\ I_{DCT}\left(i\right) \leq T\left(i\right) \end{cases} \tag{15}$$

$$B = \left[DWT_{cff}\left(1\right), DWT_{cff}\left(2\right), \cdots DWT_{cff}\left(\frac{N}{8}\right)\right] \tag{16}$$

where, index i =1, 2 ... N/8.

$$\text{Re}\, m\left(i\right) = \begin{cases} 0, if\, C\left(i\right) = W_{s2}\left(i\right) \\ 1, if\, I_{DCT}\left(i\right) \le L\left(i\right) \end{cases} \tag{17}$$

- Then apply IDWT up to two levels of decomposition and replace the value of T (i) in DWT$_{cff}$ using fifth step. I$_e$ is the image after embedment of the information. Hence image encryption has been done.

2. Watermark Extraction Process

The watermark can be extracted by performing the extraction process which is the reverse of embedding process. Then confirm barcode readability.

Experimental Results

We have taken MATLAB 2013a simulator for the demonstration purpose using 'x_ray.bmp' image of size 64 x 64 as shown in Figure 15. We have used Visual Basic 2012 for barcode decoding. The details of patient Aditi Sahay has been taken (as shown in Figure 13) and barcode has been generated as shown in Figure 14. After embedding the medical image with encrypted patient information, we got Figure 16.

The process of generating medical information and patient information from the extracted watermark is shown in the figures (Figure 17 to 20).

To detect the similarity between two images and extraction watermark images, we are using two parameters i. e. Peak Signal to Noise Ratio (PSNR) and Normal Correlation (NC) which is given in the Equations 18 and 20.

Figure 13. Patient information

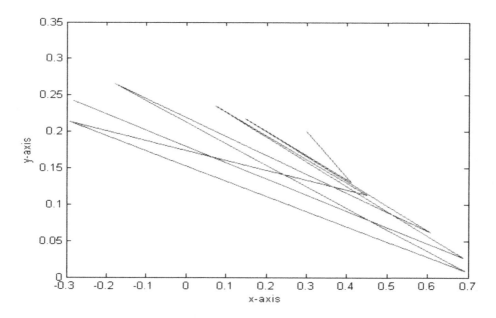

Figure 14. Encrypted patient information

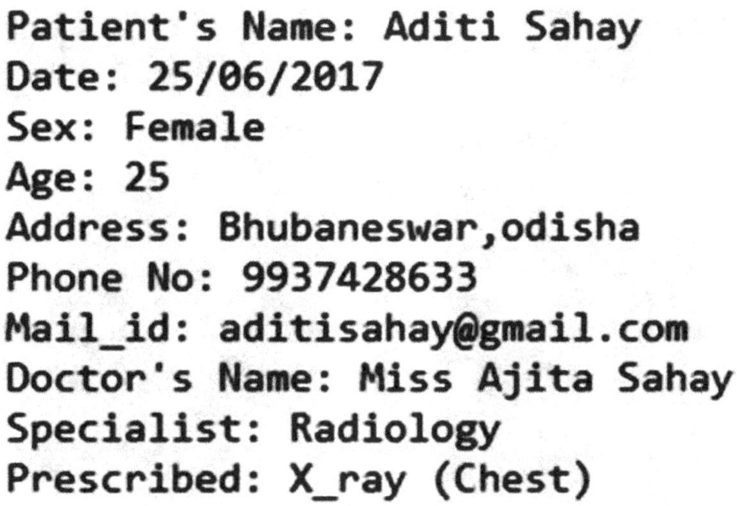

Patient's Name: Aditi Sahay
Date: 25/06/2017
Sex: Female
Age: 25
Address: Bhubaneswar,odisha
Phone No: 9937428633
Mail_id: aditisahay@gmail.com
Doctor's Name: Miss Ajita Sahay
Specialist: Radiology
Prescribed: X_ray (Chest)

Figure 15. Patient medical image

$$PSNR = 10log_{10}\left(\frac{N*N}{MSE}\right) \qquad (18)$$

$$MSE = \frac{1}{N*N}\sum_{I=0}^{M-1}\sum_{j=0}^{N-1}\left[\left\{x\left(i,j\right)-y\left(i,j\right)\right\}^2\right] \qquad (19)$$

$$NC = \frac{1}{W_H W_H}\sum_{i=1}^{W_H}\sum_{j=1}^{W_W}W\left(i,j\right)*W'\left(i,j\right) \qquad (20)$$

Figure 16. Embedment of medical image with encrypted patient information

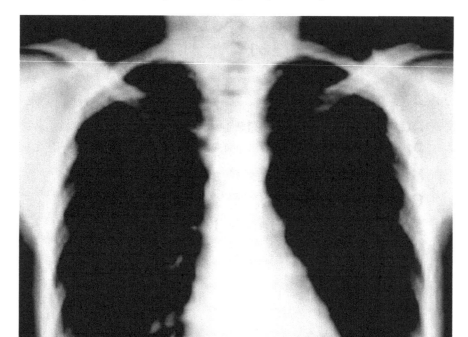

Figure 17. Final encrypted image

N x N is the size of image and MSE stands for mean square error between extracted image and the original image

For experimental purpose we take a data set of patient personal details and encode that details by using bar code ECC200. The encoded form is then embedded as watermarked image by using DCT and DWT. This helps to provide the more security in the medical fields. The result analysis is given in Table 1.

Figure 18. Extracted medical image

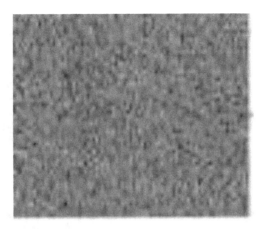

Figure 19. Extracted barcode

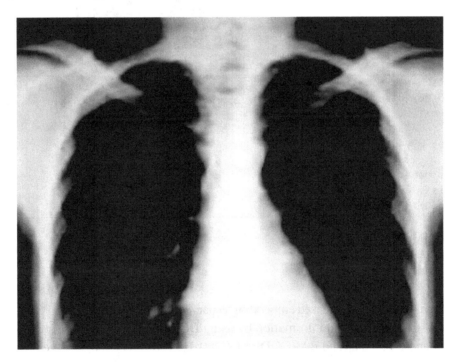

Figure 20. Extracted patient information

Table 1. Result Analysis

Patient Information	Medical Image	PSNR	NC
Patient's Name: Aditi Sahay Date: 25/06/2017 Sex: Female Age: 25 Address: Bhubaneswar,odisha Phone No: 9937428633 Mail_id: aditisahay@gmail.com Doctor's Name: Miss Ajita Sahay Specialist: Radiology Prescribed: X_ray (Chest)		47.15	0.925
Patient's Name: Riya Sahay Date: 29/06/2017 Sex : Female Address : Banagalore,Marathahalli Phone no: 09945327844 Mail_id : riya1234@gmal.com Doctor's name: Miss Ajita Sahay Specialist: Gynecologist Prescribed : Ultra Sound		47.20	0.940
Patient's Name: Sonali Sahay Date: 25/06/2017 Sex : Female Address : Banagalore,BTM first phase Phone no: 09946490799 Mail_id : riya1234@gmal.com Doctor's name: Miss Dimpi Sahay Specialist: Gynecologist Prescribed : Ultra Sound		47.80	0.917

CONCLUSION

This model helps us to achieve increased embedding capacity with maintaining high PSNR values which shows the details of the embedded information by using DCT and DWT. Image encryption is done by using 2D Gaussian iterated map and BARCODE ECC200. Here, the personal data is encoded in barcode whereas the medical image is encrypted using 2D Gauss iterated function. Then the encrypted image and barcode are embedded using DCT and DWT. On the basis of experimental result which gives higher PNSR value and higher NC value proves that our approach provides better security.

REFERENCES

Abraham, J., & Paul, V. (2014). Image Watermarking using DCT in Selected Pixel Regions. *IEEE International Conference on Control, Instrumentation, Communication and Computational Technologies*, 398-402. 10.1109/ICCICCT.2014.6992994

Agrawal, R., & Sharma, M. (2016). Medical Image Watermarking Technique in the Application of E-diagnosis using M-Ary Modulation. *Elsevier International Conference on Computational Modelling and Security, Procedia Computer Science*, 85, 648-655.

AlShaikh, M., Laouamer, L., Nana, L., & Pascu, A. (2016, January). A Novel CT Scan Images Watermarking Scheme in DWT Transform Coefficients. *International Journal of Computer Science and Network Security*, 16(1), 62–71.

Dai, Y., & Wang, X. (2012). Medical Image Encryption based on a Composition of Logistic Maps and Chebyshev Maps. *IEEE International Conference on Information and Automation*. 10.1109/ICInfA.2012.6246810

Giokoumaki, A., Pavlopoulos, S., & Koutouris, D. (2003). A Medical Image Watermarking Scheme based on Wavelet Transform. *IEEE International Conference on Engineering in Medicine and Biology Society*. 10.1109/IEMBS.2003.1279900

Kabi, K. K., Saha, B. J., Pradhan, C., & Bisoi, A. K. (2014). Comparative Study of Image Encryption using 2D Chaotic Map. *IEEE International Conference on Information Systems and Computer Networks*, 105-108. 10.1109/ICISCON.2014.6965227

Liu, L., & Miao, S. (2016, March). A New Image Encryption Algorithm based on Logistic Chaotic Map with Varying Parameter. *SpringerPlus*. PMID:27066326

Liu, X., & Li, S. (2010). An Adaptive Chaotic Encrypted Binary Image Digital Watermarking Algorithm based on DCT. *IEEE International Conference on Intelligent Computing and Integrated Systems*, 149-153. 10.1109/ICISS.2010.5656801

Nambutdee, A., & Airphaiboon, S. (2015). Medical Image Encryption based on DCT-DWT Domain Combining 2D-Data Matrix Barcode. *IEEE Biomedical Engineering International Conference*.

Pisarchik, A. N. (2012). *Chaotic Map Cryptography and Security. In Horizons in Computer Science* (Vol. 4). Springer.

Pradhan, C., Rath, S., & Bisoi, A. K. (2012). Non Blind Digital Watermarking Technique using DWT and Cross Chaos. *Elsevier International Conference on Communication, Computing & Security, Procedia Technology*, 6, 897-904. 10.1016/j.protcy.2012.10.109

Pradhan, C., Saha, B. J., & Kabi, K. K. (2014). Blind Watermarking Techniques using DCT and Arnold 2D Cat Map for Color Images. *IEEE International Conference on Communication and Signal Processing*, 26-30.

Puech, W., & Rodrigues, J. M. (2005). Crypto-Compression of Medical Images by Selective Encryption of DCT. *European Signal Processing Conference*.

Sahay, A., & Pradhan, C. (2017). Multidimensional Comparative Analysis of Image Encryption using Gauss Iterated and Logistic Maps. *IEEE International Conference on Communication and Signal Processing*.

Singh, Kumar, Singh, & Mohan. (2017). *Medical Image Watermarking*. Springer.

Wang, Q., Ding, Q., Zhang, Z., & Ding, L. (2008). Digital Image Encryption Research based on DWT and Chaos. *IEEE International Conference on Natural Computation*, 494-498. 10.1109/ICNC.2008.105

Zhou, Y., Bao, L., & Philip Chen, C. L. (2014). A New 1D Chaotic System for Image Encryption. *Signal Processing, Elsevier*, 97(Apr), 172–182. doi:10.1016/j.sigpro.2013.10.034

Zhou, Z., Shi, W., Bao, Y., & Yang, M. (2010). A Gaussian Function based Chaotic Neural Network. *IEEE International Conference on Computer Application and System Modeling*, 203-206.

Compilation of References

2016. ISO 27799:2016. (n.d.). *Health Informatics – Information Security Management in Health using ISO/IEC 27002*. Available: https://www.iso.org/standard/62777.html

Abbas, Abo-Zahhad, Ahmed, & Farrag. (2015). *Heart-ID: human identity recognition using heart sounds based on modifying mel-frequency cepstral features*. Academic Press. 10.1049/iet-bmt.2015.0033

Abdelaziz, A. K., Nafaa, M., & Salim, G. (2013). Survey of Routing Attacks and Countermeasures in Mobile Ad Hoc Networks. Computer Modelling Simulation (UKSim).

Abraham, J., & Paul, V. (2014). Image Watermarking using DCT in Selected Pixel Regions. *IEEE International Conference on Control, Instrumentation, Communication and Computational Technologies*, 398-402. 10.1109/ICCICCT.2014.6992994

Acharjee, S., Ray, R., Chakraborty, S., Nath, S., & Dey, N. (2014, July). Watermarking in motion vector for security enhancement of medical videos. In *Control, Instrumentation, Communication and Computational Technologies (IC-CICCT), 2014 International Conference on* (pp. 532-537). IEEE. 10.1109/ICCICCT.2014.6993019

Aggarwal, C. (2005). On k-Anonymity and the Curse of Dimensionality. *Proc. Int'l Conf. Very Large Data Bases (VLDB)*, 901-909.

Agrawal, D., & Aggarwal, C. C. (2001). On the design and quantification of privacy preserving data mining algorithms. *Proc. of the 20th ACM Symposium on Principles of Database Systems (PODS)*, 247–255. 10.1145/375551.375602

Agrawal, R., & Sharma, M. (2016). Medical Image Watermarking Technique in the Application of E-diagnosis using M-Ary Modulation. *Elsevier International Conference on Computational Modelling and Security, Procedia Computer Science, 85*, 648-655.

Ahmad, M., ul-Hassan, M., Shafi, I., & Osman, F. (2012). Classification of tumours in human brain MRI using wavelet and support vector machine. *IOSR Journal of Computer Engineering, 8*(2), 25-31.

Ahrens, T., & Rutherford, K. (1993). *Essentials of Oxygenation*. Boston: Jones & Barlett.

Akay, M., Akay, Y. M., Welkowitz, W., & Lewkowicz, S. (1994). Investigating the effects of vasodilator drugs on the turbulent sound caused by femoral artery stenosis using short-term Fourier and wavelet transform methods. *IEEE Transactions on Biomedical Engineering, 41*(10), 921–928. doi:10.1109/10.324523 PMID:7959798

Akay, Y. M., Akay, M., Welkowitz, W., & Kostis, J. (1994). Noninvasive detection of coronary artery disease. *IEEE Engineering in Medicine and Biology Magazine, 13*(5), 761–764. doi:10.1109/51.334639

Al Ameen & Kwak. (n.d.). Social Issues in Wireless Sensor Networks with Healthcare Perspective. *The International Arab Journal of Information Technology, 8*(1).

Alajmi,N. (2014). Wireless Sensor Networks Attacks and Solutions. *International Journal of Computer Science and Information Security*.

Alan. (2011). 5 Most Popular Two-Factor Authentication Security Devices. *Technology Bloggers*. Retrieved From http://www.technologybloggers.org/technology/5-most-popular-two-factor-authentication-security-devices/

Ali, T. J., Aziz, A., Akhtar, P., & Bhatti, M. I. (2009). A framework for secure access to medical images. *2009 International Conference on Bioinformatics, Computational Biology, Genomics and Chemoinformatics (BCBGC-09)*.

Al-Kadi & Watson. (2008). Texture analysis of aggressive and nonaggressive lung tumor CE CT images. IEEE Transactions on Biomedical Engineering, 55(7), 1822-1830.

Alnajim, A., & Munro, M. (2009). An Anti-Phishing Approach that Uses Training Intervention for Phishing Websites Detection. *6th IEEE International Conference on Information Technology - New Generations (ITNG)*.

AlShaikh, M., Laouamer, L., Nana, L., & Pascu, A. (2016, January). A Novel CT Scan Images Watermarking Scheme in DWT Transform Coefficients. *International Journal of Computer Science and Network Security*, 16(1), 62–71.

Amar, J., Neidzwski, J., Wald, A., & Finck, A. D. (1989). Neidzwski, A. Wald and A. D. Finck, "Fluorescent light interferes with pulse oximetry. *Journal of Clinical Monitoring*, 5(2), 135–136. doi:10.1007/BF01617888 PMID:2656924

Amar, Y. B., Trabelsi, I., Dey, N., & Bouhlel, S. (2016). Euclidean Distance Distortion Based Robust and Blind Mesh Watermarking. *International Journal of Interactive Multimedia and Artificial Intelligence*, 4(2), 46. doi:10.9781/ijimai.2016.428

Amar, Y. B., Trabelsi, I., Dey, N., Shi, F., Satapathy, S. C., & Bouhlel, M. S. (2017). Robust Watermarking of Polygonal Meshes Based on Vertex Norms Variance Distortion. *Journal of Global Information Management*, 25(4), 46–60. doi:10.4018/JGIM.2017100104

Amazon. (2017). *Healthcare Providers and Insurers in the Cloud*. Retrieved 7 13, 2017, from Amazon web services: https://aws.amazon.com/health/providers-and-insurers/

American cancer society, cancer facts and figures. (2013). New York, NY: American Cancer Society.

American Cancer Society. (2014). *Cancer facts & figures*. Author.

American Cancer Society. (2017). *Breast Cancer Statistics*. Retrieved from http://pressroom.cancer.org/BreastCancerStats2017

American College of Radiology (ACR). (1998). *Illustrated breast imaging reporting and data system* (3rd ed.). Reston, VA: BI-RADS.

American Hospital Association. (2015, January). The Promise of Telehealth for Hospitals, Health Systems, and Their Communities. *Trend Watch*.

Amos, C. (2017). *Biomedical data science*. Retrieved June 29, 2017, from Geisel School of Medicine: https://bmds.dartmouth.edu/biomedical-data-science

Anderson, N. R.-H., Lee, E. S., Brockenbrough, J. S., Minie, M. E., Fuller, S., Brinkley, J., & Tarczy-Hornoch, P. (2007). Issues in Biomedical Research Data Management and Analysis: Needs and Barriers. *Journal of the American Medical Informatics Association*, 14(4), 478–488. doi:10.1197/jamia.M2114 PMID:17460139

Anderson, R. J. (1996). *Security in Clinical Information Systems*. University of Cambridge.

Angelidis, P. A. (1994). MR image compression using a wavelet transform coding algorithm. *Magnetic Resonance Imaging*, *12*(7), 1111–1120. doi:10.1016/0730-725X(94)91243-P PMID:7997098

Anthony, T., & Velte, T. J. (2010). *Cloud Computing A practical Approach.* New Delhi: McGraw Hill.

Aoyagi, T., Kishi, M., Yamaguchi, K., & Watanabe, S. (1974). Improvement of an ear-piece oximeter. Proc. Abstracts of 13th Annu. Japanese Soc. Med. Electro. Biologic Eng., 90-91.

Appari, A., & Johnson, M. E. (2010). *Information Security and Privacy in Healthcare: Current State of Research* (Vol. 6). Int. J. Internet and Enterprise Management.

Arena, E. T., Rueden, C. T., Hiner, M. C., Wang, S., Yuan, M., & Eliceiri, K. W. (2016). Quantitating the cell: Turning images into numbers with ImageJ. *Wiley Interdisciplinary Reviews. Developmental Biology*, *6*(2). doi:10.1002/wdev.260 PMID:27911038

Arijit Kumar, P., Nilanjan, D., & Sourav, S. (2014). A hybrid reversible watermarking technique for color biomedical images. In Computational Intelligence and Computing Research. New Delhi: IEEE.

Arndt, R. Z. (2017). *Bupa breach affects more than half a million customers.* Retrieved From http://www.modernhealthcare.com/article/20170713/NEWS/170719949/bupa-breach-affects-more-than-half-a-million-customers

Atakli, I. M., Hu, H., Chen, Y., Ku, W.S., & Su, Z. (2008). Malicious node detection in wireless sensor networks using weighted trust evaluation. *Proceedings of the Symposium on Simulation of Systems Security.*

Ayman, A., Qahwaji, R. S., Aqel, M. J., Hussam, A., & Salehand, M. H. (2006). Efficient Pre-processing of USF and MIAS Mammogram Images. *Journal of Computational Science*, *3*(2), 67–75.

Ayres, F. J., & Rangayyan, R. M. (2003). Characterization of Architectural Distortion in Mammograms. In *Proceedings of the 25" Annual International Conference of the IEEE EMB* (Vol 1, pp. 886-889). Cancun, Mexico: IEEE. 10.1109/IEMBS.2003.1279907

Azure, M. (2017). *What is cloud computing?* Retrieved 7 2, 2017, from Micrososft Azure: https://azure.microsoft.com/en-in/overview/what-is-cloud-computing/

Ba, H., Gao, X., Zhang, X., & He, Z. (2014). Protecting Data Privacy from Being Inferred from High Dimensional Correlated Data. In *Proceedings of the 2014 IEEE/WIC/ACM International Joint Conferences on Web Intelligence (WI) and Intelligent Agent Technologies (IAT)* . IEEE Computer Society. 10.1109/WI-IAT.2014.139

Bagchi & Shroff. (2005). LITEWORP: A Lightweight Countermeasure for the Wormhole Attack in Multi hop Wireless Networks. *Proceedings of the International Conference on Dependable Systems and Networks.*

Balakumaran, T., & Vennila, I. (2011). *Detection of Microcalcification Clusters in Digital Mammograms using Multiresolution based Foveal Algorithm.* Paper presented at IEEE International 2011 World Congress on Information and Communication Technologies. 10.1109/WICT.2011.6141323

Balasubramaniyan, J. S., Garcia-Fernandez, J. O., Isacoff, D., & Spafford, E. (1998). An architecture for intrusion detection using autonomous agents. In *ACSAC'98: Proceedings of the 14th Annual Computer Security Applications Conference.* IEEE Computer Society.

Banerjee, Chakraborty, Dey, Pal, & Ray. (2015, February). High Payload Watermarking using Residue Number System. *I.J. Image, Graphics and Signal Processing*, 1-8.

Banerjee, S., Mishra, M., & Mukherjee, A. (2016). Segmentation and detection of first and second heart sounds (S1 and S2) using variational mode decomposition. *IEEE EMBS conference on biomedical engineering and science (IECBES)*, 565-570.

Bao, Chen, Chang, & Cho. (2012). Hierarchical Trust Management for Wireless Sensor Networks and its Applications to Trust-Based Routing and Intrusion Detection. *IEEE Transactions on Network and Service Management*.

Barker, S. J., Tremper, K. K., & Hyatt, J. (1989). Effects of methemoglobinemia on pulse oximetry and mixed venous oximetry. *Anesthesiology*, 70(1), 112–117. doi:10.1097/00000542-198901000-00021 PMID:2912291

Barros, A. K., Mansour, A., & Ohnishi, N. (1998). Removing artifacts from electrocardiographic signals using independent components analysis. *Neurocomputing*, 22(1), 173–186. doi:10.1016/S0925-2312(98)00056-3

Bauer, S., May, C., Dionysiou, D., Stamatakos, G., Buchler, P., & Reyes, M. (2012). Multiscale modeling for image analysis of brain tumour studies. *IEEE Transactions on Biomedical Engineering*, 59(1), 25–29. doi:10.1109/TBME.2011.2163406 PMID:21813362

Baura, G. D. (2002). *System theory and practical applications of biomedical signals, IEEE press series on biomedical engineering*. John Wiley & Sons.

Baur, H., Engelmann, U., Saurbier, F., Schroter, A., Baur, U., & Menizer, H. (1997). How to Deal with Security Issues in Teleradiology. *Computer Methods and Programs in Biomedicine*, 53(1), 1–8. doi:10.1016/S0169-2607(96)01798-1 PMID:9113462

Belkhede, M., Gulhane, V., & Bajaj, P. (2012). Biometric Mechanism for enhanced Security of Online Transaction on Android system: A Design Approach. In *Proc* (pp. 1193–1197). ICACT.

Bemmel, J. H. V. (1984). The structure of medical informatics. *Medical Informatics*, 9(3-4), 175–180. doi:10.3109/14639238409015187 PMID:6390014

Bennett & Lanning. (2007). The Netflix Prize. *Proceedings of KDD Cup and Workshop 2007*.

Beritelli, F., & Spadaccini, A. (2011). *Human Identity Verification based on Heart Sounds: Recent Advances and Future Directions*. Academic Press.

Beritelli, F., & Serrano, S. (2007). Biometric Identification based on Frequency Analysis of Cardiac Sounds. *IEEE Transactions on Information Forensics and Security*, 2(3), 596–604. doi:10.1109/TIFS.2007.902922

Beritelli, F., & Spadaccini, A. (2009a). Heart sounds quality analysis for automatic cardiac biometry applications. *Proceedings of the 1st IEEE International Workshop on Information Forensics and Security*. 10.1109/WIFS.2009.5386481

Beritelli, F., & Spadaccini, A. (2009b). Human Identity Verification based on Mel Frequency Analysis of Digital Heart Sounds. *Proceedings of the 16th International Conference on Digital Signal Processing*. 10.1109/ICDSP.2009.5201109

Beritelli, F., & Spadaccini, A. (2010a). An improved biometric identification system based on heart sounds and gaussian mixture models. *Proceedings of the 2010 IEEE Workshop on Biometric Measurements and Systems for Security and Medical Applications*, 31–35 10.1109/BIOMS.2010.5610442

Beritelli, F., & Spadaccini, A. (2010b). A statistical approach to biometric identity verification based on heart sounds. *Proceedings of the Fourth International Conference on Emerging Security Information, Systems and Technologies (SECURWARE2010)*, 93–96. 10.1109/SECURWARE.2010.23

Berman, J. J. (2007). *Biomedical informatics*. Sudbury, MA: Jones and Barlett Publishers.

Bezdek, J. C., Hall, L. O., & Clarke, L. P. (1993). Review of MR image segmentation techniques using pattern recognition. *Medical Physics*, *20*(4), 1033–1048. doi:10.1118/1.597000 PMID:8413011

Bhadauria, H. S., & Dewal, M. L. (2011, March). Performance evaluation of curvelet and wavelet based denoising methods on brain computed tomography images. In *Emerging Trends in Electrical and Computer Technology (ICETECT), 2011 International Conference on* (pp. 666-670). IEEE. 10.1109/ICETECT.2011.5760201

Bhadauria, H. S., Dewal, M. L., & Anand, R. S. (2011, February). Comparative analysis of curvelet based techniques for denoising of computed tomography images. In *Devices and Communications (ICDeCom), 2011 International Conference on* (pp. 1-5). IEEE. 10.1109/ICDECOM.2011.5738492

Bhadauria, H. S., & Dewal, M. L. (2013). Medical image denoising using adaptive fusion of curvelet transform and total variation. *Computers & Electrical Engineering*, *39*(5), 1451–1460. doi:10.1016/j.compeleceng.2012.04.003

Bhaladhare & Jinwala. (2016). Novel Approaches for Privacy Preserving Data Mining in *k*-Anonymity Model. *Journal of Information Science and Engineering*, *32*(1), 63–78.

Bhardwaj, N., Nara, S., Malik, S., & Singh, G. (2016). *Analysis of ECG Signal Denoising Algorithms in DWT and EEMD Domains*. Academic Press.

Bhattacherjee, A., Roy, S., Paul, S., Roy, P., Kausar, N., & Dey, N. (2016). Classification Approach for Breast Cancer Detection Using Back Propagation Neural Network: A Study. In W. B. A. Karaa & N. Dey (Eds.), Biomedical Image Analysis and Mining Techniques for Improved Health Outcomes. Academic Press. doi:10.4018/978-1-4666-8811-7.ch010

Biswas, D., Das, P., Maji, P., Dey, N., & Chaudhuri, S. S. (2013). Visible watermarking within the region of non-interest of medical images based on fuzzy c-means nd harris corner detection. ICCSEA, SPPR, CSIA, WimoA, 161–168.

Biswas, D., Das, P., Maji, P., Dey, N., & Chaudhuri, S. S. (2013). Visible watermarking within the region of non-interest of medical images based on fuzzy c-means and Harris corner detection. *Proceedings of the Third International Conference on Computer Science, Engineering & Applications*, 161-168. 10.5121/csit.2013.3517

Biswas, S. K., & Mukherjee, D. P. (2011). Recognizing Architectural Distortion in Mammogram: A Multiscale Texture Modeling Approach with GMM. *IEEE Transactions on Biomedical Engineering*, *58*(7), 2023–2030. doi:10.1109/TBME.2011.2128870 PMID:21421429

Blanes, I., Serra-Sagrista, J., Marcellin, M. W., & Bartrina-Rapesta, J. (2012). Divide-and-conquer strategies for hyperspectral image processing: A review of their benefits and advantages. *IEEE Signal Processing Magazine*, *29*(3), 71–81. doi:10.1109/MSP.2011.2179416

Blazek & Schultz-Ehrenburg. (1996). Quantitative Photoplethysmography: Basic facts and examination tests for evaluating peripheral vascular functions. *VDI Verlog*, *20*(192).

Boliek, M. (2002). JPEG 2000 Image Coding System: Core Coding System. *ISO/IEC*.

Borie, J. C., Puech, W., & Dumas, M. (2004). Crypto-Compression System for Secure Transfer of Medical Images. *2nd Medical Image and Signal Processing*.

Borko Furht, A. E. (2010). *Hand Book on Cloud Computing*. London: Springer. doi:10.1007/978-1-4419-6524-0

Boujelben, A., Tmar, H., Abid, M., & Mnif, J. (2012). Automatic Diagnosis of Breast Tissue. *Advances in Cancer Management*. Retrieved from: http://www.intechopen.com

Boukerch, A., Xu, L., & El-Khatib, K. (2007). Trust-based security for wireless ad hoc and sensor networks. *Computer Communications*, *30*(11-12), 2413–2427. doi:10.1016/j.comcom.2007.04.022

Bowes, W. A. III, Corke, B. C., & Hulka, J. (1989). Pulse oximetry: A review of the theory, accuracy, and clinical applications. *Obstetrics and Gynecology*, *74*(3 Pt 2), 541–546. PMID:2668828

Boyinbode, O., Le, H., Mbogho, A., Takizawa, M., & Poliah, R. (2010). A Survey on Clustering Algorithms for Wireless Sensor Networks. Network-Based Information Systems (NBiS).

Bozeman, W. P., Myers, R. A., & Barish, R. A. (1997). Confirmation of pulse oximetry gap in carbonmonoxide poisoning. *Annals of Emergency Medicine*, *30*(5), 608–611. doi:10.1016/S0196-0644(97)70077-5 PMID:9360570

Brinkman, R., & Zijlstra, W. G. (1949). Determination and continuous registration of the percentage oxygen saturation in clinical conditions. *Archivum Chirurgicum Neerlandicum*, *1*, 177–183. PMID:15398660

Brown, M., & Vender, J. S. (1988). Noninvasive oxygen monitoring. *Critical Care Clinics*, *4*(3), 493–509. PMID:3063350

Bruce, E. N. (2001). *Biomedical signal processing and signal modeling*. John Wiley & Sons.

Bruylants, T., Munteanu, A., & Schelkens, P. (2015). Wavelet based volumetric medical image compression. *Signal Processing Image Communication*, *31*, 112–133. doi:10.1016/j.image.2014.12.007

Butun, I., Morgera, S. D., & Sankar, R. (2015). A Surevy of Intrusion Detection Systems in Wireless Sensor Networks. *IEEE Communications Surveys and Tutorials*, 266–282.

Canan, S., Ozbay, Y., & Karhk. (1997). A Method for Removing Low Varying Frequency Trend from ECG Signal. *Proc. IEEE 2nd International Biomedical Engineering Days*, 144-146.

Candès, E. J. (2003). What is... a curvelet? *Notices of the American Mathematical Society*, *50*(11), 1402–1403.

Candes, E. J., Demanet, L., Donoho, D., & Ying, L. (2006). Fast discrete curvelet transforms. *Multiscale Modeling & Simulation*, *5*(3), 861–899. doi:10.1137/05064182X

Carmen, S., Javier, D., Begoña, A., & Rangayyan, R. M. (2001). *Use Of 2d Linear Prediction Error to Detect Microcalcifications In Mammograms*. Retrieved from: citeseerx.ist.psu.edu/viewdoc/download

Carpenter, A. E., Jones, T. R., Lamprecht, M. R., Clarke, C., Kang, I. H., Friman, O., ... Golland, P. (2006). CellProfiler: Image analysis software for identifying and quantifying cell phenotypes. *Genome Biology*, *7*(10), R100. doi:10.1186/gb-2006-7-10-r100 PMID:17076895

Castro, D. (2009). *Explaining International Health IT Leadership*. Washington, DC: Information Technology and Innovation Foundation.

Castro, D. (2009). The Role of Information Technology in Medical Research. *Atlanta Conference on Science, Technology and Innovation Policy*.

Chakraborty, S., Chatterjee, S., Dey, N., Ashour, A. S., & Hassanien, A. E. (2017). Comparative approach between singular value decomposition and randomized singular value decomposition-based watermarking. In *Intelligent Techniques in Signal Processing for Multimedia Security* (pp. 133–149). Springer International Publishing. doi:10.1007/978-3-319-44790-2_7

Chang, C. H., Ko, H. J., & Chang, K. M. (2010). Cancellation of high-frequency noise in ECG signals using adaptive filter without external reference. In Biomedical Engineering and Informatics (BMEI), (Vol. 2, pp. 787-790). IEEE. doi:10.1109/BMEI.2010.5639953

Chang, Yu, & Vetterli. (2000). Adaptive wavelet thresholding for image Denoising and compression. *Image Processing, IEEE Transactions on, 9*(9), 1532–1546.

Chan, M. M., Chan, M. M., & Chan, E. D. (2003). What is the effect of finger nail polish on pulse oximetry? *Chest, 123*(6), 2163–2164. doi:10.1378/chest.123.6.2163 PMID:12796214

Chao, H., Hsu, C., & Miaou, S. (2002). A Data Hiding Technique with Authentication, Integration, and Confidentiality for Electronic Patient Records. *IEEE Transactions on Information Technology in Biomedicine, 6*(1), 46–53. doi:10.1109/4233.992161 PMID:11936596

Chaudhuri, P. N., Bhattacharya, S., & Dey, S. (2016). Baseline Drift Correction in Standard ECG Signals Using Centroid Based Approach. *International Journal of Engineering Science*, 3310.

Chen & Chien. (2011). Flexible Hardware Architecture of Hierarchical K-Means Clustering for Large Cluster Number. *IEEE Transactions on Very Large Scale Integration (VLSI) Systems, 19*(8).

Chen, H., Wu, H., & Zhou, X. (2007). Agent based Trust model in wireless sensor networks. In *Eight AICS International Conference on software Engineering, Artificial Intelligence, Networking and Parrallel Distributed Computing*. IEEE.

Chen, B.-W., Lin, P.-C., Wang, J.-F., Kuan, T.-W., & Chou, C.-H. (2015). Memory-efficient buffering method and enhanced reference template for embedded automatic speech recognition system. *IET Computers & Digital Techniques, 9*(3), 153–164. doi:10.1049/iet-cdt.2014.0008

Cheney, F. W. (1990). *The ASA closed claims study after the pulse oximeter* (Vol. 54). ASA Newsletter.

Cheng, G., Guo, S., Yang, Y., & Wang, Y. (2015). *Replication attack detection with monitor nodes in clustered wireless sensor networks. In IEEE 34th International Performance*. IPCCC.

Cheriguene, S., Azizi, N., Zemmal, N., Dey, N., Djellali, H., & Farah, N. (2016). Optimized Tumor Breast Cancer Classification Using Combining Random Subspace and Static Classifiers Selection Paradigms. In A. E. Hassanien, C. Grosan, & T. M. Fahmy (Eds.), *Applications of Intelligent Optimization in Biology and Medicine. Intelligent Systems Reference Library* (Vol. 96). Cham: Springer; doi:10.1007/978-3-319-21212-8_13

Cheung, S., Chiu, D., & Ho, C. (2008). The Use of Digital Watermarking for Intelligence Multimedia Document Distribution. *Journal of Theoretical and Applied Electronic Commerce Research, 3*(3), 103–118. doi:10.4067/S0718-18762008000200008

Chiu, D., Hung, P., Cheng, V., & Kafeza, E. (2007, January). Protecting the Exchange of Medical Images in Healthcare Process Integration with Web Services. In *System Sciences, 2007. HICSS 2007. 40th Annual Hawaii International Conference on* (pp. 131 – 131). IEEE. 10.1109/HICSS.2007.451

Chiu, H. S., & Lui, K. (2006). DelPHI: Wormhole Detection Mechanism for Ad Hoc Wireless Networks. *Proceedings of International Symposium on Wireless Pervasive Computing*. 10.1109/ISWPC.2006.1613586

Choudhry, M. S., Puri, A., & Kapoor, R. (2016). Removal of baseline wander from ECG signal using cascaded Empirical Mode Decomposition and morphological functions. In Signal Processing and Integrated Networks (SPIN), (pp. 769-774). IEEE. doi:10.1109/SPIN.2016.7566803

Claessens, J., Dem, V., Cock, D., Preneel, B., & Vandewalle, J. (2002). On the Security of Today's On-line Electronic Banking Systems. *Computers & Security, 21*(3), 253–265. doi:10.1016/S0167-4048(02)00312-7

Coatrieux, G., Maitre, H., Sankur, B., Rolland, Y. & Collorec, R. (2000). Relevance of Watermarking in Medical Imaging. *Proceedings of Information Technology Applications in Biomedicine*, 250 – 255.

Cohen, A., & Wardsworth, N. A. (1972). Light emitting diode skin reflectance oximeter. *Medical & Biological Engineering, 10*(3), 385–391. doi:10.1007/BF02474218 PMID:5043486

Collection Development Manual of the National Library of Medicine. (2004). 4th ed.). Bethesda, MD: U.S. Dept. of Health and Human Services, Public Health Service, National Institutes of Health, National Library of Medicine.

Conn, J. (2011). *Tricare reports data breach affecting 4.9 million patients.* Retrieved from http://www.modernhealthcare.com/article/20110929/NEWS/110929951

Cote, J., Goldstein, E. A., Buschman, W. H., & Hoaglin, D. C. (1988). The effect of nail polish on pulse oximetry. *Anesthesia and Analgesia, 67*(7), 683–686. PMID:3382042

Cox, I., Miller, M., & Bloom, J. (2000). Watermarking Applications and Their Properties. *Proceedings of the International Conference on Information Technology: Coding and Computing – ITCC 2000, 6 – 10.*

Cox, I., Miller, M., Bloom, J., Fridrich, J., & Kalker, T. (2007). *Digital Watermarking and Steganography.* Burlington: Elsevier.

Craigen, D., Diakun-Thibault, N., & Purse, R. (2014). Defining Cyber security. *Technology Innovation Management Review., 4*(10), 13–21.

Daemen, J., & Rijmen, V. (2011). *The design of Rijndael: AES - the advanced encryption standard.* Berlin: Springer.

Dahab, D. A., Ghoniemy, D. S. A., & Selim, G. A. (2012). Automated brain tumour detection and identification using image processing and probabilistic neural network techniques. *International Journal of Image Processing and Visual Communication, 1*(2), 1–8.

Dai, Y., & Wang, X. (2012). Medical Image Encryption based on a Composition of Logistic Maps and Chebyshev Maps. *IEEE International Conference on Information and Automation.* 10.1109/ICInfA.2012.6246810

Dalenius, T., & Reiss, S. P. (1982). Data-Swapping: A Technique for Disclosure Control. *Journal of Statistical Planning and Inference, 6*(1), 73–85. doi:10.1016/0378-3758(82)90058-1

Das, H., Jena, A. K., Nayak, J., Naik, B., & Behera, H. S. (2015). A Novel PSO Based Back Propagation Learning-MLP (PSO-BP-MLP) for Classification. In Computational Intelligence in Data Mining: Vol. 2. Smart Innovation, Systems and Technologies. Springer. doi:10.1007/978-81-322-2208-8_42

Das, H., Naik, B., Pati, B., & Panigrahi, C. R. (2014). A Survey on Virtual Sensor Networks Framework. *International Journal of Grid and Distributed Computing, 7*(5), 121–130. doi:10.14257/ijgdc.2014.7.5.11

Das, Jena, Nayak, & Naik, & Behera. (2014). A novel PSO based back propagation learning-MLP (PSO-BP-MLP) for Classification. *Computational Intelligence in Data Mining, 2,* 461–471.

Das, S., & Kundu, M. (2012, January). Effective Management of Medical Information through a Novel Blind Watermarking Technique. *Journal of Medical Systems, 36*(5), 3339–3351. doi:10.100710916-012-9827-1 PMID:22327385

Daubechies, I. (1998). Orthonormal bases of compactly supported wavelets. *Communications on Pure and Applied Mathematics, 41*(7), 909–996. doi:10.1002/cpa.3160410705

Daugman, J. G. (1989). Entropy reduction and decorrelation in visual coding by oriented neural receptive fields. *IEEE Transactions on Biomedical Engineering, 36*(1), 107–114. doi:10.1109/10.16456 PMID:2921058

Davis, J. (2017). *Phishing attack on UC Davis Health breaches data on 15,000 patients.* Retrieved From http://www.healthcareitnews.com/news/phishing-attack-uc-davis-health-breaches-data-15000-patients

Debi Acharjya & Anitha. (2017). A Comparative Study of Statistical and Rough Computing Models in Predictive Data Analysis. *International Journal of Ambient Computing and Intelligence Archive, 8*(2), 32-51.

Debi Acharjya. (2017). A Comparative Study of Statistical and Rough Computing Models in Predictive Data Analysis. *International Journal of Ambient Computing and Intelligence, 8*(2). doi:10.4018/IJACI.2017040103

Deka, B., & Bora, P. K. (2013). Removal of correlated speckle noise using sparse and Over complete representations. *Biomedical Signal Processing and Control, 8*(6), 520–533. doi:10.1016/j.bspc.2013.05.003

Denning, D. E. R. (1982). *Cryptography and data Security.* Menlo Park, CA: Addison-Wesley Publishing Company.

Dettori, L., & Semler, L. (2007). A comparison of wavelet, ridgelet, and curvelet-based texture classification algorithms in computed tomography. *Computers in Biology and Medicine, 37*(4), 486–498. doi:10.1016/j.compbiomed.2006.08.002 PMID:17054933

Devarakonda, A. K. (2010). Security Solutions to the Phishing: Transactions Based on Security Questions and Image. In BAIP 2010, CCIS 70 (pp. 565–567). Springer-Verlag.

Dey & Santhi. (n.d.). Intelligent Techniques in Signal Processing for Multimedia Security. In *Computational Intelligence and Complexity.* Springer.

Dey, Ashour, Chakraborty, & Hassanien. (2016). Watermarking in Bio-medical Signal Processing. *Intelligent Techniques in Signal Processing For Multimedia Security.* DOI: 0.1007/978-3-319-44790-2_16

Dey, N., & Dey, G. (2014). Feature Analysis of Blind Watermarked Electromyogram Signal in Wireless Telemonitoring. Concepts and Trends in healthcare Information Systems, 205-229.

Dey, N., & Samanta, S. (2014). Optimization of Watermarking In Biomedical Signal, with 38 Reads. LAP Lambert Academic Publishing.

Dey, N., Acharjee, S., Biswas, D., & Das, A. (2012). Medical Information Embedding in Compressed Watermarked Intravascular Ultrasound Video. *Scientific Bulletin of the Politehnica University of Timisoara - Transactions on Electronics and Communications, 57*(71).

Dey, N., Biswas, D., Roy, A., Das, A., & Chaudhuri, S. (2012, November). DWT-DCT-SVD based Blind Watermarking Technique of Gray Image in Electrooculogram Signal. *2012 12th International Conference on Intelligent Systems Design and Applications (ISDA),* 680 – 685.

Dey, N., Nandi, B., Das, P., Das, A., & Chaudhuri, S. S. (2013). Retention of Electrocardiogram Features Insignificantly Devalorized As an Effect Of Watermarking For a Multi-Modal Biometric Authentication System. Advances in Biometrics for Secure Human Authentication and Recognition, 175–212. Doi:10.1201/b1624710

Dey, Samanta, Yang, Das, & Choudhuri. (2005). Optimization of scaling factors in electrocardiogram signal watermarking using cuckoo Search. *International Journal of Bio Inspire Computation.*

Dey, Solanki, & Tamane. (2017). *Privacy and Security Policies in Big Data.* IGI Global.

Dey, N. (2017). *Intelligent Techniques in Signal Processing for Multimedia Security, book* (V. Santhi, Ed.). Springer International Publishing. doi:10.1007/978-3-319-44790-2

Dey, N., Ashour, A. S., Chakraborty, S., Banerjee, S., Gospodinova, E., Gospodinov, M., & Hassanien, A. E. (2017). Watermarking in Biomedical Signal Processing. In *Intelligent Techniques in Signal Processing for Multimedia Security* (pp. 345–369). Springer International Publishing. doi:10.1007/978-3-319-44790-2_16

Dey, N., Das, P., Chaudhuri, S. S., & Das, A. (2012). Feature analysis for the blind-watermarked electroencephalogram signal in wireless telemonitoring using Alattar's method. *Proceedings of the Fifth International Conference on Security of Information and Networks,* 87-94. 10.1145/2388576.2388588

Dey, N., Das, P., Roy, A., Das, A., & Chaudhuri, S. (2012, October). DWT-DCT-SVD based Intravascular Ultrasound Video Watermarking. *2012 World Congress on Information and Communication Technologies (WICT)*, 224 – 229. 10.1109/WICT.2012.6409079

Dey, N., Mukhopadhyay, S., Das, A., & Chaudhuri, S. S. (2012, July). Analysis of P-QRS-T Components Modified by Blind Watermarking Technique Within the Electrocardiogram Signal for Authentication in Wireless Telecardiology Using DWT. *I.J. Image. Graphics and Signal Processing, 2012*(7), 33–46. doi:10.5815/ijigsp.2012.07.04

Dey, N., Pal, M., & Das, A. (2012, May-June). A Session Based Blind Watermarking Technique within the NROI of Retinal Fundus Images for Authentication Using DWT, Spread Spectrum and Harris Corner Detection. *International Journal of Modern Engineering Research, 2*(3), 749–757.

Dey, N., Roy, A. B., Das, A., & Chaudhuri, S. S. (2012). Stationary Wavelet Transformation Based Self-recovery of Blind-Watermark from Electrocardiogram Signal in Wireless Telecardiology. In S. M. Thampi, A. Y. Zomaya, T. Strufe, J. M. Alcaraz Calero, & T. Thomas (Eds.), *Recent Trends in Computer Networks and Distributed Systems Security. SNDS 2012. Communications in Computer and Information Science* (Vol. 335). Berlin: Springer. doi:10.1007/978-3-642-34135-9_35

Dhanelekshmi, M., & Phadke, A. C. (2013). Classification Using Fractal Features of Well-Defined Mammographic Masses Using Power Spectral Analysis and Differential Box Counting Approaches. In L. Suresh, S. Dash, & B. Panigrahi (Eds.), *Artificial Intelligence and Evolutionary Algorithms in Engineering Systems, Advances in Intelligent Systems and Computing* (pp. 495–501). New Delhi: Springer. doi:10.1007/978-81-322-2135-7_53

Dhillon, Jindal, & Girdhar. (2011). A novel threshold technique for Eliminating speckle noise in ultrasound images. *International Conference on Modelling, Simulation and Control, IPCSIT, 10.*

DICOM. (2009). *DICOM, Part 15: Security and System Management Profiles, PS 3.15 – 2009.* Available: ftp://medical.nema.org/medical/dicom/2009/

Dimpi Rani, R. K. (2014, June). A Comparative Study of SaaS, PaaS and IaaS in Cloud Computing. *International Journal of Advanced Research in Computer Science and Software Engineering, 4*(6), 458–461.

Do, M. N. (2002). *Directional multiresolution image representations.* Academic Press.

Do, M. N., & Vetterli, M. (2005). The contourlet transform: An efficient directional multiresolution image representation. *IEEE Transactions on Image Processing, 14*(12), 2091–2106. doi:10.1109/TIP.2005.859376 PMID:16370462

Domingo-Ferrer, J., & Torra, V. (2008). A critique of k-anonymity and some of its enhancements, *Proc. of the 3rd International Conference on Availability, Reliability and Security (ARES)*, 990–993. 10.1109/ARES.2008.97

Donoho, D. L. (1995). De-noising by soft thresholding. *IEEE Trans. Inform. Theory, 41*(3), 613–627.

Donoho, D. L., & Johnstone, I. M. (1995). Adapt to unknown smoothness via wavelet shrinkage. *Journal of the American Statistical Association, 90*(432), 1200–1224. doi:10.1080/01621459.1995.10476626

Dorsch, J. A., & Dorsch, S. E. (1999). *Understanding anaesthesia equipment.* Baltimore, MD: Williams & Wilkins.

Dragomiretskiy, K., & Zosso, D. (2014). Variational Mode Decomposition. IEEE Trans. On Signal Processing, 62(3), 531-544.

Du, J., & Li, J. (2011). A Study of Security Routing Protocol For Wireless Sensor Network. *International Conference on Instrumentation, Measurement, Computer, Communication and Control.* 10.1109/IMCCC.2011.68

ECG Signal. (n.d.). Available at https://physionet.org/physiobank/database/#ecg

El-Baz, A. (2012). Appearance based diagnostic system for early assessment of malignant lung nodules. Proceedings of the IEEE International Conference on Image Processing, 533-536.

El-Baz. (2010). Appearance analysis for diagnosing malignant lung nodules. *Proceedings of the International Symposium on Biomedical Imaging.*

Elhaj, F. A., Salim, N., Harris, A. R., Swee, T. T., & Ahmed, T. (2016). Arrhythmia recognition and classification using combined linear and nonlinear features of ECG signals. *Computer Methods and Programs in Biomedicine, 127,* 52–63. doi:10.1016/j.cmpb.2015.12.024 PMID:27000289

Elhossiny, I., Nirmeen, A. E., & Fatma, A. O. (2016). *Task Scheduling Algorithm in Cloud Computing Environment Based on Cloud Pricing Models. In Computer Applications & Research.* Cairo, Egypt: IEEE.

Eltoukhy, M. M., Faye, I., & Samir, B. B. (2010). A comparison of wavelet and curvelet for breast cancer diagnosis in digital mammogram. *Computers in Biology and Medicine, 40*(4), 384–391. doi:10.1016/j.compbiomed.2010.02.002 PMID:20163793

English, C., & Nixon, P. (2002). Dynamic trust Models for Ubiquitous Computing Environment. Presented at *Ubicomp security workshop.*

Epstein, M., Pasieka, M., Lord, W., Wong, S., & Mankovich, N. (1998). Security for the Digital Information Age of Medicine: Issues, Applications, and Implementation. *Journal of Digital Imaging, 11*(1), 33–44. doi:10.1007/BF03168723 PMID:9502324

Esmaeili, M., Rabbani, H., & Dehnavi, A. M. (2012). Automatic optic disk boundary extraction by the use of curvelet transform and deformable variational level set model. *Pattern Recognition, 45*(7), 2832–2842. doi:10.1016/j.patcog.2012.01.002

Evangelista, G. (1994). Comb and multiplexed wavelet transforms and their applications to signal processing. *IEEE Transactions on Signal Processing, 42*(2), 292–303. doi:10.1109/78.275603

Falconer, R. J., & Robinson, B. J. (1990). Comparison of pulse oximeters: Accuracy at low arterial pressure in volunteers. *BJA, 65*(4), 552–557. doi:10.1093/bja/65.4.552 PMID:2248826

Fallahpour, M., Megias, D., & Ghanbari, M. (2009). High Capacity, Reversible Data Hiding in Medical Images. *16th IEEE International Conference on Image Processing (ICIP),* 4241 – 4244. 10.1109/ICIP.2009.5413711

Fan, L., & Jin, H. (2015). A Practical Framework for Privacy-Preserving Data Analytics. In *Proceedings of the 24th International Conference on World Wide Web (WWW '15).* ACM. 10.1145/2736277.2741122

Fan, Z., & Hongbin, Z. (2004). Digital Watermarking Capacity and Reliability. *Proceedings of IEEE International Conference on e-Commerce Technology,* 295 – 298.

Fatema, N., Brad, R. (2014). Security Requirements, Counterattacks and Projects in Healthcare Applications Using WSNs - A Review. *International Journal of Computer Networking and Communication, 2*(2).

Fatemian, S. Z., & Hatzinakos, D. (n.d.). *A Wavelet-Based Approach to Electrocardiogram (ECG) and Phonocardiogram (PCG)* (Ph.D. dissertation). University.

Fatemi, M., & Sameni, R. (2017). An Online Subspace Denoising Algorithm for Maternal ECG Removal from Fetal ECG Signals. *Iranian Journal of Science and Technology. Transaction of Electrical Engineering, 41*(1), 65–79. doi:10.100740998-017-0018-4

Fatima, A. (2011). E-Banking Security Issues – Is There A Solution in Biometrics? *Journal of Internet Banking and Commerce, 16*(2).

Fengli, Z., & Yijing, B. (2015). ARM-Based Privacy Preserving for Medical Data Publishing. *Cloud Computing and Security: First International Conference, ICCCS 2015*. 10.1007/978-3-319-27051-7_6

Feng, R., Xu, X., Zhou, X., & Wan, J. (2011). A trust evaluation algorithm for wireless sensor networks based on node behaviors and d-s evidence theory. *Sensors (Basel)*, *11*(12), 1345–1360. doi:10.3390110201345 PMID:22319355

Fluck, R. R. Jr, Schroeder, C., Frani, G., Kropf, B., & Engbretson, B. (2003). Does ambient light affect the accuracy of pulse oximetry? *Respiratory Care*, *48*(7), 677–680. PMID:12841858

Foo, S. Y., Stuart, G., Harvey, B., & Meyer-Baese, A. (2002). Neural network-based EKG pattern recognition. *Engineering Applications of Artificial Intelligence*, *15*(3), 253–260. doi:10.1016/S0952-1976(02)00041-6

Forouzan, B. A. (2008). *Data Communications & Networking* (4th ed.). New York: Tata McGraw- Hill.

Forouzan, B. A., & Mukhopadhyay, D. (2010). *Cryptography and Network Security*. New Delhi, India: Tata McGraw-Hill.

Fotopoulos, V., Stavrinou, M., & Skodras, A. (2008). Medical Image Authentication and Self-Correction through an Adaptive Reversible Watermarking Technique. *8th IEEE International Conference on Bioinformatics and Bioengineering*, 1 – 5. 10.1109/BIBE.2008.4696803

Fouad, K. M., Hassan, M. B., & Hassan, M. F. (2016). User Authentication based on Dynamic Keystroke Recognition. International Journal of Ambient Computing and Intelligence, 7(2).

Fouad, K. M., Hassan, B. M., & Hassan, M. F. (2017). User Authentication based on Dynamic Keystroke Recognition. *Identity Theft: Breakthroughs in Research and Practice*. doi:10.4018/978-1-5225-0808-3.ch019

Francesco, E., Giuliana, D., & Luigi, P. (2009). A Summary of Genomic Databases: Overview and Discussion. In Bioinformatice Data and Applications (pp. 37-59). Springer-Verlag Berlin.

Franciszek, B., Bram, S., Chirstian, W., Michael, G., Klaus, M.-H., Hans-peter, M., ... Joanna, P. (2017). MiMSeg - an algorithm for automated detection of tumor tissue on NMR apparent diffusion coefficient maps. *Information Sciences*, *384*, 235–248. doi:10.1016/j.ins.2016.07.052

Frazier, M. W. (1999). *An Introduction to Wavelets through Linear Algebra*. Springer.

Fung, Wang, Chen, & Yu. (2010). Privacy-preserving data publishing: A survey of recent developments. *ACM Comput. Surv., 42*(4). DOI:10.1145/1749603.1749605

G¨orgel, P., Sertbas, A., & Ucan, O. N. (2013). Mammographical mass detection and Classification using local seed region growing–spherical wavelet transform (lsrg–swt) hybrid Scheme. *Computers in Biology and Medicine*, *43*(6), 765–774. doi:10.1016/j.compbiomed.2013.03.008 PMID:23668353

Galbally, J., & Satta, R. (2015). *Three-dimensional and two-and-a-half-dimensional face recognition spoofing using three-dimensional printed models*. IET Biometrics.

Galldiks, N., Law, I., Pope, W. B., Arbizu, J., & Langen, K.-J. (2017). The use of amino acid PET and conventional MRI for monitoring of brain tumor therapy. *NeuroImage. Clinical*, *13*, 386–394. doi:10.1016/j.nicl.2016.12.020 PMID:28116231

Game, S., & Raut, C. (2014). Protocols for Detection of Node Replication Attack on Wireless sensor Network. *IOSR Journal of Computer Engineering*, 1-11.

Ganong, W. F. (1993). *Review of Medical Physiology* (16th ed.). Norwalk, CT: Appleton & Lange.

Gautam, G., & Kumar, D. (2013). Biometric system for heart sound using wavelet based feature set. *International conference on communication & signal processing (ICCSP)*, 551-555. 10.1109/iccsp.2013.6577115

Gebäck, T., & Koumoutsakos, P. (2009). Edge detection in microscopy images using curvelets. *BMC Bioinformatics*, *10*(1), 75. doi:10.1186/1471-2105-10-75 PMID:19257905

George Suciu, S. H. (2013). Cloud Computing as Evolution of Distributed Computing – A Case Study. *Informações Econômicas*, *7*(4), 109–122. doi:10.12948/issn14531305/17.4.2013.10

Georgia, M. A. D., Kaffashi, F., Jacono, R. J., & Loparo, K. A. (2015). Information Technology in Critical Care: Review of Monitoring and Data Acquisition Systems for Patient Care and Research. *The Scientific World Journal*. PMID:25734185

Ghada, S., Ahmad, K., & Qosai, K. (2016). ANN and Adaboost application for automatic detection of microcalcifications in breast cancer. *The Egyptian Journal of Radiology and Nuclear Medicine*, *47*(4), 1803–1814. doi:10.1016/j.ejrnm.2016.08.020

Gholami, B., Norton, I., Eberlin, L. S., & Nathalie, Y. R. A. (2013). A statistical modeling approach for tumour-type identification in surgical neuropathology using tissue mass spectrometry imaging. *IEEE Journal of Biomedical and Health Informatics*, *17*(3), 734–744. doi:10.1109/JBHI.2013.2250983 PMID:24592474

Giokoumaki, A., Pavlopoulos, S., & Koutouris, D. (2003). A Medical Image Watermarking Scheme based on Wavelet Transform. *IEEE International Conference on Engineering in Medicine and Biology Society*. 10.1109/IEMBS.2003.1279900

Gladis PushpaRathi, V.P., & Palani, S. (2011). Detection and characterization of brain tumour using segmentation based on HSOM Wavelet packet feature spaces and ANN. *Proceedings of the Third International Conference on Electronics Computer Technology.*

Goldberg, A. (1988). *A History of Personal Workstations*. New York: ACM Press.

Goldie, E. A. G. (1942). Device for continuous indication of oxygen saturation of circulating blood in man. *Journal of Scientific Instruments*, *19*(2), 23–25. doi:10.1088/0950-7671/19/2/302

Goldwasser, S., & Bellare, M. (2008, July). *Lecture Notes on Cryptography*. Available: http://cseweb.ucsd.edu/~mihir/papers/gb.html

Gonzalez, R. C., & Woods, R. E. (2008). *Digital Image Processing* (3rd ed.). Pearson.

Google. (2017, June 29). *Archival Cloud Storage: Nearline & Coldline*. Retrieved July 12, 2017, from Google Cloud Platform: https://cloud.google.com/storage/archival/

Gorgel, P., Sertbas, A., & Ucan, O. N. (2010). A wavelet-based mammographic image denoising and enhancement with homomorphic filtering. *Journal of Medical Systems*, *34*(6), 993–1002. doi:10.100710916-009-9316-3 PMID:20703608

Graham, S., Estrin, D., Horvitz, E., Kohane, I., Mynatt, E., & Sim, I. (2010). *Information Technology Research Challenges for Healthcare: From Discovery to Delivery:* A white paper prepared for the Computing Community Consortium committee of the Computing Research Association. Retrieved From http://cra.org/ccc/resources/ccc-led-whitepapers/

Greenes, R. A., & Shortliffe, E. H. (1990). *Medical informatics. An emerging academic discipline and institutional priority. JAMA, 263(8)*, 1114–1120. Retrieved from https://www.ncbi.nlm.nih.gov/pubmed/2405204

Greiner, A. C., & Knebel, E. (2003). *Health Professions Education: A Bridge to Quality. Institute of Medicine of the national Academice*. Washington, DC: The National Academies Press.

Guo, Q., Ruiz, V., Shao, J., & Guo, F. (2005). A novel approach to mass abnormality detection in mammographic images. In *Proceedings of the IASTED International Conference on Biomedical Engineering*, (pp. 180-185). Innsbruck, Austria: IASTED.

Guo, L., Zhao, L., Wu, Y., Li, Y., Xu, G., & Yan, Q. (2011). Tumour detection in MR images using one-class immune feature weighted SVMs. *IEEE Transactions on Magnetics*, *47*(10), 3849–3852. doi:10.1109/TMAG.2011.2158520

Gupta, V., & Sangroha, D. (n.d.). Protection against packet drop attack. *Advances in Engineering and Technology Research (ICAETR)*.

Guttman, B., & Roback, E. (1995). *An Introduction to Computer Security: The NIST Handbook*. Special Publication. doi:10.6028/NIST.SP.800-12

Habib. (2009). *A Computer aided diagnosis system (CAD) for the detection of pulmonary nodules on CT scans*. Systems and Biomedical Engineering Department, Faculty of Engineering, Cairo University.

Hajeb Mohammad Alipour, S., Rabbani, H., & Akhlaghi, M. R. (2012). Diabetic retinopathy grading by digital curvelet transform. *Computational and Mathematical Methods in Medicine*. PMID:23056148

Hanning, C. D., & Alexander-Williams, J. M. (1995). Pulse oximetry: A practical review. *BMJ (Clinical Research Ed.)*, *311*(7001), 367–370. doi:10.1136/bmj.311.7001.367 PMID:7640545

Heady, R., & Lugar, G. (2009). *MThe architecture of a network level intrusion detection system. Technical report*. Albuquerque, NM: University of New Mexico.

He, G., Sugahara, T., Miyamoto, Y., Fujinaga, T., Noguchi, H., Izumi, S., ... Yoshimoto, M. (2012, August). A 40 nm 144 mW VLSI Processor for Real-Time 60-kWord Continuous Speech Recognition. *IEEE Transactions on Circuits and Systems. I, Regular Papers*, *59*(8).

Henschke, C., Sone, S., Markowitz, S., Tockman, M., Shaham, D., Zulueta, J., ... Klippenstein, D. (2005). *CT screening for lung cancer: The relationship of disease stage to tumor size Lung Cancer*. Elsevier.

Herndon, C., Uzelac, I., Farmer, J. T., & Fenton, F. (2016). Computational ECG reconstruction and validation from high-resolution optical mapping. In *Computing in Cardiology Conference (CinC)*, (pp. 713-716). IEEE.

Hertzman, B. (1938). The blood supply of various skin areas as estimated by the photoelectric plethysmograph. *The American Journal of Physiology*, *124*(2), 328–340. doi:10.1152/ajplegacy.1938.124.2.328

HHS.gov. (2013). *Summary of the HIPAA Security Rule*. Retrieved July 29, 2017, from https://www.hhs.gov/hipaa/for-professionals/security/laws-regulations/index.html

Ho, J. (2009). Distributed Detection Replica Cluster Attacks in Sensor Networks using Sequential Analysis. *Distributed Detection Replica Cluster Performance, Computing and Commuincations Conference (IPCCC)*.

Horecker, L. (1943). The absorption spectra of hemoglobin and its derivatives in the visible and near infra-red regions. *The Journal of Biological Chemistry*, *148*(1), 173–183.

Huang, H. K. (2014). *PACS and Imaging Informatics: Basic Principles and Applications* (2nd ed.). Wiley-Blackwell.

Huang, M., Yang, W., Wu, Y., Jiang, J., Chen, W., & Feng, Q. (2014). Brain tumour segmentation based on local independent projection-based classification. *IEEE Transactions on Biomedical Engineering*, *61*(10), 2633–2645. doi:10.1109/TBME.2014.2325410 PMID:24860022

Huch, A., Huch, R., Konig, V., Neuman, M. R., Parker, D., Yount, J., & Lubbers, D. (1988). Limitations of pulse oximetry (letter). *Lancet*, *1*(8581), 357–358. doi:10.1016/S0140-6736(88)91148-8 PMID:2893163

Ipsita Kar, I., Parida, R. N. R., & Das, H. (2016). *Energy aware scheduling using genetic algorithm in cloud data centers. In Electrical, Electronics, and Optimization Techniques*. IEEE.

Ishmanov, F. (2013). *Trust management system in wireless sensor networks: Design considerations and research challenges*. Transaction Emerging Telecommunication Techno.

Isin, A., Direkoglu, C., & Sah, M. (2016). Review of MRI-based brain tumour image segmentation using deep learning methods. *Procedia Computer Science, 102*, 317–324. doi:10.1016/j.procs.2016.09.407

ITIE Academy. (n.d.). *Blog on Biomedical Signal & Medical Image Processing*. Retrieved From http://itieacademy.com/resources/blog/biomedical-signal-image-processing/

Ivan, C., & Iker, G. (2017). MRI segmentation fusion for brain tumor detection. *Information Fusion, 36*, 1–9. doi:10.1016/j.inffus.2016.10.003

Iwano, S., Nakamura, T., Kamioka, Y., & Ishigaki, T. (2005). Computer-aided diagnosis: a shape classification of pulmonary nodules imaged by high-resolution CT. Computerized Medical Imaging and Graphics, 29(7), 565-570.

Iwano, S., Nakamura, T., Kamioka, Y., Ikeda, M., & Ishigaki, T. (2008). Computer-aided differentiation of malignant from benign solitary pulmonary nodules imaged by high-resolution CT. *Computerized Medical Imaging and Graphics, 32*(5), 416–422. doi:10.1016/j.compmedimag.2008.04.001 PMID:18501556

Jafari-Khouzani, K. (2014). MRI upsampling using feature-based nonlocal means approach. *IEEE Transactions on Medical Imaging, 33*(10), 1969–1985. doi:10.1109/TMI.2014.2329271 PMID:24951680

Jain, A. K., Ross, A. A., & Prabhakar, S. (2004). An introduction to biometric recognition. *IEEE Transactions on Circuits and Systems for Video Technology, 14*(2), 4–20. doi:10.1109/TCSVT.2003.818349

Jain, S., Gupta, S., & Thenua, R. K. (2011). A review on Advancements in Biometrics. *International Journal of Electronics and Computer Science Engineering., 1*(3), 853–859.

Janakiraman, S., Rajasoundaran, S., & Narayanasamy, P. (2012). *The Model- Dynamic and Flexible Intrusion Detection Protocol for high error rate Wireless Sensor Networks based on data flow. In Computing, Communication and Applications (ICCCA)*. Tamilnadu, India: Dindigul.

Javid, T. (2017). How to read DICOM in R with oro.dicom? [Web log post]. Retrieved July 30, 2017, from http://tariqjavid72.blogspot.com/2017/07/how-to-read-dicom-in-r-with-orodicom.html

Jayanthi, A. (2016). *Ransomware encrypts data at Keck Medicine of USC, no ransom paid*. Retrieved From http://www.beckershospitalreview.com/healthcare-information-technology/ransomware-encrypts-data-at-keck-medicine-of-usc-no-ransom-paid.html

Jiang, I., Han, G., Wang, F., Shu, L., & Guizani, M. (2015). Han, G.; Wang, F.; Shu, L.; Guizani, M. "An efficient distributed trust model for wireless sensor networks. *IEEE Transactions on Parallel and Distributed Systems, 26*(5), 1228–1237. doi:10.1109/TPDS.2014.2320505

Jin, H., & Chen, H. (2008). Lightweight session key management scheme in Sensor Networks. Future Generation Communication and Networking (FGCN 2007).

Jorgenson, D., Pyette, P., Davis, J. M., Connor, K., & Blobel, B. (2014). *HL7 Standard: Privacy, Access and Security Services (PASS) - Security Labeling Service, Release 1.0*. Academic Press.

Jos'e, V. (2010). Adaptive non-local means denoising of MR images with spatially varying noise Levels. *Journal of Magnetic Resonance Imaging, 31*(1), 192–203. doi:10.1002/jmri.22003 PMID:20027588

José, S., & Bruno, R. (2005). *Detection of Calcifications in Digital Mammograms using Wavelet Analysis and Contrast Enhancement*. Paper presented at IEEE conference, Faro, Portugal.

Jubran, A. (1999). Pulse oximetry. *Critical Care (London, England)*, *3*(2), R11–R17. doi:10.1186/cc341 PMID:11094477

Judith Hurwitz, R. B. (2016). cloud Computing for dummies (J. Jensen, Ed.). Delhi, India: A Wiley Brand.

Kabi, K. K., Saha, B. J., Pradhan, C., & Bisoi, A. K. (2014). Comparative Study of Image Encryption using 2D Chaotic Map. *IEEE International Conference on Information Systems and Computer Networks*, 105-108. 10.1109/ICIS-CON.2014.6965227

Kabir, M. E., Wang, H., & Bertino, E. (2011, February). Md. Enamul Kabir, Hua Wang, and Elisa Bertino: (2011). Efficient systematic clustering method for *k*-anonymization. *Acta Informatica*, *48*(1), 51–66. doi:10.100700236-010-0131-6

Kalakota, R., & Whinston, A. B. (1997). Electronic Commerce- A Manager's Guide. Addison Wesley.

Kalayci, T., & Ozdamar, O. (1995). Wavelet preprocessing for automated neural network detection of EEG spikes. *IEEE Engineering in Medicine and Biology Magazine*, *14*(2), 160–166. doi:10.1109/51.376754

Kalker, T., Haitsma, J., & Oostveen, J. C. (2001). Issues with Digital Watermarking and Perceptual Hashing. *Proceedings of the Society for Photo-Instrumentation Engineers*, *4518*, 189–197. doi:10.1117/12.448203

Kalman, R., & Bucy, R. (1961). New results in linear filtering and prediction theory. *Trans. ASME, Ser. D. Journal of Basic Engineering*, *83*(1), 95–107. doi:10.1115/1.3658902

Kania, M., Fereniec, M., & Maniewski, R. (2007). Wavelet denoising for multi-lead high resolution ECG signals. *Measurement Science Review*, *7*(4), 30–33.

Karahaliou, A., Skiadopoulos, S., Boniatis, I., Sakellaropoulos, P., Likaki, E., Panayiotakis, G., & Costaridou, L. (2007). Texture analysis of tissue surrounding microcalcifications on mammograms for breast cancer diagnosis. *The British Journal of Radiology*, *80*(956), 648–656. doi:10.1259/bjr/30415751 PMID:17621604

Karuna, K., & Joshi, A. (2013). Automatic detection and severity analysis of brain tumours using GUI in MATLAB. *International Journal of Research in Engineering and Technology*, *2*(10), 586–594. doi:10.15623/ijret.2013.0210092

Kasper, D. L. (2005). *Harrison's principles of internal medicine* (16th ed.). McGraw-Hill.

Kaur, N. (2015). A survey on online banking system attacks and its countermeasures. *International Journal of Computer Science and Network Security, 15*(3).

Kaur, M., Sarangal, M., & Nayyar, A. (2014). Simulation of Jelly Fish Periodic Attack in Mobile Ad hoc Networks. *International Journal of Computer Trends and Technology*, *15*(1), 20–22. doi:10.14445/22312803/IJCTT-V15P104

Kausar, N., Abdullah, A., Samir, B. B., Palaniappan, S., AlGhamdi, B. S., & Dey, N. (2016). Ensemble Clustering Algorithm with Supervised Classification of Clinical Data for Early Diagnosis of Coronary Artery Disease. *Journal of Medical Imaging and Health Informatics*, *6*(1), 78–87. doi:10.1166/jmihi.2016.1593

Kekre, H. B., Sarode, T., Gharge, S., & Raut, K. (2010). Detection of Cancer Using Vector Quantization for Segmentation. *International Journal of Computers and Applications*, *4*(9), 14–19. doi:10.5120/856-1199

Khadra, L., Dickhaus, H., & Lipp, A. (1993). Representations of ECG—late potentials in the time treauencvDlane. *Journal of Medical Engineering & Technology*, *17*(6), 228–231. doi:10.3109/03091909309006330 PMID:8169939

Khadra, L., Matalgah, M., El-Asir, B., & Mawagdeh, S. (1991). The wavelet transform and its applications to phonocardiogram signal analysis. *Medical Informatics*, *16*(3), 271–277. doi:10.3109/14639239109025301 PMID:1758216

Kifer, D., & Gehrke, J. (2006). Injecting Utility into Anonymized Data Sets. *Proc. ACM SIGMOD Int'l Conf. Management of Data (SIGMOD)*, 217-228.

Kim, J. G., Xia, M., & Liu, H. (2005, March/April). Extinction coefficients of hemoglobin for near-infrared spectroscopy of tissue. *IEEE Engineering in Medicine and Biology Magazine*, *24*(2), 118–121. doi:10.1109/MEMB.2005.1411359 PMID:15825855

Kishore, P., Rao, M., Prasad, C., & Kumar, D. (2016, March). Medical Image Watermarking: Run through Review. *Journal of Engineering and Applied Sciences (Asian Research Publishing Network)*, *11*(5), 2882–2899.

Kissel, R. (Ed.). (2013). *Glossary of key information security terms*. Gaithersburg, MD: U.S. Dept. of Commerce, National Institute of Standards and Technology. doi:10.6028/NIST.IR.7298r2

Kouras, N., Boutana, D., & Bendir, M. (2012). Wavelet based segmentation and time-frequency characterization of some abnormal heart sound signals. *24th International conference on microelectronics (ICM)*, 1-4.

Kowear, M. K., & Yadev, S. (2012). Brain tumour detection and segmentation using histogram thresholding. *International Journal of Engineering and Advanced Technology*, *1*(4), 16–20.

Kriti, V. J., Dey, N., & Kumar, V. (2016). PCA-PNN and PCA-SVM Based CAD Systems for Breast Density Classification. In Applications of Intelligent Optimization in Biology and Medicine. Springer.

Kuan, Wang, Wang, Lin, & Gu. (2012). VLSI Design of an SVM Learning Core on Sequential Minimal Optimization Algorithm. *IEEE Transactions on Very Large Scale Integration (VLSI) Systems, 20*(4).

Kumar, A., Mahapatra, K., Kabi, B., & Routray, A. (2015). A novel approach of Speech Emotion Recognition with prosody, quality and derived features using SVM classifier for a class of North-Eastern Languages. *IEEE 2nd International Conference on Recent Trends in Information Systems*.

Kumar, D., Carvalho, P., Antunes, M., Henriqus, J., Maldonado, M., Schmidt, R., & Habetha, J. (2006). Wavelet transform and simplicity based on heart murmurs and segmentation. *Computers in Cardiology*, *33*, 173–176.

Kundu, M., Nasipuri, M., & Basu, D. K. (2000). Knowledge-based ECG interpretation: A critical review. *Pattern Recognition*, *33*(3), 351–373. doi:10.1016/S0031-3203(99)00065-5

Kutscher, B., & Conn, J. (2014). *Chinese hackers hit Community Health Systems; others vulnerable*. Retrieved From http://www.modernhealthcare.com/article/20140818/NEWS/308189946

Kutter, M., & Petitcolas, F. (1999, January). A Fair Benchmark for Image Watermarking Systems. *Electronics Imaging'99. Security, and Watermarking of Multimedia Contents*, *3657*, 1–14.

Laine, A. F., Schuler, S., Fan, J., & Huda, W. (1994). Mammographic feature enhancement by multiscale analysis. *IEEE Transactions on Medical Imaging*, *13*(4), 725–740. doi:10.1109/42.363095 PMID:18218551

Lampson, B. (2004). Computer Security in the Real World. *IEEE Computer*, *37*(6), 37–46. doi:10.1109/MC.2004.17

Langelaar, G., Setyawan, I., & Lagendijk, R. (2000, September). Watermarking of Digital Image and Video Data – A State of Art Review. *IEEE Signal Processing Magazine*, *17*(5), 20–46. doi:10.1109/79.879337

Langton, J. A., & Hanning, C. D. (1990). Effect of motion artefact on pulse oximeters: Evaluation of four instruments and finger probes. *British Journal of Anaesthesia*, *65*(4), 564–570. doi:10.1093/bja/65.4.564 PMID:2248828

Lee, M. C., Wiemker, R., & Boroczky, L. (2010). Computer aided diagnosis of pulmonary nodules using a two-step approach for feature selection and classifier ensemble construction. *Artificial Intelligence in Medicine*, *50*(1), 43–53. doi:10.1016/j.artmed.2010.04.011 PMID:20570118

Lee, M. H., Shyu, K. K., Lee, P. L., Huang, C. M., & Chiu, Y. J. (2011). Hardware Implementation of EMD Using DSP and FPGA for Online Signal Processing. *IEEE Transactions on Industrial Electronics*, *58*(6), 2473–2481. doi:10.1109/TIE.2010.2060454

LeFevre, K., DeWitt, D. J., & Ramakrishnan, R. (2005). Incognito: efficient full-domain K-anonymity. In *Proceedings of the 2005 ACM SIGMOD international conference on Management of data (SIGMOD '05)*. ACM. 10.1145/1066157.1066164

LeFevre, K., DeWitt, D. J., & Ramakrishnan, R. (2006). Mondrian Multidimensional K-Anonymity. *22nd International Conference on Data Engineering (ICDE'06)*, 25-25. 10.1109/ICDE.2006.101

Li. (2004). Dynamics of vascular system. World scientific publishing Co. Pte. Ltd.

Li, C., Zheng, C., & Tai, C. (1995). Detection of ECG characteristic points using wavelet transforms. *IEEE Transactions on Biomedical Engineering*, *42*(1), 21–28. doi:10.1109/10.362922 PMID:7851927

Lichman, M. (2013). *UCI Machine Learning Repository*. Irvine, CA: University of California, School of Information and Computer Science.

Liew, S., & Zain, J. (2010). Experiment of Tamper Detection and Recovery Watermarking in PACS. *Second International Conference on Computer Research and Development*, 387 – 390. 10.1109/ICCRD.2010.37

Li, M., Koutsopoulos, I., & Poovendran, R. (2010). Optimal Jamming attack strategies and Network Defense Policies in Wireless Senosr Networks. *IEEE Transactions on Mobile Computing*, 1119–1133.

Lima, C. S., & Cardoso, M. J. (2007). *Phonocardiogram segmentation by using Hidden Markov Models*. The 5th IASTED International conference in Biomedical Engineering, BioMED, Austria.

Li, T., Li, N., Zhang, J., & Molloy, I. (2012). Slicing: A New Approach for Privacy Preserving Data Publishing. *IEEE Transactions on Knowledge and Data Engineering*, *24*(3), 561–574. doi:10.1109/TKDE.2010.236

Liu, L., & Miao, S. (2016, March). A New Image Encryption Algorithm based on Logistic Chaotic Map with Varying Parameter. *SpringerPlus*. PMID:27066326

Liu, S., Babbs, C. F., & Delp, E. J. (2001). Multiresolution Detection of Spiculated Lesions in Digital Mammograms. *IEEE Transactions on Image Processing*, *10*(6), 874–884. doi:10.1109/83.923284

Liu, X., & Li, S. (2010). An Adaptive Chaotic Encrypted Binary Image Digital Watermarking Algorithm based on DCT. *IEEE International Conference on Intelligent Computing and Integrated Systems*, 149-153. 10.1109/ICISS.2010.5656801

Li, Y., Zhang, A., & Liang, Y. (2013). *Improvement of leach Protocol for Wireless Sensor Networks. In Instrumentation, Measurement, Computer, Communication and Control*. Shenyang, China: IMCCC.

Lopez, J., & Roman, R. (2010). Trust management system for WSN: Best Practices. *Computer Communications*. doi:10.1016/j.comcom.2010.02.006

Lori, M. K. A. (2009). Data Security in the World of Cloud Computing. *IEEE Security & Privacy*, *7*(4), 1-64.

Lu, Wei, Qian, & Jain. (2001). Learning-based pulmonary nodule detection from mutliscale CT data. *IEEE Transactions on Medical Image*.

Lucier, B. J., Kallergi, M., Qian, W., DeVore, R. A., Clark, R. A., Saff, E. B., & Clarke, L. P. (1994). Wavelet compression and segmentation of digital mammograms. *Journal of Digital Imaging*, *7*(1), 27–38. doi:10.1007/BF03168476 PMID:8172976

M.D John Eng. (2014). *ROC Analysis: Web-based Calculator for ROC Curves*. Retrieved from http://www.rad.jhmi.edu/jeng/javarad/roc/JROCFITi.html

Machanavajjhala, A., Gehrke, J., Kifer, D., & Venkitasubramaniam, M. (2006). *ℓ*-Diversity: Privacy Beyond k-Anonymity. *Proc. Int'l Conf. Data Eng. (ICDE)*, 24.

Maglaveras, N., Stamkopoulos, T., Diamantaras, K., Pappas, C., & Strintzis, M. (1998). ECG pattern recognition and classification using non-linear transformations and neural networks: A review. *International Journal of Medical Informatics*, *52*(1), 191–208. doi:10.1016/S1386-5056(98)00138-5 PMID:9848416

Mahmood, A. (2015, July). *Adaptive Approaches for Medical Imaging Security* (Ph.D. Thesis). University of Guelph, Canada.

Mahmoodabadi, S. Z., Ahmadian, A., & Abolhasani, M. D. (2005). ECG feature extraction using Daubechies wavelets. In *Proceedings of the fifth IASTED International conference on Visualization, Imaging and Image Processing* (pp. 343-348). Academic Press.

Maidamwar & Chavhan. (2012). A Survey on Security Issues to Detect wormhole Attack in Wireless Sensor network. *International Journal on Ad Hoc Networking Systems*.

Maitra, I. K., Nag, S., & Bandopadhyay, S. (2011). *Techniques for preprocessing of digital mammogram*. Elsevier Computer Methods and Programs in Biomedicine; doi:10.1016/j.cmpb.2011.05.007

Ma, J., & Plonka, G. (2009). Computing with curvelets: From image processing to turbulent flows. *Computing in Science & Engineering*, *11*(2), 72–80. doi:10.1109/MCSE.2009.26

Maji, U., & Pal, S. (2016). Emperical mode decomposiiton vs varaiational mode decomposition on ECG signal processin: A comparative study. *International conference on advance in computing, communications and informatics (ICACCI)*, 1129-1134.

Majumder, S., Pal, S., & Dutta, P. K. (2009). A comparative study for disease identification from heart auscultation using FFT, cepstrum and DCT correlation coefficients. In *13th International conference on biomedical engineering IFMBE proceedings* (vol. 23). Springer. 10.1007/978-3-540-92841-6_185

Mallat, S. G. (1989). Multifrequency channel decompositions of images and wavelet models. *IEEE Transactions on Acoustics, Speech, and Signal Processing*, *37*(12), 2091–2110. doi:10.1109/29.45554

Mallet, S. G. (1989). A Theory for Multiresolution Signal Decomposition: The Wavelet Representation. *IEEE Transactions on Pattern Analysis and Machine Intelligence*, *11*(7), 674–693. doi:10.1109/34.192463

Manirajan, R., & Sathishkumar, R.K. (2015). Sleep/Wake Scheduling for Target Coverage Problem in Wireless Sensor Networks. *International Journal of Advanced Research in Computer and Communication Engineering*.

Marĉelja, S. (1980). Mathematical description of the responses of simple cortical cells. *JOSA*, *70*(11), 1297–1300. doi:10.1364/JOSA.70.001297 PMID:7463179

Martínez, J. P., Almeida, R., Olmos, S., Rocha, A. P., & Laguna, P. (2004). A wavelet-based ECG delineator: Evaluation on standard databases. *IEEE Transactions on Biomedical Engineering*, *51*(4), 570–581. doi:10.1109/TBME.2003.821031 PMID:15072211

Marx, V. (2013, June). Biology: The big challenges of big data. *Nature*, *498*(7453), 255–260. doi:10.1038/498255a PMID:23765498

Mateo, J., Torres, A. M., Aparicio, A., & Santos, J. L. (2016). An efficient method for ECG beat classification and correction of ectopic beats. *Computers & Electrical Engineering*, *53*, 219–229. doi:10.1016/j.compeleceng.2015.12.015

Matsubaraa, T., Ichikawa, T., Hara, T., Fujita, H., Kasai, S., Endo, T., & Iwase, T. (2003). Automated detection methods for architectural distortions around skinline and within mammary gland on mammograms. *International Congress Series*, *1256*, 950–955. doi:10.1016/S0531-5131(03)00496-5

Matsumoto, T., Matsumoto, H., Yamada, K., & Hoshino, S. (2002). Impact of artificial gummy fingers on fingerprint systems. *Proceedings of the Society for Photo-Instrumentation Engineers*, *4677*, 275–289. doi:10.1117/12.462719

MedPix™ Medical Image Database. (n.d.). Available at http://rad.usuhs.mil/medpix/medpix.html, https://medpix.nlm.nih.gov/home

Megalan, L. L., Ranjith, A., & Thandaiah, R. P. (2012). Analysis of Mammogram Images using Active Contour Segmentation process and Level Set Method. *International Journal of Emerging Technology and Advanced Engineering*, *2*(2), 204–207.

Mehdy, Ng, Shair, Md Saleh, & Gomes. (2017). *Artificial Neural Networks In Image Processing for Early Detection of Breast Cancer*. Hindawi Computational And Mathematical Methods in Medicine. 10.1155/2017/2610628\

Mencattini, A., Salmeri, M., Casti, P., & Pepe, M. L. (2011). Automatic breast masses boundary extraction in digital mammography using spatial fuzzy c-means clustering and active contour models. In *Proceedings of Conference on Medical Measurement and Applications, on Medical Imaging* (pp. 632-637). Academic Press. 10.1109/MeMeA.2011.5966747

Mencattini, A., Rabottino, G., Salmeri, M., Lojacono, R., & Colini, E. (2008). Breast Mass Segmentation in Mammographic Images by an Effective Region Growing Algorithm. In J. Blanc-Talon, S. Bourennane, W. Philips, D. Popescu, & P. Scheunders (Eds.), Lecture Notes in Computer Science: Vol. 5259. *Advanced Concepts for Intelligent Vision Systems* (pp. 948–957). Berlin: Springer. doi:10.1007/978-3-540-88458-3_86

Mendelson, Y. (1992). Pulse oximetry: Theory and applications for noninvasive monitoring. *Clinical Chemistry*, *38*(9), 1601–1607. PMID:1525987

Merrick, E. B., & Hayes, T. J. (1976). Continuous, non-invasive measurements of arterial blood oxygen levels. *Hewlett-packard J.*, *28*(2), 2–9.

Meste, O., Rix, H., Caminal, P., & Thakor, N. V. (1994). Ventricular late potentials characterization in time-frequency domain by means of a wavelet transform. *IEEE Transactions on Biomedical Engineering*, *41*(7), 625–634. doi:10.1109/10.301729 PMID:7927383

Mexiane, M. A. (2009). Current Concepts in imaging and management of the solitary pulmonary nodule. *Le Journal Medical Libanais*.

Meyer, Y. (1993). *Wavelets: Algorithm and Applications*. Philadelphia: Society for Industrial and Applied Mathematics, SIAM.

Mhetre, N. A., Deshpande, A. V., & Mahalle, P. N. (2016). Trust Management Model based on Fuzzy Approach for Ubiquitous Computing. *International Journal of Ambient Computing and Intelligence, 7*(2). doi:10.4018/IJACI.2016070102

Milchevski, A., & Gusev, M. (2017). Improved pipelined Wavelet implementation for filtering ECG signals. *Pattern Recognition Letters*, *95*, 85–90. doi:10.1016/j.patrec.2017.06.005

Millenson, M. L. (1997). *Demanding Medical Excellence*. Chicago: University of Chicago Press.

Miller, R. D. (2005). *Miller's anesthesia* (6th ed.). Philadelphia: Elsevier Churchill Livingstone.

Millikan, G. A. (1942). The oximeter, an instrument for measuring continuously the arterial saturation of arterial blood in man. *The Review of Scientific Instruments, 13*(10), 434–444. doi:10.1063/1.1769941

Ming-Sian, L., Chong-Guang, C., Chiun-Li, C., & Shih-Hua, L. (2013). Stroke area detection using texture feature and iFuzzyLDA algorithm. *International Journal of Electronics and Electrical Engineering, 1*(2), 1–4.

Mini, M. G., Devassia, V. P., & Thomas, T. (2004). Multiplexed wavelet transform technique for detection of micro-calcification in digitized mammograms. *Journal of Digital Imaging, 17*(4), 285–291. doi:10.100710278-004-1020-8 PMID:15692872

Miri, M. S., & Mahloojifar, A. (2011). Retinal image analysis using curvelet transform and multistructure elements morphology by reconstruction. *IEEE Transactions on Biomedical Engineering, 58*(5), 1183–1192. doi:10.1109/TBME.2010.2097599 PMID:21147592

Mishra, A. K., & Turuk, A. K. (2015). A Comparative Analysis of Node Replica Detection Scheme in Wireless Sensor Networks. *Journal of Network and Computer Applications*, 21–32.

Mohammad, Y., & Adnan, A. A. (2018). Improving Privacy and Security of User Data in Location Based Services. *Ambient Computing and Intelligence, 9*(1), 24.

Momani. (2008). *Bayesian Methods for modeling and Management of trust in WSN* (Ph.D Thesis). University of Technology, Sydney, Australia.

Mostafa, S., El-Sheimy, N., Tolba, A., Abdelkader, F., & Elhindy, H. (2010). Wavelet packets based blind watermarking for Medical Image Management. *The Open Biomedical Engineering Journal, 4*(1), 93–98. doi:10.2174/1874120701004010093 PMID:20700520

Mudigonda, N. R., Rangayyan, R. M., & Leo, D. J. E. (2001). Detection of Breast Masses in Mammograms by Density Slicing and Texture Flow-Field Analysis. *IEEE Transactions on Medical Imaging, 20*(12), 1225–1227. doi:10.1109/42.974917 PMID:11811822

Mukesh, K., & Mehta, K. K. (2011). A texture based tumour detection and automated segmentation of MRI brain tumour images. *International Journal of Computer Technology and Applications, 2*(4), 855–859.

Musen, M. A., & Bemmel, J. H. V. (1999). *Handbook of medical informatics.* Retrieved From: http://www.mieur.nl/mihandbook/r_3_3/handbook/homepage_self.htm

Mustaqeem, A., Javed, A., & Fatima, T. (2012). An efficient brain tumour detection algorithm using watershed and thresholding based segmentation. *International Journal of Image. Graphics and Signal Processing, 10,* 34–39. doi:10.5815/ijigsp.2012.10.05

Nagpal, S., Bhushan, S., & Mahajan, M. (2016, April). An Enhanced Digital Image Watermarking Scheme for Medical Images using Neural Network, DWT, and RSA. *International Journal of Modern Education and Computer Science, 4*(4), 46–56. doi:10.5815/ijmecs.2016.04.06

Nakagawa, S., Wang, L., & Ohtsuka, S. (2012, May). Speaker Identification and Verification by Combining MFCC and Phase Information. *IEEE Transactions on Audio, Speech, and Language Processing, 20*(4), 1085–1095. doi:10.1109/TASL.2011.2172422

Nakajima, K., Tamura, T., & Miike, H. (1996). Monitoring of heart and respiratory rates by photoplethysmography using a digital filtering technique. *Medical Engineering & Physics, 18*(5), 365–372. doi:10.1016/1350-4533(95)00066-6 PMID:8818134

Nambutdee, A., & Airphaiboon, S. (2015). Medical Image Encryption based on DCT-DWT Domain Combining 2D-Data Matrix Barcode. *IEEE Biomedical Engineering International Conference*.

Nandi, R. J., Nandi, A. K., Rangayyan, R. M., & Scutt, D. (2006). Classification of breast masses in mammograms using genetic programming and feature selection. *Medical & Biological Engineering & Computing, 44*(8), 683–694. doi:10.100711517-006-0077-6 PMID:16937210

Nandi, S., Roy, S., Dansana, J., Karaa, W. B. A., Ray, R., Chowdhury, S. R., ... Dey, N. (2014). Cellular automata based encrypted ECG-hash code generation: An application in inter human biometric authentication system. *International Journal of Computer Network and Information Security, 6*(11), 1–12. doi:10.5815/ijcnis.2014.11.01

National Research Council. (1997). *For the Record. Protecting electronic health information*. Washington, DC: National Academy Press.

Nazir, B., & Hasbullah, H. (2011). Dynamic sleep scheduling for minimizing delay in Wireless Sensor Network. *Electronics, Communications and Photonics Conference (SIECPC)*.

NEMA PS3 / ISO 12052. (2017). *Digital Imaging and Communications in Medicine (DICOM) Standard*. Rosslyn, VA, USA: National Electrical Manufacturers Association (NEMA). Available at http://medical.nema.org/

Nergiz, M. E., Atzori, M., & Clifton, C. (2007). Hiding the Presence of Individuals from Shared Databases. *Proc. ACM SIGMOD Int'l Conf. Management of Data (SIGMOD)*, 665-676. 10.1145/1247480.1247554

Nidhi, G., & Pritee, K. (2017). A non-invasive and adaptive CAD system to detect *brain tumor* from T2-weighted MRIs using customized Otsu's thresholding with prominent features and supervised learning. *Signal Processing Image Communication, 59*, 18–26. doi:10.1016/j.image.2017.05.013

NIH, Working Group on Biomedical Computing. (1999). *The Biomedical Information Science and Technology Initiative*. Retrieved from https://acd.od.nih.gov/documents/reports/060399_Biomed_Computing_WG_RPT.htm

Nikolaev, N. (2000). Wavelet Domain Wiener Filtering for ECG Denoising using improved Signal Estimate. *Proc. IEEE, 4*, 3578-3581. 10.1109/ICASSP.2000.860175

Ninghui, L., Tiancheng, L., & Venkatasubramanian, S. (2007). t-Closeness: Privacy beyond k-anonymity and ℓ-diversity. *Proceedings - International Conference on Data Engineering*, 106-115.

Nithya, R., & Santhi, B. (2011). Mammogram classification using maximum difference feature selection method. *Journal of Theoretical and Applied Information Technology, 33*(2), 197–204.

Nyeem, H., Boles, W., & Boyd, C. (2013). A Review of Medical Image Watermarking Requirements for Teleradiology. *Journal of Digital Imaging, 26*(2), 326–343. doi:10.100710278-012-9527-x PMID:22975883

O'Hara, M.E. (2017). Thousands of Patient Records Leaked in New York Hospital Data Breach. *News by NBC*. Retrieved From http://www.nbcnews.com/news/us-news/thousands-patient-records-leaked-hospital-data-breach-n756981

Obaidat, M. S. (1993). Phonocardiogram signal Analysis: Technique and performance comparison. *Journal of Medical Engineering & Technology, 17*(6), 221–227. doi:10.3109/03091909309006329 PMID:8169938

Oliver, A., Torrent, A., Xavier, L., Meritxell, T., Lidia, T., Melcior, S., ... Reyer, Z. (2012). Automatic microcalcification and cluster detection for digital and digitized mammograms. *Elsevier Knowledge Based System, 28*, 68–75. doi:10.1016/j.knosys.2011.11.021

Open Government Data (OGD) of India. (n.d.). Retrieved from https://data.gov.in/

Paar, C., & Pelzl, J. (2010). Hash Functions: Understanding Cryptography. Springer Berlin Heidelberg.

Paar, C., & Pelzl, J. (2010). *Understanding Cryptography: A Textbook for Students and Practitioners*. Berlin: Springer Berlin. doi:10.1007/978-3-642-04101-3

Pal, A., Dey, N., Samanta, S., Das, A., & Chaudhuri, S. (2013, December). A Hybrid Reversible Watermarking Technique for Color Biomedical Images. *IEEE International Conference on Computational Intelligence and Computing Research (ICCIC)*, 1 – 6. 10.1109/ICCIC.2013.6724177

Panigrahi, C. R., Sarkar, J. L., Pati, B., & Das, H. (2005). S2S: A Novel Approach for Source to Sink Node Communication in Wireless Sensor Networks. In R. Prasath, A. Vuppala, & T. Kathirvalavakumar (Eds.), Lecture Notes in Computer Science: Vol. 9468. *Mining Intelligence and Knowledge Exploration*. Cham: Springer.

Panigrahi, C. R., Sarkar, J., Pati, B., & Das, H. (2016). S2S: a novel approach for source to sink node communication in wireless sensor networks. *International Conference on Mining Intelligence and Knowledge Exploration*.

Panigrahi, C. R., Tiwary, M., Pati, B., & Das, H. (2016). Big Data and Cyber Foraging: Future Scope and Challenges. In B. Mishra, S. Dehuri, E. Kim, & G. N. Wang (Eds.), *Techniques and Environments for Big Data Analysis. Studies in Big Data* (Vol. 17). Cham: Springer. doi:10.1007/978-3-319-27520-8_5

Parah, S. A., Sheikh, J. A., Dey, N., & Bhat, G. M. (2017). Realization of a New Robust and Secure Watermarking Technique Using DC Coefficient Modification in Pixel Domain and Chaotic Encryption. *Journal of Global Information Management*, 25(4), 80–102. doi:10.4018/JGIM.2017100106

Parra, C., Iftekharuddin, K. M., & Kozma, R. (2003). Automated brain data segmentation and pattern recognition using ANN. *Proceedings of the Second International Conference on Computational Intelligence, Robotics and Autonomous Systems (CIRAS)*.

Patel, V. L., & Kaufman, D. R. (1998). Medical Informatics and the Science of Cognition. *Journal of the American Medical Informatics Association*, 5(6), 493–502. Retrieved From: https://www.ncbi.nlm.nih.gov/pmc/articles/PMC61330/

Pathak, G., Nishar, R., Shah, H., & Gajera, P. (2015). Study of Anti-Phishing on Internet Banking. *International Journal of Innovative and Emerging Research in Engineering*, 2(2).

Patil, R. C., & Bhalchandra, A. S. (2012). Brain tumour extraction from MRI images using MATLAB. *International Journal of Electronics, Communication & Soft Computing in Science & Engineering*, 2(1), 1–4.

Pelechrinis, K., Lliofotou, M., & Krishnamurthy, S. V. (2011). *Denial of Service Attacks in Wireless Networks: The Case of Jammers*. IEEE Communications Surverys & Tutorials.

Peng, Kuan, Lin, Wang, & Wu. (2015). Trainable and Low-Cost SMO Pattern Classifier Implemented via MCMC and SFBS Technologies. *IEEE Transactions on Very Large Scale Integration (VLSI) Systems*, 23(10).

Pennebaker, W. B., & Mitchell, J. L. (1992). *JPEG: Still image data compression standard*. Springer Science & Business Media.

Phadke, A. C., & Rege, P. P. (2013a). Classification of Architectural Distortion from Other Abnormalities in Mammograms. *International Journal of Application or Innovation in Engineering & Management*, 2(2), 42-48.

Phadke, A. C., & Rege, P. P. (2014). Comparison of SVM & ANN Classifier for Mammogram classification Using ICA features. *WIT Transaction on Information and Communication Technologies*, 49, 499-506. doi: 10.2495/ ICIE20130581

Phadke, A. C., & Rege, P. P. (2015). Fusion of Local and Global Features for Classification of Abnormality in Mammograms. *Sadhana - Academy Proceedings in Engineering Science*, 41(4), 385-395. doi: 10.1007/s12046-016-0482-y

Phadke, A. C., & Rege, P. P. (2013b). Detection and Classification of microcalcifications using Discrete Wavelet Transform. *International Journal of Emerging Trends and Technologies in Computer Science*, 2(4), 130–134.

Phua, K., Chen, J., Dat, T. H., & Shue, L. (2008). Heart sound as a biometric. *Pattern Recognition*, 41(3), 906–919. doi:10.1016/j.patcog.2007.07.018

PHYSIONET Homepage. (n.d.). Retrieved from https://physionet.org/physiobank/database/challenge/2016/training.zip

Pinkas, B. (2002). Cryptographic techniques for privacy-preserving data mining. *ACM SIGKDD Explorations Newsletter*, 4(2), 12–19. doi:10.1145/772862.772865

Pisarchik, A. N. (2012). *Chaotic Map Cryptography and Security. In Horizons in Computer Science* (Vol. 4). Springer.

Plummer, J. L., Zakaria, A. Z., Ilsley, A. H., Fronsko, R. R. L., & Owen, H. (1995). Evaluation of the influence of movement on saturation readings from pulse oximeters. *Anaesthesia*, 50(5), 423–426. doi:10.1111/j.1365-2044.1995. tb05998.x PMID:7793549

Polanyi, M. L., & Hehir, R. M. (1960). New reflection oximeter. *The Review of Scientific Instruments*, 31(4), 401–403. doi:10.1063/1.1716990

Pole, Y. (2002). Evolution of the pulse oximeter. *International Congress Series*, 1242, 137–142. doi:10.1016/S0531-5131(02)00803-8

Pradhan, C., Rath, S., & Bisoi, A. K. (2012). Non Blind Digital Watermarking Technique using DWT and Cross Chaos. *Elsevier International Conference on Communication, Computing & Security, Procedia Technology*, 6, 897-904. 10.1016/j.protcy.2012.10.109

Pradhan, C., Saha, B. J., & Kabi, K. K. (2014). Blind Watermarking Techniques using DCT and Arnold 2D Cat Map for Color Images. *IEEE International Conference on Communication and Signal Processing*, 26-30.

Preneel, B. (2003, February). *Analysis and Design of Cryptographic Hash Functions*. Ph.D. Thesis. Available: http://homes.esat.kuleuven.be/~preneel/phd_preneel_feb1993.pdf

Puech, W., & Rodrigues, J. M. (2005). Crypto-Compression of Medical Images by Selective Encryption of DCT. *European Signal Processing Conference*.

Que, D., Wen, X., & Chen, B. (2009). PACS Model based on Digital Watermarking and its Core Algorithms. *MIPPR 2009 – Medical Imaging, Parallel Processing of Images, and Optimization Techniques: 6th International Symposium on Multispectral Image Processing and Pattern Recognition*.

Rabbani, H., Nezafat, R., & Gazor, S. (2009). Wavelet-domain medical image denoising using bivariate laplacian mixture model. *IEEE Transactions on Biomedical Engineering*, 56(12), 2826–2837. doi:10.1109/TBME.2009.2028876 PMID:19695984

Rahman, M. Z. U., Shaik, R. A., & Reddy, D. R. K. (2011). Efficient sign based normalized adaptive filtering techniques for cancelation of artifacts in ECG signals: Application to wireless biotelemetry. *Signal Processing*, 91(2), 225–239. doi:10.1016/j.sigpro.2010.07.002

Rajesh, N., & Selvakumar, A. L. (2015). Hiding personalised anonymity of attributes using privacy preserving data mining. *Int. J. Advanced Intelligence Paradigms*, 7(3/4), 394–402. doi:10.1504/IJAIP.2015.073717

Rakshit, M., & Das, S. (2017). An improved EMD based ECG denoising method using adaptive switching mean filter. In *Signal Processing and Integrated Networks (SPIN), 4th International Conference on* (pp. 251-255). Academic Press. 10.1109/SPIN.2017.8049954

Rangayyan, R. M. (2002). *Biomedical signal analysis: A case study approach*. Singapore: John Wiley & Sons.

Rangayyan, R. M., Oloumi, F., & Nguyen, T. M. (2010). Fractal Analysis of Contours of Breast Masses in Mammograms via the Power Spectra of their Signatures. In *Proceedings of the 32nd Annual International Conference of the IEEE EMBS* (pp. 6737-6740). Buenos Aires, Argentina: IEEE. 10.1109/IEMBS.2010.5626017

Rao, P. T., Rao, S. K., Manikanta, G., & Kumar, S. R. (2016). Distinguishing normal and abnormal ECG signal. *Indian Journal of Science and Technology, 9*(10).

Rashed, E. A., Ismail, A. I., & Zaki, S. I. (2007). Multiresolution mammogram analysis in multilevel decomposition. *Elsevier Pattern Recognition Letters, 28*(2), 286–292. doi:10.1016/j.patrec.2006.07.010

Rassam, M. A., Maarof, M. A., & Zainal, A. (2012). A Survey of Intrusion Detection Schemes in Wireless Sensor Networks. *American Journal of Applied Sciences*.

Rathi, S., & Inamdar, V. (2012, August). Medical Images Authentication through Watermarking preserving ROI. *Health Informatics – International Journal (Toronto, Ont.), 1*(1), 27–42.

Reddy, K. A., Bai, J. R., George, B., Mohan, N. M., & Kumar, V. J. (2006). Virtual instrument for the measurement of haemo-dynamic parameters using photoplethysmograph. *Proc. 23rd Int. Conf. IEEE, IMTC-2006*, 1167-1171. 10.1109/IMTC.2006.328443

Reddy, K. A., George, B., Mohan, N. M., & Kumar, V. J. (2008, May). A Novel method of measurement of oxygen saturation in arterial blood. *Proc. 25rd IEEE International Instrumentation and Measurement Technology Conf., I2MTC-2008*, 1627-1630. 10.1109/IMTC.2008.4547304

Reddy, K. A., George, B., Mohan, N. M., & Kumar, V. J. (2009). A novel calibration–free method of measurement of oxygen saturation in arterial blood. *IEEE Transactions on Instrumentation and Measurement, 58*(5), 1699–1705. doi:10.1109/TIM.2009.2012934

Reddy, K. A., & Kumar, V. J. (2011, May). A Novel model based method of measurement of oxygen saturation in arterial blood. *Proc. of 28th IEEE International Instrumentation and Measurement Technology Conf., I2MTC-2011*, 1-5.

Ries, A. L., Prewitt, L. M., & Johnson, J. J. (1989). Skin color and ear oximetry. *Chest, 96*(2), 287–290. doi:10.1378/chest.96.2.287 PMID:2752811

Rindfleisch, T. C. (1997). Privacy, information technology, and health care. *Communications of the ACM, 40*(8), 93–100. doi:10.1145/257874.257896

Rioul, O., & Duhamel, P. (1992). Fast algorithms for discrete and continuous wavelet transforms. *IEEE Transactions on Information Theory, 38*(2), 569–586. doi:10.1109/18.119724

Roadknight, C., Parrott, L., Boyd, N., & Marshall, I. (2005). A novel approach for real-time data management in wireless sensor networks. *International Journal of Distributed Sensor Networks, 1*(2), 215–225. doi:10.1080/15501320590966468

Rouse, M. (2016, September). *What is your strategy for selectively performing data backup?* Retrieved 06 20, 2017, from TechTerget: http://searchdatabackup.techtarget.com/definition/backup

Roy, S., & Pal, A. (2017, February). A Robust Blind Hybrid Image Watermarking Scheme in RDWT-DCT domain using Arnold Scrambling. *Multimedia Tools and Applications, 76*(3), 3577–3616. doi:10.100711042-016-3902-4

Rudin, L. I., Osher, S., & Fatemi, E. (1992). Nonlinear total variation based noise removal algorithms. *Physica D. Nonlinear Phenomena, 60*(1-4), 259–268. doi:10.1016/0167-2789(92)90242-F

Ruotsalainen, P. (2010). Privacy and Security in Teleradiology. *European Journal of Radiology, 73*(1), 31–35. doi:10.1016/j.ejrad.2009.10.018 PMID:19914020

Rusch, T. L., Sankar, R., & Scharf, J. E. (1996). Signal processing methods for pulse oximetry. *Computers in Biology and Medicine, 26*(2), 143–159. doi:10.1016/0010-4825(95)00049-6 PMID:8904288

Ruttimann, U. E., Unser, M. A., Rio, D. E., & Rawlings, R. R. (1993, June). Use of the wavelet transform to investigate differences in brain PET images between patient groups. In *SPIE's 1993 International Symposium on Optics, Imaging, and Instrumentation* (pp. 192-203). International Society for Optics and Photonics. 10.1117/12.146601

Sabri & Kamoun. (2016). *GRPW-MuS-S: A Secure Enhanced Trust Aware Routing against Wormhole Attacks in Wireless Sensor Networks.* Academic Press.

Sadar, A. R., & Sahoo, R. R. (2014). Intelligent Intrusion Detection System in WSN. *Proceeding of the 3rd Int. Conf. on Front. of Intelligence Computation (FICTA).*

Saha, M., Naskar, M. K., & Chatterji, B. N. (2015). Soft, hard and block thresholding techniques for denoising of mammogram images. *Journal of the Institution of Electronics and Telecommunication Engineers, 61*(2), 186–191. doi:10.1080/03772063.2015.1009394

Sahambi, J. S., Tandon, S. N., & Bhatt, R. K. P. (1997). Using wavelet transforms for ECG characterization. An on-line digital signal processing system. *IEEE Engineering in Medicine and Biology Magazine, 16*(1), 77–83. doi:10.1109/51.566158 PMID:9058586

Sahay, A., & Pradhan, C. (2017). Multidimensional Comparative Analysis of Image Encryption using Gauss Iterated and Logistic Maps. *IEEE International Conference on Communication and Signal Processing.*

Saltanat, N., Hossain, M. A., & Alam, M. S. (2010). An Efficient Pixel Value based Mapping Scheme to Delineate Pectoral Muscle from Mammograms. In *Proceedings of the IEEE 2010 conference on Bio-inspired Computing: Theories and Applications (BIC-TA)* (pp. 1510-1517). IEEE. 10.1109/BICTA.2010.5645272

Salva-Garau, F., & Stojanovic, M. (2003). Multi-Cluster Protocol for Ad-hoc Mobile Underwater Acoustic Network. *IEEE OCEANS'03 Conference.*

Samarati, P. (2001). Protecting Respondents' Identities in Microdata Release. *IEEE Transactions on Knowledge and Data Engineering, 13*(6), 1010–1027. doi:10.1109/69.971193

Sameni, R. (2008). *Extraction of fetal cardiac signals from an array of maternal abdominal recordings* (Doctoral dissertation). Institute National Polytechnique de Grenoble-INPG, Sharif University of Technology (SUT).

Sampat, M. P., & Bovik, A. C. (2003). Detection of Spiculated Lesions in mammograms. In *Proceedings of the 25th Annual International Conference of the IEEE Engineering in Medicine and Biology Society* (Vol. 1, pp. 810-813). IEEE.

Sánchez, D., Batet, M., & Viejo, A. (2014, December). Utility-preserving privacy protection of textual healthcare documents. *Journal of Biomedical Informatics, 52*(C), 189–198. doi:10.1016/j.jbi.2014.06.008 PMID:24998814

Sara & Kumar. (2017). Breast Cancer Detection using Image Processing Techniques. *Oriental Journal of Computer Science & Technology, 10*(2), 391-399.

Sarin, S., Shields, D. A., Scurr, J. H., & Smith, P. D. C. (1992). Photoplethysmography: A valuable noninvasive tool in the assessment of venous dysfunction? *Journal of Vascular Surgery, 16*(2), 154–162. doi:10.1016/0741-5214(92)90103-F PMID:1495139

Saritha, C., Sukanya, V., & Murthy, Y. N. (2008). ECG signal analysis using wavelet transforms. *Bulg. J. Phys, 35*(1), 68–77.

Sarkar, Soumya, & Sangaiah. (2017). Configuring a Trusted Cloud Service Model for Smart City Exploration Using Hybrid Intelligence. *International Journal of Ambient Computing and Intelligence, 8*(3).

Sarkar, G., & Saha, G. (2010). Real Time Implementation of Speaker Identification System with Frame Picking Algorithm. *Elsevier, Procedia Computer Science, 2,* 173–180. doi:10.1016/j.procs.2010.11.022

Sarkar, J. L. (2015). A Novel Approach for Real-Time Data Management in Wireless Sensor Networks. *Proceedings of 3rd International Conference on Advanced Computing, Networking and Informatics,* 599-607.

Sarkar, M., Banerjee, S., & Badr, Y. (2017). Configuring a Trusted Cloud Service Model for Smart City Exploration Using Hybrid Intelligence. *International Journal of Ambient Computing and Intelligence, 8*(3). doi:10.4018/IJACI.2017070101

Sarkar, M., Banerjee, S., & Sangaiah, A. (2017). Trust Management Model based on Fuzzy Approach for Ubiquitous Computing. *International Journal of Ambient Computing and Intelligence.*

Sasidhar, B., Ramesh Babu, D. R., Ravishankar, M., & Bhaskar Rao, N. (2013). Automated Segmentation of Lung Regions using Morphological Operators in CT Scan. *International Journal of Scientific and Engineering Research, 4*(9).

Savner, J., & Gupta, V. (2014). *Clustering Of Mobile Ad-hoc Networks: An approach for black hole prevention. In Issues and Challenges in Intelligent Computing Techniques.* Ghaziabad, India: ICICT.

Saxena, S., Mishra, S., & Singh, M. (2013). Clustering Based on Node Density in Hetergeneous Under-Water Sensor Networks. *Information Technology and Computer Science,* 49-55.

Saxena, S. C., Kumar, V., & Hamde, S. T. (2002). Feature extraction from ECG signals using wavelet transforms for disease diagnostics. *International Journal of Systems Science, 33*(13), 1073–1085. doi:10.1080/00207720210167159

Sayan, C., Prasenjit, M., Arijit, K. P., Debalina, B., & Nilanjan, D. (2014) Reversible Color Image Watermarking Using Trigonometric Functions. Electronic Systems Signal Processing and Computing Technologies.

Sayed, A. M., Zaghloul, E., & Nassef, T. M. (2016). Automatic classification of breast tumours using features extracted from magnetic resonance images. *Procedia Computer Science, 95,* 392–398. doi:10.1016/j.procs.2016.09.350

Saylor, J. W. (2003). Neonatal and pediatric pulse oximetry. *Respiratory Care, 48*(4), 386–398. PMID:12667266

Scheller, M. S., Unger, R. J., & Kelner, M. J. (1986). Effects of intravenously administered dyes on pulse oximetry readings. *Anesthesiology, 65*(5), 550–552. doi:10.1097/00000542-198611000-00023 PMID:3777490

Schematic diagram of normal sinus rhythm for a human heart as seen on ECG. (n.d.). Wikimedia Common, Public Domain. Retrieved June 15, 2017, from http://commons.wikimedia.org/wiki/File%3ASinusRhythmLabels.svg

Schiff, S. J., Aldroubi, A., Unser, M., & Sato, S. (1994). Fast wavelet transformation of EEG. *Electroencephalography and Clinical Neurophysiology, 91*(6), 442–455. doi:10.1016/0013-4694(94)90165-1 PMID:7529683

Schiff, S. J., Milton, J. G., Heller, J., & Weinstein, S. L. (1994). Wavelet transforms and surrogate data for electroencephalographic spike and seizure localization. *Optical Engineering (Redondo Beach, Calif.), 33*(7), 2162–2169. doi:10.1117/12.172248

Schnapp, L. M., & Cohen, N. H. (1990). Pulse oximetry: Uses and abuses. *Chest, 98*(5), 1244–1250. doi:10.1378/chest.98.5.1244 PMID:2225973

Schneier, B. (1996). Applied Cryptography (2nd ed.). John Wiley & Sons, Inc.

Schwarz, D., Kasparek, T., Provaznik, I., & Jarkovsky, J. (2007). A deformable registration method for automated morphometry of MRI brain images in neuropsychiatric research. *IEEE Transactions on Medical Imaging*, *26*(4), 452–461. doi:10.1109/TMI.2007.892512 PMID:17427732

Secker, C., & Spiers, P. (1997). Accuracy of pulse oximetry in patients with low systematic vascular resistance. *Anaesthesia*, *52*(2), 127–130. doi:10.1111/j.1365-2044.1997.32-az0062.x PMID:9059094

Sehgal, A., Goel, S., Mangipudi, P., Mehra, A., & Tyagi, D. (2016). Automatic brain tumour segmentation and extraction in MR images. *Proceedings of the IEEE Conference on Advances in Signal Processing (CASP)*.

Sekelj, P., Johnson, A. L., Hoff, H. E., & Scherch, P. M. (1951). A photoelectric method for the determination of arterial oxygen saturation in man. *American Heart Journal*, *42*(6), 826–848. doi:10.1016/0002-8703(51)90055-5 PMID:14885079

Seshadri, N. P. G., Geethanjali, B., & Kumar, S. P. (2016). Analysis of heart sounds using time-frequency visual representations. *International Journal of Biomedical Engineering and Technology*, *21*(3), 205–228. doi:10.1504/IJBET.2016.078283

Severinghaus, J. W., & Astrup, P. B. (1986). History of blood gas analysis-VI. Oximetry. *Journal of Clinical Monitoring*, *2*(4), 270–288. doi:10.1007/BF02851177 PMID:3537215

Shah, S. A. A., Laude, A., Faye, I., & Tang, T. B. (2016). Automated microaneurysm detection in diabetic retinopathy using curvelettransform. *Journal of Biomedical Optics*, *21*(10), 101404–101404. doi:10.1117/1.JBO.21.10.101404 PMID:26868326

Shao, D. (2016). Noncontact monitoring of blood oxygen saturation using camera and dual-wavelength imaging system. *Biomedical Engineering. IEEE Transactions on*, *63*, 1091–1098. PMID:26415199

Sharma, M., Dwivedi, S., & Garg, R.B. (2015). Let It Encrypt (LIE). *International Journal of Computer Applications*, *128*(8).

Sharma, P., Diwakar, M., & Choudhary, S. (2012). Application of edge detector for brain tumour detection. *International Journal of Computers and Applications*, *58*(16), 21–25. doi:10.5120/9366-3820

Sharvari, C. T., Vijender, K. S., Pati, B., & Madhuri, S. J. (2017). The Basics of Big Data and Security Concerns. In *Privacy and Security Policies in Big Data*. IGI Global.

Shen, Yu, & Chuang. (2011). Computer Aided Diagnosis for Pulmonary Nodule on Low-Dose Computed Tomography (LDCT) using Density Features. In *Eighth International Conference Computer Graphics, Imaging and Visualization*. IEEE.

Shen, S., Sandham, W., Granat, M., & Sterr, A. (2005). MRI fuzzy segmentation of brain tissue using neighborhood attraction with neural network optimization. *IEEE Transactions on Information Technology in Biomedicine*, *9*(3), 459–467. doi:10.1109/TITB.2005.847500 PMID:16167700

Shen, S., Sandhom, W. A., Gramat, M. H., Dempsey, M. F., & Patterson, J. (2003). A new approach to brain tumour diagnosis using fuzzy logic based genetic programming. *Proceedings of the 25th Annual International Conference of the IEEE Engineering in Medicine and Biology Society*. 10.1109/IEMBS.2003.1279903

Shortliffe, E. H., & Blois, M. S. (2006). The computer meets medicine and biology: the emergence of a discipline. In E. H. Shortliffe (Ed.), *Biomedical informatics: computer applications in health care and biomedicine. Springer Science* (pp. 3–45). New York, NY: Business Media, LLC. doi:10.1007/0-387-36278-9_1

Sidi, A., Paulus, D. A., Rush, W., Gravenstein, N., & Davis, R. F. (1987). Methylene blue and indocyanine green artifactually lower pulse oximetry readings of oxygen saturation: Studies in dogs. *Journal of Clinical Monitoring*, *3*(4), 249–256. PMID:3681358

Simmons, G. J. (2016). Cryptology. In *Encyclopædia Britannica*. Encyclopædia Britannica, Inc.

Sinex, J. E. (1999). Pulse oximetry: Principles and limitations. *The American Journal of Emergency Medicine, 17*(1), 59–68. doi:10.1016/S0735-6757(99)90019-0 PMID:9928703

Singh, A. (2015, May). *Some New Techniques of Improved Wavelet Domain Watermarking for Medical Images* (Ph.D. Thesis). NIT Kurukshetra.

Singh, Kumar, Singh, & Mohan. (2017). *Medical Image Watermarking*. Springer.

Singh, Singh, & Singh. (2016). WHRT: A Hybrid Technique For Detecting Of Wormhole Attack in Wireless Sensor Networks. In *Mobile Information Systems*. Hindawi Publishing Corporation.

Singh. (2012). A Survey of different techniques for detection of wormhole attack in Wireless Sensor Network. *International Journal of Scientific and Engineering Research*.

Singh, M., & Das, R. (2012). *A survey of Different techniques for Detection of Wormhole attack in Wireless Sensor Network*. IJSER.

Singh, S., Singh, R., Singh, A., & Siddiqui, T. (2018). SVD-DCT based Medical Image Watermarking in NSCT Domain. In *Quantum Computing: An Environment for Intelligent Large Scale Real Application* (pp. 467–488). Cham: Springer. doi:10.1007/978-3-319-63639-9_20

Sing, K., & Singh, G. (2014). A trust based Approach for Detection and Prevention of Wormhole Attack in MANET. *International Journal of Computers and Applications*.

Solmaz, A., & Farshad, T. (2017). Detection of Brain Tumor in 3D MRI Images using Local Binary Patterns and Histogram Orientation Gradient. *Neurocomputing, 219*, 526–535. doi:10.1016/j.neucom.2016.09.051

Song, N., Qian, L., & Li, X. (2005). Wormhole Attacks Detection in Wireless Ad Hoc Networks: A Statistical Analysis Approach. *Proceedings of the 19th IEEE International Parallel and Distributed Processing Symposium*. 10.1109/IPDPS.2005.471

Sornmo, L. S., & Laguna, P. (2005). *Bioelectrical signal processing in cardiac and neurological applications*. Elsevier Academic Press.

Srinath, M. D., Rajasekaran, P. K., & Viswanathan, R. (2003). *Introduction to Statistical Signal Processing and Applications*. Pearson Education.

Stallings, W. (2011). *Cryptography and Network Security Principles and Practices (5th ed.)*. Pearson Education.

Stead, W. W., & Lin, S. H. (2009). *Computational Technology for Effective Health Care: Immediate Steps and Strategic Directions*. Washington, DC: The National Academies Press.

Strickland, R. N., & Hahn, H. I. (1996). Wavelet transforms for detecting microcalcifications in mammograms. *IEEE Transactions on Medical Imaging, 15*(2), 218–229. doi:10.1109/42.491423 PMID:18215904

Suchetha. (2017). A comparative analysis of EMD based filtering methods for 50 Hz noise cancellation in ECG signal. *Journal of Medical Informatics Unlocked, 8*(1), 54-59.

Suchetha, M. (2017). A Novel Approach for the Reduction of 50Hz Noise in Electrocardiogram using Variational Mode Decomposition. *International Journal of Current Signal Transduction Therapy, 12*(1), 39–48. doi:10.2174/1574362412666170307092351

Suckling, J., Astley, S., Betal, D., Cerneaz, N., Dance, D. R., & Kok, S. L. (1994). International Congress Series: Vol. 1069. *The Mammographic Image Analysis Society Digital Mammogram Database.* Excerpta Medica. Available at http://peipa.essex.ac.uk/info/mias.html

Sugantharathnam, M. D., & Manimegalai, D. (2011). The curvelet approach for denoising in various imaging modalities using different shrinkage rules. *International Journal of Computers and Applications, 29*(7), 36–42. doi:10.5120/3575-4933

Sun, H., Chen, W., & Gong, J. (2013). An improved empirical mode decomposition-wavelet algorithm for phonocardiogram signal denoising and its application in the first and second heart sound extraction. *6th International conference on Biomedical Engineering and informatics*, 187-191. 10.1109/BMEI.2013.6746931

Suzuki, K., Li, F., Sone, S., & Doi, K. (2005). Computer-aided diagnostic scheme for distinction between benign and malignant nodules in thoracic low-dose CT by use of massive training artificial neural network. IEEE Transactions on Medical Imaging, 24(9), 1138-1150.

Sweeney, L. (2002). k-Anonymity: A Model for Protecting Privacy. *Int'l J. Uncertainty Fuzziness and Knowledge-Based Systems, 10*(5), 557–570. doi:10.1142/S0218488502001648

Takatani, S., & Ling, J. (1994). Optical oximetry sensors for whole blood and tissue. *IEEE Engineering in Medicine and Biology Magazine, 13*(June/July), 347–357. doi:10.1109/51.294005

Tamane, S., Kumar Solanki, V., & Dey, N. (2017). Privacy and Security Policies in Big Data. *Advances in Information Security, Privacy, and Ethics*, 305.

Tamane, S., Solanki, V. K., & Dey, N. (2017). *Privacy and Security Policies in Big Data.* doi:10.4018/978-1-5225-2486-1

Tanachaiwiwat, S., Bhindwale, R., & Helmy, A. (2004). Location-centric isolation of misbehavior and trust routing in energy-constrained sensor networks. *IEEE International Conference on Performance, Computing, and Communications.* 10.1109/PCCC.2004.1395061

Tao, Y., Xiao, X., Li, J., & Zhang, D. (2008). On Anti-Corruption Privacy-Preserving Publication. In *Proc. ICDE 08* (pp. 725–734). IEEE Computer Society.

Tarkoma, S., Rothenberg, C.E., & Lagerspetz, E. (2011). Theory and Practice of Bloom Filters for Distributed Systems. *IEEE Communication Surveys & Tutorials*, 131-155.

Thakkar, F., & Srivastava, V. (2017, February). A Blind Medical Image Watermarking: DWT-SVD based Robust and Secure Approach for Telemedicine Applications. *Multimedia Tools and Applications, Springer, 76*(3), 3669–3697. doi:10.100711042-016-3928-7

Thanki, R. & Kothari, A. (2016, July). Digital Watermarking – Technical Art of Hiding a Message. *Intelligent Analysis of Multimedia Information*, 426 – 460.

Thanki, R., Borra, S., Dwivedi, V. & Borisagar, K. (2017). An Efficient Medical Image Watermarking Scheme based on FDCuT – DCT. *Engineering Science and Technology, an International Journal, 20*(4), 1366 – 1379.

The home of the U.S. Government's open data. (n.d.). Retrieved from https://www.data.gov/

Tian, Wang, Huang, Ning, Wang, Liu, & Tang. (2008). The digital database for breast ultrasound image. *Joint International Conference on Information Sciences.*

Timp, S., & Karssemeijer, N. (2004). A new 2D segmentation method based on dynamic programming applied to computer aided detection in mammography. *Medical Physics, 31*(5), 958–971. doi:10.1118/1.1688039 PMID:15191279

Tiwari, M., Veer Arya, K., Choudhari, R., & Sidharth Choudhary, K. (2009). Designing Intrusion Detection to Detect Black hole and Selective Forwarding Attack in WSN based on local Information. *Fourth International Conference on Computer Sciences and Convergence Information Technology.* 10.1109/ICCIT.2009.290

Tomar,G.S., Kevre,P., & Shrivastava,L. (2015). Energy model based performance analysis of cluster based wireless sensor network. *International Journal of Reliable Information and Assurance.*

Tripathi, M., Gaur, M. S., Laxmi, V., & Battula, R. B. (2013). Energy efficient LEACH-C protocol for wireless sensor network. *Third International Conference on Computational Intelligence and Information Technology (CIIT).* 10.1049/cp.2013.2620

Trivedi, N. S., Ghouri, A. F., Shah, N. K., Lai, E., & Barker, S. J. (1997). Effects of motion, ambient light and hypoperfusion on pulse oximeter function. *Journal of Clinical Anesthesia, 9*(3), 179–183. doi:10.1016/S0952-8180(97)00039-1 PMID:9172022

Tsiakoulis, P., Potamianos, A., & Dimitriadis, D. (2010, June). Spectral Moment Features Augmented by Low Order Cepstral Coefficients for Robust ASR. *IEEE Signal Processing Letters, 17*(6), 551–554. doi:10.1109/LSP.2010.2046349

Tyagi, S., & Subhranil, Q. P. R. (2017). Trust based Dynamic multicast group routing ensuring reliability for ubiquitous environment in MANET's. *International Journal of Ambient Computing and Intelligence, 8*(1). doi:10.4018/IJACI.2017010104

Under Standing E. C. G. Filtering. (2014). Retrieved from http://www.ems12lead.com/2014/03/10/understanding-ecg-filtering/#sthash.AlhGhgBb.dpuf

Unser, M. A., Aldroubi, A., & Gerfen, C. R. (1993, November). Multiresolution image registration procedure using spline pyramids. In *SPIE's 1993 International Symposium on Optics, Imaging, and Instrumentation* (pp. 160-170). International Society for Optics and Photonics.

Unser, M., & Aldroubi, A. (1996). A review of wavelets in biomedical applications. *Proceedings of the IEEE, 84*(4), 626–638. doi:10.1109/5.488704

Unser, M., Aldroubi, A., & Eden, M. (1992). On the asymptotic convergence of B-spline wavelets to Gabor functions. *IEEE Transactions on Information Theory, 38*(2), 864–872. doi:10.1109/18.119742

US Government. (1996, July). *The Health Insurance Portability and Accountability Act (HIPAA).* Available: https://www.hhs.gov/hipaa/index.html

US Government. (2010, October). *Code of Federal Regulations – Title 45, subtitle A – Department of Health and Human Services, part 164 – Security and Privacy.* Available: https://www.gpo.gov/fdsys/pkg/CFR-2010-title45-vol1/pdf/CFR-2010-title45-vol1.pdf

Varshney, T., Sharma, T., & Sharma, P. (2014). *Implementation of Watchdog Protocol with AODV in Mobile Ad Hoc Network. In Communication Systems and Network Technologies.* Bhopal, India: CSNT.

Venkatram, N., Reddy, L., & Kishore, P. (2014, August). Blind Medical Image Watermarking with LWT-SVD for Telemedicine Applications. *WSEAS Transactions on Signal Processing, 10,* 288–300.

Verkruysse, W., Bartula, M., Bresch, E., Rocque, M., Meftah, M., & Kirenko, I. (2017). Calibration of contactless pulse oximetry. *Anesthesia and Analgesia, 124*(1), 136–145. doi:10.1213/ANE.0000000000001381 PMID:27258081

Vibha, S. V., & Rege, P. P. (2007). Malignancy texture classification in digital mammograms based on Chebyshev moments and log polar transformation. *ICGST-BIME Journal, 7*(1), 29–35.

Vijai Anand, S. K. (2010). *Segmentation coupled textural feature classification for lung tumor prediction*. ICCCCT. doi:10.1109/ICCCCT.2010.5670607

Voloshynovskiy, S., Koval, O., Beekhof, F., & Pun, T. (2009, January). Conception and Limits of Robust Perceptual Hashing: towards Side Information assisted Hash Functions. Media Forensics and Security. doi:10.1117/12.805919

Von Borries, R. F., Pierluissi, J. H., & Nazeran, H. (2006). Wavelet transform-based ECG baseline drift removal for body surface potential mapping. In Engineering in Medicine and Biology Society, (pp. 3891-3894). IEEE.

Wang, H., Huang, L., & Zhao, X. (2007). Automated detection of masses in digital mammograms based on pyramid. In *Proceedings of the 2007 International Conference on Wavelet Analysis and Pattern Recognition* (pp. 2-4). Beijing, China: Academic Press. 10.1109/ICWAPR.2007.4420660

Wang, L., Zhu, M., Deng, L., & Yuan, X. (2010). Automatic pectoral muscle boundary detection in mammograms based on Markov chain and active contour model. *Journal of Zhejiang University-Science C (Computers & Electronics), 11*(2), 111-118.

Wang, P., Kim, Y., & Soh, C. B. (2005). Feature extraction based on mel-scaled wavelet transform for heart sound analysis. *IEEE Engineering in medicine and biology 27th annual conference*, 7572-7575. 10.1109/IEMBS.2005.1616264

Wang, P., Kim, Y., Ling, L. H., & Soh, C. B. (2005). First heart sound detection for phonocardiogram segmentation. *IEEE Engineering in medical and biology 27th annual conference*, 5519-5522. 10.1109/IEMBS.2005.1615733

Wang, Q., Ding, Q., Zhang, Z., & Ding, L. (2008). Digital Image Encryption Research based on DWT and Chaos. *IEEE International Conference on Natural Computation*, 494-498. 10.1109/ICNC.2008.105

Wang, T. C., & Karayiannis, N. B. (1998). Detection of Microcalcifications in Digital Mammograms Using Wavelets. *IEEE Transactions on Medical Imaging, 17*(4), 498–509. doi:10.1109/42.730395 PMID:9845306

Webster, J. G. (1997). *Design of pulse oximeters*. Taylor & Francis Group. doi:10.1887/0750304677

Welch, J., Ford, P., Teplick, R., & Rubsamen, R. (1991). The Massachusetts General Hospital-Marquette Foundation hemodynamic and electrocardiographic database–comprehensive collection of critical care waveforms. *Clinical Monitoring, 7*(1), 96–97.

Weng, L., Amsaleg, L., & Furon, T. (2016). Privacy-Preserving Outsourced Media Search. *IEEE Transactions on Knowledge and Data Engineering, 28*(10), 2738–2751. doi:10.1109/TKDE.2016.2587258

Wheeler, D., & Needham, R. (1995). TEA, a tiny encryption algorithm. In *Proceedings of the 1995 Fast Software Encryption Workshop*. Springer-Verlag.

Whitcher, B. (2015). Rigorous - DICOM Input / Output [R package oro.dicom version 0.5.0]. Retrieved July 31, 2017, from https://CRAN.R-project.org/package=oro.dicom

White, P. F., & Boyle, W. A. (1989). Nail polish and oximetry. *Anesthesia and Analgesia, 68*(4), 546–547. doi:10.1213/00000539-198904000-00030 PMID:2929991

Widrow, B., Glover, J. R., McCool, J. M., Kaunitz, J., Williams, C. S., Hearn, R. H., ... Goodlin, R. C. (1975). Adaptive noise canceling: Principles and applications. *Proceedings of the IEEE, 63*(12), 692–1716. doi:10.1109/PROC.1975.10036

Widrow, B., & Stearns, S. D. (2000). *Adaptive Signal Processing*. Englewood Cliffs, NJ: Prentice Hall International.

Wiener, N. (1949). *Extrapolation, Interpolation and Smoothing of Stationary Time Series with Engineering Applications*. Wiley.

Williams, A. J. (1998). ABC of oxygen: Assessing and interpreting arterial blood gases and acid-base balance. *BMJ (Clinical Research Ed.), 317*(7167), 1213–1216. doi:10.1136/bmj.317.7167.1213 PMID:9794863

Wood, E. H., & Geraci, J. E. (1949). Photoelectric determination of arterial oxygen saturation in man. *The Journal of Laboratory and Clinical Medicine, 34*, 387–401. PMID:18113925

Wukitsch, M. W., Petterson, M. T., Tobler, D. R., & Pologe, J. A. (1988). Pulse oximetry: Analysis of theory, technology, and practice. *Journal of Clinical Monitoring, 4*(4), 290–301. doi:10.1007/BF01617328 PMID:3057122

Wu, X., & Memon, N. (1997). Context-based, adaptive, lossless image coding. *IEEE Transactions on Communications, 45*(4), 437–444. doi:10.1109/26.585919

Xia, D., & Vlajic, N. (2007). *Near-Optimal Node Clustering in Wireless sensor Networks for Environment Monitoring.* Niagara Falls, Canada: Advanced Information Networking and Applications. doi:10.1109/AINA.2007.97

Xiao, X., & Tao, Y. (2006). Personalized privacy preservation. *Proc. Of ACM International Conference on Management of Data (SIGMOD).*

Xiao, X., & Tao, Y. (2007). m-invariance: Towards privacy preserving re-publication of dynamic datasets. *ACM SIGMOD International Conference on Management of Data*, 689–700. 10.1145/1247480.1247556

Xiaoyun, D., Xuejia, L., & Hongbo, Y. (2004). *Collisions for Hash Functions MD4, MD5, HAVAL-128, and RIPEMD.* Academic Press.

Xu, L., & Yan, Y. (2004). Wavelet based Removal of Sinusoidal Interference from a Signal. *Measurement Science & Technology, 15*(9), 1779–1786. doi:10.1088/0957-0233/15/9/015

Yadav, T., & Mehra, R. (2016). Denoising and SNR improvement of ECG signals using wavelet based techniques. In *Next Generation Computing Technologies (NGCT)*, (pp. 678-682). IEEE. doi:10.1109/NGCT.2016.7877498

Yadav, O. P., & Ray, S. (2016). Smoothening and Segmentation of ECG Signals Using Total Variation Denoising–Minimization-Majorization and Bottom-Up Approach. *Procedia Computer Science, 85*, 483–489. doi:10.1016/j.procs.2016.05.195

Yamin, & Abdulaziz, & AbiSen. (2017). Improving Privacy and Security of User Data in Location Based Services. *International Journal of Ambient Computing and Intelligence, 9*(1).

Yamin, M., & Sen, A. A. A. (2018). Improving Privacy and Security of User Data in Location Based Services. *International Journal of Ambient Computing and Intelligence, 9*(1), 19–42. doi:10.4018/IJACI.2018010102

Yang, X., Wang, K., & Shamma, S. A. (1992). Auditory representations of acoustic signals. *IEEE Transactions on Information Theory, 38*(2), 824–839. doi:10.1109/18.119739

Yassin, N. (2015, November). Digital Watermarking for Telemedicine Applications: A Review. *International Journal of Computers and Applications, 129*(17), 30–37. doi:10.5120/ijca2015907183

Yu, N., Cao, L., Fang, W., & Li, X., (2003). Practical Analysis of Watermarking Capacity. *International Conference on Communication Technology, 2*, 1872 – 1877.

Zaman, Obimbo, & Dara. (2016). A Novel Differential Privacy Approach that Enhances Classification Accuracy. In *Proceedings of the Ninth International C* Conference on Computer Science & Software Engineering (C3S2E '16).* ACM. DOI: 10.1145/2948992.2949027

Zarzoso, V., & Nandi, A. K. (2001). Noninvasive fetal electrocardiogram extraction: Blind separation versus adaptive noise cancellation. *IEEE Transactions on Biomedical Engineering, 48*(1), 12–18. doi:10.1109/10.900244 PMID:11235584

Zemmal, N., Azizi, N., Dey, N., & Sellami, M. (2016). Adaptive Semi Supervised Support Vector Machine Semi Supervised Learning with Features Cooperation for Breast Cancer Classification. *Journal of Medical Imaging and Health Informatics*, *6*(1), 53–62. doi:10.1166/jmihi.2016.1591

Zhang & Chen. (2016). A speaker model clustering method based on space position. *International Journal of Advanced Computer Research, 6.*

Zhang, L., Dong, W., Zhang, D., & Shi, G. (2010). Two-stage image denoising By principal component analysis with local pixel grouping. *Pattern Recognition*, *43*(4), 1531–1549. doi:10.1016/j.patcog.2009.09.023

Zhao, Z.-D., & Chen, Y.-Q. (2006). A New Method for Removal of Baseline Wander and Power Line Interference in ECG Signals. *Machine Learning and Cybernetics, 2006 International Conference on,* 4342-4347. 10.1109/ICMLC.2006.259082

Zhou, X. Q., Huang, H. K., & Lou, S. L. (2000, February). Secure Method for Sectional Image Archiving and Transmission. Medical Imaging 2000: PACS Design and Evaluation: Engineering and Clinical Issues, 390 – 399.

Zhou, W., Rockwood, T., & Sagetong, P. (2002). Non-repudiation Oblivious Watermarking Scheme for Secure Digital Video Distribution. *IEEE Workshop on Multimedia Signal Processing*, 343 – 346.

Zhou, Y., & Bai, J. (2007). Atlas-based fuzzy connectedness segmentation and intensity non-uniformity correction applied to brain MRI. *IEEE Transactions on Biomedical Engineering*, *54*(1), 122–129. doi:10.1109/TBME.2006.884645 PMID:17260863

Zhou, Y., Bao, L., & Philip Chen, C. L. (2014). A New 1D Chaotic System for Image Encryption. *Signal Processing, Elsevier*, *97*(Apr), 172–182. doi:10.1016/j.sigpro.2013.10.034

Zhou, Z., Shi, W., Bao, Y., & Yang, M. (2010). A Gaussian Function based Chaotic Neural Network. *IEEE International Conference on Computer Application and System Modeling*, 203-206.

Zhu, H., Tian, S., & Lü, K. (2015). Privacy-Preserving Data Publication with Features of Independent -Diversity. *The Computer Journal*, *58*(4), 549–571. doi:10.1093/comjnl/bxu102

Zijlstra, W. G., Buursma, A., & Meeuwsen-van der Roest, W. P. (1991). Absorption spectra of human fetal and adult oxyhemoglobin, de-oxyhemoglobin, carboxyhemoglobin and methemoglobin. *Clinical Chemistry*, *37*(9), 1633–1638. PMID:1716537

Znaidi, W., Minier, M., & Ubeda, S. (2013). Hierarchical Node Replication Attacks Detection in Wireless Sensor Networks. *International Journal of Distributed Sensor Networks*, 12.

About the Contributors

Chittaranjan Pradhan is working at School of Computer Engineering, KIIT University, India. He obtained his Bachelors, Masters and PhD degree in Computer Science & Engineering stream. His research includes Information Security, Image Processing, Data Analytics and Multimedia Systems. Dr. Pradhan has published more than 40 articles in the national and international journals and conferences. Also, he has been associated to a number of events organized at national and international level. He is also associated with various educational and research societies like IACSIT, ISTE, UACEE, CSI, IET, IAENG, ISCA etc. He has also experience of more than 10 years in teaching and research activities.

Himansu Das is working as an as Assistant Professor in the School of Computer Engineering, KIIT University, Bhubaneswar, Odisha, India. He has received his B. Tech and M. Tech degree from Biju Pattnaik University of Technology (BPUT), Odisha, India. He has published several research papers in various international journals and conferences. He has also edited several books of international repute. He is associated with different international bodies as Editorial/Reviewer board member of various journals and conferences. He is a proficient in the field of Computer Science Engineering and served as an organizing chair, publicity chair and act as member of program committees of many national and international conferences. He is also associated with various educational and research societies like IACSIT, ISTE, UACEE, CSI, IET, IAENG, ISCA etc., His research interest includes Grid Computing, Cloud Computing, and Machine Learning. He has also 10 years of teaching and research experience in different engineering colleges.

Bighnaraj Naik is an Assistant Professor in the Department of Computer Applications, Veer Surendra Sai University of Technology, Burla, Odisha, India. He received his Doctoral degree from the Department of Computer Sc. Engineering & Information Technology, Veer Surendra Sai University of Technology, Burla, Odisha, India, Master degree from Institute of Technical Education and Research, SOA University, Bhubaneswar, Odisha, India and Bachelor degree from National Institute of Science and Technology, Berhampur, Odisha, India, in 2016, 2009 and 2006 respectively. He has published more than 40 research papers in various reputed peer reviewed International Conferences, Referred Journals and Book Chapters. He has more than eight years of teaching experience in the field of Computer Science and Information Technology. He is the life member of International Association of Engineers (Hongkong). His area of interest includes Data Mining, Soft Computing, etc. He is the recipient of "Young Faculty in Engineering" award for the year 2017 from Centre of Advance Research and Design, VIFA-2017, Chennai, India, for exceptional academic records and research excellence in the area of Computer Science and Engineering. He has been serving as an active member of reviewer committee of various reputed peer reviewed journals such as Swarm and Evolutionary Computation, Elsevier, Journal of King Saud University, Elsevier, International Journal of Computational System Engineering, Inderscience, International Journal of Swarm Intelligence, Inderscience, International Journal of Computational Science and Engineering, Inderscience, International Journal of Data Science, Inderscience, etc. Currently, He is serving as Editor of the book entitled "Information Security in Biomedical Signal Processing", Publisher: IGI-Global, USA. Also He is the Guest Editor of International Journal of Computational Intelligence Studies, Inderscience Publication, and International Journal of Data Science and Analytics, Springer. He is associated with many International Conference in the capacity of Convenor, Program Committee Member, Session Chair and Volume editor.

Nilanjan Dey received his Ph. D. Degree from Jadavpur University, India, in 2015. He is an Assistant Professor in the Department of Information Technology, Techno India College of Technology, Kolkata, W.B., India. He holds an honorary position of Visiting Scientist at Global Biomedical Technologies Inc., CA, USA and Research Scientist of Laboratory of Applied Mathematical Modeling in Human Physiology, Territorial Organization of- Scientific and Engineering Unions, Bulgaria. Associate Researcher of Laboratoire RIADI, University of Manouba, Tunisia. His research topic is Medical Imaging, Data mining, Machine learning, Computer Aided Diagnosis, Atherosclerosis etc. He is the Editor-in-Chief of International Journal of Ambient Computing and Intelligence (IGI Global), US, International Journal of Rough Sets and Data Analysis (IGI Global), US, the International Journal of Synthetic Emotions (IGI Global), US, (Co-EinC) and International Journal of Natural Computing Research (IGI Global), US. Series Editor (Co.) of Advances in Ubiquitous Sensing Applications for Healthcare (AUSAH), Elsevier, Advances in Geospatial Technologies (AGT) Book Series, (IGI Global), US, Executive Editor of International Journal of Image Mining (IJIM), Inderscience, Associated Editor of IEEE Access and International Journal of Information Technology, Springer. He has 20 books and more than 200 research articles in peer-reviewed journals and international conferences. He is the organizing committee member of several international conferences including ITITS, W4C, ICMIR, FICTA, ICICT, etc.

* * *

Joe Virgin A. is pursuing M.E. degree in Communication Systems from Anna University, Chennai.

Poornima B. is Professor and Head of Information Science Department at Bapuji Institute of Engineering and Technology, located in the central part of Karnataka, India. Her research area includes Artificial Intelligence, Data Warehouse and Data Mining. She has published papers in nine reputed international journals. She has completed AICTE funded RPS project. Presently she is guiding six research scholars. She is a life member of Indian Society for Technical Education.

Shashidhara Bola is an assistant professor in Department of CSE, Dayananda Sagar College of Engineering, Bangalore.

Komal R. Borisagar received B.E. degree in Electronics and Communication from C. U. Shah Engineering College, Saurashtra University, Rajkot, Gujarat, India in 2002 and M.E. degree in Communication System Engineering from Changa Institute of Technology, Gujarat University, and Ahmedabad in 2008. In 2012, she received her doctoral degree from the Department of Electronics and Communication

Engineering, JJT University, Rajasthan. She has teaching experience of over 10 years. She is working as Assistant Professor at Electronics & Communication Department, Atmiya Institute of Technology and Science, Rajkot. Her areas of interest are wireless communication, speech processing and signal & image processing.

Surekha Borra is currently a Professor in the Department of ECE, K. S. Institute of Technology, Bangalore, India. She earned her Doctorate in Image Processing from Jawaharlal Nehru Technological University, Hyderabad, India, in 2015. Her research interests are in the areas of Image and Video Analytics, Machine Learning, Biometrics and Remote Sensing. She has published 4 book chapters and 22 research papers to her credit in refereed & indexed journals, and conferences at international and national levels. Her international recognition includes her professional memberships & services in refereed organizations, programme committees, editorial & review boards, wherein she has been a guest editor for 2 journals and reviewer for journals published by IEEE, IET, Elsevier, Taylor & Francis, Springer, IGI-Global etc. She has received Woman Achiever's Award from The Institution of Engineers (India), for her prominent research and innovative contribution (s)., Woman Educator & Scholar Award for her contributions to teaching and scholarly activities, Young Woman Achiever Award for her contribution in Copyright Protection of Images.

B. N. Chatterji obtained BTech (Hons) (1965) and Phd (1970) in Electronics and Electrical Communication Engineering of IIT, Kharagpur. He did Post Doctoral work at University of Erlangen-Nurenberg, Germany during 1972-73. He worked with Telerad Pvt Ltd, Bombay (1965), Central Electronics Research Institute, Pilani (1966) and IIT, Kharagpur as faculty member during 1967-2005. He was Professor during 1980-2005, Head of the Department during 1987-1991, Dean Academic Affairs during 1994-1997 and Member of Board of Governors of IIT, Kharagpur during 1998-2000. He has published more than 150 journal papers, 200 conference papers and four books. He was Chairman of four International Conferences and ten National conferences. He has coordinated 25 short term courses and was the chief investigator of 24 Sponsored Projects. He is the Fellow/Life Member/Member of eight Professional Societies. He has received ten National Awards on the basis of his Academic/Research contributions. His areas of interests are Pattern Recognition, Image Processing, Signal Processing, Parallel Processing and Control Systems.

Satya Ranjan Dash is an Associate Professor in School of Computer Applications, KIIT University, Bhubaneswar, India. He received his MCA degree from Jorhat Engineering College, Dibrugarh University, Assam and M.Tech. degree in Computer Science from Utkal University, Odisha. He received his Ph.D. in Computer Science from Utkal University, Bhubaneswar, Odisha in 2015. His research interest includes Machine Learning, Bioinformatics and Cloud Computing.

Umashankar Ghugar received his B.E degree in IT from Utkal University,Bhubaneswar in 2006 and M.Tech degree in Computer Science from Fakir Mohan University,Balasore in 2012. He has 07 years of Teaching experience and Now He is PhD Scholar in the Department of Computer Science, Berhampur University,Orissa. His research interests are in Computer Networks such as Wireless Sensor Network and Network security. He is currently a member of IACSIT, CSTA, IAENG and IRED. He has published 03 International journal papers and 02 are under review process.

Tariq Javid is currently working as Associate Professor and Chairman, Department of Biomedical Engineering, Hamdard University, Pakistan. He has more than 20 years of experience in academics and healthcare industry. His research interests include image processing and information security.

Adalarasu Kanagasabai received the B.E. degree in Electronics and Instrumentation Engineering from Bharathiar University, Coimbatore, Tamilnadu, India, in 1998 and the Ph.D. degree in driver fatigue measurements from Indian Institute of Technology Madras, India, in 2010. At present, he is an Associate Professor in the School of Electrical and Electronics Engineering at Sastra University (Deemed), Thanjavur, Tamilnadu His research interests include cognitive neuroscience, industrial human safety and ergonomics testing of vehicles.

Ashoka Reddy Komalla studied Bachelor of Engineering in Electronics & Instrumentation Engineering at Kakatiya Institute of Technology & Science, Warangal (KITSW) and received B.Tech degree in 1992 from Kakatiya University, Warangal, Telangana. He received M.Tech degree in 1994 from Jawaharlal Nehru Technological University, Kakinada (JNTUK), Andhra Pradesh. He did research on Pulse Oximeters and received PhD in Electrical Engineering in 2008 from Indian Institute of Technology Madras (IITM), Chennai, India. He received Innovative Research Project award in 2008 from Indian National Academy of Engineering (INAE) for his PhD work. His teaching and research interests include signal processing for communications, biomedical signal processing and instrumentation. He has authored over 25 research papers in refereed journals and more than 70 papers in conferences proceedings. He is a reviewer for IEEE Transactions on Measurements & Instrumentation, IEEE transactions on Biomedical Engineering, IEEE Sensors Journal. He is also a member of IEEE, life member of ISTE, member IETE and member CSI. Under his guidance 6 scholars received Ph.D and 3 more are pursuing their PhD Currently, Dr. Reddy is a Professor in the department of Electronics & Communication Engineering at KITSW.

Swanirbhar Majumder is currently serving as an Associate Professor in the Department of IT at Tripura University since 2017. Previously he worked at NERIST since 2006 as Assistant Professor. He got his PhD, PG and UG degrees from Jadavpur University, University of Calcutta and North Eastern Hill University respectively. He has contributed as an author in various research publications in the field of Biomedical Signal Processing, Image Processing, Embedded Systems, and Soft Computing.

Takhellambam Gautam Meitei received his Bachelor Degree in Electronics and Communication Engineering from National Institute of Technology Manipur in 2014. He is currently pursuing his Masters Degree (2016-18) in Electronics and Communication at NERIST. He has a keen research interest in Biomedical Signal processing, image processing and digital circuits.

Jagannath Mohan is an Associate Professor in the School of Electronics Engineering at Vellore Institute of Technology (VIT), Chennai, India. He obtained his Ph.D. from Indian Institute of Technology Madras, Chennai in the year 2012. He has served the position of Senior Project Officer at Indian Institute of Technology Madras, Chennai, India. He is the recipient of Best Circuit Faculty of the Year 2017 from the South Indian Association of Scientists, Developers and Faculties Award. He has been conferred Young Faculty Award (Specialization in Biomedical Engineering) for the year 2016 from the Venus International Foundation, Chennai. He received Indira Gandhi Sadbhavna Gold Medal Award for

Individual Achievement and Service to the Nation from Global Economic Progress and Research Association, India, 2014. He has more than 60 research articles published in various reputed conferences and journals. His research interest includes ergonomics, biomedical instrumentation systems, biomechanics, control systems, mechatronic systems and robotics.

M. K. Naskar received both the B.Tech and M. Tech degrees from E & ECE Department, IIT, Kharagpur and the PhD degree from Jadavpur University. He served as a faculty member in RIT, Jamshedpur and REC, Durgapur from 1991–1996 and 1996–1999 respectively. He is currently working as Professor in the Department of Electronics and Telecommunication Engineering at Jadavpur University, Kolkata, India and is in-charge of the Advanced Digital and Embedded Systems Lab. His research interests include mobile ad-hoc networks, wireless sensor networks, optical networks, embedded systems and digital image processing.

S. Selva Nidhyananthan received his B.E degree in Electronics and Communication Engineering from Manonmanium Sundaranar University, Tirunelveli, in 1999, M.E. degree in Communication Systems from Anna University, Chennai, in 2005 and Ph.D degree in Speech Processing from Anna University, Chennai, in 2014. He has 14 years of teaching experience and he is currently working as Associate Professor in the department of Electronics and Communication Engineering at Mepco Schlenk Engineering College, Sivakasi, Tamil Nadu, India. His current research interest includes Signal Processing and Image Processing & Information Retrieval. He is the Editorial Review Board member of IGI Global International Journal of Information Security and Privacy (IJISP). He is a member of IETE and ISTE.

Anuradha C. Phadke received the BE and ME degree from Walchand College of Engineering, Sangli, India in 1993 and 1995 respectively and the Ph.D. degree for research work titled "Development of algorithms for diagnosis of breast cancer using digital Mammogram Analysis", in 2016 from Savitribai Phule Pune University (SPPU). Research work is carried out under the esteemed guidance of Dr. Priti P. Rege at research centre College of Engineering, Pune. Since 1995 she has been with Maharashtra Institute of Technology, Pune, India where she is currently working as Associate Professor at Department of Electronics and Telecommunication Engineering. She has published and presented several papers in leading national and international conferences, journals and published two books. She was recipient of "Ideal Teacher Award" by Maharashtra Academy of Engineering & Education Research, Pune for Sept. 2011.

Jayaram Pradhan started his teaching career as Computer Sc lecturer at Bhopal University in the year 1985 after completing M.Phil Computer Sc from J.N.U,New Delhi. He joined in the department of CSEA, REC Rourkela in the year 1986 where he completed his doctorial dissertation under Sambalpur University. In the year 1993 he joined in the department of Computer Science Berhampur University and worked as founder Head of the department. During more than three decade experience he has offered different courses to DCA, MCA, BE, M.Tech students, beside guided many M.Tech, Ph.D scholars, published many papers, reviewed different manuscripts of journals, adjudicated several M.Tech/Ph.D thesis of other Indian University, design many courses, deliver several talk at different Universities with in India and abroad. Now He is the PG Council Chairman of Berhampur University, Orissa. In addition he has much academic administrative assignment during this period. His present research interests include designing of Algorithms, Cryptography and computationally hard problems.

Shantha Selva Kumari R. received her B.E degree in Electronics and Communication Engineering from Bharathiyar University, in 1987, M.S. degree in Electronics and Control from Birla Institute of Technology, Pilani, in 1994 and Ph.D degree in Bio Signal Processing from Manonmanium Sundaranar University, Tirunelveli, in 2008. She has 30 years of teaching experience and she is currently working as Senior Professor & Head in the department of Electronics and Communication Engineering at Mepco Schlenk Engineering College, Sivakasi, TamilNadu. Her current research interest includes Signal Processing, Wavelets and its Applications and Neural Networks.She has serving as Reviewer/Editorial Board Member for many reputed Journals and Conferences. Received Best Subject Award in Computer Engineering Division (IE India) in the Year 2007, Received Best Teacher Award from IMS Learning Resources Pvt. Ltd in the Year 2009. She is a Life Member in Indian Society for Technical Education (ISTE), Life Fellow Member in Institute of Electronics and Telecommunication Engineers (IETE) and Life Member in Computer Society of India (CSI).

Priti P. Rege received the B.E. and M.E.(Gold medal) degrees from Devi Ahilya University of Indore, India, and the Ph.D. degree from the University of Pune, India, in 2002. Since 1989, she has been with the College of Engineering Pune, where she is currently working as Head and Professor in the Department of Electronics and Telecommunications. Her research interests include signal processing and pattern recognition. Several of her papers have appeared in leading journals and conferences. Dr. Rege was the recipient of Nagarkar Fellowship for carrying out research in sub-band coding of images and Best Faculty Award by Cognizant for the year 2012-13 and Prof. SVC Aiya award for Excellence in Telecom Education for the year 2016-17. She has 31 years of teaching experience and has published more than 100 papers in reputed national and international conferences/refereed journals. She is senior member of IEEE, Fellow IETE and member of the IET.

Manas Saha did B.E (Electronics) and M.Tech from Nagpur University and Jadavpur University respectively. He completed his PhD from Jadavpur University in the field of biomedical imaging. He serves the department of Electronics and Communication Engineering, Siliguri Institute of Technology, Siliguri in the capacity of Assistant Professor. His research interests include medical image processing and computer vision.

Annapurna Samantaray received her MCA degree from SOA University, Bhubaneswar, Odisha and has received her M.Tech(Data Mining) . degree from Indraprastha Institute of Information Technology, Delhi (IIIT-D).

Sharad Saxena did Ph. D. (CSE) 2012 and M. Tech. (CE) in 2009. He has nearly 50 International publications in the area of Ad-hoc and sensor networks. He has guided 10 M. Tech. Dissertations and four Ph.D. till date. His research interest includes Wireless Sensor Networks, IoT, and Mobile Computing, with a focus on Mobile Ad-Hoc and sensor Networks. Presently he is working as Assistant Professor in the department of Computer Science at Thapar University, Patiala, Punjab, India.

Mukta Sharma holds M. Phil (Computer Science), M. Tech (IT), M. Sc (CS), PGDCA. Currently she is pursuing Ph. D in Computer Applications from Teerthanker Mahaveer University, Moradabad. She has submitted her thesis. She has more than fifteen years experience of teaching in various undergraduate & postgraduate courses of Indian Universities like DTU, GGSIP University, MCRP, Kurukshetra,

IASE, PTU & UPTU etc. She has co-authored a book titled "Web Technologies: Planning, Designing, and Development of Websites", Galgotia Publications Ltd. She has authored a chapter titled "Services of Mobile Commerce", in Securing Transactions and Payment Systems for M-Commerce, IGI Global, and ISSN: 1935-2700 with Advances in E-Business Research (AEBR) book series, Lee (Western Illinois University, USA). To her credit, she has various research papers published in national and international Journals/ conferences like IEEE, IJATES (YMCA), Amity University, JNU, TMU etc. She has contributed various book reviews.

Asim Syed Sheeraz is Biodesign Engineer in KIIT University, He has done his MSc Biomedical Engineering (2013), University of Dundee, UK and BE Medical Electronics (2011), Visvesvaraya Technological University, India.

Sinam Ajitkumar Singh received his B.Tech in Electronics and Communication Engineering and Masters Degree in VLSI & Embedded System, from National Institute of Technology Manipur in 2014 and 2016 respectively. He is currently a Research scholar at NERIST. His research interest includes Biomedical Signal Processing and Circuit design.

Amandip Sinha has completed his B.tech in CSE from JIS college which is under WBUT university in 2015.He is working in Amdocs company with 1 year 7 months of experience.

Rohit Thanki is recently doctorate from the Department of E.C.E., C. U. Shah University, Wadhwan City, India. His research interests are in the areas of Digital Watermarking, Copyright Protection, Biometrics System, Security, Compressive Sensing, Digital Image and Video Analytics, Medical Imaging, and Digital VLSI Design. He has published 2 books, 4 book chapters and 35 research papers to his credit in referred & indexed journals, and conferences at international and national levels. His international recognition includes his professional memberships & services in refereed organizations, programme committees and reviewer for journals published by IEEE, Elsevier, Taylor & Francis, Springer, IGI Global, etc.

Babangida Zubairu is a research scholar currently undergoing Ph.D Computer Science studies from Jaipur National University,Jaipur, India; he obtained M.Sc Computer Science from Bayero University Kano, Nigeria. His research interest includes computer networks, intelligent transportation system and System Security. He is two times best paper award, AICE 2014 and REDSET 2016 and He has chapter contribution in the published book title Innovations in Computational Intelligence, Springer 2017.

Index

Purchase Print, E-Book, or Print + E-Book

IGI Global books can now be purchased from three unique pricing formats:
Print Only, E-Book Only, or Print + E-Book. Shipping fees apply.

www.igi-global.com

Recommended Reference Books

ISBN: 978-1-4666-9661-7
© 2016; 308 pp.
List Price: $200

ISBN: 978-1-5225-1016-1
© 2017; 345 pp.
List Price: $200

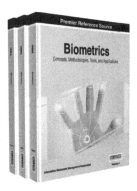

ISBN: 978-1-5225-0983-7
© 2017; 1,852 pp.
List Price: $2,200

ISBN: 978-1-5225-0808-3
© 2017; 442 pp.
List Price: $345

ISBN: 978-1-4666-8793-6
© 2016; 548 pp.
List Price: $335

ISBN: 978-1-4666-8387-7
© 2015; 408 pp.
List Price: $325

Looking for free content, product updates, news, and special offers?
Join IGI Global's mailing list today and start enjoying exclusive perks sent only to IGI Global members.
Add your name to the list at **www.igi-global.com/newsletters.**

Publishing Information Science and Technology Research Since 1988

www.igi-global.com   Sign up at www.igi-global.com/newsletters   f facebook.com/igiglobal   t twitter.com/igiglobal

Stay Current on the Latest Emerging Research Developments

Become an IGI Global Reviewer for Authored Book Projects

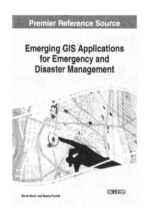

The overall success of an authored book project is dependent on quality and timely reviews.

In this competitive age of scholarly publishing, constructive and timely feedback significantly decreases the turnaround time of manuscripts from submission to acceptance, allowing the publication and discovery of progressive research at a much more expeditious rate. Several IGI Global authored book projects are currently seeking highly qualified experts in the field to fill vacancies on their respective editorial review boards:

Applications may be sent to:
development@igi-global.com

Applicants must have a doctorate (or an equivalent degree) as well as publishing and reviewing experience. Reviewers are asked to write reviews in a timely, collegial, and constructive manner. All reviewers will begin their role on an ad-hoc basis for a period of one year, and upon successful completion of this term can be considered for full editorial review board status, with the potential for a subsequent promotion to Associate Editor.

If you have a colleague that may be interested in this opportunity, we encourage you to share this information with them.

www.igi-global.com

InfoSci®-Books

A Database for Information Science and Technology Research

Maximize Your Library's Book Collection!

Invest in IGI Global's InfoSci®-Books database and gain access to hundreds of reference books at a fraction of their individual list price.

The InfoSci®-Books database offers unlimited simultaneous users the ability to precisely return search results through more than 80,000 full-text chapters from nearly 3,900 reference books in the following academic research areas:

Business & Management Information Science & Technology • Computer Science & Information Technology
Educational Science & Technology • Engineering Science & Technology • Environmental Science & Technology
Government Science & Technology • Library Information Science & Technology • Media & Communication Science & Technology
Medical, Healthcare & Life Science & Technology • Security & Forensic Science & Technology • Social Sciences & Online Behavior

Peer-Reviewed Content:
• Cutting-edge research
• No embargoes
• Scholarly and professional
• Interdisciplinary

Award-Winning Platform:
• Unlimited simultaneous users
• Full-text in XML and PDF
• Advanced search engine
• No DRM

Librarian-Friendly:
• Free MARC records
• Discovery services
• COUNTER4/SUSHI compliant
• Training available

To find out more or request a free trial, visit:
www.igi-global.com/eresources

IGI Global
DISSEMINATOR OF KNOWLEDGE
www.igi-global.com

www.igi-global.com

IGI Global Proudly Partners with

Enhance Your Manuscript with eContent Pro International's Professional
Copy Editing Service

Expert Copy Editing

eContent Pro International copy editors, with over 70 years of combined experience, will provide complete and comprehensive care for your document by resolving all issues with spelling, punctuation, grammar, terminology, jargon, semantics, syntax, consistency, flow, and more. In addition, they will format your document to the style you specify (APA, Chicago, etc.). All edits will be performed using Microsoft Word's Track Changes feature, which allows for fast and simple review and management of edits.

Additional Services

eContent Pro International also offers fast and affordable proofreading to enhance the readability of your document, professional translation in over 100 languages, and market localization services to help businesses and organizations localize their content and grow into new markets around the globe.

IGI Global Authors Save 25% on eContent Pro International's Services!

Scan the QR Code to Receive Your 25% Discount

The 25% discount is applied directly to your eContent Pro International shopping cart when placing an order through IGI Global's referral link. Use the QR code to access this referral link. eContent Pro International has the right to end or modify any promotion at any time.

Email: customerservice@econtentpro.com

econtentpro.com

Information Resources Management Association

Advancing the Concepts & Practices of Information Resources
Management in Modern Organizations

Become an IRMA Member

Members of the **Information Resources Management Association (IRMA)** understand the importance
of community within their field of study. The Information Resources Management Association is an ideal
venue through which professionals, students, and academicians can convene and share the latest industry
innovations and scholarly research that is changing the field of information science and technology.
Become a member today and enjoy the benefits of membership as well as the opportunity to collaborate
and network with fellow experts in the field.

IRMA Membership Benefits:

- **One FREE Journal Subscription**

- **30% Off Additional
  Journal Subscriptions**

- **20% Off Book Purchases**

- Updates on the latest events and research on
  Information Resources Management through
  the IRMA-L listserv.

- Updates on new open access and downloadable
  content added to Research IRM.

- A copy of the Information Technology Management
  Newsletter twice a year.

- A certificate of membership.

IRMA Membership $195

Scan code or visit **irma-international.org** and begin by
selecting your free journal subscription.

Membership is good for one full year.

www.irma-international.org

Printed in the United States
By Bookmasters